Introduction to Literature

GINN LITERATURE SERIES

Robert A. Bennett, *Senior Author*

INTRODUCTION TO LITERATURE

EXPLORING LITERATURE

UNDERSTANDING LITERATURE

TYPES OF LITERATURE

AMERICAN LITERATURE

ENGLISH LITERATURE

SCHOONER AT SUNSET *Winslow Homer*

Introduction to Literature

Betty Yvonne Welch
Denver Public Schools

Robert A. Bennett
San Diego City Schools

CONSULTANTS

Robert E. Beck, *English Consultant*
John Swett Unified School District
Crockett, California

Sharon L. Belshaw, *English Instructor*
Hopkins Junior High School
Fremont, California

Mary Gloyne Byler, *Consultant*
Association on American Indian Affairs
New York, New York

Kenneth L. Chambers, *Asst. Professor*
Black Studies Department
Wellesley College
Wellesley, Massachusetts

Barbara Z. Chasen
Instructional Support Team
Boston Public Schools
Boston, Massachusetts

Paula Grier, *Education Consultant*
Intercultural Development Research Association
San Antonio, Texas

Nicolás Kanellos, *Editor*
Revista Chicano-Riqueña
University of Houston
Houston, Texas

Ann Rayson, *Asst. Professor*
Department of English
University of Hawaii at Manou
Honolulu, Hawaii

Ginn and Company

Acknowledgments

Grateful acknowledgment is made to the following publishers, authors, and agents for permission to use and adapt copyrighted materials:

American Bible Society for "David and Goliath" (Chapter 17 of the First Book of Samuel). Scripture quotations in this volume are from the *Good News Bible*—Old Testament. Copyright © American Bible Society 1976. Used by permission.

Brandt & Brandt Literary Agents, Inc., for "The Most Dangerous Game" by Richard Connell. Copyright, 1924 by Richard Connell. Copyright renewed, 1952 by Louise Fox Connell. Reprinted by permission of Brandt & Brandt Literary Agents, Inc.

Doubleday & Company, Inc., for "The Small Miracle" by Paul Gallico. Copyright 1950 by Paul Gallico. Reprinted by permission of Doubleday & Company, Inc. Also for the poem "Direction" by Alonzo Lopez from *The Whispering Wind* edited by Terry Allen. Copyright © 1972 by The Institute of American Indian Arts. Reprinted by permission of Doubleday & Company, Inc. Also for the poem beginning "A trout leaps high" ("The World Upside Down") by Onitsura from *An Introduction to Haiku* by Harold G. Henderson. Copyright © 1958 by Harold G. Henderson. Reprinted by permission of Doubleday & Company, Inc. Also for "The Gift of the Magi" from *The Four Million* by O. Henry. Copyright 1904. Published by Doubleday.

Farrar, Straus & Giroux, Inc., for "Charles" by Shirley Jackson. Reprinted by permission of Farrar, Straus and Giroux, Inc., "Charles" from *The Lottery* by Shirley Jackson. Copyright © 1943, 1944, 1947, 1948, 1949 by Shirley Jackson. Copyright renewed © 1971, 1972, 1975, 1976, 1977 by Laurence Hyman, Barry Hyman, Mrs. Sarah Webster and Mrs. Joanne Schnurer.

Harcourt Brace Jovanovich, Inc., for "All Stories Are Anansi's" from *The Hat Shaking Dance and Other Ashanti Tales from Ghana,* © 1957 by Harold Courlander. Reprinted by permission of Harcourt Brace Jovanovich, Inc. Also for "The Apprentice" by Dorothy Canfield Fisher. Copyright 1947 by Curtis Publishing Company; renewed 1975 by Downe Publishing, Inc. Reprinted from *Four-Square* by Dorothy Canfield Fisher by permission of Harcourt Brace Jovanovich, Inc. Also for "The Pacing Goose" by Jessamyn West. Copyright 1945, 1973 by Jessamyn West. Reprinted from her volume *The Friendly Persuasion* by permission of Harcourt Brace Jovanovich, Inc. Also for the poem "Rural Dumpheap" by Melville Cane. Copyright 1938, 1966 by Melville Cane. Reprinted from his volume *And Pastures New* by permission of Harcourt Brace Jovanovich, Inc. Also for the poem "Song of the Settlers" by Jessamyn West. Copyright 1947, 1975 by Jessamyn West. Reprinted from her volume *A Mirror for the Sky* by permission of Harcourt Brace Jovanovich, Inc.

Harper & Row, Publishers, Inc., for "Pygmalion and Galatea" from *The Magic and the Sword* by Miriam Cox; Copyright © 1960, 1956 by Harper & Row, Publishers, Inc. Also for "Urashima" from the book *The Three Treasures* by Miriam Cox, copyright © 1964 by Harper & Row, Publishers, Inc. Also for "The Cheyenne Account of How the World Was Made" by Mary Little Bear Inkanish, pp. 21–26 in *American Indian Mythology* by Alice Marriott and Carol K. Rachlin. Copyright © 1968 by Alice Marriott and Carol K. Rachlin. Also for "Through the Tunnel" from *The Habit of Loving* by Doris Lessing (Thomas Y. Crowell). Copyright © 1955, 1957 by Doris Lessing. Originally appeared in *The New Yorker*. Also for "The Inspiration of Mr. Budd" from *In the Teeth of the Evidence* by Dorothy L. Sayers. Copyright 1940 by Dorothy Leigh Sayers Fleming. Also for "The Celebrated Jumping Frog of Calaveras County" from *Sketches New and Old* by Mark Twain—Harper & Row. Also for the text of the poem "Sara Cynthia Sylvia Stout Would Not Take the Garbage Out" from *Where the Sidewalk Ends: the Poems and Drawings of Shel Silverstein*. Copyright © 1974 by Shel Silverstein. All reprinted by permission of Harper & Row, Publishers, Inc.

Holt, Rinehart and Winston for the poem "Oh, when I was in love with you" from "A Shropshire Lad"—Authorized Edition—from *The Collected Poems of A. E. Housman*. Copyright 1939, 1940, © 1965 by Holt, Rinehart and Winston. Copyright © 1967, 1968 by Robert E. Symons. Reprinted by permission of Holt, Rinehart and Winston, Publishers.

Houghton Mifflin Company for "Baldur the Beautiful" from *Legends of the North* by Olivia E. Coolidge published by Houghton Mifflin Company. Copyright 1951 by Olivia E. Coolidge. Reprinted by permission. Also for "Phaëton, Son of Apollo" from *Greek Myths* by Olivia E. Coolidge published by Houghton Mifflin Company. Copyright 1949 and © renewed 1977 by Olivia E. Coolidge. Reprinted by permission. Also for "The First Snowfall" from *The Complete Poetical Works of James Russell Lowell*, published by Houghton Mifflin Company.

International Creative Management for the play "Grandpa and the Statue" by Arthur Miller. Reprinted by permission of International Creative Management. Copyright © 1945, 1973 by Arthur Miller. Also for the poem "Elizabeth Blackwell" from *Independent Voices* by Eve Merriam, published by Atheneum Publishers. Reprinted by permission of Eve Merriam c/o International Creative Management. Copyright © 1968 Eve Merriam.

Little, Brown and Company for *The Third Gift* by Jan Carew. Text Copyright © 1974 by Jan Carew. By permission of Little,

Acknowledgments continue on page 610.

Table of Contents

5 Plays

6 Poems

NARRATIVE POEMS

BALLADS

7 Myths, Fables, and Folktales

8 The Novel

Introduction to Literature

Courage

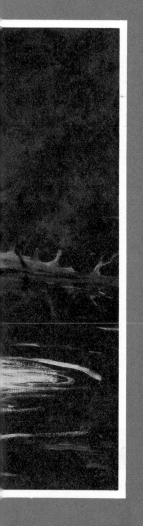

COURAGE

In Hindustan, according to ancient legend, there lived a man called Hassim. Seeking wisdom, Hassim spent many years alone in the mountains, fasting and praying and meditating about good ways to live. When he had acquired wisdom, he journeyed to the city to preach. In the crowded marketplace he began to talk to the people about wisdom, but no one listened. Instead, everyone was talking excitedly and looking upward.

There, high above the marketplace, a tightrope walker balanced himself on one foot. Suddenly, the babble of voices stopped; the spectators held their breath. The acrobat leaped into the air, flipped head over heels, and landed with both feet on the tightrope.

When the performance was over, Hassim again began to preach. But now, instead of preaching about wisdom, he spoke to the people about courage. "Live with daring!" he cried. "Live with danger. Seek to excel in what you do!"

The tightrope walker had taught Hassim, the wise man, a lesson.

As Hassim was talking to the people, he felt something gently pulling the hem of his robe. Looking down, he saw a handsome young woman. "Yes, my child?" inquired Hassim. "Please, Master," asked the young woman, "can you show me the way to the Institute? Without difficulty have I come from my village, a three-day journey from here. But in this crowded marketplace I am confused because, you see, I am blind. Can you show me the way?"

"You are blind, and yet alone you have journeyed a hundred miles from your home?" Hassim was amazed.

"Oh, yes," stated the young woman. "But at the Institute I shall not be alone, for I shall learn how to help others who are blind."

"What courage!" exclaimed Hassim to the crowd.

Like the acrobat, the blind girl had taught Hassim a lesson. COURAGE!

There was only one way to leave Ship-Trap Island. Rainsford knew he would need all the reasoning power he could muster. But more than that—if he was to survive—he would need courage!

The Most Dangerous Game

RICHARD CONNELL

"OFF THERE to the right—some-where—is a large island," said Whitney. "It's rather a mystery—"

"What island is it?" Rainsford asked.

"The old charts call it 'Ship-Trap Island,'" Whitney replied. "A suggestive name, isn't it? Sailors have a curious dread of the place. I don't know why. Some superstition—"

"Can't see it," remarked Rainsford, trying to peer through the dank tropical night that was palpable[1] as it pressed its thick warm blackness in upon the yacht.

"You've good eyes," said Whitney, with a laugh, "and I've seen you pick off a moose moving in the brown fall bush at four hundred yards, but even you can't see four miles or so through a moonless Caribbean night."

"Nor four yards," admitted Rainsford. "Ugh! It's like moist velvet."

"It will be light enough in Rio," promised Whitney. "We should make it in a few days. I hope the jaguar guns have come from Purdey's. We should have some good hunting up the Amazon. Great sport, hunting."

"The best sport in the world," agreed Rainsford.

"For the hunter," amended Whitney. "Not for the jaguar."

"Don't talk rot, Whitney," said Rainsford. "You're a big-game hunter, not a philosopher. Who cares how a jaguar feels?"

"Perhaps the jaguar does," observed Whitney.

"Bah! They've no understanding."

"Even so, I rather think they understand one thing at least—fear. The fear of pain and the fear of death."

"Nonsense," laughed Rainsford. "This hot weather is making you soft, Whitney. Be a realist. The world is made up of two classes—the hunters and the hunted. Luckily, you and I are hunters. Do you think we've passed that island yet?"

"I can't tell in the dark. I hope so."

"Why?" asked Rainsford.

"The place has a reputation—a bad one."

"Cannibals?" suggested Rainsford.

"Hardly. Even cannibals wouldn't live in such a God-forsaken place. But it's got into sailor lore, somehow. Didn't you notice that

---

1 **palpable** (pal′ pə bəl): readily noticed by one's senses.

the crew's nerves seem a bit jumpy today?"

"They were a bit strange, now you mention it. Even Captain Nielsen—"

"Yes, even that tough-minded old Swede, who'd go up to the devil himself and ask him for a light. Those fishy blue eyes held a look I never saw there before. All I could get out of him was: 'This place has an evil name among seafaring men, sir.' Then he said to me, very gravely: 'Don't you feel anything?'—as if the air about us was actually poisonous. Now, you mustn't laugh when I tell you this—I did feel something like a sudden chill.

"There was no breeze. The sea was as flat as a plate-glass window. We were drawing near the island then. What I felt was a—a mental chill—a sort of sudden dread."

"Pure imagination," said Rainsford. "One superstitious sailor can taint the whole ship's company with his fear."

"Maybe. But sometimes I think sailors have an extra sense that tells them when they are in danger. Sometimes I think evil is a tangible thing—with wave lengths, just as sound and light have. An evil place can, so to speak, broadcast vibrations of evil. Anyhow, I'm glad we're getting out of this zone. Well, I think I'll turn in now, Rainsford."

"I'm not sleepy," said Rainsford. "I'm going to smoke another pipe up on the afterdeck."

"Good night, then, Rainsford. See you at breakfast."

"Right. Good night, Whitney."

There was no sound in the night as Rainsford sat there, but the muffled throb of the engine that drove the yacht swiftly through the darkness, and the swish and ripple of the wash of the propeller.

Rainsford, reclining in a steamer chair, indolently puffed on his favorite brier. The sensuous drowsiness of the night was on him.

"It's so dark," he thought, "that I could sleep without closing my eyes; the night would be my eyelids—"

An abrupt sound startled him. Off to the right he heard it, and his ears, expert in such matters, could not be mistaken. Again he heard the sound, and again. Somewhere, off in the blackness, someone had fired a gun three times.

Rainsford sprang up and moved quickly to the rail, mystified. He strained his eyes in the direction from which the reports had come, but it was like trying to see through a blanket. He leaped upon the rail and balanced himself there, to get greater elevation; his pipe, striking a rope, was knocked from his mouth. He lunged for it; a short, hoarse cry came from his lips as he realized he had reached too far and had lost his balance. The cry was pinched off short as the blood-warm waters of the Caribbean Sea closed over his head.

He struggled up to the surface and tried to cry out, but the wash from the speeding yacht slapped him in the face and the salt water in his open mouth made him gag and strangle. Desperately he struck out with strong strokes after the receding lights of the yacht, but he stopped before he had swum fifty feet. A certain cool-headedness had come to him; it was not the first time he had been in a tight place. There was a chance that his cries could be heard by someone aboard the yacht, but that chance was slender, and grew more slender as the yacht raced on. He wrestled himself out of his clothes, and shouted with all his power. The lights of the yacht became faint and ever-vanishing fireflies; then they were blotted out entirely by the night.

Rainsford remembered the shots. They had come from the right, and doggedly he swam in that direction, swimming with slow, deliberate strokes, conserving his strength. For a seemingly endless time he fought the sea. He began to count his strokes desperately; he could do possibly a hundred more and then—

Rainsford heard a sound. It came out of the darkness, a high, screaming sound, the sound of an animal in an extremity of anguish and terror.

He did not recognize the animal that made the sound; he did not try to; with fresh vitality he swam toward the sound. He heard it again; then it was cut short by another noise, crisp, staccato.

"Pistol shot," muttered Rainsford, swimming on.

Ten minutes of determined effort brought another sound to his ears—the most welcome he had ever heard—the muttering and growling of the sea breaking on a rocky shore. He was almost on the rocks before he saw them; on a night less calm he would have been shattered against them. With his remaining strength he dragged himself from the swirling waters. Jagged crags appeared to jut up into the opaqueness; he forced himself upward, hand over hand. Gasping, his hands raw, he reached a flat place at the top. Dense jungle came down to the very edge of the cliffs. What perils that tangle of trees and underbrush might hold for him did not concern Rainsford just then. All he knew was that he was safe from his enemy, the sea, and that utter weariness was on him. He flung himself down at the jungle edge and tumbled headlong into the deepest sleep of his life.

When he opened his eyes he knew from the position of the sun that it was late in the afternoon. Sleep had given him new vigor; a sharp hunger was picking at him. He looked about him, almost cheerfully.

"Where there are pistol shots, there are men. Where there are men, there is food," he thought. But what kind of men, he wondered, in so forbidding a place? An unbroken front of snarled and jagged jungle fringed the shore.

He saw no sign of a trail through the closely knit web of weeds and trees; it was easier to go along the shore, and Rainsford floundered along by the water. Not far from where he had landed, he stopped.

Some wounded thing, by the evidence a large animal, had thrashed about in the underbrush; the jungle weeds were crushed down and the moss was lacerated;[2] one patch of weeds was stained crimson. A small, glittering object not far away caught Rainsford's eye and he picked it up. It was an empty cartridge.

"A twenty-two," he remarked. "That's odd. It must have been a fairly large animal, too. The hunter had his nerve to tackle it with a light gun. It's clear that the brute put up a fight. I suppose the first three shots I heard was when the hunter flushed his quarry[3] and wounded it. The last shot was when he trailed it here and finished it."

He examined the ground closely and found what he had hoped to find—the print of hunting boots. They pointed along the cliff in the direction he had been going. Eagerly he hurried along, now slipping on a rotten log or a loose stone, but making headway; night was beginning to settle down on the island.

Bleak darkness was blacking out the sea and jungle when Rainsford sighted the lights. He came upon them as he turned a crook in the coast line, and his first thought was that he had come upon a village, for there were

---

2 **lacerated** (las′ ə rāt′ ed): cut and bruised.
3 **flushed his quarry**: forced the hunted animal out of hiding

many lights. But as he forged along he saw to his great astonishment that all the lights were in one enormous building—a lofty structure with pointed towers plunging upward into the gloom. His eyes made out the shadowy outlines of a palatial château;[4] it was set on a high bluff, and on three sides of it cliffs dived down to where the sea licked greedy lips in the shadows.

"Mirage," thought Rainsford. But it was no mirage, he found, when he opened the tall spiked iron gate. The stone steps were real enough; the massive door with a leering gargoyle[5] for a knocker was real enough; yet

---

4 **palatial château** (pə lā′ shəl sha tō′): magnificent castle.

5 **gargoyle** (gär′ goil): an animal or human figure carved out of stone and given a hideous face.

about it all hung an air of unreality.

He lifted the knocker, and it creaked up stiffly, as if it had never before been used. He let it fall, and it startled him with its booming loudness. He thought he heard footsteps within; the door remained closed. Again Rainsford lifted the heavy knocker, and let it fall. The door opened then, opened as suddenly as if it were on a spring, and Rainsford stood blinking in the river of glaring gold light that poured out. The first thing Rainsford's eyes discerned was the largest man Rainsford had ever seen—a gigantic creature, solidly made and black-bearded to the waist. In his hand the man held a long-barrel revolver, and he was pointing it straight at Rainsford's heart.

Out of the snarl of beard two small eyes regarded Rainsford.

"Don't be alarmed," said Rainsford, with a smile which he hoped was disarming. "I'm no robber. I fell off a yacht. My name is Sanger Rainsford of New York City."

The menacing look in the eyes did not change. The revolver pointed as rigidly as if the giant were a statue. He gave no sign that he understood Rainsford's words, or that he had even heard them. He was dressed in uniform, a black uniform trimmed with gray astrakhan.[6]

"I'm Sanger Rainsford of New York," Rainsford began again. "I fell off a yacht. I am hungry."

The man's only answer was to raise with his thumb the hammer of his revolver. Then Rainsford saw the man's free hand go to his forehead in a military salute, and he saw him click his heels together and stand at attention. Another man was coming down the broad marble steps, an erect, slender man in evening clothes. He advanced to Rainsford and held out his hand.

In a cultivated voice marked by a slight accent that gave it added precision and deliberateness, he said: "It is a very great pleasure and honor to welcome Mr. Sanger Rainsford, the celebrated hunter, to my home."

Automatically Rainsford shook the man's hand.

"I've read your book about hunting snow leopards in Tibet, you see," explained the man. "I am General Zaroff."

Rainsford's first impression was that the man was singularly handsome; his second was that there was an original, almost bizarre quality about the general's face. He was a tall man past middle age, for his hair was a vivid white; but his thick eyebrows and pointed military mustache were as black as the night from which Rainsford had come. His eyes, too, were black and very bright. He had high cheekbones, a sharp-cut nose, a spare, dark face, the face of a man used to giving orders, the face of an aristocrat. Turning to the giant in uniform, the general made a sign. The giant put away his pistol, saluted, withdrew.

"Ivan is an incredibly strong fellow," remarked the general, "but he has the misfortune to be deaf and dumb. A simple fellow, but, I'm afraid, like all his race, a bit of a savage."

"Is he Russian?"

"He is a Cossack," said the general, and his smile showed red lips and pointed teeth. "So am I."

"Come," he said, "we shouldn't be chatting here. We can talk later. Now you want clothes, food, rest. You shall have them. This is a most restful spot."

Ivan had reappeared, and the general spoke to him with lips that moved but gave forth no sound.

---

6 **astrakhan** (as′ trə kən): lamb's wool that is tightly curled.

"Follow Ivan, if you please, Mr. Rainsford," said the general. "I was about to have my dinner when you came. I'll wait for you. You'll find that my clothes will fit you, I think."

It was to a huge, beam-ceilinged bedroom with a canopied bed big enough for six men that Rainsford followed the silent giant. Ivan laid out an evening suit, and Rainsford, as he put it on, noticed that it came from a London tailor who ordinarily cut and sewed for none below the rank of duke.

The dining room to which Ivan conducted him was in many ways remarkable. There was a medieval magnificence about it: it suggested a baronial hall of feudal times with its oaken panels, its high ceiling, its vast refectory table where twoscore men could sit down to eat. About the hall were the mounted heads of many animals—lions, tigers, elephants, moose, bears; larger or more perfect specimens Rainsford had never seen. At the great table the general was sitting, alone.

"You'll have a cocktail, Mr. Rainsford," he suggested. The cocktail was surpassingly good; and, Rainsford noted, the table appointments were of the finest, the linen, the crystal, the silver, the china.

They were eating *borsch,* the rich, red soup with sour cream so dear to Russian palates. Half apologetically General Zaroff said: "We do our best to preserve the amenities of civilization here. Please forgive any lapses. We are well off the beaten track, you know. Do you think the champagne has suffered from its long ocean trip?"

"Not in the least," declared Rainsford. He was finding the general a most thoughtful and affable host, a true cosmopolite.[7] But

there was one small trait of the general's that made Rainsford uncomfortable. Whenever he looked up from his plate he found the general studying him, appraising him.

"Perhaps," said General Zaroff, "you were surprised that I recognized your name. You see, I read all books on hunting published in English, French, and Russian. I have but one passion in my life, Mr. Rainsford, and it is the hunt."

"You have some wonderful heads here," said Rainsford as he ate a particularly well cooked filet mignon. "That Cape buffalo is the largest I ever saw."

"Oh, that fellow. Yes, he was a monster."

"Did he charge you?"

"Hurled me against a tree," said the general. "Fractured my skull. But I got the brute."

"I've always thought," said Rainsford, "that the Cape buffalo is the most dangerous of all big game."

For a moment the general did not reply; he was smiling his curious red-lipped smile. Then he said slowly: "No. You are wrong, sir. The Cape buffalo is not the most dangerous big game." He sipped his wine. "Here in my preserve on this island," he said in the same slow tone, "I hunt more dangerous game."

Rainsford expressed his surprise. "Is there big game on this island?"

The general nodded. "The biggest."

"Really?"

"Oh, it isn't here naturally, of course. I have to stock the island."

"What have you imported, General?" Rainsford asked. "Tigers?"

The general smiled. "No," he said. "Hunting tigers ceased to interest me some years ago. I exhausted their possibilities, you see. No thrill left in tigers, no real danger. I live for danger, Mr. Rainsford."

---

7 **cosmopolite** (koz mop′ə līt): a person who has been around and who feels at home in any country.

The general took from his pocket a gold cigarette case and offered his guest a long black cigarette with a silver tip; it was perfumed and gave off a smell like incense.

"We will have some capital hunting, you and I," said the general. "I shall be most glad to have your society."

"But what game——" began Rainsford.

"I'll tell you," said the general. "You will be amused, I know. I think I may say, in all modesty, that I have done a rare thing. I have invented a new sensation. May I pour you another glass of port, Mr. Rainsford?"

"Thank you, General."

The general filled both glasses, and said: "God makes some men poets. Some He makes kings, some beggars. Me He made a hunter. My hand was made for the trigger, my father said. He was a very rich man with a quarter of a million acres in the Crimea, and he was an ardent sportsman. When I was only five years old he gave me a little gun, specially made in Moscow for me, to shoot sparrows with. When I shot some of his prize turkeys with it, he did not punish me; he complimented me on my marksmanship. I killed my first bear in the Caucasus when I was ten. My whole life has been one prolonged hunt. I went into the army—it was expected of noblemen's sons—and for a time commanded a division of Cossack cavalry, but my real interest was always the hunt. I have hunted every kind of game in every land. It would be impossible for me to tell you how many animals I have killed."

The general puffed at his cigarette.

"After the debacle[8] in Russia I left the country, for it was imprudent for an officer of the Czar to stay there. Many noble Russians lost everything. I, luckily, had invested heavily in American securities, so I shall never have to open a tearoom in Monte Carlo or drive a taxi in Paris. Naturally, I continued to hunt—grizzlies in your Rockies, crocodiles in the Ganges, rhinoceroses in East Africa. It was in Africa that the Cape buffalo hit me and laid me up for six months. As soon as I recovered I started for the Amazon to hunt jaguars, for I had heard they were unusually cunning. They weren't." The Cossack sighed. "They were no match at all for a hunter with his wits about him, and a high-powered rifle. I was bitterly disappointed. I was lying in my tent with a splitting headache one night when a terrible thought pushed its way into my mind. Hunting was beginning to bore me! And hunting, remember, had been my life. I have heard that in America businessmen often go to pieces when they give up the business that has been their life."

"Yes, that's so," said Rainsford.

The general smiled. "I had no wish to go to pieces," he said. "I must do something. Now, mine is an analytical mind, Mr. Rainsford. Doubtless that is why I enjoy the problems of the chase."

"No doubt, General Zaroff."

"So," continued the general, "I asked myself why the hunt no longer fascinated me. You are much younger than I am, Mr. Rainsford, and have not hunted as much, but you perhaps can guess the answer."

"What was it?"

"Simply this: hunting had ceased to be what you call 'a sporting proposition.' It had become too easy. I always got my quarry. Always. There is no greater bore than perfection."

The general lit a fresh cigarette.

"No animal had a chance with me any more. That is no boast; it is a mathematical certainty. The animal had nothing but his legs and his instinct. Instinct is no match for

---

8 **debacle** (di bak′ əl): calamity; collapse. (General Zaroff is referring to the Russian Revolution of 1917.)

reason. When I thought of this it was a tragic moment for me, I can tell you."

Rainsford leaned across the table, absorbed in what his host was saying.

"It came to me as an inspiration what I must do," the general went on.

"And that was?"

The general smiled the quiet smile of one who has faced an obstacle and surmounted it with success. "I had to invent a new animal to hunt," he said.

"A new animal? You are joking."

"Not at all," said the general. "I never joke about hunting. I needed a new animal. I found one. So I bought this island, built this house, and here I do my hunting. The island is perfect for my purposes—there are jungles with a maze of trails in them, hills, swamps—"

"But the animal, General Zaroff?"

"Oh," said the general, "it supplies me with the most exciting hunting in the world. No other hunting compares with it for an instant. Every day I hunt, and I never grow bored now, for I have a quarry with which I can match my wits."

Rainsford's bewilderment showed in his face.

"I wanted the ideal animal to hunt," explained the general. "So I said: 'What are the attributes of an ideal quarry?' And the answer was, of course: 'It must have courage, cunning, and, above all, it must be able to reason.'"

"But no animal can reason," objected Rainsford.

"My dear fellow," said the general, "there is one that can."

"But you can't mean——" gasped Rainsford.

"And why not?"

"I can't believe you are serious, General Zaroff. This is a grisly joke."

"Why should I not be serious? I am speaking of hunting."

"Hunting? General Zaroff, what you speak of is murder."

The general laughed with entire good nature. He regarded Rainsford quizzically. "I refuse to believe that so modern and civilized a young man as you seem to be harbors romantic ideas about the value of human life. Surely your experiences in the war——" He stopped.

"Did not make me condone cold-blooded murder," finished Rainsford stiffly.

Laughter shook the general. "How extraordinarily droll you are!" he said. "One does not expect nowadays to find a young man of the educated class, even in America, with such a naive, and, if I may say so, mid-Victorian point of view. It's like finding a snuffbox in a limousine. Ah, well, doubtless you had Puritan ancestors. So many Americans appear to have had. I'll wager you'll forget your notions when you go hunting with me. You've a genuine new thrill in store for you, Mr. Rainsford."

"Thank you, I'm a hunter, not a murderer."

"Dear me," said the general, quite unruffled, "again that unpleasant word. But I think I can show you that your scruples are quite ill-founded."

"Yes?"

"Life is for the strong, to be lived by the strong, and, if needs be, taken by the strong. The weak of the world were put here to give the strong pleasure. I am strong. Why should I not use my gift? If I wish to hunt, why should I not? I hunt the scum of the earth—sailors from tramp ships—lascars, blacks, Chinese, whites, mongrels—a thoroughbred horse or hound is worth more than a score of them."

"But they are men," said Rainsford hotly.

"Precisely," said the general. "That is why I use them. It gives me pleasure. They can reason, after a fashion. So they are dangerous."

"But where do you get them?"

The general's left eyelid fluttered down in a wink. "This island is called Ship-Trap," he answered. "Sometimes an angry god of the high seas sends them to me. Sometimes, when Providence is not so kind, I help Providence a bit. Come to the window with me."

Rainsford went to the window and looked out toward the sea.

"Watch! Out there!" exclaimed the general, pointing into the night. Rainsford's eyes saw only blackness, and then, as the general pressed a button, far out to sea Rainsford saw the flash of lights.

The general chuckled. "They indicate a channel," he said, "where there's none: giant rocks with razor edges crouch like a sea monster with wide-open jaws. They can crush a ship as easily as I crush this nut." He dropped a walnut on the hardwood floor and brought his heel grinding down on it. "Oh, yes," he said casually, as if in answer to a question, "I have electricity. We try to be civilized here."

"Civilized? And you shoot down men?"

A trace of anger was in the general's black eyes, but it was there for but a second, and he said, in his most pleasant manner: "Dear me, what a righteous young man you are! I assure you I do not do the thing you suggest. That would be barbarous. I treat these visitors with every consideration. They get plenty of good food and exercise. They get into splendid physical condition. You shall see for yourself tomorrow."

"What do you mean?"

"We'll visit my training school," smiled the general. "It's in the cellar. I have about a dozen pupils down there now. They're from the Spanish bark *San Lucar* that had the bad luck to go on the rocks out there. A very inferior lot, I regret to say. Poor specimens and more accustomed to the deck than to the jungle."

He raised his hand, and Ivan, who served as waiter, brought thick Turkish coffee. Rainsford, with an effort, held his tongue in check.

"It's a game, you see," pursued the general blandly. "I suggest to one of them that we go hunting. I give him a supply of food and an excellent hunting knife. I give him three hours' start. I am to follow, armed only with a pistol of the smallest caliber and range. If my quarry eludes me for three whole days, he wins the game. If I find him"—the general smiled—"he loses."

"Suppose he refuses to be hunted."

"Oh," said the general, "I give him his option, of course. He need not play that game if he doesn't wish to. If he does not wish to hunt, I turn him over to Ivan. Ivan once had the honor of serving as official knouter[9] to the Great White Czar, and he has his own ideas of sport. Invariably, Mr. Rainsford, invariably they choose the hunt."

"And if they win?"

The smile on the general's face widened. "To date I have not lost," he said.

Then he added, hastily: "I don't wish you to think me a braggart, Mr. Rainsford. Many of them afford only the most elementary sort of problem. Occasionally I strike a tartar.[10] One almost did win. I eventually had to use the dogs."

"The dogs?"

---

9 **knouter** (nout′ ər): one who whips—flogs—prisoners.
10 **tartar** (tär′ tər): a violent, savage person.

"This way, please. I'll show you."

The general steered Rainsford to a window. The lights from the windows sent a flickering illumination that made grotesque patterns on the courtyard below, and Rainsford could see moving about there a dozen or so huge black shapes; as they turned toward him, their eyes glittered greenly.

"A rather good lot, I think," observed the general. "They are let out at seven every night. If anyone should try to get into my house—or out of it—something extremely regrettable would occur to him." He hummed a snatch of song from the Folies Bergère.[11]

"And now," said the general, "I want to show you my new collection of heads. Will you come with me to the library?"

"I hope," said Rainsford, "that you will excuse me tonight, General Zaroff. I'm really not feeling at all well."

"Ah, indeed?" the general inquired solicitously. "Well, I suppose that's only natural, after your long swim. You need a good, restful night's sleep. Tomorrow you'll feel like a new man, I'll wager. Then we'll hunt, eh? I've one rather promising prospect——"

Rainsford was hurrying from the room.

"Sorry you can't go with me tonight," called the general. "I expect rather fair sport—a big, strong black. He looks resourceful— Well, good night, Mr. Rainsford; I hope that you have a good night's rest."

The bed was good and the pajamas of the softest silk, and he was tired in every fiber of his being, but nevertheless Rainsford could not quiet his brain with the opiate of sleep. He lay, eyes wide open. Once he thought he heard stealthy steps in the corridor outside his room. He sought to throw open the door; it would not open. He went to the window and looked out. His room was high up in one of the towers. The lights of the château were out now, and it was dark and silent, but there was a fragment of sallow moon, and by its wan light he could see, dimly, the courtyard; there, weaving in and out in the pattern of shadow, were black, noiseless forms; the hounds heard him at the window and looked up, expectantly, with their green eyes. Rainsford went back to the bed and lay down. By many methods he tried to put himself to sleep. He had achieved a doze when, just as morning began to come, he heard, far off in the jungle, the faint report of a pistol.

General Zaroff did not appear until luncheon. He was dressed faultlessly in the tweeds of a country squire. He was solicitous about the state of Rainsford's health.

"As for me," sighed the general, "I do not feel so well. I am worried, Mr. Rainsford. Last night I detected traces of my old complaint."

To Rainsford's questioning glance the general said: "Ennui. Boredom."

Then, taking a second helping of *crêpes suzette,*[12] the general explained: "The hunting was not good last night. The fellow lost his head. He made a straight trail that offered no problems at all. That's the trouble with these sailors; they have dull brains to begin with, and they do not know how to get about in the woods. They do excessively stupid and obvious things. It's most annoying. Will you have another glass of Chablis, Mr. Rainsford?"

---

11 **Folies Bergère** (fō′ lēz ber jher′): a Paris stage spectacle noted for the beautiful costumes worn by the participants.

12 *crêpes suzette* (krāp sü zet′): thin pancakes rolled in a sauce made from fruit and set ablaze for serving.

"General," said Rainsford firmly, "I wish to leave this island at once."

The general raised his thickets of eyebrows; he seemed hurt. "But, my dear fellow," the general protested, "you've only just come. You've had no hunting——"

"I wish to go today," said Rainsford. He saw the dead black eyes of the general on him, studying him. General Zaroff's face suddenly brightened.

He filled Rainsford's glass with venerable Chablis from a dusty bottle.

"Tonight," said the general, "we will hunt—you and I."

Rainsford shook his head. "No, General," he said. "I will not hunt."

The general shrugged his shoulders and delicately ate a hothouse grape. "As you wish, my friend," he said. "The choice rests entirely with you. But may I not venture to suggest that you will find my idea of sport more diverting than Ivan's?"

He nodded toward the corner to where the giant stood, scowling, his thick arms crossed on his hogshead of chest.

"You don't mean——" cried Rainsford.

"My dear fellow," said the general, "have I not told you I always mean what I say about hunting? This is really an inspiration. I drink to a foeman worthy of my steel—at last."

The general raised his glass, but Rainsford sat staring at him.

"You'll find this game worth playing," the general said enthusiastically. "Your brain against mine. Your woodcraft against mine. Your strength and stamina against mine. Outdoor chess! And the stake is not without value, eh?"

"And if I win——" began Rainsford huskily.

"I'll cheerfully acknowledge myself defeated if I do not find you by midnight of the third day," said General Zaroff. "My sloop will place you on the mainland near a town."

The general read what Rainsford was thinking.

"Oh, you can trust me," said the Cossack. "I will give you my word as a gentleman and a sportsman. Of course you, in turn, must agree to say nothing of your visit here."

"I'll agree to nothing of the kind," said Rainsford.

"Oh," said the general, "in that case— But why discuss it now? Three days hence we can discuss it over a bottle of Veuve Clicquot, unless——"

The general sipped his wine.

Then a businesslike air animated him. "Ivan," he said to Rainsford, "will supply you with hunting clothes, food, a knife. I suggest you wear moccasins; they leave a poorer trail. I suggest too that you avoid the big swamp in the southeast corner of the island. We call it Death Swamp. There's quicksand there. One foolish fellow tried it. The deplorable part of it was that Lazarus followed him. You can imagine my feelings, Mr. Rainsford. I loved Lazarus; he was the finest hound in my pack. Well, I must beg you to excuse me now. I always take a siesta after lunch. You'll hardly have time for a nap, I fear. You'll want to start, no doubt. I shall not follow till dusk. Hunting at night is so much more exciting than by day, don't you think? *Au revoir,*[13] Mr. Rainsford, *au revoir.*"

General Zaroff, with a deep, courtly bow, strolled from the room.

From another door came Ivan. Under one arm he carried khaki hunting clothes, a haversack of food, a leather sheath containing a long-bladed hunting knife; his right hand rested on a cocked revolver thrust in the crimson sash about his waist. . . .

---

13 *Au revior* (ō rə vwär'): farewell until we meet again. (A French term.)

Rainsford had fought his way through the bush for two hours. "I must keep my nerve. I must keep my nerve," he said through tight teeth.

He had not been entirely clear-headed when the château gates snapped shut behind him. His whole idea at first was to put distance between himself and General Zaroff, and, to this end, he had plunged along, spurred on by the sharp rowels[14] of something very like panic. Now he had got a grip on himself, had stopped, and was taking stock of himself and the situation.

He saw that straight flight was futile; inevitably it would bring him face to face with the sea. He was in a picture with a frame of water, and his operations, clearly, must take place within that frame.

"I'll give him a trail to follow," muttered Rainsford, and he struck off from the rude path he had been following into the trackless wilderness. He executed a series of intricate loops; he doubled on his trail again and again, recalling all the lore of the fox hunt, and all the dodges of the fox. Night found him leg-weary, with hands and face lashed by the branches, on a thickly wooded ridge. He knew it would be insane to blunder on through the dark, even if he had the strength. His need for rest was imperative and he thought: "I have played the fox; now I must play the cat of the fable." A big tree with a thick trunk and outspread branches was nearby, and, taking care to leave not the slightest mark, he climbed up into the crotch, and stretching out on one of the broad limbs, after a fashion, rested. Rest brought him new confidence and almost a feeling of security. Even so zealous a hunter as General Zaroff could not trace him there, he told himself;

only the devil himself could follow that complicated trail through the jungle after dark. But, perhaps, the general was a devil—

An apprehensive night crawled slowly by like a wounded snake, and sleep did not visit Rainsford, although the silence of a dead world was on the jungle. Toward morning, when a dingy gray was varnishing the sky, the cry of some startled bird focused Rainsford's attention in that direction. Something was coming through the bush, coming slowly, carefully, coming by the same winding way Rainsford had come. He flattened himself down on the limb, and through a screen of leaves almost as thick as tapestry, he watched. The thing that was approaching him was a man.

It was General Zaroff. He made his way along with his eyes fixed in utmost concentration on the ground before him. He paused, almost beneath the tree, dropped to his knees and studied the ground. Rainsford's impulse was to hurl himself down like a panther, but he saw that the general's right hand held something small and metallic—an automatic pistol.

The hunter shook his head several times, as if he were puzzled. Then he straightened up and took from his case one of his black cigarettes; its pungent incenselike smoke floated up to Rainsford's nostrils. Rainsford held his breath. The general's eyes had left the ground and were traveling inch by inch up the tree. Rainsford froze there, every muscle tensed for a spring. But the sharp eyes of the hunter stopped before they reached the limb where Rainsford lay; a smile spread over his brown face. Very deliberately he blew a smoke ring into the air; then he turned his back on the tree and walked carelessly away, back along the trail he had come. The swish of the underbrush against

---

14 **rowels** (rou′ elz): small wheels with spurs.

his hunting boots grew fainter and fainter.

The pent-up air burst hotly from Rainsford's lungs. His first thought made him feel sick and numb. The general could follow a trail through the woods at night; he could follow an extremely difficult trail; he must have uncanny powers; only by the merest chance had the Cossack failed to see his quarry.

Rainsford's second thought was even more terrible. It sent a shudder of cold horror through his whole being. Why had the general smiled? Why had he turned back?

Rainsford did not want to believe what his reason told him was true, but the truth was as evident as the sun that had by now pushed through the morning mists. The general was playing with him! The general was saving him for another day's sport! The Cossack was the cat; he was the mouse. Then it was that Rainsford knew the full meaning of terror.

"I will not lose my nerve. I will not."

He slid down from the tree, and struck off again into the woods. His face was set and he forced the machinery of his mind to function. Three hundred yards from his hiding place he stopped where a huge dead tree leaned precariously on a smaller, living one. Throwing off his sack of food, Rainsford took his knife from its sheath and began to work with all his energy.

The job was finished at last, and he threw himself down behind a fallen log a hundred feet away. He did not have to wait long. The cat was coming again to play with the mouse.

Following the trail with the sureness of a bloodhound came General Zaroff. Nothing escaped those searching black eyes, no crushed blade of grass, no bent twig, no mark, no matter how faint, in the moss. So intent was the Cossack on his stalking that he was upon the thing Rainsford had made before

he saw it. His foot touched the protruding bough that was the trigger. Even as he touched it, the general sensed his danger and leaped back with the agility of an ape. But he was not quite quick enough; the dead tree, delicately adjusted to rest on the cut living one, crashed down and struck the general a glancing blow on the shoulder as it fell; but for his alertness, he must have been smashed beneath it. He staggered, but he did not fall; nor did he drop his revolver. He stood there, rubbing his injured shoulder, and Rainsford, with fear again gripping his heart, heard the general's mocking laugh ring through the jungle.

"Rainsford," called the general, "if you are within sound of my voice, as I suppose you are, let me congratulate you. Not many men know how to make a Malay man catcher. Luckily for me, I too have hunted in Malacca. You are proving interesting, Mr. Rainsford. I am going now to have my wound dressed; it's only a slight one. But I shall be back. I shall be back."

When the general, nursing his bruised shoulder, had gone, Rainsford took up his flight again. It was flight now, a desperate, hopeless flight, that carried him on for some hours. Dusk came, then darkness, and still he pressed on. The ground grew softer under his moccasins; the vegetation grew ranker, denser; insects bit him savagely. Then, as he stepped forward, his foot sank into the ooze. He tried to wrench it back, but the muck sucked viciously at his foot as if it were a giant leech. With a violent effort, he tore his foot loose. He knew where he was now. Death Swamp and its quicksand.

His hands were tight closed as if his nerve were something tangible that someone in the darkness was trying to tear from his grip. The softness of the earth had given him an idea.

He stepped back from the quicksand a dozen feet or so and, like some huge prehistoric beaver, he began to dig.

Rainsford had dug himself in in France when a second's delay meant death. That had been a placid pastime compared to his digging now. The pit grew deeper; when it was above his shoulders, he climbed out and from some hard saplings cut stakes and sharpened them to a fine point. These stakes he planted in the bottom of the pit with the points sticking up. With flying fingers he wove a rough carpet of weeds and branches and with it he covered the mouth of the pit. Then, wet with sweat and aching with tiredness, he crouched behind the stump of a lightning-charred tree.

He knew his pursuer was coming; he heard the paddling sound of feet on the soft earth, and the night breeze brought him the perfume of the general's cigarette. It seemed to Rainsford that the general was coming with unusual swiftness; he was not feeling his way along, foot by foot. Rainsford, crouching there, could not see the general, nor could he see the pit. He lived a year in a minute. Then he felt an impulse to cry aloud with joy, for he heard the sharp crackle of the breaking branches as the cover of the pit gave way; he heard the sharp scream of pain as the pointed stakes found their mark. He leaped up from his place of concealment. Then he cowered back. Three feet from the pit a man was standing, with an electric torch in his hand.

"You've done well, Rainsford," the voice of the general called. "Your Burmese tiger pit has claimed one of my best dogs. Again you score. I think, Mr. Rainsford, I'll see what you can do against my whole pack. I'm going home for a rest now. Thank you for a most amusing evening."

At daybreak Rainsford, lying near the swamp, was awakened by a sound that made him know that he had new things to learn about fear. It was a distant sound, faint and wavering, but he knew it. It was the baying of a pack of hounds.

Rainsford knew he could do one of two things. He could stay where he was and wait. That was suicide. He could flee. That was postponing the inevitable. For a moment he stood there, thinking. An idea that held a wild chance came to him, and, tightening his belt, he headed away from the swamp.

The baying of the hounds drew nearer, then still nearer, nearer, ever nearer. On a ridge Rainsford climbed a tree. Down a watercourse, not a quarter of a mile away, he could see the bush moving. Straining his eyes, he saw the lean figure of General Zaroff; just ahead of him Rainsford made out another figure whose wide shoulders surged through the tall jungle weeds; it was the giant Ivan, and he seemed pulled forward by some unseen force; Rainsford knew that Ivan must be holding the pack in leash.

They would be on him any minute now. His mind worked frantically. He thought of a native trick he had learned in Uganda. He slid down the tree. He caught hold of a springy young sapling and to it he fastened his hunting knife, with the blade pointing down the trail; with a bit of wild grapevine he tied back the sapling. Then he ran for his life. The hounds raised their voices as they hit the fresh scent. Rainsford knew now how an animal at bay feels.

He had to stop to get his breath. The baying of the hounds stopped abruptly, and Rainsford's heart stopped too. They must have reached the knife.

He shinned excitedly up a tree and looked back. His pursuers had stopped. But the hope that was in Rainsford's brain when he

climbed died, for he saw in the shallow valley that General Zaroff was still on his feet. But Ivan was not. The knife, driven by the recoil of the spring tree, had not wholly failed.

Rainsford had hardly tumbled to the ground when the pack took up the cry again.

"Nerve, nerve, nerve!" he panted, as he dashed along. A blue gap showed between the trees dead ahead. Ever nearer drew the hounds. Rainsford forced himself on toward the gap. He reached it. It was the shore of the sea. Across a cove he could see the gloomy gray stone of the château. Twenty feet below him the sea rumbled and hissed. Rainsford hesitated. He heard the hounds. Then he leaped far out into the sea. . . .

When the general and his pack reached the place by the sea, the Cossack stopped. For some minutes he stood regarding the blue-green expanse of water. He shrugged his shoulders. Then he sat down, took a drink of brandy from a silver flask, lit a perfumed

cigarette, and hummed a bit from "Madame Butterfly."

General Zaroff had an exceedingly good dinner in his great paneled dining hall that evening. With it he had a bottle of Pol Roger and half a bottle of Chambertin. Two slight annoyances kept him from perfect enjoyment. One was the thought that it would be difficult to replace Ivan; the other was that his quarry had escaped him; of course, the American hadn't played the game—so thought the general as he tasted his after-dinner liqueur. In his library he read, to soothe himself, from the works of Marcus Aurelius. At ten he went up to his bedroom. He was deliciously tired, he said to himself, as he locked himself in. There was a little moonlight, so, before turning on his light, he went to the window and looked down at the courtyard. He could see the great hounds, and he called: "Better luck another time," to them. Then he switched on the light.

A man, who had been hiding in the curtains of the bed, was standing there.

"Rainsford!" screamed the general. "How did you get here?"

"Swam," said Rainsford. "I found it quicker than walking through the jungle."

The general sucked in his breath and smiled. "I congratulate you," he said. "You have won the game."

Rainsford did not smile. "I am still a beast at bay," he said, in a low, hoarse voice. "Get ready, General Zaroff."

The general made one of his deepest bows. "I see," he said. "Splendid! One of us is to furnish a repast for the hounds. The other will sleep in this very excellent bed. On guard, Rainsford.". . .

He had never slept in a better bed, Rainsford decided.

Discussion

1. How did Rainsford outwit General Zaroff? How, in your opinion, was it possible for Rainsford to get back to the château and into Zaroff's bedroom without being detected?

2. Why had General Zaroff become bored with hunting? What "new animal" did he invent to keep from being bored? In what sense could the new animal be called "the most dangerous game"?

3. What happened to General Zaroff? How do you know?

4. In outwitting General Zaroff, how did Rainsford reveal unusual courage? In what other situations did Rainsford show himself to be a courageous man?

5. In your opinion, which of the two men—Rainsford or Zaroff—was the smarter, the cleverer? Why?

6. To enjoy a fast-paced story like this one, you need to follow the action closely. Where did the opening incident occur? What connection did that incident have with the rest of the story? How did Rainsford get to Ship-Trap Island? What alarming discoveries did he make in his talks with Zaroff? What tricks did Rainsford use in the jungle to try to outwit Zaroff? Where were the two men just before the story ended?

7. Throughout the story the author develops a feeling of increasing terror. How does the name "Ship-Trap Island" contribute to that feeling? How does Ivan add to that feeling? What other persons, animals, and places in the story contribute to the feeling of terror? Give specific examples from the story.

Vocabulary

When you meet an unfamiliar word while reading, what do you do to find its meaning? Context clues can often help you figure out what that word means. CONTEXT CLUES are hints about a word's meaning given by the surrounding familiar words.

Here is an example from "The Most Dangerous Game": "They were eating *borsch,* the rich, red soup with sour cream . . . " In this case, the words that follow *borsch* state that it is a soup, that it is rich, that it is red, and that it is served with sour cream.

Not all context clues state the meanings of new words that clearly. Look at this example: " . . . Hunting had ceased to be what you call 'a sporting proposition.' It had become too easy. I always got my *quarry.*" In this case, you must analyze and reason to figure out the meaning of the unfamiliar word:

1. *Quarry* is somehow related to hunting.

2. *Always* getting *quarry* makes hunting *too easy* and keeps hunting from being "a sporting proposition." What fits the circumstances that are described?

Analysis and reasoning will tell you that a good synonym is *prey,* the thing being hunted. Notice that context clues can be given either before or after the unfamiliar word.

Below are four sentences from "The Most Dangerous Game." Each one contains an *italicized* word. Use context clues to figure out the meaning of each word. Write your answer on a separate sheet of paper. After each answer, tell whether the context clues state the meaning clearly or require analysis and reasoning.

1. So I said: "What are the *attributes* of an ideal quarry?" And the answer was, of course: "It must have courage, cunning, and, above all, it must be able to reason."

2. Rainsford noted the table *appointments* were of the finest, the linen, the crystal, the silver, the china.

3. He leaped up from his place of concealment. Then he *cowered* back.

4. Rainsford had dug himself in in France when a second's delay meant death. That had been a *placid* pastime compared to his digging now.

Richard Connell 1893–1949

As a boy, Richard Connell covered baseball games, writing for his father's daily newspaper in Poughkeepsie, New York. Connell said, "I was ten years old and got ten cents a game. I have been a professional writer ever since." At sixteen he became city editor. While attending Harvard University, he edited the *Daily Crimson* and the *Lampoon.*

After writing in New York for a few years and serving in France in World War I, Connell lived in London, Paris, and New York. In 1925, he and his writer wife moved to Beverly Hills, California, where he lived and wrote for the rest of his life. Connell published over 300 stories and several novels.

Courage

DUDLEY RANDALL

There are degrees of courage.
One man is not afraid to die.
A second is not afraid to kill.
A third is not afraid to be merciful.

Discussion

1. The first line of the poem could mean that there are three *kinds* of courage. But a closer look at that word *degrees* suggests that there are better synonyms for it than the word *kinds*. What word (or words) would you use? Why?

2. In what ways, do you think, can there be *degrees* of courage? Give some examples.

3. The poet suggests that "to be merciful" is the highest degree of courage. Do you agree or disagree? Why?

Dudley Randall 1914—

Dudley Randall is a well-known Black poet and the founder-editor of a unique publishing company. Broadside Press prints poems on single sheets, like old-fashioned broadside posters, and these are sold individually. Each poem is printed in colors and style appropriate for the subject of the poem. Randall's intent is to present poems as they were written, one at a time, rather than bound into books.

Courage is for everybody! It takes courage to face danger without flinching. It takes courage to venture into the unknown—to try something new. It also takes courage to continue to struggle day after day after day to turn a lifelong dream into a reality. Just look for example, at Mary McLeod Bethune.

Born in South Carolina in 1875, Mary McLeod was the fifteenth child of parents who had once been slaves. Somehow she seemed different from her brothers and sisters. As her mother once said, "She'll go far or break her heart."

To read and learn so that she could serve her people was Mary McLeod's greatest ambition. When she was eleven, a school for Black children opened in Mayesville, South Carolina. By the time she was fourteen, Mary had mastered every subject taught in that little school. With the help of a woman from Denver, Mary won a scholarship to a girls' school in Concord, North Carolina. Because of her determination to continue her education, she managed to enroll at Chicago's Moody Bible Institute, where she was the only Black student. Upon her graduation, Mary returned to Mayesville to teach the Black children of that community.

A born teacher, Mary McLeod now began her struggle to open the doors of educational opportunity to all of her people. This is the story of that struggle.

Mary McLeod Bethune: Woman of Courage

DOROTHY NATHAN

AFTER SEVERAL YEARS of teaching at Haines, Mary moved on to the Kendall Institute in Sumter, North Carolina, where she continued to dream about opening a school of her own. Here she met and married a fellow teacher, Alburtus Bethune. The young couple moved to Savannah, Georgia, where their son Albert was born, and then on to Palatka, Florida.

Except for a short time while Albert was tiny, Mrs. Bethune continued to teach. While she taught, she took steps to make her dream come true. Later she wrote, "When I accumulated a bit of money I was off on an exploring trip, seeking a location where a new school would do the greatest good for the greatest number."

On one of her exploring trips Mrs. Bethune found a community in desperate need of a school: Daytona, Florida. Daytona was a booming vacation city. Wealthy white people were beginning to flock there in wintertime, to enjoy the warm climate and the fine beach. Railroad tracks were going down, and big resort hotels were going up. Hundreds of Negro families were pouring into Daytona, lured by the work on railroad gangs and building crews, in hotel kitchens and wealthy homes. Without training, the children of these people faced lives of the same ugly sort their parents were trapped in.

Alburtus was reluctant to move again, but Mary always did what she set out to do. She tidied up the two-room cottage and fixed some food. She packed clothes for herself and little Albert. And she got her husband to promise that he might come on to Daytona later—if Mary wasn't forced to return home first. Then with all the cash they had on hand—$1.50—she set forth down the road with little Albert to beg a ride to Daytona, seventy miles away.

When they got to Daytona Mrs. Bethune and Albert stayed with a hospitable family while Mary got her bearings. The neighbors she talked to were not encouraging.

"How can you begin to do any good with just one puny school!" they said. "Negroes who forget their place just get into trouble around here."

Mrs. Bethune listened but did not hear. She roamed the Negro section of town, looking for a place for her school. Down at the edge of the city, close to the ocean, next to a dumping ground, she found a ramshackle cottage. The porch floor sagged and the paint was gone, but the building had four rooms downstairs and three above, and it was for rent . . . for eleven dollars a month. . . .

Next Mrs. Bethune, with little Albert tagging along at her side, toured the construction camps looking for pupils. Not too many of these workers were interested in an education for their children, or had the money to spare. But she found five girls, aged eight to twelve, whose parents were willing to pay a tuition fee of fifty cents a week.

Mrs. Bethune spent hours scouring every dump heap in town. She was looking for pieces of lumber, broken furniture, old lamps and washtubs, cracked mirrors—anything that could be used. She knocked at the back doors of white people's houses, begging for anything from pennies to nails. Some people gave her money. Others let her cart off their chipped dishes, torn linens, extra pots.

Everything was cleaned and mended, and Mrs. Bethune repaired and furnished the cottage with these bits and pieces. Later she described it: "I lay awake nights, contriving how to turn peach baskets into chairs. People laughed at my makeshifts. The members of my own race called after me: 'There goes the beggar!' And many white folks gave me their leftovers just to get rid of me."

Mrs. Bethune burned logs and carefully collected charred splinters to use instead of pencils. She never passed a hen house without stopping to collect feathers to use as pens. She made ink by squeezing elderberries. She turned a packing case into a desk for herself, and decorated it with a bit of printed cretonne.[1] "This was all part of the training," she said, "to salvage, to reconstruct, to make bricks without straw."[2]

But even the remarkable Mrs. Bethune could not manage entirely without cash. She found a way to earn money by using a friend's kitchen to bake toothsome batches of sweet-potato pies. She took the fragrant hot pies down to the construction camps and sold them by the slice.

With the girls' help, Mrs. Bethune gathered moss from live-oak trees and stuffed it into sacks to make mattresses. She carefully dusted off her library and laid it out on the packing-case desk. Six books! There was a Bible, a blue-backed speller, a geography book and one on algebra, a songbook and one volume of poetry by John Greenleaf Whittier. This last was a lovely leather-bound edition. Alburtus had given it to her, back in their courting days.

In one month the cottage was ready. The Daytona Educational and Industrial Training School for Negro Girls opened its doors on October 3, 1904. There was a simple ceremony first, before a handful of well-wishers.

"This is a new kind of school," said Mrs. Bethune to her friends. "I am going to teach my girls crafts and home-making. I am going to teach them to earn a living. They will be trained in head, hand, and heart: their heads to think, their hands to work, and their hearts to have faith."

Standing outdoors in front of the cottage, Mrs. Bethune led her five pupils and Albert in the singing of the 23rd Psalm: "The Lord is my Shepherd, I shall not want. . . ."

She offered a brief prayer: "We thank Thee, Lord, for this school building. Let these girls enter to learn; let them depart to serve."

Then the principal and her charges marched inside and Mrs. Bethune settled down to hoe the long, hard row that lay ahead. She had an empty purse, to be sure, but her fund of zeal was so immense no bank could hope to hold it.

Life at school fell into a regular channel: half a day for lessons, half a day for work to keep body and soul together. Mrs. Bethune continued to bake her sweet-potato pies. She rode a patched-up bicycle across the peninsula into the handsome part of town and sold her pies to guests at the resort hotels.

---

1 **cretonne** (krĕ′ ton): unglazed cotton or linen cloth.
2 **make bricks without straw**: a reference to work done by the Israelites when they were in bondage in ancient Egypt.

Mrs. Bethune made friends with some of the resort people. A few of the gentlemen developed the habit of taking a morning stroll down to the hotel entrance. There they would buy a piece of sweet-potato pie and chat with the deep-voiced woman who sold it. She was stout and broad-featured, but there was a shining quality about her that made beauty unimportant. Some white people began to feel it was entirely respectable to be interested in a school for Negro children—especially if the children learned humbleness and service along with a little simple arithmetic and reading.

Mrs. Bethune did not quarrel with their idea. She knew her girls had to learn to cook and serve, because jobs such as these were the only ones open to them when they grew up. But in her heart she was still dreaming—dreaming of the day when people of her race could take their full places in the community. Someday her students would go forth to become business leaders and scientists, statesmen and nurses and doctors, lawyers and teachers, contributing to the community according to their abilities.

A dignified gentleman named James N. Gamble became one of Mrs. Bethune's steadiest pie customers. She often described her school to him. Its main building was called Faith Hall, she said. It contained a library and a chapel as well as schoolrooms and living quarters. "I would like you to become one of the school's trustees," she told him.

One morning just before the end of the winter tourist season, a stately limousine drew up before the school and a chauffeur helped Mr. Gamble step out. He looked around. Faith Hall? A beautifully planted campus? Uniformed students?

What Mr. Gamble saw was an outside shed rigged up near the cottage to serve as a kitchen. Several of the girls were peeling hot sweet potatoes, dropping them into a steaming pot for Mrs. Bethune to mash. One girl was reading aloud from the geography book. Little Albert played quietly under a nearby tree.

Mrs. Bethune took off her apron and walked to greet Mr. Gamble. They looked one another in the eye. "And where is the school of which you want me to be trustee?" Mr. Gamble said sternly.

"In my mind and in my soul," answered Mary Bethune. "I am asking you to be trustee of a glorious dream, trustee of the hope I have in my heart for my people."

There was another moment of silence. Then Mr. Gamble reached for his checkbook. "I'll be back next winter," he said, writing out a check, "and I hope to be present on that day when your Faith Hall is dedicated."

Mrs. Bethune's school grew quickly, and so did her problems. She added grades as she added pupils. In less than two years there were two hundred and fifty pupils and four teachers. Many of the pupils lived at the school. So did the teachers, who were each paid $3.50 a week besides room and board. Many a dinner was nothing more than black-eyed peas and hominy grits. Mrs. Bethune rented another shack next door to her first cottage, but she was in desperate need of space, supplies, and money.

When Mrs. Bethune's shoes wore through, she cut new soles out of cardboard. She trained her girls to sing Negro folk songs and spirituals and sent them out into the community to sing for money. Soon it was fashionable to invite them to sing in white churches, hotels, and private drawing rooms for the entertainment of guests.

Mrs. Bethune redoubled her appeals: "I learned . . . that one of my most important jobs was to be a good beggar! I rang doorbells and tackled cold prospects without a lead. I wrote articles for whoever would print them, distributed leaflets, rode interminable miles of dusty roads on my old bicycle, invaded churches, clubs, lodges, chambers of commerce. If a prospect refused to make a contribution, I would say, 'Thank you for your time.' No matter how deep my hurt, I always smiled. I refused to be discouraged, for neither God nor man can use a discouraged person."

By this time the school offered night classes for adults three times a week. These men and women had daytime jobs as janitors, garbage collectors, cleaning women, and the like. They were often able to bring Mrs. Bethune such treasures as old newspapers, discarded clothes, a sack of corn meal, an abandoned ice-cream freezer. Sometimes they even had money for the school, slipped to them by "the lady of the house," who admired Mrs. Bethune's courage but didn't dare support a Negro school openly.

"I was supposed to keep the balance of the funds for my own pocket, but there never was any balance—only a yawning hole," said Mrs. Bethune. "At last I saw that our only solution was to stop renting space and to buy and build our own college."

Where? Again Mrs. Bethune combed the possible neighborhood from one end to another. Finally she settled on a swampy dumping ground on Oak Street. . . . She located the owner.

"What, you want to buy that dump heap?" he asked.

"I don't see a dump heap!" said Mrs. Bethune. "I see thousands of boys and girls, walking through open doors."

They settled on a price of two hundred dollars, with a down payment of five dollars. "He never knew it, but I didn't have five dollars," Mrs. Bethune wrote later. "I promised to be back in a few days with the initial payment. I raised this sum selling ice-cream and sweet-potato pies to the workmen on construction jobs, and I took the owner his money in small change wrapped in my handkerchief."

Some of the workmen were also friends of Mrs. Bethune's school. In their free time they helped her drain the swamp. They burned all the trash that would burn, and buried the rest. Mrs. Bethune described the way she "hung on to contractors' coattails, begging for loads of sand and secondhand bricks." She went around to carpenters, mechanics, and plasterers, inviting them to parties at the school. They came, ate her delicious desserts, joined in some singing, and then "first thing you know, those men got in the mood to do a bit of work for me, on the spot, free of charge. After a while, those coffee parties of mine became sort of famous."

And so, slowly but surely, a four-story wooden building with an open front porch took shape. As soon as there was a roof over part of it, Mrs. Bethune moved students in. Now and then, whenever she ran out of funds, work stopped until she raised more money. But in two years the building had been "prayed up, sung up, and talked up," and in 1907 Faith Hall officially opened. "Enter to Learn," said a motto over the front entrance. Inside the same door were the words, "Depart to Serve."

With the help of her pupils and one hired man, Mrs. Bethune filled in the rest of the swamp by the school and planted a garden. Soon they had sugar cane and sweet potatoes, snap beans and strawberries. The finest specimens were sold from a wooden roadside stand. People drove miles to this out-of-the-way place to buy succulent fruits and vegetables.

While people bought produce, Mrs. Bethune exercised her talent for persuasion. One tourist from Ridgewood, New Jersey, contributed seventy-five dollars. Mrs. Bethune promptly bought a cow and courteously named it "Ridgewood." A Longmeadow, Massachusetts, lady contributed another cow and it was suitably called "Longmeadow." Soon the school owned a mule and three pigs.

The job of running the school grew until it became impossible for one person to manage everything. At about this time, Mrs. Bethune named one of the four teachers, Mrs. Frances Keyser, as acting principal. This gave Mrs. Bethune time to concentrate on the vital job of finding money.

But Mrs. Bethune continued to keep her own bright eyes on what was going on in the classrooms. The girls could expect her to pop in and out, asking questions that were embarrassing if they hadn't done their homework. And woe to the pupil who walked past a scrap of paper. Mrs. Bethune would materialize out of nowhere and say, "How can you pass litter without picking it up! Don't be lazy!"

Mrs. Bethune inspected rooms regularly, to see that beds were made, closets neat, and girls themselves well washed and tidy. She had a habit of tacking up her handwritten mottoes on schoolroom walls. "Blessed is he that readeth," they would say, or "Speak softly, save your voice for songs of praise."

Everybody cleaned, sewed, learned to bake bread, prepare and serve delicious food, and sing. The singing was so successful in raising money for the school that Mrs. Bethune often took her neatly uniformed group on singing tours in the North.

Now the school's curriculum ran through high school. It was turning out graduates trained for homemaking, teaching, and nursing. But Faith Hall was full to overflowing almost as soon as it was built. Another building was urgently needed.

As usual, Mrs. Bethune found the money. A large brick building went up. It was called White Hall because most of the money for it was given by a man named Thomas H. White. . . .

During the same period, Mrs. Bethune found time to sponsor various other projects. One day, at school, she was called to the bedside of a student weeping with pain. The young Negro doctor who came hurrying over said, "She has acute appendicitis. She needs an immediate operation."

There was no hospital in Daytona Beach where Negro doctors could operate or Negro patients could recover. Mrs. Bethune hurried to a white surgeon and begged him to help her sick youngster. Moved by her desperate pleading, the doctor agreed.

But when Mrs. Bethune visited the girl in the hospital the next day, she found Clara lying on a drafty back-porch cot. It was hard for her to recover from the operation when she felt sickened by smells from the adjoining kitchen.

This was a call to action for Mrs. Bethune. She located another cottage to buy. She figured up costs for an operating table, instruments, two beds, sheets, blankets—five thousand dollars would do it. As usual, her pleading letters went out across the country, written to everybody she could think of. In a month she had the money, and in two months the tiny two-bed hospital stood ready to serve. She named it McLeod Hospital, to honor her now-dead father.

The day McLeod Hospital opened, Mary Bethune allowed herself one very special luxury: She sent a railroad ticket to her mother. Old Patsy McLeod had never been on a train, had never set eyes on her grandson Albert, had never seen Faith Hall, with its trim grounds and abundant gardens. Now she came to enjoy these pleasures. She saw her daughter Mary, loved and respected, guiding the lives of hundreds of energetic, hopeful young people. . . .

Mrs. Bethune knew that Negroes must vote if they were to take their full places in the community, . . . and so she moved stanchly forward in her fight to get her people to the polls. She held night classes in civics. She rode her old bicycle up and down the streets of the colored quarter, urging citizens to pay their poll tax.[3] By prodding and lecturing, begging and praying, she managed to get almost a hundred Negro citizens in Volusia County registered to vote. Eleven of them were teachers from her own school, for "the Susan B. Anthony amendment," allowing women to vote, had just been added to the law of the land. . . .

In 1923 Mrs. Bethune's school merged with a men's college, Cookman Institute, operated by the Methodist Episcopal Church. Mrs. Bethune remained as president of the new Bethune-Cookman Junior College with its 600 students, 32 teachers, and 14 buildings on 32 acres of campus.

She was nearing fifty, an age when most people begin to slow up. But Mrs. Bethune was never like most people. She lived to be almost eighty, and her last thirty years were busier, if possible, than her first half a century.

Mrs. Bethune often worked until midnight, and then called her secretary again at four o'clock in the morning. Once, when Mrs. Bethune was over seventy, a sculptor named Ruth Brall was trying to sketch her. Mrs. Brall complained that she lost ten pounds whisking around after her subject. Finally she had to say, "Please, Mrs. Bethune. I can work all day, or all night; I can't do both."

Mrs. Bethune was in great demand as a speaker. One year she talked at more than five hundred meetings in forty states. She was an imposing figure with her white hair, her majestic bulk, and the heavy cane she always carried "for swank." But it was her message that people came to hear, her eloquence as she asked the country to "let my people go."

"In order to know which way a tree is growing," she said, "we must watch its upper branches: those of the race who have accomplished something and are leaders. The race should be judged by that group rather than the masses who have not had their chance to develop."

Wherever she went, Mrs. Bethune told her own people, "Walk proudly in the light! Faith ought not to be a puny thing. If we believe, we should believe like giants." Young people adored her, and she became known as "the First Lady" of her race.

She was a close friend of another "First Lady," Mrs. Eleanor Roosevelt. President Franklin Delano Roosevelt often made use of Mrs. Bethune's wisdom and knowledge. He named her Director of Negro Affairs when he established a National Youth Administration to help young people find employment during the severe business depression of the 1930s. He appointed her Special Civilian Assistant when he set up the first United States Women's Army Corps during World War II. She was a frequent visitor to the

---

3 **poll tax** (pōl′ taks): a tax, usually of a modest sum, levied on every person—usually only the male citizens in a community—over 21. In many communities one was obliged to pay the poll tax before he could vote. Such use of a poll tax is now illegal throughout the United States.

White House. President Roosevelt said he was always glad to see Mrs. Bethune because she never asked anything for herself.

Mrs. Bethune told her friends, "I never walk through the White House door without wondering how all this happened to a child from the cotton fields."

All her life, wherever she went, Mrs. Bethune insisted on her rights as a human being. Often, traveling around the country, she would run into restaurant owners who would not serve her, elevator men who would not let her ride, train conductors who would rudely say, "Gimme your ticket, Auntie!" Mrs. Bethune would smile and ask, "And which one of my sister's children are you?". . .

When the first meeting of the United Nations was held in San Francisco in April of 1945, Mrs. Bethune was present. She was deeply interested in this newly forming organization with its determination "to reaffirm faith in fundamental human rights, in the dignity and worth of the human person, in the equal rights of men and women and of nations large and small."

In all her life's work Mrs. Bethune had been part of the progress of the Negro race. She was delighted to be able to say now, "I have come to the point where I can embrace all humanity—not just the people of my race or another race. I just love people."

The recently widowed Mrs. Eleanor Roosevelt was at the United Nations meeting, too. She gave Mrs. Bethune one of President Roosevelt's canes, as a memento of their long, warm friendship.

Mrs. Bethune used this cane until the day she died. It was in her hand one hot morning in 1950 when she walked slowly down the dirt road in Mayesville, South Carolina. She had returned to her old home town for one last look around.

Many things were changed. There was not a trace of the cabin her father had built. All the faces were different in the sharecroppers' shanties. But down at the end of the road, next to the railroad tracks, Miss Wilson's old school was still standing. It was pitifully shabby. It was still—sixty years later—the only school open to the Negro children of Mayesville.

But, by God's gift, the aged, ailing Mrs. Bethune lived long enough to know that Miss Wilson's old school would not need to stand much longer. On May 17, 1954, the Supreme Court of the United States ruled that Negro children and white children across the nation must be allowed to go to school together.

And so, when Mary McLeod Bethune's heart stopped beating on May 18, 1955, she died in the peace of a dream that would soon be real: "There is no such thing as Negro education—only education. I want my people to prepare themselves bravely for life, not because they are Negroes, but because they are men."

Discussion

1. What was Mary McLeod Bethune's lifelong dream?

2. To turn her dream into reality, Mary McLeod Bethune had to overcome a number of obstacles—large and small. What, in your judgment, were the three chief obstacles she had to overcome?

3. In what ways did Mrs. Bethune earn money for her school?

4. Mrs. Bethune's first school in Daytona was in a rented "ramshackle" cottage. What did she hope to teach the students at this school? What motto served as a guide for all of Mrs. Bethune's students—those in later years, as well as those in the early years? What does the motto mean? How important do you think it is?

5. How did Mr. Gamble help Mrs. Bethune realize her dream? How did others help?

6. In the construction of Faith Hall, Mrs. Bethune remarked that the building had been "prayed up, sung up, and talked up." What does she mean?

7. In her later years, what important projects besides education was Mrs. Bethune involved in?

8. Sixty years after Mary McLeod Bethune taught in the little school in Mayesville, South Carolina, it was still the only school in the town open to Black children. What happened in 1954 to change that situation?

CONTEXT CLUES are familiar words or details in writing that either state clearly or give hints about the meaning of an unfamiliar word. For example, in "Mary McLeod Bethune" you read this sentence: "I lay awake nights, *contriving* how to turn peach baskets into chairs." That sentence gives you two clues to the meaning of *contriving:* 1. "Turning peach baskets into chairs" tells you that Mrs. Bethune was inventive to think of converting cheap objects into a substitute for expensive ones. 2. "I lay awake nights" tells you that she was carefully planning to solve her problem. Together, these clues show that Mrs. Bethune was figuring out an original scheme or plan, and that is what *contriving* means: "planning in an inventive, clever way."

In each group of words below, condensed from "Mary McLeod Bethune," context clues can give you a good idea of the meaning of the *italicized* word. On a separate sheet of paper, write the meaning that the context clues point to. Then, after each answer list the context clue or clues that helped you choose that meaning.

1. She found a *ramshackle* cottage. The porch floor sagged and the paint was gone. The cottage was falling to pieces.

2. Not too many of these workers were interested in education, or had the money to spare. But she found five girls whose parents were willing to pay a *tuition* fee of fifty cents a week.

3. They settled on a down payment of five dollars. Mrs. Bethune wrote later: "I promised to be back in a few days with the *initial* payment."

4. She was an *imposing* figure with her white hair, her majestc bulk, and the heavy cane she always carried "for swank."

5. "Walk proudly in the light. Faith ought not to be a *puny* thing. If we believe, we should believe like giants."

Dorothy Nathan

Dorothy Nathan was born in a small town near Portland, Oregon. She received an education degree from the University of California. After teaching for several years, she worked in a social agency. She raised three children and began writing when her children went to college. In 1964, she published *Women of Courage.*

The Courage That My Mother Had

EDNA ST. VINCENT MILLAY

The courage that my mother had
Went with her, and is with her still:
Rock from New England quarried,
Now granite in a granite hill.

The golden brooch my mother wore   5
She left behind for me to wear;
I have no thing I treasure more:
Yet, it is something I could spare.

Oh, if instead she'd left to me
The thing she took into the grave!—   10
That courage like a rock, which she
Has no more need of, and I have.

1. In the first stanza, the speaker in the poem explains that her mother, who had died, took something with her. What is it? Yet in the second stanza, the speaker points out that her mother had left something behind. What is that?

2. How does the speaker feel about what was taken and what was left behind? Why?

3. The poem speaks of courage as if it were a rock. In what ways is courage like a rock?

Edna St. Vincent Millay 1892—1950

Edna St. Vincent Millay first became famous when she was part of the New York City Greenwich Village scene in the 1920s. It was a time when many young writers and artists were, as she said, "very, very poor and very, very merry." Millay was recognized as the voice of youth, determined to burn their candles at both ends. Her poems shocked older people, but people her own age identified with her daring verses about liberated women.

Even though her fame declined, Millay continued to write sonnets and other poems from her homes in the Berkshires of New York and her native Maine.

You'd think that anybody with any sense would hesitate a good long time before picking a fight with someone nine feet tall! But could it be that a lowly shepherd boy from Bethlehem—David was his name—knew something that the giant Goliath didn't know?

David and Goliath

1 SAMUEL: 17

THE PHILISTINES gathered for battle in Socoh, a town in Judah; they camped at a place called Ephes Dammim, between Socoh and Azekah. Saul and the Israelites assembled and camped in Elah Valley, where they got ready to fight the Philistines. The Philistines lined up on one hill and the Israelites on another, with a valley between them.

A man named Goliath, from the city of Gath, came out from the Philistine camp to challenge the Israelites. He was over nine feet tall and wore bronze armor that weighed about 125 pounds and a bronze helmet. His legs were also protected by bronze armor, and he carried a bronze javelin slung over his shoulder. His spear was as thick as the bar on a weaver's loom, and its iron head weighed about fifteen pounds. A soldier walked in front of him carrying his shield. Goliath stood and shouted at the Israelites, "What are you doing there, lined up for battle? I am a Philistine, you slaves of Saul! Choose one of your men to fight me. If he wins and kills me, we will be your slaves; but if I win and kill

him, you will be our slaves. Here and now I challenge the Israelite army. I dare you to pick someone to fight me!" When Saul and his men heard this, they were terrified.

David was the son of Jesse, who was an Ephrathite from Bethlehem in Judah. Jesse had eight sons, and at the time Saul was king, he was already a very old man. His three oldest sons had gone with Saul to war. The oldest was Eliab, the next was Abinadab, and the third was Shammah. David was the youngest son, and while the three oldest brothers stayed with Saul, David would go back to Bethlehem from time to time, to take care of his father's sheep.

Goliath challenged the Israelites every morning and evening for forty days.

One day Jesse said to David, "Take a half-bushel of this roasted grain and these ten loaves of bread and hurry with them to your brothers in the camp. And take these ten cheeses to the commanding officer. Find out how your brothers are getting along and bring back something to show that you saw them and that they are well. King Saul, your brothers, and all the other Israelites are in Elah Valley fighting the Philistines."

David got up early the next morning, left someone else in charge of the sheep, took the food, and went as Jesse had told him to. He arrived at the camp just as the Israelites were going out to their battle line, shouting the war cry. The Philistine and the Israelite armies took positions for battle, facing each other. David left the food with the officer in charge of the supplies, ran to the battle line, went to his brothers, and asked how they were getting along. As he was talking with them, Goliath came forward and challenged the Israelites as he had done before. And David heard him. When the Israelites saw Goliath, they ran away in terror. "Look at him!" they said to each other. "Listen to his challenge! King Saul has promised to give a big reward to the man who kills him; the king will also give him his daughter to marry and will not require his father's family to pay taxes."

David asked the men who were near him, "What will the man get who kills this Philistine and frees Israel from this disgrace? After all, who is this heathen Philistine to defy the army of the living God?" They told him what would be done for the man who killed Goliath.

Eliab, David's oldest brother, heard David talking to the men. He became angry with David and said, "What are you doing here? Who is taking care of those sheep of yours out there in the wilderness? You smart aleck, you! You just came to watch the fighting!"

"Now what have I done?" David asked. "Can't I even ask a question?" He turned to another man and asked him the same question, and every time he asked, he got the same answer.

Some men heard what David had said, and they told Saul, who sent for him. David said to Saul, "Your Majesty, no one should be afraid of this Philistine! I will go and fight him."

"No," answered Saul. "How could you fight him? You're just a boy, and he has been a soldier all his life!"

"Your Majesty," David said, "I take care of my father's sheep. Any time a lion or a bear carries off a lamb, I go after it, attack it, and rescue the lamb. And if the lion or bear turns on me, I grab it by the throat and beat it to death. I have killed lions and bears, and I will do the same to this heathen Philistine, who has defied the army of the living God. The Lord has saved me from lions and bears; he will save me from this Philistine."

"All right," Saul answered. "Go, and the Lord be with you." He gave his own armor to David for him to wear: a bronze helmet, which he put on David's head, and a coat of armor. David strapped Saul's sword over the armor and tried to walk, but he couldn't, because he wasn't used to wearing them. "I can't fight with all this," he said to Saul. "I'm not used to it." So he took it all off. He took his shepherd's stick and then picked up five smooth stones from the stream and put them in his bag. With his sling ready, he went out to meet Goliath.

The Philistine started walking toward David, with his shield bearer walking in front of him. He kept coming closer, and when he got a good look at David, he was filled with scorn for him because he was just a nice, good-looking boy. He said to David, "What's that stick for? Do you think I'm a dog?" And he called down curses from his god on David. "Come on," he challenged David, "and I will give your body to the birds and animals to eat."

David answered, "You are coming against

me with sword, spear, and javelin, but I come against you in the name of the Lord Almighty, the God of the Israelite armies, which you have defied. This very day the Lord will put you in my power; I will defeat you and cut off your head. And I will give the bodies of the Philistine soldiers to the birds and animals to eat. Then the whole world will know that Israel has a God, and everyone here will see that the Lord does not need swords or spears to save his people. He is victorious in battle, and he will put all of you in our power."

Goliath started walking toward David again, and David ran quickly toward the Philistine battle line to fight him. He reached into his bag and took out a stone, which he slung at Goliath. It hit him on the forehead and broke his skull, and Goliath fell face downward on the ground. And so, without a sword, David defeated and killed Goliath with a sling and a stone! He ran to him, stood over him, took Goliath's sword out of its sheath, and cut off his head and killed him.

When the Philistines saw that their hero was dead, they ran away. The men of Israel and Judah shouted and ran after them, pursuing them all the way to Gath and to the gates of Ekron. The Philistines fell wounded all along the road that leads to Shaaraim, as far as Gath and Ekron. When the Israelites came back from pursuing the Philistines, they looted their camp. David got Goliath's head and took it to Jerusalem, but he kept Goliath's weapons in his own tent.

When Saul saw David going out to fight Goliath, he asked Abner, the commander of his army, "Abner, whose son is he?"

"I have no idea, Your Majesty," Abner answered.

"Then go and find out," Saul ordered.

So when David returned to camp after killing Goliath, Abner took him to Saul. David was still carrying Goliath's head. Saul asked him, "Young man, whose son are you?"

"I am the son of your servant Jesse from Bethlehem," David answered.

Discussion

1. In what way was David's preparation for battle different from Goliath's.

2. How was Goliath armed for battle?

3. How do you explain David's victory over Goliath?

4. What specific lines from the narrative give evidence of David's faith—faith in God and in himself? How does having faith give a person strength?

Composition

1. In your own words, describe the fight between David and Goliath. Describe the action as if you were relating the story to someone who has never heard it before. Keep your account brief. Do not be concerned with what David said of Goliath or with what happened before their encounter. Tell only about the fight itself.

2. How much courage does it take for a person to speak up for what he or she thinks is right? In a paragraph or two, tell about an incident in which someone does just that. The incident might involve yourself or somebody you know, or it might be one you make up. In your account:

—briefly describe the situation
—tell what the person does
—tell what happens as a result
—point out why the person's action does or does not take courage.

Vocabulary

Writings from a long time ago sometimes seem difficult for us to understand. Such writings often contain unfamiliar vocabulary, long sentences, and unusual arrangements of words within sentences. When reading a selection that presents such problems, you should read slowly and look for ways to PARAPHRASE each sentence that gives you trouble. To paraphrase means to "restate in your own words."

A. Here are two sentences from "David and Goliath" that have already been paraphrased for you. Read each one carefully. Then turn back to the selection and find the original version of each sentence. On a separate sheet of paper, copy each sentence as it was first written.

1. Goliath, a Philistine from Gath, was a warrior who stood about nine feet, nine inches tall.

2. If I win the fight, the people of Israel will be our slaves. But if your warrior wins, the Philistines will become the slaves of Israel.

B. Paraphrase each sentence below. Use the glossary or a dictionary to find definitions of unfamiliar words.

1. David was the youngest son, and while the three oldest brothers stayed with Saul, David would go back to Bethlehem from time to time, to take care of his father's sheep.

2. David left the food with the officer in charge of the supplies, ran to the battle line, went to his brothers, and asked how they were getting along.

3. He kept coming closer, and when he got a good look at David, he was filled with scorn for him because he was just a nice, good-looking boy.

4. David answered, "You are coming against me with sword, spear, and javelin, but I come against you in the name of the Lord Almighty, the God of the Israelite armies. . . .

If, as the saying goes, "hope springs eternal,"
does it also give you courage?

Hope

EMILY DICKINSON

Hope is the thing with feathers
That perches in the soul,
And sings the tune without the words,
And never stops at all,

And sweetest in the gale is heard;   5
And sore must be the storm
That could abash[1] the little bird
That kept so many warm.

I've heard it in the chillest land,
And on the strangest sea;   10
Yet, never, in extremity,
It asked a crumb of me.

---

1 **abash** (ə bash′): shame.

1. The speaker compares hope to what living creature?
2. How is hope like the creature it is compared to? How can hope keep a person warm?
3. How is it possible for hope to sing "sweetest in the gale"?
4. According to the poet, what does hope ask in return for the encouragement it brings?

Emily Dickinson 1830—1886

In Amherst, Massachusetts, where she spent her life, Emily Dickinson was considered an oddity. She was well-educated but rather nonconforming as a pupil. As a young girl, she was social and well-liked. In her twenties, however, she changed into a recluse who dressed only in white and secretly wrote more than seventeen hundred poems.

She wrote many short poems, often on small scraps of paper, and kept them hidden. She did allow a few poems to be published while she lived, but most were printed after her death.

They were but three small vessels alone on an endless, uncharted sea. Yet they were not doomed; they were not lost. Westward, ever westward, lay their course. An adventure into the unknown? Yes, it was that. But even more, it was an adventure in courage!

First Crossing of the Atlantic

SAMUEL ELIOT MORISON

B Y THE SECOND day of August, 1492, everything at last was ready. That night every man and boy of the fleet confessed his sins, received absolution, and made his communion at the church of Palos, which by happy coincidence was dedicated to Saint George, patron saint of Genoa. Columbus went on board his flagship in the small hours of Friday the third and gave the signal to get under way. Before the sun rose, all three vessels had anchors aweigh, and with sails hanging limp from their yards were floating down the Rio Tinto on the morning ebb, using their long sweeps to maintain steerageway.[1] As they swung into the Saltés and passed La Rábida close aboard, they could hear the friars chanting the ancient hymn *Iam lucis orto sidere*[2] with its haunting refrain *Et nunc et in perpetuum*,[3] which we render "Evermore and evermore. . . ."

Columbus's plan for the voyage was simple, and its simplicity insured his success. Not for him the boisterous head winds, the monstrous seas and the dark, unbridled waters of the North Atlantic, which had already baffled so many Portuguese. He would run south before the prevailing northerlies[4] to the Canary Islands, and there make, as it were, a right-angle turn; for he had observed on his African voyages that the winter winds in the latitude of the Canaries blew from the east, and that the ocean around them, more often than not, was calm as a millpond. An even better reason to take his departure from the Canaries was their position astride latitude 28 degrees North, which, he believed, cut Japan, passing en route the mythical Isle of Antilia,[5] which would make a good break in the westward passage. Until about a hundred years ago when chronometers became generally available to find longitude, sailors always tried to find the latitude of their destination

---

1 **using** . . . **steerageway**: using long oars to give the ships sufficient speed for easy steering.
2 *Iam lucis orto sidere*: a Latin phrase meaning "the stars of light already rising."
3 *Et nunc et in perpetuum*: a Latin phrase meaning "Now and forever."

Abridged from Chapter VI of CHRISTOPHER COLUMBUS by Samuel Eliot Morison.

---

4 **northerlies**: winds blowing from the north.
5 **mythical** . . . **Antilia**: fabled land that Europeans once believed was located in the unknown West.

and then would "run their westing" (or easting) down until they hit it. That is what Columbus proposed to do with respect to Japan, which he had figured out to be only 2400 nautical miles due west of the Canaries.

The first leg of the voyage was made in less than a week. Then, within sight of the Grand Canary, the fleet ran into a calm that lasted two or three days. Columbus decided to send *Pinta* into Las Palmas for some needed repairs while *Santa María* and *Niña* went to Gomera, westernmost of the Canaries that the Spaniards had wrested from their native inhabitants. At Gomera the Captain General (as we should call Columbus on this voyage before he made Admiral) sent men ashore to fill extra water casks, buy breadstuffs and cheese, and put a supply of native beef in pickle. He then sailed to Las Palmas to superintend *Pinta's* repairs and returned with her to Gomera.

On September 2 all three ships were anchored off San Sebastián, the port of that island. Columbus then met for the first time Doña Beatriz de Bobadilla, widow of the former captain of the island. Beatriz was a beautiful lady still under thirty, and Columbus is said to have fallen in love with her; but if that is true, he did not love her warmly enough to tarry to the next full moon. Additional ship's stores were quickly hoisted on board and struck below, and on September 6, 1492, the fleet weighed anchor for the last time in the Old World. They had still another island to pass, the lofty Ferro or Hierro. Owing to calms and variables[6] Ferro and the 12,000-foot peak of Tenerife were in sight until the ninth, but by nightfall that day, every trace of land had sunk below the eastern horizon, and the three vessels were alone on an uncharted ocean. Columbus himself gave out the course: "West; nothing to the north, nothing to the south."

Before going into the details of the voyage, let us see how those vessels were navigated, and how a day was passed at sea. Celestial navigation[7] was then in its infancy, but rough estimates of latitude could be made from the height of the North Star above the horizon and its relation to the two outer stars (the "Guards") of the Little Dipper. A meridian altitude[8] of the sun, applied to available tables of the sun's declination, also gave latitude, by a simple formula. But the instruments of observation—a solid wood or brass quadrant and the seaman's astrolabe—were so crude, and the movement of a ship threw them off to such an extent, that most navigators took their latitude sights ashore. Columbus relied almost completely on "dead reckoning," which means plotting your course and position on a chart from the three elements of direction, time and distance.

The direction he had from one or more compasses which were similar to those used in small craft until recently—a circular card graduated to the 32 points (N, N by E, NNE, NE by N, NE, and so on), with a lodestone[9] under the north point, mounted on a pin and enclosed in a binnacle with gimbals[10] so it could swing freely with the motion of the ship. Columbus's standard compass was mounted on the poop deck where the officer of the watch could see it. The helmsman, who steered with a heavy tiller attached

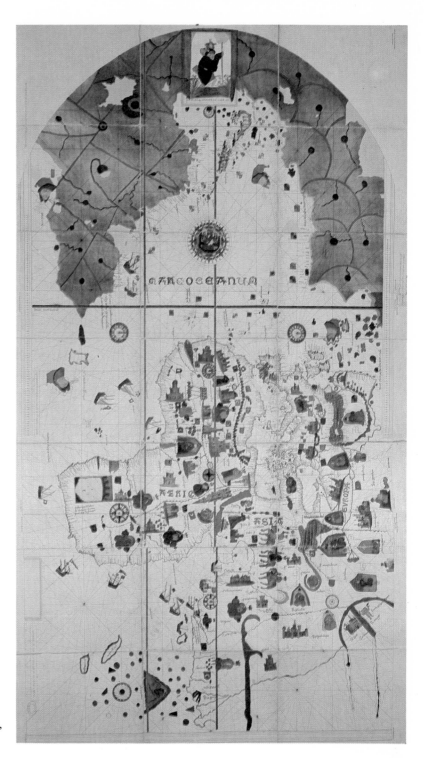

A map of the world
by Juan de la Cosa,
pilot-navigator on Columbus' ship,
the *Nina*.

directly to the rudder head, was below decks and could see very little. He may have had another compass to steer by, but in the smaller vessels, at least, he was conned[11] by the officer of the deck and kept a steady course by the feel of the helm. On a sailing vessel you can do that; it would be impossible in any power craft.

Time on the vessels of that day was measured by a half-hour glass which hung from a beam so the sand could flow freely from the upper to the lower half. As soon as the sand was all down, a ship's boy turned the glass and the officer of the deck recorded it by making a stroke on a slate. Eight glasses made a watch; the modern ship's bells were originally a means of marking the glasses. This half-hour-glass time could be corrected daily in fair weather by noting the moment when the sun lay due south, which was local noon.

Distance was the most variable of these three elements. Columbus had no ship log or other method of measuring the speed of his vessels. He and the watch officers merely estimated it and noted it down. By carefully checking Columbus's Journal of his First Voyage, Captain J. W. McElroy ascertained that he made an average 9 per cent overestimate of his distance. This did not prevent his finding the way home, because the mistake was constant, and time and course were correct. It only resulted in Columbus placing the islands of his discovery farther west than they really were.

Even after making the proper reduction for this overestimate, the speed of his vessels is surprising. Ships of that day were expected to make 3 to 5 knots[12] in a light breeze, up to

9 1/2 in a strong, fair gale, and at times to be capable of 12 knots. In October 1492, on the outward passage, the Columbus fleet made an average of 142 miles per day for five consecutive days, and the best day's run, 182 miles, averaged 8 knots. On the homeward passage, in February 1493, *Niña* and *Pinta* covered 198 miles one day, and at times hit it up to 11 knots. Any yachtsman today would be proud to make the records that the great Admiral did on some of his transatlantic crossings in the 15th century. Improvements in sailing vessels since 1492 have been more in seaworthiness and comfort than in speed.

One reason Columbus always wanted two or more vessels was to have someone to rescue survivors in case of sinking. But he made an unusual record for that era by never losing a ship at sea, unless we count the *Santa María*, grounded without loss of life. Comforts and conveniences were almost totally lacking. Cooking was done on deck over a bed of sand in a wooden firebox protected from the wind by a hood. The diet was a monotonous one of salt meat, hardtack and dried peas. For drink they had wine, while it lasted, and water in casks, which often went bad. Only the Captain General and the ships' captains had cabins with bunks; the others slept where they could, in their clothes. . . .

On September 9, the day he dropped the last land below the horizon, Columbus decided to keep a true reckoning of his course for his own use and a false one to give out to the people, so that they would not be frightened at sailing so far from land. But, owing to his overestimate of speed, the "false" reckoning was more nearly correct than the "true"!

During the first ten days (September 9 to 18), the easterly trade wind blew steadily, and the fleet made 1163 nautical miles westing. This was the honeymoon of the voyage.

---

11 **conned:** directed.
12 **knots:** A knot is a measure of speed; it is equal to moving one nautical mile (6080 feet) per hour, or about 1.85 kilometers per hour.

Que era plazer grande el gusto de las mañanas— "What a delight was the savor of the mornings!" wrote Columbus in his Journal. That entry speaks to the heart of anyone who has sailed in the trades; it recalls the beauty of the dawn, kindling clouds and sails' rose color, the smell of dew drying on a wooden deck, and, something Columbus didn't have, the first cup of coffee. Since his ships were at the northern edge of the northeast trades, where the wind first strikes the water, the sea was smooth, and the air, remarked the Captain General in his Journal, was "like April in Andalusia; the only thing wanting was to hear the song of the nightingale." But there were plenty of other birds following the ships: the little Mother Carey's chickens, dabbling for plankton in the bow waves and wakes; the boatswain bird, so called (as old seamen used to say) because it carries a marlinspike in its tail; the man-of-war or frigate bird, "thou ship of the air that never furl'st thy sails," as Walt Whitman[13] wrote; and when the fleet passed beyond the range of these birds, the big Jaeger gulls gave it a call. During this period the fleet encountered its first field of sargassum or gulfweed and found that it was no hindrance to navigation. "Saw plenty weed" was an almost daily notation in the Captain General's log. The gulfweed bothered him much less than observing a westerly variation of the compass,[14] for in European waters the variation is always easterly.

On September 19, only ten days out from Ferro, the fleet temporarily ran into an area of variable winds and rain. It was near the point on Columbus's chart where the fabled island of Antilia should have been, and all hands expected to sight land. The Captain General even had the deep-sea lead hove,[15] and found no bottom at 200 fathoms;[16] no wonder, since the ocean is about 2300 fathoms deep at the point he had reached. But the seamen who, on the tenth day of the northeast trades, were beginning to wonder whether they could ever beat back home were cheered by the change of wind.

During the next five days only 234 miles were made good. During this spell of moderate weather it was easy to converse from ship to ship and to talk about this or that island, St. Brendan's or Antilia, which they might pick up. In the middle of one of these colloquies,[17] a seaman of *Pinta* gave the "Land Ho!" and everyone thought he saw an island against the setting sun. Columbus fell on his knees to thank God, ordered *Gloria in excelsis Deo* to be sung by all hands, and set a course for the island. But at dawn no island was visible; there was none. It was simply a cloud bank above the western horizon resembling land, a common phenomenon at sea. Martín Alonso Pinzón apparently wished to beat about and search for this island, but Columbus refused, because, he said, "his object was to reach the Indies, and if he delayed, it would not have made sense."

The trade wind now returned, but moderately, and during the six days September 26 to October 1, the fleet made only 382 miles. Under these circumstances the people began to mutter and grumble. Three weeks was probably more than they had ever been

---

13 **Walt Whitman:** American poet who lived from 1819 to 1892.
14 **westerly variation of the compass:** a reference to a compass error resulting from that difference between the magnetic North Pole and the true North Pole.

15 **deep-sea lead** (led) **hove:** deep-sea weight thrown overboard to measure depth.
16 **200 fathoms:** one fathom equals 6 feet; thus 200 fathoms is 1200 feet deep.
17 **colloquies** (kol′ e kwēz): conversations.

outside sight of land before. They were all getting on each other's nerves, as happens even nowadays on a long voyage to a known destination. There was nothing for the men to do in the light wind except to follow the ship's routine, and troll for fish. Grievances, real or imaginary, were blown up; cliques[18] were formed; Spain was farther away every minute, and what lay ahead? Probably nothing, except in the eye of that cursed Genoese. Let's make him turn back, or throw him overboard!

On the first day of October the wind increased, and in five days (October 2 to 6) the fleet made 710 miles. On the sixth, when they had passed longitude 65 degrees West and actually lay directly north of Puerto Rico, Martín Alonso Pinzón shot his agile *Pinta* under the flagship's stern and shouted, "Alter course, sir, to southwest by west . . . Japan!" Columbus did not understand whether Martín Alonso meant that he thought they had missed Japan and should steer southwest by west for China, or that Japan lay in that direction; but he knew and Pinzón knew that the fleet had sailed more than 2400 miles which, according to their calculations, lay between the Canaries and Japan. Naturally Columbus was uneasy, but he held to the west course magnetic, which, owing to the variation for which he did not allow, was about west by south, true.

On October 7, when there was another false landfall, great flocks of birds passed over the ships, flying westsouthwest; this was the autumn migration from eastern North America to the West Indies. Columbus decided that he had better follow the birds rather than his chart, and changed course accordingly that evening. That was "good joss";[19] it was his shortest course to the nearest

land. Now, every night, the men were heartened by seeing against the moon (full on October 5) flocks of birds flying their way. But by the tenth, mutiny flared up again. No land for thirty-one days. Even by the phony reckoning which Columbus gave out they had sailed much farther west than anyone had expected. Enough of this nonsense, sailing west to nowhere; let the Captain General turn back or else! Columbus, says the record, "cheered them as best he could, holding out good hope of the advantages they might gain; and, he added, it was useless to complain, *since he had come to go to the Indies, and so had to continue until he found them, with Our Lord's help.*"

That was typical of Columbus's determination. Yet even he, conscious of divine guidance, could not have kept on indefinitely without the support of his captains and officers. According to one account, it was Martín Alonso Pinzón who cheered him by shouting, *Adelante! Adelante!* which an American poet has translated, "Sail on! Sail on!" But, according to Oviedo, one of the earliest historians who talked with the participants, it was Columbus alone who persuaded the Pinzóns and La Cosa to sail on, with the promise that if land were not found within three days, he would turn back. If this version is correct, as I believe it is, the Captain General's promise to his captains was made on October 9. Next day the trade wind blew fresher, sending the fleet along at 7 knots; it so continued on the eleventh, with a heavy following sea. But signs of land, such as branches of trees with green leaves and flowers, became so frequent that the people were content with their Captain General's decision, and the mutinous mutterings died out in the keen anticipation of making a landfall in the Indies.

---

18 **cliques** (klēks): small, closely knit groups of people.
19 **good joss**: slang for good luck.

As the sun set under a clear horizon October 11, the northeast trade breezed up to gale force, and the three ships tore along at 9 knots. But Columbus refused to shorten sail, since his promised time was running out. He signaled everyone to keep a particularly sharp watch, and offered extra rewards for first landfall in addition to the year's pay promised by the Sovereigns. That night of destiny was clear and beautiful with a late rising moon, but the sea was the roughest of the entire passage. The men were tense and expectant, the officers testy and anxious, the Captain General serene in the confidence that presently God would reveal to him the promised Indies.

At 10 P.M., an hour before moonrise, Columbus and a seaman, almost simultaneously, thought they saw a light "like a little wax candle rising and falling." Others said they saw it too, but most did not; and after a few minutes it disappeared. Volumes have been written to explain what this light was or might have been. To a seaman it requires no explanation. It was an illusion, created by overtense watchfulness. When uncertain of your exact position, and straining to make a night landfall, you are apt to see imaginary lights and flashes and to hear nonexistent bells and breakers.

On rush the ships, pitching, rolling, throwing spray—white waves at their bows and white wakes reflecting the moon. *Pinta* is perhaps half a mile in the lead, *Santa María* on her port quarter, *Niña* on the other side. Now one, now another forges ahead, but they are all making the greatest speed of which they are capable. With the sixth glass of the night watch, the last sands are running out of an era that began with the dawn of history. A few minutes now and destiny will turn up a glass the flow of whose sands we are

still watching. Not since the birth of Christ has there been a night so full of meaning for the human race.

At 2 A.M., October 12, Rodrigo de Triana, lookout on *Pinta*, sees something like a white cliff shining in the moonlight, and sings out, *Tierra! tierra!* "Land! land!" Captain Pinzón verifies the landfall, fires a gun as agreed, and shortens sail to allow the flagship to catch up. As *Santa María* approaches, the Captain General shouts across the rushing waters, "Señor Martín Alonso, you *did* find land! Five thousand maravedis for you as a bonus!"

Yes, land it was this time, a little island of the Bahamas group. The fleet was headed for the sand cliffs on its windward side and would have been wrecked had it held course. But these seamen were too expert to allow that to happen. The Captain General ordered sail to be shortened and the fleet to jog off and on until daylight, which was equivalent to a southwesterly drift clear of the island. At dawn they made full sail, passed the southern point of the island and sought an opening on the west coast, through the barrier reef. Before noon they found it, sailed into the shallow bay now called Long or Fernandez, and anchored in the lee of the land, in five fathoms.

Here on a gleaming beach of white coral occurred the famous first landing of Columbus. The Captain General (now by general consent called Admiral) went ashore in the flagship's boat with the royal standard of Castile displayed, the two Captains Pinzón in their boats, flying the banner of the Expedition—the green crowned cross on a white field. "And, all having rendered thanks to Our Lord, kneeling on the ground, embracing it with tears of joy for the immeasurable mercy of having reached it, the Admiral rose and gave this island the name *San Salvador*"—Holy Savior.

1. Why did the men aboard Columbus's ships threaten mutiny? How did Columbus respond? Why didn't the men carry out their threat?

2. On page 51 the author says: "With the sixth glass of the night watch, the last sands are running out of an era that began with the dawn of history. A few minutes now and destiny will turn up a glass the flow of whose sands we are still watching. Not since the birth of Christ has there been a night so full of meaning for the human race." What do you think these sentences mean?

3. How much of Columbus's success do you think was due to knowledge? to luck? to courage?

Vocabulary

Words that are made up of two or more smaller words are called COMPOUND WORDS. Here are some of the compound words found in "First Crossing of the Atlantic":

breadstuffs	honeymoon	moonlight	seaworthiness
flagship	landfall	nightfall	southwesterly
gulfweed	millpond	overestimate	yachtsman

To figure out the meaning of a compound word which you do not know, follow these steps:

1. Separate the compound word into its parts. For example: rowboat = row/boat; snowstorm = snow/storm.

2. Define each part.

3. Put these definitions together to make a temporary definition for the whole word.

4. Look at the context clues in the sentence to see whether they support your temporary definition.

A. For each compound word printed in *italics* below, follow the process which has just been described. On a separate sheet of paper, write the compound word, the meaning of each part of the word, a temporary definition for the whole word, and a *Yes* or *No*, telling whether the temporary definition fits the context.

1. Any *yachtsman* today would be proud to make the records that the great Admiral did on some of his transatlantic crossings in the 15th century.

2. He had observed on his African voyages that the winter winds in the latitude of the Canaries blew from the east, and that the ocean around them, more often than not, was calm as a *millpond.*

3. At Gomera, the Captain General . . . sent men ashore to fill extra water casks, buy *breadstuffs* and cheese, and put a supply of native beef in pickle.

4. By carefully checking Columbus's Journal of his First Voyage, Captain J. W. McElroy ascertained that he made an average 9 percent *overestimate* of his distance.

5. Improvements in sailing vessels since 1492 have been more in *seaworthiness* and comfort than in speed.

B. Choose any three other compound words from the list at the beginning of this lesson. Write a sentence using each one correctly. Include in each sentence one or more context clues to the meaning of the compound word. Underline each compound word once, and underline each context clue twice.

Samuel Eliot Morison 1886–1976

Believing that it was not enough to research history in books, Samuel Eliot Morison preferred to live and feel as much of the historical experience as he could. To write his biography of Christopher Columbus, Morison made voyages to the islands Columbus visited, checking Columbus's routes and methods. Morison became a naval officer and took part in several sea battles. He used his experiences to help him prepare a history of the U.S. Navy in World War II. His maritime history of New England was sparked by his hobby of sailing along the New England coast.

Although Morison was a world famous historian himself, he had a special interest in young, unknown historians. His advice to them was, "First and foremost, get writing."

The place: the territory of the Lakotas (Sioux) on the American Great Plains.
The time: the 1870s.
The season: spring.
The day: a day like any other spring day in a Lakota village. There were lodges to clean, and there was food to prepare. There were council meetings to attend, and there were enemies to look out for. There were pony herds to guard, and there were babies to take care of. Yes, it was just an ordinary spring day. But for Whirlwind and her thirteen-year-old grandson Shoots, it was a day they'd never forget!

How Whirlwind Saved Her Cub

DOROTHY JOHNSON

WHIRLWIND WAS a widow now. Her hair, hacked off in mourning for White Thunder, had grown out long enough to make short, ragged braids, but she no longer cared very much how she looked. The cuts made when she had gashed her arms and her legs had healed to scars. She no longer had a lodge of her own. When White Thunder died of a wasting sickness—not in battle, as he had wished—she abandoned the lodge as was proper and let other people take away everything in it.

But she had a good home with her son, Morning Rider. She was Grandmother Whirlwind, the old-woman-who-sits-by-the-door. She worked hard and took pride in her work. She was the one who told small children the old stories about the White Buffalo Maiden and the other sacred spirits just as those stories had been told to her by Grandmother Earth Medicine when she was very small. . . .

All over the huge encampment there was singing and drumming, and all over people were busy. There was much to be done, because they would move again very soon. The pony herds needed new grazing.

There was plenty of work to be done in the lodge of Morning Rider, but there were plenty of women there to do it, so Whirlwind left on a project of her own.

"I'm going to dig roots," she explained to Round Cloud Woman. "Shall I take the baby for company?"

"He has just been fed, so take him if you like," her daughter-in-law agreed. His ears had not yet been pierced,[1] so he did not have a boy name yet; his baby name was Jumps.

Whirlwind slung her baby grandson's cradleboard onto her back with the ease of long practice and went walking at a brisk pace, answering the baby when he made small sounds. She had two things hidden under her dress: her digging stick and a soft leather bag for carrying roots. She thought she knew where biscuit root would be growing—desert parsley. The roots were good to eat raw, or she might dry and grind them to make big flat cakes. The biscuit root made good mush with a wild onion cooked in it.

As a rule she liked company when she worked, but there was no point in inviting some other busy woman to come along to dig something that might not be there.

She did tell her destination to one person, her grandson Shoots, thirteen years old. She met him when he was returning on foot from his turn at guarding part of the vast pony herd.

"Your little brother is going to help me dig biscuit root over there," she said. "Don't tell anybody where we are. Let the other women be sharp-eyed and find their own roots."

Shoots smiled and promised. He patted his baby brother's cheek and said, "Ho, warrior, old man chief. Take care of Grandmother." The baby jumped in his buckskin wrappings and cooed.

The biscuit root was plentiful on flat ground under a cutbank, just out of sight of the lodges. Whirlwind carefully propped the

---

1 **ears . . . pierced:** The piercing of the ear lobes took place in a ceremony making the Lakota child an accepted member of the tribe.

baby's cradleboard against a rock so the sun wouldn't shine in the child's face. Then, talking to him quietly, she began to dig skillfully, filling her buckskin bag, stooping and kneeling and rising again like a young woman. She was not young, she had lived through fifty-six winters, but she was strong and happy and healthy.

Her back was toward the baby when she heard him shriek with glee. She turned instantly—and saw a dreadful thing. Between her and the baby was another kind of baby, an awkward little bear cub, the cub of the frightfully dangerous grizzly bear. The cub itself was harmless, but the old-woman bear, its mother, must be near, and she would protect her child.

Whirlwind did not even think of danger to herself. She ran to save *her* cub. She snatched up the baby on his cradleboard and threw him, with all her strength, above her head toward the level top of the cutbank.

At that moment the old-woman bear appeared. She snarled and came running, a shambling, awkward-looking run but very fast.

Whirlwind saw with horror the cradleboard with its precious burden sliding back down the cutbank. She had been too close when she threw the baby upward. The baby was screaming. Grandmother Whirlwind ran, picked up the cradleboard, ran back a few steps, and then threw hard again. This time the bundle stayed up there.

Whirlwind ran again toward the cutbank and climbed as fast as she could, digging into the dirt frantically with clutching fingers and digging toes.

The upper part of her body was on the flat ground and she was gripping a small tree as she tried to pull up her legs. Just then the old-woman grizzly reached up and tore at

Shoots was an untried boy. He had never even asked to go along with a war party to do errands for men of proved courage, to watch how a man should act. He had only thought of going on the hill to starve and thirst and lament to the Powers, praying for a powerful spirit helper.[2] He had not yet done this thing. He believed his heart was strong. That day he found out.

He was only playing when he heard the she-bear snarl. He was practicing a stealthy approach, intending to startle Grandmother Whirlwind. He was creeping quietly through thin brush, pretending that she was an enemy. He did not really expect to surprise her; she was usually very alert. She would scold when she discovered what he was up to, and then she would laugh at him because she had caught him.

He saw a bundle fly through the air and slide down the cutbank. It happened too fast for him to see that it was the cradleboard with his baby brother. He heard fast movement in the weeds as Whirlwind ran back and threw the cradleboard again. He stood up, mouth open, just as she scrambled up the bank. With horror he saw the old-woman bear's claws rake her struggling legs.

With his heart in his mouth he did the best thing he could think of. He dropped his bow and grabbed the cub with both hands, so that it squalled with fear and pain. Then he threw it hard—past its mother.

Hearing her child cry, the woman bear whirled away from the cutbank to protect her cub. Shoots snatched up his bow; it was a good one, as strong as he could pull, and in a

the legs with curved claws as long as a big man's middle finger.

Whirlwind thought, I am dead—but my cub is safe if the sow bear does not come up here. No, I am not dead yet. I have something more to do. She screamed as hard as she could.

And her scream was heard.

---

2 going on the hill . . . powerful spirit helper: When a Lakota boy became old enough, he underwent initiation rites—a period of fasting—so that he could be looked on as a man and a warrior.

quiver on his shoulder he had six hunting arrows tipped with sharpened iron. At his waist he had a good steel knife.

But his enemy was better armed, with twenty immensely long, curved, sharp, death-dealing claws and a mouthful of long, sharp teeth, and she weighed more than five times as much as he did. She was protected by thick fur. Shoots was almost naked.

He stood his ground and fired his arrows at her, fast but very carefully. Few grizzlies had ever been killed by one man alone; there were true tales of some bears killing men even after they should have been dead themselves. The woman bear yelled in pain and fury. She batted at the arrows deep in her flesh. She bit at them. But she kept coming.

Then Shoots did the last thing he could do, because it was too late to run. While the grizzly fought at the arrows, especially one that had gone into her left eye, he leaped on her back. With all his strength he sank his good steel knife into her throat, through the heavy fur and hide.

Then, as Grandmother Whirlwind had done, he clambered up the cutbank while the bear groped and swiped at him. He wondered why he could not see very well. He wondered who was screaming. He wondered if this was the day he was going to die.

Whirlwind, lying helpless with the calf of one leg torn away, screamed louder when she saw him with blood running down his face, but he did not even know blood was there.

She cried, "Take the baby and run!" in so commanding a voice that he never thought of doing otherwise. With the cradled baby under one arm, he ran toward the camp, howling for help, but stumbling.

His yells were heard. Two men on horseback lashed their ponies and met him. One seized the squalling baby. The other pulled

Shoots up behind him on the pony. They rode fast toward where Whirlwind lay.

They leaped off—the one with the baby hung the cradleboard on a tree branch—and Shoots tumbled off. He had just realized that there was something he ought to do to prove his valor. He did something that his people talked about for many years afterward. While the men knelt by Whirlwind, he slid down the cutbank, picked up his bow, and struck the bear with it. She was coughing and dying. He shouted, as warriors do, "I, Shoots, have killed her! I count the first coup!"[3]

Whirlwind and the men above heard him say it. They shouted in wonder and admiration. For a man to kill a grizzly without help was a very great thing indeed, and he had actually gone back into danger to count coup and claim the credit that was due him. He had counted coup against an armed enemy, after he was wounded, although he had never gone to war before that day. Now he was entitled to wear an eagle feather upright in his hair for first coup, a feather tipped with red paint because he had been wounded in battle.

He was the one who rode toward camp for more help while the two men stayed with Whirlwind and did what they could to make her comfortable. A crowd of people came hurrying after he delivered his message. There were women on horseback with poles and hides to make a pony drag for Whirlwind, because a great chunk of the muscles in the calf of one leg had been torn out by the she-bear's claws. There were men riding and boys riding, leading horses. More women brought supplies to help the wounded, and a

---

3 **count** . . . **coup** (kü): to strike or touch an enemy in a battle, thus showing bravery. To count coup was an act deserving honor.

medicine woman came with them, carrying her bundle of magic things. Round Cloud Woman came riding, crying, and Morning Rider came at a hard gallop to see about his mother and his infant son.

Whirlwind fought them off, so keyed up and triumphant that she did not yet feel much pain. "Let me carry my grandchild!" she ordered when Round Cloud tried to take him away.

"I saved your cub," Whirlwind kept boasting, laughing and proud. "And Shoots saved us both. He is not a cub any more. He is a warrior!" She tried to make a victory trill in his honor, but as they lifted her gently onto the pony drag[4] she fainted.

Morning Rider himself attended to the wound of his son Shoots, who did not even remember when the old-woman bear had slashed his forehead. The boy was able to laugh as he said, "She tried to scalp me!"

Morning Rider covered the wound with clotted blood from the bear and tied the flap of skin down with a strip of buckskin around the boy's head. He remarked fondly, "You will have a big scar there. The girls will keep asking you to tell how you got it. I am very proud of you."

Now maybe Grandmother Whirlwind would stop treating him like a little boy, to be ordered around.

He heard her shouting, laughing: "Behold Shoots—he is a warrior. He fought a grizzly bear and killed her."

Shoots shouted back, "Behold Whirlwind! She is a warrior. She was wounded in battle."

He began to sing a praise song for her, although he was feeling weak all of a sudden.

She laughed hysterically. "I am a warrior who was wounded while running away! Take the hide of the enemy—it belongs to Shoots."

Women were skinning out the dead, bloody bear and fighting with a horse that reared, not wanting to carry the hide on its back. The medicine woman filled a big dish with bear blood. She washed the great wound on Whirlwind's leg with water, chanting prayers. She covered the wound with the bear's thickening blood and then cut a big piece of the bear's hide, covering the wound and the blood with the raw side of the fresh hide.

She said with pity, "My friend, I think you will have trouble walking—always, as long as you live. But nobody will ever forget how you saved your son's cub today."

They killed the great bear's cub and cut off its claws to make a necklace for the baby when he grew older. They cut off the immense claws of the woman bear; these were for Shoots. Not long afterward, when he went out to lament for a vision, his dream was a powerful one and when he made up his protective medicine bag, one of the claws was in it. The others he wore for a necklace when he dressed up.

That night the people had a victorious kill dance over the bloody hides of the great bear and the little one. Morning Rider rode around the camp circle leading a fine horse to give away, with Shoots riding beside him. Morning Rider sang:

"A bear killed a woman long ago.
A bear killed a mother long ago.
Now the woman's son has avenged her.
The warrior son has avenged his mother!"

Morning Rider gave the fine horse to a very brave old warrior, who gave Shoots a new name. The warrior shouted, "The boy

---

4 **pony drag**: a small platform-like device that was dragged along the ground when attached to and pulled by a pony or a horse. The principle of the wheel was unknown.

Shoots counted first coup on a grizzly bear and killed her to save two people. So I give him an honorable name. Kills Grizzly is his name!"

Grandmother Whirlwind lay on her bed, smiling as she listened to the singing and the triumphant drumming of the kill dance in honor of Shoots—no, now she must remember to call him Kills Grizzly. Her daughter was with her, and the medicine woman, who used all her spells and prayers and medicines to try to ease the pain. No matter how Whirlwind lay, with her foot propped up, the pain was very great, but her pride was greater.

"It does not hurt," she said. "It is nothing." She pretended to sleep.

Brings Horses stayed, and Morning Rider's wives came back with their sleepy children. They spoke softly but were full of talk that Whirlwind wanted to hear: about how everyone was honoring Shoots for his courage and talking about how brave Whirlwind herself was.

"Everybody wants to see you," one of them remarked, smiling, "but we refused them all—all except one, who will come soon."

They were hurrying around, Whirlwind noticed, to tidy up the lodge—her work, but she could not do it now. It must be an important visitor or the women would not be so careful to have everything neat and nice this late at night, with the baby and the little girl, Reaches Far, asleep.

Men's voices came nearer, two men. One was Morning Rider; his mother did not recognize the other one. Morning Rider entered and ushered in his companion. He said, "This is Whirlwind Woman, my mother. She saved my baby son."

The other man stood looking down at her.

He smiled a little and said, "I am Crazy Horse."

Whirlwind gasped. For once in her life, she had nothing to say. This was the great man, the quiet one, whose very presence made the hearts of his people big.

Morning Rider told her, "I have asked Crazy Horse to name the baby, and he agrees. When the boy is old enough, we will have the ear-piercing ceremony. But today Crazy Horse will give my youngest son a name."

Round Cloud Woman brought the sleeping infant. She was shaking with excitement.

Crazy Horse looked long at the sleeping little face. Then he touched the child's forehead and said, "I give you a name that you can make great in honor of your grandmother, who saved you, and your brother, who counted first coup on the bear. I name the child She Throws Him."

A murmur of delight went up among Morning Rider's family: "Thank you, friend, thank you!"

Round Cloud Woman said to her child, "Wake up, She Throws Him, so that sometime you can say you looked on the face of Crazy Horse the day he gave you your name." The baby opened his eyes, yawned, and went to sleep again.

Now Whirlwind thought of something to say: "My son has forgotten his manners. I did not raise him right. He has not asked our visitor to sit down in the place of honor beside him."

The two men chuckled, and Morning Rider explained, "I asked him before we came, but he thought he would not stay long enough. Will the visitor sit down and smoke?"

Crazy Horse would. Morning Rider filled and lighted the sacred pipe and smoked it to the Powers of the six directions. Then he passed it to Crazy Horse, who did the same and gave back the sacred pipe.

"I wish also to speak to the warrior woman," he said. "Grandmother, how is it with you in your pain?" He used the term "grandmother" in the sense of great respect.

"Not so bad," she replied stoutly, as a warrior should.

Crazy Horse stood up, then knelt beside her and looked into her face. "I give you a name, too, Grandmother. Your name is Saved Her Cub."

Then he nodded and left the lodge, leaving Whirlwind speechless for the second time that day.

When she got her wits back, she complained happily, "But I am too old to remember another name for myself!"

Morning Rider replied, "Others will remember."

Discussion

1. Who, in your opinion, is more important in the story—Whirlwind or Shoots? Why? Perhaps you feel that the two characters are equally important. If so, why?

2. When Whirlwind saw the bear cub, what did she do? Why?

3. It seems that in no way did Whirlwind threaten the bear cub. Why, then, did the "old-woman bear" attack Whirlwind?

4. Do you agree or disagree that both Whirlwind and Shoots showed great courage in what they did? Why?

5. How was Shoots honored for what he did? How was Whirlwind honored for what she did? Do you think that all this acclaim was deserved or undeserved? Why?

Vocabulary

When you learn a new word, you can often learn other forms of the same word—almost automatically. For example, when you first learned that *courage* means "bravery," you almost automatically learned that *courageous* means "brave." *Courage* became *courageous* by the addition of *-ous,* a SUFFIX.

A suffix is any letter—or group of letters—that can be attached to the end of a word, changing the way in which the word can be used. The suffix *-ous* changes *courage,* a noun (naming word), into *courageous,* an adjective (describer of nouns):

Whirlwind and Shoots showed *courage.*
Shoots and Whirlwind were *courageous.*

The suffix *-ous* means "possessing, having, or full of." Another suffix often used to change nouns into adjectives is *-al,* meaning "connected with."

A. 1. On a separate sheet of paper, add the suffix -*ous* to each of the following nouns from "How Whirlwind Saved Her Cub." Check the glossary or a dictionary for the correct spelling of each adjective.

danger   valor   wonder

2. Write a short sentence for each of the nouns listed above and for each of the adjectives you created by adding the suffix.

B. 1. Add the suffix -*al* to each of the following nouns from the same story. Check the glossary or a dictionary for the correct spelling.

magic   medicine   ceremony

2. Write a short sentence for each noun listed above and for each adjective you created by adding the suffix.

Dorothy Johnson 1905 —

Dorothy Johnson has received several interesting honors for her stories about the West she knows so well. She was "adopted" as a member of the Blackfoot tribe, with the name "Kills in Both Places." Her hometown, Whitefish, Montana, made her honorary police chief.

Johnson began writing about the West when she returned there after a fifteen year residence in the East. Critics have often commented about the honesty and realism of her situations and characters. One has said, "These are Western stories with a difference, told by a woman who grew up in the country she writes about. Miss Johnson is a Grade A storyteller and her people—men or women, Indians or whites—definitely come alive."

Several television shows and movies have been based on her stories, including "The Man Who Shot Liberty Valence" and "A Man Called Horse."

Living your life . . . Running a race . . .
Effort . . . Determination . . . Courage
. . . Could it be that somehow they are all
related?

To James

FRANK HORNE

Do you remember
How you won
That last race . . . ?
How you flung your body
At the start . . .   5
How your spikes
Ripped the cinders
In the stretch . . .
How you catapulted
Through the tape . . .   10
Do you remember . . . ?
Don't you think
I lurched with you
Out of those starting holes . . . ?
Don't you think   15
My sinews tightened
At those first
Few strides . . .
And when you flew into the stretch
Was not all my thrill   20
Of a thousand races
In your blood . . . ?
At your final drive
Through the finish line
Did not my shout   25
Tell of the
Triumphant ecstasy
Of victory . . . ?

Live
As I have taught you   30
To run, Boy—
It's a short dash
Dig your starting holes
Deep and firm
Lurch out of them   35
Into the straightaway
With all the power
That is in you
Look straight ahead
To the finish line   40
Think only of the goal
Run straight
Run high
Run hard
Save nothing   45

And finish
With an ecstatic burst
That carries you
Hurtling
Through the tape   50
To victory. . . .

Discussion

1. At what point in the poem does the speaker turn from remarks about running a race to remarks about living one's life?

2. Using your own words, summarize the advice that the speaker gives James.

3. Note that the poem is in two parts. The second part contains the speaker's advice. What, then, is the purpose of the first part (lines 1–28)?

Frank S. Horne 1899—1974

Frank S. Horne put his athletic knowledge to good use in his poetry. After winning varsity letters in track at the City College of New York, Horne kept a fresh memory of the excitement and feel of a race well run. He wrote "To James" and other poems using athletic challenges as symbols for life. Ironically, the optimistic poem "To James" is part of a group titled "Letters Found Near a Suicide." These poems are written by a man preparing for his death, addressing the many people in his life. The attitude in "To James" is more typical of Horne's philosophy than the other, more bitter poems in the collection.

Yes, Grandmother did have the law on her side. And—yes—Grandmother also believed in being honest. But in this situation, how could she have it both ways?

I'll Give You Law

MOLLY PICON

WHEN I READ the newspaper, there is always a must section in it that I never pass by. This is the lost and found advertisements usually buried in the back pages. This is a habit I picked up from my grandmother. She always took a keen interest in who had lost what, and who was honestly reporting on items found. She could people a whole colony from just a couple of advertisements.

"Lost—one black puppy with a white patch around its eye. Answers to the name 'Spot.' Please call Beaver 6–5000. Reward."

From this my grandmother would draw for me a picture of a child sobbing itself to sleep at night, of parents out searching the streets anxiously, calling in hopeless voices, "Here, Spot. Come on, Spot. Here, boy."

The picture was so visual to both of us we used to sit there with tears in our eyes, willing Spot to answer, wanting the child to cry with joy and not in sorrow.

"Lost—a white platinum ring, inscribed 'To J. from W., forever thine.' Ring not valuable but of sentimental value. Reward."

My grandmother would analyze the situation for me.

"What kind of woman is she to lose a ring like that?" Grandma would cry sternly. "In the first place, how could it fall off her finger?"

"Maybe it was loose?" I would suggest helpfully.

"Loose? Why should it be loose?" Grandma was not going to accept any of my flimsy excuses. "She didn't have a little string in the house she could wind around the ring so it could fit? Don't give me such stories."

"Maybe she took it off in a washroom when she was washing her hands and then she forgot it," I would then suggest.

"A ring like that you don't take off, and if you take it off, you don't forget it. I'm only sorry for that W., whoever he is. A bargain he hasn't got in her, believe me."

"But, Bubba, how do we know that J. is a woman and W. is a man. Maybe J. is the man and W. is the woman, and *she* gave *him* the ring."

My grandmother was openly amused at such naïveté.

"A lady to give a man a ring?" Absolutely out of the question. My grandmother wouldn't accept it even as a premise.

"Maybe it was a wedding ring," I argued. "Sometimes people have double ring ceremonies."

For the sake of argument, Grandma would concede.

"All right. So J. is the man. So it was a wedding ring. So what kind of a man loses his wedding ring? A good-for-nothing loafer. So what does she need him for? She should let him go with the ring together."

In no time at all, my grandmother would get into a rage at the perfidy of this man, who thought so little of his marriage vows that he didn't have the decency to hang on to his wedding band.

We speculated about all the lost items with equal interest. We wondered about the found items as well, visualizing the happy claimants, and the honest finders handsomely rewarded. At such moments, God was in Heaven, and all was right with the world.

And then one day, we moved swiftly from the land of fantasy to a world of realities. My grandmother found something!

"What is it? What is it?" I asked, hopping with excitement.

"A lavaliere!"[1] My grandmother was absolutely overwhelmed. She had never found anything in her life, and now, here in her hand, was this magnificent lavaliere.

"It must be very expensive," I said, running my fingers over it.

"A fortune," my grandmother said positively. She held it up against her. "A regular fortune," she breathed.

"Are you going to keep it?" I asked.

She gave me a sharp look. If the thought entered her mind, she wasn't going to admit it to me.

---

1 **lavaliere** (lăv ə lēr'): jewelry hanging on a ribbon or chain that is worn around the neck.

"Am I going to keep it?" she asked. "Such a question." She threw her shawl over her head.

"Where are you going?" I asked. "Can I go too?"

"I'm going to the police station. Let them worry about it. You can't come," she added firmly. "A police station is not respectable."

At the police station, the property clerk informed her politely that if the lavaliere was not claimed within ninety days, the police department would turn the jewelry over to her, and she would be its rightful and legal owner. He took her name and address and wrote it down. They would let her know, he said indifferently.

"Oh, I hope nobody claims it," I said fervently. "Oh, Bubba, I hope whoever lost it doesn't even know they lost it."

Such a dilemma for my grandmother. If ever she yearned for anything, it was for this lavaliere. On the other hand, her active imagination conjured up for her such tearful scenes that she couldn't wait for the loser to come and claim her property.

She could not compromise with her stern standards. She advertised in the local paper, running the advertisement for three days. Then she had to abandon this, because money spent for anything but food was both wasteful and sinful. During that three-day period, we waited literally with our hearts in our mouths. Every time there was a knock at the door, we could see the lavaliere leaving us forever. Meanwhile, my grandmother took to haunting the police station and the property clerk. She would first observe all the amenities. How are you, she would ask, and how is the family? In the beginning he would dismiss this with a curt fine we haven't heard don't call on us we'll let you know attitude. But my grandmother began to take a personal interest in the policemen at the precinct. After all, she visited them daily. It wasn't like they were strangers, she would tell me. She knew their names and the names of their wives and the names of their children. She knew at any given moment what child was suffering from what childhood disease, how hard it was to make ends meet on a policeman's salary, what policeman was going to night school to study law and improve his station in life, what policeman was smarting at being passed over when promotions were handed out. Only the property clerk held out. When he would look up and see my grandmother, he would mutter and groan.

"Mrs. Ostrow," he would say, "don't you have anything to do at home?"

"Why don't I have something to do at home?" my grandmother would regard him scornfully. "You think I like to come here day after day?"

"So why do you come?" he would ask logically.

"To see what I have to see," she would tell him cryptically.

And then she would demand to see the lavaliere with "my own eyes." And then she would subject him to a searching interrogation. Who had come today, and what had they claimed, and wasn't it possible the lavaliere had belonged to one of the people who had come, and had he told anybody about it, and if he was keeping it such a big secret, how could anybody know he had it in the first place?

As fervently as I prayed that no one would show up, he prayed that someone—anyone—would.

"Ninety days," he would cry, clutching his hair. "I'll never survive it."

"Bubba," I once asked, "why *do* you go there every day? Don't you trust him?"

"Trust him?" My grandmother smiled at such innocence.

"But he's a policeman. And he's right in the police station," I protested. "What could he do?"

My grandmother didn't want to fill my mind with sordid stories of what could happen to a policeman in a police station. After all, he might have been an officer, but at the same time he was only a man. Man is weak, and temptation is strong. My grandmother could not visualize a man so strong-minded as to be able to resist the golden lure presented by such a collection of lost treasures.

I never knew that ninety days could last so long. But eventually the ninetieth day arrived, bringing with it much excitement and expectation. My grandmother and I dressed as though we were going to a party. She was going to allow me to go with her for the presentation. On the way we discussed her immense good fortune.

"When I die," she said to me, "I want you to have it."

"Please, Bubba," I said, uncomfortably. It seemed like a grim note to inject in an otherwise cloudless day.

"No," she insisted seriously. "I want you to have it. It will be like a—what is the word I want, Malkele?"

"An heirloom?"

"That's the word." She pounced on it with satisfaction. "And when you die, your children will have it."

In two sentences, my grandmother had disposed of us both.

At the police station, my grandmother was greeted with happy smiles, even from the property clerk. I should say, especially from the property clerk. It was the happiest day of his life.

When my grandmother finally held the

lavaliere in her hand, her eyes misted over. She couldn't speak, but she nodded her head tremulously at the policemen.

"Don't be a stranger," they urged her. "Don't wait till you find something before you drop in."

"Such nice boys," my grandmother said, as we left the station. She touched her eyes with her handkerchief. "Such good boys, *even him*," she said, referring to the property clerk. "He had his eye on it, but out of respect, he didn't touch it." I believed my grandmother. I didn't see how that property clerk could have looked at that lavaliere for

ninety days and so nobly fought off temptation.

When we got home, my grandmother promptly put the lavaliere on.

"I'll wear it night and day," she vowed. "I'll never take it off." For a week she was as good as her word.

Then one day there came a knock at the door, and tragedy swept in, escorted by an embarrassed and harassed property clerk from the police station.

"Where is it?" cried the woman he had brought to the door. She looked at my grandmother. "My lavaliere she's wearing,"

she cried in horror, pointing to my grandmother.

My grandmother looked at both of them, appalled. Her hand went up automatically to clutch the lavaliere.

"It's mine," she said. "You told me, after ninety days . . ."

"That's right," the property clerk said promptly. "Legally it is yours. That's what I've been trying to tell this lady. She didn't claim it in ninety days, and the law says . . ."

"I'll give you law," the lady shouted vigorously, pounding him on the arm. "Does the law ask me where was I the past ninety days? Does the law say after ninety days thieves and murderers can do whatever they want? Law! I'll give you law!"

"Please, lady," the property clerk pleaded. "Let's try to be calm."

"Calm!" she took up the cry. "I'll give you calm!"

My grandmother entered the fray briskly.

"So much commotion," she said. "You want the neighbors to think we're killing you on the doorstep? Come inside." She urged them in and closed the door. "So if you'll stop talking and tell me where you were," she said, guiding the distracted woman to a seat, "we'll listen and we'll be the same good friends."

"Where was I?" the woman said, shaking her head. "My daughter was having her baby, so she says to me, 'Ma,' she says, 'if you don't come, I won't have it, that's all.' Scared to death with the first child. Wait till she's had six, like me."

"I had eleven," my grandmother topped her quietly.

"Eleven! So I don't have to tell you," the woman continued. "So I had to go to Scranton yet—a husband takes it into his head to

make a living in Scranton," she added in a parenthetical note of disbelief. "With all the children I had to go. One month in advance, just in case. And then, with God's help, the baby comes. Now she's afraid to hold it; it might break. And she's afraid to wash it. It might come apart in the water. And she's afraid to feed it. It throws up on her. One month. Two months. Finally I say to her, 'Rebeccah,' I say, 'enough is enough already. Whatever you'll do you'll do.'"

My grandmother was already making tea for everybody, bustling about the kitchen, putting crackers and jam on the table.

"The young people today," she commented, sympathetically.

"So when I come back, I first realized my lavaliere is gone. I'm not hung with jewelry, and between you and me and the lamp post," she added confidentially to my grandmother, "I need a lavaliere like I need a hole in the head. But when I need a little extra money in an emergency, that lavaliere saves my life."

"How does it save you life?" I asked, intrigued.

She made a face, lifting her eyebrows eloquently to the grownups present.

"I bring it to the pawnshop and whatever few pennies he gives me . . ."

"The pawnshop!" I was indignant. "She doesn't even *wear* it, Bubba," I said passionately. "Don't give it back. You don't have to. The law says you don't have to."

"That's right," the property clerk said instantly. He was on his second cup of tea and using my grandmother's jam as if the jar had an endless bottom.

The woman opened her mouth to protest, but my grandmother forestalled her by holding up her hand for silence.

"Malkele," she said gently, "there is a law here, too." She laid her hand tenderly on my heart. "Look in your heart and tell me. Suppose it was your lavaliere. Suppose you lost it and somebody else found it. Ninety days, a thousand days . . . how would you feel?"

"I would want it back," I answered honestly, "no matter how."

She spread her hands out eloquently.

"So?" she asked me.

"That's not fair," I burst out.

"Fair? Who said anything about fair?" She reached up and took off the lavaliere. She fondled it for a moment, and then handed it over to the woman.

"Why should I complain?" she asked no one in particular and shrugged philosophically. "For three months I lived in a dream, and for five days I lived like a queen. Is that bad?"

Discussion

1. Why did Grandmother decide to return the lavaliere to its original owner? In your opinion, was that decision a good one or a misguided one? Why?

2. How important is the lavaliere to Grandmother when she finds it? How important is it to her during the 90-day waiting period? How important is it once she finally has it?

3. What is the original owner's attitude toward the lavaliere? How does her attitude differ from Grandmother's?

4. What does the original owner mean when she cries, "I'll give you law."?

5. How does Molly's feeling about returning the lavaliere differ from Grandmother's? How does Grandmother help Molly understand why the lavaliere should be returned? What is Molly's response?

6. How does Grandmother's action in returning the lavaliere show her to be woman of courage?

Vocabulary

A suffix is any letter or group of letters added to the end of a word to form a different word. The new word will relate closely in meaning to the original, but it will be used differently. The two words cannot be substituted for each other in a sentence.

One suffix is -ant which can mean "a person who does something." An example of the use of this suffix is seen in these two sentences based on "I'll Give You Law."

Grandmother hoped no one would *claim* the lavaliere.
A *claimant* appeared after the ninety-day time limit had run out.

Adding the suffix *-ant* changes *claim,* a verb (action word), into *claimant,* a noun (naming word). Another suffix that can change a verb into a noun is *-er,* when it means "one who," or "that which."

A. 1. On a separate sheet of paper, add the suffix *-ant* to each of the following verbs. Remember: Spellings of words may change slightly when suffixes are added. Always check your glossary or a dictionary for the correct spelling.

    assist   serve   dispute

  2. Write a short sentence for each of the verbs listed above and for each of the nouns you created by adding the suffix.

B. 1. Add the suffix *-er* to each of the following verbs, changing the spelling when necessary:

    read   own   find   lose

  2. Write a short sentence for each of the verbs listed above and for each of the nouns you created by adding the suffix.

Molly Picon 1898 —

Molly Picon has been famous for many years as a comedienne, actress, and singer. She is called the "Darling of the Yiddish Stage." She began her career at the age of five in Philadelphia, when she won the prize of a five-dollar gold piece at a children's amateur night. During her high school years, she sang between reels at the local movie houses. She traveled with a Yiddish acting company and became a star.

A petite woman, Picon was not a typical leading lady for the serious dramas which were popular in the Yiddish theater at that time. Her husband, a producer, wrote plays to fit her size and comic talent. She became famous in the play "Yankele" which has been called the "Peter Pan of the Yiddish theater." After that, she entertained enthusiastic audiences all over the world. She has performed in French, German, and English as well as Yiddish.

Picon and her husband were among the first entertainers to go to postwar Europe, hoping to bring some cheer to surviving Jews. They visited hospitals and orphanages. She commented, "It was a difficult emotional experience—but gratifying in retrospect. We heard people laugh who hadn't laughed in seven years."

1 COURAGE

Discussion

1. Look back over the ten selections that make up this unit. Which selection, in your opinion, best illustrates the meaning and the exercise of courage? Why?

2. Several selections in the unit concern women. Which ones? What is the problem that each of those women faces? In what way does courage reflect the general attitude toward life—the "quality of mind"—of each of those women?

3. In each of the following selections, what might have been the outcome had the main character NOT had courage?
   a. "The Most Dangerous Game" d. "First Crossing of the Atlantic"
   b. "Mary McLeod Bethune" e. "How Whirlwind. . . Cub"
   c. "David and Goliath" f. "I'll Give You Law"

4. Some of the selections in this unit suggest rewards that can be gained by acting courageously. Which selections? What are some of the rewards?

Composition

1. Of the people you have met in this unit, which one do you think is the most impressive in demonstrating courage? When you have made your choice, write a composition in which you (a) identify that person and (b) supply evidence from the appropriate story or poem to support your decision. Consider the general situation that your chosen person faced. Consider, too, the extent to which he or she was aware of any danger or hardship. Finally, describe how he or she demonstrated courage in his or her handling of the situation.

2. At sometime during your life, you, yourself, no doubt have had to exercise courage, or you know of someone who did demonstrate courage. In a composition, briefly describe the situation that called for the exercise of courage. Then explain how you (or someone else) demonstrated courage. Finally, tell how it feels to have lived through that experience.

2

Determination

DETERMINATION

Disaster loomed along the Paru! The creatures living along that tributary of the mighty Amazon were in danger of losing their homes. Worse than that, they were in danger of drowning!

It seems that some years back, a family of rubber trees had found the south bank of the Paru so much to their liking that they immediately put down roots. And then they multiplied. Before long, there were so many aunts, uncles, nieces, nephews, cousins, and distant cousins—you just wouldn't believe! Naturally, the need for more and more living space became acute. In time, scouts reported that the north bank of the river was up for grabs. And so the rubber trees—particularly the distant cousins—began moving across. What with their trunks and their roots and all, they soon had almost dammed the river. Indeed, the once robust Paru had become a mere trickle. The Paru itself was becoming a lake!

Alarmed about the rising waters, the creatures living along the Paru met in conference.

"Paruvians!" cried the self-important Jaguar, who was also the self-appointed moderator, "something must be done to restore the current of our river. And it must be done fast, or we'll all surely drown!" He lashed his spotted tail.

"It's those pesky rubber trees," snapped the red Coati. "They've got to go!" And with that she sank her teeth into the trunk of one of the not-so-distant cousins.

"But how?" whined the Cayman, shedding a crocodile tear. (Secretly, he welcomed the prospect of dining on his drowning neighbors.)

"Well, I guess I could squeeze them to death," offered the Anaconda.

"But that'll take too long," snorted the Collared Peccary. "I think we ought to—"

"Neighbors," interrupted the Army Ant, waving her antennae in a businesslike manner, "my family and I are at your disposal. Just show us where to start."

"You?" scoffed the Jaguar. "You little pipsqueak, what good can *you* do?"

"Give her a chance!" Both the Coati and the Collared Peccary were insistent.

Thus encouraged, the Army Ant gave a sharp whistle. Immediately the entire family appeared. They swarmed over the trunk of the nearest rubber tree.

Taking his cue from the Army Ant, the Jaguar sprang to another rubber tree, biting it and clawing at its roots. But in an instant he was spitting out the bitter roots and shaking his mud-caked paws. And besides that, his beautiful spotted coat had become soiled.

"What's the use?" he snarled. "It isn't worth all this. I'm off to find a new home." And with that, he disappeared.

"My snout just isn't made to uproot rubber trees," asserted the Cayman primly. And she crawled to a sunny spot on the river bank and went to sleep.

The Anaconda, who had wrapped himself around three rubber trees, was squeezing them so vigorously that his entire body had turned crimson. Yet the rubber trees still stood—defiantly.

"Timber-r-r!" suddenly shouted the Coati as she raced out of the way of a falling rubber tree.

"Those Army Ants mean business," declared the Collared Peccary. "Woops, there goes *another* rubber tree!"

Two rubber trees, had indeed fallen.

The Army Ant paused, wiped her brow, and eyed the rubber trees still blocking the river.

"Hm," she observed to her companions, "only forty-five more to go. If we apply ourselves, we can finish before sundown."

And sure enough, within minutes, down went two more rubber trees.

Now *that's* DETERMINATION!

Who'd ever think of having a pet goose! Eliza Birdwell would; that's who. What's more, she'd even go to court—just to keep that goose. No matter what else you might say about Eliza, she was determined!

The Pacing Goose

JESSAMYN WEST

J ESS SAT IN THE KITCHEN at the long table by the west window where in winter he kept his grafting tools: the thin-bladed knife, the paper sweet with the smell of beeswax and the resin, the boxes of roots and scions.[1] Jess was a nurseryman[2] and spring meant for him not only spirits flowering—but the earth's. A week more of moderating weather and he'd be out, still in gum boots, but touching an earth that had thawed, whose riches were once again fluid enough to be sucked upward, toward those burgeonings[3] which by summer would have swelled into Early Harvests, Permains and Sweet Bows.

Spring's a various season, Jess thought, no two years the same: comes in with rains, mud deep enough to swallow horse and rider; comes in cold, snow falling so fast it weaves a web; comes in with a warm wind blowing about thy ears and bringing a smell of some-thing flowering, not here, but southaways, across the Ohio, maybe, in Kentucky. Nothing here now but a smell of melting snow—which is no smell at all, but a kind of prickle in the nose, like a bygone sneeze. Comes in so various, winter put by and always so welcome.

"And us each spring so much the same."

"Thee speaking to me, Jess?"

"Nothing thee'd understand, Eliza."

Spring made Jess discontented with the human race—and with women, if anything more than men. It looked as if spring put them all in the shade: the season so resourceful and they each year meeting it with nothing changed from last year; digging up roots from the same sassafras thicket, licking sulphur and molasses from the same big-bowled spoon.

Behind him the table was set for supper, plates neatly turned to cover the bone-handled knives and forks, spoon vase aglitter with steel well burnished by brick dust, dishes of jam with more light to them than the sun, which was dwindling away, peaked and overcast outside his window.

---

1 scions (sī′ ənz): shoots ready for planting.
2 nurseryman: owner of a plant nursery, where plants and trees are raised for sale.
3 burgeonings (bûr′ jən ingz): new growths.

"Spring opening up," he said, "and nobody in this house so much as putting down a line of poetry."

Eliza, who was lifting dried-peach pies from a hot oven, said nothing. She set the four of them in a neat row on the edge of her kitchen cabinet to cool, and slid her pans of cornbread into the oven. Then she turned to Jess, her cheeks red with heat, and her black eyes warm with what she had to say. "Thee'd maybe relish a nice little rhyme for thy supper, Jess Birdwell."

Jess sighed, then sniffed the pies, so rich with ripe peach flavor that the kitchen smelled like a summer orchard, nothing lacking but the sound of bees. "Now, Eliza," he said, "thee knows I wouldn't have thee anyways altered. Thee . . ."

"Thee," Eliza interrupted him, "is like all men. Thee wants to have thy poetry and eat it too."

Jess wondered how what he'd felt about spring, a season with the Lord's thumbprint fresh on it, could've led to anything so un-springlike as an argument about a batch of dried-peach pies.

"Eliza," he said firmly, "I didn't mean thee. Though it's crossed my mind sometimes as strange that none of the boys have ever turned, this time of year, to rhyming."

"Josh writes poems," Eliza said.

"Thee ever read what Josh writes, Eliza?" Eliza nodded.

Ah, well, Jess thought, no use at this date to tell her what's the difference.

Eliza looked her husband over carefully.

"Jess Birdwell," she said, "thee's full of humors.[4] Thy blood needs thinning. I'll boil thee up a good cup of sassafras tea."

Jess turned away from the green and gold sunset and the patches of snow it was gilding and fairly faced the dried-peach pies and Eliza, who was dropping dumplings into a pot of beans.

"That's just it, Eliza," he said. "That's just the rub."

Eliza gave him no encouragement, but he went on anyway. "Earth alters, season to season, spring comes in never two times the same, only us pounding on steady as pump bolts and not freshened by so much as a grass blade."

"Jess, thee's got spring fever."

"I could reckon time and temperature, each spring, by the way thee starts honing for geese. 'Jess, don't thee think we might have a few geese?' It's a tardy spring," Jess said. "Snow still on the ground and not a word yet from thee about geese."

Eliza pulled a chair out from the table and sat. "Jess, why's thee always been so set against geese?"

"I'm not set against geese. It's geese that's set against farming. They can mow down a half acre of sprouting corn while thee's trying to head them off—and in two minutes they'll level a row of pie plant it's taken two years to get started. No, Eliza, it's the geese that's against me."

"If thee had tight fences . . ." Eliza said.

"Eliza, I got tight fences, but the goose's never been hatched that'll admit fences exist. And an old gander'd just as soon go through a fence as hiss—and if he can't find a hole or crack in a fence he'll lift the latch."

"Jess," said Eliza flatly, "thee don't like geese."

"Well," said Jess, "I wouldn't go so far's to say I didn't like them, but I will say that if there's any meaner, dirtier animal, or one that glories in it more, I don't know it. And a thing I've never been able to understand about thee, Eliza, is what thee sees in the shifty-eyed birds."

"Geese," said Eliza, with a dreaminess unusual to her, "march along so lordly like . . . they're pretty as swans floating down a branch . . . in fall they stretch out their necks and honk to geese passing overhead as if they's wild. My father never had any trouble raising geese and I've heard him say many a time that there's no better food for a brisk morning than a fried goose egg."

Jess knew, with spring his topic, he'd ought to pass over Eliza's father and his fried goose egg but he couldn't help saying, "A fried goose egg always had a kind of bloated look to me, Eliza"—but then he went on fast. "The season's shaping up," he said. "I can see thee's all primed[5] to say, 'Jess, let's get a setting of goose eggs.'"

Eliza went over to the bean kettle and began to lift out dumplings. "It's a forwarder season than thee thinks, Jess," she said. "I got a setting under a hen now."

Jess looked at his wife. He didn't know what had made him want spring's variety in a human being—nor Eliza's substituting doing for asking. And speaking of it just now, as he had, made opposition kind of ticklish.

"When'd thee set them?" he asked finally.

"Yesterday," said Eliza.

"Where'd thee get the eggs?"

"Overbys'," said Eliza. The Overbys were their neighbors to the south.

"Well, they got enough for a surety," Jess said, "to give a few away."

---

4 **full of humors:** moody.

5 **primed** (prīmd): prepared.

"The Overbys don't give anything away, as thee knows. I paid for them. With my own money," Eliza added.

"How many?" Jess asked.

"Eight," Eliza said.

Jess turned back to his window. The sun had set, leaving a sad green sky and desolate black and white earth. "Five acres of corn gone," he calculated.

"Thee said," Eliza reminded him, "that what thee wanted was a little variety in me. 'Steady as a pump bolt,' were thy words."

"I know I did," Jess admitted glumly. "I talk too much."

"Draw up thy chair," Eliza said placidly, not contradicting him; "here's Enoch and the boys."

Next morning after breakfast Jess and Enoch left the kitchen together. The sun was the warmest the year had yet produced and the farm roofs were steaming; south branch, swollen by melting snow, was running so full the soft lap of its eddies[6] could be heard in the barnyard; a rooster tossed his voice into the bright air, loud and clear as if aiming to be heard by every fowl in Jennings County.

"Enoch," said Jess to his hired man, "what's thy feeling about geese?"

Enoch was instantly equipped, for the most part, with feelings on every subject. Geese was a homelier topic than he'd choose himself to enlarge upon, not one that could be much embellished[7] nor one on which Mr. Emerson,[8] so far's he could recall, had ever expressed an opinion. "In the fall of the year," he said, "long about November or December, there's nothing tastier on the table than roast goose."

"Goose on the table's not what I mean," Jess said. "I was speaking of goose on the hoof. Goose nipping off a stand of corn, Enoch, goose roistering round, honking and hissing so's thee can't hear thyself think, goose eyeing thee like a snake on stilts."

Enoch gazed at his employer for a few seconds. "Mr. Birdwell," he said, "I think that if they's an ornery bird, it's a goose. Ornery and undependable."

"I'm glad we's so like minded about them," Jess said. "Otherwise, I'd not like to ask thee to do this little job." He pulled a long darning needle from beneath the lapel of his coat.

Enoch eyed it with some mistrust. "I can't say's I've ever been handy with a needle, Mr. Birdwell."

"Thee'll be handy enough for this," Jess said with hearty conviction. "To come to it, Enoch, Eliza's set eight goose eggs. Next year with any luck she'd have two dozen. And so on. More and more. Feeling the way thee does, Enoch, about geese it's no more'n fair to give thee a chance to put a stop to this before it goes too far. One little puncture in each egg with this and the goose project's nipped in the bud and Eliza none the wiser."

"I'm mighty awkward with my hands," said Enoch, "doing fine work. Ticklish job like this I might drop an egg and break it."

"Enoch," said Jess, "thee's not developing a weakness for geese, is thee?"

"It ain't the geese," said Enoch frankly, "it's your wife. She's been mighty clever[9] to me and if she's got her heart set on geese, it'd go against the grain to disappoint her. Whyn't you do it, Mr. Birdwell?"

"Same reason," said Jess, "only more of them—and if Eliza ever asks if I tampered with that setting of eggs I figure on being able

---

6 **eddies** (ed' ēz): currents of water.
7 **embellished** (em bel' ishd): made more interesting.
8 **Mr. Emerson**: Ralph Waldo Emerson, 19th-century American poet and essayist.

9 **clever**: good-natured.

to say No." Jess held the needle nearer Enoch, who looked at it but still made no motion to take it.

"Likely no need to do a thing," Enoch said. "Two to one those eggs'll never hatch anyways. Overbys' such a fox-eared tribe they more'n likely sold her bad eggs to begin with."

"Thee's knowed about this," Jess asked, "all along?"

"Yes," Enoch said.

"Here's the needle," Jess said.

"You look at this," Enoch inquired, "not so much as a favor asked as a part of the day's work with orders from you?"

"Yes," Jess said, "that's about the way I look at it."

Enoch took the needle, held it somewhat gingerly, and with the sun glinting across its length, walked slowly toward the chickenhouse.

It takes thirty days for a goose egg to hatch, and the time, with spring work to be done, went fast. The hen Eliza had picked was a good one and kept her mind strictly on her setting. Eliza kept her mind on the hen, and Jess and Enoch found their minds oftener than they liked on Eliza and her hoped-for geese.

At breakfast on the day the geese were due to break their shells Jess said, "If I's thee, Eliza, I wouldn't bank too much on them geese. I heard Enoch say a while back he wouldn't be surprised if not an egg hatched. Thought the eggs were likely no good."

Enoch was busy pouring coffee into a saucer, then busy cooling it, but Eliza waited until he was through. "Did thee say that, Enoch?"

Enoch looked at Jess. "Yes," he said, "I kind of recollect something of the sort."

"What made thee think so, Enoch?"

"Why," said Jess, for Enoch was busy with his coffee again, "it was the Overbys. Enoch's got a feeling they's kind of unreliable. Fox-eared, I think thee said, Enoch, didn't thee?"

Enoch's work took him outside almost at once and Jess himself said, "If thee'll just give me a little packet of food, Eliza, I won't trouble thee for anything at noon. I'm going to be over'n the south forty and it'll save time coming and going."

Eliza was surprised for Jess'd usually come twice as far for a hot dinner at midday, but she made him fried ham sandwiches and put them and some cold apple-turnovers in a bag.

"It's a pity thee has to miss thy dinner," she told him, but Jess only said, "Press of work, press of work," and hurriedly departed.

Jess came home that evening through the spring twilight, somewhat late, and found a number of things to do at the barn before he went up to the house. When he entered the kitchen nothing seemed amiss—lamps ruddy, table set, stove humming, and beside the stove a small box over which Eliza was bending. Jess stopped to look—and listen; from inside the box was coming a kind of birdlike peeping, soft and not unpleasant. Reluctantly he walked to Eliza's side. There, eating minced boiled egg, and between bites lifting its beak to Eliza, it seemed, and making those chirping sounds he'd heard was a gray-gold gosling.

Eliza looked up pleasantly. "Enoch was right," she said. "The eggs were bad. Only one hatched. I plan to call it Samantha," she told Jess. "It's a name I've always been partial to."

"Samantha," said Jess without any enthusiasm whatever for either name or gosling. "How's thee know it's a she?"

"I don't," said Eliza, "but if it's a gander it's a name easily changed to Sam."

Enoch came in just then with a load of wood for the kitchen woodbox. "Enoch," asked Jess, "has thee seen Samantha—or Sam?"

Enoch mumbled but Jess understood him to say he had.

"It was my understanding, Enoch, that thy opinion was that all those eggs were bad."

"Well, Mr. Birdwell," said Enoch, "a man could make a mistake. He could count wrong."

"A man ought to be able to count to eight without going astray," Jess said.

Eliza was paying no attention to either of them; she was making little tweeting sounds herself, bending over the chirping gosling. "Does thee know," she asked Jess, "that this is the first pet I ever had in my life?"

"Thee's got Ebony," Jess said.

"I don't mean a caged pet," Eliza said, "but one to walk beside thee. I'm reconciled the others didn't hatch. With eight I'd've had to raise geese for the table. With one only I can make Samantha a pure pet."

A pure pet was what she made of her: Samantha ate what the family ate, with the exception of articles which Eliza thought might be indigestible and would risk on humans but not on her goose. Cake, pie, corn-on-the-cob, there was nothing too good for Samantha. From a big-footed, gold-downed gosling she swelled, almost at once, like a slack sail which gets a sudden breeze, into a full-rounded convexity.[10]

"Emphasis on the vexity," Jess said when he thought of this. Samantha was everything he'd disliked in the general run of geese, with added traits peculiar to herself, which vexed[11] him. Because she was fed at the

doorstep, she was always underfoot. No shout, however loud, would move her before she's ready to move. If she's talked to too strong she'd flail you with her wings and pinch the calf of your leg until for some days it would look to be mortifying.[12] She'd take food out of children's hands and the pansies Jess had planted in a circle at the base of the Juneberry tree she sheared so close that there was not a naked stem left to show for all his work. And when not being crossed in any way, Jess simply looking at her and meditating, trying to fathom[13] Samantha's fascination for Eliza, the goose would suddenly extend her snakelike neck, and almost touching Jess, hiss with such a hint of icy disapprobation[14] that Jess would involuntarily recoil.

But she was Eliza's pure pet, no two ways about that, and would lift her head for Eliza to scratch, and walk beside her with the lordly roll of the known elect.

"There was some goddess," Enoch remembered, "who always had a big bird with

---

10 **convexity** (con veks′ ə ti): curve.
11 **vexed**: annoyed.

12 **mortifying** (môr′ tə fī ing): infected with gangrene.
13 **fathom**: understand.
14 **disapprobation** (dis ap rō bā′ shən): disapproval; dislike.

her." Jess supposed Enoch was thinking of Juno and her peacock, but the reference didn't convince him that a goose was a suitable companion for any goddess—let alone Eliza, and he couldn't honestly feel much regret when one evening toward the end of November Eliza told him Samantha was missing. "She'll turn up," Jess said. "That bird's too ornery to die young."

Eliza said nothing, but next evening she proved Jess was right. "Samantha's over at Overbys'," she said.

"Well, did thee fetch her home?" Jess asked.

"No," said Eliza with righteous indignation, "they wouldn't let me. They said they had forty geese—and forty's what they got now, and they don't think Samantha's there. They provoked me so, Jess, I told them they'd sold me seven bad eggs and now they try to take the eighth away from me."

Jess felt a little abashed at this, but he asked, "How can thee be so sure Samantha's there? She might've been carried off by a varmint."

Eliza was scornful. "Thee forgets I hand-raised Samantha from a gosling. I'd know her among four hundred—let alone forty."

"Whyn't thee buy her back then," Jess asked, "if that's the only way?"

"After what I said about their eggs," Eliza answered sadly, "the Overbys say they don't want any more dealings with me."

Eliza mourned so for the lost Samantha that first Enoch and then Jess went over to the Overbys' but no one there would admit the presence of a visiting goose—forty they had, and forty you could see by counting was what they had now. Short of force there didn't seem any way of getting Samantha home again.

When Eliza heard the Overbys were going to sell geese for Christmas eating she was frantic. "Jess," she said, "I just can't bear to think of Samantha, plucked naked and resting on a table waiting to be carved. She used to sing as sweet as any bird when she was little, and she'd walk by my side taking the air. She's the only goose I ever heard of," Eliza remembered mournfully, "who'd drink tea."

In Jess's opinion a goose'd eat anything at either end of the scale, but he didn't suppose this was a suitable time to mention it to Eliza. "Eliza," he said, "short of me and Enoch's going over there and using force on old man Overby—or sneaking over at night and breaking into their chicken pen, I don't know how in the world we're going to get Samantha back for thee."

"We could sue," said Eliza.

"Thee mean go to law?" Jess asked, astounded. Quakers stayed out of courts, believing in amicable settlements without recourse to law.

"Yes," said Eliza. "I'd do it for Samantha. I'd think it my duty. Going to law'd be a misery for us . . . but not so lasting a misery as being roasted would be for Samantha."

Jess couldn't deny this, but he said, "I'd have to think it over. I've never been to law yet in my life and suing for a gone goose don't seem to me a very likely place to start."

Next morning Eliza served a good but silent breakfast, not sitting herself to eat with the rest of her family.

"Thee feeling dauncy,[15] Eliza?" Jess asked.

"I just can't eat," she said, "for thinking of Samantha."

Labe and Mattie had tears in their eyes. Little Jess was mournfully bellowing. Enoch looked mighty glum. Jess felt ashamed to be swallowing victuals in the midst of so much sorrow. Eliza stood at the end of the stove

---

15 **dauncy** (dôn' si): sickly.

where the gosling's box had rested for the first few weeks of its life, looking down, as if remembering how it had sung and lifted its beak to her.

Jess couldn't stand it. "Eliza," he said, "if thee wants to go through with it I'll go to Vernon and fee a lawyer for thee. Thee'll have to go to court, be on the witness stand—and even then I misdoubt thee'll ever get thy goose back. Does thee still want me to do it?"

Eliza came to the table and stood with her hand on Jess' shoulder. "Yes, Jess," she said, "I want thee to do it."

Jess went to Vernon, fee'd a lawyer, had a restraining order put on the Overbys so they couldn't sell or kill the goose Eliza said was Samantha, and awaited with misgivings the day of the trial. It came in mid-December.

Eliza, Jess and Enoch rode to the trial through a fall of light, fresh snow. Brilliant sunlight, crisp air, glittering snow, and Rome's spirited stepping made the occasion, in spite of its purpose, seem festive. Eliza made it seem festive. Jess, who did not forget its purpose, regarded her with some wonder. He couldn't say what it was about her—dress and bonnet appeared to be simply her First Day[16] best—but she had a holiday air.

He considered it his duty to warn her. "Eliza," he said, "thee understands thee's not going to Meeting?[17] They're not going to sit silent while thee tells them how much thee loves Samantha and how she sang when young and drank tea. Old man Overby'll have his say and he's got a lawyer hired for no other purpose than to trip thee up."

Eliza was unimpressed. "What's our lawyer fee'd for, Jess?" she asked.

Jess took another tack. "Eliza," he told her,

"I don't figger thee's got a chance in a thousand to get Samantha back."

"This is a court of justice, isn't it?" Eliza asked.

"Yes," Jess said.

"Then there's no need for thee to fash[18] thyself, Jess Birdwell. I'll get Samantha back."

Not getting Samantha back wasn't what fashed Jess—he reckoned he could bear up under that mighty well. What fashed him was the whole shooting match. . . . In some few cases, matters of life and death, going to court might be necessary, and he could imagine such. But a suit over a goose named Samantha wasn't one of them. And poor Eliza. Law to her was all Greek and turkey tracks . . . and here she was bound for court as chipper as if she was Chief Justice Taney[19] himself. Jess sighed and shook his head. Getting shut of Samantha would be no hardship for him, but he was downcast for Eliza's sake and the way she'd have to turn homeward empty-handed.

In the courtroom hard, clear light reflected upward from the snow fell onto what Jess thought were hard faces: courthouse hangers on; farmers whose slackening work made the diversion[20] of a trial an inviting possibility; lovers of oddity who figured a tilt between a Quaker female, preacher, to boot, and an old sinner like Milt Overby over the ownership of a goose ought to produce some enlivening quirks. They stared at Eliza, exchanged salutes with Milt Overby and inspected Samantha who in her crate awaited the court's decision.

The two lawyers, Jess considered to be on a par. Nothing fancy, either one . . . old

---

16 **First Day:** Sunday.
17 **Meeting:** Quaker religious service.

18 **fash:** trouble.
19 **Chief Justice Taney:** Roger Brooke Taney (tô′ nĭ), Chief Justice of the United States Supreme Court, 1836 - 1864.
20 **diversion** (də vėr′ zhən): pleasant change.

roadsters both, gone gray in service and with a knowledge of their business. The circuit judge was something else, unaccountably young, jug-eared and dressed more sprightly than a groom for his own wedding. A city whippersnapper, born and trained north of the Mississinewa, and now, in Jess's opinion, setting a squeamish foot in backwoods provinces, and irked to find himself trying so trifling a case. Didn't know a goose from a guinea hen, like as not, and would consider tossing a coin a more suitable manner of settling such a matter—just as near right in the end—and his valuable time saved.

Eliza, Jess saw, was of no such opinion. She, too, was scanning the young judge, and Jess, who knew her, saw from the look on her face that she was taken by him. A neat, thin, pious boy—far from home—he looked, no doubt to her; a young man who could do with better cooking and more regular eating.

The young man rapped the court to order. Spitting and shuffling slackened and in a high, precise voice he read, "Birdwell versus Overby. Charge, petty larceny. Appropriation and willful withholding of goose named Samantha." The name Samantha seemed to somewhat choke him, but he got it out.

"Ready for Birdwell," said Mr. Abel Samp, Eliza's lawyer.

"Ready for Overby," said the defendant's lawyer.

Eliza was the first witness on the stand. Jess sometimes forgot what a good-looking woman Eliza was, but the interest shown on lifted faces all about him refreshed his memory.

"Swear the plaintiff in," the judge said.

Eliza, in her sweet voice, spoke directly to the judge. "I don't swear," she said.

The judge explained that profanity was not asked for. "I understood," said Eliza, "that thee wasn't asking for profanity. No one would think that of thee. But we Quakers do not take oaths in court. We affirm."[21]

"Permit Mrs. Birdwell to affirm," said the judge. Eliza affirmed.

Mr. Samp then proceeded to question Eliza as to Samantha's birth and habits.

"Judge," Eliza began.

"Address the judge," Mr. Samp said, "as Your Honor."

"We Quakers," Eliza told the judge, gently, "do not make use of such titles. What is thy name? I think thee'll go far in our state and thy name's one I'd like to know."

The judge appeared somewhat distraught, undecided as to whether to make the tone of the court brisk and legal (if possible) or to follow Eliza's lead of urbane[22] sociability.

"Pomeroy," he said and made a slight bow in Eliza's direction.

Eliza returned the bow, deeper and with more grace. "Friend Pomeroy," she said, "it is indeed a pleasure to know thee."

Samantha's story as Eliza told it to Friend Pomeroy was surprisingly terse.[23] Affecting, and losing nothing by Eliza's telling, but to the point.

"Mrs. Birdwell," said Samp, "how long have you had an acquaintanceship with geese and their habits?"

"Since I was a child," Eliza said. "My father was a great fancier of geese."

"And you think you could identify this goose Samantha, which you admit in looks was similar to the defendant's?"

"I could," Eliza said with much authority.

Mr. Samp, to Jess's surprise, left the matter there. "Take the witness," he said to

---

21 **affirm** (ə fėrm´): declare something to be true.
22 **urbane** (ėr bān´): well-mannered.
23 **terse**: short and to the point; brief.

Overby's lawyer—but the counsel for the defendant was in no hurry to cross-examine Eliza. Instead he put his client on the stand.

"Farewell, Samantha," Jess said to Enoch.

"You relieved?" Enoch asked.

"Putting Eliza first," Jess said, "as I do, no."

Milt Overby, whose natural truculence[24] was somewhat stimulated by a nip he'd had to offset snappy weather, bellowed his way through his testimony. At one juncture he set the judge aright when he asked some elementary questions concerning the habits and configurations of geese. "Where in tarnation you from?" he snorted. "What they mean sending us judges down here who don't know Toulouse from Wyandotte,[25] or goose from gander?"

The young judge used voice and gavel to quiet the guffawing which filled the courtroom and the trial proceeded. A number of witnesses for both sides were brought to the stand and while it was shown that Overbys had maybe eaten a goose or two and neglected out of pure fondness for the creatures to count them as among the departed, still nobody had been able to positively identify Samantha.

Mr. Overby's lawyer seemed somewhat loath to cross-examine Eliza, but he put her on the stand. She'd said she knew geese and her testimony had been direct and positive. "Mrs. Birdwell," he said, "how can you be so sure your goose was with my client's geese?"

Eliza's black eyes rested confidingly upon the judge. "Friend Pomeroy," she said, "I raised Samantha from a gosling."

Jess sighed. "Here it comes," he said, "how that goose could sing and drink tea."

Eliza continued, "And there's one thing about her that always set her apart from every other goose."

"Yes, Mrs. Birdwell," said Judge Pomeroy, who was inclined to forget, with Eliza on the stand, that he was in a courtroom.

"Samantha," said Eliza, with much earnestness, "from the day she was born had a gait unlike any other goose I ever saw and one that set her apart from all her Overby connections. I picked her out at once when I went over there, because of it. Thee couldn't've missed it, Friend Pomeroy."

"Yes, Mrs. Birdwell," said the judge with interest in his voice.

"Samantha," said Eliza, "was a born pacer.[26] Thee knows what a pacer is?"

"Certainly," said Judge Pomeroy. "A pacer," he repeated with no surprise—and with obvious pleasure that Eliza'd hit upon so clear and differentiating an aspect of her goose and one that made identification possible.

A titter was mounting through the courtroom—Judge Pomeroy lifted his head. He had no desire to be further instructed as to the history, habits and breeds of geese, and he liked to see a trial settled by some such little and too often overlooked subtlety.[27] Judge Pomeroy brought down his gavel. "The court awards decision in favor of the plaintiff.[28] Case dismissed." While the silence that followed on his words still prevailed Judge Pomeroy stepped briskly and with obvious pleasure out through the rear door.

Jess was also brisk about departure. No use lingering until friend Pomeroy had been more thoroughly informed as to gaits in

---

24 **truculence** (truk' yə lens): fierce bullying.
25 **Toulouse . . . Wyandotte:** Toulouse is a French breed of fowl; Wyandotte is American.

26 **pacer:** that is, she moved with slow, regular steps.
27 **subtlety** (sut' əl tē): fine distinction.
28 **plaintiff:** one who files the complaint in the lawsuit.

general and geese in particular. Mid-afternoon's a quiet time in any season. In winter with snow on the ground, no leaves to rustle and bare limbs rigid as rock against a cloudless sky, the hush is deepest of all. Nothing broke that hush in the surrey, except the squeak of leather and snow, the muffled footfalls of Rome Beauty. Jess and Eliza, on the front seat, rode without speaking. Enoch, in the back, seemed to meditate. Even Samantha in her crate at Enoch's feet was silent.

Maple Grove Nursery was in sight before Jess spoke. "Eliza," he said, "would thee mind telling me—did thee ever see a trotting goose?"

Enoch ceased to meditate and listened. He had been wondering about this himself.

"Certainly not," said Eliza. "Thee knows as well as I, Jess Birdwell, an animal can't trot without hind feet and forefeet."

"So far, Eliza," Jess said, "we see eye to eye. Now maybe thee'd tell me—did thee ever see a goose that didn't pace?"

Eliza was truly amazed, it seemed. "Why, Jess," she said, "an ordinary goose just walks—but Samantha paces."

Jess was silent for a spell. "What'd thee say the difference is?"

"It's the swing, Jess Birdwell," said Eliza, "same as in a horse that nature's formed for a pacer . . . it's the natural bent, the way the spirit leads the beast to set his feet down. Samantha's a natural pacer."

That seemed as far as they'd likely get on the subject and Jess joined Enoch in meditation. In the barnyard, before she went up to the house, Eliza said, like an old hand at the business, "Attending court whettens the appetite. It's a little early but I thought if thee'd relish it"—and she looked at Jess and Enoch, never sparing a glance for Samantha, as if her menfolk's welfare was her sole concern—"I'd

stir us up a bite to eat. Hot tea and fresh sweetcakes, say. Might fry a little sausage and open some cherry preserves. If thee'd relish it," she repeated.

Jess wasn't taken in, but he'd relish it, and so would Enoch, and they both said so. They hustled with the unhitching so they could uncrate Samantha and note her progress with eyes newly instructed as to what made a pacer. Jess dumped her in the snow, and Enoch tapped her with his hat: Samantha made for the back door.

"By sugar," said Jess, "Eliza's right. She paces." Samantha had the smooth roll of a racker[29]—there were no two ways about it. At heart she was a pacer, and what two legs could do in that line, Samantha accomplished.

"With four legs," Enoch said, "you could enter her in any county fair—rack[30] on," he cried with enthusiasm. As they followed Samantha to the house, Enoch, for whom any event existed chiefly in its after aspects as a cud for rumination, asked, "How you feel in respect of court trials, now, Mr. Birdwell?"

---

29 **racker:** that is, she moved with the regular gait of a horse.
30 **rack:** a framework to which animals are fastened for feeding.

"I'm still against them," Jess said, "though they's three things this trial's taught me I might never otherwise have learned. Two's about women."

Enoch revered[31] all knowledge and he had a notion that information on this subject might have a more than transcendental[32] value. "What's the two things you learned about women, Mr. Birdwell?"

"Well, Enoch, I learned first, dependability's woman's greatest virtue. Steady as a pump bolt, day in, day out. When thee finds a woman like that, Enoch, don't try to change her. Not even in spring."

"No, sir," said Enoch, "I won't."

"Second, when it's a case of woman and the law—thee don't need to waste any worry on the woman."

"No, sir," said Enoch again.

When they reached the back steps, Enoch asked, "I understood you to say you'd learned three things, Mr. Birdwell. What's the third about?"

"Hired men," said Jess.

Enoch was taken aback, but he'd asked for it. "Yes, Mr. Birdwell," he said.

"Never hire one," Jess told him, "till thee finds out first if he can count to eight. Save thyself a lot of trouble that way, Enoch."

"How's I to know the eighth'd turn out to be Samantha?" Enoch asked.

Samantha herself, who was waiting at the doorstep for an expected tidbit, reached out and, unhampered by either boots or work pants, nipped Enoch firmly through his thin Sunday best.

"Thee say something, Enoch?" Jess asked.

Enoch had but he didn't repeat it. Instead he said, "Pacer or no pacer, that's Samantha," and the two of them stepped out of the snow into the warm kitchen, scented with baking sweetcakes and frying sausage.

---

31 **revered** (rə vērd'): respected highly; honored.
32 **transcendental** (tran sən den' təl): theoretical; difficult to understand.

Discussion

1. At the beginning of the story, Jess Birdwell expresses some dissatisfaction with life. Why? How does Eliza feel about her life?

2. Where and why does Jess introduce geese into the conversation? How does Jess feel about geese? How does Eliza feel about them? What has she done as a result of that feeling?

3. At one point in the story Jess asks, "Enoch, what's thy feeling toward geese?" What do you think is the purpose of his question? What are Enoch's true feelings about geese?

4. Why do you think the author skips thirty days between the time that Jess and Enoch put their plan into action and the scene in which they next appear? Why does the author have Jess leave for the entire day, not coming back to the house for his usual midday dinner? Why is he surprised when he does finally come home?

What does he mean in his remark to Enoch: "A man ought to be able to count to eight without going astray"?

5. Why, in your opinion, is Eliza willing to take the Samantha case to court? How can she distinguish Samantha from other geese? Why do you think the judge awards the goose to Eliza?

6. What are three things that Jess learns from the trial? What is the purpose of his remark to Enoch: "Never hire one [a man] till thee finds out first if he can count to eight"? What is the significance of Enoch's response?

7. Though the story seems to focus on the disagreement between a man and a woman over the suitability of a goose as a pet, the author is actually making an important observation about human nature. What do you think she is saying?

Composition

1. As you have seen, Eliza is a woman of determination. Yet Jess, too, shows himself to have determination. Choose either Eliza or Jess. Then in a short composition, tell in your own words why she or he is a determined person.

2. To Jess, a goose is a mean destroyer of crops and flowers. To Eliza, a goose is a lordly creature, a worthwhile pet. In your opinion, is what Jess did about the goose eggs fair and honest? Remember; he is concerned about the safety of his farm. In a short composition, give your appraisal of Jess's actions. Is he right, or is he wrong in what he does? Why?

Jessamyn West 1907 —

Jessamyn West's first book, *The Friendly Persuasion,* is a portrait of Indiana Quaker life during the Civil War. West used her own Quaker childhood in Indiana as a starting point for presenting her characters. Her other books and stories have been quite varied in focus.

West says that the four cornerstones of her life are "family, words on paper (this means books and writing), the world of nature (weeds, wind, buzzards, clouds), and privacy." One time she spent several months in a house trailer, just to be by herself. When she came out, she had written a book of recollections about her life.

Mother to Son

LANGSTON HUGHES

Well, son, I'll tell you:
Life for me ain't been no crystal stair.
It's had tacks on it,
And splinters,
And boards torn up,   5
And places with no carpet on the floor—
Bare.
But all the time
I'se been a-climbin' on,
And reachin' landin's,   10
And turnin' corners,
And sometimes goin' in the dark
Where there ain't been no light.
So, boy, don't you turn back.
Don't you set down on the steps   15
'Cause you finds it's kinder hard.
Don't you fall now—
For I'se still goin', honey,
I'se still climbin',
and life for me ain't been no crystal stair.   20

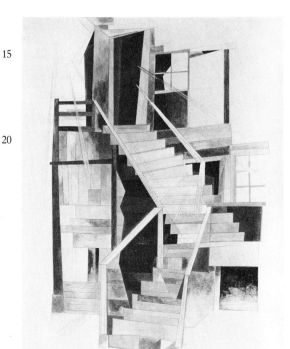

STAIRS, PROVINCETOWN 1920 *Charles Demuth*

1. In this pep talk to her son, the Mother is actually making a comparison. What two things is she comparing?
2. What do you think these words and phrases stand for: "tacks," "splinters," "boards torn up," and "places with no carpet on the floor"?
3. What do you understand these words to mean: "reachin' landin's," "turnin' corners," and "sometimes goin' in the dark/Where there ain't been no light"?
4. Why does the Mother tell her son, "don't you turn back./Don't you set down on the steps"?
5. At one point, the Mother says: "Life for me ain't been no crystal stair." What does she mean?
6. Explain how the Mother's words do or do not show determination.

Langston Hughes 1902—1967

Langston Hughes was an outstanding writer of Harlem during its literary re-awakening in the 1920s. After graduating from high school in Cleveland, Ohio, Hughes worked at odd jobs in New York, Paris, and at sea. His literary break came when he was working as a busboy at a hotel in Washington. The well-known poet Vachel Lindsay was dining at the hotel. Hughes left three of his poems beside Lindsay's plate, and Lindsay later publicized them by including them at a reading of his own work. With this favorable introduction, Hughes became a well-known poet by the time he was twenty-four.

Hughes wrote about racial injustice and social struggle. The humor he used usually served a serious purpose. His poems reflected folk dialect; rhythms of jazz, blues, and spirituals; and social commentary.

It was determination that would make the difference—and stamina, too. One of them might then be lucky enough to stand for a moment where no one had ever stood before. Could any one of the eight men meet that challenge? Did any one of them have the stamina—and the determination?

Top Man

JAMES RAMSEY ULLMAN

THE GORGE BENT. The walls fell steeply away, and we came out on the edge of a bleak boulder-strewn valley. *And there it was.*

Osborn saw it first. He had been leading the column, threading his way slowly among the huge rock masses of the gorge's mouth. Then he came to the first flat bare place and stopped. He neither pointed nor cried out, but every man behind him knew instantly what it was. The long file sprang taut, like a jerked rope. As swiftly as we could, but in complete silence, we came out one by one into the open space where Osborn stood and raised our eyes with his.

In the records of the Indian Topographical Survey it says: "Kalpurtha: altitude 27,930 ft. The highest peak in the Garhwal Himalayas. Also known as K₃. A Tertiary formation of sedimentary limestone . . ."

There were men among us who had spent months of their lives—in some cases years—reading, thinking, planning about what now lay before us; but at that moment statistics and geology, knowledge, thought and plans,

were as remote and forgotten as the far-away western cities from which we had come. We were men bereft[1] of everything but eyes, everything but the single electric perception: *there it was!*

Before us the valley stretched into miles of rocky desolation. To right and left it was bounded by low ridges, which, as the eye followed them, slowly mounted and drew closer together, until the valley was no longer a valley at all, but a narrowing, rising corridor between the cliffs. What happened then I can describe only as a stupendous crash of music. At the end of the corridor and above it—so far above it that it shut out half the sky—hung the blinding white mass of K₃.

It was like the many pictures I had seen, and at the same time utterly unlike them. The shape was there, and the familiar distinguishing features: the sweeping skirt of glaciers; the monstrous vertical precipices of the face and the jagged ice line of the east ridge;

---

1 **bereft** (bi reft′): deprived.

finally the symmetrical summit pyramid that transfixed the sky. But whereas in the pictures the mountain had always seemed unreal—a dream-image of cloud, snow and crystal—it was now no longer an image at all. It was a mass: solid, palpable, appalling. We were still too far away to see the windy whipping of its snowplumes or to hear the cannonading of its avalanches, but in that sudden silent moment every man of us was for the first time aware of it not as a picture in his mind, but as a thing, an antagonist.[2] For all its twenty-eight thousand feet of lofty grandeur it seemed, somehow, less to tower than to crouch—a white-hooded giant, secret and remote, but living. Living and on guard.

I turned my eyes from the dazzling glare and looked at my companions. Osborn still stood a little in front of the others. He was absolutely motionless, his young face tense and shining, his eyes devouring the mountain as a lover's might devour the form of his beloved. One could feel in the very set of his body the overwhelming desire that swelled in him to act, to come to grips, to conquer. A little behind him were ranged the other white men of the expedition: Randolph, our leader, Wittmer and Johns, Dr. Schlapp and Bixler. All were still, their eyes cast upward. Off to one side a little stood Nace, the Englishman, the only one among us who was not staring at K$_3$ for the first time. He had been the last to come up out of the gorge and stood now with arms folded on his chest, squinting at the great peak he had known so long and fought so tirelessly and fiercely. His lean British face, under its mask of stubble and windburn, was expressionless. His lips were a thin line, and his eyes seemed almost shut. Behind the sahibs[3] ranged the porters,

bent forward over their staffs, their brown seamed faces straining upward from beneath their loads.

For a long while no one spoke or moved. The only sounds were the soft hiss of our breathing and the pounding of our hearts.

Through the long afternoon we wound slowly between the great boulders of the valley and at sundown pitched camp in the bed of a dried-up stream. The porters ate their rations in silence, wrapped themselves in their blankets and fell asleep under the stars. The rest of us, as was our custom, sat close about the fire that blazed in the circle of tents, discussing the events of the day and the plans for the next. It was a flawlessly clear Himalayan night, and K$_3$ tiered up into the blackness like a gigantic beacon lighted from within. There was no wind, but a great tide of cold air crept down the valley from the ice fields above, penetrating our clothing, pressing gently against the canvas of the tents.

"Another night or two and we'll be needing the sleeping bags," commented Randolph.

Osborn nodded. "We could use them tonight would be my guess."

Randolph turned to Nace. "What do you say, Martin?"

The Englishman puffed at his pipe a moment. "Rather think it might be better to wait," he said at last.

"Wait? Why?" Osborn jerked his head up.

"Well, it gets pretty nippy high up, you know. I've seen it thirty below at twenty-five thousand on the east ridge. The longer we wait for the bags, the better acclimated[4] we'll get."

Osborn snorted. "A lot of good being acclimated will do, if we have frozen feet."

---

2 **antagonist** (an tag′ ə nist): opponent.
3 **sahibs** (sä′ hibz): masters.

4 **acclimated** (ə klī′ mə təd): used to the weather and the climate.

"Easy, Paul, easy," cautioned Randolph. "It seems to me Martin's right."

Osborn bit his lip, but said nothing. The other men entered the conversation, and soon it had veered to other matters: the weather, the porters and pack animals, routes, camps and strategy, the inevitable inexhaustible topics of the climber's world.

There were all kinds of men among the eight of us, men with a great diversity of background and interest. Sayre Randolph whom the Alpine Club had named leader of our expedition, had for years been a well-known explorer and lecturer. Now in his middle fifties, he was no longer equal to the grueling physical demands of high climbing, but served as planner and organizer of the enterprise. Wittmer was a Seattle lawyer, who had recently made a name for himself by a series of difficult ascents in the Coast Range of British Columbia. Johns was an Alaskan, a fantastically strong able sour-dough,[5] who had been a ranger in the U.S. Forestry Service and had accompanied many famous Alaskan expeditions. Schlapp was a practicing physician from Milwaukee, Bixler a government meteorologist with a talent for photography. I, at the time, was an assistant professor of geology at an eastern university.

Finally, and pre-eminently,[6] there were Osborn and Nace. I say "pre-eminently," because even at this time, when we had been together as a party for little more than a month, I believe all of us realized that these were the two key men of our venture. None, to my knowledge, ever expressed it in words, but the conviction was nonetheless there that if any of us were eventually to stand on the summit of K_3, it would be one of them or

both. They were utterly dissimilar men. Osborn was twenty-three and a year out of college, a compact buoyant mass of energy and high spirits. He seemed to be wholly unaffected by either the physical or mental hazards of mountaineering and had already, by virtue of many spectacular ascents in the Alps and Rockies, won a reputation as the most skilled and audacious[7] of younger American climbers. Nace was in his forties—lean, taciturn, introspective.[8] An official in the Indian Civil Service, he had explored and climbed in the Himalayas for twenty years. He had been a member of all four of the unsuccessful British expeditions to K_3, and in his last attempt had attained to within five hundred feet of the summit, the highest point which any man had reached on the uncon-quered giant. This had been the famous tragic attempt in which his fellow climber and lifelong friend, Captain Furness, had slipped and fallen ten thousand feet to his death. Nace never mentioned his name, but on the steel head of his ice ax were engraved the words: TO MARTIN FROM JOHN. If fate were to grant that the ax of any one of us should be planted upon the summit of K_3, I hoped it would be this one.

Such were the men who huddled about the fire in the deep still cold of a Himalayan night. There were many differences among us, in temperament as well as in background. In one or two cases, notably that of Osborn and Nace, there had already been a certain amount of friction, and as the venture con-tinued and the struggles and hardships of the actual ascent began, it would, I knew, in-crease. But differences were unimportant. What mattered—all that mattered—was that

---

5 **sourdough** (sour′ dō): prospector; explorer.
6 **pre-eminently** (prē em′ ə nənt lē): most importantly.

7 **audacious** (ô dā′ shəs): daring.
8 **taciturn/introspective** (tas′ ə turn / in trō spek′ tiv): not inclined to talk/thoughtful.

our purpose was one: to conquer the monster of rock and ice that now loomed above us in the night; to stand for a moment where no man, no living thing, had ever stood before. To that end we had come from half a world away, across oceans and continents to the fastnesses[9] of inner Asia. To that end we were prepared to endure cold, exhaustion and danger, even to the last extremity of human endurance. . . . Why? . . . There is no answer, and at the same time every man among us knew the answer; every man who has ever looked upon a great mountain and felt the fever in his blood to climb and conquer knows the answer. George Leigh Mallory, greatest of mountaineers, expressed

9 **fastnesses**: strongholds; places that are very difficult to reach.

it once and for all when he was asked why he wanted to climb unconquered Everest.

"I want to climb it," said Mallory, "because it is there."

Day after day we crept on and upward. Sometimes the mountain was brilliant above us, as it had been when we first saw it; sometimes it was partially or wholly obscured by tiers of clouds. The naked desolation of the valley was unrelieved by any motion, color or sound, and, as we progressed, the great rock walls that enclosed it grew so high and steep that its floor received the sun for less than two hours each day. The rest of the time it lay in ashen half-light, its gloom intensified by the dazzling brilliance of the ice slopes above. As long as we remained there we had the sensation of imprisonment; it was like being trapped at the

bottom of a deep well or in a sealed court between tall skyscrapers. Soon we were thinking of the ascent of the shining mountain not only as an end in itself, but as an escape.

In our nightly discussions around the fire our conversation narrowed more and more to the immediate problems confronting us, and during them I began to realize that the tension between Osborn and Nace went deeper than I had at first surmised.[10] There was rarely any outright argument between them—they were both far too able mountain men to disagree on fundamentals—but I saw that at almost every turn they were rubbing each other the wrong way. It was a matter of personalities, chiefly. Obsorn was talkative, enthusiastic, optimistic, always chafing to be up and at it, always wanting to take the short straight line to the given point. Nace, on the other hand, was matter-of-fact, cautious, slow. He was the apostle of trial and error and watchful waiting. Because of his far greater experience and intimate knowledge of K$_3$ Randolph almost invariably followed his advice, rather than Osborn's, when a difference of opinion arose. The younger man usually capitulated[11] with good grace, but I could tell that he was irked.

During the days in the valley I had few occasions to talk privately with either of them, and only once did either mention the other in any but the most casual manner. Even then, the remarks they made seemed unimportant and I remember them only in view of what happened later.

My conversation with Osborn occurred first. It was while we were on the march, and Osborn, who was directly behind me, came up suddenly to my side. "You're a geologist, Frank," he began without preamble.[12] "What do you think of Nace's theory about the ridge?"

"What theory?" I asked.

"He believes we should traverse under it from the glacier up. Says the ridge itself is too exposed."

"It looks pretty mean through the telescope."

"But it's been done before. He's done it himself. All right, it's tough—I'll admit that. But a decent climber could make it in half the time the traverse will take."

"Nace knows the traverse is longer," I said. "But he seems certain it will be much easier for us."

"Easier for *him* is what he means." Osborn paused, looking moodily at the ground. "He was a great climber in his day. It's a shame a man can't be honest enough with himself to know when he's through." He fell silent and a moment later dropped back into his place in line.

It was that same night, I think, that I awoke to find Nace sitting up in his blanket and staring at the mountain.

"How clear it is," I whispered.

The Englishman pointed. "See the ridge?"

I nodded, my eyes fixed on the great twisting spine of ice that climbed into the sky. I could see now, more clearly than in the blinding sunlight, its huge indentations and jagged wind-swept pitches.[13] "It looks impossible," I said.

"No, it can be climbed. Trouble is, when you've made it you're too done in for the summit."

---

10 **surmised** (sŭr mīzd′): guessed, imagined.
11 **capitulated** (kə pit′ yə lā ted): gave in; agreed.

12 **preamble** (prē′ am bəl): beginning remarks; introduction.
13 **pitches:** slopes.

"Osborn seems to think its shortness would make up for its difficulty."

Nace was silent a long moment before answering. Then for the first and only time I heard him speak the name of his dead companion. "That's what Furness thought," he said quietly. Then he lay down and wrapped himself in his blanket.

For the next two weeks the uppermost point of the valley was our home and workshop. We established our base camp as close to the mountain as we could, less than half a mile from the tongue of its lowest glacier, and plunged into the arduous tasks of preparation for the ascent. Our food and equipment were unpacked, inspected and sorted, and finally repacked in lighter loads for transportation to more advanced camps. Hours were spent poring over maps and charts and studying the intricate heights above us through telescope and binoculars. Under Nace's supervision, a thorough reconnaissance of the glacier was made and the route across it laid out; then began the backbreaking labor of moving up supplies and establishing the chain of camps.

Camps I and II were set up on the glacier itself, in the most sheltered sites we could find. Camp III we built at its upper end, as near as possible to the point where the great rock spine of K_3 thrust itself free of ice and began its precipitous[14] ascent. According to our plans, this would be the advance base of operations during the climb. The camps to be established higher up, on the mountain proper, would be too small and too exposed to serve as anything more than one or two nights' shelter. The total distance between the base camp and Camp III was only fifteen miles, but the utmost daily progress of our porters was five miles, and it was essential that we should never be more than twelve hours' march from food and shelter. Hour after hour, day after day, the long file of men wound up and down among the hummocks and crevasses of the glacier, and finally the time arrived when we were ready to advance.

Leaving Dr. Schlapp in charge of eight porters at the base camp, we proceeded easily and on schedule, reaching Camp I the first night, Camp II the second, and the advance base the third. No men were left at Camps I and II, inasmuch as they were designed simply as caches[15] for food and equipment; and furthermore we knew we would need all the man power available for the establishment of the higher camps on the mountain proper.

---

14 **precipitous** (prĕ sip′ ə təs): steep.
15 **caches** (kash′ ĕz): hiding places.

For more than three weeks now the weather had held perfectly, but on our first night at the advance base, as if by malignant[16] prearrangement of nature, we had our first taste of the fury of a high Himalayan storm. It began with great streamers of lightning that flashed about the mountain like a halo; then heavily through the weird glare snow began to fall. The wind rose. At first it was only sound—a remote, desolate moaning in the night high above us—but soon it descended, sucked down into the deep valley as if into an enormous funnel. Hour after hour it howled about the tents with hurricane frenzy, and the wild flapping of the canvas dinned in our ears like machine-gun fire.

16 **malignant** (mə lig' nənt): evil; intending evil.

There was no sleep for us that night or the next. For thirty-six hours the storm raged without lull, while we huddled in the icy gloom of the tents, exerting our last ounce of strength to keep from being either buried alive or blown into eternity. At last, on the third morning, it was over, and we came out into a world transformed by a twelve-foot cloak of snow. No single landmark remained as it had been before, and our supplies and equipment were in the wildest confusion. Fortunately there had not been a single serious injury, but it was another three days before we had regained our strength and put the camp in order.

Then we waited. The storm did not return, and the sky beyond the ridges gleamed flawlessly clear; but night and day we could hear the thunder of avalanches on the mountain above us. To have ventured so much as one step into that savage vertical wilderness before the new-fallen snow froze tight would have been suicidal. We chafed[17] or waited patiently, according to our individual temperaments, while the days dragged by.

It was late one afternoon that Osborn returned from a short reconnaissance up the ridge. His eyes were shining and his voice jubilant.

"It's tight," he cried. "Tight as a drum. We can go!" All of us stopped whatever we were doing. His excitement leapt like an electric spark from one to another. "I went about a thousand feet, and it's sound all the way. What do you say, Sayre? Tomorrow?"

Randolph hesitated, then looked at Nace.

"Better give it another day or two," said the Englishman.

Osborn glared at him. "Why?" he challenged.

"It's generally safer to wait until—"

"Wait! Wait!" Osborn exploded. "Don't you ever think of anything but waiting? Man, the snow's firm, I tell you!"

"It's firm down here," Nace replied quietly, "because the sun hits it only two hours a day. Up above it gets the sun for twelve hours. It may not have frozen yet."

"The avalanches have stopped."

"That doesn't necessarily mean it will hold a man's weight."

"It seems to me that Martin's point—" Randolph began.

Osborn wheeled on him. "Sure," he snapped. "I know. Martin's right. The cautious bloody English are always right. Let him have his way, and we'll be sitting here chewing our nails until the mountain falls down on us." His eyes flashed to Nace. "Maybe with a little less of that bloody cautiousness you English wouldn't have made such a mess of Everest. Maybe your pals Mallory and Furness wouldn't be dead."

"Osborn!" commanded Randolph sharply.

The youngster stared at Nace for another moment, breathing heavily. Then abruptly he turned away.

The next two days were clear and windless, but we still waited, following Nace's advice. There were no further brushes between him and Osborn, but an unpleasant air of restlessness and tension hung over the camp. I found myself chafing almost as impatiently as Osborn himself for the moment when we would break out of that maddening inactivity and begin the assault.

At last the day came. With the first paling of the sky a roped file of men, bent almost double beneath heavy loads, began slowly to climb the ice slope, just beneath the jagged line of the east ridge. In accordance with prearranged plan, we proceeded in relays, this first group consisting of Nace, Johns, myself, and eight porters. It was our job to ascend approximately two thousand feet in a day's climbing and establish Camp IV at the most level and sheltered site we could find. We would spend the night there and return to the advance base next day, while the second relay, consisting of Osborn, Wittmer, and eight more porters, went up with their loads. This process was to continue until all necessary supplies were at Camp IV, and then the whole thing would be repeated between Camps IV and V and V and VI. From VI, at an altitude of about 26,000 feet, the ablest and fittest men—presumably Nace and Osborn—would make the direct assault on the summit. Randolph and Bixler were to remain at the advance base throughout the operations, acting as directors and co-ordin-

---

17 **chafed** (chāft): complained; fretted.

ators. We were under the strictest orders that any man—sahib or porter—who suffered illness or injury should be brought down immediately.

How shall I describe those next two weeks beneath the great ice ridge of K$_3$? In a sense there was no occurrence of importance, and at the same time everything happened that could possibly happen, short of actual disaster. We established Camp IV, came down again, went up again, came down again. Then we crept laboriously higher. With our axes we hacked uncountable thousands of steps in the gleaming walls of ice. Among the rocky outcroppings of the cliffs we clung to holds and strained at ropes until we thought our arms would spring from their sockets. Winds swooped down on us, battered us and passed, and the air grew steadily colder and more difficult to breathe. One morning two of the porters awoke with their feet frozen black; they had to be sent down. A short while later Johns developed an uncontrollable nosebleed and was forced to descend to a lower camp. Wittmer was suffering from racking headaches and I from a continually dry throat. But providentially,[18] the one enemy we feared the most in that icy gale-lashed hell did not again attack us. No snow fell. And day by day, foot by foot, we ascended.

It is during ordeals like this that the surface trappings of a man are shed and his secret mettle[19] laid bare. There were no shirkers or quitters among us—I had known that from the beginning—but now, with each passing day, it became more manifest[20] which were the strongest and ablest among us. Beyond all argument, these were Osborn and Nace.

Osborn was magnificent. All the boyish impatience and moodiness which he had exhibited earlier were gone, and, now that he was at last at work in his natural element, he emerged as the peerless mountaineer he was. His energy was inexhaustible, his speed, both on rock and ice, almost twice that of any other man in the party. He was always discovering new routes and short cuts. Often he ascended by the ridge itself, instead of using the traverse beneath it, as had been officially prescribed; but his craftsmanship was so sure and his performance so brilliant that no one ever thought of taking him to task. Indeed, there was such vigor, buoyancy, and youth in everything he did that it gave heart to all the rest of us.

In contrast, Nace was slow, methodical, unspectacular. Since he and I worked in the same relay, I was with him almost constantly, and to this day I carry in my mind the clear image of the man: his tall body bent almost double against shimmering slopes of ice; his lean brown face bent in utter concentration on the problem in hand, then raised searchingly to the next; the bright prong of his ax rising, falling, rising, falling with tireless rhythm, until the steps in the glassy incline were so wide and deep that the most clumsy of the porters could not have slipped from them had he tried. Osborn attacked the mountain head on. Nace studied it, sparred with it, wore it down. His spirit did not flap from his sleeve like a pennon;[21] it was deep inside him—patient, indomitable.[22]

The day soon came when I learned from him what it is to be a great mountaineer. We were making the ascent from Camp IV to V, and an almost perpendicular ice wall had

---

18 **providentially** (prov ə dent' shə lē): luckily, miraculously.
19 **mettle**: stamina; ability to withstand hardship.
20 **more manifest**: plainer; more obvious.

21 **pennon** (pen' ən): flag; banner.
22 **indomitable** (in dom' it ə bəl): unconquerable.

made it necessary for us to come out for a few yards on the exposed crest of the ridge. There were six of us in the party, roped together, with Nace leading, myself second, and four porters bringing up the rear. The ridge at this particular point was free of snow, but razor-thin, and the rocks were covered with a smooth glaze of ice. On either side the mountain dropped away in sheer precipices of five thousand feet.

Suddenly the last porter slipped. I heard the ominous scraping of boot nails behind me and, turning, saw a gesticulating[23] figure plunge sideways into the abyss. There was a scream as the next porter was pulled off too. I remember trying frantically to dig into the ridge with my ax, realizing at the same time it would no more hold against the weight of the falling men than a pin stuck in a wall. Then I heard Nace shout, "Jump!" As he said it, the rope went tight about my waist, and I went hurtling after him into space on the opposite side of the ridge. After me came the nearest porter. . . .

What happened then must have happened in five yards and a fifth of a second. I heard myself cry out, and the glacier, a mile below, rushed up at me, spinning. Then both were blotted out in a violent spasm, as the rope jerked taut. I hung for a moment, an inert mass, feeling that my body had been cut in two; then I swung in slowly to the side of the mountain. Above me the rope lay tight and motionless across the crest of the ridge, our weight exactly counterbalancing that of the men who had fallen on the far slope.

Nace's voice came up from below. "You chaps on the other side!" he shouted. "Start climbing slowly. We're climbing too."

In five minutes we had all regained the ridge. The porters and I crouched panting on the jagged rocks, our eyes closed, the sweat beading our faces in frozen drops. Nace carefully examined the rope that again hung loosely between us.

"All right, men," he said presently. "Let's get on to camp for a cup of tea."

Above Camp V the whole aspect of the ascent changed. The angle of the ridge eased off, and the ice, which lower down had covered the mountain like a sheath, lay only in scattered patches between the rocks. Fresh enemies, however, instantly appeared to take the place of the old. We were now laboring at an altitude of more than 25,000 feet—well above the summits of the highest surrounding peaks—and day and night, without protection or respite,[24] we were buffeted by the fury of the wind. Worse than this was that the atmosphere had become so rarified it could scarcely support life. Breathing itself was a major physical effort, and our progress upward consisted of two or three painful steps followed by a long period of rest in which our hearts pounded wildly and our burning lungs gasped for air. Each of us carried a small cylinder of oxygen in his pack, but we used it only in emergencies and found that, while its immediate effect was salutary,[25] it left us later even worse off than before. My throat dried and contracted until it felt as if it were lined with brass. The faces of all of us, under our beards and windburn, grew haggard and strained.

But the great struggle was now mental as much as physical. The lack of air induced a lethargy[26] of mind and spirit; confidence and the powers of thought and decision waned,

---

23 **gesticulating** (je stik′ yə lāt ing): gesturing; suddenly motioning.

24 **respite** (res′ pit): relief.
25 **salutary** (sal′ yə ter ē): helpful; beneficial.
26 **lethargy** (leth′ ər jē): inaction; laziness.

and dark foreboding crept out from the secret recesses of the subconscious. The wind seemed to carry strange sounds, and we kept imagining we saw things which we knew were not there. The mountain, to all of us, was no longer a mere giant of rock and ice; it had become a living thing, an enemy, watching us, waiting for us, hostile, relentless, and aware. Inch by inch we crept upward through that empty forgotten world above the world, and only one last thing remained to us of human consciousness and human will: to go on. To go on.

On the fifteenth day after we had first left the advance base we pitched Camp VI at an altitude of almost 26,000 feet. It was located near the uppermost extremity of the east ridge, directly beneath the so-called shoulder of the mountain. On the far side of the shoulder the vast north face of K_3 fell sheer to the glaciers, two miles below. And above it and to the left rose the symmetrical bulk of the summit pyramid. The topmost rocks of its highest pinnacle were clearly visible from the shoulder, and the intervening two thousand feet seemed to offer no insuperable obstacles.

Camp VI, which was in reality no camp at all, but a single tent, was large enough to accommodate only three men. Osborn established it with the aid of Wittmer and one porter; then, the following morning, Wittmer and the porter descended to Camp V, and Nace and I went up. It was our plan that Osborn and Nace should launch the final assault—the next day, if the weather held—with myself in support, following their progress through binoculars and going to their aid or summoning help from below if anything went wrong. As the three of us lay in the tent that night, the summit seemed already within arm's reach, victory securely in our grasp.

Then the blow fell. With malignant timing, which no power on earth could have made us believe was a simple accident of nature, the mountain hurled at us its last line of defense. It snowed.

For a day and a night the great flakes drove down upon us, swirling and swooping in the wind, blotting out the summit, the shoulder, everything beyond the tiny white-walled radius of our tent. Hour after hour we lay in our sleeping bags, stirring only to eat or to secure the straining rope and canvas. Our feet froze under their thick layers of wool and rawhide. Our heads and bodies throbbed with a dull nameless aching, and time crept over our numbed minds like a glacier. At last, during the morning of the following day, it cleared. The sun came out in a thin blue sky, and the summit pyramid again appeared above us, now whitely robed in fresh snow. But still we waited. Until the snow either froze or was blown away by the wind, it would have been the rashest courting of destruction for us to have ascended a foot beyond the camp. Another day passed. And another.

By the third nightfall our nerves were at the breaking point. For hours on end we had scarcely moved or spoken, and the only sounds in all the world were the endless moaning of the wind outside and the harsh sucking noise of our breathing. I knew that, one way or another, the end had come. Our meager food supply was running out; even with careful rationing there was enough left for only two more days.

Presently Nace stirred in his sleeping bag and sat up. "We'll have to go down tomorrow," he said quietly.

For a moment there was silence in the tent. Then Osborn struggled to a sitting position and faced him.

"No," he said.

"There's still too much loose snow above. We can't make it."

"But it's clear. As long as we can see—"

Nace shook his head. "Too dangerous. We'll go down tomorrow and lay in a fresh supply. Then we'll try again."

"Once we go down we're licked. You know it."

Nace shrugged. "Better to be licked than—" The strain of speech was suddenly too much for him and he fell into a paroxysm[27] of coughing. When it had passed there was a long silence.

Suddenly Osborn spoke again. "Look, Nace," he said, "I'm going up tomorrow."

The Englishman shook his head.

"I'm going—understand?"

For the first time since I had known him I saw Nace's eyes flash in anger. "I'm the senior member of this group," he said. "I forbid you to go!"

Osborn jerked himself to his knees, almost upsetting the tiny tent. "You forbid me? This may be your fifth time on the mountain, and all that, but you don't *own* it! I know what you're up to. You haven't got it in you to make the top yourself, so you don't want anyone else to make it. That's it, isn't it? Isn't it?" He sat down again suddenly, gasping for breath.

Nace looked at him with level eyes. "This mountain has beaten me four times," he said softly. "It killed my best friend. It means more to me to climb it than anything else in the world. Maybe I'll make it and maybe I won't. But if I do, it will be as a rational, intelligent human being—not as a fool throwing my life away."

He collapsed into another fit of coughing and fell back in his sleeping bag. Osborn, too, was still. They lay there inert,[28] panting, too exhausted for speech.

It was hours later that I awoke from dull, uneasy sleep. In the faint light I saw Nace fumbling with the flap of the tent.

"What is it?" I asked.

"Osborn. He's gone."

The words cut like a blade through my lethargy. I struggled to my feet and followed Nace from the tent.

Outside, the dawn was seeping up the eastern sky. It was very cold, but the wind had fallen and the mountain seemed to hang suspended in a vast stillness. Above us the summit pyramid climbed bleakly into space, like the last outpost of a spent and lifeless planet. Raising my binoculars, I swept them over the gray waste. At first I saw nothing but rock and ice; then, suddenly, something moved.

"I've got him," I whispered.

---

27 **paroxysm** (par' ək siz əm): fit; spasm.

28 **inert** (in ėrt'): motionless.

As I spoke, the figure of Osborn sprang into clear focus against a patch of ice. He took three or four slow upward steps, stopped, went on again. I handed the glasses to Nace.

The Englishman squinted through them, returned them to me, and re-entered the tent. When I followed he had already laced his boots and was pulling on his outer gloves.

"He's not far," he said. "Can't have been gone more than half an hour." He seized his ice ax and started out again.

"Wait," I said. "I'm going with you."

Nace shook his head. "Better stay here."

"I'm going with you," I said.

He said nothing further, but waited while I made ready. In a few moments we left the tent, roped up, and started off.

Almost immediately we were on the shoulder and confronted with the paralyzing two-mile drop of the north face; but we negotiated the short exposed stretch without mishap and in ten minutes were working up the base of the summit pyramid. The going here was easier, in a purely climbing sense: the angle of ascent was not steep, and there was firm rock for hand- and foot-holds between the patches of snow and ice. Our progress, however, was creepingly slow. There seemed to be literally no air at all, and after almost every step we were forced to rest, panting and gasping as we leaned forward against our axes. My heart swelled and throbbed with every movement until I thought it would explode.

The minutes crawled into hours, and still we climbed. Presently the sun came up. Its level rays streamed across the clouds, far below, and glinted from the summits of distant peaks. But, although the pinnacle of K_3 soared a full three thousand feet above anything in the surrounding world, we had scarcely any sense of height. The wilderness of mountain valley and glacier that spread beneath us to the horizon was flattened and remote, an unreal insubstantial landscape seen in a dream. We had no connection with it, or it with us. All living, all awareness, purpose and will, were concentrated in the next step, and the next; to put one foot before the other; to breathe; to ascend. We struggled on in silence.

I don't know how long it was since we had left the camp—it might have been two hours, it might have been six—when we suddenly sighted Osborn. We had not been able to find him again since our first glimpse through the binoculars; but now, unexpectedly and abruptly, as we came up over a bulge of rock, there he was. He was at a point only a few yards above us, where the mountain steepened into an almost vertical wall. The smooth surface directly in front of him was obviously unclimbable, but two alternate routes were presented. To the left, a chimney cut obliquely[29] across the wall, forbiddingly steep, but seeming to offer adequate holds. To the right was a gentle slope of snow that curved upward and out of sight behind the rocks. As we watched, Osborn ascended to the edge of the snow, stopped, and probed it with his ax. Then, apparently satisfied that it would bear his weight he stepped out on the slope.

I felt Nace's body tense. "Paul!" he cried out.

His voice was too weak and hoarse to carry. Osborn continued his ascent.

Nace cupped his hands and called his name again, and this time Osborn turned. "Wait!" cried the Englishman.

Osborn stood still, watching us, as we struggled up the few yards to the edge of the

---

29 **obliquely** (ō blēk′ lē): in a sloping or slanting line.

snow slope. Nace's breath came in shuddering gasps, but he climbed faster than I had ever seen him climb before.

"Come back!" he called. "Come off the snow!"

"It's all right. The crust is firm," Osborn called back.

"But it's melting. There's—" Nace paused, fighting for air. "There's nothing underneath!"

In a sudden sickening flash I saw what he meant. Looked at from directly below, at the point where Osborn had come to it, the slope on which he stood appeared as a harmless covering of snow over the rocks. From where we were now, however, a little to one side, it could be seen that it was in reality no covering at all, but merely a cornice or unsupported platform clinging to the side of the mountain. Below it was not rock, but ten thousand feet of blue air.

"Come back!" I cried. "Come back!"

Osborn hesitated, then took a downward step. But he never took the next. For in that same instant the snow directly in front of him disappeared. It did not seem to fall or to break away. It was just soundlessly and magically no longer there. In the spot where Osborn had been about to set his foot there was now revealed the abysmal drop of the north face of K_3.

I shut my eyes, but only for a second, and when I reopened them Osborn was still, miraculously, there. Nace was shouting, "Don't move! Don't move an inch!"

"The rope—" I heard myself saying.

The Englishman shook his head. "We'd have to throw it, and the impact would be too much. Brace yourself and play it out." As he spoke, his eyes were traveling over the rocks that bordered the snow bridge. Then he moved forward.

I wedged myself into a cleft in the wall and let out the rope which extended between us. A few yards away Osborn stood in the snow, transfixed, one foot a little in front of the other. But my eyes now were on Nace. Cautiously, but with astounding rapidity, he edged along the rocks beside the cornice. There was a moment when his only support was an inch-wide ledge beneath his feet, another where there was nothing under his feet at all, and he supported himself wholly by his elbows and hands. But he advanced steadily, and at last reached a shelf wide enough for him to turn around on. At this point he was perhaps six feet away from Osborn.

"It's wide enough here to hold both of us," he said in a quiet voice. "I'm going to reach out my ax. Don't move until you're sure you have a grip on it. When I pull, jump."

He searched the wall behind him and found a hold for his left hand. Then he slowly extended his ice ax, head foremost, until it was within two feet of Osborn's shoulder. "Grip it!" he cried suddenly. Osborn's hands shot out and seized the ax. "Jump!"

There was a flash of steel in the sunlight and a hunched figure hurtled inward from the snow to the ledge. Simultaneously another figure hurtled out. The haft of the ax jerked suddenly from Nace's hand, and he lurched forward and downward. A violent spasm convulsed my body as the rope went taut. Then it was gone. Nace did not seem to hit the snow; he simply disappeared through it, soundlessly. In the same instant the snow itself was gone. The frayed, yellow end of broken rope spun lazily in space. . . .

Somehow my eyes went to Osborn. He was crouched on the ledge, where Nace had been a moment before, staring dully at the ax he held in his hands. Beyond his head, not

two hundred feet above, the white untrod-den pinnacle of K₃ stabbed the sky.

Perhaps ten minutes passed, perhaps a half hour. I closed my eyes and leaned forward motionless against the rock, my face against my arm. I neither thought nor felt; my body and mind alike were enveloped in a suffocating numbness. Through it at last came the sound of Osborn moving. Looking up, I saw he was standing beside me.

"I'm going to try for the top," he said tonelessly.

I merely stared at him.

"Will you come?"

"No," I said.

Osborn hesitated; then turned and began slowly climbing the steep chimney above us. Halfway up he paused, struggling for breath. Then he resumed his laborious upward progress and presently disappeared beyond the crest.

I stayed where I was, and the hours passed. The sun reached its zenith above the peak and sloped away behind it. And at last I heard above me the sound of Osborn returning. As I looked up, his figure appeared at the top of the chimney and began the descent. His clothing was in tatters, and I could tell from his movements that only the thin flame of his will stood between him and collapse. In another few minutes he was standing beside me.

"Did you get there?" I asked dully.

He shook his head. "I couldn't make it," he answered. "I didn't have what it takes."

We roped together silently and began the descent to the camp.

There is nothing more to be told of the fifth assault on K₃—at least not from the experiences of the men who made it. Osborn and I reached Camp V in safety, and three days later the entire expedition gathered at the advance base. It was decided, in view of the tragedy that had occurred, to make no further attempt on the summit, and by the end of the week we had begun the evacuation of the mountain.

It remained for another year and other men to reveal the epilogue.[30]

The summer following our attempt a combined English-Swiss expedition stormed the peak successfully. After weeks of hardship and struggle they attained the topmost pinnacle of the giant, only to find that what should have been their great moment of triumph was, instead, a moment of the bitterest disappointment. For when they came out at last upon the summit they saw that they were *not* the first. An ax stood there. Its haft was embedded in rock and ice and on its steel head were the engraved words: TO MARTIN FROM JOHN.

They were sporting men. On their return to civilization they told their story, and the name of the conqueror of K₃ was made known to the world.

---

30 **epilogue** (ep′ ə lôg): conclusion to the events that have been described.

Discussion

1. Which member of the expedition actually made it to the top of K_3? How do you know?

2. Who are the two principal members of the expedition? In what ways are they different? In what ways are they alike?

3. In what mountain range does K_3 lie? How high is K_3?

4. How had Nace acquired the ice ax he carries? What is inscribed on the ax head? What part does the ax play in saving Osborn's life?

5. The narrator of this account, the "I," is himself a member of the expedition. What advantage or disadvantage do you see in that fact? What incident does the narrator witness that makes him realize more than ever how expert a mountaineer Nace was?

6. As Nace, Osborn, and the narrator prepare for the final assault on K_3, what happens? Why does Nace say that they would "have to go down tomorrow"? How does Osborn respond? What is the result?

7. In what ways does the struggle to conquer K_3 become as much a mental struggle as it is a physical struggle?

Vocabulary

The author of "Top Man" uses geological (earth-science) and other terms widely known among mountain-climbers, but these terms may be new to you. Context clues do not provide keys to the meanings of many of these words. Yet knowledge of these words is needed for full appreciation of the selection. One good way to determine the meanings of these words is to apply the technique called PARAPHRASING. When you paraphrase, you restate portions of a story in your own words.

Here is an example of paraphrasing:

ORIGINAL: The porters ate their rations in silence.
PARAPHRASE: Without talking, the people hired to carry the climbers' equipment ate the shares of food that were passed out to them.

The purpose of paraphrasing is not to make things short, but to make them clear.

The sample paraphrase given above follows three steps:

1. Pick out the unfamiliar words (*porter* and *rations*) and look them up in the glossary or a dictionary.

2. Review the sentence in the selection to make sure that the definition of each word really applies here.

3. Reword the whole sentence, using simple expressions.

On a separate sheet of paper, follow these same steps, and paraphrase each sentence below.

1. Day after day, the long file of men wound up and down among the hummocks and crevasses of the glacier.

2. Above and to the left rose the symmetrical bulk of the summit pyramid.

3. The shape was there, and the features: the sweeping skirt of glaciers; the monstrous vertical precipices of the face and the jagged ice line of the east ridge; finally the pyramid that transfixed the sky.

James Ramsey Ullman 1907–1971

When he graduated from Princeton, James Ullman had an ambition popular with writers of his time. He "took off for Paris with the twin purposes of getting a job as a foreign correspondent and writing the Great American Novel." He was unable to achieve either purpose, however, and returned to New York, arriving on the day of the 1929 stock market crash.

After working as a reporter and theatrical producer, in 1939 Ullman turned to full-time writing and traveling. He traveled to all parts of the globe and wrote about most of them. Some of his novels were set in the Amazon, the South Pacific, and several mountain ranges.

James Ullman realized the ambition of his lifetime when, in the spring of 1963, he became a member of the first American expedition to climb Mount Everest. His history of that expedition and his fiction about mountain climbing won high praise from mountain climbers and literary critics alike. He wrote with the special insight of an expert.

Lucinda Matlock

EDGAR LEE MASTERS

I went to the dances at Chandlerville,
And played snap-out at Winchester.
One time we changed partners,
Driving home in the moonlight of middle June,
And then I found Davis.   5
We were married and lived together for seventy years,
Enjoying, working, raising the twelve children,
Eight of whom we lost
Ere I had reached the age of sixty.
I spun, I wove, I kept the house, I nursed the sick,   10
I made the garden, and for holiday
Rambled over the fields where sang the larks,
And by Spoon River gathering many a shell,
And many a flower and medicinal weed—
Shouting to the wooded hills, singing to the green valleys.   15
At ninety-six I had lived enough, that is all,
And passed to a sweet repose.
What is this I hear of sorrow and weariness,
Anger, discontent and drooping hopes?
Degenerate[1] sons and daughters,   20
Life is too strong for you—
It takes life to love Life.

---

1 **degenerate** (dē gen′ ə rət): weak; degraded.

Discussion

1. Would you or would you not have enjoyed being a member of Lucinda Matlock's family? Explain your answer.

2. Would you or would you not include determination among Lucinda Matlock's traits? Why?

3. Beginning with line 18—"What is this I hear of sorrow and weariness"—her words take on a different tone. Why, do you think, does she say what she does in lines 18–21?

4. What do you think is the meaning of the last line?

Vocabulary

One good way to keep in mind the meaning of an unfamiliar word is to learn a familiar SYNONYM for the word. A synonym is any word that means nearly the same as another word. Stated another way, a synonym is any word that can replace another word in a sentence without changing the meaning of the sentence.

Look at the word *rambled* in the poem "Lucinda Matlock," for example.

> I made the garden, and for holiday
> *Rambled* over the fields where sang the larks . . .

One synonym for *rambled* is *wandered. Wandered* can take the place of *rambled* in the poem. The two are synonymous, and you can keep the first word in mind to help you remember the second.

Below are three short sections of "Lucinda Matlock." Each section contains an *italicized* word. That word is probably unfamiliar to you. Replace each unfamiliar word with one of the three familiar synonyms printed below. Use context clues to decide which to use, but check the glossary or a dictionary if necessary. On a separate sheet of paper, copy both the *italicized* word and the familiar synonym.

weak   before   rest

1. We were married and lived together for seventy years,
   Enjoying, working, raising the twelve children,
   Eight of whom we lost
   Ere I had reached the age of sixty.
2. At ninety-six I had lived enough, that is all,
   And passed to a sweet *repose.*
3. *Degenerate* sons and daughters,
   Life is too strong for you. . . .

Edgar Lee Masters 1868—1950

Edgar Lee Masters grew up in Lewistown and Petersburg, Illinois, the Spoon River country he later made famous. He became a lawyer with his father's firm but abruptly left to practice law in Chicago.

Even in the city, he vividly remembered all sides of the small town life he had just left. To that memory, he wrote *Spoon River Anthology.* This collection of verse tells the life of Spoon River in the epitaphs of people who were buried in Masters' hometown cemeteries. Out of family tales, neighborhood gossip, and the visible successes and failures of the individuals, Masters wove their stories of tragedies and triumphs. Together, the poems show the whole fabric of life of small-town America.

There was so little to go on—Grandma and the other relatives talking on the front porch about "The African"—several strange-sounding words beginning with k. Yet it was these bits of information that prompted Alex Haley's search—a search that spanned three continents and more than thirty years!

My Furthest-Back Person—"The African"

ALEX HALEY

MY GRANDMA Cynthia Murray Palmer lived in Henning, Tennessee (pop. 500), about 50 miles north of Memphis. Each summer as I grew up there, we would be visited by several women relatives who were mostly around Grandma's age, such as my Great Aunt Liz Murray who taught in Oklahoma, and Great Aunt Till Merriweather from Jackson, Tennessee, or their considerably younger niece, Cousin Georgia Anderson from Kansas City, Kansas, and some others. Always after the supper dishes had been washed, they would go out to take seats and talk in the rocking chairs on the front porch, and I would scrunch down, listening, behind Grandma's squeaky chair, with the dusk deepening into night and the lightning bugs flicking on and off above the now shadowy honeysuckles. Most often they talked about our family—the story had been passed down for generations—until the whistling blur of lights of the southbound Panama Limited train *whooshing* through Henning at 9:05 P.M. signaled our bedtime.

So much of their talking of people, places and events I didn't understand: For instance, what was an "Ol' Massa," and "Ol' Missus" or a "plantation"? But early I gathered that white folks had done lots of bad things to our folks, though I couldn't figure out why. I guessed that all that they talked about had happened a long time ago, as now or then Grandma or another, speaking of someone in the past, would excitedly thrust a finger toward me, exclaiming, "Wasn't big as *this* 'un!" And it would astound me that anyone as old and grey-haired as they could relate to my age. But in time my head began both a recording and picturing of the more graphic scenes they would describe, just as I also visualized David killing Goliath with his slingshot, Old Pharaoh's army drowning, Noah and his ark, Jesus feeding that big multitude with nothing but five loaves and two fishes, and other wonders that I heard in my Sunday school lessons at our New Hope Methodist Church.

The furthest-back person Grandma and the others talked of—always in tones of awe, I noticed—they would call "The African." They said that some ship brought him to a place that they pronounced "'Naplis." They said that then some "Mas' John Waller" bought him for his plantation in "Spotsylvania County, Virginia." This African kept on escaping, the fourth time trying to kill the "hateful po' cracker" slavecatcher, who gave him a choice of punishment. This African took a foot being chopped off with an ax against a tree stump, they said, and he was about to die. But his life was saved by "Mas' John's" brother—"Mas' William Waller," a doctor who was so furious about what had happened that he bought the African for himself and gave him the name "Toby."

Crippling about, working in "Mas' William's" house and yard, the African in time met "the big house cook named Bell," and there was born a girl named Kizzy. As she grew up, her African daddy often showed her different kinds of things, telling her what they were in his native tongue. Pointing at a banjo, for example, the African uttered, *"ko"*; or pointing at a river near the plantation, he would say *Kamby Bolong.* Many of his strange words started with a *"k"* sound, and the little, growing Kizzy learned gradually that they identified different things.

When addressed by other slaves as "Toby," the master's name for him, the African said angrily that his name was *"Kintay."* And as he gradually learned English, he told young Kizzy some things about himself—for instance, that he was not far from his village, chopping wood to make himself a drum, when four men had surprised, overwhelmed, and kidnapped him.

So Kizzy's head held much about her African daddy when at age 16 she was sold away onto a much smaller plantation in North Carolina. Her first child, a boy, she named George. And Kizzy told her boy all about his African grandfather. George grew up to be such a gamecock fighter that he was called "Chicken George," and people would come from all over and "bet big money" on his cockfights. He and Matilda, another of Lea's slaves, had seven children, and he told them the stories and strange sounds of their African great-grandfather. And one of those children, Tom, became a blacksmith who was bought away by a "Mas' Murray" for his tobacco plantation in Alamance County, North Carolina.

There Tom met Irene, a weaver on the plantation. She also bore seven children, and Tom now told them all about their African great-great-grandfather, the faithfully passed-down knowledge of his sounds and stories having become by now the family's prideful treasure.

The youngest of that second set of seven children was a girl, Cynthia, who became my maternal Grandma (which today I can only see as fated). Anyway, all of this is how I was growing up in Henning at Grandma's, listening from behind her rocking chair as she and the other visiting old women talked of that African (never then comprehended as *my* great-great-great-great-grandfather) who said his name was *"Kin-tay,"* and said *"ko"* for banjo, *"Kamby Bolong"* for river, and a jumble of other *"k"*-beginning sounds that Grandma privately muttered, most often while making beds or cooking, and who also said that near his village he was kidnapped while chopping wood to make himself a drum.

The story had become nearly as fixed in my head as in Grandma's by the time Dad and Mama moved me and my two younger brothers, George and Julius, away from Henning to be with them at the small black agricultural and mechanical college in Normal, Alabama, where Dad taught.

To compress my next 25 years: When I was 17 Dad let me enlist as a mess boy in the U.S. Coast Guard. I became a ship's cook out in the South Pacific during World War II, and at night down by my bunk I began trying to write sea adventure stories, mailing them off to magazines and collecting rejection slips for eight years before some editors began purchasing and publishing occasional stories. By 1949 the Coast Guard had made me its first "journalist"; finally with 20 years' service, I retired at the age of 37, determined to make a full-time career of writing. . . .

Then one Saturday in 1965 I happened to be walking past the National Archives building in Washington. Across the interim[1] years I had thought of Grandma's old stories—otherwise I can't think what diverted me up the Archives' steps. And when a main reading room desk attendant asked if he could help me, I wouldn't have dreamed of admitting to him some curiosity hanging on from boyhood about my slave forbears. I kind of mumbled that I was interested in census records of Alamance County, North Carolina, just after the Civil War.

The microfilm rolls were delivered, and I turned them through the machine with a building sense of intrigue, viewing in different census takers' penmanship an endless parade of names. After about a dozen microfilmed rolls, I was beginning to tire, when in utter astonishment I looked upon the names of Grandma's parents: Tom Murray, Irene Murray . . . older sisters of Grandma's as well—every one of them a name that I'd heard countless times on her front porch.

It wasn't that I hadn't believed Grandma. You just *didn't* not believe my Grandma. It was simply so uncanny[2] actually seeing those names in print and in official U.S. Government records.

During the next several months I was back in Washington whenever possible, in the Archives, the Library of Congress, the Daughters of the American Revolution Library. (Whenever black attendants understood the idea of my search, documents I requested reached me with miraculous speed.) In one source or another during 1966 I was able to document at least the highlights of the cherished family story. I would have given anything to have told Grandma, but, sadly, in 1949 she had gone. So I went and told the only survivor of those Henning frontporch storytellers: Cousin Georgia Anderson, now in her 80's in Kansas City, Kansas. Wrinkled, bent, not well herself, she was so overjoyed, repeating to me the old stories and sounds; they were like Henning echoes: "Yeah, boy, that African say his name was '*Kin-tay*'; he say the banjo was '*ko*,' an' the river '*Kamby-Bolong*, an' he was off choppin' some wood to make his drum when they grabbed 'im!" Cousin Georgia grew so excited we had to stop her, calm her down, "You go 'head, boy! Your grandma an' all of 'em—they up there watching what you do!"

That week I flew to London on a magazine assignment. Since by now I was steeped in the old, in the past, scarcely a tour guide missed me—I was awed at so many historical places and treasures I'd heard of and read of. I

---

1 **interim** (in' tər im): between.

2 **uncanny**: eerie; mysterious.

came upon the Rosetta stone[3] in the British Museum, marveling anew at how Jean Champollion, the French archaeologist, had miraculously deciphered[4] its ancient demotic and hieroglyphic[5] texts. . . .

The thrill of that just kept hanging around in my head. I was on a jet returning to New York when a thought hit me. Those strange, unknown-tongue sounds, always part of our family's old story . . . they were obviously bits of our original African *"Kin-tay's"* native tongue. What specific tongue? Could I somehow find out?

Back in New York, I began making visits to the United Nations Headquarters lobby; it wasn't hard to spot Africans. I'd stop any I could, asking if my bits of phonetic sounds held any meaning for them. A couple of dozen Africans quickly looked at me, listened, and took off—understandably dubious[6] about some Tennesseean's accent alleging[7] "African" sounds.

My research assistant, George Sims (we grew up together in Henning), brought me some names of ranking scholars of African linguistics.[8] One was particularly intriguing: a Belgian- and English-educated Dr. Jan Vansina; he had spent his early career living in West African villages, studying and tape-recording countless oral histories that were narrated by certain very old African men; he had written a standard textbook, *The Oral Tradition.*

So I flew to the University of Wisconsin to see Dr. Vansina. In his living room I told him every bit of the family story in the fullest detail that I could remember it. Then, intensely, he queried me about the story's relay across the generations, about the gibberish of *"k"* sounds Grandma had fiercely muttered to herself while doing her housework, with my brothers and me giggling beyond her hearing at what we had dubbed "Grandma's noises."

Dr. Vansina, his manner very serious, finally said, "These sounds your family has kept sound very probably of the tongue called 'Mandinka.'"

I'd never heard of any "Mandinka." Grandma just told of the African saying *"ko"* for banjo, or *"Kamby Bolong"* for a Virginia river.

Among Mandinka stringed instruments, Dr. Vansina said, one of the oldest was the *"kora."*

"Bolong," he said, was clearly Mandinka for "river." Preceded by *"Kamby,"* it very likely meant "Gambia River."

Dr. Vansina telephoned an eminent Africanist colleague, Dr. Philip Curtin. He said that the phonetic *"Kin-tay"* was correctly spelled *"Kinte,"* a very old clan that had originated in Old Mali. The Kinte men traditionally were blacksmiths, and the women were potters and weavers.

I knew I must get to the Gambia River.

The first native Gambian I could locate in the U.S. was named Ebou Manga, then a junior attending Hamilton College in upstate Clinton, New York. He and I flew to Dakar, Senegal, then took a smaller plane to

---

3 **Rosetta stone:** a stone tablet found in 1799 near the Egyptian town of Rosetta. On the tablet are carved three kinds of writing—Greek, hieroglyphic (the picture writing of the ancient Egyptians), and Demotic (sign writing used by the descendants of the ancient Egyptians). By comparing the Greek words (which scholars understood) with the hieroglyphics, scholars were able to understand the meaning of that ancient Egyptian picture writing. The Rosetta stone is now a treasure of the British Museum in London.

4 **deciphered** (di sī′ fərd): figured out.

5 **demotic and hieroglyphic** (di mä′ tik / hī rō glif′ ik): forms of ancient Egyptian picture writing.

6 **dubious** (dü′ bi əs): unsure.

7 **alleging** (ə lej′ ing): suggesting.

8 **linguistics** (lin gwis′ tiks): study of the structure of language.

Yundum Airport, and rode in a van to Gambia's capital, Bathurst. Ebou and his father assembled eight Gambia government officials. I told them Grandma's stories, every detail I could remember, as they listened intently, then reacted. "'Kamby Bolong' of course is Gambia River!" I heard. "But more clue is your forefather's saying his name was 'Kinte.'" Then they told me something I would never even have fantasized—that in places in the back country lived very old men, commonly called *griots,* who could tell centuries of the histories of certain very old family clans. As for *Kintes,* they pointed out to me on a map some family villages, Kinte-Kundah, and Kinte-Kundah Janneh-Ya, for instance.

The Gambian officials said they would try to help me. I returned to New York, dazed. It is embarrassing to me now, but despite Grandma's stories, I'd never been concerned much with Africa, and I had the routine images of African people living mostly in exotic jungles. But a compulsion now laid hold of me to learn all I could, and I began devouring books about Africa, especially about the slave trade. Then one Thursday's mail contained a letter from one of the Gambian officials, inviting me to return there.

Monday I was back in Bathurst. It galvanized[9] me when the officials said that a *griot* had been located who told the *Kinte* clan history—his name was Kebba Kanga Fofana. To reach him, I discovered, required a modified safari: renting a launch to get upriver, two land vehicles to carry supplies by a roundabout land route, and employing finally 14 people, including three interpreters and four musicians, since a *griot* would not speak the revered clan histories without background music.

The boat *Baddibu* vibrated upriver, with me acutely tense: Were these Africans maybe viewing me as but another of the pith-helmets?[10] After about two hours, we put in at James Island, for me to see the ruins of the once British-operated James Fort. Here two centuries of slave ships had loaded thousands of cargoes of Gambian tribespeople. The crumbling stones, the deeply oxidized swivel cannon, even some remnant links of chain seemed all but impossible to believe. Then we continued upriver to the left-bank village of Albreda, and there put ashore to continue on foot to Jaffure, village of the *griot.* Once more we stopped, for me to see *toubob kolong,* "the white man's well," now almost filled in, in a swampy area with abundant, tall, saw-toothed grass. It was dug two centuries ago to "17 men's height deep" to insure survival drinking water for long-driven, famishing coffles of slaves.[11]

Walking on, I kept wishing that Grandma could hear how her stories had led me to the *"Kamby Bolong."* (Our surviving storyteller Cousin Georgia died in a Kansas City hospital during this same morning, I would learn later.) Finally, Juffure village's playing children, sighting us, flashed an alert. The 70-odd people came rushing from their circular, thatch-roofed, mud-walled huts, with goats bounding up and about, and parrots squawking from up in the palms. I sensed him in advance somehow, the small man amid them, wearing a pillbox cap and an off-white robe—the *griot.* Then the interpreters went to him, as the villagers thronged around me.

---

9 **galvanized** (gal' vən īzd): excited.

10 **pith-helmets:** foreign tourists (a reference to the fact that most tourists to equatorial Africa wear white pith helmets).
11 **coffles** (kôf' əlz) **of slaves:** trains of slaves chained together.

And it hit me like a gale wind: every one of them, the whole crowd, was *jet black.* An enormous sense of guilt swept me—a sense of being some kind of hybrid . . . a sense of being impure among the pure. It was an awful sensation.

The old *griot* stepped away from my interpreters and the crowd quickly swarmed around him—all of them buzzing. An interpreter named A. B. C. Salla came to me; he whispered: "Why they stare at you so, they have never seen here a black American." And that hit me: I was symbolizing for them twenty-five millions of us they had never seen. What did they think of me—of us?

Then abruptly the old *griot* was briskly walking toward me. His eyes boring into mine, he spoke in Mandinka, as if instinctively I should understand—and A. B. C. Salla translated:

"Yes . . . we have been told by the forefathers . . . that many of us from this place are in exile . . . in that place called America . . . and in other places."

I suppose I physically wavered, and they thought it was the heat; rustling whispers went through the crowd, and a man brought me a low stool. Now the whispering hushed—the musicians had softly begun playing *kora* and *balafon,* and a canvas sling lawn seat was taken by the *griot,* Kebba Kanga Fofana, aged 73 "rains" (one rainy season each year). He seemed to gather himself into a physical rigidity, and he began speaking the *Kinte* clan's ancestral oral history; it came rolling from his mouth across the next hours . . . 17th- and 18th-century *Kinte* lineage details, predominantly what men took wives; the children they "begot," in the order of their births; those children's mates and children.

Events frequently were dated by some proximate[12] singular physical occurrence. It was as if some ancient scroll were printed indelibly within the *griot's* brain. Each few sentences or so, he would pause for an interpreter's translation to me. I distill here the essence:

The *Kinte* clan began in Old Mali, the men generally blacksmiths ". . . who conquered fire," and the women potters and weavers. One large branch of the clan moved to Mauretania, from where one son of the clan, Kairaba Kunta Kinte, a Moslem Marabout holy man, entered Gambia. He lived first in the village of Pakali N'Ding; he moved next to Jiffarong village; ". . . and then he came here, into our own village of Juffure."

In Juffure, Kairaba Kunte Kinte took his first wife, ". . . a Mandinka maiden, whose name was Sireng. By her, he begot two sons, whose names were Janneh and Saloum. Then he got a second wife, Yaisa. By her, he begot a son, Omoro."

The three sons became men in Juffure. Janneh and Saloum went off and found a new village, Kinte-Kundah Janneh-Ya. "And then Omoro, the youngest son, when he had 30 rains, took as a wife a maiden, Binta Kebba.

"And by her, he begot four sons—Kunta, Lamin, Suwadu, and Madi. . . ."

Sometimes, a "begotten," after his naming, would be accompanied by some later-occurring detail, perhaps as ". . . in time of big water (flood), he slew a water buffalo." Having named those four sons, now the *griot* stated such a detail.

"About the time the king's soldiers came, the eldest of these four sons, Kunta, when he had about 16 rains, went away from

---

12 **proximate** (prok' sə mət): near; close; at the same time.

this village, to chop wood to make a drum . . . and he was never seen again. . . ."

Goose-pimples the size of lemons seemed to pop all over me. In my knapsack were my cumulative notebooks, the first of them including how in my boyhood, my Grandma, Cousin Georgia and the others told of the African *"Kin-tay"* who always said he was kidnapped near his village—while chopping wood to make a drum. . . .

I showed the interpreter, he showed and told the *griot,* who excitedly told the people; they grew very agitated. Abruptly then they formed a human ring, encircling me, dancing and chanting. Perhaps a dozen of the women carrying their infant babies rushed in toward me, thrusting the infants into my arms—conveying, I would later learn, "the laying on of hands . . . through this flesh which is us, we are you, and you are us." The men hurried me into their mosque, their Arabic praying later being translated outside: "Thanks be to Allah for returning the long lost from among us." Direct descendants of Kunta Kinte's blood brothers were hastened, some of them from nearby villages, for a family portrait to be taken with me, surrounded by actual ancestral sixth cousins. More symbolic acts filled the remaining day.

When they would let me leave, for some reason I wanted to go away over the African land. Dazed, silent in the bumping Land Rover, I heard the cutting staccato of talking drums. Then when we sighted the next village, its people came thronging to meet us. They were all—little naked ones to wizened elders—waving, beaming, amid a cacophony[13] of crying out; and then my ears

identified their words: *"Meester Kinte! Meester Kinte!"*

Let me tell you something: I am a man. But I remember the sob surging up from my feet, flinging up my hands before my face and bawling as I had not done since I was a baby . . . the jet-black Africans were jostling, staring . . . I didn't care, with the feelings surging. If you really knew the odyssey[14] of us millions of black Americans, if you really knew how we came in the seeds of our forefathers, captured, driven, beaten, inspected, bought, branded, chained in foul ships, if you really knew, you needed weeping. . . .

Back home, I knew that what I must write, really, was our black saga,[15] where any individual's past is the essence of the millions'. Now flat broke, I went to some editors I knew, describing the Gambian miracle, and my desire to pursue the research; Doubleday contracted to publish, and Reader's Digest to condense the projected book; then I had advances[16] to travel further.

What ship brought Kinte to Grandma's "'Naplis" (Annapolis, Maryland, obviously)? The old *griot's* time reference to "king's soldiers" sent me flying to London. Feverish searching at last identified, in British Parliament records, "Colonel O'Hare's Forces," dispatched in mid-1767 to protect the then British-held James Fort whose ruins I'd visited. So Kunta Kinte was down in some ship probably sailing later that summer from the Gambia River to Annapolis.

Now I feel it was fated that I had taught myself to write in the U.S. Coast Guard. For

---

13 **cacophony** (kə kof′ ə ni): discordant sounds; confusion of sounds.

14 **odyssey** (od′ ə sē): a long wandering.
15 **saga** (sä′ gə): long story.
16 **advances:** sums of money given an author prior to publication of the book.

My Furthest-Back Person — "The African" **119**

the sea dramas I had concentrated on had given me years of experience searching among yellowing old U.S. maritime records. So now in English 18th-century marine records I finally tracked ships reporting themselves in and out to the Commandant of the Gambia River's James Fort. And then early one afternoon I found that a *Lord Ligonier* under a Captain Thomas Davies had sailed on the Sabbath of July 5, 1767. Her cargo: 3,265 elephants' teeth, 3,700 pounds of beeswax, 800 pounds of cotton, 32 ounces of Gambian gold, and 140 slaves; her destination: "Annapolis."

That night I recrossed the Atlantic. In the Library of Congress the *Lord Ligonier's* arrival was one brief line in "Shipping in the Port of Annapolis—1748–1775." I located the author, Vaughan W. Brown, in his Baltimore brokerage office. He drove to Historic Annapolis, the city's historical society, and found me further documentation of her arrival on Sept. 29, 1767. (Exactly two centuries later, Sept. 29, 1967, standing, staring seaward from an Annapolis pier, again I knew tears). More help came in the Maryland Hall of Records. Archivist Phebe Jacobsen found the *Lord Ligonier's* arriving customs declaration listing, "98 Negroes"— so in her 86-day crossing, 42 Gambians had died, one among the survivors being 16-year-old Kunta Kinte. Then the microfilmed Oct. 1, 1767, *Maryland Gazette* contained, on page two, an announcement to prospective buyers from the ship's agents, Daniel of St. Thos. Jenifer and John Ridout (the Governor's secretary): "from the River GAMBIA, in AFRICA . . . a cargo of choice, healthy SLAVES. . . ."

Discussion

1. Briefly describe the evening ritual at Grandma Palmer's when relatives came. What did Haley do at these gatherings? Did he or didn't he understand every detail in the family's story? What made a lasting impression on him?

2. Alex Haley says that the African became angry when others addressed him as "Toby." Why? What was his real name? Why, do you think, his real name was so important to him?

3. Which one of the African's "unknown-tongue sounds" turned out to be the single more important clue to discovering his ancestral village? Why?

4. At several points in his research and his travels, Haley admits to being overcome by powerful emotions. Why, at one point, does he experience "an enormous sense of guilt"? Why, at two other points, does he weep?

5. How did Haley's service in the Coast Guard contribute to his career as a writer?

6. Basing your opinion on this selection, how dependable would you say the "oral tradition" is? Under what circumstances might it be most dependable? least dependable?

7. What do you understand by the title—"My Furthest-Back Person—'The African'"?

Vocabulary

A glossary, as you know, is like a miniature dictionary made up for a particular book. Both a glossary and a dictionary serve as guides not only to the meanings and spellings of words, but also to their pronunciations. PRONUNCIATION is shown in parentheses ( ) directly following each alphabetically listed word. For example:

pro•nun•ci•a•tion (prə•nun′sē•ā′shən) *n.* one way of pronouncing.

In the sample glossary entry above, you can see two kinds of accent marks, light (′) and heavy (′). If capital letters had been used to show what those accent marks mean, then the pronunciation might read this way: prə•NUN•sē•Ā•shən.

You can see other small marks placed above various vowels to show how each one of those should sound. At the bottom of the first page of the glossary, you will find a key to the sounds for these marks, called diacritical marks:

u in the second syllable, *nun,* sounds like the *u* in *cup;*
ē in the third syllable, *se,* sounds like the *e* in *equal;*
ā in the fourth syllable sounds like the *a* in *age.*

In addition, the key shows that ə is pronounced like the *a* in the word *about*.

1. On a separate sheet of paper, make three columns labeled as follows:

   Word   Pronunciation   Meaning

2. In the column at the left, labeled "Word," copy each of these words from "My Furthest-Back Person," leaving four or five spaces below each one:
   archaeology
   archive
   cacophony
   hieroglyphic
   linguistics

3. In the middle column, labeled "Pronunciation," copy the pronunciation of each word exactly as it is given in the glossary of this book or in a dictionary. Be sure to include both accent marks and diacritical marks. (As you copy these pronunciations, whisper the words to yourself several times for practice.)

4. In the column at the right, write what the glossary or a dictionary says each word means.

Alex Haley 1921 ——

Alex Haley is best known for his monumental book *Roots,* which traces the history of his family from the earliest known ancestor, Kunte Kinte. When Haley's book was televised in 1977, it was regarded as a landmark in America's race relations. Through this story, Black and white Americans realized that they have a common heritage that links them to their own ancestors and to each other.

Haley spent more than ten years researching and writing the book. He felt compelled to complete it, both for his own family and for the symbolic history it presented for the millions of Americans of African descent. Haley says, "I intend my book to be a buoy for Black self-esteem—and a reminder that we are all children of the same Creator." Haley believes, "You can never enslave somebody who knows who he is."

Rural Dumpheap

MELVILLE CANE

This rusty mound of cans,
This scatter of tires and pans,
This litter of mattresses and twisted springs,
This rotting refuse, these abandoned things
Malodorously[1] flung,—this impudent pile   5
That dares to choke the current, to defile
The innocent season,—all are man's.

Man's inhumanity to sod
Makes countless snowdrops mourn,
And every gentle seed that's born   10
Gives battle for a dishonored god.

Within the heap and darkly, heaves
The growing mutiny of leaves,
While down the valley bird to bird
Relays the rallying word,   15
And courage calls on every breeze
To armies of anemones,[2]
And triumph scales the parapet,[3]
A host of violet.

O man, where is thy victory?   20
Despite this blight of tins,
The fern persists and cleaves and wins,
And, gladly, spring begins.

---

1 **Malodorously** (mal ō′ dər əs li): causing an offensive odor.
2 **anemones** (ə nem′ ə nēz): type of flowers.
3 **parapet** (par′ ə pet): protective wall.

Discussion

1. What does the poet see that causes him to speak out?

2. What is "the innocent season" (line 7)? What does "sod" (line 8) mean?

3. In the third stanza (lines 12-19) the poet suggests that a battle is taking place. Who is fighting whom?

4. What connection does this poem have with the central theme of this unit—*determination?*

Melville Cane 1879——1980

On his hundredth birthday in April, 1979, Melville Cane was honored by his alma mater, Columbia University. The unusual celebration included an exhibit of his writings and some of the mementos he acquired during his career.

After entering Columbia as a freshman in 1896, Cane earned his law degree and began practicing copyright law in New York. Before he practiced law, however, he had written light verse for magazines and the lyrics for a varsity operetta. Cane has continued to "practice law for seven decades and poetry for even longer." Over the years he has advised famous writers such as T. S. Elliot, Thomas Wolfe, Sinclair Lewis, and William Saroyan.

*Of course there are times when things seem
tough—even hopeless. What do you do? Give
up? Or do you "bear down"?*

Fable for When There's No Way Out

MAY SWENSON

Grown too big for his skin,
and it grown hard,

without a sea and atmosphere—
he's drunk it all up—

his strength's inside him now,   5
but there's no room to stretch.

He pecks at the top
but his beak's too soft;

though instinct and ambition shoves,
he can't get through.   10

Barely old enough to bleed
and already bruised!

In a case this tough
what's the use

if you break your head   15
instead of the lid?

Despair tempts him
to just go limp:

Maybe the cell's
already a tomb,   20

and beginning end
in this round room.

Still, stupidly he pecks
and pecks, as if from under

his own skull—   25
yet makes no crack . . .

No crack until
he finally cracks,

and kicks and stomps.
What a thrill   30

and shock to feel
his little gaff[1] poke

through the floor!
A way he hadn't known or meant.

Rage works if reason won't.   35
When locked up, bear down.

---

1 **gaff**: head.

Discussion

1. What's the poem about—that is, what's going on? How do you know?
2. Which lines suggest that the "he" in the poem is tempted to give up?
3. How does the "he" in the poem finally free himself?
4. What do you understand by the last two lines? What implication do those lines have for anyone who is facing what seems like a hopeless situation?

May Swenson 1919——

May Swenson writes poetry so that she can learn and teach about reality. She feels, "The experience of poetry is based on a craving to get through the curtains of things as they *appear,* to things as they *are,* and then into the larger, wilder space of things as they are *becoming.*" Her critics agree that she succeeds in her aims. One critic has said, "Miss Swenson's distinction is that she is able to make her reader see clearly what he has merely looked at before."

One method Swenson uses to help "her reader see clearly" is to arrange her poems in unusual shapes. The reader must then look at the entire poem if he or she is to understand the meaning of all the words of the poem.

Anton van Leeuwenhoek actually lived in the Netherlands from 1632 to 1723. Though he was a merchant, it was his "outside" interest that made him a man of distinction.

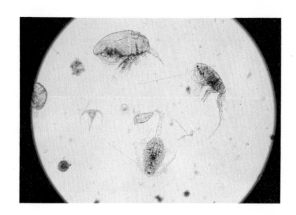

The Microscope

MAXINE KUMIN

Anton Leeuwenhoek[1] was Dutch.
He sold pincushions, cloth, and such.
The waiting townsfolk fumed and fussed
As Anton's dry goods gathered dust.

He worked, instead of tending store,   5
At grinding special lenses for
A microscope. Some of the things
He looked at were:
                  mosquitoes' wings,
the hairs of sheep, the legs of lice;   10
the skin of people, dogs, and mice;
ox eyes, spiders' spinning gear,
fishes' scales, a little smear
of his own blood,
                and best of all,   15
the unknown, busy, very small
bugs that swim and bump and hop
inside a simple water drop.

Impossible! Most Dutchmen said.
This Anton's crazy in the head.   20
We ought to ship him off to Spain.
He says he's seen a housefly's brain.
He says the water that we drink
Is full of bugs. He's mad, we think!

They called him dumkopf, which means   25
    dope.
That's how we got the microscope.

---

1 **Leeuwenhoek** (lā′ vən hùk): Anton van Leeuwenhoek (1632 - 1723) was a Dutch naturalist whose interests led to his investigation of objects too small to be seen clearly by the naked eye.

1. Where did Anton Leeuwenhoek's real interest lie?

2. How did the townspeople regard Anton? How do you explain their attitude?

3. What do you understand by the last two lines of the poem?

Vocabulary

Many English words are based upon ROOT WORDS drawn from other languages, such as Latin and Greek. Knowing about root words and the ways in which they relate to words in English can be useful in vocabulary development.

You already know, for example, that a *microscope* is "an instrument that enlarges a person's view of tiny objects." But just for a moment, assume this: You are now seeing the word *microscope* for the first time. However, you already know these two ancient Greek root words:

mikro = "smallest unit"   *skop* = "to see"

Your knowledge of those root words will not give you the full meaning of this new word, *microscope*. But it will make it possible for you to figure out that a microscope is something related to "seeing small." Knowing the two root words will help you remember the definition of *miscroscope* when you find the meaning in a glossary or dictionary.

A. 1. On a separate sheet of paper, copy the words *mikro* and *skop* with their meanings. Then copy the six additional root words below and their meanings:

tele = "far, or distant"	*meter* = "measure, or measurer"
stereo = "depth; three dimensions"	
seismo = "shaking" (of earth)	*film* = "photograph"
	cosmos = "world"

2. Using the meanings of the various root words given in step one, figure out each of the following words. Write each meaning next to the word.

telescope	micrometer
stereoscope	microfilm
seismoscope	microcosm

B. From the glossary or a dictionary, copy the full definition of each word above.

An old saying has it that faith can "move mountains." But, for Pepino, mountains were not the problem. It was other people that he needed to move. How could faith move them?

The Small Miracle

PAUL GALLICO

APPROACHING ASSISI via the chalky, dusty road that twists its way up Monte Subasio, now revealing, now concealing the exquisite little town, as it winds its way through olive and cypress groves, you eventually reach a division where your choice lies between an upper and a lower route.

If you select the latter, you soon find yourself entering Assisi through the twelfth-century archway of the denticulated[1] door of St. Francis. But if, seduced by the clear air, the wish to mount even closer to the canopy of blue Italian sky and expose still more of the delectable view of the rich Umbrian valley below, you choose the upper way, you and your vehicle eventually become inextricably entangled in the welter of humanity, oxen, goats, bawling calves, mules, fowl, children, pigs, booths, and carts gathered at the market place outside the walls.

It is here you would be most likely to encounter Pepino, with his donkey Violetta, hard at work, turning his hand to anything whereby a small boy and a strong, willing beast of burden could win for themselves the crumpled ten and twenty lira notes[2] needed to buy food and pay for lodging in the barn of Niccolo the stableman.

Pepino and Violetta were everything to each other. They were a familiar sight about Assisi and its immediate environs—the thin brown boy, ragged and barefooted, with the enormous dark eyes, large ears, and close-cropped, upstanding hair, and the dust-colored little donkey with the Mona Lisa[3] smile.

Pepino was ten years old and an orphan, his father, mother, and near relatives having been killed in the war. In self-reliance, wisdom, and demeanor he was, of course, much older, a circumstance aided by his independence, for Pepino was an unusual orphan in that having a heritage[4] he need rely on no one. Pepino's heritage was Violetta.

She was a good, useful and docile donkey, alike as any other with friendly, gentle eyes,

---

1 **denticulated** (den tik′ yə lā təd): covered with small pointed parts that jut out from the surface.

2 **lira** (lir′ ə) **notes**: paper money. Ten lira equal about one cent; twenty lira, about two cents.
3 **Mona Lisa** (mō′ nə lē′ zə): Leonardo da Vinci's famous painting of a Florentine woman with an unusual smile.
4 **heritage** (her′ ə tij): something acquired from a parent or grandparent or ancestor.

soft taupe-colored[5] muzzle, and long, pointed brown ears, with one exception that distinguished her. Violetta had a curious expression about the corners of her mouth, as though she were smiling gently over something that amused or pleased her. Thus, no matter what kind of work, or how much she was asked to do, she always appeared to be performing it with a smile of quiet satisfaction. The combination of Pepino's dark lustrous eyes and Violetta's smile was so harmonious that people favored them and they were able not only to earn enough for their keep but, aided and advised by Father Damico, the priest of their parish, to save a little as well.

There were all kinds of things they could do—carry loads of wood or water, deliver purchases carried in the panniers[6] that thumped against Violetta's sides, hire out to help pull a cart mired in the mud, aid in the olive harvest, and even, occasionally, help some citizen who was too encumbered with wine to reach his home on foot, by means of a four-footed taxi with Pepino walking beside to see that the drunkard did not fall off.

But this was not the only reason for the love that existed between boy and donkey, for Violetta was more than just the means of his livelihood. She was mother to him, and father, brother, playmate, companion, and comfort. At night, in the straw of Niccolo's stable, Pepino slept curled up close to her when it was cold, his head pillowed on her neck.

Since the mountainside was a rough world for a small boy, he was sometimes beaten or injured, and then he could creep to her for comfort and Violetta would gently nuzzle his bruises. When there was joy in his heart, he shouted songs into her waving ears; when he was lonely and hurt, he could lean his head against her soft, warm flank and cry out his tears.

On his part, he fed her, watered her, searched her for ticks and parasites, picked stones from her hoofs, scratched and groomed and curried her, lavished affection on her, particularly when they were alone, while in public he never beat her with the donkey stick more than was necessary. For this treatment Violetta made a god of Pepino, and repaid him with loyalty, obedience, and affection.

Thus, when one day in the early spring Violetta fell ill, it was the most serious thing that had ever happened to Pepino. It began first with an unusual lethargy that would respond neither to stick nor caresses, nor the young, strident voice urging her on. Later Pepino observed other symptoms and a visible loss of weight. Her ribs, once so well padded, began to show through her sides. But most distressing, either through a change in the conformation of her head, due to growing thinner, or because of the distress of the illness, Violetta lost her enchanting and lovable smile.

Drawing upon his carefully hoarded reserves of lira notes and parting with several of the impressive denomination of a hundred, Pepino called in Dr. Bartoli, the vet.

The vet examined her in good faith, dosed her, and tried his best; but she did not improve and, instead, continued to lose weight and grow weaker. He hummed and hawed then and said, "Well, now, it is hard to say. It might be one thing, such as the bite of a fly new to this district, or another, such as a germ settling in the intestine." Either way, how could one tell? There had been a similar

---

5 **taupe** (tōp)-**colored**: brownish gray.
6 **panniers** (pan′ yərz): large baskets.

case in Foligno and another in a far-away town. He recommended resting the beast and feeding her lightly. If the illness passed from her and God willed, she might live. Otherwise, she would surely die and there would be an end to her suffering.

After he had gone away, Pepino put his cropped head on Violetta's heaving flank and wept unrestrainedly. But then, when the storm, induced by the fear of losing his only companion in the world, had subsided, he knew what he must do. If there was no help for Violetta on earth, the appeal must be registered above. His plan was nothing less than to take Violetta into the crypt beneath the lower church of the Basilica of St. Francis, where rested the remains of the Saint who had so dearly loved God's creations, including all the feathered and the four-footed brothers and sisters who served Him. There he would beg St. Francis to heal her. Pepino had no doubt that the Saint would do so when he saw Violetta.

These things Pepino knew from Father Damico, who had a way of talking about St. Francis as though he were a living person who might still be encountered in his frayed cowl,[7] bound with a hemp cord at the middle, merely by turning a corner of the Main Square in Assisi or by walking down one of the narrow, cobbled streets.

And besides, there was a precedent. Giani, his friend, the son of Niccolo the stableman, had taken his sick kitten into the crypt and asked St. Francis to heal her, and the cat had got well—at least half well, anyway, for her hind legs still dragged a little; but at least she had not died. Pepino felt that if Violetta were to die, it would be the end of everything for him.

Thereupon, with considerable difficulty, he persuaded the sick and shaky donkey to rise, and with urgings and caresses and minimum use of the stick drove her through the crooked streets of Assisi and up the hill to the Basilica of St. Francis. At the beautiful twin portal of the lower church he respectfully asked Fra Bernard, who was on duty there, for permission to take Violetta down to St. Francis, so that she might be made well again.

Fra Bernard was a new monk, and, calling Pepino a young and impious scoundrel, ordered him and his donkey to be off. It was strictly forbidden to bring livestock into the church, and even to think of taking an ass into the crypt of St. Francis was a desecration.[8] And besides, how did he imagine she would get down there when the narrow, winding staircase was barely wide enough to accommodate humans in single file, much less four-footed animals? Pepino must be a fool as well as a shiftless rascal.

As ordered, Pepino retreated from the portal, his arm about Violetta's neck, and bethought himself of what he must do next to succeed in his purpose, for while he was disappointed at the rebuff he had received, he was not at all discouraged.

Despite the tragedy that had struck Pepino's early life and robbed him of his family, he really considered himself a most fortunate boy, compared with many, since he had acquired not only a heritage to aid him in earning a living but also an important precept by which to live.

This maxim, the golden key to success, had been left with Pepino, together with bars of chocolate, chewing gum, peanut brittle, soap, and other delights, by a corporal in the United States Army who had, in the six

---

7 **frayed cowl**: threadbare cloak—the type of cloak worn by a monk.

8 **desecration** (des ə krā′ shən): irreverent, outrageous act.

months he had been stationed in the vicinity of Assisi, been Pepino's demigod and hero. His name was Francis Xavier O'Halloran, and what he told Pepino before he departed out of his life forever was, "If you want to get ahead in this world, kid, don't never take no for an answer. Get it?" Pepino never forgot this important advice.

He thought now that his next step was clear; nevertheless, he went first to his friend and adviser, Father Damico, for confirmation.

Father Damico, who had a broad head, lustrous eyes, and shoulders shaped as though they had been especially designed to support the burdens laid upon them by his parishioners, said, "You are within your rights, my son, in taking your request to the lay Supervisor and it lies within his power to grant or refuse it."

There was no malice[9] in the encouragement he thus gave Pepino, but it was also true that he was not loath[10] to see the Supervisor brought face to face with an example of pure and innocent faith. For in his private opinion that worthy man was too much concerned with the twin churches that formed the Basilica and the crypt as a tourist attraction. He, Father Damico, could not see why the child should not have his wish, but, of course, it was out of his jurisdiction. He was, however, curious about how the Supervisor would react, even though he thought he knew in advance.

However, he did not impart his fears to Pepino and merely called after him as he was leaving, "And if the little one cannot be got in from above, there is another entrance from below, through the old church, only it has been walled up for a hundred years. But it could be opened. You might remind the Supervisor when you see him. He knows where it is."

Pepino thanked him and went back alone to the Basilica and the monastery attached to it and asked permission to see the Supervisor.

This personage was an accessible[11] man, and even though he was engaged in a conversation with the Bishop, he sent for Pepino, who walked into the cloister gardens where he waited respectfully for the two great men to finish.

The two dignitaries were walking up and down, and Pepino wished it were the Bishop who was to say yea or nay to his request, as he looked the kindlier of the two, the Supervisor appearing to have more the expression of a merchant. The boy pricked up his ears, because, as it happened, so they were speaking of St. Francis, and the Bishop was just remarking with a sigh, "He has been gone too long from this earth. The lesson of his life is plain to all who can read. But who in these times will pause to do so?"

The Supervisor said, "His tomb in the crypt attracts many to Assisi. But in a Holy Year, relics are even better. If we but had the tongue of the Saint, or a lock of his hair, or a fingernail."

The Bishop had a far-away look in his eyes, and he was shaking his head gently. "It is a message we are in need of, my dear Supervisor, a message from a great heart that would speak to us across the gap of seven centuries to remind us of The Way." And here he paused and coughed, for he was a polite man and noticed that Pepino was waiting.

9 **malice** (mal′ əs): ill will.
10 **loath** (lōth): unwilling.

11 **accessible** (ak ses′ ə bəl): easy to reach.

The Supervisor turned also and said, "Ah yes, my son, what is it that I can do for you?"

Pepino said, "Please, sir, my donkey Violetta is very sick. The Doctor Bartoli has said he can do nothing more and perhaps she will die. Please, I would like permission to take her into the tomb of Saint Francis and ask him to cure her. He loved all animals, and particularly little donkeys. I am sure he will make her well."

The Supervisor looked shocked. "A donkey. In the crypt. However did you come to that idea?"

Pepino explained about Giani and his sick kitten, while the Bishop turned away to hide a smile.

But the Supervisor was not smiling. He asked, "How did this Giani succeed in smuggling a kitten into the tomb?"

Since it was all over, Pepino saw no reason for not telling, and replied, "Under his coat, sir."

The Supervisor made a mental note to warn the brothers to keep a sharper eye out for small boys or other persons with suspicious-looking lumps under their outer clothing.

"Of course we can have no such goings on," he said. "The next thing you know, everyone would be coming, bringing a sick dog, or an ox, or a goat, or even a pig. And then where should we end up? A veritable sty."

"But, sir," Pepino pleaded, "no one need know. We would come and go so very quickly."

The Supervisor's mind played. There was something touching about the boy—the bullet head, the enormous eyes, the jug-handle ears. And yet, what if he permitted it and the donkey then died, as seemed most likely if Dr. Bartoli had said there was no further hope? Word was sure to get about, and the shrine would suffer from it. He wondered what the Bishop was thinking and how *he* would solve the problem.

He equivocated:[12] "And besides, even if we were to allow it, you would never be able to get your donkey around the turn at the bottom of the stairs. So, you see, it is quite impossible."

"But there is another entrance," Pepino said. "From the old church. It has not been used for a long time, but it could be opened just this once—couldn't it?"

The Supervisor was indignant. "What are you saying—destroy church property? The entrance has been walled up for over a century, ever since the new crypt was built."

The Bishop thought he saw a way out and said gently to the boy, "Why do you not go home and pray to Saint Francis to assist you? If you open your heart to him and have faith, he will surely hear you."

"But it wouldn't be the same," Pepino cried, and his voice was shaking with the sobs that wanted to come. "I must take her where Saint Francis can see her. She isn't like any other old donkey—Violetta has the sweetest smile. She does not smile any more since she has been so ill. But perhaps she would, just once more for Saint Francis. And when he saw it he would not be able to resist her, and he would make her well. I know he would!"

The Supervisor knew his ground now. He said, "I am sorry, my son, but the answer is no."

But even through his despair and the bitter tears he shed as he went away, Pepino knew that if Violetta was to live he must not take no for an answer.

"Who is there, then?" Pepino asked of Father Damico later. "Who is above the Supervisor and my lord the Bishop who might tell them to let me take Violetta into the crypt?"

Father Damico's stomach felt cold as he thought of the dizzying hierarchy[13] between Assisi and Rome. Nevertheless, he explained as best he could, concluding with, "And at the top is His Holiness, the Pope himself. Surely his heart would be touched by what has happened if you were able to tell him, for he is a great and good man. But he is busy with important weighty affairs, Pepino, and it would be impossible for him to see you."

Pepino went back to Niccolo's stable, where he ministered to Violetta, fed and watered her, and rubbed her muzzle a hundred times. Then he withdrew his money from the stone jar buried under the straw and counted it. He had almost three hundred lire.[14] A hundred of it he set aside and promised to his friend Giani if he would look after Violetta, while Pepino was gone, as if she were his own. Then he patted her once more, brushed away the tears that had started again at the sight of how thin she was, put on his jacket, and went out on the high road, where, using his thumb as he had learned from Corporal Francis Xavier O'Halloran, he got a lift in a lorry[15] going to Foligno and the main road. He was on his way to Rome to see the Holy Father.

Never had any small boy looked quite so infinitesimal[16] and forlorn as Pepino standing in the boundless and almost deserted, since it was early in the morning, St. Peter's Square.

---

12 **equivocated** (ē kwiv′ ə kāt əd): avoided giving a firm, definite answer.

13 **hierarchy** (hī′ ə rär kē): a ruling body of church officers organized into ranks, each rank subordinate to the one above it.

14 **lire** (lir′ā): the plural form of *lira*. Three hundred lire equal about 36 cents.

15 **lorry** (lôr′ ē): truck.

16 **infinitesimal** (in fin ə tes′ ə məl): small and unimportant.

Everything towered over him—the massive dome of St. Peter's, the obelisk of Caligula, the Bernini colonnades.[17] Everything contrived to make him look pinched and miserable in his bare feet, torn trousers, and ragged jacket. Never was a boy more overpowered, lonely, and frightened, or carried a greater burden of unhappiness in his heart.

For now that he was at last in Rome, the gigantic proportions of the buildings and monuments, their awe and majesty, began to sap his courage, and he seemed to have a glimpse into the utter futility and hopelessness of his mission. And then there would arise in his mind a picture of the sad little donkey who did not smile any more, her heaving flanks and clouded eyes, and who would surely die unless he could find help for her. It was thoughts like these that enabled him finally to cross the piazza[18] and timidly approach one of the smaller side entrances to the Vatican.

The Swiss guard, in his slashed red, yellow, and blue uniform, with his long halberd,[19] looked enormous and forbidding. Nevertheless, Pepino edged up to him and said, "Please, will you take me to see the Pope? I wish to speak to him about my donkey Violetta, who is very ill and may die unless the Pope will help me."

The guard smiled, not unkindly, for he was used to these ignorant and innocent requests, and the fact that it came from a dirty, ragged little boy, with eyes like ink pools and a round head from which the ears stood out like the handles of a cream jug,

made it all the more harmless. But, nevertheless, he was shaking his head as he smiled, and then said that His Holiness was a very busy man and could not be seen. And the guard grounded his halberd with a thud and let it fall slantwise across the door to show that he meant business.

Pepino backed away. What good was his precept in the face of such power and majesty? And yet the memory of what Corporal O'Halloran had said told him that he must return to the Vatican yet once again.

At the side of the piazza he saw an old woman sitting under an umbrella, selling little bouquets and nosegays of spring flowers—daffodils and jonquils, snowdrops and white narcissus, Parma violets and lilies of the valley, vari-colored carnations, pansies, and tiny sweetheart roses. Some of the people visiting St. Peter's liked to place these on the altar of their favorite saint. The flowers were crisp and fresh from the market, and many of them had glistening drops of water still clinging to their petals.

Looking at them made Pepino think of home and Father Damico and what he had said of the love St. Francis had for flowers. Father Damico had the gift of making everything he thought and said sound like poetry. And Pepino came to the conclusion that if St. Francis, who had been a holy man, had been so fond of flowers, perhaps the Pope, who according to his position was even holier, would love them, too.

For fifty lire he bought a tiny bouquet in which a spray of lilies of the valley rose from a bed of dark violets and small red roses crowded next to yellow pansies all tied about with leaf and feather fern and paper lace.

From a stall where postcards and souvenirs were sold, he begged pencil and paper, and laboriously composed a note:

---

17 **massive dome . . . colonnades:** important buildings and monuments in St. Peter's Square.
18 **piazza** (pē ät′ zə): Italian word for square or plaza.
19 **halberd** (hal′ bərd): battle-ax and pike on a handle about six feet long.

Dear and most sacred Holy Father: These flowers are for you. Please let me see you and tell you about my donkey Violetta who is dying and they will not let me take her to see Saint Francis so that he may cure her. I live in the town of Assisi, but I have come all the way here to see you.

Your loving Pepino.

Thereupon, he returned to the door, placed the bouquet and the note in the hand of the Swiss guard, and begged, "Please take these up to the Pope. I am sure he will see me when he receives the flowers and reads what I have written."

The guard had not expected this. The child and the flowers had suddenly placed him in a dilemma[20] from which he could not extricate himself in the presence of those large and trusting eyes. However, he was not without experience in handling such matters. He had only to place a colleague[21] at his post, go to the Guard Room, throw the flowers and the note into the wastepaper basket, absent himself for a sufficient length of time, and then return to tell the boy that His Holiness thanked him for the gift of the flowers and regretted that press of important business made it impossible for him to grant him an audience.

This little subterfuge[22] the guard put into motion at once; but when he came to completing the next-to-last act in it, he found to his amazement that somehow he could not bring himself to do it. There was the wastepaper basket, yawning to receive the offering, but the little nosegay seemed to be glued to

his fingers. How gay, sweet, and cool the flowers were. What thoughts they brought to his mind of spring in the green valleys of his far-off canton of Luzern.[23] He saw again the snow-capped mountains of his youth, the little gingerbread houses, the grey, soft-eyed cattle grazing in the blossom-carpeted meadows, and he heard the heart-warming tinkling of their bells.

Dazed by what had happened to him, he left the Guard Room and wandered through the corridors, for he did not know where to go or what to do with his burden. He was eventually encountered by a busy little Monsignor, one of the vast army of clerks and secretaries employed in the Vatican, who paused, astonished at the sight of the burly guard helplessly contemplating a tiny posy.

And thus occurred the minor miracle whereby Pepino's plea and offering crossed the boundary in the palace that divided the

---

20 **dilemma** (də lem′ ə): a situation that presents a choice between two equally unattractive courses of action.
21 **colleague** (kol′ lēg): associate; here, another Swiss Guard.
22 **subterfuge** (sub′ tər fyüj): trick.

23 **canton of Luzern:** a section of Switzerland.

mundane[24] from the spiritual, the lay from the ecclesiastical.[25]

For to the great relief of the guard, the Monsignor took over the burning articles that he had been unable to relinquish; and this priest they touched, too, as it is the peculiar power of flowers that while they are universal and spread their species over the world, they invoke in each beholder the dearest and most cherished memories.

In this manner, the little bouquet passed on and upward from hand to hand, pausing briefly in the possession of the clerk of the Apostolic Chamber, the Privy Almoner, the Papal Sacristan, the Master of the Sacred Palaces, the Papal Chamberlain. The dew vanished from the flowers; they began to lose their freshness and to wilt, passing from hand to hand. And yet they retained their magic, the message of love and memories that rendered it impossible for any of these intermediaries to dispose of them.

Eventually, then, they were deposited with the missive[26] that accompanied them on the desk of the man for whom they had been destined. He read the note and then sat there silently contemplating the blossoms. He closed his eyes for a moment, the better to entertain the picture that arose in his mind of himself as a small Roman boy taken on a Sunday into the Alban Hills, where for the first time he saw violets growing wild.

When he opened his eyes at last, he said to his secretary, "Let the child be brought here. I will see him."

Thus it was that Pepino at last came into the presence of the Pope, seated at his desk in his office. Perched on the edge of a chair next to him, Pepino told the whole story about Violetta, his need to take her into the tomb of St. Francis, about the Supervisor who was preventing him, and all about Father Damico, too, and the second entrance to the crypt, Violetta's smile, and his love for her—everything, in fact, that was in his heart and that now poured forth to the sympathetic man sitting quietly behind the desk.

And when, at the end of half an hour, he was ushered from the presence, he was quite sure he was the happiest boy in the world. For he had not only the blessing of the Pope, but also, under his jacket, two letters, one addressed to the lay Supervisor of the Monastery of Assisi and the other to Father Damico. No longer did he feel small and overwhelmed when he stepped out on to the square again past the astonished but delighted Swiss guard. He felt as though he could give one leap and a bound and fly back to his Violetta's side.

Nevertheless, he had to give heed to the more practical side of transportation. He inquired his way to a bus that took him to where the Via Flaminia became a country road stretching to the north, then plied his thumb backed by his eloquent eyes, and before nightfall of that day, with good luck, was home in Assisi.

After a visit to Violetta had assured him that she had been well looked after and at least was no worse than she had been before his departure, Pepino proudly went to Father Damico and presented his letters as he had been instructed to do.

The Father fingered the envelope for the Supervisor and then, with a great surge of warmth and happiness, read the one addressed to himself. He said to Pepino, "Tomorrow we will take the Supervisor's letter to him. He will summon masons and the old

---

24 **mundane** (mun' dān): worldly.
25 **lay . . . ecclesiastical** (iklē zē as' ti kəl): church officials who are not ordained priests or ministers.
26 **missive** (mis' iv): note; letter.

door will be broken down and you will be able to take Violetta into the tomb and pray there for her recovery. The Pope himself has approved it."

The Pope, of course, had not written the letters personally. They had been composed with considerable delight and satisfaction by the Cardinal-Secretary, backed by Papal authority, who said in his missive to Father Damico:

Surely the Supervisor must know that in his lifetime the blessed Saint Francis was accompanied to chapel by a little lamb that used to follow him about Assisi. Is an *asinus* any less created by God because his coat is rougher and his ears longer?

And he wrote also of another matter, which Father Damico imparted to Pepino in his own way.

He said, "Pepino, there is something you must understand before we go to see the Abbot. It is your hope that because of your faith in St. Francis he will help you and heal your donkey. But had you thought, perhaps, that he who dearly cared for all of God's creatures might come to love Violetta so greatly that he would wish to have her at his side in Eternity?"

A cold terror gripped Pepino as he listened. He managed to say, "No, Father, I had not thought—"

The priest continued: "Will you go to the crypt only to ask, Pepino, or will you also, if necessary, be prepared to give?"

Everything in Pepino cried out against the possibility of losing Violetta, even to someone as beloved as St. Francis. Yet when he raised his stricken face and looked into the lustrous eyes of Father Damico, there was something in their depths that gave him the courage to whisper, "I will give—if I must. But, oh, I hope he will let her stay with me just a little longer."

The clink of the stonemason's pick rang again and again through the vaulted chamber of the lower church, where the walled-up door of the passageway leading to the crypt was being removed. Nearby waited the Supervisor and his friend the Bishop, Father Damico, and Pepino, large-eyed, pale, and silent. The boy kept his arms about the neck of Violetta and his face pressed to hers. The little donkey was very shaky on her legs and could barely stand.

The Supervisor watched humbly and impassively while broken bricks and clods of mortar fell as the breach widened and the freed current of air from the passage swirled the plaster dust in clouds. He was a just man for all his weakness, and had invited the Bishop to witness his rebuke.

A portion of the wall proved obstinate. The mason attacked the archway at the side to weaken its support. Then the loosened masonry began to tumble again. A narrow passageway was effected, and through the opening they could see the distant flicker of the candles placed at the altar wherein rested the remains of St. Francis.

Pepino stirred towards the opening. Or was it Violetta who had moved nervously, frightened by the unaccustomed place and noises? Father Damico said, "Wait," and Pepino held her; but the donkey's uncertain feet slipped on the rubble and then lashed out in panic, striking the side of the archway where it had been weakened. A brick fell out. A crack appeared.

Father Damico leaped and pulled boy and animal out of the way as, with a roar, the side of the arch collapsed, laying bare a piece of the old wall and the hollow behind it before everything vanished in a cloud of dust.

But when the dust settled, the Bishop, his eyes starting from his head, was pointing to something that rested in a niche of the hollow just revealed. It was a small, grey, leaden box. Even from there they could see the year 1226, when St. Francis died, engraved on the side, and the large initial *F*.

The Bishop's breath came out like a sigh, "Ah, could it be? The legacy of Saint Francis! Fra Leo mentions it. It was hidden away centuries ago, and no one has ever been able to find it since."

The Supervisor said hoarsely, "The contents! Let us see what is inside—it may be valuable!"

The Bishop hesitated. "Perhaps we had best wait. For this is in itself a miracle, this finding."

But Father Damico, who was a poet and to whom St. Francis was a living spirit, cried, "Open it, I beg of you! All who are here are humble. Surely Heaven's Plan has guided us to it."

The Abbot held the lantern. The mason with his careful, honest workman's hands deftly loosed the bindings and pried the lid of the airtight box. It opened with an ancient creaking of its hinge and revealed what had been placed there more than seven centuries before.

There was a piece of hempen cord, knotted as though, perhaps, once it had been worn about the waist. Caught in the knot, as fresh as though it had grown but yesterday, was a single sprig of wheat. Dried and preserved, there lay, too, the stem and starry flower of a mountain primrose and, next to it, one downy feather from a tiny meadow bird.

Silently the men stared at these objects from the past to try to read their meaning, and Father Damico wept, for to him they brought the vivid figure of the Saint, half-

blinded, worn and fragile, the cord knotted at his waist, singing, striding through a field of wheat. The flower might have been the first discovered by him after a winter's snow, and addressed as "Sister Cowslip," and praised for her tenderness and beauty. As though he were transported there, Father Damico saw the little field bird fly trustingly to Francis' shoulder and chirrup and nestle there and leave a feather in his hand. His heart was so full he thought he could not bear it.

The Bishop, too, was close to tears as, in his own way, he interpreted what they had found. "Ah, what could be clearer than the

messsage of the Saint? Poverty, love, and faith. This is his bequest to all of us."

Pepino said, "Please, lords and sirs, may Violetta and I go into the crypt now?"

They had forgotten him. Now they started up from their contemplation of the touching relics.

Father Damico cleared the tears from his eyes. The doorway was freed now, and there was room for boy and donkey to pass. "Ah, yes," he said. "Yes, Pepino. You may enter now. And may God go with you."

The hoofs of the donkey went sharply *clip-clop, clip-clop* on the ancient flagging of the passageway. Pepino did not support her

now, but walked beside, hand just resting lightly and lovingly on her neck. His round, cropped head with the outstanding ears was held high, and his shoulders were bravely squared.

And to Father Damico it seemed, as they passed, whether because of the uneven light and the dancing shadows, or because he wished it so, that the ghost, the merest wisp, the barest suspicion of a smile had returned to the mouth of Violetta.

Thus the watchers saw boy and donkey silhouetted against the flickering oil lamps and altar candles of the crypt as they went forward to complete their pilgrimage of faith.

1. What was Pepino's "heritage"? How did this "heritage" allow Pepino to be independent? What was Pepino's attitude toward—how did he feel about—his "heritage"?

2. What caused Pepino to think he should take Violetta to the crypt of Saint Francis of Assisi? Whatever made him think he *could* do so?

3. In seeking permission to take Violetta to St. Francis's crypt, Pepino found that he had to deal with several levels of authority. How did Father Damico respond to Pepino's request? How did Fra Bernard respond? the Supervisor? the Bishop?

4. Of what importance was Francis Xavier O'Halloran in Pepino's life?

5. Why did Pepino go to Rome to see the Pope? What chance did he, a poor ten-year-old boy, have of getting in to see such an important person? How did he manage to do so? What was the Pope's response?

6. As the stonemason worked to break through the blocked entrance, the wall collapsed. When the dust settled, what did the small group discover? What mementos of Saint Francis did they find? Of what importance are the mementos?

7. As Pepino and Violetta passed through the opening into the crypt, what did Father Damico think he saw? What might this incident suggest?

8. What *was* the small miracle? What part did determination play in that miracle?

Composition

1. Was determination an important or an unimportant element in Pepino's success? In a short composition, give your answer to that question. Be sure to tell why you think as you do by referring to specific events in the story. Conclude your composition with a restatement of your first sentence.

2. Corporal Francis Xavier O'Halloran told Pepino never to "take no for an answer." In a short composition, explain whether you think O'Halloran's advice is worth following or not worth following. Support your opinion by giving at least three reasons for thinking as you do. Conclude your composition by restating your position. For example, you might say something like this: "For these reasons, I think that O'Halloran's advice is well worth following (or not worth following)."

2 DETERMINATION

Discussion

1. Reading and discussing the selections making up this unit have no doubt given you a clear understanding of the meaning of determination. Explain briefly what determination means to you.

2. Of the eleven selections in this unit, which one do you think best demonstrates the importance of determination in achieving one's goals? Be prepared to defend your choice.

3. When you come right down to it, all of the selections in this unit involve a determination to succeed. Yet a number of the selections deal with other facets of determination:
   a. Which selections deal with a determination to see that right is done?
   b. Which selections deal with a determination to live life to its fullest?
   c. Which selections deal with a determination to persevere in spite of seemingly overwhelming odds?
   d. Which selections deal with a determination to do the job one has set for oneself?

Composition

1. Of the persons you met in this unit, which one impressed you most in his or her demonstration of determination? Write a composition of one or more pages in which you (a) identify that person and (b) supply evidence from the appropriate selection to support your choice. Consider the total situation that your chosen person faced. Consider, too, the obstacles he or she had to overcome in achieving success. Finally, consider how he or she showed determination in his or her handling of the situation.

2. At some time during your life you have demonstrated determination to attain the goal you sought. (Or perhaps you know of someone else who showed such determination.) In a composition of one or more pages, briefly describe the situation in which it was necessary to exercise determination to gain success. Then explain how you (or someone else) demonstrated the necessary determination to get what you wanted. Finally, tell how it feels to have had such an experience.

3

Plot and Character

PLOT AND CHARACTER

Although a storyteller's main purpose is to entertain you, he or she also seeks to take you out of your own world into another. In doing so, he or she tells you about what happens (action) to someone (character) somewhere (setting). Over the years that storytellers have been plying their craft, they have developed ways of spinning their yarns that are sure to capture and hold your attention.

You know, of course, that the things storytellers tell about need not actually have happened. But the accounts of those things must be so convincing that you *believe* they have. Expert storytellers, for example, have convinced many readers/listeners that the Pied Piper of Hamelin could have charmed all the children of the town, or that Alice could have fallen down a rabbit hole.

What kind of magic do storytellers practice to make their tales convincing? No magic; just this: Every expert storyteller creates his or her story *by organizing a series of related incidents into a* PLOT. He or she doesn't just tell you about what happens; to do so would be mere reporting. Instead, the expert storyteller *selects*—from all the things that happened—*only those incidents that are important to the story itself*. And then he or she connects those incidents in a way that makes sense. The plot of a story, in other words, is like a chain of events, each link joined logically to the next.

But the related events that make up the plot of a story don't just happen all by themselves. *Someone* or *something* is involved in them. In other words, every storyteller focuses on a central CHARACTER, or central characters, who are involved in the plot in two ways: (1) They can cause things to happen, and (2) they can react to—that is, do and say things as a result of—the things that happen.

Plot and character! They are the essential ingredients that every storyteller uses in every story.

The night was tailor-made for what he wanted—a chance to fish, a time to be alone. But the night was also harboring something else—something he hadn't counted on!

The Sea Devil

ARTHUR GORDON

THE MAN CAME out of the house and stood quite still, listening. Behind him, the lights glowed in the cheerful room, the books were neat and orderly in their cases, the radio talked importantly to itself. In front of him, the bay stretched dark and silent, one of the countless lagoons that border the coast where Florida thrusts its great green thumb deep into the tropics.

It was late in September. The night was breathless; summer's dead hand still lay heavy on the land. The man moved forward six paces and stood on the seawall. He dropped his cigarette and noted where the tiny spark hissed and went out. The tide was beginning to ebb.

Somewhere out in the blackness a mullet[1] jumped and fell back with a sullen splash. Heavy with roe,[2] they were jumping less often now. They would not take a hook, but a practiced eye could see the swirls they made in the glassy water. In the dark of the moon a skilled man with a cast net might take half a

dozen in an hour's work. And a big mullet makes a meal for a family.

The man turned abruptly and went into the garage, where his cast net hung. He was in his late twenties, wide-shouldered and strong. He did not have to fish for a living, or even for food. He was a man who worked with his head, not with his hands. But he liked to go casting alone at night.

He liked the loneliness and the labor of it. He liked the clean taste of salt when he gripped the edge of the net with his teeth, as a cast netter must. He liked the arching flight of sixteen pounds of lead and linen against the starlight, and the weltering crash of the net into the unsuspecting water. He liked the harsh tug of the retrieving rope around his wrist, and the way the net came alive when the cast was true, and the thud of captured fish on the floorboards of the skiff.

He liked all that because he found in it a reality that seemed to be missing from his twentieth-century job and from his daily life. He liked being the hunter, skilled and solitary and elemental. There was no conscious cruelty in the way he felt. It was the way things had been in the beginning.

---

1 **mullet** (mul′ ət): a salt-water food fish.
2 **roe** (rō): the mullet's eggs.

The man lifted the net down carefully and lowered it into a bucket. He put a paddle beside the bucket. Then he went into the house. When he came out, he was wearing swimming trunks and a pair of old tennis shoes. Nothing else.

The skiff, flat-bottomed, was moored off the seawall. He would not go far, he told himself. Just to the tumbledown dock half a mile away. Mullet had a way of feeding around old piling after dark. If he moved quietly, he might pick up two or three in one cast close to the dock. And maybe a couple of others on the way down or back.

He shoved off and stood motionless for a moment, letting his eyes grow accustomed to the dark. Somewhere out in the channel a porpoise blew with a sound like steam escaping. The man smiled a little; porpoises were his friends. Once, fishing in the Gulf, he had seen the charter-boat captain reach overside and gaff a baby porpoise through the sinewy part of the tail. He had hoisted it aboard, had dropped it into the bail well, where it thrashed around puzzled and unhappy. And the mother had swum alongside the boat and under the boat and around the boat, nudging the stout planking with her back, slapping it with her tail, until the man felt sorry for her and made the captain let the baby porpoise go.

He took the net from the bucket, slipped the noose in the retrieving rope over his wrist, pulled the slipknot tight. It was an old net, but still serviceable; he had rewoven the rents made by underwater snags. He coiled the thirty-foot rope carefully, making sure there were no kinks. A tangled rope, he knew, would spoil any cast.

The basic design of the net had not changed in three thousand years. It was a mesh circle with a diameter of fourteen feet.

It measured close to fifteen yards around the circumference and could, if thrown perfectly, blanket a hundred and fifty square feet of sea water. In the center of this radial trap was a small iron collar where the retrieving rope met the twenty-three separate drawstrings leading to the outer rim of the net. Along this rim, spaced an inch and a half apart, were the heavy lead sinkers.

The man raised the iron collar until it was a foot above his head. The net hung soft and pliant and deadly. He shook it gently, making sure that the drawstrings were not tangled, that the sinkers were hanging true. Then he eased it down and picked up the paddle.

The night was black as a witch's cat; the stars looked fuzzy and dim. Down to the southward, the lights of a causeway made a yellow necklace across the sky. To the man's left were the tangled roots of a mangrove swamp; to his right, the open waters of the bay. Most of it was fairly shallow, but there were channels eight feet deep. The man could not see the old dock, but he knew where it was. He pulled the paddle quietly through the water, and the phosphorescence glowed and died.

For five minutes he paddled. Then, twenty feet ahead of the skiff, a mullet jumped. A big fish, close to three pounds. For a moment it hung in the still air, gleaming dully. Then it vanished. But the ripples marked the spot, and where there was one there were often others.

The man stood up quickly. He picked up the coiled rope, and with the same hand grasped the net at a point four feet below the iron collar. He raised the skirt to his mouth, gripped it strongly with his teeth. He slid his free hand as far as it would go down the circumference of the net so that he had three points of contact with the mass of cordage and metal. He made sure his feet were planted solidly. Then he waited, feeling the tension that is older than the human race, the fierce exhilaration of the hunter at the moment of ambush, the atavistic desire[3] to capture and kill and ultimately consume.

A mullet swirled, ahead and to the left. The man swung the heavy net back, twisting his body and bending his knees so as to get more upward thrust. He shot it forward, letting go simultaneously with rope hand and with teeth, holding a fraction of a second longer with the other hand so as to give the net necessary spin, impart the centrifugal force[4] that would make it flare into a circle. The skiff ducked sideways, but he kept his balance. The net fell with a splash.

The man waited for five seconds. Then he began to retrieve it, pulling in a series of sharp jerks so that the drawstrings would gather the net inward, like a giant fist closing on this segment of the teeming sea. He felt the net quiver, and knew it was not empty. He swung it, dripping, over the gunwale, saw the broad silver side of the mullet quivering, saw too the gleam of a smaller fish. He looked closely to make sure no stingray was hidden in the mesh, then raised the iron collar and shook the net out. The mullet fell with a thud and flapped wildly. The other victim was an angelfish, beautifully marked, but too small to keep. The man picked it up gently and dropped it overboard. He coiled the rope, took up the paddle. He would cast no more until he came to the dock.

The skiff moved on. At last, ten feet apart, a pair of stakes rose up gauntly out of the

night. Barnacle-encrusted, they once had marked the approach from the main channel. The man guided the skiff between them, then put the paddle down softly. He stood up, reached for the net, tightened the noose around his wrist. From here he could drift down upon the dock. He could see it now—a ruined skeleton in the starshine. Beyond it a mullet jumped and fell back with a flat, liquid sound. The man raised the edge of the net, put it between his teeth. He would not cast at a single swirl, he decided; he would wait until he saw two or three close together. The skiff was barely moving. He felt his muscles tense themselves, awaiting the signal from the brain.

Behind him in the channel he heard the porpoise blow again, nearer now. He

---

3 **atavistic** (at ə vis′ tik) **desire**: a craving like that of one's early ancestors.
4 **centrifugal** (sen trif′ yu gəl) **force**: a tendering that impels something outward from the center.

frowned in the darkness. If the porpoise chose to fish this area, the mullet would scatter and vanish. There was no time to lose.

A school of sardines surfaced suddenly, skittering along like drops of mercury. Something, perhaps the shadow of the skiff, had frightened them. The old dock loomed very close. A mullet broke water just too far away; then another, nearer. The man marked the spreading ripples and decided to wait no longer.

He swung back the net, heavier now that it was wet. He had to turn his head, but out of the corner of his eye he saw two swirls in the black water just off the starboard bow. They were about eight feet apart, and they had the sluggish oily look that marks the presence of something big just below the surface. His conscious mind had no time to function, but instinct told him that the net was wide enough to cover both swirls if he could alter the direction of his cast. He could not halt the swing, but he shifted his feet slightly and made the cast off balance. He saw the net shoot forward, flare into an oval, and drop just where he wanted it.

Then the sea exploded in his face. In a frenzy of spray, a great horned thing shot like a huge bat out of the water. The man saw the mesh of his net etched against the mottled blackness of its body, and he knew, in the split second in which thought was still possible, that those twin swirls had been made not by two mullet, but by the wing tips of the giant ray of the Gulf Coast, *Manta birostris,* also known as clam cracker, devil ray, sea devil.

The man gave a hoarse cry. He tried to claw the slipknot off his wrist, but there was no time. The quarter-inch line snapped taut. He shot over the side of the skiff as if he had roped a runaway locomotive. He hit the water headfirst and seemed to bounce once. He plowed a blinding furrow for perhaps ten yards. Then the line went slack as the sea devil jumped again. It was not the full-grown manta of the deep Gulf, but it was close to nine feet from tip to tip and it weighed over a thousand pounds. Up into the air it went, pearl-colored underbelly gleaming as it twisted in a frantic effort to dislodge the clinging thing that had fallen upon it. Up into the starlight, a monstrous survival from the dawn of time.

The water was less than four feet deep. Sobbing and choking, the man struggled for a foothold on the slimy bottom. Sucking in great gulps of air, he fought to free himself from the rope. But the slipknot was jammed deep into his wrist; he might as well have tried to loosen a circle of steel.

The ray came down with a thunderous splash and drove forward again. The flexible net followed every movement, impeding it hardly at all. The man weighed a hundred and seventy-five pounds, and he was braced for the shock, and he had the desperate strength that comes from looking into the blank eyes of death. It was useless. His arm straightened out with a jerk that seemed to dislocate his shoulder; his feet shot out from under him; his head went under again. Now at last he knew how the fish must feel when the line tightens and drags him toward the alien element that is his doom. Now he knew.

Desperately he dug the fingers of his free hand into the ooze, felt them dredge a futile channel through broken shells and the ribbonlike sea grasses. He tried to raise his head, but could not get it clear. Torrents of spray choked him as the ray plunged toward deep water.

His eyes were of no use to him in the foam-streaked blackness. He closed them tight, and at once an insane sequence of pictures flashed through his mind. He saw his wife sitting in their living room, reading, waiting calmly for his return. He saw the mullet he had just caught, gasping its life away on the floorboards of the skiff. He saw the cigarette he had flung from the seawall touch the water and expire with a tiny hiss. He saw all these things and many others simultaneously in his mind as his body fought silently and tenaciously for its existence. His hand touched something hard and closed on it in a death grip, but it was only the sharp-edged helmet of a horseshoe crab, and after an instant he let it go.

He had been underwater perhaps fifteen seconds now, and something in his brain told him quite calmly that he could last another forty or fifty, and then the red flashes behind his eyes would merge into darkness, and the water would pour into his lungs in one sharp, painful shock, and he would be finished.

This thought spurred him to a desperate effort. He reached up and caught his pinioned wrist with his free hand. He doubled up his knees to create more drag. He thrashed his body madly, like a fighting fish, from side to side. This did not disturb the ray, but now one of the great wings tore through the mesh, and the net slipped lower over the fins projecting like horns from below the nightmare head, and the sea devil jumped again.

And once more the man was able to get his feet on the bottom and his head above water, and he saw ahead of him the pair of ancient stakes that marked the approach to the channel. He knew that if he was dragged much beyond those stakes, he would be in eight feet of water, and the ray would go down to hug the bottom as rays always do, and then no power on earth could save him. So in the moment of respite[5] that was granted him, he flung himself toward them. For a moment he thought his captor yielded a bit. Then the ray moved off again, but more slowly now, and for a few yards the man was able to keep his feet on the bottom. Twice he hurled himself back against the rope with all his strength, hoping that something would break. But nothing broke. The mesh of the net was ripped and torn, but the draw lines were strong, and the stout perimeter cord threaded through the sinkers was even stronger.

The man could feel nothing now in his trapped hand—it was numb—but the ray could feel the powerful lunges of the unknown thing that was trying to restrain it. It drove its great wings against the unyielding water and forged ahead, dragging the man and pushing a sullen wave in front of it.

The man had swung as far as he could toward the stakes. He plunged toward one and missed it by inches. His feet slipped and he went down on his knees. Then the ray swerved sharply and the second stake came right at him. He reached out with his free hand and caught it.

He caught it just above the surface, six or eight inches below high-water mark. He felt the razor-sharp barnacles bite into his hand, collapse under the pressure, drive their tiny slime-covered shell splinters deep into his flesh. He felt the pain, and he welcomed it, and he made his fingers into an iron claw that would hold until the tendons were severed or the skin was shredded from the bone. The ray felt the pressure increase with a jerk that stopped it dead in the water. For a moment all was still as the tremendous forces came into equilibrium.[6]

Then the net slipped again, and the perimeter cord came down over the sea devil's eyes, blinding it momentarily. The great ray settled to the bottom and braced its wings against the mud and hurled itself forward and upward.

The stake was only a four-by-four of creosoted pine, and it was old. Ten thousand tides had swirled around it. Worms had bored; parasites had clung. Under the crust of barnacles it still had some heart left, but not enough. The man's grip was five feet above the floor of the bay; the leverage was too great. The stake snapped off at its base.

The ray lunged upward, dragging the man and the useless timber. The man had his lungs full of air, but when the stake snapped he thought of expelling the air and inhaling the water so as to have it finished quickly. He thought of this, but he did not do it. And then, just at the channel's edge, the ray met the porpoise coming in.

The porpoise had fed well this night and was in no hurry, but it was a methodical creature and it intended to make a sweep around the old dock before the tide dropped too low. It had no quarrel with any ray, but it feared no fish in the sea, and when the great black shadow came rushing blindly and unavoidably, it rolled fast and struck once with its massive horizontal tail.

---

5 respite (res′ pit): pause.

6 equilibrium (ē kwə lib′ rē əm): balance.

The blow descended on the ray's flat body with a sound like a pistol shot. It would have broken a buffalo's back, and even the sea devil was half stunned. It veered wildly and turned back toward shallow water. It passed within ten feet of the man, face down in the water. It slowed and almost stopped, wing tips moving faintly, gathering strength for another rush.

The man had heard the tremendous slap of the great mammal's tail and the snorting gasp as it plunged away. He felt the line go slack again, and he raised his dripping face, and he reached for the bottom with his feet. He found it, but now the water was up to his neck. He plucked at the noose once more with his lacerated hand, but there was no strength in his fingers. He felt the tension come back into the line as the ray began to move again, and for half a second he was tempted to throw himself backward and fight as he had been doing, pitting his strength against the vastly superior strength of the brute.

But the acceptance of imminent death had done something to his brain. It had driven out the fear, and with the fear had gone the panic. He could think now, and he knew with absolute certainty that if he was to make any use of this last chance that had been given him, it would have to be based on the one faculty that had carried man to his pre-eminence above all beasts: the faculty of reason. Only by using his brain could he possibly survive, and he called on his brain for a solution, and his brain responded. It offered him one.

He did not know whether his body still had the strength to carry out the brain's commands, but he began to swim forward, toward the ray that was still moving hesitantly away from the channel. He swam forward, feeling the rope go slack as he gained on the creature.

Ahead of him he saw the one remaining stake, and he made himself swim faster until he was parallel with the ray and the rope trailed behind both of them in a deep U. He

swam with a surge of desperate energy that came from nowhere, so that he was slightly in the lead as they came to the stake. He passed on one side of it; the ray was on the other.

Then the man took one last deep breath, and he went down under the black water until he was sitting on the bottom of the bay. He put one foot over the line so that it passed under his bent knee. He drove both his heels into the mud, and he clutched the slimy grass with his bleeding hand, and he waited for the tension to come again.

The ray passed on the other side of the stake, moving faster now. The rope grew taut again, and it began to drag the man back toward the stake. He held his prisoned wrist close to the bottom, under his knee, and he prayed that the stake would not break. He felt the rope vibrate as the barnacles bit into it. He did not know whether the rope would crush the barnacles or whether the barnacles would cut the rope. All he knew was that in five seconds or less he would be dragged into the stake and cut to ribbons if he tried to hold on, or drowned if he didn't.

He felt himself sliding slowly, and then faster, and suddenly the ray made a great leap forward, and the rope burned around the base of the stake, and the man's foot hit it hard. He kicked himself backward with his remaining strength, and the rope parted and he was free.

He came slowly to the surface.

Thirty feet away the sea devil made one tremendous leap and disappeared into the darkness. The man raised his wrist and looked at the frayed length of rope dangling from it. Twenty inches, perhaps. He lifted his other hand and felt the hot blood start instantly, but he didn't care. He put this hand on the stake above the barnacles and held onto the good, rough, honest wood. He heard a strange noise, and realized that it was himself sobbing.

High above, there was a droning sound, and looking up, he saw the nightly plane from New Orleans inbound for Tampa. Calm and serene, it sailed, symbol of man's proud mastery over nature. Its lights winked red and green for a moment; then it was gone.

Slowly, painfully, the man began to move through the placid water. He came to the skiff at last and climbed into it. The mullet, still alive, slapped convulsively with its tail. The man reached down with his torn hand, picked up the mullet, let it go.

He began to work on the slipknot doggedly with his teeth. His mind was almost a blank, but not quite. He knew one thing. He knew he would do no more casting alone at night. Not in the dark of the moon. No, not he.

Discussion

1. What situation forced the man to have to fight for his life?

2. Even as he fought for his life, the man struggled to think clearly—to control his panic. How did he free himself from the net and the ray?

3. Why, in your opinion, did the man let the mullet go?

4. Some readers have said that the airplane overhead (at the end of the story) represents human "mastery over nature." Do you think the man in the story would agree or disagree that human beings have gained mastery over nature? Why?

Writer's Craft

The plot of every story you have ever read involves a struggle of some kind. That struggle could be a difference of opinion, a sports contest, a fist fight, or a war. Such a struggle is called the CONFLICT. It is the basic element of the story. No conflict, no story worth telling. It's that simple.

Naturally, if there's a conflict, there have to be people or things pitted against one another. In short, there have to be opposing forces. Those forces might consist of one person working against another person in some way. Or they might consist of an element of nature working against a person. For example, Sue Hanson wants to swim the English Channel. But the tides, the ocean currents, and the winds may work against her. The opposing forces, then, are Sue and Nature. The conflict lies between them.

1. In "The Sea Devil," what is the conflict? What opposing forces do you find?
2. What lines in the story indicate the beginning of the conflict?
3. What lines in the story indicate that the conflict has been resolved?
4. What is the importance of the story up to the point where the conflict begins?
5. Suppose that the man had simply caught the mullet he had expected to catch and then had gone home. What would probably be your reaction?

Vocabulary

In our language many words have several definitions. When a word can be defined in various ways, it is said to have MULTIPLE MEANINGS. For example, think about the way the meaning of *paddle* differs in each of these sentences:

1. The man eased his net down into the boat and then picked up the *paddle*.
2. My little brother can't swim, but he certainly can *paddle*.
3. The coach says if you skip practice again, she'll *paddle* you.

The dictionary lists all the definitions for each multiple-meaning word, but there is only one reliable way to choose the definition that is intended: You do that by examining the context clues that surround the word.

On a separate sheet of paper, write the definition for each multiple-meaning word given in *italics* in the sentences below. The sentences are arranged in pairs. In each pair, the first sentence deals with something that happens in "The Sea Devil." If you need help, use a dictionary.

1. a. The man put on his swimming *trunks* and a pair of old shoes.
   b. The bark was thick on the *trunks* of the trees.

2. a. He liked to get into his boat and go out *casting* on the bay at night.
   b. Most of the voters are *casting* their ballots for Laura Chang.

3. a. He told himself he would go no farther out than the *dock* half a mile away.
   b. The boss threatened to *dock* the employees' salaries.

4. a. He gripped the edge of the *net* with his teeth.
   b. According to those figures, your *net* profit for the year has dropped by twenty percent.

5. a. He had rewoven *rents* made by underwater snags.
   b. The small house *rents* for $175.00 a month.

Arthur Gordon 1912 ——

Arthur Gordon was born in Savannah, Georgia, where he now lives when he is not traveling. His hobbies are fishing, boating, hunting, and tennis. His stories are often centered around these sports.

Gordon has written over two hundred stories for magazines, most recently for *Guideposts*. Many of his stories and articles have been inspirational. Among the six books he has written is a biography of the Reverend Norman Vincent Peale.

Good-by, Grandma

RAY BRADBURY

SHE WAS A WOMAN with a broom or a dustpan or a washrag or a mixing spoon in her hand. You saw her cutting pie-crust in the morning, humming to it, or you saw her setting out the baked pies at noon or taking them in, cool, at dusk. She rang porcelain cups like a Swiss bell ringer, to their place. She glided through the halls as steadily as a vacuum machine, seeking, finding, and setting to rights. She made mirrors of every window, to catch the sun. She strolled but twice through any garden, trowel[1] in hand, and the flowers raised their quivering faces upon the warm air in her wake. She slept quietly and turned no more than three times in a night, as relaxed as a white glove to which, at dawn, a brisk hand will return. Waking, she touched people like pictures, to set their frames straight.

But, now . . . ?

"Grandma," said everyone. "Great-grandma."

Now it was as if a huge sum in arithmetic were finally drawing to an end. She had stuffed turkeys, chickens, squabs, gentlemen, and boys. She had washed ceilings, walls, invalids, and children. She had laid linoleum, repaired bicycles, wound clocks, stoked furnaces, swabbed iodine on ten thousand grievous wounds. Her hands had flown all around about and down, gentling this, holding that, throwing baseballs, swinging bright croquet mallets, seeding black earth, or fixing covers over dumplings, ragouts,[2] and children wildly strewn by slumber. She had pulled down shades, pinched out candles, turned switches, and—grown old. Looking back on thirty billions of things started, carried, finished and done, it all summed up, totaled out; the last decimal was placed, the final zero swung slowly into line. Now, chalk in hand, she stood back from life a silent hour before reaching for the eraser.

"Let me see now," said Great-grandma. "Let me see. . . ."

With no fuss or further ado, she traveled the house in an ever-circling inventory, reached the stairs at last, and, making no special announcement, she took herself up three flights to her room where, silently, she

---

1 **trowel** (trou' əl): a hand tool for digging up small plants and for light gardening.

2 **ragouts** (rə güz'): highly seasoned stews of meat and vegetables.

laid herself out like a fossil imprint under the snowing cool sheets of her bed and began to die.

Again the voices:

"Grandma! Great-grandma!"

The rumor of what she was doing dropped down the stair well, hit, and spread ripples through the rooms, out doors and windows, and along the street of elms to the edge of the green ravine.

"Here now, here!"

The family surrounded her bed.

"Just let me lie," she whispered.

Her ailment could not be seen in any microscope; it was a mild but ever-deepening tiredness, a dim weighting of her sparrow body; sleepy, sleepier, sleepiest.

As for her children and her children's children—it seemed impossible that with such a simple act, the most leisurely act in the world, she could cause such apprehension.

"Great-grandma, now listen—what you're doing is no better than breaking a lease. This house will fall down without you. You must give us at least a year's notice!"

Great-grandma opened one eye. Ninety years gazed calmly out at her physicians like a dust-ghost from a high cupola[3] window in a fast-emptying house. "Tom . . . ?"

The boy was sent, alone, to her whispering bed.

"Tom," she said, faintly, far away, "in the Southern Seas there's a day in each man's life when he knows it's time to shake hands with all his friends and say good-by and sail away, and he does, and it's natural—it's just his time. That's how it is today. I'm so like you sometimes, sitting through Saturday mati-

nees until nine at night when we send your dad to bring you home. Tom, when the time comes that the same cowboys are shooting the same Indians on the same mountaintop, then it's best to fold back the seat and head for the door, with no regrets and no walking backward up the aisle. So, I'm leaving while I'm still happy and still entertained."

Douglas was summoned next to her side.

"Grandma, who'll shingle the roof next spring?"

Every April for as far back as there were calendars, you thought you heard woodpeckers tapping the housetop. But no, it was Great-grandma somehow transported, singing, pounding nails, replacing shingles, high in the sky!

"Douglas," she whispered, "don't ever let anyone do the shingles unless it's fun for them."

"Yes'm."

"Look around come April, and say, 'Who'd like to fix the roof?' And whichever face lights up is the face you want, Douglas. Because up there on that roof you can see the whole town going toward the country and the country going toward the edge of the earth and the river shining, and the morning lake, and birds on the trees down under you, and the best of the wind all around above. Any one of those should be enough to make a person climb a weather vane some spring sunrise. It's a powerful hour, if you give it half a chance. . . ."

Her voice sank to a soft flutter.

Douglas was crying.

She roused herself again. "Now, why are you doing that?"

"Because," he said, "you won't be here tomorrow."

---

3 **cupola** (kyü′ pə lə): small domed structure built on the top of a building.

She turned a small hand mirror from herself to the boy. He looked at her face and himself in the mirror and then at her face again as she said, "Tomorrow morning I'll get up at seven and wash behind my ears; I'll run to church with Charlie Woodman; I'll picnic at Electric Park; I'll swim, run barefoot, fall out of trees, chew spearmint gum . . . Douglas, Douglas, for shame! You cut your fingernails, don't you?"

"Yes'm."

"And you don't yell when your body makes itself over every seven years or so, old cells dead and new ones added to your fingers and your heart. You don't mind that, do you?"

"No'm."

"Well, consider then, boy. Any man saves fingernail clippings is a fool. You ever see a snake bother to keep his peeled skin? That's about all you got here today in this bed is fingernails and snake skin. One good breath would send me up in flakes. Important thing is not the me that's lying here, but the me that's sitting on the edge of the bed looking back at me, and the me that's downstairs cooking supper, or out in the garage under the car, or in the library reading. All the new parts, they count. I'm not really dying today. No person ever died that had a family. I'll be around a long time. A thousand years from now a whole township of my offspring will be biting sour apples in the gumwood shade. That's my answer to anyone asks big questions! Quick now, send in the rest!"

At last the entire family stood, like people seeing someone off at the rail station, waiting in the room.

"Well," said Great-grandma, "there I am. I'm not humble, so it's nice seeing you standing around my bed. Now next week there's late gardening and closet-cleaning and clothes-buying for the children to do. And since that part of me which is called, for convenience, Great-grandma, won't be here to step it along, those other parts of me called Uncle Bert and Leo and Tom and Douglas, and all the other names, will have to take over, each to his own."

"Yes, Grandma."

"I don't want any Halloween parties here tomorrow. Don't want anyone saying anything sweet about me; I said it all in my time and my pride. I've tasted every victual and danced every dance; now there's one last tart I haven't bit on, one tune I haven't whistled. But I'm not afraid. I'm truly curious. Death won't get a crumb by my mouth I won't keep and savor.[4] So don't you worry over me. Now, all of you go, and let me find my sleep. . . ."

Somewhere a door closed quietly.

"That's better." Alone, she snuggled luxuriously down through the warm snowbank of linen and wool, sheet and cover, and the colors of the patchwork quilt were bright as the circus banners of old time. Lying there, she felt as small and secret as on those mornings eighty-some-odd years ago when, wakening, she comforted her tender bones in bed.

A long time back, she thought, I dreamed a dream, and was enjoying it so much when someone wakened me, and that was the day when I was born. And now? Now, let me see. . . . She cast her mind back. Where was I? she thought. Ninety years . . . how to take up the thread and the pattern of that lost dream again? She put out a small hand. *There.* . . . Yes, that was it. She smiled. Deeper in the warm snow hill she turned her head upon her pillow. That was better. Now,

---

4 **savor** (sā′ vər): taste with pleasure.

yes, now she saw it shaping in her mind quietly, and with a serenity like a sea moving along an endless and self-refreshing shore. Now she let the old dream touch and lift her from the snow and drift her above the scarce-remembered bed.

Downstairs, she thought, they are polishing the silver, and rummaging the cellar, and dusting in the halls. She could hear them living all through the house.

"It's all right," whispered Great-grandma, as the dream floated her. "Like everything else in this life, it's fitting."

And the sea moved her back down the shore.

Discussion

1. Grandma knew that her life was coming to an end. How did she adjust to that knowledge? How did she help her family adjust?

2. Why does Grandma advise Douglas not to "let anyone do the shingles unless it's fun . . ."?

3. Toward the end of the story (page 160), Grandma says: "I'm not really dying today. No person ever died that had a family." What do you think she meant?

Writer's Craft

What kind of story would you have if it didn't involve anyone or anything? Well, it wouldn't be—couldn't be—much of a story! Every story has to be about something. Every story, in other words, must have a CENTRAL CHARACTER—a person or an animal or something about whose fortunes you are concerned. Like the conflict in a story, a central character is essential because in every story something happens to somebody or to something.

Of course, there can be other CHARACTERS, too. But those characters are usually involved in helping or hindering the central character in some way, and so they are less important.

1. Who is the central character in "Good-by, Grandma"?

2. Why is that person the central character?

3. What other characters figure in the story? Why are they needed?

1. Grandma is a woman whose attitude toward death is different from that held by many people. She calmly accepts death, seeing it as a natural part of life. Because of her attitude toward death, Grandma does not fear it. Write a paragraph in which you agree or disagree with Grandma's attitude toward death. State your position—that is, state whether you agree or disagree—and then give your reasons for taking that position. Make sure that each of your sentences supports your position. Conclude your paragraph by restating your position. For example, you might conclude by saying something like this: "For these reasons I (agree, disagree) with Grandma's attitude—that death is a necessary part of life and need not be feared."

2. Grandma was loved and respected by every member of her family. In your opinion, what traits or characteristics make a person an ideal family member? In a paragraph or two, describe such a person. Be sure to explain why each of your chosen traits or characteristics is important.

Grandma could see part of her own self—her own existence—in each member of her family. Besides that, she could see that changes take place in every living body as it "makes itself over. . . ."

Most words, like people, are members of families. And words may be said to undergo changes of form as well—although not "every seven years." The name for the changes that words undergo as they take their places in word families is INFLECTION. Nouns can be inflected to show number and possession. For example:

1. grandma   2. grandmas   3. grandma's   4. grandmas'

You can immediately see an unmistakable family resemblance among these words. Yet when they are used in sentences, each one is different.

1. Douglas said good-by to his grandma. (singular nominative)
2. We all said good-by to our grandmas. (plural nominative)
3. Douglas rearranged his grandma's pillow. (singular possessive)
4. We all rearranged our grandmas' pillows. (plural possessive)

Verbs can be inflected to show number and tense. For example:
He climbs. They climb. She climbed yesterday.

Adjectives and adverbs can be inflected to show comparison. For example:
May is lucky. Elena is luckier. Ayanna is luckiest.
Kamau left early. Juan left earlier than Kamau. Robert left earliest.

Pronouns are inflected to show their function. For example:
As a subject: he, she, they   As an object: him, her, them   As possessives: his, hers, their.

A. On a separate sheet of paper, write one short sentence for each inflected form listed below as shown in the "grandma" sentences on page 162.

1. child (singular noun); children (plural noun); child's (singular possessive); children's (plural possessive)

2. sleepy (adjective); sleepier (comparative adjective); sleepiest (superlative adjective)

3. stuff (present-tense verb); stuffed (past-tense verb)

4. he (nominative pronoun); him (objective pronoun); his (possessive pronoun)

B. Make a list of as many inflected forms as you can think of for each word below.

boy (noun)   dream (verb)
quiet (adjective)   I (pronoun)

Ray Bradbury 1920——

Ray Bradbury claims that he has been living in a fantasy world for most of his life. He became interested in writing when he was seven years old. Someone read him Poe's stories and the Oz books. He collected Tarzan and Buck Rogers comic strips, learned to be a magician, and wrote stories on his first typewriter when he was twelve. He wrote and illustrated his own stories for years. When he was twenty-one, he sold his first story. Strangely, this master of science fiction has never learned to drive a car and has never flown in an airplane.

Bradbury is well known for his stories and novels of fantasy and science fiction. He often presents problems of the future in his stories to make people think about what might happen. He says, "Science fiction is a wonderful hammer. I intend to use it if and when necessary to bark a few shins or knock a few heads, in order to make people leave people alone."

FIGURE ON PORCH *Richard Diebenkorn*

No one was forcing him to do it. Yet Jerry knew it was the toughest test he had ever had to face. Could he pass it?

Through the Tunnel

DORIS LESSING

GOING TO THE SHORE on the first morning of the vacation, the young English boy stopped at a turning of the path and looked down at a wild and rocky bay, and then over the crowded beach he knew so well from other years. His mother walked on in front of him, carrying a bright striped bag in one hand. Her other arm, swinging loose, was very white in the sun. The boy watched that white, naked arm, and turned his eyes, which had a frown behind them, toward the bay and back again to his mother. When she felt he was not with her, she swung around. "Oh, there you are, Jerry!" she said. She looked impatient, then smiled. "Why, darling, would you rather not come with me? Would you rather—" She frowned, conscientiously worrying over what amusements he might secretly be longing for, which she had been too busy or too careless to imagine. He was very familiar with that anxious, apologetic smile. Contrition[1] sent him running after her. And yet, as he ran, he looked back over his shoulder at the wild bay; and all morning, as he played on the safe beach, he was thinking of it.

---

1 **contrition** (kən trish′ ən): sincere regret.

Next morning, when it was time for the routine of swimming and sunbathing, his mother said, "Are you tired of the usual beach, Jerry? Would you like to go somewhere else?"

"Oh, no!" he said quickly, smiling at her out of that unfailing impulse of contrition—a sort of chivalry. Yet, walking down the path with her, he blurted out, "I'd like to go and have a look at those rocks down there."

She gave the idea her attention. It was a wild-looking place, and there was no one there; but she said, "Of course, Jerry. When you've had enough, come to the big beach. Or just go straight back to the villa, if you like." She walked away, that bare arm, now slightly reddened from yesterday's sun, swinging. And he almost ran after her again, feeling it unbearable that she should go by herself, but he did not.

She was thinking, Of course he's old enough to be safe without me. Have I been keeping him too close? He mustn't feel he ought to be with me. I must be careful.

He was an only child, eleven years old. She was a widow. She was determined to be neither possessive nor lacking in devotion. She went worrying off to her beach.

As for Jerry, once he saw that his mother had gained her beach, he began the steep descent to the bay. From where he was, high up among red-brown rocks, it was a scoop of moving bluish green fringed with white. As he went lower, he saw that it spread among small promontories[2] and inlets of rough, sharp rock, and the crisping, lapping surface showed stains of purple and darker blue. Finally, as he ran sliding and scraping down the last few yards, he saw an edge of white surf and the shallow, luminous movement of water over white sand, and, beyond that, a solid, heavy blue.

He ran straight into the water and began swimming. He was a good swimmer. He went out fast over the gleaming sand, over a middle region where rocks lay like discolored monsters under the surface, and then he was in the real sea—a warm sea where irregular cold currents from the deep water shocked his limbs.

When he was so far out that he could look back not only on the little bay but past the promontory that was between it and the big beach, he floated on the buoyant surface and looked for his mother. There she was, a speck of yellow under an umbrella that looked like a slice of orange peel. He swam back to shore, relieved at being sure she was there, but all at once very lonely.

On the edge of a small cape that marked the side of the bay away from the promontory was a loose scatter of rocks. Above them, some boys were stripping off their clothes. They came running, naked, down to the rocks. The English boy swam toward them, but kept his distance at a stone's throw. They were of that coast; all of them were burned smooth dark brown and speaking a language he did not understand. To be with them, of them, was a craving that filled his whole body. He swam a little closer; they turned and watched him with narrowed, alert dark eyes. Then one smiled and waved. It was enough. In a minute, he had swum in and was on the rocks beside them, smiling with a desperate, nervous supplication.[3] They shouted cheerful greetings at him; and then, as he preserved his nervous, uncomprehending smile, they understood that he was a foreigner strayed from his own beach, and they proceeded to forget him. But he was happy. He was with them.

They began diving again and again from a high point into a well of blue sea between rough, pointed rocks. After they had dived and come up, they swam around, hauled themselves up, and waited their turn to dive again. They were big boys—men, to Jerry. He dived, and they watched him; and when he swam around to take his place, they made way for him. He felt he was accepted and he dived again, carefully, proud of himself.

Soon the biggest of the boys poised himself, shot down into the water, and did not come up. The others stood about, watching. Jerry, after waiting for the sleek brown head to appear, let out a yell of warning; they looked at him idly and turned their eyes back toward the water. After a long time, the boy came up on the other side of a big dark rock, letting the air out of his lungs in a sputtering gasp and a shout of triumph. Immediately the rest of them dived in. One moment, the morning seemed full of chattering boys; the next, the air and the surface of the water were empty. But through the heavy blue,

---

2 **promontories** (prom′ ən tôr ēz): high points of land extending from the coast into the water.

3 **supplication** (sup lə kā′ shən): an earnest, humble request; an entreaty.

dark shapes could be seen moving and groping.

Jerry dived, shot past the school of underwater swimmers, saw a black wall of rock looming at him, touched it, and bobbed up at once to the surface, where the wall was a low barrier he could see across. There was no one visible; under him, in the water, the dim shapes of the swimmers had disappeared. Then one, and then another of the boys came up on the far side of the barrier of rock, and he understood that they had swum through some gap or hole in it. He plunged down again. He could see nothing through the stinging salt water but the blank rock. When he came up the boys were all on the diving rock, preparing to attempt the feat again. And now, in a panic of failure, he yelled up, in English, "Look at me! Look!" and he began splashing and kicking in the water like a foolish dog.

They looked down gravely, frowning. He knew the frown. At moments of failure, when he clowned to claim his mother's attention, it was with just this grave, embarrassed inspection that she rewarded him. Through his hot shame, feeling the pleading grin on his face like a scar that he could never remove, he looked up at the group of big brown boys on the rock and shouted, *"Bonjour! Merci! Au revoir! Monsieur, monsieur!"*[4] while he hooked his fingers round his ears and waggled them.

Water surged into his mouth; he choked, sank, came up. The rock, lately weighted with boys, seemed to rear up out of the water as their weight was removed. They were flying down past him, now, into the water; the air was full of falling bodies. Then the

rock was empty in the hot sunlight. He counted one, two, three. . . .

At fifty, he was terrified. They must all be drowning beneath him, in the watery caves of the rock! At a hundred, he stared around him at the empty hillside, wondering if he should yell for help. He counted faster, faster, to hurry them up, to bring them to the surface quickly, to drown them quickly—anything rather than the terror of counting on and on into the blue emptiness of the morning. And then, at a hundred and sixty, the water beyond the rock was full of boys blowing like brown whales. They swam back to the shore without a look at him.

He climbed back to the diving rock and sat down, feeling the hot roughness of it under his thighs. The boys were gathering up their bits of clothing and running off along the shore to another promontory. They were leaving to get away from him. He cried openly, fists in his eyes. There was no one to see him, and he cried himself out.

It seemed to him that a long time had passed, and he swam out to where he could see his mother. Yes, she was still there, a yellow spot under an orange umbrella. He swam back to the big rock, climbed up, and dived into the blue pool among the fanged and angry boulders. Down he went, until he touched the wall of rock again. But the salt was so painful in his eyes that he could not see.

He came to the surface, swam to shore and went back to the villa to wait for his mother. Soon she walked slowly up the path, swinging her striped bag, the flushed, naked arm dangling beside her. "I want some swimming goggles," he panted, defiant and beseeching.

She gave him a patient, inquisitive look as she said casually, "Well, of course, darling."

But now, now, now! He must have them

4 *Bonjour . . . monsieur:* French for "Hello! Thank you! Good-by! Sir, Sir!"

this minute, and no other time. He nagged and pestered until she went with him to a shop. As soon as she had bought the goggles, he grabbed them from her hand as if she were going to claim them for herself, and was off, running down the steep path to the bay.

Jerry swam out to the big barrier rock, adjusted the goggles, and dived. The impact of the water broke the rubber-enclosed vacuum, and the goggles came loose. He understood that he must swim down to the base of the rock from the surface of the water. He fixed the goggles tight and firm, filled his lungs, and floated, face down, on the water. Now, he could see. It was as if he had eyes of a different kind—fish eyes that showed everything clear and delicate and wavering in the bright water.

Under him, six or seven feet down, was a floor of perfectly clean, shining white sand, rippled firm and hard by the tides. Two grayish shapes steered there, like long, rounded pieces of wood or slate. They were fish. He saw them nose toward each other, poise motionless, make a dart forward, swerve off, and come around again. It was like a water dance. A few inches above them the water sparkled as if sequins were dropping through it. Fish again—myriads of minute fish, the length of his fingernail, were drifting through the water, and in a moment he could feel the innumerable tiny touches of them against his limbs. It was like swimming in flaked silver. The great rock the big boys had swum through rose sheer out of the white sand—black, tufted lightly with greenish weed. He could see no gap in it. He swam down to its base.

Again and again he rose, took a big chestful of air, and went down. Again and again he groped over the surface of the rock, feeling it, almost hugging it in the desperate need to find the entrance. And then, once, while he was clinging to the black wall, his knees came up and he shot his feet out forward and they met no obstacle. He had found the hole.

He gained the surface, clambered about the stones that littered the barrier rock until he found a big one, and, with this in his arms, let himself down over the side of the rock. He dropped, with the weight, straight to the sandy floor. Clinging tight to the anchor of stone, he lay on his side and looked in under the dark shelf at the place where his feet had gone. He could see the hole. It was an irregular, dark gap; but he could not see deep into it. He let go of his anchor, clung with his hands to the edges of the hole, and tried to push himself in.

He got his head in, found his shoulders jammed, moved them in sidewise, and was inside as far as his waist. He could see nothing ahead. Something soft and clammy touched his mouth; he saw a dark frond moving against the grayish rock, and panic filled him. He thought of octopuses, of clinging weed. He pushed himself out backward and caught a glimpse, as he retreated, of a harmless tentacle of seaweed drifting in the mouth of the tunnel. But it was enough. He reached the sunlight, swam to shore, and lay on the diving rock. He looked down into the blue well of water. He knew he must find his way through that cave, or hole, or tunnel, and out the other side.

First, he thought, he must learn to control his breathing. He let himself down into the water with another big stone in his arms, so that he could lie effortlessly on the bottom of the sea. He counted. One, two, three. He counted steadily. He could hear the movement of blood in his chest. Fifty-one, fifty-two. . . . His chest was hurting. He let go of the rock and went up into the air. He saw that the sun was low. He rushed to the villa and found his mother at her supper. She said only "Did you enjoy yourself?" and he said "Yes."

All night the boy dreamed of the water-filled cave in the rock, and as soon as breakfast was over he went to the bay.

That night, his nose bled badly. For hours he had been under water, learning to hold his breath, and now he felt weak and dizzy. His mother said, "I shouldn't overdo things, darling, if I were you."

That day and the next, Jerry exercised his lungs as if everything, the whole of his life, all that he would become, depended upon it. Again his nose bled at night, and his mother insisted on his coming with her the next day. It was a torment to him to waste a day of his careful self-training, but he stayed with her on that other beach, which now seemed a place for small children, a place where his mother might lie safe in the sun. It was not his beach.

He did not ask for permission, on the following day, to go to his beach. He went, before his mother could consider the complicated rights and wrongs of the matter. A day's rest, he discovered, had improved his count by ten. The big boys had made the passage while he counted a hundred and sixty. He had been counting fast, in his fright. Probably now, if he tried, he could get through the long tunnel, but he was not going to try yet. A curious, most unchildlike persistence, a controlled impatience, made him wait. In the meantime, he lay underwater on the white sand, littered now by stones he had brought down from the upper air, and studied the entrance to the tunnel. He knew every jut and corner of it, as far as it was possible to see. It was as if he already felt its sharpness about his shoulders.

He sat by the clock in the villa, when his mother was not near, and checked his time. He was incredulous[5] and then proud to find he could hold his breath without strain for two minutes. The words "two minutes," authorized by the clock, brought close the adventure that was so necessary to him.

In another four days, his mother said casually one morning, they must go home. On the day before they left, he would do it. He would do it if it killed him, he said defiantly to himself. But two days before they were to leave—a day of triumph when he increased his count by fifteen—his nose bled so badly that he turned dizzy and had to lie limply over the big rock like a bit of seaweed, watching the thick red blood flow on to the rock and trickle slowly down to the sea. He was frightened. Supposing he turned dizzy in the tunnel? Supposing he died there, trapped? Supposing—his head went around, in the hot sun, and he almost gave up. He thought he would return to the house and lie down, and next summer, perhaps, when he had another year's growth in him—*then* he would go through the hole.

But even after he had made the decision, or thought he had, he found himself sitting up on the rock and looking down into the water; and he knew that now, this moment, when his nose had only just stopped bleeding, when his head was still sore and throbbing—this was the moment when he would try. If he did not do it now, he never would. He was trembling with fear that he would not go; and he was trembling with horror at that long, long tunnel under the rock, under the sea. Even in the open sunlight, the barrier rock seemed very wide and very heavy; tons of rock pressed down on where he would go. If he died there, he would lie until one

---
5 **incredulous** (in krej′ ə ləs): doubting; skeptical.

day—perhaps not before next year—those big boys would swim into it and find it blocked.

He put on his goggles, fitted them tight, tested the vacuum. His hands were shaking. Then he chose the biggest stone he could carry and slipped over the edge of the rock until half of him was in the cool, enclosing water and half in the hot sun. He looked up once at the empty sky, filled his lungs once, twice, and then sank fast to the bottom with the stone. He let it go and began to count. He took the edges of the hole in his hands and drew himself into it, wriggling his shoulders in sidewise as he remembered he must, kicking himself along with his feet.

Soon he was clear inside. He was in a small rockbound hole filled with yellowish-gray water. The water was pushing him up against the roof. The roof was sharp and pained his back. He pulled himself along with his hands—fast, fast—and used his legs as levers. His head knocked against something; a sharp pain dizzied him. Fifty, fifty-one, fifty-two. . . . He was without light, and the water seemed to press upon him with the weight of rock. Seventy-one, seventy-two. . . . There was no strain on his lungs. He felt like an inflated balloon, his lungs were so light and easy, but his head was pulsing.

He was being continually pressed against the sharp roof, which felt slimy as well as sharp. Again he thought of octopuses, and wondered if the tunnel might be filled with weed that could tangle him. He gave himself a panicky, convulsive kick forward, ducked his head, and swam. His feet and hands moved freely, as if in open water. The hole must have widened out. He thought he must be swimming fast, and he was frightened of banging his head if the tunnel narrowed.

A hundred, a hundred and one. . . . The water paled. Victory filled him. His lungs were beginning to hurt. A few more strokes and he would be out. He was counting wildly; he said a hundred and fifteen, and then, a long time later, a hundred and fifteen again. The water was a clear jewel-green all around him. Then he saw, above his head, a crack running up through the rock. Sunlight was falling through it, showing the clean, dark rock of the tunnel, a single mussel shell, and darkness ahead.

He was at the end of what he could do. He looked up at the crack as if it were filled with air and not water, as if he could put his mouth to it to draw in air. A hundred and fifteen, he heard himself say inside his head—but he had said that long ago. He must go on into the blackness ahead, or he would drown. His head was swelling, his lungs cracking. A hundred and fifteen, a hundred and fifteen pounded through his head, and he feebly clutched at rocks in the dark, pulling himself forward, leaving the brief space of sunlit water behind. He felt he was dying. He was no longer quite conscious. He struggled on in the darkness between lapses into unconsciousness. An immense, swelling pain filled his head, and then the darkness cracked with an explosion of green light. His hands, groping forward, met nothing; and his feet, kicking back, propelled him out into the open sea.

He drifted to the surface, his face turned up to the air. He was gasping like a fish. He felt he would sink now and drown; he could not swim the few feet back to the rock. Then he was clutching it and pulling himself up on to it. He lay face down, gasping. He could see nothing but a red-veined, clotted dark. His eyes must have burst, he thought; they were full of blood. He tore off his goggles and a gout of blood went into the sea. His nose was bleeding, and the blood had filled the goggles.

He scooped up handfuls of water from the cool, salty sea, to splash on his face, and did not know whether it was blood or salt water he tasted. After a time, his heart quieted, his eyes cleared, and he sat up. He could see the local boys diving and playing half a mile away. He did not want them. He wanted nothing but to get back home and lie down.

In a short while, Jerry swam to shore and climbed slowly up the path to the villa. He flung himself on his bed and slept, waking at the sound of feet on the path outside. His mother was coming back. He rushed to the bathroom, thinking she must not see his face with bloodstains, or tearstains, on it. He came out of the bathroom and met her as she walked into the villa, smiling, her eyes lighting up.

"Have a nice morning?" she asked, laying her hand on his warm brown shoulder.

"Oh, yes, thank you," he said.

"You look a bit pale," And then, sharp and anxious, "How did you bang your head?"

"Oh, just banged it," he told her.

She looked at him closely. He was strained; his eyes were glazed-looking. She was worried. And then she said to herself, Oh, don't fuss! Nothing can happen. He can swim like a fish.

They sat down to lunch together.

"Mummy," he said, "I can stay under water for two minutes—three minutes, at least." It came bursting out of him.

"Can you, darling?" she said. "Well, I shouldn't overdo it. I don't think you ought to swim any more today."

She was ready for a battle of wills, but he gave in at once. It was no longer of the least importance to go to the bay.

Discussion

1. Why did Jerry feel he had to swim through the tunnel? Do you think he was right or wrong? Why?

2. Would you agree or disagree that Jerry's mother was genuinely concerned about him? Do you think she was right or wrong in permitting him to go to the bay by himself? Why?

3. In what way are the local boys necessary to the story? Why did Jerry act foolish in front of them?

4. After Jerry had swum through the tunnel, why was it no longer important to him to go back to the bay and swim through again?

5. Jerry did not tell his mother of his accomplishment. Why?

Writer's Craft

If you have read "The Most Dangerous Game" (page 5), you will no doubt remember these sentences:

> At daybreak Rainsford, lying near the swamp, was awakened by a sound that made him know that he had new things to learn about fear. . . . It was the baying of a pack of hounds. . . . The baying of the hounds grew

nearer, then still nearer, nearer, ever nearer. . . . They would be on him any minute now. His mind worked frantically. . . . "Nerve, nerve, nerve!" he panted, as he dashed along. . . . Ever nearer drew the hounds. Rainsford forced himself to the gap. He reached it. . . . Twenty feet below him the sea rumbled and hissed. Rainsford hesitated. He heard the hounds. . . .

What effect do those sentences have on you? What emotion do you feel as you read them? Well, if you are like most of us, you read these sentences with increasing emotional tension—with increasing alarm. Can Rainsford escape the hounds? Can he survive a leap into the sea?

When a storywriter's words and sentences cause an increasing concern and arouse an increasing emotional tension, they cause the reader to care about what happens. We say, then, that the writer is building SUSPENSE. It is the skillful development of suspense in a story that causes the reader to want to read on, that keeps the reader on the edge of the seat. All expert storywriters develop suspense in their stories, building greater and greater tension so that the reader is swept along to the very end.

1. In "Through the Tunnel," how does the counting that Jerry does—"fifty, fifty-one . . . seventy-one, seventy-two . . . a hundred, a hundred and one"—build suspense?

2. What other events in the story help build suspense?

Doris Lessing 1919—

Doris Lessing is a British citizen who was born in Iran when her father managed a bank there. When she was five, the family moved to Southern Rhodesia. As one of the few white children in a segregated society, Lessing had a rather lonely childhood. She says she was unhappy then, but now she is thankful that she had so much time for reading and for walking in the African bush country.

Lessing enjoys the self-discovery that comes with writing. In order to write, she must explore her own thoughts. She says, "I am always surprised at what I find in myself, and this to me is the most rewarding part of being a writer."

The Inspiration of Mr. Budd

DOROTHY SAYERS

WANTED   **£500[1] REWARD**   WANTED

"The evening messenger, ever anxious to further the ends of justice, has decided to offer the above reward to any person who shall give information leading to the arrest of the man, William Strickland, alias Bolton, who is wanted by the police in connection with the murder of the late Emma Strickland at 59 Acacia Crescent, Manchester.

DESCRIPTION OF THE WANTED MAN

"The following is the official description of William Strickland: Age 43; height 6 ft. 1 or 2 in.; complexion rather dark; hair silver-grey and abundant, may dye same; full grey mustache and beard, may now be clean-shaven; eyes light grey, rather close-set; hawk nose; teeth strong and white, displays them somewhat prominently when laughing; left upper eyetooth stopped with gold; left thumbnail disfigured by a recent blow.

"Speaks in rather loud voice; quick, decisive manner. Good address.

"May be dressed in a grey or dark blue lounge suit, with stand-up collar (size 15) and a soft felt hat.

"Absconded[2] 5th inst., and may have left, or will endeavor to leave, the country."

WANTED   WANTED

MR. BUDD READ the description through carefully once again and sighed. It was in the highest degree unlikely that William Strickland should choose his small and unsuccessful saloon, out of all the barbers' shops in London, for a haircut or a shave, still less for "dyeing same"; even if he was in London, which Mr. Budd saw no reason to suppose.

Three weeks had gone by since the murder, and the odds were a hundred to one that William Strickland had already left a country too eager with its offer of free hospitality. Nevertheless, Mr. Budd committed the description, as well as he could, to memory. It was a chance—just as the Great Crossword Tournament had been a chance, just as the Ninth Rainbow Ballot had been a chance, and the Bunko Poster Ballot, and the Monster Treasure Hunt organized by the *Evening Clarion*. Any headline with money in it could attract Mr. Budd's fascinated eye in

---

1 **£500**: 500 pounds; about $1,125.00.

2 **Absconded** (ab skon′ dəd): left hurriedly and secretly.

these lean days, whether it offered a choice between fifty thousand pounds down and ten pounds a week for life, or merely a modest hundred or so.

It may seem strange, in an age of shingling and bingling,[3] Mr. Budd should look enviously at Complete Lists of Prizewinners. Had not the hairdresser across the way, who only last year had eked out his mean ninepences with the yet meaner profits on cheap cigarettes and comic papers, lately bought out the greengrocer next door, and engaged a staff of exquisitely coiffed assistants to adorn his new "Ladies' Hairdressing Department" with its purple and orange curtains, its two rows of gleaming marble basins, and an apparatus like a Victorian chandelier for permanent waving?

Had he not installed a large electric sign surrounded by a scarlet border that ran round and round perpetually, like a kitten chasing its own tail? Was it not his sandwich-man[4] even now patrolling the pavement with a luminous announcement of Treatment and Prices? And was there not at this moment an endless stream of young ladies hastening into those heavily-perfumed parlors in the desperate hope of somehow getting a shampoo and a wave "squeezed in" before closing-time?

If the reception clerk shook a regretful head, they did not think of crossing the road to Mr. Budd's dimly lighted window. They made an appointment for days ahead and waited patiently, anxiously fingering the bristly growth at the back of the neck and the straggly bits behind the ears that so soon got out of hand.

Day after day Mr. Budd watched them flit in and out of the rival establishment, willing, praying even, in a vague, ill-directed manner, that some of them would come over to him; but they never did.

And yet Mr. Budd knew himself to be the finer artist. He had seen shingles turned out from over the way that he would never have countenanced, let alone charged three shillings and sixpence for. Shingles with an ugly hard line at the nape, shingles which were a slander on the shape of a good head or brutally emphasized the weak points of an ugly one; hurried, conscienceless shingles, botched work, handed over on a crowded afternoon to a girl who had only served a three years' apprenticeship and to whom the final mysteries of "tapering" were a sealed book.

And then there was the "tinting"—his own pet subject, which he had studied *con amore*[5]—if only those too-sprightly matrons would come to him! He would gently dissuade them from that dreadful mahogany dye that made them look like metallic robots—he would warn them against that widely advertised preparation which was so incalculable in its effects; he would use the cunning skill which long experience had matured in him—tint them with the infinitely delicate art which conceals itself.

Yet nobody came to Mr. Budd but the navvies[6] and the young loungers and the men who plied their trade beneath the naphtha-flares[7] in Wilton Street.

And why could not Mr. Budd also have burst out into marble and electricity and swum to fortune on the rising tide?

The reason is very distressing, and, as it

---

3 **shingling and bingling:** ways of cutting women's hair.
4 **sandwich-man:** a person carrying two pieces of advertising, each glued to a board. The two boards are connected with ropes, leather, or cloth to fit over the man's shoulders. Thus he carries one advertising board in front and the other in back. He himself is sandwiched between them.

5 *con amore* (kōn ə môr′ ā): Italian for "with love."
6 **navvies** (nav′ ēz): British slang for "unskilled workers."
7 **naphtha-flares** (naf′ thə): street lights that use naphtha gasoline, a highly flammable liquid.

fortunately has no bearing on the story, shall be told with merciful brevity.

Mr. Budd had a younger brother, Richard, whom he had promised his mother to look after. In happier days Mr. Budd had owned a flourishing business in their native town of Northampton, and Richard had been a bank clerk. Richard had got into bad ways (poor Mr. Budd blamed himself dreadfully for this). There had been a sad affair with a girl, and a horrid series of affairs with bookmakers, and then Richard had tried to mend bad with worse by taking money from the bank. You need to be very much more skillful than Richard to juggle successfully with bank ledgers.

The bank manager was a hard man of the old school: he prosecuted. Mr. Budd paid the bank and the bookmakers, and saw the girl through her trouble while Richard was in prison, and paid for their fares to Australia when he came out, and gave them something to start life on.

But it took all the profits of the hairdressing business, and he couldn't face all the people in Northampton any more, who had known him all his life. So he had run to vast London, the refuge of all who shrink from the eyes of their neighbors, and bought this little shop in Pimlico,[8] which had done fairly well, until the new fashion which did so much for other hairdressing businesses killed it for lack of capital.

That is why Mr. Budd's eye was so painfully fascinated by headlines with money in them.

He put the newspaper down, and as he did so, caught sight of his own reflection in the glass and smiled, for he was not without a sense of humor. He did not look quite the man to catch a brutal murderer single-handed. He was well on in the middle forties—a trifle paunchy, with fluffy pale hair, getting a trifle thin on top (partly hereditary, partly worry, that was), five feet six at most, and soft-handed, as a hairdresser must be.

Even razor in hand, he would hardly be a match for William Strickland, height six feet one or two, who had so ferociously battered his old aunt to death, so butcherly hacked her limb from limb, so horribly disposed of her remains in the copper.[9] Shaking his head dubiously, Mr. Budd advanced to the door, to cast a forlorn eye at the busy establishment over the way, and nearly ran into a bulky customer who dived in rather precipitately.

"I beg your pardon, sir," murmured Mr. Budd, fearful of alienating ninepence; "just stepping out for a breath of fresh air, sir. Shave, sir?"

The large man tore off his overcoat without waiting for Mr. Budd's obsequious[10] hands.

"Are you prepared to die?" he demanded abruptly.

The question chimed in so alarmingly with Mr. Budd's thoughts about murder that for a moment it quite threw him off his professional balance.

"I beg your pardon, sir," he stammered, and in the same moment decided that the man must be a preacher of some kind. He looked rather like it, with his odd, light eyes, his bush of fiery hair and short, jutting chin-beard. Perhaps he even wanted a subscription. That would be hard, when Mr. Budd had already set him down as ninepence, or, with tip, possibly even a shilling.

"Do you do dyeing?" said the man impatiently.

---

8 **Pimlico** (pim' li kō): a section of London.

9 **copper**: a large copper kettle used for cooking or for laundering.
10 **obsequious** (ob sē' kwē əs): obedient because one hopes to gain something.

"Oh!" said Mr. Budd, relieved, "yes, sir, certainly, sir."

A stroke of luck, this. Dyeing meant quite a big sum—his mind soared to seven-and-sixpence.

"Good," said the man, sitting down and allowing Mr. Budd to put an apron about his neck. (He was safely gathered in now—he could hardly dart away down the street with a couple of yards of white cotton flapping from his shoulders.)

"Fact is," said the man, "my young lady doesn't like red hair. She says it's conspicuous. The other young ladies in her firm make jokes about it. So, as she's a good bit younger than I am, you see, I like to oblige her, and I was thinking perhaps it could be changed into something quieter, what? Dark brown, now—that's the color she has a fancy for. What do you say?"

It occurred to Mr. Budd that the young ladies might consider this abrupt change of coat even funnier than the original color, but in the interests of business he agreed that dark brown would be very becoming and a great deal less noticeable than red. Besides, very likely there was no young lady. A woman, he knew, will say frankly that she wants different colored hair for a change, or just to try, or because she fancies it would suit her, but if a man is going to do a silly thing he prefers, if possible, to shuffle the responsibility on to someone else.

"Very well, then," said the customer, "go ahead. And I'm afraid the beard will have to go. My young lady doesn't like beards."

"A great many young ladies don't, sir," said Mr. Budd. "They're not so fashionable nowadays as they used to be. It's very fortunate that you can stand a clean shave very well, sir. You have just the chin for it."

"Do you think so?" said the man, examining himself a little anxiously. "I'm glad to hear it."

"Will you have the mustache off as well, sir?"

"Well, no—no, I think I'll stick to that as long as I'm allowed to, what?" He laughed loudly, and Mr. Budd approvingly noted well-kept teeth and a gold stopping. The customer was obviously ready to spend money on his personal appearance.

In fancy, Mr. Budd saw this well-off and gentlemanly customer advising all his friends to visit "his man"—"wonderful fellow—wonderful—round at the back of Victoria Station—you'd never find it by yourself—only a little place, but he knows what he's about—I'll write it down for you." It was imperative that there should be no fiasco.[11] Hair-dyes were awkward things—there had been a case in the paper lately.

"I see you have been using a tint before, sir," said Mr. Budd with respect. "Could you tell me—?"

"Eh?" said the man. "Oh, yes—well, fact is, as I said, my fiancée's a good bit younger than I am. As I expect you can see I began to go grey early—my father was just the same—all our family—so I had it touched up—streaky bits restored, you see. But she doesn't take to the color, so I thought, if I have to dye it at all, why not a color she does fancy while we're about it, what?"

It is a common jest among the unthinking that hairdressers are garrulous.[12] This is their wisdom. The hairdresser hears many secrets and very many lies. In his discretion he occupies his unruly tongue with the weather and the political situation, lest, restless with

---

11 **fiasco** (fē as′ kō): humiliating failure.
12 **garrulous** (gar′ ə ləs): talkative.

inaction, it plunge unbridled into a mad career of inconvenient candor.

Lightly holding forth upon the caprices of the feminine mind, Mr. Budd subjected his customer's locks to the scrutiny of trained eye and fingers. Never—never in the process of Nature could hair of that texture and quality have been red. It was naturally black hair, prematurely turned, as some black hair will turn, to a silvery grey. However, that was none of his business. He elicited the informa-tion he really needed—the name of the dye formerly used, and noted that he would have to be careful. Some dyes do not mix kindly with other dyes.

Chatting pleasantly, Mr. Budd lathered his customer, removed the offending beard, and executed a vigorous shampoo, preliminary to the dyeing process. As he wielded the roaring drier, he reviewed Wimbledon, the Silk-tax and the Summer Time Bill—at that moment threatened with sudden strangulation—and passed naturally on to the Manchester murder.

"The police seem to have given it up as a bad job," said the man.

"Perhaps the reward will liven things up a bit," said Mr. Budd, the thought being naturally uppermost in his mind.

"Oh, there's a reward, is there? I hadn't seen that."

"It's in tonight's paper, sir. Maybe you'd like to have a look at it."

"Thanks, I should."

Mr. Budd left the drier to blow the fiery bush of hair at its own wild will for a moment, while he fetched the *Evening Messenger*. The stranger read the paragraph carefully and Mr. Budd, watching him in the glass, after the disquieting manner of his craft, saw him suddenly draw back his left hand, which was resting carelessly on the arm of the chair, and thrust it under the apron.

But not before Mr. Budd had seen it. Not before he had taken conscious note of the horny, misshapen thumbnail. Many people had such an ugly mark, Mr. Budd told himself hurriedly—there was his friend, Bert Webber, who had sliced the top of his thumb right off in a motorcycle chain—his nail looked very much like that. . . .

The man glanced up, and the eyes of his reflection became fixed on Mr. Budd's face with a penetrating scrutiny—a horrid warning that the real eyes were steadfastly interrogating the reflection of Mr. Budd.

"Not but what," said Mr. Budd, "the man is safe out of the country, I reckon. They've put it off too late."

The man laughed in a pleasant way.

"I reckon they have," he said. Mr. Budd wondered whether many men with smashed left thumbs showed a gold left upper eyetooth. Probably there were hundreds of men

like that going about the country. Likewise with silver-grey hair ("may dye same") and aged about forty-three. Undoubtedly.

Mr. Budd folded up the drier and turned off the gas. Mechanically he took up a comb and drew it through the hair that never, never in the process of Nature had been that fiery red.

There came back to him, with an accuracy which quite unnerved him, the exact number and extent of the brutal wounds inflicted upon the Manchester victim—an elderly lady, rather stout, she had been. Glaring through the door, Mr. Budd noticed that his rival over the way had closed. The streets were full of people. How easy it would be—

"Be as quick as you can, won't you?" said the man, a little impatiently, but pleasantly enough. "It's getting late; I'm afraid it will keep you overtime."

"Not at all, sir," said Mr. Budd. "It's of no consequence—not the least."

No—if he tried to bolt out of the door, his terrible customer would leap upon him, drag him back, throttle his cries, and then with one frightful blow like the one he had smashed in his aunt's skull with—

Yet surely Mr. Budd was in a position of advantage. A decided man would do it. He would be out in the street before the customer could disentangle himself from the chair. Mr. Budd began to edge round towards the door.

"What's the matter?" said the customer.

"Just stepping out to look at the time, sir," said Mr. Budd, meekly pausing. (Yet he might have done it then, if he only had the courage to make the first swift step that would give the game away.)

"It's five-and-twenty past eight," said the man, "by tonight's broadcast. I'll pay extra for the overtime."

"Not on any account," said Mr. Budd. Too late now, he couldn't make another effort. He vividly saw himself tripping on the threshold—falling—the terrible fist lifted to smash him into a pulp. Or, perhaps, under the familiar white apron, the disfigured hand was actually clutching a pistol.

Mr. Budd retreated to the back of the shop, collecting his materials. If only he had been quicker—more like a detective in a book—he would have observed that thumbnail, that tooth, put two and two together, and run out to give the alarm while the man's beard was wet and soapy and his face buried in the towel. Or he could have dabbed lather in his eyes—nobody could possibly commit a murder or even run away down the street with his eyes full of soap.

Even now—Mr. Budd took down a bottle, shook his head, and put it back on the shelf—even now, was it really too late? Why could he not take a bold course? He had only to open a razor, go quietly up behind the unsuspecting man, and say in a firm, loud, convincing voice: "William Strickland, put up your hands. Your life is at my mercy. Stand up till I take your gun away. Now walk straight out to the nearest policeman." Surely, in his position, that was what Sherlock Holmes would do.

But as Mr. Budd returned with a little trayful of requirements, it was borne in upon him that he was not of the stuff of which great man-hunters are made. For he could not seriously see that attempt "coming off." Because if he held the razor to the man's throat and said: "Put up your hands," the man would probably merely catch him by the wrists and take the razor away. And greatly as Mr. Budd feared his customer unarmed, he felt it would be a perfect crescendo[13] of madness to put a razor into his hands.

Or, supposing he said, "Put up your hands," and the man just said, "I won't." What was he to do next? To cut his throat then and there would be murder, even if Mr. Budd could possibly have brought himself to do such a thing. They could not remain there, fixed in one position, till the boy came to do out the shop in the morning.

Perhaps the policeman would notice the light on and the door unfastened and come in? Then he would say, "I congratulate you, Mr. Budd, on having captured a very dangerous criminal." But supposing the policeman didn't happen to notice—and Mr. Budd would have to stand all the time, and he would get exhausted and his attention would relax, and then—

After all, Mr. Budd wasn't called upon to arrest the man himself. "Information leading to arrest"—those were the words. He would be able to tell them the wanted man had been there, that he would now have dark brown hair and mustache and no beard. He might even shadow him when he left—he might—

It was at this moment that the great Inspiration came to Mr. Budd.

As he fetched a bottle from the glass-fronted case he remembered, with odd vividness, an old-fashioned wooden paper-knife that had belonged to his mother. Between sprigs of blue forget-me-not, hand-painted, it bore the inscription "Knowledge Is Power."

A strange freedom and confidence were vouchsafed to Mr. Budd; his mind was alert; he removed the razors with an easy, natural

---

13 **crescendo** (krə shen′ dō): here, peak.

movement, and made nonchalant conversation as he skillfully applied the dark-brown tint.

The streets were less crowded when Mr. Budd let his customer out. He watched the tall figure cross Grosvenor Place and climb on to a 24 bus.

"But that was only his artfulness," said Mr. Budd, as he put on his hat and coat and extinguished the lights carefully; "he'll take another at Victoria, like as not, and be making tracks from Charing Cross or Waterloo."[14]

He closed the shop door, shook it, as was his wont, to make sure that the lock had caught properly, and in his turn made his way, by means of a 24, to the top of Whitehall.[15]

The policeman was a little condescending at first when Mr. Budd demanded to see "somebody very high up," but finding the little barber insist so earnestly that he had news of the Manchester murderer, and that there wasn't any time to lose, he consented to pass him through.

Mr. Budd was interviewed first by an important-looking inspector in uniform, who listened very politely to his story and made him repeat very carefully about the gold tooth and the thumbnail and the hair which had been black before it was grey or red and was now dark-brown.

The inspector then touched a bell, and said, "Perkins, I think Sir Andrew would like to see this gentleman at once," and he was taken to another room, where sat a very shrewd, genial gentleman in mufti,[16] who heard him with even greater attention, and called in another inspector to listen too, and to take down a very exact description of—yes, surely the undoubted William Strickland as he now appeared.

"But there's one thing more," said Mr. Budd—"and I'm sure to goodness," he added, "I hope, sir, it is the right man, because if it isn't it'll be the ruin of me—"

He crushed his soft hat into an agitated ball as he leaned across the table, breathlessly uttering the story of his great betrayal.

"Tzee—z-z-z—tzee—tzee—z-z—tzee—z-z—."

"Dzoo—dz-dz-dz—dzoo—dz—dzoo—dzoo—dz—."

"Tzee—z—z."

The fingers of the wireless operator on the packet[17] *Miranda* bound for Ostend[18] moved swiftly as they jotted down the messages of the buzzing wireless mosquito-swarms.

One of them made him laugh.

"The Old Man'd better have this, I suppose," he said.

The Old Man scratched his head when he read and rang a little bell for the steward. The steward ran down to the little round office where the purser was counting his money and checking it before he locked it away for the night. On receiving the Old Man's message, the purser put the money quickly into the safe, picked up the passenger list, and departed aft. There was a short consultation, and the bell was rung again—this time to summon the head steward.

"Tzee—z-z—tzeez-z-z—tzee—tzee—z—tzee."

---

14 **Victoria** . . . **Charing Cross** . . . **Waterloo:** large railroad stations in London.
15 **Whitehall:** an important London thoroughfare on which many government offices are located.
16 **mufti** (muf' tē): civilian clothes.

---

17 **packet** (pak' it): a small ship that runs on a regular route, carrying mail and passengers.
18 **Ostend:** a city in Belgium.

All down the Channel, all over the North Sea, up to the Mersey Docks, out into the Atlantic soared the busy mosquito-swarms. In ship after ship the wireless operator sent his message to the captain, the captain sent for the purser, the purser sent for the head steward, and the head steward called his staff about him. Huge liners, little packets, destroyers, sumptuous private yachts—every floating thing that carried aerials—every port in England, France, Holland, Germany, Denmark, Norway, every police center that could interpret the mosquito message, heard, between laughter and excitement, the tale of Mr. Budd's betrayal. Two Boy Scouts at Croydon, practicing their Morse with a home-made valve set, decoded it laboriously into an exercise book.

"Cripes," said Jim to George, "what a joke! D'you think they'll get the beggar?"

The *Miranda* docked at Ostend at at 7 A.M. A man burst hurriedly into the cabin where the wireless operator was just taking off his headphones.

"Here!" he cried; "this is to go. There's something up and the Old Man's sent over for the police. The Consul's coming on board."

The wireless operator groaned, and switched on his valves.[19]

"Tzee—z—tzee——" a message to the English police.

"Man on board answering to description. Ticket booked name of Watson. Has locked himself in cabin and refuses to come out. Insists on having hairdresser sent out to him. Have communicated Ostend police. Await instructions."

The Old Man, with sharp words and authoritative gestures, cleared a way through the excited little knot of people gathered about First Class Cabin No. 36. Several passengers had got wind of "something up." Magnificently he herded them away to the gangway with their bags and suitcases. Sternly he bade the stewards and the boy, who stood gaping with his hands full of breakfast dishes, to stand away from the door. Terribly he commanded them to hold their tongues. Four or five sailors stood watchfully at his side. In the restored silence, the passenger in No. 36 could be heard pacing up and down the narrow cabin, moving things, clattering, splashing water.

Presently came steps overhead. Somebody arrived, with a message. The Old Man nodded. Six pairs of Belgian police boots came tiptoeing down the companion. The Old Man glanced at the official paper held out to him and nodded again.

"Ready?"

"Yes."

The Old Man knocked at the door of No. 36.

"Who is it?" cried a harsh, sharp voice.

"The barber is here, sir, that you sent for."

"Ah!" There was relief in the tone. "Send him in alone, if you please. I—I have had an accident."

"Yes, sir."

At the sound of the bolt being cautiously withdrawn, the Old Man stepped forward. The door opened a chink, and was slammed to again, but the Old Man's boot was firmly wedged against the jamb. The policemen surged forward. There was a yelp and a shot which smashed harmlessly through the window of the first-class saloon, and the passenger was brought out.

"Strike me pink!" shrieked the boy; "strike me pink if he ain't gone green in the night!"

---

19 **switched on his valves:** turned on the radio transmitter.

The Inspiration of Mr. Budd **181**

Green!

Not for nothing had Mr. Budd studied the intricate mutual reactions of chemical dyes. In the pride of his knowledge he had set a mark on his man, to mark him out from all the billions of this overpopulated world. Was there a port in all Christendom where a murderer might slip away, with every hair on him green as a parrot—green mustache, green eyebrows, and that thick, springing shock of hair, vivid, flaring midsummer green?

Mr. Budd got his five hundred pounds. The *Evening Messenger* published the full story of his great betrayal. He trembled, fearing this sinister fame. Surely no one would ever come to him again.

On the next morning an enormous blue limousine rolled up to his door, to the immense admiration of Wilton Street. A lady, magnificent in musquash[20] and diamonds, swept into the saloon.

"You are Mr. Budd, aren't you?" she cried. "The great Mr. Budd? Isn't it too wonderful? And now, dear Mr. Budd, you must do me a favor. You must dye my hair green, at once. Now. I want to be able to say I'm the very first to be done by you. I'm the Duchess of Winchester, and that awful Melcaster woman is chasing me down the street—the cat!"

If you want it done, I can give you the number of Mr. Budd's parlors in Bond Street. But I understand it is a terribly expensive process.

---

20 **musquash** (mus kwosh′): muskrat fur coat.

Discussion

1. At what point did you first suspect that the man who came to Mr. Budd's shop was the murderer, William Strickland? What other clues given by the author convinced you that it was, indeed, the murderer who was in Mr. Budd's shop?

2. What is Mr. Budd's "Inspiration"?

3. Mr. Budd firmly believed that knowledge gives a person power. What did Mr. Budd know that would insure the murderer's capture?

4. How was the murderer finally captured? What part did Mr. Budd play in the capture?

5. Although the story concerns the capture of a murderer, an event that ordinarily would be treated in a serious, businesslike manner, the author uses humor throughout. What examples of humor do you find? What purpose do you think the author's humor serves?

Writer's Craft As the events of the plot unfold, and as the conflict becomes sharper, the tension—the suspense—builds. But it can't go on building forever. At some point in the story, something has to happen to permit the central character to reach—or fail to reach—his or her goal. In short, the conflict must have a *turning point*. Such a turning point is the CLIMAX of the story. It's the point where the reader's interest is the most intense. It's the point just before the reader breathes a sigh of relief, knowing how things will turn out.

In the story "Through the Tunnel," for example, the climax occurs at this point: " . . . and then the darkness cracked with an explosion of green light. His hands, groping forward, met nothing; and his feet, kicking back, propelled him out into the open sea." Here is the turning point in the story. Now the reader knows that Jerry has swum through the tunnel safely and will be all right.

1. Where does the climax occur in "The Inspiration of Mr. Budd"? Why is the point you have identified the climax of the story?

2. What important events build to the climax?

3. What events follow the climax?

Vocabulary Dorothy Sayers uses a "Wanted" poster as a prefix to "The Inspiration of Mr. Budd." A PREFIX is "anything put before another thing." In language, a prefix is "one or more letters put before a word to change its meaning in some way."

One of the most familiar and often-used prefixes in English is *un-*. This prefix can change the meaning of a word in several ways—all of them negative. The two chief changes this prefix can make are these:

1. to show opposite meaning (*un*happy), or reversed meaning (*un*lock)

2. to show release from (*un*earth), or removal from (*un*seat)

A. In each sentence at the top of page 184, one word that starts with the prefix *un-* is *italicized*. On a separate sheet of paper, copy the word. Then tell whether the prefix places the word in category (1) or in category (2) explained above. Use a dictionary if necessary.

1. Mr. Budd considered his barber shop *unsuccessful.*
2. William Strickland entered the shop and *unfastened* his collar.
3. Mr. Budd was *uncertain* what to do when he first saw Strickland's smashed left thumbnail.
4. Mr. Budd was greatly relieved that his customer was *unarmed.*
5. Later, Strickland was filled with *unbridled* anger when he discovered that his dyed hair had turned green.

B. For each *italicized* word above, give an ANTONYM, a word that has either an exactly opposite or approximately opposite meaning.

C. In some of the words printed below, the *un-* at the beginning is *not* a prefix; it is a part of the word itself. Below your answers for Exercise B, make two columns, side by side. In the column at the left, copy the words below which start with *un-* as a prefix. In the column at the right, copy the words which start with *un-* as part of the word itself. Use a dictionary if you need help.

untie   untroubled   unanimous   under
uncle   unruly   unnerved   uniform

Dorothy Sayers 1893—1957

Dorothy Sayers, one of the first women to earn a degree at Oxford University, is best remembered for her detective character, Lord Peter Wimsey. Just as she was an extraordinary woman, her favorite detective was also unusual for his profession. Lord Peter Wimsey was a wealthy Englishman who occasionally quoted Latin sayings, wore a monocle, and lived the life of a gentleman. Sayers had a genius for setting up unusual problems for him, and she told his tales with a fine sense of humor.

Besides being a highly respected writer of detective mysteries, Sayers was considered a leading authority on all detective fiction. She occasionally wrote analyses of actual murder cases for the police. She worked well with the concept first expressed by Poe, but which she refined: "When you have eliminated all the impossibilities, then, whatever remains, however improbable, must be the truth."

Of course you've heard about courtship—the special attention a young man and a young woman give each other when they have come to know each other pretty well. Courtship usually leads to engagement and marriage. It's a practice you'll find the world over. But it's also a practice that varies from country to country—even from community to community.

In Hidalgo, a community in north central Mexico, Porfirio Rodriguez had had his eye on Alma Orona for some time. What's more, Porfirio had planned his courtship strategy carefully—so very carefully. And now—at last—everything was ready. . . .

The Street of the Three Crosses

JOSEPHINA NIGGLI

THE MOON HUNG like a silver crescent behind the blue belfry of the pink church, and the sky was night indigo with a silver sheen. At the four corners of the Plaza of Independence hung oil lanterns, throwing their small circles of yellow light on the broad cement walk.

Beyond this walk, in the center of the plaza, the bitter orange trees were heavy with fruit; the limes were in blossom, and their sweet perfume drenched the music-filled air—for the orchestra was playing in the bandstand.

Clusters of women moved counterclockwise on the street side; the men clockwise on the orchestra side. Some of the older people sat on benches, or on straight chairs hired from the "Sunday Evening Plaza Chair Association," a concern owned by Porfirio, the carver of wood, Pepe Gonzalez, and Andrés Treviño.

Although the orchestra conductor was urging his men to play as loudly as possible, the shrill voices of the plaza crowd were louder still. Above the noise rose the high tones of the candymaker, calling his wares: "Almond paste, nut cheese, candies of burnt milk, of sweet potato, of cactus heart. Who will buy my candies? Almond paste! Nut cheese!" And when he paused, the town gardener would take up the refrain with "Carnations, roses, gardenias! Buy flowers for

your mother, your sister, your sweetheart, your wife! Carnations for her mouth, roses for her heart, gardenias for her hair!"

As the gardener wandered through the crowd, his white trousers flapping around his thin brown legs and his straw hat set well back on his head to show he was an honest man, Porfirio stopped him.

"Eh, Don Serapio, give me a small gift of flowers."

The old man chuckled, tipping his head to one side. "A gift, is it? Wood is your trade, flowers mine. Let me see the color of your money."

"Now, Don Serapio," Porfirio protested, "you know I am a poor soul. I have not the wealth of Pepe Gonzalez, that son of a cheese factory. One little gift of flowers is not much to ask."

Don Serapio rolled his eyes toward heaven and ran his tongue over his teeth. His tray needed mending, and he had intended to take it to Porfirio the next day. That job would cost about fifty centavos.[1] A bouquet of flowers cost ten centavos. . . .

He beamed and said, "Listen to me, Porfirio. Every man knows the worth of his own blanket. This tray of mine needs mending. In exchange for such labor I will give you a bouquet of flowers. Is it agreed?"

Porfirio answered eagerly, "But naturally, Don Serapio. Bring your tray tomorrow. And now I want your most beautiful gardenia— one with a very loud smell."

For forty centavos' profit, the gardener handed over a waxen white flower. As Porfirio hurried across one of the cement paths, Don Serapio chuckled and fell into step with Don Nacho. It was whispered in the town

that because of his great stomach, the mayor had not seen his own feet for the past ten years.

"That Porfirio," said Don Serapio, and recounted the little episode. He finished with, "Someday he will learn that his fine deals always lose him money. Much cheaper to pay out the coins and be done with it. Forty centavos that ten-centavo flower cost him, but Porfirio thinks he got it for nothing. What a magnificent intellect."

"Flowers," said Don Nacho thoughtfully. "So Porfirio makes deals for flowers, does he? And for whom were the flowers?"

Don Serapio's mouth dropped open. "I never thought to ask him!" He slapped his palm against his forehead. "San Benedito, is it possible that Porfirio, that tightfisted man, is rolling the eye at some girl?"

When Don Nacho laughed, his stomach quivered in sympathy. "And you the finest gossip in Hidalgo. Every man knows the worth of his own blanket, you said!" Still laughing, he passed on with the crowd.

---

1 **fifty centavos** (sen tä′ vōz): about three cents.

Porfirio found his friend Andrés Treviño walking with Nena Santos and Alma Orona. He knew that to join them was impossible. Two boys and two girls walking together would create a scandal. But sitting in a chair beside her mother was Don Nacho's homely daughter, Chela. He hurried to her and whispered. She nodded, and a moment later joined the promenade. Porfirio sat impatiently beside Doña Mariliria, waiting for the group of three girls and a boy to encircle the plaza and return to where he was sitting, so that no gossip could connect his name with Chela's.

He sat very straight on one of his own chairs, the gardenia tightly gripped in his hot palm.

"That is a pretty flower," said Don Nacho's fragile wife.

Porfirio smiled weakly at her. If she continued to admire it, he, of politeness, must offer it to her, and he knew enough of women to know she would not refuse.

"It is a poor thing," he said quickly. "Already it is wilting."

"Do you like gardenias?" she asked with a mischievous gleam in her eye. She wondered what excuse he would make to keep from giving it to her. Porfirio's love of money was famous not only in Hidalgo, but through all the five villages strung along the banks of the Sabinas River.

"The little doctor," he said hastily, "tells me that gardenia perfume is very good for weakness of the chest."

"Have you a weakness of the chest?"

Porfirio squirmed on the hard straight chair. "No, not exactly. But I might have. Better to prevent sickness than to pay doctors' bills."

"Indeed, yes," said Doña Mariliria, hiding a smile behind her large black net fan and winking at Pepe Gonzalez, who came up to them.

"Eh, Porfirio, have you paid for that chair?"

"Why should I pay for it? I own it."

"Not that chair," said Pepe, with a sly glance at Doña Mariliria. "That one belongs to me. Your chairs are on the other side of the plaza."

"Come now, Pepe, is this a kind thing? Do not you and Andrés and I own all the chairs? Besides, the money would go to the Association. Why should I pay money to myself?"

"And steal the rightful share that belongs to Andrés and myself?" Pepe flung up his hands in a scandalized gesture. "I ask you, Doña Mariliria, is that fair, is that honest? Every Sunday night we divide the profits between us in three equal sections. Is it right that one should have more than the other two?"

"But I don't have more than you," Porfirio snapped. "If the money is not there at all, how can I have more nothing than you do? That is foolish."

Doña Mariliria tapped him on the arm with her fan. "But if you were not sitting in the chair, someone else would sit on it, paying ten centavos for the privilege. In that way you deprive your partners of three and one-half centavos each."

"A small amount, true," said Pepe. "But if all of us sat in our chairs, how could we make a profit?"

Porfirio sprang to his feet. "There is your chair," he cried. "It is cheaper to stand. Soon you will be charging me for the air I breathe!"

At this moment he saw his group coming toward him, and with a curt bow to Doña Mariliria, he hurried to join them. With careful management he contrived to walk between Chela and Alma Orona. To his prejudiced eyes Chela's homeliness, her large nose, heavy black brows, and wide, full-lipped mouth, pointed up the serene prettiness of Alma, with her large clear eyes, her heavy black hair worn in a crown of braids, and her skin warmed by the sun to a dark gold.

The gardenia slipped from his fingers to Alma's. She gave him a quick sideways glance, and he said with careful innocence, "Don Nacho says the moon will be late tonight."

Andrés Treviño said, "Pablo the goatherd told me that a late moon gives the goats moon madness."

There was a gasp of protest from Nena Santos. "Andrés Treviño! And you a good Christian talking to Pablo the goatherd! Have you no care for your soul, and he the son of Grandfather Devil?"

While Andrés was trying to explain to Nena that it was impossible to be a goat owner without having traffic with goatherds, Porfirio asked Alma if she would be at her window later in the evening.

"If you come with musicians," she whispered wickedly.

"Ay, but Alma, musicians cost money."

"So! Am I so worthless then?" With a toss of her head she separated herself from the group and walked away with Chela. Nena gave a little scream at finding herself alone with two men and darted after them. Andrés and Porfirio stared moodily at each other.

"That Nena Santos," Andrés mourned. "Why is it given to a man to be afflicted by a stubborn woman?"

"To your own troubles," retorted Porfirio, moving toward the bandstand. "I have enough of my own."

But Don Alonso, the orchestra leader, who knew Porfirio's bargaining ways, was adamant. To play the rooster[2] cost five pesos. It had always cost five pesos, and he did not see why it should be cheaper for the woodcarver.

"But five pesos," Porfirio wailed, "is a lot of money for thirty minutes' work. And when the music is done, what do I have left?"

"The smiles of a woman," said Don Alonso promptly, who had often parried this argument. "That should be enough for any man."

"Five pesos," mourned Porfirio. Ay me, that is a fortune—a very fortune."

"For two pesos," said Don Alonso, "I could give you a guitar and a violin. But a proper rooster is played with five men. Of course, if you want your girl to think herself worth only two pesos. . . ."

Porfirio shuddered. Alma Orona was as proud as the mountains. If she thought he put her value so low, she would never speak to him again. And he loved Alma Orona. He really loved her. He loved her more than the two hundred pesos he had saved to buy her

---

2 **play the rooster:** seranade a young woman.

trousseau[3] and rebuild a house and shop for their married life. But during the time he had saved those two hundred pesos, he had not counted upon all the extra money it seemed a courtship needed. For example, these five pesos, thrown, as it were, on a musical wind.

"I can't pay five pesos," he cried desperately. "I can't, Don Alonso."

Don Alonso looked over his shoulder at his musicians and winked. As one man they winked back at him.

"In the new casino they are building," said Don Alonso smoothly, "it would be a nice thing to have an orchestra-stand at the far end of the patio, as I have told you many times."

"But the committee says it would be a useless extravagance."

"The committee lacks a musical soul. Should you erect such a platform. . . ."

"But that would take lumber!"

"Of course," said Don Alonso, shrugging his unconcern, "if you prefer to pay us five silver pesos cash, we will be glad to play. . . ."

"One moment," said Porfirio, wrinkling his forehead in a desperate endeavor to think. "One little moment. I have some lumber left over from the making of two coffins. It might be possible—it might be just possible."

"A stand," said Don Alonso, "to seat seven men, and sufficient room for me to walk about."

"At the southern end of the patio . . . yes," said Porfirio, "it is possible. And you will play for me?"

"In return for a really fine stand," said the harp player, "perhaps we could excel ourselves and give you all of us tonight."

"All of you," Porfirio breathed happily, looking around at the seven faces—eight, with Don Alonso. "Including the drum?"

"Including," said Don Alonso grandly, "the saxophone."

It seemed to Porfirio that time moved slowly forward to the hour of the serenade. The free benches were occupied, and he was afraid to sit in one of his own chairs for fear Pepe Gonzalez or Andrés Treviño would demand payment of him. His legs ached from standing, and he was thankful when Bob Webster[4] invited him to his house for a glass of wine.

"To the ending of a year," Bob said in toast, and Porfirio echoed him.

"So you are leaving Hidalgo, Don Bob?"

"At this hour next month I will be on the blue Gulf."

"*Ay*, that will be a grand thing. But the valley will miss you."

Bob said with an air of surprise, "And I will miss the valley. Sometimes I almost wish I didn't have to leave."

Bob poured another glass of sherry for Porfirio.

"Enough, enough," murmured the young man. "Already my brain clouds, and I will have no words to speak to Alma Orona. Wine makes me stupid and sleepy."

"A *tequilito*, perhaps?"

"Thank you, Don Bob, but—well, a little one. This is my first playing of the rooster. I shake with nerves."

Bob laughed and gave him a small glass of tequila. Porfirio poured some salt on his palm, licked it, tossed the tequila down his throat, and ended by sucking a lemon. "Wine is for women," he said firmly, "but tequila puts heart in a man."

---

3 trousseau (trü′ sō): a bride's linens and clothes.

4 **Bob Webster**: an American who had gone to the Mexican town of Hidalgo to supervise the operation of a cement quarry.

He rose and solemnly embraced Bob. "My good friend, when you leave Hidalgo, I will light a candle for you. I will even weep a little." With a formal bow, he walked steadily out of the house to meet Don Alonso and the orchestra members.

The men grouped themselves near the house of Alma Orona on the Street of the Three Crosses. Pepe Gonzalez had come along to offer his advice.

"Now, Porfirio, you stand there beneath the window. Don Alonso, the musicians, and I will stand across the street."

Porfirio looked at his friend suspiciously. "But that window belongs to the house of old Don Ursulo. Alma Orona's is there."

"Nonsense! How can you tell the difference?"

"By the color. Alma's house is pink and green. Don Ursulo's is blue and red."

"'By the color,' he says." Pepe turned to the musicians. "At night he thinks he can tell the difference in color. Has he not remarkable eyes? And only today I was reading in a book that under moonlight nothing has color—nothing."

"I don't care," said Porfirio stubbornly. "I'm not going to play the rooster in front of the wrong house."

Don Alonso said gravely, his eyes twinkling behind his thick-lensed glasses, "There is a true way to distinguish the houses. Only this afternoon Don Ursulo said that of all pieces, his favorite was the North American jazz piece 'Yes, We Have No Bananas.' If we play it, it will bring him purring to the door. Then we will know to whom the window belongs."

"A most excellent idea," said Pepe, who had heard Don Ursulo on the subject of bananas.

Porfirio, his head buzzing from the effects

of the tequila and wine, rolled his eyes from Pepe's face to Don Alonso's. Although Pepe was his very good friend, Porfirio never quite trusted him. But at last he nodded his head. "Very well. Play the jazz. We will see what happens."

"But first," said Pepe quickly, "you are too far from the window. Stand closer so that you can hear Alma's sighs. Remember, she is too shy a maiden to open the window immediately. Oh, and take off your hat, Porfirio. You are serenading a young lady, not drinking beer in the saloon."

When Porfirio was placed to Pepe's satisfaction, the cheesemaker's son hastily retired to the safety of the musicians' group. At a nod from Don Alonso, the violins released a wailing note of warning; then the harp added its rippling sound, the drums and flutes joined in; and finally the precious saxophone, ordered from a North American mail-order house and entrusted to Don Alonso's fifteen-year-old son, took up the melody. "Yes, We Have No Bananas" ricocheted[5] down the narrow Street of the Three Crosses.

----

5 **ricocheted** (rik ə shād′): bounced from one surface to another.

Suddenly the window was flung open. Old Don Ursulo, in lavender nightgown and bright pink nightcap, swung up a pail of water and flung it with full force over Porfirio's head. The woodcarver, his mouth open ready to voice lovers' phrases, stood immobile in surprise, the water running down his face and dripping from his shoulders. The music came to a jerking pause.

As Porfirio slowly turned around, musicians, Don Alonso, and Pepe Gonzalez whirled and ran up the street, stumbling and pushing against each other, harp, guitars, and violins clutched for safety against their owners' stomachs. They did not pause for breath until they were safely crouching behind the bar in the Saloon of the Devil's Laughter. Then Pepe emitted a choked snort, and they pounded each other's backs and laughed until the tears came.

But Porfirio, left alone, water dripping in a pool about his feet, was not laughing. He slowly put on his hat and trudged home, his heels dragging in the dirt. He realized with mournful certainty that his playing of the rooster for Alma Orona had entered the pages of Hidalgo's history.

Discussion

1. How did Pepe Gonzalez, Don Alonso, and the musicians trick Porfirio? What happened as a result? Was their practical joke an example of fair play, or did they go too far? Why?

2. Porfirio stands out as the central character of the story. What three traits do you think best describe him? Refer to incidents in the story to support your answers.

3. So that his or her story will represent real life accurately, an author often includes factual information. This story, for example, permits you to "see" some courtship customs as practiced in Hidalgo. Which of those customs do you find different from American courtship customs you know about?

4. What do you understand by the phrase "playing the rooster"? Why will Porfirio's experience of "playing the rooster" be entered in the "pages of Hidalgo's history"?

Writer's Craft

In every story, as you know, something happens to someone (or to something). But whatever it is that happens doesn't happen in a vacuum. It occurs at a definite time in a definite place. It is that time and place which make up a story's SETTING.

Setting plays an important part in the way you read a story. Different settings can arouse different feelings. For example, a story that takes place in a cemetery on a dark, windy night is sure to affect you differently than does a story which takes place at a football game on a bright, crisp Saturday afternoon.

What's more, the setting influences what you can expect from a story. For example, from a story that takes place at the present time in the Amazon jungle, you might well expect the main character to become involved with jaguars, anteaters, and even hostile tribes. But you would hardly expect to find those same things in a story in the frozen wastes of the Antarctic!

1. "The Street of the Three Crosses" takes place in a town in north central Mexico. But what is the precise setting of the story? Where and when does most of the action occur?

2. How does the setting increase your understanding of the events in the story? Could these events have occurred in your community or in your neighborhood? Why or why not?

3. The setting of the story is especially vivid because of its many specific details of color, sound, taste, and smell. Find several examples of each kind of specific detail.

Vocabulary

Writers perform many challenging tasks. One of these tasks is to choose words that express the exact meaning that the writers want to give. This task is more difficult when a word has many SYNONYMS. A synonym is a word that has almost the same meaning as another word. Naturally, the more synonyms a person has to select from, the harder the choice becomes.

Imagine the process that the author of "The Street of the Three Crosses" might have gone through as she chose the *italicized* word in the following sentence:

> "Old Don Ursulo. . . swung up a pail of water and *flung* it with full force over Porfirio's head."

Look at a few of the synonyms the author could have chosen: *threw, propelled, tossed, pitched, hurled, cast,* and *launched.* Why do you think Josephina Niggli chose *flung* instead? These might have been among her reasons: (1) *Threw* is a very ordinary word. It would not make a particularly strong impression on the reader. (2) *Propelled,* on the other hand, may be too unusual; it could call too much attention to itself. Besides, *propelled* suggests the action of a machine rather than that of a person. (3) *Tossed* generally means a playful activity instead of an angry one, like Don Ursulo's. (4) For many readers, *pitched* is associated with baseball. Each of the other synonyms seems to have some fault that made it unsuitable. But *flung*—which means "threw with great strength"—clearly expresses the exact idea the author had in mind.

A. Below are ten sentences based on "The Street of the Three Crosses." In each sentence, three synonyms are printed in parentheses ( ). Without going back to the story, pick out the one synonym that seems to express the author's meaning most clearly. Do the exercise on a separate sheet of paper.

1. The moon hung like a silver crescent behind the (*top, belfry, tower*) of the pink church.
2. Porfirio was well known as a (*tightfisted, thrifty, budget-conscious*) man.
3. At the doctor's Porfirio (*wiggled, squirmed, turned*) in the hard, straight chair.
4. There was a (*breath, inhalation, gasp*) of protest from Nena Santos.
5. Andrés mourned, "Why is it given to a man to be (*bothered, martyred, afflicted*) by a stubborn woman?"

6. Time moved slowly forward to the hour of the (*serenade, concert, performance*).

7. Don Alonso's eyes (*flickered, shone, twinkled*) behind his thick-lensed glasses.

8. In Porfirio's head, there was a (*vibration, buzzing, noise*) from the tequila.

9. The musicians (*put, clutched, held*) their instruments against their stomachs for safety as they ran up the street.

10. Porfirio slowly put his hat on and (*trudged, walked, strolled*) home.

B. On the same sheet of paper, give your reasons for making the choices you did in Exercise A.

Josephina Niggli 1910——

Josephina Niggli has written many plays and stories about life in Mexico. She was born in Monterrey, Mexico, the daughter of Frederick Ferdinand and Goldie (Morgan) Niggli. Her education and career have been international. After graduating from colleges in Texas and North Carolina, she studied drama in England with the Old Vic Theater School.

Niggli teaches and writes in the United States now, but she travels to England nearly every year.

The Duvitches were a new family in town. What's more, they seemed different from other neighbor families. Playing a practical joke on them might be fun. Who would know who had played the joke? Besides, who would care?

The Strangers That Came to Town

AMBROSE FLACK

THE FIRST OF APRIL came dark and stormy, with silver whips of lightning cracking open the lowering clouds that seemed to skim the treetops. My brother Tom and I, recovering from chest colds, tired of reading and listening to the radio, turned to the big living-room window of our house on Syringa Street.

"Here they come, Mother," cried Tom when a big truck drove up in the teeming rain and stopped in front of the empty cottage across the street.

Mother hurried in from the kitchen and we three looked out. That truck, we knew, contained the Duvitch family and all their earthly possessions.

Mr. Duvitch and the biggest boy carefully helped Mrs. Duvitch from the seat and walked her into the house, supporting her all the way. Another big boy, carrying a well-bundled baby, followed. A stream of young Duvitches, accompanied by a big brown houndlike dog, poured out of the back of the truck and stood in a huddle in the rain.

The barnyard sounds we heard escaped from two crates of hens the Duvitches had fetched along and from a burlap bag in which a small flock of ducks had been stowed. While the livestock made noises according to its kind, the Duvitches were quiet—almost solemn. They showed no elation at finding themselves in a new neighborhood and a very pretty neighborhood at that.

All afternoon Mother, Tom, and myself had been watching out for them, with rather mixed emotions. For the Duvitches were immigrants and the first of their nationality to settle in our small smug town. Coming to our obscure part of the state a year before, they had moved into a rotting old farmhouse two miles north of town, long abandoned. After the slashing hurricane of mid-March, the moss-rotten dwelling looked like the house in the fairy tale that remained standing only because it did not know which way to fall and the Duvitches were forced to give it up.

"I wonder if Mrs. Duvitch is ill," murmured Mother, looking through the rain at the dreary street scene.

"She must be," said Tom. "I wonder if it'll be all right for Andy and me to help 'em move in their stuff."

This request, as Mother well knew, was

not inspired by genuine feeling for the Duvitches but by curiosity and she shook her head. It was a strict family rule that any illness which kept us out of school would automatically keep us indoors.

But the Duvitches got along very well without help from us. As it turned out, they were old hands at moving. For years before coming to America they had been on the move, to escape starvation, separation, possible assassination. Every child capable of two-legged locomotion pitched in and helped carry the things from the truck. In no time at all, it seemed, the truck was empty and the Duvitches were shut up tight in their new home.

That was the signal for Mother to step into the kitchen. She returned swathed[1] in her hooded raincoat, carrying a basket containing a vacuum jug of chicken soup, a baked tuna-fish dish, steaming hot, a loaf of fresh bread, and a chocolate cake. These she took to the house across the street and gave basket and all to the boy who answered her knock. It wasn't her plan to stop for a visit that day but to wait a week or so and call when the Duvitches were all settled.

The next day when the three of us—Mother, Tom, and myself—were having lunch, we heard a faint tap at the back door. I answered it and there stood a pale dark-eyed boy, looking very solemn, holding our basket. It contained the empty vacuum jug, casserole dish, and cake plate, all of which shone, and a tiny very shapely potted rose tree, in exquisite pink-tipped bud, the handsomest plant—and the only plant of its kind—ever seen in that neighborhood.

"I send them a few scraps of food," murmured Mother, a few seconds later, deeply touched, "and get this queenly gift!"

That was our last traffic with the Duvitch family for over two years. When Mother stopped to visit them a week after their coming, the little girl who opened the door a few inches said, "Mamma sick; she stay in bed today." Mrs. Duvitch never crossed the street to our house and Mother, a rather formal woman, made no further attempts to see the family. But Father disagreed when she remarked that she thought the Duvitches probably wished to be left alone.

Syringa Street seemed to be a friendly street. It was a crooked maple-shady country lane that wound through the town without losing its charm. The sidewalk here and there was almost lost in weeds and the ditches, in places, were brightened by clumps of orange day lilies. Widely spaced cottages, some of them smothered in vines, only seemed to make the neighborhood more rural. There were brilliant flower gardens, vegetable plots, fruit trees—and a few henhouses. The children, who enjoyed all the benefits of country life while actually living in town, were quite numerous. Behind the facades[2] of the street's dwellings there was probably no more greed, envy, superstition, or intolerance than lurked behind the doors of any average dwelling in any average American town. The cardinal[3] virtues, no doubt, were all represented. Yes, Syringa Street seemed to be a friendly street.

But the Duvitches were marked people. They were the one struggling family in a prosperous community—and poverty, amid prosperity, is often embarrassing and irritating to the prosperous. They were considered unattractive physically. They were so meek! The Duvitches never fought back.

The women started in on Mrs. Duvitch because she "never showed her face." It is true; she was rarely if ever seen in the

---

1 **swathed** (swāᵀHd): wrapped.

2 **facades** (fə säd′): fronts.
3 **cardinal** (kärd′ ən əl): chief, most important.

daytime, emerging from her dwelling only after dark in warm weather, to sit on the veranda, where she found privacy behind the ragged trumpet creeper.[4] But this gave rise to the rumor that she was the victim of an obscure skin disease and that every morning she shook scales out of the bed sheet. (When my father heard that one, he went out to the pantry and mixed himself a tall drink.)

Mr. Duvitch, too, was classified as an untouchable. His job, a rather malodorous[5] one, was with the local rendering plant[6] as a laborer. It followed that the Syringa Street young, meeting him on the street, sometimes stopped their noses as they passed him by—a form of torment all the more acute when Mr. Duvitch had to share it with the children that happened to be with him.

Black hard luck seemed to be their lot.

A few weeks after they moved to Syringa Street they suffered a tragedy they were all summer in recovering from—Mr. Duvitch lost two weeks' pay while gathering mushrooms in Tamarack Swamp. Inside of a year and a half, three Duvitch boys had lost, among them, by various mishaps, two fingers, one eye and an ear lobe. They were forever being cut up, bruised, mutilated by things falling, breaking, cracking, and exploding.

A mild case of typhoid, mass cases of whooping cough and measles—all plagued the family within a year of their arrival. Their only bright spot here was Dr. Switzer, one of the town's kindliest souls. He declined to accept fees, but was several times seen leaving the Duvitch cottage, carrying off a handsome house plant and looking very

pleased. The Duvitches' dog, Kasimar, acted just like the family to which he belonged—like one of the world's poorest canine relations. He seemed to be afraid of his own shadow and no one had ever heard him bark or growl.

Because they cast their eyes on the sidewalk as one passed them by and spoke only when spoken to, the young Duvitches, like their parents, were considered antisocial. They were regarded as born scavengers too, for they spent hours foraging[7] in the town dump, where they often picked up their footgear, some of their pants and shirts and furnishings for the house as well. They went on country excursions to gather watercress, dandelion greens, mushrooms, and wild berries; and the few apples and tomatoes they occasionally concealed under their blouses didn't make the farmers on whom they poached much poorer. Tom and I raided tomato patches and robbed apple trees just for the fun of it.

That first September four Duvitches—Irving, Benny, Abe and Esther—registered at the local grammar school. Mrs. Lovejoy, the principal, said they were bright, conscientious, pathetically eager but almost pathologically[8] shy. Before she could put a stop to it, some of their classmates scoffed at the leaf-lard-and-black-bread sandwiches they ate for lunch, huddled in one corner of the recreation room, dressed in their boiled-out ragpickers' clothes. After school they headed straight for home, never lingering on the playground.

Even the tradesmen to whom the Duvitches gave good money were either curt with them or downright rude. Mrs. Frithjof

---

4. **trumpet creeper:** a climbing plant with trumpet-shaped flowers.

5. **malodorous** (mal ō′ dər əs): ill-smelling.

6. **rendering plant:** a business operation making industrial fats and oils from livestock carcasses.

7. **foraging** (fôr′ ij ing): searching for food or for useful items.

8. **pathologically** (path ə loj′ ə kə lē): unhealthily.

Kinsella, the proprietor of the general store and a big jolly Viking who could be heard two blocks away, extended credit to almost everybody in town and had a way of insulting her customers so heartily that they all loved her for it. The Duvitches, however, Mrs. Kinsella very carefully *did not insult* (a form of insult in itself) and neither did she extend them credit.

But Mother, remembering the potted rose tree, always had a friendly word and a smile for the young Duvitches when she saw them and a bone for Kasimar when he found courage to venture across the road. Father was the only man on Syringa Street who tipped his hat to sixteen-year-old pockmarked Maria Duvitch, otherwise quite pretty, when he met her coming home from her piece-work job in Miller's Box Factory. It may have been that their European travail[9] made it easy for them to endure such a trifle as humiliation in America.

"I think," said Father one fine Saturday morning in July two years after the Duvitches had come to Syringa Street, "that it

9 **travail** (trə vāl'): troubles; torment.

would be very pleasant for Andy, Tom, and myself to pitch our tent out at Durston's Pond and spend the night. We could fish and swim. That is," he added, "if Mother can spare us."

"I can spare you very well," Mother said cheerfully.

She had a notion it did menfolk good to get away from their women occasionally and in this instance the sacrifice came easily, because camp life was little to her liking. She packed a hamper of food, Tom and I fetched the tent from the attic, and Father looked over his fishing tackle. An hour after lunch we were driving through rolling farm country out to Durston's Pond, four miles north of town.

We often had the serene little lake all to ourselves, but on our arrival that afternoon we found half a dozen male Duvitches in possession. They had been fishing for several hours, casting from the shore, dropping their lines over the wooden bridge that spanned Cat Creek where it flowed into the pond and trolling for bass from a flat-bottomed rowboat.

Tom and I, Philistines[10] like our friends, ignored the Duvitch boys but Father went up to Mr. Duvitch, who was fishing from the shore, and put out his hand.

"Good afternoon, Mr. Duvitch! It's nice to see you and the boys here. What a beautiful day! Are Mrs. Duvitch and the girls all well?"

Mr. Duvitch was a little fellow, a lean starveling of a man with watery blue eyes and a kicked-about look. Gratitude for being agreeably noticed showed in his mosquito-bitten face as he took Father's hand and his tremulous smile showed broken teeth.

"I know the mosquitoes are biting," Father went on pleasantly, "but are the fish?"

Proudly, oh, so proudly, Mr. Duvitch exhibited the catch that would probably feed his family for the better part of a week: a fine mess of bass, perch, and sunfish, all of them alive, as far as I could see, and swimming around in the oaken washtub in which they had been dropped. Father gave Mr. Duvitch hearty congratulations and said we couldn't hope to do as well but that we'd try.

We three pitched the tent on a little knoll over the pond, and then Father, with a happy sigh, lay down on the blanket for a nap in the sun. Tom and I played a game of chew-the-peg on the grassy bank above the water and, later on, made several trips to the tent, for the camera, the field glasses, the sun lotion. On a trip for a cold drink from the vacuum jug and to fetch towels and soap, we stopped to look again at the Duvitches' catch of fish.

Mr. Duvitch and the boys had moved away and were fishing in a small arm of the pond below us. None of them seemed visible. Tom and I, our glances meeting over the big cake of soap in my hand, were similarly and wickedly inspired—the thing was irresistible.

We held a brief whispering conversation; and then egged on by him and quite willing on my own, I played a shameful trick on the Duvitches, the memory of which will come back to the end of my days to plague me. Without considering further, I dropped the cake of soap into the tub of fish.

"Let's go," whispered Tom after we had watched the soap sink to the bottom.

We swam out to the raft, diving and frolicking in the deep water. After a while the Duvitches, calling it a day, assembled at a spot on the shore below our tent, happy in the knowledge of a good catch to take home.

In a little while Tom and I could hear their muffled exclamations of disbelief and dismay. Father woke up and joined our neighbors in a conclave,[11] looking down at the tub of fish near his feet. After a few moments he produced the whistle he carried on all our country excursions and blew it piercingly three times, the proclamation of emergency. This meant that Tom and I must come at once.

---

10 **Philistines** (fil' ə stēnz): here, insensitive persons.

11 **conclave** (kon' klāv): private meeting.

Looking as guilty as we felt, we swam in and joined the group gathering around the tub. In the midst of our stricken neighbors stood Father, holding the half-melted cake of soap in his palm silently but accusingly, for the fish had perished miserably in the soapy water and were unfit to eat. Not only had Tom and I snatched precious food from their mouths but we had brazenly[12] advertised the contempt[13] in which we held them.

Father's eyes were narrow slits of blue fire in his white face. I had never seen him so angry. One look at Tom and me told him everything. Words would have been superfluous[14] and my brother and I bowed our heads in acknowledgment of our guilt.

"You will begin," Father said in a voice I didn't recognize, "by saying you're sorry."

Our stunned neighbor wiped his blinking eyes as he listened to our mumbled words, which Father made us repeat when they were inaudible. But there was no hostility, no animosity[15] toward us in the man, and it was obvious also that he considered himself too humble to receive an apology, finding it, like most of life's troubles, a mockery to be endured without protest. His sons showed no resentment, either, only a kind of resignation in their minds, which carried almost atavistic memories[16] of century-old oppression by country barons and landed gentry.

One-eyed Manny Duvitch, as it turned out, had told Father he had seen me drop something in the tub of fish (before he learned that it had been a cake of soap). Now he looked guiltier than Tom and I. Because he had been the witness and accuser, it was as if he considered himself to be the troublemaker, deserving the punishment. The two real culprits were the young lords of the ruling manor, with unlimited license, exempt from chastisement.[17] To Manny, the fortunate, the well-to-do, were also the privileged.

"Do you realize," said Father coldly, looking from Tom to me, "that in certain primitive communities the sort of stunt you've pulled would be punishable by death?"

Tom and I did not reply.

"Turn over the tub," said Father abruptly, addressing us as if we were strangers.

We turned it over. The gray soapy water ran away in bubbly rivulets, disappearing in the coarse mat of turf, and the poisoned fish lay exposed on the grass—quiet, strangled, open-mouthed—and somehow looking as if they were mutely[18] protesting their horrid, unnatural fate.

"Count the fish," Father ordered us, his voice like steel.

Tom and I got down on our knees.

"How many are there?" demanded Father.

"Sixty-one," I said.

"How many bass?"

"Twelve."

Father handed Mr. Duvitch two dollars, the price of a day's rental of the rowboat. Then, looking both the avenging angel and executioner, he ordered Tom and me, with our tackle and bait, off the land we had disgraced—into exile, out on Durston's Pond.

"And you are not to come back," he gave out in the same steely tones, "until you've caught sixty-one fish to repay Mr. Duvitch.

12 **brazenly** (brā′ zən lē): boldly and impudently.
13 **contempt** (kən tempt′): scorn; disdain.
14 **superfluous** (sù pėr′ flü əs): unnecessary.
15 **animosity** (an əm os′ ə tē): ill-will; resentment.
16 **atavistic** (at ə vis′ tik) **memories**: memories inherited from one's ancestors.

17 **chastisement** (cha′ stiz mənt): punishment.
18 **mutely** (myüt′ lē): silently.

See to it that among them you bring in at least a dozen bass."

Father stepped up to the tent on the knoll to fetch our shirts and dungarees. These he rolled into a tight ball and shot like a bolt into the rowboat. He then turned his back to us and, thus disowned, Tom and I lost no time in rowing out on the pond. Father's decisions, even with Mother present, were never reversed and swift execution, from which there was no appeal, followed his sentences.

Out in the middle of the big pond we dropped anchor, threaded our steel rods and, baiting our hooks, began to fish. I knew that if it took us all summer to catch them, we dared not set foot ashore without sixty-one fish. Almost at once Tom pulled in a good-sized bass and ten minutes later two yellow perch were added to our string. The crestfallen Duvitches went home. Father threw himself on the blanket, furiously smoking a cigar. That was about four in the afternoon.

Oh, the mosquitoes! They were bad enough at the time, and while the light held, but after we had been fishing for three hours and had caught eight fish, they swarmed out of the dark Hades of swampland surrounding the pond like Lucifer's[19] angels, in legions.

After an hour of it we wanted to leap overboard. They got in our ears, our noses, our eyes, even in our mouths, and nestling in our hair, they bit through to our scalps. I remembered tales of Indian prisoners in Alaska, stripped by their captors and turned loose on the tundra, where they died of the mosquitoes in two hours. Several times we slipped over the side of the boat, immersing ourselves in the water to escape the blood-thirsty clouds. The night dragged on while the whining swarms grew thicker.

"Andy, what time is it?"

"Ten o'clock, Tom."

"Is that all?" Tom groaned and pulled in another bass and killed six or eight mosquitoes in one slap. Two hours passed and midnight was ghostly on Durston's Pond.

The moon, bright as day, sailed high in the purple sky, dimming the starfire, casting a great white shaft of quivering radiance on the water, but it was all hideous. The big yellow disk sank in a gauzy cloudbank, then disappeared for good and the stars shone out with renewed splendor.

"Andy, what *time* is it?"

"Two o'clock, Tom."

The treetops whispered as if in conspiracy against us. Owls hooted—mockingly we thought—and bats circled over our heads, making us feel thoroughly damned. Our only solace was the campfire Father kept burning near the tent, which flared like a beacon light in the dark. We went on fishing as our tormentors bit and sang. Each hour was an eternity of frenzy and I fairly panted for the light of dawn to come, but even now I cannot decide which was worse, that night with the mosquitoes on Durston's Pond or the following day in the blistering heat.

"Andy—"

"It's four o'clock, Tom, and we've got sixteen fish."

Dawn came but even I, a highly impressionable youngster of seventeen, did not enjoy that calm effulgent[20] majesty of daybreak. A long stretch on Durston's Pond, under the July sun, still faced us.

The rising sun was red, casting glimmering circles of rose-colored light on the windless surface of the pond. The mosquitoes thinned, the fish continued to bite. But as we fished, the sun mounted steadily and by eleven it

---

19 **Lucifer's** (lü′ sə fərz): the Devil's.

20 **effulgent** (i ful′ jənt): radiant.

had fulfilled its awful prophecy and became a ball of fire in the cloudless skies. Tom and I began to bake in the heat waves that shimmered over the pond and we were steamed in the scalding, vapory mist.

"I wish it was night again, Andy," groaned Tom after sweating out two hours of it. "This is worse than the mosquitoes."

"At least we won't get any infections from our bites, Tom," I said feebly. "The sun's cauterizing[21] them."

"We might get sunstrokes, though. We're liable to, without our hats. But I don't care if I do. I'd rather be unconscious."

Tom was only fifteen and I think he hated me that day. I, the older, should have been his protector against participation in crime, not his accomplice. I wanted to row him in, then come back to finish the business alone, but there on the green Eden-like shore stood Father—the archangel bearing the fiery sword, stationed by the Lord at the gates of Paradise to bar the way.

Tom and I weighed our hooks down to the deep cold water. We caught two more bass and half a dozen sunfish.

By one o'clock groups of people gathered on the shore, for word of the drama that was being enacted on Durston's Pond had spread through the town. Some of the visitors praised Father for his stern discipline; others berated him. He went right on reading his magazine and smoking his cigar, as indifferent to their praise as he was to their criticism.

Local fishermen who knew the lake and something about the angling ability of the average youngster made gloomy estimates as to the possible length of our exile on the water. A few had us fishing until the snow flew. They made bets too. Would Tom and I have the guts to stick it out? Most of the bets were against us.

But we sat there in the rowboat, without food, through the hottest day of the summer.

No breeze stirred. No cloud obscured the sun. Even the bird life of the swamp, usually a medley of song, was silent and dead. Tom was drooping visibly in the glare and I tried hard not to look at his scorched face.

Between three and four we dropped lines in a school of yellow perch and pulled up no less than twenty. The bass continued to bite in the deep black holes off the swamp, which bristled with tree trunks. Benumbed, half-blinded, moving like automatons,[22] Tom and I geared ourselves for the home stretch.

When the sun, dropping low, had lost its fury and the hard blue enamel of the sky began to pale, I pulled up the thirteenth bass, which was our sixty-first fish.

Turned lobster-red, fairly devoured, famished, and drooping from lack of sleep, we put together our rods and with our remaining strength rowed to where Father was waiting.

He received us coolly, making no comment on our condition. At once he asked to see the fish and we held them up by the strings.

"Count them," he said.

Obviously we would receive permission to land only when we had produced the required number, which was the price of our freedom.

"Sixty-one," said Tom.

"Including thirteen bass," I added.

"Very good," said Father in businesslike tones. "We will now restore to Mr. Duvitch his rightful property."

Tom and I took care not to play the part

---

21 **cauterizing** (kô′ tə rīz ing): searing.

22 **automatons** (ô tom′ ə tonz): automatic machines; robots.

of triumphant heroes, even of redeemed sinners—that would not have suited our parent. Certainly, in appearance, we were more damned than redeemed. But when we tottered out of the rowboat something in me was quietly rejoicing. I guessed that Father was secretly proud of our fortitude and I realized, too, that all through the night he had suffered with us.

We walked through the crowd of visitors on the lake shore, climbed into the car, and silently drove to the Duvitch cottage. Mrs. Duvitch and the children were not visible, but we found Mr. Duvitch sitting on the porch.

When he saw Tom and me and we silently handed him the strings of fish, he gulped and swallowed hard. For a moment he could not speak. Then, in a voice that was raw with emotion, he protested that he had not wished us to suffer so. Suppose we had fallen overboard in the dark?

"Will you shake hands with the boys?" asked Father.

Instead, Mr. Duvitch broke down. My brother and I did not know where to look and during those moments we suffered more acutely than we had suffered in the clouds of mosquitoes and under the broiling sun. After our neighbor had composed himself, he seized our hands and bowed his head over them. There was something Biblical, like a picture in the Old Testament, in the man's gesture. Anyway, it was my greatest lesson in humility.

When Mother, who had heard about our exile on the pond from a neighbor, saw us she burst into tears. She tried to embrace us but we drew back painfully. While she was rubbing salves and ointments on our seared backs and necks, somebody knocked at the kitchen door and Father opened it to find Mrs. Duvitch standing there, her face and skin as undefiled as the Virgin's—the first time she had crossed the street to our house.

In her pale swaying hand Mrs. Duvitch held a porcelain teacup, ornamented with pink rosebuds and golden leaves—a relic from the old country and, as it turned out, her most cherished possession.

Her voice, thin and wispy from fright and shock, was difficult to follow. But we gathered that she had brought the teacup over as a peace offering and as a plea for our forgiveness to her family for the living purgatory,[23] no matter whose fault, through which my brother and I had passed. When Mother declined the teacup and assured Mrs. Duvitch that she would not have it otherwise with Tom and me, our neighbor, unable to find her tongue, made a little eloquent sign with her hands that was for thanks and that looked like a silent blessing. She quietly turned and went away; and again I felt that I had witnessed a scene from the Old Testament.

Mother continued her ministrations to Tom and me and put us to bed. Despite our skin, which stuck to sheet and pillowcase, we slept like creatures drugged.

"It is high time," Tom and I heard Father say calmly, sanely, to Mother around noon next day when we woke up, "for this senseless feeling against the Duvitches to stop, and I'm willing to do still more to stop it. Tonight we are having supper with them. I've just seen Mr. Duvitch and he remarked that since Andy and Tom caught the fish, he'd feel better if we all shared in them. I suggested a fish-fry picnic supper and with a few hints from me, and some encouragement, he invited us over. It may be an ordeal but we ought to be able to bear it."

We walked across the street at six o'clock,

---

23 **purgatory** (pėr′ gə tôr ē): prolonged punishment.

not knowing what to expect. All the Duvitches, dressed in their Sunday best, bright
and flushed and shining as we had never seen
them, received us at the door as if we had
been royalty. They looked at Tom and me
and delicately looked away—I shuddered
when I thought of what my brother and I
would have had to endure had this been any
other family.

Instead of a wretched abode we found a
scantily furnished home that shone with
cleanliness and smelled of spicy garden pinks.
In its almost barren simplicity there was
something comely.[24] A few of the stands,
chairs, and tables had the intimate quality of
what is fashioned by the human hand. These,
together with odds and ends the family had
brought from the old country and others
resurrected from the town dump and
mended, painted, waxed, and polished, made
for a kind of native household harmony. The
house plants (no window was without several) delighted Mother. Mrs. Duvitch was
raising little orange and lemon trees from
seed and experimenting with a pineapple
plant growing in a butter tub.

At once we were conscious of a remarkable
difference in the demeanor[25] of the family.
The children, thrilled by their first party, by
the family's first recognition in this country,
kept showing their pleasure in wide, delighted smiles. I couldn't believe they were
the same timid, downcast youngsters one met
on the street and saw in school; they seemed
to have been touched by a wand. The Duvitches' home was their castle: sustained and
animated by the security of its four walls,
shut away from a world of contempt and
hostility, they were complete human beings.
In their own house their true personalities
emerged.

As the host Mr. Duvitch was a man we
were seeing for the first time. Overjoyed to
have neighbors in his house, he was so full of
himself that I was conscious of an invisible
stature in him which made him seem quite as
tall as Father. He beamed and feasted his eyes
on us. Saying very little, he managed to make
us feel a great deal and he constantly sought
his wife's eyes with glances of delight over the
wonder of what was happening.

David, the oldest boy, helped his father
serve a bottle of homemade blackberry wine.

We ate fried fish and good food of the
American picnic variety at a long plank table
set out in the back yard under an apple tree.
The young Duvitches passed things politely,
never helping themselves first: and their
thanks upon receiving a dish were almost
ceremonial. They waited patiently for their
plates and ate every scrap of food.

Father kept the conversation going. His
every word was listened to, every childish
eye riveted on him while he spoke.

Tom and I, fascinated by the family's
metamorphosis,[26] almost forgot about our
blisters and our stings. As Father told stories
and jokes, we discovered that the Duvitches
had a gift for gaiety, for laughter, all but
extinguished but still capable of resurrection.
They were merry people who had suffered
too much. How strange to see the boys and
girls throw back their heads and laugh when
Father said something that was funny, but
not terribly funny.

After supper we were ushered to the open
summer kitchen, the coolest room in the
house, for entertainment.

David played folk songs on his accordion.
Mr. Duvitch turned out to be an amateur
ventriloquist; he made the dog Kasimar talk
Polish, the cat Jan talk Russian, and a doll

---

24 **comely** (kum′ lē): pleasant; attractive.
25 **demeanor** (di mēn′ ər): behavior.

26 **metamorphosis** (met ə môr′ fə sis): change;
transformation.

named Sophia talk English. Mrs. Duvitch read aloud to us, translating as she went along, a letter her mother had received from the great actress Modjeska, whom her family had known long ago.

I could tell that the Duvitches were a great revelation to Father and that he had enjoyed the evening tremendously.

"To think," he murmured as if talking to himself, while we were crossing the street, "that they should turn out to be gentle people of cultivation and accomplishment. Looked down on and ignored by their inferiors!"

I like to believe that the oil paintings of George Washington, Abraham Lincoln, and Thomas Jefferson, which hung in our living room, helped to establish the Duvitches in our community. Even the fountain tinkling in the lily pool in our garden might have helped. In that town, oil paintings and flowing fountains were the symbols of wealth and aristocracy. Only a few mansions on Sycamore Hill were adorned with such.

Because our home was graced with these symbols, we had always been classified with the town's great, which gave us such prestige in the neighborhood that people often followed our lead. Obviously the Duvitches were important in Father's eyes, shown by the rigorous sentence he had imposed on Tom and me for our misuse of them. Added to that, we had recognized the family by taking a meal with them in their own house. People, often persuaded to accept what we accepted, to believe what we believed, began to think the Duvitches must really count, after all. Most of our neighbors decided that if they were good enough for a highly educated man like Father (the only college graduate on Syringa Street), they were good enough for them. The galvanized[27] community began to look upon things in a different light and it soon became the fashion to give the Duvitches the favorable nod.

Mother invited Mrs. Duvitch to a tea party, where her delicate manners, and the fine needlework which engaged her, won the approval of the local housewives who were present. On hot days our neighbor asked one of her big boys to carry the pineapple plant (which Mother had advertised well), into the back yard; and since botanical rarities were irresistible in that town of gardens, people were soon stopping by the fence for a look at the tropical specimen. After a while Mrs. Duvitch found courage to ask these people into her house and, if Mr. Duvitch was at home, he told the visitors stories about life in the old country. It was then that the neighborhood learned about the family's European past.

The children ceased stopping their noses when Mr. Duvitch passed them by and it wasn't long before the young Duvitches were able to enjoy outside companionship when they found time to play. They blossomed out in school and they were soon shining in school plays and festivals. Even Kasimar began to take on the ways of an American dog, daring to bark and growl on occasion.

Nathan Duvitch, who was seventeen, could throw and hit a baseball as far as anybody his age in town. When I learned this, and let it be known, he was asked to join one of the local ball clubs. David, invited to play his accordion at a country dance, turned out to be a magician with the instrument and ended up being one of the community's most popular players. Mrs. Frithjof Kinsella gave one-eyed Manny an after-school job in her store and later on told Mother he was worth three boys put together.

The community presently had reason to be grateful for Mrs. Duvitch's presence. It turned out that she had a great gift for nursing, and no fear of death, no fear of disease, contagious or otherwise. In times of severe illness Dr. Switzer often suggested that she be sent for—her own girls could take over at home. There were almost no nurses in town and the nearest hospital was over a hundred miles away. When Mrs. Duvitch quietly slipped into a sickroom, she never failed to bring along a sedative[28] influence, a kind of sanity. After an hour or two of her serene presence, the patient was calmed and comforted and the family reassured.

People began to turn to the Duvitches in all kinds of trouble. A boy who got in a bad scrape, a bitter family quarrel, a baby who had come into the world deformed—the elder Duvitches, with their old-world wisdom and gift for accepting the inevitable, could sit by the hour and argue gently and convincingly against disgrace, false pride, grief, fear.

Most surprising of all, Mr. Duvitch, in one respect, turned out to be characteristically American. One Saturday afternoon when my ball team was playing Nathan's, Father met him in the local ball park.

"Chust like de American boy," Mr. Duvitch exploded when Nathan made a timely hit that drove in two runs. Our neighbor choked with pride and went on: "Nathan's battering averich three hunnert twenty-seven!"

---

27 **galvanized** (gal′ və nīzd): aroused.

28 **sedative** (sed′ ə tiv): calming; quieting.

On a cold snowy afternoon in winter Mr. Duvitch stopped at our house and presented Father (who had enormous hands, much bigger than any of the Duvitches') with a handsome pair of leather mittens, lined with fur, which had a slightly acrid,[29] ashy odor.

29 acrid (ak' rid): bitter.

"No doubt one of the boys resurrected them from a heap of ashes in the dump," remarked Father, drawing on the mittens, which fitted perfectly. "Why should I value them any the less? *Who* would have dreamed that the Duvitches would have so much more to offer us than we have to offer them?"

Discussion

1. How are the Duvitches different from the other families in Andy's neighborhood?

2. Two years after the Duvitches move to Syringa Street, they still have no friends. How do they limit their chances to make friends? How do the neighbors treat them? Why?

3. What trick do Andy and Tom play on the Duvitches? What do the Duvitches do when they discover what has happened? Why?

4. Why is Andy's father so angry at what his two sons have done? What punishment does he impose on them? Do you think that that punishment was fair or unfair? Why?

5. The trick that Andy and Tom play on the Duvitches has at least one good result. What is it?

6. At the picnic supper, what does Andy's family discover about the Duvitches? What changes gradually occur in the Duvitches themselves?

7. At the end of the story, how is Andy different from the kind of person he was at the beginning? Why is he different?

Writer's Craft

Why do people do what they do? There are always reasons. One man, for example, buys a subcompact car because he wants to spend less for gasoline. A woman becomes a landscape gardener because she likes to be outdoors, working with plants. You are late for school because you overslept because you stayed up late to watch a TV special—because. . . . You see—there are always reasons.

Similarly, in every well-written story, there have to be reasons for whatever the characters do. Otherwise, what they do—indeed, the story itself—would not be believable. That's why competent writers give special attention to the MOTIVATION of their characters. They know how important it is for the reader to understand the causes that account for the behavior of their characters.

1. At the beginning of the story, why do the Duvitches keep to themselves, seeming not to want to be friendly?

2. For what reasons do the Duvitches change their behavior? How does the author make those changes believable?

3. Why do Andy and Tom drop the cake of soap in the Duvitches' tub of fish? Is their behavior believable? Why or why not?

4. Why does Andy and Tom's father punish the two boys as he does? Is it believable that a father would treat his sons as Andy's father does? Why or why not?

Composition

1. Andy is the character who tells about the events in "The Strangers That Came to Town." That is, we see the events through his eyes. But suppose that Andy's father or Tom or Mr. Duvitch were to tell the story. How would their versions differ from Andy's? Imagine that you are one of those persons. Write your account of the main events in the story as *you* experience them.

2. Have you ever changed your mind about a person? Most of us have. In a paragraph or two, describe why you changed your mind about someone. Briefly give your first impressions of the person. Then as you came to know that person better, show how you changed your mind about him or her. Be sure to make it clear why you changed your mind.

Vocabulary

Context clues are hints given by surrounding words about the general meaning of an unfamiliar word. One good place to look for such hints is in WORD-SERIES CONTEXT CLUES. A word-series is any group of three or more successive words. For example:

a lion, a tiger, a giraffe, and an ibex

Even if you had never seen the word *ibex* before, you should be able to tell that it is an animal because it is being introduced in a word series listing other animals. The context clues do not tell you what an *ibex* looks like or what kind of animal it is, but they do provide you with a general category to put *ibex* into. Therefore, they give you the general meaning of the word.

A. On a separate sheet of paper, use word-series context clues by giving the category of all *italicized* words in the following sentences:

1. *Typhoid*, *whooping cough*, and *measles* all struck the family.

2. They were forever being *cut up, bruised,* and *mutilated.*

3. They gathered *watercress, dandelion greens, mushrooms,* and *wild berries.*

4. Mr. Duvitch exhibited his catch: *bass, perch,* and *sunfish.*

5. The Duvitches argued gently against *disgrace, false pride, grief,* and *fear.*

B. Each sentence below contains an *italicized* word from "The Strangers That Came to Town." Write the word-series context clues for each word. Then write the category in which the *italicized* word belongs.

EXAMPLE: I saw a lion, a tiger, and an ibex.
ANSWER: lion, tiger, ibex—animals

1. For two years, the Duvitches received nothing but insults, ridicule, and *contempt* from most of their neighbors.

2. In the calm, quiet, *serene* surroundings of Durston's Pond, Andy and Tom played a particularly cruel prank on the immigrant family.

3. Their father felt that no ordinary scolding, no everyday penalty, no routine *chastisement* would be enough to make up for what his sons had done.

4. When the townspeople found out how their father was punishing the two boys, some thought he was doing the right thing; but others disapproved, criticized, and *berated* him.

5. It surprised the other people on Syringa Street to discover that the Duvitches deserved admiration for their cleanliness, talent, good humor, and *fortitude.*

Ambrose Flack 1902——

Ambrose Flack was raised in Syracuse, New York, the son of a family whose idol was Theodore Roosevelt. Two of Flack's stories, "Theodore Roosevelt and My Green-Gold Fountain Pen" and "The President's Advice," describe the family's reverence for the President, as well as the family's dedication to each other.

Thirteen! When you are thirteen, are you still a child? Are you a young adult? Or are you neither one?

Peg was thirteen. She knew she had put her childhood behind her. But somehow her parents didn't. How to convince them that she was more a young woman than a child—that was the problem.

The Apprentice

DOROTHY CANFIELD FISHER

THE DAY HAD BEEN one of the unbearable ones, when every sound had set her teeth on edge like chalk creaking on a blackboard, when every word her father or mother said to her or did not say to her seemed an intentional injustice. And of course, it would happen as the end to such a day, that just as the sun went down back of the mountain and the long twilight began, she noticed that Rollie was not around.

Tense with exasperation at what her mother would say, she began to call him in a carefully casual tone—she would simply explode if Mother got going—"Here, Rollie! He-ere, boy! Want to go for a walk, Rollie?" Whistling to him cheerfully, her heart full of wrath at the way the world treated her, she made the rounds of his haunts; the corner of the woodshed, where he liked to curl up on the wool of Father's discarded old windbreaker; the hay barn, the cow barn, the sunny spot on the side porch—, no Rollie.

Perhaps he had sneaked upstairs to lie on her bed where he was not supposed to go—not that *she* would have minded! That rule was a part of Mother's fussiness, part too of Mother's bossiness. It was *her* bed, wasn't it? But was she allowed the say-so about it? Not on your life. They *said* she could have things the way she wanted in her own room, now she was in her teens, but—her heart raged against unfairness as she took the stairs stormily, two steps at a time, her pigtails flopping up and down on her back. If Rollie was on her bed, she was just going to let him stay right there, and Mother could say what she wanted to.

But he was not there. The bedspread and pillow were crumpled, but not from his weight. She had flung herself down to cry there that afternoon. And then she couldn't. Every nerve in her had been twanging discordantly, but she couldn't cry. She could only lie there, her hands doubled up hard, furious that she had nothing to cry about. Not really. She was too big to cry just over

Father's having said to her, severely, "I told you if I let you take the chess set you were to put it away when you got through with it. One of the pawns was on the floor of our bedroom this morning. I stepped on it. If I'd had my shoes on, I'd have broken it."

Well, he *had* told her to be sure to put them away. And although she had forgotten and left them, he hadn't said she mustn't ever take the set again. No, the instant she thought about that, she knew she couldn't cry about it. She could be, and she was, in a rage about the way Father kept on talking, long after she'd got his point, "It's not that I care so much about the chess set," he said, just leaning with all his weight on being right, "it's because if you don't learn how to take care of things, you yourself will suffer for it, later. You'll forget or neglect something that will be really important, for *you*. We have to try to teach you to be responsible for what you've said you'll take care of. If we . . ." on and on, preaching and preaching.

She heard her mother coming down the hall, and hastily shut her door. She had a right to shut the door to her own room, hadn't she? She had *some* rights, she supposed, even if she was only thirteen and the youngest child. If her mother opened it to say, smiling, "What are you doing in here that you won't want me to see?" she'd say—she'd just say—

She stood there, dry-eyed, by the bed that Rollie had not crumpled, and thought, "I hope Mother sees the spread and says something about Rollie—I just hope she does."

But her mother did not open the door. Her feet went steadily on along the hall, and then, carefully, slowly, down the stairs. She probably had an arm full of winter things she was bringing down from the attic. She was probably thinking that a tall, thirteen-year-old daughter was big enough to help with a chore like that. But she wouldn't *say* anything. She would just get out that insulting look of a grown-up silently putting up with a crazy unreasonable kid. She had worn that expression all day; it was too much to be endured.

Up in her bedroom behind her closed door the thirteen-year-old stamped her foot in a rage, none the less savage and heartshaking because it was mysterious to her.

But she had not located Rollie. Before she would let her father and mother know she had lost sight of him, forgotten about him, she would be cut into little pieces. They would not scold her, she knew. They would

do worse. They would look at her. And in their silence she would hear droning on reproachfully what they had said when the sweet, woolly collie-puppy had first been in her arms and she had been begging to keep him for her own.

How warm he had felt! Astonishing how warm and alive a puppy was compared to a doll! She had never liked her dolls much, after she had held Rollie, feeling him warm against her breast, warm and wriggling, bursting with life, reaching up to lick her face—he had loved her from that first instant. As he felt her arms around him, his beautiful eyes had melted in trusting sweetness. As they did now, whenever he looked at her. "My dog is the only one in the whole world who *really* loves me," she thought passionately.

Even then, at the very minute when as a darling baby dog he was beginning to love her, her father and mother were saying, so cold, so reasonable—gosh! how she *hated* reasonableness!—"Now, Peg, remember that, living where we do, with sheep on the farms around us, it is a serious responsibility to have a collie dog. If you keep him, you've got to be the one to take care of him. You'll have to be the one to train him to stay at home. We're too busy with you children to start bringing up a puppy, too." Rollie, nestling in her arms, let one hind leg drop awkwardly. It must be uncomfortable. She looked down at him tenderly, tucked his dangling leg up under him and gave him a hug. He laughed up in her face—he really did laugh, his mouth stretched wide in a cheerful grin.

Her parents were saying, "If you want him, you can have him. But you must be responsible for him. If he gets to running sheep, he'll just have to be shot, you know that."

They had not said, aloud, "Like the Wilsons' collie." They never mentioned that awfulness—her racing unsuspectingly down across the fields just at the horrible moment when Mr. Wilson shot their collie caught in the very act of killing sheep. They probably thought that if they never spoke about it, she would forget it—*forget* the crack of that rifle, and the collapse of the great beautiful dog! Forget the red red blood spurting from the hole in his head. She hadn't forgotten. She never would. She knew as well as they did, how important it was to train a collie-puppy about sheep. They didn't need to rub it in like that. They always rubbed everything in. She had told them, fervently, indignantly, that *of course* she would take care of him, be responsible for him, teach him to stay at home. Of course, of course. *She* understood!

And now, this afternoon, when he was six months old, tall, rangy, powerful, standing up far above her knee, nearly to her waist, she didn't know where he was. But of course he must be somewhere around. He always was. She composed her face to look natural and went downstairs to search the house. He was probably asleep somewhere. She looked every room over carefully. Her mother was nowhere visible. It was safe to call him again, to give the special piercing whistle which always brought him racing to her, the white-feathered plume of his tail waving in elation that she wanted him.

But he did not answer. She stood still on the front porch to think.

Could he have gone up to their special place in the edge of the field where the three young pines, their branches growing close to the ground, make a triangular, walled-in space, completely hidden from the world. Sometimes he went up there with her. When she lay down on the dried grass to dream, he too lay down quietly, his head on his paws, his beautiful eyes fixed adoringly on her. He entered into her every mood. If she wanted to be quiet, all right, he did too.

It didn't seem as though he would have gone alone there. Still—She loped up the steep slope of the field rather fast, beginning to be anxious.

No, he was not there. She stood, irresolutely, in the roofless, green-walled triangular hide-out, wondering what to do next.

Then, before she knew what thought had come into her mind, its emotional impact knocked her down. At least her knees crumpled under her. Last Wednesday the Wilsons had brought their sheep down to the home farm from the upper pasture! She herself had seen them on the way to school, and like an idiot had not thought of Rollie. She had seen them grazing on the river meadow.

She was off like a racer at the crack of the starting pistol, her long, strong legs stretched in great leaps, her pigtails flying. She took the short cut down to the upper edge of the meadow, regardless of the brambles. Their thorn-spiked, wiry stems tore at her flesh, but she did not care. She welcomed the pain. It was something she was doing for Rollie, for her Rollie.

She was tearing through the pine woods now, rushing down the steep, stony path, tripping over roots, half-falling, catching herself just in time, not slackening her speed. She burst out on the open knoll above the river meadow, calling wildly, "Rollie, here, Rollie, here, boy! here! here!" She tried to whistle, but she was crying too hard to pucker her lips. She had not, till then, known she was crying.

There was nobody to see or hear her. Twilight was falling over the bare knoll. The sunless evening wind slid down the mountain like an invisible river, engulfing her in cold. Her teeth began to chatter. "Here, Rollie, here boy, here!" She strained her eyes to look down into the meadow to see if the sheep were there. She could not be sure. She stopped calling him as if he were a dog, and called out his name despairingly, as if he were her child, "Rollie! oh, *Rollie*, where are you!"

The tears ran down her cheeks in streams. She sobbed loudly, terribly. Since there was no one to hear, she did not try to control herself. "Hou! hou! hou!" she sobbed, her face contorted grotesquely. "Oh, Rollie! Rollie! Rollie!" She had wanted something to cry about. Oh, how terribly now she had something to cry about.

She saw him as clearly as if he were there beside her, his muzzle and gaping mouth all smeared with the betraying blood (like the Wilsons' collie). "But he didn't *know* it was wrong!" she screamed like a wild creature. "Nobody *told* him it was wrong. It was my fault. I should have taken better care of him. I will now. I will!"

But no matter how she screamed, she could not make herself heard. In the cold gathering darkness, she saw him stand, poor, guiltless victim of his ignorance, who should have been protected from his own nature, his soft eyes looking at her with love, his splendid plumed tail waving gently. "It was my fault. I promised I would bring him up. I should have *made* him stay at home. I was responsible for him. It was my fault."

But she could not make his executioners hear her. The shot rang out, Rollie sank down, his beautiful liquid eyes glazed, the blood spurting from the hole in his head—like the Wilsons' collie. She gave a wild shriek, long, soul-satisfying, frantic. It was the scream at sudden, unendurable tragedy of a mature, full-blooded woman. It drained dry

the girl of thirteen. She came to herself. She was standing on the knoll, trembling and quaking with cold, the darkness closing in on her.

Her breath had given out. For once in her life she had wept all the tears there were in her body. Her hands were so stiff with cold she could scarcely close them. How her nose was running! Simply streaming down her upper lip. And she had no handkerchief. She lifted her skirt, fumbled for her slip, stopped, blew her nose on it, wiped her eyes, drew a long quavering breath—and heard something! Far off in the distance, a faint sound, like a dog's muffled bark.

She whirled on her heels and bent her head to listen. The sound did not come from the meadow below the knoll. It came from back of her higher up, from the Wilsons' maple grove. She held her breath. Yes, it came from there.

She began to run again, but now she was not sobbing. She was silent, absorbed in her effort to cover ground. If she could only live to get there, to see if it really were Rollie. She ran steadily till she came to the fence and went over this in a great plunge. Her skirt caught on a nail. She impatiently pulled at it, not hearing or not heeding the long sibilant tear as it came loose. She was in the dusky maple woods, stumbling over the rocks as she ran. As she tore on up the slope, she heard the bark again, and knew it was Rollie's.

She stopped short and leaned weakly against a tree. She was sick with the breathlessness of her straining lungs, sick in the reaction of relief, sick with anger at Rollie, who had been here having a wonderful time while she had been dying, just dying in terror about him.

For she could now not only hear that it was Rollie's bark. She could hear, in the dog language she knew as well as he, what he was saying in those excited yips—that he had run a woodchuck into a hole in the tumbled stone wall, that he almost had him, that the intoxicating wild-animal smell was as close to him—almost—as if he had his jaws on his quarry. Yip! Woof! Yip! Yip!

The wildly joyful quality of the dog-talk enraged the girl. She had been trembling in exhaustion. Now it was indignation. So that was where he had been—when *she* was *killing* herself trying to take care of him. Plenty near enough if he had paid attention to hear her calling and whistling to him. Just so set on having his foolish good time, he never thought to listen for her call.

She stooped to pick up a stout stick. She would teach him. She was hot with anger. It was time he had something to make him remember to listen. She started forward on a run.

But after a few steps she stopped, stood thinking. One of the things to remember about collies, everybody knew that, was that a collie who had been beaten was never "right" again. His spirit was broken. "Anything but a broken-spirited collie," she had often heard a farmer say that. They were no good after that.

She threw down her stick. Anyhow, she thought, he was really too young to know that he had done wrong. He was still only a puppy. Like all puppies, he got perfectly crazy over wild-animal smells. Probably he truly hadn't heard her calling and whistling.

All the same, all the same—she stood stock-still, staring intently into the twilight—you couldn't let a puppy grow up just as he wanted to. It wouldn't be safe—for *him*. Somehow she would have to make him understand that he mustn't go off this way, by himself. He must be trained to know how to do what a good dog does—not because *she* wanted to, but for his own sake.

She walked on now, steady, purposeful, gathering her inner strength together, Olympian[1] in her understanding of the full meaning of the event.

When he heard his own special young god approaching, he turned delightedly and ran to meet her, panting, his tongue hanging out. His eyes shone. He jumped up on her in an ecstasy of welcome and licked her face.

She pushed him away. Her face and voice were grave. "No, Rollie, *no!*" she said severely, "you're *bad*. You know you're not to go off in the woods without me! You are—a—*bad—dog*."

He was horrified. Stricken into misery. He stood facing her, frozen. The gladness went out of his eyes, the waving plume of his tail slowly lowered to slinking, guilty dejection.

"I know you were all wrapped up in that woodchuck. But that's no excuse. You *could* have heard me, calling you, whistling for you, if you'd paid attention," she went on. "You've got to learn, and I've got to teach you."

With a shudder of misery he lay down, his tail stretched out limp on the ground, his head flat on his paws, his ears drooping—ears ringing with the doomsday awfulness of the voice he loved and revered. To have it speak so to him, he must have been utterly wicked. He trembled, he turned his head away from her august look of blame, he groveled[2] in remorse for whatever mysterious sin he had committed.

As miserable as he, she sat down by him. "I don't *want* to scold you. But I have to! I have to bring you up right, or you'll get shot, Rollie. You mustn't go away from the house without me, do you hear, *never.*"

His sharp ears, yearning for her approval, caught a faint over-tone of relenting affection in her voice. He lifted his eyes to her, humbly, soft in imploring fondness.

"Oh, Rollie!" she said, stooping low over him, "I *do* love you. I do. But I *have* to bring you up. I'm responsible for you, don't you see."

He did not see. Hearing sternness, or something else he did not recognize, in the beloved voice, he shut his eyes tight in sorrow, and made a little whimpering lament in his throat.

She had never heard him cry before. It was too much. She sat down by him and drew his head to her, rocking him in her arms, soothing him with inarticulate[3] small murmurs.

He leaped in her arms and wriggled happily as he had when he was a baby; he reached up to lick her face as he had then. But he was no baby now. He was half as big as she, a great, warm, pulsing, living armful of love. She clasped him closely. Her heart was brimming full, but calmed, quiet. The blood flowed in equable gentleness all over her body. She was deliciously warm. Her nose was still running, a little. She sniffed and wiped it on her sleeve.

It was almost dark now. "We'll be late to supper, Rollie," she said, responsibly. Pushing him gently off she stood up. "Home, Rollie, home."

Here was a command he could understand. At once he trotted along the path

---

1 **Olympian** (ō lim' pē ən): polite and gracious, but in a lofty, aloof way.
2 **groveled** (gruv' əld): cringed; crawled.

3 **inarticulate** (in är tik' yə lit): sounds that have no meaning; meaningless.

towards home. His tail, held high, waved plumelike. His short dog-memory had forgotten the suffering just back of him.

Her human memory was longer. His prancing gait was as carefree as a young child's. She plodded behind him like a serious adult. Her very shoulders seemed bowed by what she had lived through. She felt, she thought, like an old, old woman of thirty. But it was all right now, she knew she had made an impression on him.

When they came out into the open pasture, Rollie ran back to get her to play with him. He leaped around her in circles, barking in cheerful yawps, jumping up on her, inviting her to run a race with him, to throw him a stick, to come alive.

His high spirits were ridiculous. But infectious. She gave one little leap to match his. Rollie took this as a threat, a pretend, play-threat. He planted his forepaws low and barked loudly at her, laughing between yips. He was so funny, she thought, when he grinned that way. She laughed back, and gave another mock-threatening leap at him. Radiant that his sky was once more clear, he sprang high on his steel-spring muscles in an explosion of happiness, and bounded in circles around her.

Following him, not noting in the dusk where she was going, she felt the grassy slope drop steeply. Oh, yes, she knew where she was. They had come to the rolling-down hill just back of the house. All the kids rolled down there, even the little ones, because it was soft grass without a stone. She had rolled down that slope a million times—years and years before, when she was a kid herself, six or seven years ago. It was fun. She remembered well the whirling dizziness of the descent, all the world turning crazily over and over. And the delicious giddy staggering when you first stood up, the earth still spinning under your feet.

"All right, Rollie, let's go," she cried, and flung herself down in the rolling position, her arms straight up over her head.

Rollie had never seen this skylarking before. It threw him into almost hysterical amusement. He capered around the rapidly rolling figure, half scared, mystified, enchanted.

His wild, frolicsome barking might have come from her own throat, so accurately did it sound the way she felt—crazy, foolish—like a little kid, no more than five years old, the age she had been when she had last rolled down that hill.

At the bottom she sprang up, on muscles as steel-strong as Rollie's. She staggered a little, and laughed aloud.

The living-room windows were just before them. How yellow lighted windows looked when you were in the darkness going home. How nice and yellow. Maybe Mother had waffles for supper. She was a swell cook, Mother was, and she certainly gave her family all the breaks, when it came to meals.

"Home, Rollie, home!" She burst open the door to the living room. "Hi, Mom, what you got for supper?"

From the kitchen her mother announced coolly, "I hate to break the news to you, but it's waffles."

"Oh, *Mom*!" she shouted in ecstasy.

Her mother could not see her. She did not need to. "For goodness' sakes, go and wash," she called.

In the long mirror across the room she saw herself, her hair hanging wild, her long bare legs scratched, her broadly smiling face dirt-streaked, her torn skirt dangling, her dog laughing up at her. Gosh, was it a relief to feel your own age, just exactly thirteen years old.

1. Why is Peg alarmed when she cannot find Rollie? Why doesn't he hear her calling him?
2. Peg's parents want her to be a responsible person. In what way does Peg show that she has assumed responsibility for Rollie?
3. While Peg is searching for Rollie, she picks up a stick. Why, in your opinion, does she do that? Then, just a moment later, she throws it away. Why?
4. Peg is thirteen years old. In what places in the story does she feel thirty years old? five years old? What situation in each instance makes her feel as she does?
5. At the beginning of the story, how does Peg feel about her parents? After her alarm at the possibility of losing Rollie, Peg's attitude toward her parents changes. How does it change? Why does it change?
6. What is an "apprentice"? In what way can Peg be considered an apprentice?

Writer's Craft

Chances are that you are often asked what you think of someone. At such times, you pick out the person's traits and characteristics that have impressed you, and you describe him or her in terms of these traits. You are, in effect, CHARACTERIZING that person. All good story writers do the same thing. That is, they let you know what kind of persons their characters are. One good way of doing so is to show you what the characters think, say, and do. In "The Apprentice," for example, you read this passage:

> She strained her eyes to look down into the meadow to see if the sheep were there. She could not be sure. She stopped calling him as if he were a dog, and called out his name despairingly, as if he were her child, "Rollie! oh, *Rollie,* where are you!"

In this passage, the author is showing you that Peg is a very anxious, almost desperate person who thinks she may have lost a pet that she loves very much. It is through CHARACTERIZATION like this that you come to understand the kind of person a story character is.

1. What seems to play the most important part in the author's characterization of Peg? Why?
2. Point out three things that Peg does that help to show you the kind of person she is.

Composition

1. In "The Apprentice," the author shows you what Peg thinks, says, and does. In your opinion, is Peg a convincing thirteen-year-old? Write a brief composition in which you agree or disagree that the author has made Peg seem like a true-to-life thirteen-year-old girl. Support your opinion with examples from the story. Make each sentence support the stand you take. Conclude your composition by reaffirming the position you have taken.

2. At the beginning of "The Apprentice," you know that Peg resents the way her parents lecture her about assuming responsibility. Later, events make her wish that she had been more attentive to her parents' wishes. Tell about an incident in your own life when you didn't follow your parents' wishes (or the wishes of another adult), but later wished you had. Explain what you had been asked to do. Tell what you did that was not what you had been asked to do. Describe briefly how that situation made you feel. End your composition by explaining what you learned from the experience.

Dorothy Canfield Fisher 1879–1958

Dorothy Canfield Fisher effectively combined her dedications to scholarship, human causes, and her own family life.

When she was ten, Fisher spent a year in Paris and learned to speak French fluently. She later earned a doctorate in French, but her interest in the French people went beyond studies. During World War I she wrote to a friend, "I cannot bear this sitting off in a safe corner any longer." She and her husband and two children left Vermont to add their energies to the resistance in France. While her husband worked in the ambulance service, Fisher organized a Braille print shop and managed a home for sick children in southern France. After the war, she helped organize the Children's Crusade for Children. Under this program, children in the United States collected pennies for the child war victims in Europe.

Later, Fisher worked for children's rights and urged other women to use the power gained with the newly won voting privilege. She wrote books about education and became the first woman elected to the Vermont board of education.

FOX HUNT *Winslow Homer*

For a pet fox, Bandit had earned himself quite a reputation. Could it be that his name was responsible?

Last Cover

PAUL ANNIXTER

I'M NOT SURE I can tell you what you want to know about my brother; but everything about the pet fox is important, so I'll tell all that from the beginning.

It goes back to a winter afternoon after I'd hunted the woods all day for a sign of our lost pet. I remember the way my mother looked up as I came into the kitchen. Without my speaking, she knew what had happened. For six hours I had walked, reading signs, looking for a delicate print in the damp soil or even a hair that might have told of a red fox passing that way—but I had found nothing.

"Did you go up in the foothills?" Mom asked.

I nodded. My face was stiff from held-back tears. My brother, Colin, who was going on twelve, got it all from one look at me and went into a heartbroken, almost silent, crying.

Three weeks before, Bandit, the pet fox Colin and I had raised from a tiny kit, had disappeared, and not even a rumor had been heard of him since.

"He'd have had to go off soon anyway," Mom comforted. "A big, lolloping fellow like him, he's got to live his life same as us. But he may come back. That fox set a lot of store by you boys in spite of his wild ways."

"He set a lot of store by our food, any-way," Father said. He sat in a chair by the kitchen window mending a piece of harness. "We'll be seeing a lot more of that fellow, never fear. That fox learned to pine for table scraps and young chickens. He was getting to be an egg thief, too, and he's not likely to forget that."

"That was only pranking when he was little," Colin said desperately.

From the first, the tame fox had made tension in the family. It was Father who said we'd better name him Bandit, after he'd made away with his first young chicken.

"Maybe you know," Father said shortly. "But when an animal turns to egg sucking he's usually incurable. He'd better not come pranking around my chicken run again."

It was late February, and I remember the bleak, dead cold that had set in, cold that was a rare thing for our Carolina hills. Flocks of sparrows and snowbirds had appeared to peck hungrily at all that the pigs and chickens didn't eat.

"This one's a killer," Father would say of a morning, looking out at the whitened barn roof. "This one will make the shoats squeal."

A fire snapped all day in our cookstove and another in the stone fireplace in the living room, but still the farmhouse was never warm. The leafless woods were bleak and empty, and I spoke of that to Father when I came back from my search.

"It's always a sad time in the woods when the seven sleepers are under cover," he said.

"What sleepers are they?" I asked. Father was full of woods lore.

"Why, all the animals that have got sense enough to hole up and stay hid in weather like this. Let's see, how was it the old rhyme named them?

Surly bear and sooty bat,
Brown chuck and masked coon,
Chippy-munk and sly skunk,
And all the mouses
'Cept in men's houses.

"And man would have joined them and made it eight, Granther Yeary always said, if he'd had a little more sense."

"I was wondering if the red fox mightn't make it eight," Mom said.

Father shook his head. "Late winter's a high time for foxes. Time when they're out deviling, not sleeping."

My chest felt hollow. I wanted to cry like Colin over our lost fox, but at fourteen a boy doesn't cry. Colin had squatted down on the floor and got out his small hammer and nails to start another new frame for a new picture. Maybe then he'd make a drawing for the frame and be able to forget his misery. It had been that way with him since he was five.

I thought of the new dress Mom had brought home a few days before in a heavy cardboard box. That box cover would be fine for Colin to draw on. I spoke of it, and Mom's glance thanked me as she went to get it. She and I worried a lot about Colin. He was small for his age, delicate and blond, his hair much lighter and softer than mine, his eyes deep and wide and blue. He was often sick, and I knew the fear Mom had that he might be predestined.[1] I'm just ordinary, like Father. I'm the sort of stuff that can take it—tough and strong—but Colin was always sort of special.

Mom lighted the lamp. Colin began cutting his white cardboard carefully, fitting it into his frame. Father's sharp glance turned on him now and again.

"There goes the boy making another frame before there's a picture for it," he said. "It's too much like cutting out a man's suit for a fellow that's say, twelve years old. Who knows whether he'll grow into it?"

Mom was into him then, quick. "Not a single frame of Colin's has ever gone to waste. The boy has real talent, Sumter, and it's time you realized it."

"Of course he has," Father said. "All kids have 'em. But they get over 'em."

"It isn't the pox[2] we're talking of," Mom sniffed.

"In a way it is. Ever since you started talking up Colin's art, I've had an invalid for help around the place."

Father wasn't as hard as he made out, I knew, but he had to hold a balance against all Mom's frothing. For him the thing was the land and all that pertained to it. I was following in Father's footsteps, true to form, but Colin threatened to break the family tradition with his leaning toward art, with Mom "aiding and abetting him," as Father liked to put it. For the past two years she had had dreams of my brother becoming a real artist and going away to the city to study.

---

1 **predestined** (prē des′ tənd): here, intended by fate for early death.
2 **pox** (päks): chicken pox.

It wasn't that Father had no understanding of such things. I could remember, through the years, Colin lying on his stomach in the front room making pencil sketches, and how a good drawing would catch Father's eye halfway across the room, and how he would sometimes gather up two or three of them to study, frowning and muttering, one hand in his beard, while a great pride rose in Colin, and in me too. Most of Colin's drawings were of the woods and wild things, and there Father was a master critic. He made out to scorn what seemed to him a passive "white-livered" interpretation of nature through brush and pencil instead of rod and rifle.

At supper that night Colin could scarcely eat. Ever since he'd been able to walk, my brother had had a growing love of wild things, but Bandit had been like his very own, a gift of the woods. One afternoon a year and a half before, Father and Laban Small had been running a vixen through the hills with their dogs. With the last of her strength the she-fox had made for her den, not far from our house. The dogs had over-taken her and killed her just before she reached it. When Father and Laban came up, they'd found Colin crouched nearby, holding her cub in his arms.

Father had been for killing the cub, which was still too young to shift for itself, but Colin's grief had brought Mom into it. We'd taken the young fox into the kitchen, all of us, except Father, gone a bit silly over the little thing. Colin had held it in his arms and fed it warm milk from a spoon.

"Watch out with all your soft ways," Father had warned, standing in the doorway. "You'll make too much of him. Remember, you can't make a dog out of a fox. Half of that little critter has to love, but the other half is a wild hunter. You boys will mean a whole lot to him while he's kit, but there'll come a day when you won't mean a thing to him and he'll leave you shorn."

For two weeks after that Colin had nursed the cub, weaning it from milk to bits of meat. For a year they were always together. The cub grew fast. It was soon following Colin and me about the barnyard. It turned out to be a patch fox, with a saddle of darker fur across its shoulders.

I haven't the words to tell you what the fox meant to us. It was far more wonderful owning him than owning any dog. There was something rare and secret like the spirit of the woods about him, and back of his calm, straw-gold eyes was the sense of a brain the equal of a man's. The fox became Colin's whole life.

Each day, going and coming from school, Colin and I took long side trips through the woods, looking for Bandit. Wild things' memories were short, we knew; we'd have to find him soon or the old bond would be broken.

Ever since I was ten I'd been allowed to hunt with Father, so I was good at reading signs. But, in a way, Colin knew more about the woods and wild things than Father or me. What came to me from long observation, Colin seemed to know by instinct.

It was Colin who felt out, like an Indian, the stretch of woods where Bandit had his den, who found the first slim, small fox-print in the damp earth. And then, on an afternoon in March, we saw him. I remember the day well, the racing clouds, the wind rattling the tops of the pine trees and swaying the Spanish moss. Bandit had just come out of a clump of laurel; in the maze of leaves behind him we caught a glimpse of a slim red vixen, so we knew he had found a mate. She melted from sight like a shadow, but Bandit turned to watch us, his mouth open, his tongue lolling as he smiled his old foxy smile. On his thin chops, I saw a telltale chicken feather.

Colin moved silently forward, his movements so quiet and casual he seemed to be standing still. He called Bandit's name, and the fox held his ground, drawn to us with all his senses. For a few moments he let Colin actually put an arm about him. It was then I knew that he loved us still, for all of Father's warnings. He really loved us back, with a fierce, secret love no tame thing ever gave. But the urge of his life just then was toward his new mate. Suddenly, he whirled about and disappeared in the laurels.

Colin looked at me with glowing eyes. "We haven't really lost him, Stan. When he gets through with his spring sparking he may come back. But we've got to show ourselves to him a lot, so he won't forget."

"It's a go," I said.

"Promise not to say a word to Father," Colin said, and I agreed. For I knew by the chicken feather that Bandit had been up to no good.

A week later the woods were budding and the thickets were rustling with all manner of wild things scurrying on the love scent. Colin managed to get a glimpse of Bandit every few days. He couldn't get close though, for the spring running was a lot more important to a fox than any human beings were.

Every now and then Colin got out his framed box cover and looked at it, but he never drew anything on it; he never even picked up his pencil. I remember wondering if what Father had said about framing a picture before you had one had spoiled something for him.

I was helping Father with the planting now, but Colin managed to be in the woods every day. By degrees he learned Bandit's range, where he drank and rested and where he was likely to be according to the time of day. One day he told me how he had petted Bandit again, and how they had walked together a long way in the woods. All this time we had kept his secret from Father.

As summer came on, Bandit began to live up to the prediction Father had made. Accustomed to human beings, he moved without fear about the scattered farms of the region, raiding barns and hen runs that other foxes wouldn't have dared go near. And he taught his wild mate to do the same. Almost every night they got into some poultry house, and by late June Bandit was not only killing chickens and ducks but feeding on eggs and young chicks whenever he got the chance.

Stories of his doings came to us from many sources, for he was still easily recognized by the dark patch on his shoulders. Many a farmer took a shot at him as he fled and some of them set out on his trail with dogs, but they always returned home without even sighting him. Bandit was familiar with all the dogs in the region, and he knew a hundred tricks to confound them. He got a reputation that year beyond that of any fox our hills had known. His confidence grew, and he gave up wild hunting altogether and lived entirely off the poultry farmers. By September the hill farmers banded together to hunt him down.

It was Father who brought home that news one night. All time-honored rules of the fox chase were to be broken in this hunt; if the dogs couldn't bring Bandit down, he was to be shot on sight. I was stricken and furious. I remember the misery of Colin's face in the lamplight. Father, who took pride in all the ritual of the hunt, had refused to be a party to such an affair, though in justice he could do nothing but sanction[3] any sort of hunt, for Bandit, as old Sam Wetherwax put it, had been "purely getting in the Lord's hair."

The hunt began next morning, and it was the biggest turnout our hills had known. There were at least twenty mounted men in the party and as many dogs. Father and I were working in the lower field as they passed along the river road. Most of the hunters carried rifles, and they looked ugly.

Twice during the morning I went up to the house to find Colin, but he was nowhere around. As we worked, Father and I could follow the progress of the hunt by the distant hound music on the breeze. We could tell just where the hunters first caught sight of the fox and where Bandit was leading the dogs during the first hour. We knew as well as if we'd seen it how Bandit roused another fox along Turkey Branch and forced it to run for him, and how the dogs swept after it for twenty minutes before they sensed their mistake.

Noon came, and Colin had not come in to eat. After dinner Father didn't go back to the field. He moped about, listening to the hound talk. He didn't like what was on any more than I did, and now and again I caught his smile of satisfaction when we heard the broken, angry notes of the hunting horn, telling that the dogs had lost the trail or had run another fox.

I was restless, and I went up into the hills in midafternoon. I ranged the woods for miles, thinking all the time of Colin. Time lost all meaning for me, and the short day was nearing an end, when I heard the horn talking again, telling that the fox had put over another trick. All day he had deviled the

dogs and mocked the hunters. This new trick and the coming night would work to save him. I was wildly glad, as I moved down toward Turkey Branch and stood listening for a time by the deep, shaded pool where for years we boys had gone swimming, sailed boats, and dreamed summer dreams.

Suddenly, out of the corner of my eye, I saw the sharp ears and thin, pointed mask of a fox—in the water almost beneath me. It was Bandit, craftily submerged there, all but his head, resting in the cool water of the pool and the shadow of the two big beeches that spread above it. He must have run forty miles or more since morning. And he must have hidden in this place before. His knowing, crafty mask blended perfectly with the shadows and a mass of drift and branches that had collected by the bank of the pool. He was so still that a pair of thrushes flew up from the spot as I came up, not knowing he was there.

Bandit's bright, harried[4] eyes were looking

---

3 **sanction** (sangk' shən): approve.

4 **harried** (har' ēd): worried; tormented.

right at me. But I did not look at him direct. Some woods instinct, swifter than thought, kept me from it. So he and I met as in another world, indirectly, with feeling but without sign or greeting.

Suddenly I saw that Colin was standing almost beside me. Silently as a water snake, he had come out of the bushes and stood there. Our eyes met, and a quick and secret smile passed between us. It was a rare moment in which I really "met" my brother, when something of his essence flowed into me and I knew all of him. I've never lost it since.

My eyes still turned from the fox, my heart pounding. I moved quietly away, and Colin moved with me. We whistled softly as we went, pretending to busy ourselves along the bank of the stream. There was magic in it, as if by will we wove a web of protection about the fox, a ring-pass-not that none might penetrate. It was so, too, we felt, in the brain of Bandit, and that doubled the charm. To us he was still our little pet that we had carried about in our arms on countless summer afternoons.

Two hundred yards upstream, we stopped beside slim, fresh tracks in the mud where Bandit had entered the branch. The tracks angled upstream. But in the water the wily creature had turned down.

We climbed the far bank to wait, and Colin told me how Bandit's secret had been his secret ever since an afternoon three months before, when he'd watched the fox swim downstream to hide in the deep pool. Today he'd waited on the bank, feeling that Bandit, hard pressed by the dogs, might again seek the pool for sanctuary.

We looked back once as we turned homeward. He still had not moved. We didn't know until later that he was killed that same night by a chance hunter, as he crept out from his hiding place.

That evening Colin worked a long time on his framed box cover that had lain about the house untouched all summer. He kept at it all the next day too. I had never seen him work so hard. I seemed to sense in the air the feeling he was putting into it, how he was *believing* his picture into being. It was evening before he finished it. Without a word he handed it to Father. Mom and I went and looked over his shoulder.

It was a delicate and intricate pencil drawing of the deep branch pool, and there was Bandit's head and watching, fear-filled eyes hiding there amid the leaves and shadows, woven craftily into the maze of twigs and branches, as if by nature's art itself. Hardly a fox there at all, but the place where he was—or should have been. I recognized it instantly, but Mom gave a sort of incredulous sniff.

"I'll declare," she said, "it's mazy as a puzzle. It just looks like a lot of sticks and leaves to me."

Long minutes of study passed before Father's eye picked out the picture's secret, as few men's could have done. I laid that to Father's being a born hunter. That was a picture that might have been done especially for him. In fact, I guess it was.

Finally he turned to Colin with his deep, slow smile. "So that's how Bandit fooled them all," he said. He sat holding the picture with a sort of tenderness for a long time, while we glowed in the warmth of the shared secret. That was Colin's moment. Colin's art stopped being a pox to Father right there. And later, when the time came for Colin to go to art school, it was Father who was his solid backer.

1. How does Bandit fool the hunters and their dogs?

2. How does it happen that Colin and Stan had a fox for a pet? What is their father's attitude toward the animal? How does Bandit prove different from the kind of pet a dog would have been?

3. What talent does Colin have? What is unusual about the way in which he uses that talent? Who encourages him most? How does his father's feeling about Colin's talent change?

4. What is the setting of the story? What evidence is there that the author knows a good deal about nature?

5. How does Colin's father find out about the way Bandit fooled the hunters and their dogs? What is the result of his discovery?

Writer's Craft

You know that one good way in which an author CHARACTERIZES a person in a story is to show you what that person thinks, says, and does. Another effective way is to let you know *what other characters in the story say about that person.*

For example, in "The Strangers That Came to Town," Andy makes this remark about his father:

> "I guessed that Father was secretly proud of our fortitude and I realized, too, that all through the night he had suffered with us."

From this remark, you gain some insight into the kind of person Andy's father is. The author's CHARACTERIZATION in this case is based on what one person in the story says *about* another person.

1. In "Last Cover," who tells the story? Why is he a good person to tell the story?

2. Though Bandit is an important character in the story, who is really the central character? Though you learn some things about the central character from what he says and does, most of what you know comes from what the narrator says about him. Find at least three places in the story where the narrator's remarks reveal the kind of person the main character is.

3 PLOT AND CHARACTER

Discussion

1. Read this short, short story; then answer the questions following it.

Muddy Road

ANONYMOUS

Tanzan and Ekido were once traveling together down a muddy road. A heavy rain was still falling.

Coming around a bend, they met a lovely girl in a silk kimono and sash, unable to cross the intersection.

"Come on, girl," said Tanzan at once. Lifting her in his arms, he carried her over the mud.

Ekido did not speak again until that night when they reached a lodging temple. Then he no longer could restrain himself. "We monks don't go near females," he told Tanzan, "especially not young and lovely ones. It is dangerous. Why did you do that?"

"I left the girl there," said Tanzan. "Are you still carrying her?"

   a. What events make up the plot of the story? Make sure you identify them in their proper order.

   b. Who are the characters in the story?

   c. What conflict do you find in the story? Would you characterize that conflict as one between one person and another or between a person and nature?

   d. What is the setting of the story? How does that setting influence the characters and what they do?

   e. What motivation do the two characters have for what they do?

   f. What kind of person is Tanzan? What basis do you have for your answer? What kind of person is Ekido? What basis do you have for your answer this time?

   g. Where does the climax of "Muddy Road" occur?

2. Identify the main conflict in each of the following selections: "The Sea Devil," "The Inspiration of Mr. Budd," "The Street of the Three Crosses," and "The Strangers That Came to Town." What kind of conflict is there in each story?

3. In your opinion, which one of the stories in this unit was the most suspenseful? Why?

4. In which stories does the setting have an important role in influencing the characters and the action?

5. In which stories did emphasis seem to be on the plot? In which stories did the emphasis seem to be on the characters rather than on the events? Be prepared to defend your answers.

Composition

1. At least six of the stories in this unit have to do with life within families. ("The Sea Devil" and "The Inspiration of Mr. Budd" are the two stories not mainly concerned with families.) Of which one of the families you've met in this unit would you like most to be a member? In a composition of about one page, identify that family, and then explain briefly why you find that family so appealing.

2. Conflict, as you know, constitutes the basis for the plot of every good story. *Write a brief story* (try to make it as brief as "Muddy Road") *about a conflict in which you were involved*. Perhaps you had a disagreement with someone in your family over which TV program to watch. Or perhaps you had planned to go on a picnic, only to have a downpour spoil your plans. First, identify the situation that produced the conflict. Next, show how the conflict developed toward a climax. Finally, describe the way the conflict was resolved.

4

RIBBON WITH SQUARES *Vasily Kandinsky* 1944 Collection, the Solomon R. Guggenheim Museum

The Art of Storytelling

THE ART OF STORYTELLING

Plot, character, setting—these are the essential ingredients of any story. Yet every storyteller must concern herself or himself with many other matters: If, for example, he or she wants the characters in a story to act like real people rather than like fairy-tale heroes and heroines, he or she must make it clear why those characters behave as they do. Or if a storyteller wants readers or listeners to feel a certain way about the characters or the events in a tale, he or she must choose words that will arouse the desired feeling. Or if a storyteller has something important to say about people in general or about life, he or she must make sure that everything in the story—the plot, the characters, the setting, what the characters say and do—contributes to that central idea, or theme.

To accomplish these and other purposes, the expert storyteller—like people skilled in other crafts—uses special devices (tools) and special techniques (procedures). Their effective use helps him or her make the story unforgettable. In fact, it is through their effective use that the expert storyteller makes storytelling an art.

Mad? Why would anyone think he was mad? Hadn't he planned so carefully—and moved so cautiously? But best of all, there was no trace!—Or was there?

The Telltale Heart

EDGAR ALLAN POE

TRUE!—NERVOUS—very, very dreadfully nervous I had been and am; but why *will* you say that I am mad? The disease had sharpened my senses—not destroyed—not dulled them. Above all was the sense of hearing acute. I heard all things in the heaven and in the earth. I heard many things in hell. How, then, am I mad? Hearken! and observe how healthily—how calmly I can tell you the whole story.

It is impossible to say how first the idea entered my brain; but once conceived, it haunted me day and night. Object there was none. Passion there was none. I loved the old man. He had never wronged me. He had never given me insult. For his gold I had no desire. I think it was his eye! yes, it was this! One of his eyes resembled that of a vulture—a pale blue eye, with a film over it. Whenever it fell upon me, my blood ran cold; and so by degrees—very gradually—I made up my mind to take the life of the old man, and thus rid myself of the eye forever.

Now this is the point. You fancy me mad. Madmen know nothing. But you should have seen *me*. You should have seen how wisely I proceeded—with what caution—with what foresight—with what dissimulation[1] I went to work! I was never kinder to the old man than during the whole week before I killed him. And every night, about midnight, I turned the latch of his door and opened it—oh, so gently! And then, when I had made an opening sufficient for my head, I put in a dark lantern, all closed, closed, so that no light shone out, and then I thrust in my head. Oh, you would have laughed to see how cunningly I thrust it in! I moved it slowly—very, very slowly, so that I might not disturb the old man's sleep. It took me an hour to place my whole head within the opening so far that I could see him as he lay upon his bed. Ha!—would a madman have been so wise as this? And then, when my head was well in the room, I undid the lantern cautiously—oh, so cautiously—cautiously (for the hinges creaked)—I undid it just so much that a single thin ray fell upon the vulture eye. And this I did for seven long

---

1 **dissimulation** (di sim yə lā' shən): deceit; deception; not indicating one's intentions.

nights—every night just at midnight—but I found the eye always closed; and so it was impossible to do the work; for it was not the old man who vexed me, but his Evil Eye. And every morning, when the day broke, I went boldly into the chamber, and spoke courageously to him, calling him by name in a hearty tone, and inquiring how he had passed the night. So you see he would have been a very profound old man, indeed, to suspect that every night, just at twelve, I looked in upon him while he slept.

Upon the eighth night I was more than usually cautious in opening the door. A watch's minute hand moves more quickly than did mine. Never before that night had I *felt* the extent of my own powers—of my sagacity.[2] I could scarcely contain my feelings of triumph. To think that there I was, opening the door, little by little, and he not even to dream of my secret deeds or thoughts. I fairly chuckled at the idea; and perhaps he heard me; for he moved on the bed suddenly, as if startled. Now you may think that I drew back—but no. His room was as black as pitch with the thick darkness (for the shutters were close fastened, through fear of robbers), and so I knew that he could not see the opening of the door, and I kept pushing it on steadily, steadily.

I had my head in, and was about to open the lantern, when my thumb slipped upon the tin fastening, and the old man sprang up in the bed, crying out—"Who's there?"

I kept quite still and said nothing. For a whole hour I did not move a muscle, and in the meantime I did not hear him lie down. He was still sitting up in the bed listening—just as I have done, night after night, hearkening to the death watches in the wall.

Presently I heard a slight groan, and I knew it was the groan of mortal terror. It was not a groan of pain or of grief—oh, no!—it was the low stifled sound that arises from the bottom of the soul when overcharged with awe. I knew the sound well. Many a night, just at midnight, when all the world slept, it has welled up from my own bosom, deepening, with its dreadful echo, the terrors that distracted me. I say I knew it well. I knew what the old man felt, and pitied him, although I chuckled at heart. I knew that he had been lying awake ever since the first slight noise, when he had turned in the bed. His fears had been ever since growing upon him. He had been trying to fancy them causeless, but could not. He had been saying to himself—"It is nothing but the wind in the chimney—it is only a mouse crossing the floor," or "it is merely a cricket which has made a single chirp." Yes, he has been trying to comfort himself with these suppositions; but he had found all in vain. *All in vain;*

2 **sagacity** (sə gas′ə tē): mental acuteness; shrewdness; cunning.

because Death, in approaching him, had stalked with his black shadow before him, and enveloped the victim. And it was the mournful influence of the unperceived[3] shadow that caused him to feel—although he neither saw nor heard—to *feel* the presence of my head within the room.

When I had waited a long time, very patiently, without hearing him lie down, I resolved to open a little—a very, very little crevice in the lantern. So I opened it—you cannot imagine how stealthily, stealthily—until, at length, a single dim ray, like the thread of the spider, shot from out of the crevice and full upon the vulture eye.

It was open—wide, wide open—and I grew furious as I gazed upon it. I saw it with perfect distinctness—all a dull blue, with a hideous veil over it that chilled the very marrow in my bones; but I could see nothing else of the old man's face or person: for I had directed the ray as if by instinct, precisely upon the damned spot.

And now have I not told you that what you mistake for madness is but over-acuteness of the senses?—now, I say, there came to my ears a low, dull, quick sound, such as a watch makes when enveloped in cotton. I knew *that* sound well too. It was the beating of the old man's heart. It increased my fury, as the beating of a drum stimulates the soldier into courage.

But even yet I refrained and kept still. I scarcely breathed. I held the lantern motionless. I tried how steadily I could maintain the ray upon the eye. Meantime the hellish tattoo[4] of the heart increased. It grew quicker and quicker, and louder and louder every instant. The old man's terror *must* have been

extreme! It grew louder, I say, louder every moment!—do you mark me well? I have told you that I am nervous: so I am. And now at the dead hour of the night, amid the dreadful silence of that old house, so strange a noise as this excited me to uncontrollable terror. Yet, for some minutes longer I refrained and stood still. But the beating grew louder, louder! I thought the heart must burst. And now a new anxiety seized me—the sound would be heard by a neighbor! The old man's hour had come! With a loud yell, I threw open the lantern and leaped into the room. He shrieked once—once only. In an instant I dragged him to the floor, and pulled the heavy bed over him. I then smiled gaily, to find the deed so far done. But, for many minutes, the heart beat on with a muffled sound. This, however, did not vex me; it would not be heard through the wall. At length it ceased. The old man was dead. I removed the bed and examined the corpse. Yes, he was stone, stone dead. I placed my hand upon the heart and held it there many minutes. There was no pulsation. He was stone dead. His eye would trouble me no more.

If still you think me mad, you will think so no longer when I describe the wise precautions I took for the concealment of the body. The night waned, and I worked hastily, but in silence. First of all I dismembered the corpse. I cut off the head and the arms and the legs.

I then took up three planks from the flooring of the chamber, and deposited all between the scantlings. I then replaced the boards so cleverly, so cunningly, that no human eye—not even *his*—could have detected anything wrong. There was nothing to wash out—no stain of any kind—no blood spot whatever. I had been too wary for that. A tub had caught all—ha! ha!

3 **unperceived** (un pėr sėvd'): not aware of through the senses; unseen.
4 **tattoo**: drumming.

When I had made an end of these labors, it was four o'clock—still dark as midnight. As the bell sounded the hour, there came a knocking at the street door. I went down to open it with a light heart—for what had I *now* to fear? There entered three men, who introduced themselves, with perfect suavity,[5] as officers of the police. A shriek had been heard by a neighbor during the night; suspicion of foul play had been aroused; information had been lodged at the police office, and they (the officers) had been deputed[6] to search the premises.

I smiled—for *what* had I to fear? I bade the gentlemen welcome. The shriek, I said, was my own in a dream. The old man, I mentioned, was absent in the country. I took my visitors all over the house. I bade them search—search *well.* I led them, at length, to *his* chamber. I showed them his treasures, secure, undisturbed. In the enthusiasm of my confidence, I brought chairs into the room, and desired them *here* to rest from their fatigues, while I myself, in the wild audacity of my perfect triumph, placed my own seat upon the very spot beneath which reposed the corpse of the victim.

The officers were satisfied. My *manner* had convinced them. I was singularly at ease.

---

5 **suavity** (swä′ və tē): smooth politeness.
6 **deputed** (də pyüt′ əd): assigned, appointed.

They sat, and while I answered cheerily, they chatted familiar things. But, ere long, I felt myself getting pale and wished them gone. My head ached, and I fancied a ringing in my ears: but still they sat and still chatted. The ringing became more distinct:—it continued and became more distinct: I talked more freely to get rid of the feeling: but it continued and gained definitiveness—until, at length, I found that the noise was *not* within my ears.

No doubt I now grew *very* pale;—but I talked more fluently,[7] and with a heightened voice. Yet the sound increased—and what could I do? It was *a low, dull, quick sound—such a sound as a watch makes when enveloped in cotton.* I gasped for breath—and yet the officers heard it not. I talked more quickly—more vehemently; but the noise steadily increased. I arose and argued about trifles, in a high key and with violent gesticulations,[8] but the noise steadily increased. Why *would* they not be gone? I paced the floor to and fro with heavy strides, as if excited to fury by the observation of the men—but the noise steadily increased. Oh God! what *could* I do? I foamed—I raved—I swore! I swung the chair upon which I had been sitting, and grated it upon the boards, but the noise arose over all and continually increased. It grew louder—louder—*louder!* And still the men chatted pleasantly, and smiled. Was it possible they heard not? Almighty God!—no, no! They heard!—they suspected!—they *knew!*—they were making a mockery of my horror!—this I thought, and this I think. But anything was better than this agony! Anything was more tolerable than this derision! I could bear those hypocritical smiles no longer! I felt that I must scream or die!—and now—again!—hark! louder! louder! louder! *louder!*—

"Villains!" I shrieked, "dissemble[9] no more! I admit the deed!—tear up the planks!—here, here!—it is the beating of his hideous heart!"

---

7 **fluently** (flü′ ənt lē): speaking easily and rapidly.
8 **gesticulations** (jə stik′ yə lā′ shənz): excited gestures.

9 **dissemble** (di sem′ bəl): hide one's true feelings; pretend.

Discussion

1. How is the murderer caught? Would you agree or disagree that, in effect, he gives himself away? Why? What part do the police play in solving the murder?

2. Why, in your opinion, does the narrator take the police to the old man's chamber?

3. Stating several times that the reader may think him a madman, the narrator asserts that he is not. In your opinion, is he a madman or isn't he? What evidence can you give to support your answer?

4. Why does the murderer show the police where he has hidden the body?

5. Where do you suppose the narrator—the "I"—is when he tells the story?

6. What is the setting of the story? Refer to specific phrases in the story to support your answer.

Here is a limerick that may or may not be familiar:

> A diner, while dining at Crewe,
> Found quite a large mouse in the stew.
>   Said the waiter, "Don't shout
>   And wave it about,
> Or the rest will be wanting one too!"

How does the limerick make you feel? Sad? Angry? Thoughtful? Amused? Jolly? How did the writer probably intend you to feel? If you replied "amused" or "jolly" to both questions, you're right. The writer is obviously having fun describing a situation that both you and he find humorous.

Now consider this passage from "Top Man":

> Cautiously, but with astounding rapidity, he edged along the rocks beside the cornice. There was a moment when his only support was an inch-wide ledge beneath his feet, another when there was nothing under his feet at all, and he supported himself wholly by his elbows and hands.

What feeling do you get from these sentences? Merriment? Gloom? Anxiety? Tension? What feeling did the writer no doubt hope you'd have? Obviously, one of anxiety and tension—even foreboding.

From these examples, you see that writers can create an *atmosphere* or a *feeling* that they want you, the reader, to share with them. Such an atmosphere or feeling is known as the MOOD of the story (or poem or play).

A story writer creates mood in several ways:

—by choosing an appropriate setting for his or her tale;
—by describing how things look and sound and feel and taste and smell;
—by selecting only those details that will trigger the intended responses in you, the reader.

It is in being aware of—in identifying—the mood of a story that you, the reader, can tune in on the writer's wave length.

1. How would you characterize the mood of "The Telltale Heart"? What specific words and phrases help establish that mood?

2. How does Poe's use of "light" and "dark" contribute to that mood?

3. How does the setting contribute to the mood?

4. Point out passages in the story where the use of sound—or the lack of it—contributes to the mood.

Composition

1. Write a brief character sketch of the narrator in "The Telltale Heart." In your sketch tell about the personality of the narrator. Is he clever? insane? criminal? devious? guilt-ridden? Be sure to cite evidence from the story to support what you say about him.

2. As you know from your discussion of previous selections and "The Telltale Heart," writers establish a mood for their stories. The story setting can contribute to the mood. Choose a particular mood you want to convey—tension? hostility? peacefulness? joy? Then develop and describe a story setting which reflects that mood. Use specific details of time and place. Do not describe a character. Write only a physical description of time and place.

Vocabulary

Now and then, everyone runs across a sentence that is not entirely clear because of one difficult word in it. When that happens to you, find a SYNONYM for the difficult word. Then re-read the sentence, thinking of that synonym. A synonym is a word that means approximately the same as another word. For example:

It is impossible to say how first the idea entered my brain; but once *conceived*, it haunted me day and night.

Context clues—hints about a word's meaning—which surround *conceived* will tell you this: A synonym for *conceived* is *formed* or *thought of*. By replacing *conceived* with a synonym, you can remove any doubt as to the meaning of the sentence.

A. In the groups of words below, *italics* call attention to difficult words that have already been replaced by synonyms. Look back through "The Telltale Heart," and find the original word Edgar Allan Poe used for each of these synonyms. Then, on a separate sheet of paper, write both the synonym and Poe's original word. Write each answer this way:

formed—conceived

1. *Purpose* there was none. *Feeling* there was none. I loved the old man.

2. Oh, you should have seen how *slyly* I *pushed* (the lantern) in!

3. So you see he would have been a very *wise* old man, indeed, to suspect . . .

4. . . . It was the low stifled sound that arises from the bottom of the soul when *overflowing* with *dread.*

5. Yes, he had been trying to comfort himself with these *theories.*

B. In this exercise, you make the substitutions. Use context clues, or, if necessary, use the glossary or a dictionary. This time, write Poe's original word first, and then write a synonym after it.

1. I *resolved* to open a little—a very, very little *crevice* in the lantern.

2. There was no *pulsation.*

3. The night *waned,* and I worked hastily, and in silence.

4. I took up three planks from the flooring of the chamber and *deposited* all between the *scantlings.*

5. . . . I myself, in the wild *audacity* of my pefect triumph, placed my own seat upon the very spot beneath which *reposed* the corpse of the victim.

Edgar Allan Poe 1809—1849

Edgar Allan Poe was the son of traveling actors who died when he was two. Mr. and Mrs. John Allan of Virginia took Poe into their home, and he added their name to his. Poe's adult life was a series of misadventures and tragedies. He attended the University of Virginia and West Point, both briefly. He married a young cousin, Virginia Clemm, who died ten years later. Despite his hard work as an editor and writer, Poe lived in poverty and worry about the future. Although he reacted violently to alcohol, he often abused it. The horrors and fears which have made his stories famous seemed to haunt his real life, too.

Critics now disagree over whether Poe had little talent or was a misunderstood genius, victimized by jealous gossip. Poe died a poor man in Baltimore, Maryland.

Yes, he was a newcomer to the school. Of course, that's not so surprising; he was only five. Even so, he had already made himself a person to be reckoned with. His name . . .

Charles

SHIRLEY JACKSON

THE DAY my son Laurie started kindergarten he renounced corduroy overalls with bibs and began wearing blue jeans with a belt; I watched him go off the first morning with the older girl next door, seeing clearly that an era of my life was ended, my sweet-voiced nursery-school tot replaced by a long-trousered, swaggering character who forgot to stop at the corner and wave good-bye to me.

He came home the same way, the front door slamming open, his cap on the floor, and the voice suddenly become raucous shouting, "Isn't anybody *here*?"

At lunch he spoke insolently to his father, spilled his baby sister's milk, and remarked that his teacher said we were not to take the name of the Lord in vain.

"How *was* school today?" I asked, elaborately casual.

"All right," he said.

"Did you learn anything?" his father asked.

Laurie regarded his father coldly. "I didn't learn nothing," he said.

"Anything," I said. "Didn't learn anything."

"The teacher spanked a boy, though," Laurie said, addressing his bread and butter. "For being fresh," he added, with his mouth full.

"What did he do?" I asked. "Who was it?"

Laurie thought. "It was Charles," he said. "He was fresh. The teacher spanked him and made him stand in a corner. He was awfully fresh."

"What did he do?" I asked again, but Laurie slid off his chair, took a cookie, and left, while his father was still saying, "See here, young man."

The next day Laurie remarked at lunch, as soon as he sat down, "Well, Charles was bad again today." He grinned enormously and said, "Today Charles hit the teacher."

"Good heavens," I said, mindful of the Lord's name, "I suppose he got spanked again?"

"He sure did," Laurie said. "Look up," he said to his father.

"What?" his father said, looking up.

"Look down," Laurie said. "Look at my thumb. Gee, you're dumb." He began to laugh insanely.

"Why did Charles hit the teacher?" I asked quickly.

"Because she tried to make him color with red crayons," Laurie said. "Charles wanted to color with green crayons so he hit the teacher and she spanked him and said nobody play with Charles but everybody did."

The third day—it was Wednesday of the first week—Charles bounced a see-saw on to the head of a little girl and made her bleed, and the teacher made him stay inside all during recess. Thursday Charles had to stand in a corner during story-time because he kept pounding his feet on the floor. Friday Charles was deprived of blackboard privileges because he threw chalk.

On Saturday I remarked to my husband, "Do you think kindergarten is too unsettling for Laurie? All this toughness and bad grammar, and this Charles boy sounds like such a bad influence."

"It'll be all right," my husband said reassuringly. "Bound to be people like Charles in the world. Might as well meet them now as later."

On Monday Laurie came home late, full of news. "Charles," he shouted as he came up the hill; I was waiting anxiously on the front

steps. "Charles," Laurie yelled all the way up the hill, "Charles was bad again."

"Come right in," I said, as soon as he came close enough. "Lunch is waiting."

"You know what Charles did?" he demanded, following me through the door. "Charles yelled so in school they sent a boy in from first grade to tell the teacher she had to make Charles keep quiet, and so Charles had to stay after school. And so all the children stayed to watch him."

"What did he do?" I asked.

"He just sat there," Laurie said, climbing into his chair at the table. "Hi, Pop, y'old dust mop."

"Charles had to stay after school today," I told my husband. "Everyone stayed with him."

"What does Charles look like?" my husband asked Laurie. "What's his other name?"

"He's bigger than me," Laurie said. "And he doesn't have any rubbers and he doesn't even wear a jacket."

Monday night was the first Parent-Teachers meeting, and only the fact that the baby had a cold kept me from going; I wanted passionately to meet Charles's mother. On Tuesday Laurie remarked suddenly, "Our teacher had a friend come to see her in school today."

"Charles's mother?" my husband and I asked simultaneously.

"Naaah," Laurie said scornfully. "It was a man who came and made us do exercises; we had to touch our toes. Look." He climbed down from his chair and squatted down and touched his toes. "Like this," he said. He got solemnly back into his chair and said, picking up his fork, "Charles didn't even *do* exercises."

"That's fine," I said heartily. "Didn't Charles want to do exercises?"

"Naaah," Laurie said. "Charles was so fresh to the teacher's friend he wasn't *let* do exercises."

"Fresh again?" I said.

"He kicked the teacher's friend," Laurie said. "The teacher's friend told Charles to touch his toes like I just did and Charles kicked him."

"What are they going to do about Charles, do you suppose?" Laurie's father asked him.

Laurie shrugged elaborately. "Throw him out of school, I guess," he said.

Wednesday and Thursday were routine; Charles yelled during story hour and hit a boy in the stomach and made him cry. On Friday Charles stayed after school again and so did all the other children.

With the third week of kindergarten Charles was an institution in our family; the baby was being a Charles when she cried all afternoon; Laurie did a Charles when he filled his wagon full of mud and pulled it through the kitchen; even my husband, when he caught his elbow in the telephone cord and pulled telephone, ashtray, and a bowl of flowers off the table, said, after the first minute, "Looks like Charles."

During the third and fourth weeks it looked like a reformation in Charles; Laurie reported grimly at lunch on Thursday of the third week, "Charles was so good today the teacher gave him an apple."

"What?" I said, and my husband added warily, "You mean Charles?"

"Charles," Laurie said. "He gave the crayons around and he picked up the books afterward and the teacher said he was her helper."

"What happened?" I asked incredulously.

"He was her helper, that's all," Laurie said, and shrugged.

"Can this be true, about Charles?" I asked my husband that night. "Can something like this happen?"

"Wait and see," my husband said cynically. "When you've got a Charles to deal with, this may mean he's only plotting."

He seemed to be wrong. For over a week Charles was the teacher's helper; each day he handed things out and he picked things up; no one had to stay after school.

"The P.T.A. meeting's next week again," I told my husband one evening. "I'm going to find Charles's mother there."

"Ask her what happened to Charles," my husband said. "I'd like to know."

"I'd like to know myself," I said.

On Friday of that week things were back to normal. "You know what Charles did today?" Laurie demanded at the lunch table, in a voice slightly awed. "He told a little girl to say a word and she said it and the teacher washed her mouth out with soap and Charles laughed."

"What word?" his father asked unwisely, and Laurie said, "I'll have to whisper it to you, it's so bad." He got down off his chair and went around to his father. His father bent his head down and Laurie whispered joyfully. His father's eyes widened.

"Did Charles tell the little girl to say *that?*" he asked respectfully.

"She said it *twice*," Laurie said. "Charles told her to say it *twice*."

"What happened to Charles?" my husband asked.

"Nothing," Laurie said. "He was passing out the crayons."

Monday morning Charles abandoned the little girl and said the evil word himself three or four times, getting his mouth washed out with soap each time. He also threw chalk.

My husband came to the door with me that evening as I set out for the P.T.A. meeting. "Invite her over for a cup of tea after the meeting," he said. "I want to get a look at her."

"If only she's there," I said prayerfully.

"She'll be there," my husband said. "I don't see how they could hold a P.T.A. meeting without Charles's mother."

At the meeting I sat restlessly, scanning each comfortable matronly face, trying to determine which one hid the secret of Charles. None of them looked to me haggard enough. No one stood up in the meeting and apologized for the way her son had been acting. No one mentioned Charles.

After the meeting I identified and sought out Laurie's kindergarten teacher. She had a plate with a cup of tea and a piece of chocolate cake; I had a plate with a cup of tea and a piece of marshmallow cake. We maneuvered up to one another cautiously, and smiled.

"I've been so anxious to meet you," I said. "I'm Laurie's mother."

"We're all so interested in Laurie," she said.

"Well, he certainly likes kindergarten," I said. "He talks about it all the time."

"We had a little trouble adjusting, the first week or so," she said primly, "but now he's a fine little helper. With occasional lapses, of course."

"Laurie usually adjusts very quickly," I said. "I suppose this time it's Charles's influence."

"Charles?"

"Yes," I said, laughing, "you must have your hands full in that kindergarten, with Charles."

"Charles?" she said. "We don't have any Charles in the kindergarten."

Discussion

1. Who is Charles? How do you know? When did you first suspect his true identity?
2. Why, in your opinion, does Laurie behave as he does at school? What technique(s) does the teacher use to try to improve his behavior? Which technique(s) prove successful? Which do not?
3. When Laurie tells his parents about the improvement in Charles's behavior, Laurie's father says, "When you've got a Charles to deal with, this may mean he's only plotting." What do you think Laurie's father means?
4. Why is Laurie's mother so anxious to attend the PTA meeting?
5. What clues do you find in Laurie's behavior toward his mother and father to make you suspect that it is *Laurie* whose behavior leaves something to be desired?

Writer's Craft

"Stupid movie!"
"What's that, Sue?"
"The TV movie—*Action at Dawn.* It was just plain stupid."
"Why?"
"It didn't get any place. *Action!!!* There was *no* action. All the characters just sat around and talked about what they'd do when the war was over. And that Jack Lapance! He can't act. All he can do is roll those calf eyes and grin and say, 'You bet.'"

Besides expressing her opinion about a TV movie, what else is Sue doing? Well, obviously, she is expressing her negative feelings about slow-paced motion pictures and second-rate actors. In doing so, she is revealing her ATTITUDE. In this case, her attitude is one of strong disapproval of anything that intentionally deceives, of anything that causes a person to feel short-changed.

All of us—in much of what we say and write—reveal our *attitudes* toward situations and events and other people. We do so through words that express our likes and dislikes, our approval and disapproval, or our indifference.

Storywriters, too, reveal their ATTITUDES (1) toward the subjects they write about and (2) toward the characters they invent. For instance, if an author writes about a situation that he or she considers hilarious, the words he or she uses to tell about that situation will naturally reveal the author's attitude. Similarly, if an author invents a character that he or she admires, that attitude of admiration will be expressed in the words used to describe that individual's personality and actions.

It is important for you to recognize a storywriter's attitude. Doing so will help put you on the inside track in your understanding and enjoyment of the story.

1. What is Shirley Jackson's (the author's) attitude toward Charles/Laurie? Support your answer by referring to specific words and expressions in the story.

2. What attitude do you think the author reveals toward Laurie's parents? Why?

Vocabulary

CONTEXT CLUES are hints about the meaning of an unfamiliar word. These hints are found among the words and ideas that surround the unfamiliar word in a sentence.

In providing general ideas about the meanings of difficult words, context clues can be extremely helpful. But just as Laurie's description of Charles leaves out the central fact of his story, context clues do not always provide key details about meaning. Now and then, context clues can even be misleading. For example:

> . . . my sweet-voiced nursery-school tot [was] replaced by a long-trousered, *swaggering* character who forgot to stop at the corner and wave good-bye to me.

In this sentence, context clues may give the impression that *swaggering* means "grown-up and businesslike," or perhaps "absentminded." However, the dictionary says that *swaggering* means "strutting; walking in a haughty, conceited way"—not "adult" at all.

In this exercise, use a separate sheet of paper to answer two questions about each *italicized* word below: What meaning do the context clues first suggest? What is the dictionary definition of the word?

1. I remarked to my husband, "Do you think kindergarten is too *unsettling* for Laurie? All this toughness, and bad grammar, and this Charles boy sounds like such a bad influence."

2. Laurie reported *grimly* at lunch on Thursday of the third week, "Charles was so good today the teacher gave him an apple."

3. At the meeting, I sat restlessly, scanning each *matronly* face, trying to determine which one hid the secret of Charles.

4. None of the mothers looked to me *haggard* enough. No one stood up and apologized for the way her son had been acting.

5. "We had a little trouble adjusting, the first week or so," she said *primly*, "but now he's a fine little helper."

Shirley Jackson 1919–1965

Shirley Jackson had an unusual talent for writing two types of stories which were very different from each other. People who have read one type have trouble believing she could write the other type, too.

"Charles" is an example of Jackson's humorous family tales, typical of her book *Life Among the Savages.* Reading these tales makes it easy to understand Jackson's saying that she writes "because it's the one chance I get to sit down."

But the other side of Jackson's talent produced horror tales which made her famous. These chilling stories present the view that even people who count themselves normal and respectable can easily become very cruel to individuals they consider odd.

Hazel Elizabeth Deborah Parker—Squeaky, to her friends—knew that she could and would win the May Day fifty-yard dash. After all, wasn't she the fastest thing on two feet? But what about her brother Raymond? Where did he fit into the picture?

Raymond's Run

TONI CADE BAMBARA

I DON'T HAVE MUCH WORK to do around the house like some girls. My mother does that. And I don't have to earn my pocket money. . . . George runs errands for the big boys and sells Christmas cards. And anything else that's got to get done, my father does. All I have to do in life is mind my brother Raymond, which is enough.

Sometimes I slip and say my little brother Raymond. But as any fool can see he's much bigger and he's older too. But a lot of people call him my little brother cause he needs looking after cause he's not quite right. And a lot of smart mouths got lots to say about that too, especially when George was minding him. But now, if anybody has anything to say to Raymond, anything to say about his big head, they have to come by me. And I don't play the dozens or believe in standing around with somebody in my face doing a lot of talking. I much rather just knock you down and take my chances even if I am a little girl with skinny arms and a squeaky voice, which

is how I got the name Squeaky. And if things get too rough, I run. And as anybody can tell you, I'm the fastest thing on two feet.

There is no track meet that I don't win the first place medal. I used to win the twenty-yard dash when I was a little kid in kindergarten. Nowadays, it's the fifty-yard dash. And tomorrow I'm subject to run the quarter-meter relay all by myself and come in first, second, and third. The big kids call me Mercury cause I'm the swiftest thing in the neighborhood. Everybody knows that—except two people who know better, my father and me. He can beat me to Amsterdam Avenue with me having a two fire-hydrant headstart and him running with his hands in his pockets and whistling. But that's private information. Cause can you imagine some thirty-five-year-old man stuffing himself into PAL shorts to race little kids? So as far as everyone's concerned, I'm the fastest and that goes for Gretchen, too, who has put out the tale that she is going to win the first-place medal this year. Ridiculous. In the second place, she's got short legs. In the third place, she's got freckles. In the first place, no one can beat me and that's all there is to it.

I'm standing on the corner admiring the weather and about to take a stroll down Broadway so I can practice my breathing exercises, and I've got Raymond walking on the inside close to the buildings, cause he's subject to fits of fantasy and starts thinking he's a circus performer and that the curb is a tightrope strung high in the air. And sometimes after a rain he likes to step down off his tightrope right into the gutter and splash around getting his shoes and cuffs wet. Then I get hit when I get home. Or sometimes if you don't watch him he'll dash across traffic to the island in the middle of Broadway and give the pigeons a fit. Then I have to go behind him apologizing to all the old people sitting around trying to get some sun and getting all upset with the pigeons fluttering around them, scattering their newspapers and upsetting the waxpaper lunches in their laps. So I keep Raymond on the inside of me, and he plays like he's driving a stage coach which is O.K. by me so long as he doesn't run me over or interrupt my breathing exercises, which I have to do on account of I'm serious about my running, and I don't care who knows it.

Now some people like to act like things come easy to them, won't let on that they practice. Not me. I'll high-prance down 34th Street like a rodeo pony to keep my knees strong even if it does get my mother uptight so that she walks ahead like she's not with me, don't know me, is all by herself on a shopping trip, and I am somebody else's crazy child. Now you take Cynthia Procter for instance. She's just the opposite. If there's a test tomorrow, she'll say something like,

"Oh, I guess I'll play handball this afternoon and watch television tonight," just to let you know she ain't thinking about the test. Or like last week when she won the spelling bee for the millionth time, "A good thing you got 'receive,' Squeaky, cause I would have got it wrong. I completely forgot about the spelling bee." And she'll clutch the lace on her blouse like it was a narrow escape. Oh, brother. But of course when I pass her house on my early morning trots around the block, she is practicing the scales on the piano over and over and over and over. Then in music class she always lets herself get bumped around so she falls accidentally on purpose onto the piano stool and is so surprised to find herself sitting there that she decides just for fun to try out the ole keys. And what do you know— Chopin's waltzes just spring out of her fingertips and she's the most surprised thing in the world. A regular prodigy. I could kill people like that. I stay up all night studying the words for the spelling bee. And you can see me any time of day practicing running.

I never walk if I can trot, and shame on Raymond if he can't keep up. But of course he does, cause if he hangs back someone's liable to walk up to him and get smart, or take his allowance from him, or ask him where he got that great big pumpkin head. People are so stupid sometimes.

So I'm strolling down Broadway breathing out and breathing in on counts of seven, which is my lucky number, and here comes Gretchen and her sidekicks: Mary Louise, who used to be a friend of mine when she first moved to Harlem from Baltimore and got beat up by everybody till I took up for her on account of her mother and my mother used to sing in the same choir when they were young girls, but people ain't grateful, so now she hangs out with the new girl Gretchen and talks about me like a dog; and Rosie, who is as fat as I am skinny and has a big mouth where Raymond is concerned and is too stupid to know that there is not a big deal of difference between herself and Ray-

mond and that she can't afford to throw stones. So they are steady coming up Broadway and I see right away that it's going to be one of those Dodge City scenes cause the street ain't that big and they're close to the buildings just as we are. First I think I'll step into the candy store and look over the new comics and let them pass. But that's chicken and I've got a reputation to consider. So then I think I'll just walk straight on through them or even over them if necessary. But as they get to me, they slow down. I'm ready to fight, cause like I said I don't feature a whole lot of chit-chat, I much prefer to just knock you down right from the jump and save everybody a lotta precious time.

"You signing up for the May Day races?" smiles Mary Louise, only it's not a smile at all. A dumb question like that doesn't deserve an answer. Besides, there's just me and Gretchen standing there really, so no use wasting my breath talking to shadows.

"I don't think you're going to win this time," says Rosie, trying to signify with her hands on her hips all salty, completely forgetting that I have whipped her behind many times for less salt than that.

"I always win cause I'm the best," I say straight at Gretchen who is, as far as I'm concerned, the only one talking in this ventriloquist-dummy routine. Gretchen smiles, but it's not a smile, and I'm thinking that girls never really smile at each other because they don't know how and don't want to know how and there's probably no one to teach us how, cause grown-up girls don't know either. Then they all look at Raymond who has just brought his mule team to a standstill. And they're about to see what trouble they can get into through him.

"What grade you in now, Raymond?"

"You got anything to say to my brother, you say it to me, Mary Louise Williams of Raggedy Town, Baltimore."

"What are you, his mother?" sasses Rosie.

"That's right, Fatso. And the next word out of anybody and I'll be *their* mother too." So they just stand there and Gretchen shifts from one leg to the other and so do they. Then Gretchen puts her hands on her hips and is about to say something with her freckle-face self but doesn't. Then she walks around me looking me up and down but keeps walking up Broadway, and her side-kicks follow her. So me and Raymond smile at each other and he says, "Gidyap" to his team and I continue with my breathing exercises, strolling down Broadway toward the ice man on 145th with not a care in the world cause I am Miss Quicksilver herself.

I take my time getting to the park on May Day because the track meet is the last thing on the program. The biggest thing on the program is the May Pole dancing, which I can do without, thank you, even if my mother thinks it's a shame I don't take part and act like a girl for a change. You'd think my mother'd be grateful not to have to make me a white organdy dress with a big satin sash and buy me new white baby-doll shoes that can't be taken out of the box till the big day. You'd think she'd be glad her daughter ain't out there prancing around a May Pole getting the new clothes all dirty and sweaty and trying to act like a fairy or a flower or whatever you're supposed to be when you should be trying to be yourself, whatever that is, which is, as far as I'm concerned, a poor Black girl who really can't afford to buy shoes and a new dress you only wear once a lifetime cause it won't fit next year.

I was once a strawberry in a Hansel and Gretel pageant when I was in nursery school and didn't have no better sense than to dance on tiptoe with my arms in a circle over my head doing umbrella steps and being a perfect fool just so my mother and father could come dressed up and clap. You'd think they'd know better than to encourage that kind of nonsense. I am not a strawberry. I do not dance on my toes. I run. That is what I am all about. So I always come late to the May Day program, just in time to get my number pinned on and lay in the grass till they announce the fifty-yard dash.

I put Raymond in the little swings, which is a tight squeeze this year and will be impossible next year. Then I look around for Mr. Pearson, who pins the numbers on. I'm really looking for Gretchen if you want to know the truth, but she's not around. The park is jam-packed. Parents in hats and corsages and breast-pocket handkerchiefs peeking up. Kids in white dresses and light-blue suits. The parkees unfolding chairs and chasing the rowdy kids from Lenox as if they had no right to be there. The big guys with their caps on backwards, leaning against the fence swirling the basketballs on the tips of their fingers, waiting for all these crazy people to clear out the park so they can play. Most of the kids in my class are carrying bass drums and glockenspiels and flutes. You'd think they'd put in a few bongos or something for real like that.

Then here comes Mr. Pearson with his clipboard and his cards and pencils and whistles and safety pins and fifty million other things he's always dropping all over the place with his clumsy self. He sticks out in a crowd because he's on stilts. We used to call him Jack and the Beanstalk to get him mad. But I'm the only one that can outrun him and get away, and I'm too grown for that silliness now.

"Well, Squeaky," he says, checking my name off the list and handing me number seven and two pins. And I'm thinking he's got no right to call me Squeaky, if I can't call him Beanstalk.

"Hazel Elizabeth Deborah Parker," I correct him and tell him to write it down on his board.

"Well, Hazel Elizabeth Deborah Parker, going to give someone else a break this year?" I squint at him real hard to see if he is seriously thinking I should lose the race on purpose just to give someone else a break. "Only six girls running this time," he continues, shaking his head sadly like it's my fault all of New York didn't turn out in sneakers. "That new girl should give you a run for your money." He looks around the park for Gretchen like a periscope in a submarine movie. "Wouldn't it be a nice gesture if you were . . . to ahhh. . . ."

I give him such a look he couldn't finish putting that idea into words. Grownups got a lot of nerve sometimes. I pin number seven to myself and stomp away, I'm so burnt. And I go straight for the track and stretch out on the grass while the band winds up with "Oh, the Monkey Wrapped His Tail Around the Flag Pole," which my teacher calls by some other name. The man on the loudspeaker is calling everyone over to the track and I'm on my back looking at the sky, trying to pretend I'm in the country, but I can't, because even grass in the city feels hard as sidewalk, and there's just no pretending you are anywhere but in a "concrete jungle" as my grandfather says.

The twenty-yard dash takes all of two minutes cause most of the little kids don't know no better than to run off the track or run the wrong way or run smack into the fence and fall down and cry. One little kid, though, has got the good sense to run straight for the white ribbon up ahead; so he wins. Then the second-graders line up for the thirty-yard dash and I don't even bother to turn my head to watch cause Raphael Perez always wins. He wins before he even begins by psyching the runners, telling them they're going to trip on their shoelaces and fall on their faces or lose their shorts or something, which he doesn't really have to do since he is very fast, almost as fast as I am. After that is the forty-yard dash which I use to run when I was in first grade. Raymond is hollering from the swings cause he knows I'm about to do my thing cause the man on the loudspeaker has just announced the fifty-yard dash, although he might just as well be giving a recipe for angel food cake cause you can hardly make out what he's sayin for the static. I get up and slip off my sweat pants and then I see Gretchen standing at the starting line, kicking her legs out like a pro. Then as I get into place I see that ole Raymond is on line on the other side of the fence, bending down with his fingers on the ground just like he knew what he was doing. I was going to yell at him but then I didn't. It burns up your energy to holler.

Every time, just before I take off in a race, I always feel like I'm in a dream, the kind of dream you have when you're sick with fever and feel all hot and weightless. I dream I'm flying over a sandy beach in the early morning sun, kissing the leaves of the trees as I fly by. And there's always the smell of apples, just like in the country when I was little and used to think I was a choo-choo train, running through the fields of corn and chugging up the hill to the orchard. And all the time I'm dreaming this, I get lighter and lighter until I'm flying over the beach again, getting blown through the sky like a feather that weighs nothing at all. But once I spread my fingers in the dirt and crouch over the Get on

Your Mark, the dream goes and I am solid again and am telling myself, Squeaky you must win, you must win, you are the fastest thing in the world, you can even beat your father up Amsterdam if you really try. And then I feel my weight coming back just behind my knees then down to my feet then into the earth and the pistol shot explodes in my blood and I am off and weightless again, flying past the other runners, my arms pumping up and down and the whole world is quiet except for the crunch as I zoom over the gravel in the track. I glance to my left and there is no one. To the right, a blurred Gretchen, who's got her chin jutting out as if it would win the race all by itself. And on the other side of the fence is Raymond with his arms down to his side and the palms tucked up behind him, running in his very own style, and it's the first time I ever saw that and I almost stop to watch my brother Raymond on his first run. But the white ribbon is bouncing toward me and I tear past it, racing

into the distance till my feet with a mind of their own start digging up footfuls of dirt and brake me short. Then all the kids standing on the side pile on me, banging me on the back and slapping my head with their May Day programs, for I have won again and everybody on 151st Street can walk tall for another year.

"In first place . . ." the man on the loudspeaker is clear as a bell now. But then he pauses and the loudspeaker starts to whine. Then static. And I lean down to catch my breath and here comes Gretchen walking back, for she's overshot the finish line too, huffing and puffing with her hands on her hips taking it slow, breathing in steady time like a real pro and I sort of like her a little for the first time. "In first place . . ." and then three or four voices get all mixed up on the loudspeaker and I dig my sneaker into the grass and stare at Gretchen who's staring back, we both wondering just who did win. I can hear old Beanstalk arguing with the man on the loudspeaker and then a few others running their mouths about what the stopwatches say. Then I hear Raymond yanking at the fence to call me and I wave to shush him, but he keeps rattling the fence like a gorilla in a cage like in them gorilla movies, but then like a dancer or something he starts climbing up nice and easy but very fast. And it occurs to me, watching how smoothly he climbs hand over hand and remembering how he looked running with his arms down to his side and with the wind pulling his mouth back and his teeth showing and all, it occurred to me that Raymond would make a very fine runner. Doesn't he always keep up with me on my trots? And he surely knows how to breathe in counts of seven cause he's always doing it at the dinner table, which drives my brother George up the wall. And

I'm smiling to beat the band cause if I've lost this race, or if me and Gretchen tied, or even if I've won, I can always retire as a runner and begin a whole new career as a coach with Raymond as my champion. After all, with a little more study I can beat Cynthia and her phony self at the spelling bee. And if I bugged my mother, I could get piano lessons and become a star. And I have a big rep as the baddest thing around. And I've got a roomful of ribbons and medals and awards. But what has Raymond got to call his own?

So I stand there with my new plans, laughing out loud by this time as Raymond jumps down from the fence and runs over with his teeth showing and his arms down to the side, which no one before him has quite mastered as a running style. And by the time he comes over I'm jumping up and down so glad to see him—my brother Raymond, a great runner in the family tradition. But of course everyone thinks I'm jumping up and down because the men on the loudspeaker have finally gotten themselves together and compared notes and are announcing "In first place—Miss Hazel Elizabeth Deborah Parker." (Dig that.) "In second place—Miss Gretchen P. Lewis." And I look over at Gretchen wondering what the "P" stands for. And I smile. Cause she's good, no doubt about it. Maybe she'd like to help me coach Raymond; she obviously is serious about running, as any fool can see. And she nods to congratulate me and then she smiles. And I smile. We stand there with this big smile of respect between us. It's about as real a smile as girls can do for each other, considering we don't practice real smiling every day, you know, cause maybe we too busy being flowers or fairies or strawberries instead of something honest and worthy of respect . . . you know . . . like being people.

Discussion

1. By the end of the story, the relationship between Squeaky and Raymond has changed quite a bit. How? What are Squeaky's plans for Raymond?

2. At the end of the race, Squeaky and Gretchen Lewis exchange smiles. How are these smiles different from their earlier smiles—those they managed when they met one afternoon on Broadway (page 252)?

3. Although Squeaky and Raymond are the main characters in the story, other people play important roles in their lives. What influence does Squeaky's father have? Squeaky's mother? Cynthia Procter? Mr. Pearson?

4. What evidence is there that accomplishments other than winning races are becoming important to Squeaky?

5. The last sentence of the story suggests that Squeaky has discovered something noteworthy about herself—and about others as well. What, in your opinion, has she discovered?

6. Why do you think the story is titled "Raymond's Run"?

Writer's Craft

Who tells the story "Raymond's Run"? Someone is sure to reply, "The author, Toni Cade Bambara." But someone else is bound to insist that Squeaky is the storyteller. Who is right? Strangely enough, *both* are.

It is true that Toni Cade Bambara wrote the story. In doing so, she invented the character of Squeaky. But then Bambara put herself in Squeaky's place—that is, she pretended to be Squeaky—and wrote the story to make it seem as if Squeaky tells you what happens. Squeaky, then, is the narrator. She is also the "I" in the story. You, the reader, see the action and the other characters *through her eyes*—from her POINT OF VIEW.

Not only is Squeaky the "I" in the story and the narrator, she is also a *participant* in the action. (In fact, she's the main character.) When the narrator of a story participates in the action as the "I" in the story, we say that the story is told from the FIRST-PERSON POINT OF VIEW.

1. In "Raymond's Run" you know what only one character is thinking. Which character? Why only that character?

2. Squeaky tells what the other characters do and say, but not what they think. Why?

3. When an author writes a story from the first-person point of view,

he or she works under certain limitations. What are some of those limitations?

4. Both "The Telltale Heart" and "Charles" are written from the first-person point of view. Do you agree or disagree with that statement? Why?

Toni Cade Bambara 1939—

Toni Cade Bambara says, "I am a young Black woman who writes, teaches, organizes, tries to learn, and tries to raise her daughter to be a correct little sister." Bambara's childhood took her to several locations including Harlem, New Jersey, and the South. She has been "a writer since childhood who nevertheless planned to be a doctor, lawyer, artist, musician, and everything else." Her varied interests and skills have taken her to study in Italy and France as well as the United States.

Bambara wants young people to take their heritage to heart. She writes, "It's a funny thing about the living history you hear in the family kitchen among the elders—it doesn't always match what you are supposed to learn from the books you read. . . . So while it is very, very important for young folks to learn how to read, to read well, to read everything in sight, it is equally important for young folks to learn to listen, to be proud of our oral tradition, our elders who tell their tales in the kitchen. For they are truth."

Faith? Yes, Lencho did indeed have faith!
Hope? Yes, you could say that Lencho had
plenty of hope. Charity? Hm . . . Well. . . .

A Letter to God

GREGORIO LOPEZ Y FUENTES

translated by DONALD A. YATES

THE HOUSE—the only one in the entire valley—sat on the crest of a low hill. From this height one could see the river and, next to the corral, the field of ripe corn dotted with the kidney bean flowers that always promised a good harvest.

The only thing the earth needed was a rainfall, or at least a shower. Throughout the morning Lencho—who knew his fields intimately—had done nothing else but scan the sky toward the northeast.

"Now we're really going to get some water, woman."

The woman, who was preparing supper, replied: "Yes, God willing."

The oldest boys were working in the field, while the smaller ones were playing near the house, until the woman called to them all: "Come for dinner. . . ."

It was during the meal that, just as Lencho had predicted, big drops of rain began to fall. In the northeast huge mountains of clouds could be seen approaching. The air was fresh and sweet.

The man went out to look for something in the corral for no other reason than to allow himself the pleasure of feeling the rain on his body, and when he returned he exclaimed: "Those aren't raindrops falling from the sky, they're new coins. The big drops are ten-*centavo* pieces and the little ones are fives. . . ."

With a satisfied expression he regarded the field of ripe corn with its kidney bean flowers, draped in a curtain of rain. But suddenly a strong wind began to blow and, together with the rain, very large hailstones began to fall. These truly did resemble new silver coins. The boys, exposing themselves to the rain, ran out to collect the frozen pearls.

"It's really getting bad now," exclaimed the man, mortified. "I hope it passes quickly."

It did not pass quickly. For an hour the hail rained on the house, the garden, the hillside, the corn-field, on the whole valley. The field was white, as if covered with salt. Not a leaf remained on the trees. The corn was totally destroyed. The flowers were gone from the kidney bean plants. Lencho's soul was filled with sadness. When the storm had passed, he stood in the middle of the field and said to his sons: "A plague of locusts would have left more than this. . . . The hail has left nothing: this year we will have no corn or beans. . . ."

That night was a sorrowful one: "All our work, for nothing! There's no one who can help us!"

"We'll all go hungry this year. . . ."

But in the hearts of all who lived in that solitary house in the middle of the valley, there was a single hope: help from God.

"Don't be so upset, even though this seems like a total loss. Remember, no one dies of hunger!"

"That's what they say: no one dies of hunger. . . ."

All through the night, Lencho thought only of his one hope: the help of God, whose eyes, as he had been instructed, see everything, even what is deep in one's conscience.

Lencho was an ox of a man, working like an animal in the fields, but still he knew how to write. The following Sunday, at daybreak, after having convinced himself that there is a protecting spirit, he began to write a letter which he himself would carry to town and place in the mail.

It was nothing less than a letter to God.

"God," he wrote, "if you don't help me, my family and I will go hungry this year. I need a hundred *pesos* in order to resow the field and to live until the crop comes, because of the hailstorm. . . ."

He wrote "To God" on the envelope, put the letter inside, and, still troubled, went to town. At the post office he placed a stamp on the letter and dropped it into the mailbox.

One of the employees, who was a postman and also helped at the post office, went to his boss, laughing heartily, and showed him the

letter to God. Never in his career as a post-man had he known that address. The post-master—a fat, amiable fellow—also broke out laughing, but almost immediately he turned serious and, tapping the letter on his desk, commented: "What faith! I wish I had the faith of the man who wrote this letter. To believe the way he believes. To hope with the confidence that he knows how to hope with. Starting up a correspondence with God!"

So, in order not to disillusion that prodigy of faith, revealed by a letter that could not be delivered, the postmaster came up with an idea: answer the letter. But when he opened it, it was evident that to answer it he needed something more than good will, ink, and paper. But he stuck to his resolution: he asked for money from his employee, he himself gave part of his salary, and several friends of his were obliged to give something "for an act of charity."

It was impossible for him to gather to-gether the hundred *pesos* requested by Len-cho, so he was able to send the farmer only a little more than half. He put the bills in an envelope addressed to Lencho and with them a letter containing only a single word as a signature:

GOD

The following Sunday Lencho came a bit earlier than usual to ask if there was a letter for him. It was the postman himself who handed the letter to him, while the post-master, experiencing the contentment of a man who has performed a good deed, looked on from the doorway of his office.

Lencho showed not the slightest surprise on seeing the bills—such was his confidence—but he became angry when he counted the money. God could not have made a mistake, nor could he have denied Lencho what he had requested!

Immediately, Lencho went up to the window to ask for paper and ink. On the public writing table, he started in to write, with much wrinkling of his brow, caused by the effort he had to make to express his ideas. When he finished, he went to the window to buy a stamp, which he licked and then affixed to the envelope with a blow of his fist.

The moment that the letter fell into the mailbox the postmaster went to open it. It said:

"God: Of the money that I asked for, only seventy pesos reached me. Send me the rest, since I need it very much. But don't send it to me through the mail, because the post office employees are a bunch of crooks. Lencho."

Discussion

1. At the beginning of the story, what is the situation concerning Lencho's crops? What does Lencho mean by calling the raindrops "new coins"?

2. What happens to cause Lencho to need 100 pesos?

3. Who actually provides the money that Lencho requested? Why, in your opinion, did that person make the effort to raise the money?

4. Why does Lencho write the second letter? How does that letter express Lencho's faith in God even more than did the first letter?

5. Is the outcome of the story what you expected, or isn't it? Why? How does that outcome add to your enjoyment of the story?

Writer's Craft

One of the first decisions a storywriter has to make concerns the point of view from which his or her story can best be told. Through whose eyes should the reader see the characters and the action?

If you have read "Raymond's Run" (page 250), you know that the story is told from the first-person point of view. The narrator and the "I" are the same person. What's more, the narrator "I" participates actively as a character in the story.

But not all stories are told from the first-person point of view. Very often the storywriter himself or herself is the narrator. In that case, the storyteller is *not* a character (a participant) in the story. Instead, he or she stands outside the story and assumes a god-like role. Because the author does have a god-like view, he or she sees and knows everything about all the characters in the story. That is, the author tells you not only what the characters say and do, but also what they think.

In adopting this point of view, the storywriter is somewhat like a puppeteer, pulling the strings to make the characters act as he or she wants them to. When a storywriter assumes a god-like role—when the writer sees and knows all—we say that he or she is telling the story from the OMNISCIENT POINT OF VIEW. *Omniscient* means "all-knowing."

1. In "A Letter to God," what are some things you learn about Lencho and the postmaster only because the story is told from the omniscient point of view?

2. Why, in your opinion, is the omniscient point of view better for telling this story than the first-person point of view would be?

3. Which point of view, do you think, is easier to use when writing a story? Why?

Vocabulary

The word PREFIX, when applied to language, is defined as "one or more letters put before a word to change the word's meaning in some way." Among the most often used prefixes in English is *re-*. When you add *re-* to the beginning of a word, the prefix can have one of two meanings:

1. "again," as in *refresh* (make fresh again) or *remodel* (make over again)
2. "back," as in *regain* (get back) or *refund* (give back)

A. Each sentence below contains an *italicized* word that starts with the prefix *re-*. On a separate sheet of paper, copy each word. Then write either **1** or **2** to show in which category described above the word belongs.

1. After the hailstorm, Lencho had to *reorganize* his plans for the future.
2. He decided that he would have to *resow* his fields.
3. In a letter, Lencho *referred* his problem to God because of the hail that had ruined the crops.
4. The *reply* Lencho got came from the postmaster instead of from God, but it contained some of the money Lencho asked for.
5. Lencho was disappointed with the amount that had been sent, and so he wrote another letter, *restating* his need.

B. In some of the following words, *re-* is used as a prefix. In others, *re-* is the beginning of the word itself. Below your answers for Exercise A, make two columns, side by side. In the column at the left, copy the words from the list below that start with *re-* as the prefix. In the column at the right, copy the words in which *re-* is the beginning of the word itself.

review	reaching
return	repeat
reverse	recognize
restful	reason

Gregorio Lopez y Fuentes 1897—1966

Gregorio Lopez y Fuentes was a Mexican novelist and poet who wrote about the rural people in his home state of Vera Cruz. He taught school in that area for a few years. Then he went to the capital as a reporter and author.

Lopez y Fuentes's best known novel is *El Indio* ("those who reap"). This book presents the rural life and customs in a primitive Indian village after the Mexican Revolution.

Weep No More, My Lady

JAMES STREET

THE MOONLIGHT symphony of swamp creatures hushed abruptly, and the dismal bog was as peaceful as unborn time and seemed to brood in its silence. The gaunt[1] man glanced back at the boy and motioned for him to be quiet, but it was too late. Their presence was discovered. A jumbo frog rumbled a warning, and the swamp squirmed into life as its denizens[2] scuttled to safety.

Fox fire[3] was glowing to the west and the bayou[4] was slapping the cypress knees when suddenly a haunting laugh echoed through the wilderness, a strange chuckling yodel ending in a weird "gro-o-o."

The boy's eyes were wide and staring. "That's it, Uncle Jess. Come on! Let's catch it!"

"Uh, oh." The man gripped his shotgun. "That ain't no animal. That's a thing."

They hurried noiselessly in the direction of the sound that Skeeter had been hearing for several nights. Swamp born and reared, they feared nothing they could shoot or outwit, so they slipped out of the morass[5] and to the side of a ridge. Suddenly, Jesse put out his hand and stopped the child, then pointed up the slope. The animal, clearly visible in the moonlight, was sitting on its haunches, its head cocked sideways as it chuckled. It was a merry and rather melodious little chuckle.

Skeeter grinned in spite of his surprise, then said, "Sh-h-h. It'll smell us."

Jesse said, "Can't nothing smell that far. Wonder what the durn thing is?" He peered up the ridge, studying the creature. He had no intention of shooting unless attacked, for Jesse Tolliver and his nephew never killed wantonly.[6]

The animal, however, did smell them and whipped her nose into the wind, crouched, and braced. She was about sixteen inches high and weighed twenty-two pounds. Her coat was red and silky, and there was a blaze of white down her chest and a circle of white

---

1 **gaunt** (gônt): thin and bony.
2 **denizens** (den′ ə zenz): inhabitants.
3 **fox fire**: phosphorescent light coming from decaying timber.
4 **bayou** (bī′ yü): a marshy, sluggish inlet of a gulf or lake or river in the south central United States.

5 **morass** (mə ras′): marsh.
6 **wantonly** (wän′ ton lē): without reason.

around her throat. Her face was wrinkled and sad, like a wise old man's.

Jesse shook his head. "Looks som'n like a mixture of bloodhound and terrier from here," he whispered. "It beats me—"

"It's a dog, all right," Skeeter said.

"Can't no dog laugh."

"That dog can." The boy began walking toward the animal, his right hand outstretched. "Heah, heah. I ain't gonna hurt you."

The dog, for she was a dog, cocked her head from one side to the other and watched Skeeter. She was trembling, but she didn't run. And when Skeeter knelt by her, she stopped trembling, for the ways of a boy with a dog are mysterious. He stroked her, and the trim little creature looked up at him and blinked her big hazel eyes. Then she turned over and Skeeter scratched her. She closed her eyes, stretched and chuckled, a happy mixture of chortle[7] and yodel.[8] Jesse ambled up, and the dog leaped to her feet and sprang between the boy and the man.

Skeeter calmed her. "That's just Uncle Jess."

Jesse, still bewildered, shook his head again. "I still say that ain't no dog. She don't smell and she don't bark. Ain't natural. And look at her! Licking herself like a cat."

"Well, I'll be a catty wampus," Skeeter said. "Never saw a dog do that before." However, he was quick to defend any mannerism of his friend and said, "She likes to keep herself clean. She's a lady and I'm gonna name her that, and she's mine 'cause I found her."

"Lady, huh?"

"No, sir. My Lady. If I name her just plain

Lady, how folks gonna know she's mine?" He began stroking his dog again. "Gee m'netty, Uncle Jess, I ain't never had nothing like this before."

"It still don't make sense to me," Jesse said. But he didn't care, for he was happy because the child was happy.

Like most mysteries, there was no mystery at all about My Lady. She was a lady, all right, an aristocratic Basenji,[9] one of those strange barkless dogs of Africa. Her ancestors were pets of the Pharaohs, and her line was well established when the now proud races of men were wandering about Europe, begging

---

7 **chortle** (chôr′ tl): sound made up of a chuckle and a snort.
8 **yodel** (yō′ dl): a falsetto singing with deep tones.

9 **Basenji** (bə sen′ jē): a small, reddish African dog that does not bark.

handouts from Nature. A bundle of nerves and muscles, she would fight anything and could scent game up to eighty yards. She had the gait of an antelope and was odorless, washing herself before and after meals. However, the only noises she could make were a piercing cry that sounded almost human and that chuckling little chortle. She could chuckle only when happy and she had been happy in the woods. Now she was happy again.

As most people judge values, she was worth more than all the possessions of Jesse and his nephew. Several of the dogs had been shipped to New Orleans to avoid the dangerous upper route, thence by motor to a northern kennel. While crossing Mississippi, My Lady had escaped from the station wagon. Her keeper had advertised in several papers, but Jesse and Skeeter never saw papers.

Skeeter said, "Come on, M'Lady. Let's go home."

The dog didn't hesitate, but walked proudly at the boy's side to a cabin on the bank of the bayou. Skeeter crumbled corn bread, wet it with potlikker,[10] and put it before her. She sniffed the food disdainfully at first, then ate it only when she saw the boy fix a bowl for his uncle. She licked herself clean and explored the cabin, sniffing the brush brooms, the piles of wild pecans and hickory nuts, and then the cots. Satisfied at last, she jumped on Skeeter's bed, tucked her nose under her paws, and went to sleep.

"Acts like she owns the place," Jesse said.

"Where you reckon she came from?" The boy slipped his overall straps from his shoulders, flexed his stringy muscles, and yawned.

"Lord knows. Circus maybe." He looked at M'Lady quickly. "Say, maybe she's a freak and run off from some show. Bet they'd give us two dollars for her."

Skeeter's face got long. "You don't aim to get rid of her?"

The old man put his shotgun over the mantel and lit his pipe. "Skeets, if you want that thing, I wouldn't get shed of her for a piece of bottom land a mile long. Already plowed and planted."

"I reckoned you wouldn't, 'cause you like me so much. And I know how you like dogs, 'cause I saw you cry when yours got killed. But you can have part of mine."

Jesse sat down and leaned back, blowing smoke into the air to drive away mosquitoes. The boy got a brick and hammer and began cracking nuts, pounding the meat to pulp so his uncle could chew it. Skeeter's yellow hair hadn't been cut for months and was tangled. He had freckles too. And his real name was Jonathan. His mother was Jesse's only sister and died when the child was born. No one thereabouts ever knew what happened to his father. Jesse, a leathery, toothless old man with faded blue eyes, took him to bring up and called him Skeeter because he was so little.

In the village, where Jesse seldom visited, folks wondered if he were fit'n to rear a little boy. They considered him shiftless and no-count. Jesse had lived all of his sixty years in the swamp, and his way of life was a torment to folks who believed life must be lived by rules. He earned a few dollars selling jumbo frogs and pelts, but mostly he just paddled around the swamp, watching things and teaching Skeeter about life.

The villagers might have tried to send Skeeter to an orphanage, but for Joe (Cash) Watson, the storekeeper. Cash was a hard

---

10 **potlikker** (pot′ lik ər): juice from meat and greens boiled together.

man, but fair. He often hunted with Jesse, and the old man had trained Cash's dogs. When there was talk of sending Skeeter away, Cash said, "You ain't gonna do it. You just don't take young'uns away from their folks." And that's all there was to it.

Jesse never coveted the "frills and furbelows[11] of damn-fool folks" and yearned for only two things—a twenty-gauge shotgun for Skeeter and a set of Roebuckers[12] for himself, as he called store-bought teeth. Cash had promised him the gun and the best false teeth in the catalogue for forty-six dollars. Jesse had saved nine dollars and thirty-seven cents.

"Someday I'm agonna get them Roebuckers," he often told Skeeter. "Then I'm gonna eat me enough roastin' ears to kill a goat. Maybe I can get a set with a couple of gold teeth in 'em. I seen a man once with six gold teeth."

Once Skeeter asked him, "Why don't you get a job with the W. P. and A.[13] and make enough money to buy them Roebuckers?"

"I don't want 'em that bad," Jesse said.

So he was happy for Skeeter to have M'Lady, thinking the dog would sort of make up for the shotgun.

The boy cracked as many nuts as his uncle wanted, then put the hammer away. He was undressing when he glanced over at his dog. "Gosh, Uncle Jess. I'm scared somebody'll come get her."

"I ain't heard of nobody losing no things around here. If'n they had, they'd been to me 'fo' now, beings I know all about dogs and the swamp."

"That's so," Skeeter said. "But you don't reckon she belonged to another fellow like me, do you? I know how I'd feel if I had a dog like her and she got lost."

Jesse said, "She didn't belong to another fellow like you. If'n she had, she wouldn't be so happy here."

Skeeter fed M'Lady biscuits and molasses for breakfast, and although the Basenji ate it, she still was hungry when she went into the swamp with the boy. He was hoping he could find a bee tree or signs of wild hogs. They were at the edge of a clearing when M'Lady's chokebore[14] nose suddenly tilted and she froze to a flash point,[15] pausing only long enough to get set. Then she darted to the bayou, at least sixty yards away, dived into a clump of reeds, and snatched a water rat. She was eating it when Skeeter ran up.

"Don't do that," he scolded. "Ain't you got no more sense than run into water after things? A snake or a 'gator might snatch you."

The Basenji dropped the rat and tucked her head. She knew the boy was displeased, and when she looked up at him her eyes were filled and a woebegone expression was on her face.

Skeeter tried to explain, "I didn't mean to hurt your feelings. Don't cry." He stepped back quickly and stared at her, at the tears in her eyes. "She *is* crying! By John Brown!" Skeeter called her and ran toward the cabin, where Jesse was cutting splinters.

"Uncle Jess! Guess what else my dog can do!"

"Whistle," the old man laughed.

---

11 **furbelows** (fėr' bə lōz): fancy, fussy trimmings on clothing.
12 **Roebuckers**: referring to mail order teeth from Sears, Roebuck and Company.
13 **W.P. and A.**: W.P.A., Works Progress Administration; in the 1930s, a federal agency that put the unemployed to work on useful public projects.

14 **chokebore** (chōk' bôr): tapered at the end.
15 **flash point**: hunting dog standing briefly with head pointed toward hidden game.

"She can cry! I declare to goodness! Not out loud, but she can cry just the same."

Jesse knew that most dogs will get watery-eyed on occasion, but not wanting to ridicule M'Lady's accomplishments, asked, "What made her cry?"

"Well, sir, we were walking along and all of a sudden she got a scent and flash pointed and then—" Skeeter remembered something.

"Then what?"

Skeeter sat on the steps. "Uncle Jess," he said slowly, "we must have been fifty or sixty yards from that rat when she smelled it."

"What rat? What's eating you?"

The child told him the story and Jesse couldn't believe it. For a dog to pick up the scent of a water rat at sixty yards simply isn't credible. Jesse reckoned Skeeter's love for M'Lady had led him to exaggerate.

Skeeter knew Jesse didn't believe the story, so he said, "Come on. I'll show you." He whistled for M'Lady.

The dog came up. "Hey," Jesse said. "That thing knows what a whistle means. Shows she's been around folks." He caught the dog's eye and commanded, "Heel!"

But M'Lady cocked her head quizzically.[16] Then she turned to the boy and chuckled softly. She'd never heard the order before. That was obvious. Her nose came up into the breeze and she wheeled.

Her curved tail suddenly was still and her head was poised.

"Flash pointing," Jesse said. "Well, I'll be a monkey's uncle!"

M'Lady held the strange point only for a second, though, then dashed toward a corn patch about eighty yards from the cabin.

Halfway to the patch, she broke her gait and began creeping. A whir of feathered lightning sounded in the corn and a covey[17] of quail exploded almost under her nose. She sprang and snatched a bird.

"Partridges!" Jesse's jaw dropped.

The child was as motionless as stone, his face white and his eyes wide in amazement. Finally he found his voice, "She was right here when she smelled them birds. A good eighty yards."

"I know she ain't no dog now," Jesse said. "Can't no dog do that."

"She's fast as greased lightning and ain't scared of nothing." Skeeter still was under the spell of the adventure. "She's a hunting dog from way back."

"She ain't no dog a-tall, I'm telling you. It ain't human." Jesse walked toward M'Lady and told her to fetch the bird, but the dog didn't understand. Instead, she pawed it. "Well," Jesse said. "One thing's certain. She ain't no bird hunter."

"She can do anything," Skeeter said. "Even hunt birds. Maybe I can make a bird dog out'n her. Wouldn't that be som'n?"

"You're batty. Maybe a coon dog, but not a bird dog. I know 'bout dogs."

"Me too," said Skeeter. And he did. He'd seen Jesse train many dogs, even pointers, and had helped him train Big Boy, Cash Watson's prize gun dog.

Jesse eyed Skeeter and read his mind.

"It can't be done, Skeets."

"Maybe not, but I aim to try. Any dog can run coons and rabbits, but it takes a pure D humdinger to hunt birds. Ain't no sin in trying, is it?"

---

16 **quizzically** (kwiz' ə klē): in a questioning, uncertain way.

17 **covey** (kuv' ē): a small flock.

"Naw," Jesse said slowly. "But she'll flush[18] birds."

"I'll learn her not to."

"She won't hold no point. Any dog'll flash point. And she'll hunt rats."

"I'm gonna learn her just to hunt birds. And I'm starting right now," Skeeter said. He started walking away, then turned. "I seen a man once train a razorback hawg to point birds. You know as good as me that if a dog's got pure D hoss sense and a fellow's got bat brains, he can train the dog to hunt birds."

"Wanta bet?" Jesse issued the challenge in an effort to keep Skeeter's enthusiasm and determination at the highwater mark.

"Yes, sir. If I don't train my dog, then I'll cut all the splinters[19] for a year. If I do, you cut 'em."

"It's a go," Jesse said.

Skeeter ran to the bayou and recovered the rat M'Lady had killed. He tied it around his dog's neck. The Basenji was indignant and tried to claw off the hateful burden. Failing, she ran into the house and under a bed, but Skeeter made her come out. M'Lady filled up then, and her face assumed that don't-no-body-love-me look. The boy steeled himself, tapped M'Lady's nose with the rat, and left it around her neck.

"You done whittled out a job for yourself," Jesse said. "If'n you get her trained, you'll lose her in the brush. She's too fast and too little to keep up with."

"I'll bell her," Skeeter said. "I'm gonna learn her ever'thing. I got us a gun dog, Uncle Jess."

The old man sat on the porch and propped against the wall. "Bud, I don't know what that thing is. But you're a thoroughbred. John dog my hide!"

If Skeeter had loved M'Lady one bit less, his patience would have exploded during the ordeal of training the Basenji. It takes judgment and infinite patience to train a bird dog properly, but to train a Basenji, that'll hunt anything, to concentrate only on quail took something more than discipline and patience. It never could have been done except for that strange affinity[20] between a boy and a dog, and the blind faith of a child.

M'Lady's devotion to Skeeter was so complete that she was anxious to do anything to earn a pat. It wasn't difficult to teach her to heel and follow at Skeeter's feet regardless of the urge to dash away and chase rabbits. The boy used a clothesline as a guide rope and made M'Lady follow him. The first time the dog tried to chase an animal, Skeeter pinched the rope around her neck just a bit and commanded, "Heel!" And when she obeyed, Skeeter released the noose. It took M'Lady only a few hours to associate disobedience with disfavor.

The dog learned that when she chased and killed a rat or rabbit, the thing would be tied around her neck. The only things she could hunt without being disciplined were quail. Of course, she often mistook the scent of game chickens for quail and hunted them, but Skeeter punished her by scolding. He never switched his dog, but to M'Lady a harsh word from the boy hurt more than a hickory limb.

Jesse watched the dog's progress and pretended not to be impressed. He never volunteered suggestions. M'Lady learned quickly, but the task of teaching her to point birds

---

18 **flush**: chase.
19 **splinters**: small, thin pieces of wood.

20 **affinity** (ə fin′ ə tē): attraction.

seemed hopeless. Skeeter knew she'd never point as pointers do, so he worked out his own system. He taught her to stand motionless when he shouted "Hup!" One day she got a scent of birds, paused or pointed for a moment as most animals will, and was ready to spring away when Skeeter said "Hup!"

M'Lady was confused. Every instinct urged her to chase the birds, but her master had said stand still. She broke, however, and Skeeter scolded her. She pouted at first, then filled up, but the boy ignored her until she obeyed the next command, then he patted her and she chuckled.

The lessons continued for days and weeks, and slowly and surely M'Lady learned her chores. She learned that the second she smelled birds she must stop and stand still until Skeeter flushed them. That she must not quiver when he shot.

Teaching her to fetch was easy, but teaching her to retrieve dead birds without damaging them was another matter. M'Lady had a hard mouth—that is, she sank her teeth into the birds. Skeeter used one of the oldest hunting tricks of the backwoods to break her.

He got a stick and wrapped it with wire and taught his dog to fetch it. Only once did M'lady bite hard on the stick, and then the wire hurt her sensitive mouth. Soon she developed a habit of carrying the stick on her tongue and supporting it lightly with her teeth. Skeeter tied quail feathers on the stick, and soon M'Lady's education was complete.

Skeeter led Jesse into a field one day and turned his dog loose. She flashed to a point almost immediately. It was a funny point and Jesse almost laughed. The dog's curved tail poked up over her back, she spraddled her front legs and sort of squatted, her nose pointing the birds, more than forty yards away. She remained rigid until the boy flushed and shot; then she leaped away, seeking and fetching dead birds.

Jesse was mighty proud. "Well, Skeets, looks like you got yourself a bird hunter."

"Yes, sir," Skeeter said. "And you got yourself a job." He pointed toward the kindling pile.

The swamp was dressing for winter when Cash Watson drove down that day to give his Big Boy a workout in the wild brush.

He fetched Jesse a couple of cans of smoking tobacco and Skeeter a bag of peppermint jawbreakers. He locked his fine pointer in the corncrib for the night and was warming himself in the cabin when he noticed M'Lady for the first time. She was sleeping in front of the fire.

"What's that?" he asked.

"My dog," said Skeeter. "Ain't she a beaut?"

"She sure is," Cash grinned at Jesse. Skeeter went out to the well and Cash asked his old friend, "What the devil kind of mutt is that?"

"Search me," said Jesse. "Skeets found her in the swamp. I reckon she's got a trace of bloodhound in her and some terrier and a heap of just plain dog."

M'Lady cocked one ear and got up and stretched; then, apparently not liking the company, turned her tail toward Cash and strutted out, looking for Skeeter.

The men laughed. "Som'n wrong with her throat," Jesse said. "She can't bark. When she tries, she makes a funny sound, sort of a cackling, chuckling yodel. Sounds like she's laughing."

"Well," Cash said, "trust a young'un to love the orner'st[21] dog he can find."

---

21 **orner'st:** most ornery; meanest.

"Wait a minute," Jesse said. "She ain't no-count. She's a bird-hunting fool."

Just then Skeeter entered and Cash jestingly said, "Hear you got yourself a bird dog, son."

The boy clasped his hands behind him and rocked on the balls of his feet as he had seen the men do. "Well, now, I'll tell you, Mr. Cash. M'Lady does ever'thing except tote the gun."

"She must be fair to middling. Why not take her out with Big Boy tomorrow? Do my dog good to hunt in a brace."

"Me and my dog don't want to show Big Boy up. He's a pretty good ol' dog."

"Whoa!" Cash was every inch a bird-dog man and nobody could challenge him without a showdown. Besides, Skeeter was shooting up and should be learning a few things about life. "Any old boiler can pop off steam." Cash winked at Jesse.

"Well, now, sir, if you're itching for a run, I'll just double-dog dare you to run your dog against mine. And anybody who'll take a dare will pull up young cotton and push a widow woman's ducks in the water."

Cash admired the boy's confidence.

"All right, son, it's a deal. What are the stakes?"

Skeeter started to mention the twenty-gauge gun he wanted but changed his mind quickly. He reached down and patted M'Lady, then looked up. "If my dog beats yours, then you get them Roebuckers for Uncle Jess."

Jesse's chest suddenly was tight. Cash glanced from the boy to the man and he, too, was proud of Skeeter. "I wasn't aiming to go that high. But all right. What do I get if I win?"

"I'll cut you ten cords of stove-wood."

"And a stack of splinters?"

"Yes, sir."

Cash offered his hand and Skeeter took it. "It's a race," Cash said. "Jesse will be the judge."

The wind was rustling the sage and there was a nip in the early-morning air when they took the dogs to a clearing and set them down. Skeeter snapped a bell around M'Lady's neck and, at a word from Jesse, the dogs were released.

Big Boy bounded away and began circling, ranging into the brush. M'Lady tilted her nose into the wind and ripped away toward the sage, her bell tinkling. Cash said, "She sure covers ground." Skeeter made no effort to keep up with her, but waited until he couldn't hear the bell, then ran for a clearing where he had last heard it. And there was M'Lady on a point.

Cash laughed out loud. "That ain't no point, son. That's a squat."

"She's got birds."

"Where?"

Jesse leaned against a tree and watched the fun.

Skeeter pointed toward a clump of sage. "She's pointing birds in that sage."

Cash couldn't restrain his mirth. "Boy, now that's what I call some pointing. Why, Skeeter, it's sixty or seventy yards to that sage."

Just then Big Boy flashed by M'Lady, his head high. He raced to the edge of the sage, caught the wind, then whipped around, freezing to a point. Cash called Jesse's attention to the point.

"That's M'Lady's point," Skeeter said. "She's got the same birds Big Boy has."

Jesse sauntered up. "The boy's right, Cash. I aimed to keep my mouth out'n this race,

but M'Lady is pointing them birds. She can catch scents up to eighty yards."

Cash said, "Aw, go on. You're crazy." He walked over and flushed the birds.

Skeeter picked one off and ordered M'Lady to fetch. When she returned with the bird, the boy patted her and she began chuckling.

Cash really studied her then for the first time. "Hey!" he said suddenly. "A Basenji! That's a Basenji!"

"A what?" Jesse asked.

"I should have known," Cash was very excited. "That's the dog that was lost by them rich Yankees. I saw about it in the paper." He happened to look at Skeeter then and wished he had cut out his tongue.

The boy's lips were compressed and his face was drawn and white. Jesse had closed his eyes and was rubbing his forehead.

Cash, trying to dismiss the subject, said, "Just 'cause it was in the paper don't make it

so. I don't believe that's the same dog, come to think of it."

"Do you aim to tell 'em where the dog is?" Skeeter asked.

Cash looked at Jesse, then at the ground. "It ain't none of my business."

"How 'bout you, Uncle Jess?"

"I ain't telling nobody nothin'."

"I know she's the same dog," Skeeter said. "On account of I just know it. But she's mine now." His voice rose and trembled. "And ain't nobody gonna take her away from me." He ran into the swamp. M'Lady was at his heels.

Cash said, "Durn my lip. I'm sorry, Jesse. If I'd kept my big mouth shut he'd never known the difference."

"It can't be helped now," Jesse said.

"'Course she beat Big Boy. Them's the best hunting dogs in the world. And she's worth a mint of money."

They didn't feel up to hunting and

returned to the cabin and sat on the porch. Neither had much to say, but kept glancing toward the swamp where Skeeter and M'Lady were walking along the bayou. "Don't you worry," he said tenderly; "ain't nobody gonna bother you."

He sat on a stump and M'Lady put her head on his knee. She wasn't worrying. Nothing could have been more contented then she was.

"I don't care if the sheriff comes down." Skeeter pulled her onto his lap and held her. "I don't give a whoop if the governor comes down. Even the President of the United States! The whole shebang can come, but ain't nobody gonna mess with you."

His words gave him courage and he felt better, but for only a minute. Then the tug-of-war between him and his conscience started.

"Once I found a Barlow knife and kept it and it was all right," he mumbled.

But this is different.

"Finders, keepers; losers, weepers."

No, Skeeter.

"Well, I don't care. She's mine."

Remember what your Uncle Jesse said.

"He said a heap of things."

Yes, but you remember one thing more than the rest. He said, "Certain things are right and certain things are wrong. And nothing ain't gonna ever change that. When you learn that, then you're fit'n to be a man." Remember, Skeeter?

A feeling of despair and loneliness almost overwhelmed him. He fought off the tears as long as he could, but finally he gave in, and his sobs caused M'Lady to peer into his face and wonder why he was acting that way when she was so happy. He put his arms around her neck and pulled her to him. "My li'l old puppy dog. Poor li'l old puppy dog. But I got to do it."

He sniffed back his tears and got up and walked to the cabin. M'Lady curled up by the fire, and the boy sat down, watching the logs splutter for several minutes. Then he said, almost in a whisper, "Uncle Jess, if you keep som'n that ain't yours, it's the same as stealing, ain't it?"

Cash leaned against the mantel and stared into the fire.

Jesse puffed his pipe slowly. "Son, that's som'n you got to settle with yourself."

Skeeter stood and turned his back to the flames, warming his hands. "Mr. Cash," he said slowly, "when you get back to your store, please let them folks know their dog is here."

"If that's how it is—"

"That's how it is," Skeeter said.

The firelight dancing on Jesse's face revealed the old man's dejection,[22] and Skeeter,

---

22 **dejection** (di jek′ shən): low spirits.

seeing it, said quickly, "It's best for M'Lady. She's too good for the swamp. They'll give her a good home."

Jesse flinched, and Cash, catching the hurt look in his friend's eyes, said, "Your dog outhunted mine, Skeets. You win them Roebuckers for your uncle."

"I don't want 'em," Jesse said, rather childishly. "I don't care if'n I never eat no roastin' ears." He got up quickly and hurried outside. Cash reckoned he'd better be going, and left Skeeter by the fire, rubbing his dog.

Jesse came back in directly and pulled up a chair. Skeeter started to speak, but Jesse spoke first. "I been doing a heap of thinking lately. You're sprouting up. The swamp ain't no place for you."

Skeeter forgot about his dog and faced his uncle, bewildered.

"I reckon you're too good for the swamp too," Jesse said. "I'm aiming to send you into town for a spell. I can make enough to keep you in fit'n clothes and all." He dared not look at the boy.

"Uncle Jess!" Skeeter said reproachfully. "You don't mean that. You're just saying that on account of what I said about M'Lady. I said it just to keep you from feeling so bad about our dog going away. Gee m'netty, Uncle Jess. I ain't ever gonna leave you." He buried his face in his uncle's shoulder. M'Lady put her head on Jesse's knee, and he patted the boy and rubbed the dog.

"Reckon I'll take them Roebuckers," he said at last. "I been wanting some for a long, long time."

Several days later Cash drove down and told them the man from the kennels was at his store. Skeeter didn't say a word, but called M'Lady and they got in Cash's car. All the way to town, the boy was silent. He held his dog's head in his lap.

The keeper took just one look at M'Lady and said, "That's she, all right. Miss Congo III." He turned to speak to Skeeter, but the boy was walking away. He got a glance at Skeeter's face, however. "I wish you fellows hadn't told me," he muttered. "I hate to take a dog away from a kid."

"He wanted you to know," Cash said.

"Mister"—Jesse closed his left eye and struck his swapping pose—"I'd like to swap you out'n that hound. Now, 'course she ain't much 'count—"

The keeper smiled in spite of himself. "If she was mine, I'd give her to the kid. But she's not for sale. The owner wants to breed her and establish her line in this country. And if she was for sale, she'd cost more money than any of us will ever see." He called Skeeter and offered his hand. Skeeter shook it.

"You're a good kid. There's a reward for this dog."

"I don't want no reward." The boy's words tumbled out. "I don't want nothing, except to be left alone. You've got your dog, mister. Take her and go on. Please." He walked away again, fearing he would cry.

Cash said, "I'll take the reward and keep it for him. Some day he'll want it."

Jesse went out to the store porch to be with Skeeter. The keeper handed Cash the money. "It's tough, but the kid'll get over it. The dog never will."

"Is that a fact?"

"Yep. I know the breed. They never forget. That dog'll never laugh again. They never laugh unless they're happy."

He walked to the post where Skeeter had tied M'Lady. He untied the leash and started toward his station wagon. M'Lady braced her front feet and looked around for the boy. Seeing him on the porch, she jerked away from the keeper and ran to her master.

She rubbed against his legs. Skeeter tried to ignore her. The keeper reached for the leash again and M'Lady crouched, baring her fangs. The keeper shrugged, a helpless gesture.

"Wild elephants couldn't pull that dog away from that boy," he said.

"That's all right, mister." Skeeter unsnapped the leash and tossed it to the keeper. Then he walked to the station wagon, opened the door of a cage, and called, "Heah, M'Lady!" She bounded to him. "Up!" he commanded. She didn't hesitate, but leaped into the cage. The keeper locked the door.

M'Lady, having obeyed a command, poked her nose between the bars, expecting a pat. The boy rubbed her head. She tried to move closer to him, but the bars held her. She looked quizzically at the bars, then tried to nudge them aside. Then she clawed them. A look of fear suddenly came to her eyes, and she fastened them on Skeeter, wistfully at

first, then pleadingly. She couldn't make a sound, for her unhappiness had sealed her throat. Slowly her eyes filled up.

"Don't cry no more, M'Lady. Ever'thing's gonna be all right." He reached out to pat her, but the station wagon moved off, leaving him standing there in the dust.

Back on the porch, Jesse lit his pipe and said to his friend, "Cash, the boy has lost his dog and I've lost a boy."

"Aw, Jesse, Skeeter wouldn't leave you."

"That ain't what I mean. He's growed up, Cash. He don't look no older, but he is. He growed up that day in the swamp."

Skeeter walked into the store and Cash followed him. "I've got that reward for you, Jonathan."

It was the first time anyone ever had called him that and it sounded like man talk.

"And that twenty-gauge is waiting for you," Cash said. "I'm gonna give it to you."

"Thank you, Mr. Cash." The boy bit his lower lip. "But I don't aim to do no more hunting. I don't never want no more dogs."

"Know how you feel. But if you change your mind, the gun's here for you."

Skeeter looked back toward the porch where Jesse was waiting, and said, "Tell you what, though. When you get them Roebuckers, get some with a couple of gold teeth in 'em. Take it out of the reward money."

"Sure, Jonathan."

Jesse joined them, and Skeeter said, "We better be getting back toward the house."

"I'll drive you down," Cash said. "But first I aim to treat you to some lemon pop and sardines."

"That's mighty nice of you," Jesse said, "but we better be gettin' on."

"What's the hurry?" Cash opened the pop.

"It's my time to cut splinters," Jesse said. "That's what I get for betting with a good man."

Discussion	1. More than anything else in the world, Skeeter wanted to keep My Lady. Explain why he decides to return her to her owner. In your opinion, does Skeeter do the right thing, or doesn't he? Why?

Discussion

1. More than anything else in the world, Skeeter wanted to keep My Lady. Explain why he decides to return her to her owner. In your opinion, does Skeeter do the right thing, or doesn't he? Why?

2. Why does Skeeter give the dog the name "My Lady"? In what ways is My Lady different from other dogs?

3. How does Skeeter train My Lady to be a "gun dog"? What bet do Skeeter and Uncle Jess make about the dog's training?

4. Who is Cash? What is his importance in the story?

5. What two clues are there in the story—before Skeeter actually does decide to give My Lady up—to suggest that the boy will, indeed, have to return the dog to its rightful owner?

6. When Skeeter says of My Lady, "She's too good for the swamp" (page 274), what is Uncle Jess's reaction? Why does he react as he does?

7. At the end of the story, after My Lady is taken away, Uncle Jess says, "Cash, the boy has lost his dog and I've lost a boy." What does Uncle Jess mean?

Writer's Craft

In some stories, authors seek only to entertain you. They simply have a good yarn to tell, and they want you to enjoy it with them. That is what can be said about "The Most Dangerous Game" (page 5), for example, and about "Charles" (page 243).

In other stories, however, the authors want to do more than entertain you. They want to show you something important about human nature or about life. Thus they develop their stories to focus on a THEME—a major idea or an understanding they want you to take away with you. In "The Pacing Goose" (page 76), for example, the author is showing you that it is natural for different people to have different points of view and that one needs to consider the points of view of others in judging what he or she says and does. And in "The Strangers That Came to Town" (page 196), the author is pointing out how harmful it is to judge others before you get to know them. These, in short, are the themes of those stories.

Although the theme of a story is seldom stated in so many words, everything the author says about the characters, about the setting, about the events—even the mood—contributes to and expresses the theme.

1. What is the theme of "Weep No More, My Lady"?
2. In what way does Uncle Jess contribute to and support the theme of the story?
3. What evidence can you find to indicate that Cash respects Skeeter for deciding to return My Lady? How does Cash's respect contribute to the theme?

Composition

1. My Lady had certain inbred hunting instincts. To make her a hunter of nothing but quail, Skeeter developed a plan to train her. In a paragraph or two, summarize the steps in Skeeter's training of My Lady.

2. As you read of Skeeter's decision to return My Lady to her legal owner, you understood the heartache involved. It would have been so easy to pretend that Cash had never told Skeeter of the owner's advertisement. It would have also been so easy for Skeeter to ignore this fact and keep My Lady. But Skeeter's conscience—"certain things are right"—would not permit him to keep the dog. In a short composition, tell about a situation in which you were torn between doing what you desired to do and doing what you knew was right.

James Howell Street 1903–1954

James Howell Street grew up with the Southerners he wrote about. He was born in Mississippi, attended schools and colleges in the South, and worked in six Southern states. After a few years as a reporter, Street became a minister for a short time. Realizing that he was "unfitted emotionally and spiritually for the Baptist ministry," he went back to journalism but remembered the experience for good story material later. He continued to report and edit news and to write stories and novels for the rest of his life. Many readers assumed from his tales that he must love hunting and dogs, but he had no personal taste for hunting and had only one dog.

In Dan'l Webster, Jim Smiley was positive he had a sure winner. After all, wasn't Dan'l the jumpingest frog in Calaveras County? But there was at least one man who didn't think Dan'l was that unusual.

The Celebrated Jumping Frog of Calaveras County

MARK TWAIN

IN COMPLIANCE WITH the request of a friend of mine, who wrote me from the East, I called on good-natured, garrulous[1] old Simon Wheeler, and inquired after my friend's friend, Leonidas W. Smiley, as requested to do, and I hereunto append[2] the result. I have a lurking suspicion that *Leonidas W. Smiley* is a myth; that my friend never knew such a personage; and that he only conjectured[3] that if I asked old Wheeler about him, it would remind him of his infamous *Jim* Smiley, and he would go to work and bore me to death with some exasperating reminiscence[4] of him as long and as tedious as it should be useless to me. If that was the design, it succeeded.

I found Simon Wheeler dozing comfortably by the barroom stove of the dilapidated tavern in the decaying mining camp of Angel's, and I noticed that he was fat and bald-headed, and had an expression of winning gentleness and simplicity upon his tranquil countenance.[5] He roused up, and gave me good day. I told him a friend of mine had commissioned me to make some inquiries about a cherished companion of his boyhood named *Leonidas W. Smiley—Rev. Leonidas W. Smiley*, a young minister of the Gospel, who he had heard was at one time a resident of Angel's Camp. I added that if Mr. Wheeler could tell me anything about this Rev. Leonidas W. Smiley, I would feel under many obligations to him.

Simon Wheeler backed me into a corner and blockaded me there with his chair, and then sat down and reeled off the monotonous narrative which follows this paragraph. He never smiled, he never frowned, he never changed his voice from the gentle-flowing key to which he tuned his initial sentence, he never betrayed the slightest suspicion of enthusiasm; but all through the interminable[6] narrative there ran a vein of impressive

---

1 **garrulous** (gar′ ə ləs): talkative.
2 **append** (ə pend′): attach.
3 **conjectured** (kən jek′ chərd): guessed.
4 **reminiscence** (rem′ə nis′ əns): a remembered experience.

5 **countenance** (koun′ tə nəns): face.
6 **interminable** (in tėr′ mə nə bəl): endless.

earnestness and sincerity, which showed me plainly that, so far from his imagining that there was anything ridiculous or funny about his story, he regarded it as a really important matter, and admired its two heroes as men of transcendent genius in *finesse*.[7] I let him go on in his own way, and never interrupted him once.

"Rev. Leonidas W. H'm, Reverend Le—well, there was a feller here once by the name of *Jim* Smiley, in the winter of '49—or maybe it was the spring of '50—I don't recollect exactly, somehow, though what makes me think it was one or the other is because I remember the big flume[8] warn't finished when he first come to the camp; but anyway, he was the curiosest man about always betting on anything that turned up you ever see, if he could get anybody to bet on the other side; and if he couldn't he'd change sides. Any way that suited the other man would suit *him*—any way just so's he got a bet, *he* was satisfied. But still he was lucky, uncommon lucky; he most always come out winner. He was always ready and laying for a chance; there couldn't be no solit'ry thing mentioned but that feller'd offer to bet on it, and take ary side you please, as I was just telling you. If there was a horse race, you'd find him flush[9] or you'd find him busted at the end of it; if there was a dog fight, he'd bet on it; if there was a cat fight, he'd bet on it; if there was a chicken fight, he'd bet on it; why, if there was two birds setting on a fence, he would bet you which one would fly first; or if there was a camp meeting, he would be there reg'lar to bet on Parson Walker, which he judged to be the best exhorter[10] about here, and so he was, too, and a good man. If he even see a straddlebug start to go anywheres, he would bet you how long it would take him to get to—to wherever he was going to, and if you took him up, he would foller that straddle-bug to Mexico but what he would find out where he was bound for and how long he was on the road. Lots of the boys here has seen that Smiley, and can tell you about him. Why, it never made no difference to *him*—he'd bet on *any* thing—the dangdest feller. Parson Walker's wife laid very sick once, for a good while, and it seemed as if they warn't going to save her; but one morning he come in, and Smiley up and asked him how she was, and he said she was considable better—thank the Lord for his inf'nite mercy—and coming on so smart that with the blessing of Prov'dence she'd get well yet; and Smiley, before he thought, says: 'Well, I'll resk two-and-a-half she don't anyway.'

"Thish-yer Smiley had a mare—the boys called her the fifteen-minute nag, but that was only in fun, you know, because, of course, she was faster than that—and he used to win money on that horse, for all she was so slow and always had the asthma, or the distemper, or the consumption, or something of that kind. They used to give her two or three hundred yards start, and then pass her under way; but always at the fag end of the race she'd get excited and desperate like, and come cavorting and straddling up, and scattering her legs around limber, sometimes in the air, and sometimes out to one side among the fences, and kicking up m-o-r-e dust and raising m-o-r-e racket with her coughing and sneezing and blowing her nose—and *always* fetch up at the stand just about a neck ahead, as near as you could cipher it down.

---

7 **transcendant** . . . *finesse* (tran sen'dənt . . . fə nes'): exceptional talent for effective behavior.
8 **flume** (flüm): deep, narrow channel through which water races.
9 **flush**: well supplied.

10 **exhorter** (eg zôrt' ėr): one who advises or urges.

"And he had a little small bull pup, that to look at him you'd think he warn't worth a cent but to set around and look ornery and lay for a chance to steal something. But as soon as money was up on him he was a different dog; his underjaw'd begin to stick out like the fo'castle of a steamboat, and his teeth would uncover and shine like the furnaces. And a dog might tackle him and bullyrag him, and bite him, and throw him over his shoulder two or three times, and Andrew Jackson—which was the name of the pup—Andrew Jackson would never let on but what *he* was satisfied, and hadn't expected nothing else—and the bets being doubled and doubled on the other side all the time, till the money was all up; and then all of a sudden he would grab that other dog jest by the j'int of his hind leg and freeze to it—not chaw, you understand, but only just grip and hang on till they throwed up the sponge, if it was a year. Smiley always come out winner on that pup, till he harnessed a dog once that didn't have no hind legs, because they'd been sawed off in a circular saw, and when the thing had gone along far enough, and the money was all up, and he come to make a snatch for his pet holt, he see in a minute how he'd been imposed on,[11] and how the other dog had him in the door, so to speak, and he 'peared surprised, and then he looked sorter discouraged-like and didn't try no more to win the fight, and so he got shucked out bad. He give Smiley a look, as much as to say his heart was broke, and it was *his* fault, for putting up a dog that hadn't no hind legs for him to take holt of, which was his main dependence in a fight, and then he limped off a piece and laid down and died. It was a good pup, was that Andrew Jackson, and would have made a name for hisself if he'd lived, for the stuff was in him and he had genius—I know it, because he hadn't no opportunities to speak of, and it don't stand to reason that a dog could make such a fight as he could under them circumstances if he hadn't no talent. It always makes me feel sorry when I think of that last fight of his'n, and the way it turned out.

"Well, thish-yer Smiley had rat-tarriers, and chicken cocks, and tomcats and all them kind of things, till you couldn't rest, and you couldn't fetch nothing for him to bet on but he'd match you. He ketched a frog one day, and took him home, and said he cal'lated[12] to educate him; and so he never done nothing for three months but set in his back yard and learn that frog to jump. And you bet you he *did* learn him, too. He'd give him a little punch behind, and the next minute you'd see that frog whirling in the air like a doughnut—see him turn one summerset, or maybe a couple, if he got a good start, and come down flat-footed and all right, like a cat. He got him up so in the matter of ketching flies, and kep' him in practice so constant, that he'd nail a fly every time as fur as he could see him. Smiley said all a frog wanted was education, and he could do 'most anything—and I believe him. Why, I've seen him set Dan'l Webster down here on this floor—Dan'l Webster was the name of the frog—and sing out, 'Flies, Dan'l, flies!' and quicker'n you could wink he'd spring straight up and snake a fly off'n the counter there, and flop down on the floor ag'in as solid as a gob of mud, and fall to scratching the side of his head with his hind foot as indifferent as if he hadn't no idea he'd been doin' any more'n any frog might do. You never see a frog so modest and

---

11 **imposed on:** here, tricked; cheated.

12 **cal'lated:** calculated; intended.

straightfor'ard as he was, for all he was so gifted. And when it come to fair and square jumping on a dead level, he could get over more ground at one straddle than any animal of his breed you ever see. Jumping on a dead level was his strong suit, you understand; and when it come to that, Smiley would ante up money on him as long as he had a red. Smiley was monstrous proud of his frog, and well he might be, for fellers that had traveled and been everywheres all said he laid over any frog that ever *they* see.

"Well, Smiley kep' the beast in a little lattice box, and he used to fetch him down town sometimes and lay for a bet. One day a feller—a stranger in the camp, he was—come acrost him with his box, and says:

"'What might it be that you've got in the box?'

"And Smiley says, sorter indifferent-like: 'It might be a parrot, or it might be a canary, maybe, but it ain't—it's only just a frog.'

"And the feller took it, and looked at it careful, and turned it round this way and that, and says: 'H'm—so 'tis. Well, what's *he* good for?'

"'Well,' Smiley says, easy and careless, 'he's good enough for *one* thing, I should judge—he can outjump any frog in Calaveras county.'

"The feller took the box again, and took another long, particular look, and give it back to Smiley, and says, very deliberate, 'Well,' he says, 'I don't see no p'ints about that frog that's any better'n any other frog.'

"'Maybe you don't,' Smiley says. 'Maybe you understand frogs and maybe you don't understand 'em; maybe you've had experience, and maybe you ain't only a amature,[13] as it were. Anyways, I've got *my* opinion, and

13 **amature:** amateur; one who is inexperienced.

I'll resk forty dollars that he can outjump any frog in Calaveras county.'

"And the feller studied a minute, and then says, kinder sad like, 'Well, I'm only a stranger here, and I 'ain't got no frog; but if I had a frog, I'd bet you.'

"And then Smiley says, 'That's all right—that's all right—if you'll hold my box a minute, I'll go and get you a frog.' And so the feller took the box, and put up his forty dollars along with Smiley's, and set down to wait.

"So he set there a good while thinking and thinking to hisself, and then he got the frog out and prized his mouth open and took a teaspoon and filled him full of quail shot—filled him pretty near up to his chin—and set him on the floor. Smiley he went to the swamp and slopped around in the mud for a long time, and finally he ketched a frog, and fetched him in, and give him to this feller, and says:

"'Now, if you're ready, set him alongside of Dan'l, with his forepaws just even with Dan'l's, and I'll give the word.' Then he says, 'One—two—three—*git!*' and him and the feller touched up the frogs from behind, and the new frog hopped off lively, but Dan'l give a heave, and hysted up his shoulders—so—like a Frenchman, but it warn't no use—he couldn't budge; he was planted as solid as a church, and he couldn't no more stir than if he was anchored out. Smiley was a good deal surprised, and he was disgusted too, but he didn't have no idea what the matter was, of course.

"The feller took the money and started away; and when he was going out at the door, he sorter jerked his thumb over his shoulder—so—at Dan'l, and says again, very deliberate, 'Well,' he says, '*I* don't see no p'ints about that frog that's any better'n any other frog.'

"Smiley he stood scratching his head and looking down at Dan'l a long time, and at last he says, 'I do wonder what in the nation that frog throw'd off for—I wonder if there ain't something the matter with him—he 'pears to look mighty baggy, somehow.' And he ketched Dan'l by the nap of the neck, and hefted him, and says, 'Why, blame my cats if he don't weigh five pound!' and turned him upside down and he belched out a double handful of shot. And then he see how it was, and he was the maddest man—he set the frog down and took out after that feller, but he never ketched him. And—"

Here Simon Wheeler heard his name called from the front yard, and got up to see what was wanted. And turning to me as he moved away, he said: "Just set where you are, stranger, and rest easy—I ain't going to be gone a second."

But, by your leave, I did not think that a continuation of the history of the enterprising vagabond *Jim* Smiley would be likely to afford me much information concerning the *Rev. Leonidas W.* Smiley, and so I started away.

At the door I met the sociable Wheeler returning, and he buttonholed me and recommenced:

"Well, thish-yer Smiley had a yaller one-eyed cow that didn't have no tail, only just a short stump like a bannanner, and—"

However, lacking both time and inclination, I did not wait to hear about the afflicted cow, but took my leave.

Discussion

1. How did the stranger outfox Jim Smiley and win the bet?

2. What do the incidents about Smiley's mare and his bull pup tell you about Jim Smiley? What other information do you find that suggests the kind of person Jim Smiley is? In what way is the story about the bull pup like the story of Dan'l Webster?

3. Repeated phrases are usually important. Twice the "feller" in the story says, "I don't see no p'ints about that frog that's any better'n any other frog." How does Smiley react to that remark the first time he hears it? How does he react the second time?

4. In this story there is a double plot: the story of the narrator ("I") and the story told by Simon Wheeler. What do you learn in the opening paragraphs about the "I"? What do you learn about Simon Wheeler?

Writer's Craft

How do you know when someone is kidding you? How can you tell when a storyteller is pulling your leg?

Well, have you heard the one about the man who was so tall he had to climb a ladder to see himself in the mirror?

And have you heard about the outstanding work of an army paint and camouflage squad? They camouflaged the fence around their army post so well that three platoons of cadets marched right through it. But that's not all. Two army carpenters spent a week searching for the broken place in that fence. And when they finally found it, they stationed a guard there night and day so that they'd know where to make repairs!

Straight facts? Not at all. Instead, both of the examples above deal with the impossible. That is, they stretch the facts to the point of EXAGGERATION. And that is what makes the stories funny.

Passing off an impossible action or impossible situation as if it were a common, everyday matter—that is, deliberately exaggerating—is one rich source of humor.

1. In "The Celebrated Jumping Frog . . . ," where does Mark Twain use exaggeration to produce humor?

2. Part of the fun of "The Celebrated Jumping Frog . . ." results from the way Simon Wheeler talks. Point out some of the peculiar expressions Simon uses. In what way do these expressions add to the humor of the story?

3. What evidence is there that the narrator's friend—the person who suggested that the "I" visit Simon Wheeler—has a sense of humor?

Vocabulary

Two different styles of English are used in "The Celebrated Jumping Frog. . . ." One is the literary style of the nineteenth centry. This style uses elaborate sentences and words of many syllables. The other is the plain style of a person who has had a limited formal education. This second style uses sentences that sound more like conversation than writing. Many of its unfamiliar words are ones that California Gold Rush miners used, but that are rarely used in modern times.

Both styles of English can be difficult to read. But one good way to overcome the problems they both create is to PARAPHRASE the sentences that are hard to understand. To paraphrase means "to restate in your own words." For example:

ORIGINAL: Simon Wheeler had an expression of *winning* gentleness and simplicity upon his *tranquil countenance.*
PARAPHRASE: Simon Wheeler had an expression of *pleasing* gentleness and simplicity on his *calm face.*

A. Below are three sentences that have already been paraphrased, or restated, from "The Celebrated Jumping Frog. . . ." Find the original version of each one in the story. Copy the three original sentences on a separate sheet of paper.

1. Doing as an Eastern friend's letter had requested, I visited good-natured, talkative Simon Wheeler, and asked about Leonidas W. Smiley. This is what I found out.

2. I have a sneaking suspicion that there's no such person as *Leonidas W.* Smiley; that my friend never knew anybody by that name; and that my friend had developed this theory: if I asked old Wheeler about Leonidas, Wheeler would recall a rascal named *Jim* Smiley; and then Wheeler would bore me to death by telling me his tiresome memories of that person . . .

3. Smiley was always ready and willing to bet; there's nothing you could mention that he wouldn't gamble on, and he would take whichever side you pleased . . .

B. Paraphrase, or restate in your own words, the following sentences from the same story. If necessary, use a dictionary to find synonyms for the difficult words.

1. Wheeler regarded the two heroes of his narrative as men of transcendent genius in *finesse.*

2. Well, Smiley kep' the beast in a little lattice box, and he used to fetch him down town sometimes and lay for a bet.

3. Jumping on a dead level was [the frog's] strong suit, you understand; and when it comes to that, Smiley would ante up money on him as long as he had a red.

4. But, by your leave, I did not think that a continuation of the history of the enterprising vagabond *Jim* Smiley would be likely to afford me much information concerning the Rev. *Leonidas W.* Smiley, and so I started away.

Mark Twain (Samuel Clemens) 1835–1910

Samuel Clemens grew up in Hannibal, Missouri, a small town on the Mississippi River. When his father died, he left school to go to work as a printer's apprentice. Commenting on his school days, Twain said, "Soap and education are not as sudden as massacre, but they are more deadly in the long run."

Years later, he became a pilot for boats on the Mississippi. There he picked up the phrase Mark Twain (meaning two fathoms deep, safe water) which he later used as his pen name.

Though Twain later traveled to and wrote about other parts of the world, his childhood provided the background for his most popular books. On the first page of *Huckleberry Finn,* young Huck introduces himself this way: "You don't know about me without you have read a book by the name of *The Adventures of Tom Sawyer;* but that ain't no matter. That book was made by Mr. Mark Twain, and he told the truth mainly. There was things which he stretched, but mainly he told the truth." Throughout his career, Twain stretched the truth humorously. One of his phrases describes him accurately. He was, "an experienced, industrious, ambitious, and often quite picturesque liar."

Gold, frankincense, and myrrh—those were the gifts the three kings brought with them on that first Christmas. But as Della and Jim Young discovered almost two thousand years later, those were not the only gifts the kings brought!

The Gift of the Magi

O. HENRY

ONE DOLLAR and eighty-seven cents. That was all. And sixty cents of it was in pennies. Pennies saved one and two at a time by bulldozing the grocer and the vegetable man and the butcher until one's cheeks burned with the silent imputation of parsimony[1] that such close dealing implied. Three times Della counted it. One dollar and eighty-seven cents. And the next day would be Christmas.

There was clearly nothing to do but flop down on the shabby little couch and howl. So Della did it. Which instigates the moral reflection[2] that life is made up of sobs, sniffles, and smiles, with sniffles predominating.

While the mistress of the home is gradually subsiding from the first stage to the second, take a look at the home. A furnished flat at $8 per week. It did not exactly beggar description, but it certainly had that word on the lookout for the mendicancy squad.[3]

In the vestibule below was a letter box into which no letter would go, and an electric button from which no mortal finger could coax a ring. Also appertaining thereunto[4] was a card bearing the name "Mr. James Dillingham Young."

The "Dillingham" had been flung to the breeze during a former period of prosperity when its possessor was being paid $30 per week. Now, when the income was shrunk to $20, the letters of "Dillingham" looked blurred, as though they were thinking seriously of contracting to a modest and unassuming D. But whenever Mr. James Dillingham Young came home and reached his flat above, he was called "Jim" and greatly hugged by Mrs. James Dillingham Young, already introduced to you as Della. Which is all very good.

Della finished her cry and attended to her cheeks with the powder rag. She stood by the window and looked out dully at a gray cat walking a gray fence in a gray back yard. Tomorrow would be Christmas Day, and she had only $1.87 with which to buy Jim a

---

1 **imputation of parsimony** (im pyə tā′ shən; pär′ sə mō nē): charge of stinginess.
2 **instigates the moral reflection**: prompts the careful conclusion.
3 **mendicancy** (men′ də kən sē) **squad**: police who search for illegal beggars.

4 **appertaining thereunto**: referring to that letter box.

present. She had been saving every penny she could for months, with this result. Twenty dollars a week doesn't go far. Expenses had been greater than she had calculated. They always are. Only $1.87 to buy a present for Jim. Her Jim. Many a happy hour she had spent planning for something nice for him. Something fine and rare and sterling—something just a little bit near to being worthy of the honor of being owned by Jim.

There was a pier glass[5] between the windows of the room. Perhaps you have seen a pier glass in an $8 flat. A very thin and very agile person may, by observing his reflection in a rapid sequence of longitudinal[6] strips, obtain a fairly accurate conception of his looks. Della, being slender, had mastered the art.

Suddenly she whirled from the window and stood before the glass. Her eyes were shining brilliantly, but her face had lost its color within twenty seconds. Rapidly she pulled down her hair and let it fall to its full length.

Now, there were two possessions of the James Dillingham Youngs in which they both took a mighty pride. One was Jim's gold watch·that had been his father's and his grandfather's. The other was Della's hair. Had the Queen of Sheba lived in the flat across the airshaft, Della would have let her hair hang out the window some day to dry just to depreciate[7] Her Majesty's jewels and gifts. Had King Solomon been the janitor, with all his treasures piled up in the basement, Jim would have pulled out his watch every time he passed, just to see him pluck at his beard from envy.

So now Della's beautiful hair fell about her, rippling and shining like a cascade of brown waters. It reached below her knee and made itself almost a garment for her. And then she did it up again nervously and quickly. Once she faltered for a minute and stood still while a tear or two splashed on the worn red carpet.

On went her old brown jacket; on went her old brown hat. With a whirl of skirts and with the brilliant sparkle still in her eyes, she fluttered out the door and down the stairs to the street.

Where she stopped the sign read: "Mme. Sofronie. Hair Goods of All Kinds." One flight up Della ran, and collected herself panting. Madame, large, too white, chilly, hardly looked the "Sofronie."

"Will you buy my hair?" asked Della.

"I buy hair," said Madame. "Take yer hat off and let's have a sight at the looks of it."

Down rippled the brown cascade.

"Twenty dollars," said Madame, lifting the mass with a practiced hand.

"Give it to me quick," said Della.

Oh, and the next two hours tripped by on rosy wings. Forget the hashed metaphor.[8] She was ransacking the stores for Jim's present.

She found it at last. It surely had been made for Jim and no one else. There was no other like it in any of the stores, and she had turned all of them inside out. It was a platinum fob chain[9] simple and chaste in design, properly proclaiming its value by substance alone and not by meretricious[10] ornamentation—as all good things should do.

---

5 **pier glass** (pēr′ glas): tall, narrow mirror designed to fit on a wall between windows.
6 **longitudinal** (lon jə tü′ də nəl): lengthwise.
7 **depreciate** (di prē′ shē āt): belittle; detract from.

8 **hashed metaphor** (met′ ə fôr): a comparison that doesn't make much sense.
9 **fob chain**: short watch chain.
10 **meretricious** (mer′ ə trish′ əs): showy like tinsel; falsely attractive.

It was even worthy of The Watch. As soon as she saw it she knew that it must be Jim's. It was like him. Quietness and value—the description applied to both. Twenty-one dollars they took from her for it, and she hurried home with the 87 cents. With that chain on his watch Jim might be properly anxious about the time in any company. Grand as the watch was, he sometimes looked at it on the sly on account of the old leather strap that he used in place of a chain.

When Della reached home her intoxication[11] gave way a little to prudence and reason. She got out her curling irons and lighted the gas and went to work repairing the ravages[12] made by generosity added to love. Which is always a tremendous task, dear friends—a mammoth task.

Within forty minutes her head was covered with tiny, close-lying curls that made her look wonderfully like a truant schoolboy. She looked at her reflection in the mirror long, carefully, and critically.

"If Jim doesn't kill me," she said to herself, "before he takes a second look at me, he'll say I look like a Coney Island chorus girl. But what could I do—oh! what could I do with a dollar and eighty-seven cents?"

At seven o'clock the coffee was made and the frying pan was on the back of the stove hot and ready to cook the chops.

Jim was never late. Della doubled the fob chain in her hand and sat on the corner of the table near the door that he always entered. Then she heard his step on the stair away down on the first flight, and she turned white for just a moment. She had a habit of saying little silent prayers about the simplest everyday things, and now she whispered: "Please, God, make him think I am still pretty."

The door opened and Jim stepped in and closed it. He looked thin and very serious. Poor fellow, he was only twenty-two—and to be burdened with a family! He needed a new overcoat and he was without gloves.

Jim stopped inside the door, as immovable as a setter at the scent of quail. His eyes were fixed upon Della, and there was an expression in them that she could not read, and it terrified her. It was not anger, nor surprise, nor disapproval, nor horror, nor any of the sentiments that she had been prepared for. He simply stared at her fixedly with that peculiar expression on his face.

Della wriggled off the table and went for him.

"Jim, darling," she cried, "don't look at me that way. I had my hair cut off and sold it because I couldn't have lived through Christmas without giving you a present. It'll grow out again—you won't mind, will you? I just had to do it. My hair grows awfully fast. Say 'Merry Christmas!' Jim, and let's be happy. You don't know what a nice—what a beautiful, nice gift I've got for you."

"You've cut off your hair?" asked Jim, laboriously, as if he had not arrived at that patent fact yet even after the hardest mental labor.

"Cut if off and sold it," said Della. "Don't you like me just as well, anyhow? I'm me without my hair, ain't I?"

Jim looked about the room curiously.

"You say your hair is gone?" he said, with an air almost of idiocy.

"You needn't look for it," said Della. "It's sold, I tell you—sold and gone, too. It's Christmas Eve, boy. Be good to me, for it went for you. Maybe the hairs of my head were numbered," she went on with a sudden serious sweetness, "but nobody could ever count my love for you. Shall I put the chops on, Jim?"

---

11 **intoxication** (in tok′ sə kā′ shən): here, excitement.
12 **ravages** (rav′ ij ez): damage.

Out of his trance Jim seemed quickly to wake. He enfolded his Della. For ten seconds let us regard with discreet scrutiny[13] some inconsequential[14] object in the other direction. Eight dollars a week or a million a year—what is the difference? A mathematician or a wit would give you the wrong answer. The magi brought valuable gifts, but that was not among them. This dark assertion[15] will be illuminated later on.

Jim drew a package from his overcoat pocket and threw it upon the table.

"Don't make any mistake, Dell," he said, "about me. I don't think there's anything in the way of a haircut or a shave or a shampoo that could make me like my girl any less. But if you'll unwrap that package you may see why you had me going a while at first."

White fingers and nimble tore at the string and paper. And then an ecstatic scream of joy; and then, alas! a quick feminine change to hysterical tears and wails, necessitating the immediate employment of all the comforting powers of the lord of the flat.

For there lay The Combs—the set of combs, side and back, that Della had worshiped for long in a Broadway window. Beautiful combs, pure tortoise shell, with jeweled rims—just the shade to wear in the beautiful vanished hair. They were expensive combs, she knew, and her heart had simply craved and yearned over them without the least hope of possession. And now, they were hers, but the tresses that should have adorned the coveted[16] adornments were gone.

But she hugged them to her bosom, and at length she was able to look up with dim eyes and a smile and say: "My hair grows so fast, Jim!"

And then Della leaped up like a little singed cat and cried, "Oh, oh!"

Jim had not yet seen his beautiful present. She held it out to him eagerly upon her open palm. The dull precious metal seemed to flash with a reflection of her bright and ardent spirit.

"Isn't it a dandy, Jim? I hunted all over town to find it. You'll have to look at the time a hundred times a day now. Give me your watch. I want to see how it looks on it."

Instead of obeying, Jim tumbled down on the couch and put his hands under the back of his head and smiled.

"Dell," said he, "let's put our Christmas presents away and keep 'em a while. They're too nice to use just at present. I sold the watch to get the money to buy your combs. And now suppose you put the chops on."

The magi, as you know, were wise men—wonderfully wise men—who brought gifts to the Babe in the manger. They invented the art of giving Christmas presents. Being wise, their gifts were no doubt wise ones, possibly bearing the privilege of exchange in case of duplication. And here I have lamely related to you the uneventful chronicle of two foolish children in a flat who most unwisely sacrificed for each other the greatest treasures of their house. But in a last word to the wise of these days let it be said that of all who give gifts these two were the wisest. Of all who give and receive gifts, such as they are wisest. Everywhere they are wisest. They are the magi.

---

13 **discreet scrutiny** (skrüt′ ə nē): tactful inspection.
14 **inconsequential** (in kon si kwen′ chəl): unimportant.
15 **assertion** (ə ser′ shən): statement; declaration.
16 **coveted** (kov′ ə təd): desired.

1. Would you say that Della and Jim have a usual or an unusual Christmas? Why? How does each of them obtain the money for the other's gift? What do they do with their gifts? What lasting gift does each receive?

2. Do you think Della sacrifices too much for Jim's present? Why or why not? Do you think Jim sacrifices too much for Della's present? Why or why not? What does their behavior suggest about the kind of persons they are?

3. What evidence is there that the story takes place a number of years ago?

4. Although the story is essentially a serious one, O. Henry does use humor—especially as concerns Della. Point out some examples of that humor.

5. Reread the last paragraph of the story. What do you think those sentences mean? Why do you think O. Henry says of Della and Jim, "They are the magi."?

6. What do you think the title means?

7. People who have read this story say that they have never forgotten it. Why, in you opinion, has the story had so much impact?

Writer's Craft

There are occasions when the story you are reading seems pretty ordinary. You feel sure that you know how things will turn out. But there are other occasions when a story has your undivided attention. The events do not follow the pattern you thought they would. Instead, the plot takes a sudden turn, and the ending is one you didn't expect. In that case, we say that the story has a SURPRISE ENDING because of an _unexpected twist_ in the plot.

1. Were you prepared or unprepared for the outcome of "The Gift of the Magi"? Why? Where does the unexpected twist in the plot occur?

2. Looking back through the story, you will have to admit that O. Henry does play fair with you. From time to time, he drops hints about the outcome. Which hints can you find?

3. Readers of this story generally agree that the ending is a good one, an appropriate one. Why, do you suppose, do they think so?

Vocabulary

When you look up a word in the dictionary, you find the word spelled in two ways: first, as it is written and second (in parentheses), as it sounds. After that you find an abbreviation that tells the word's PART OF SPEECH, or traditional classification according to its use in sentences. Here are three examples of those abbreviations:

n. = *noun,* "the name of a person, place, thing, or idea"
v. = *verb,* "a word expressing action, occurrence, or existence"
adj. = *adjective,* "a word that modifies (describes or changes) a noun or pronoun"

A. On a separate sheet of paper, copy each pair of related words from the two lists below. Look these words up in a dictionary. After each word, give its part of speech (abbreviated) and its meaning (stated as briefly as possible).

1. calculated   calculation
2. conception (idea)   conceive
3. parsimony   parsimonious
4. prudence   prudent
5. scrutiny   scrutinize

B. Below are five pairs of sentences. Each sentence contains, in parentheses ( ), one pair of the related words listed above. In each case, tell which word you think is correct. Explain your choice.

1. a. Expenses had been greater than Della had (*calculation, calculated*).
   b. Jim made a (*calculation, calculated*) to sell his watch.

2. a. In the pier glass, Della got a fairly accurate (*conception, conceive*) of her looks.
   b. Jim could (*conception, conceive*) of nothing he would like better than to sell his watch to buy a gift for Della.

3. a. These ideas came to them because of their poverty, not because of (*parsimony, parismonious*).
   b. Neither Della nor Jim was the least bit (*parsimony, parsimonious*).

4. a. If the young couple had been more (*prudence, prudent*), they would have been less generous.
   b. (*Prudence, Prudent*) would have told them: "Your gifts of love are enough. You need not give more."

5. a. But, as O. Henry suggests, it is foolish to (*scrutiny, scrutinize*) the reasons for generosity and love.
   b. Generosity and love have far more value than (*scrutiny, scrutinize*) does.

O. Henry (William Sydney Porter) 1862—1910

The name O. *Henry* is a certain indication that a story will end with an unusual twist of fate. The ending is a surprise for everyone except the readers who know O. Henry.

William Porter grew up in Greensboro, North Carolina, but later went to Texas for his health. He worked in Austin as a bookkeeper and bankteller, and in 1887, he married a Houston girl. Shortly after he began selling his stories, he was charged with embezzlement at the Austin bank. Porter fled to Honduras, where he met the outlaw, Al Jennings. The two men traveled through South America and Mexico on Jennings's stolen money. When Porter learned that his wife was seriously ill in Texas, he returned to her and to face the law. He was convicted and served more than three years of his sentence in prison before he was released for good behavior.

Porter probably borrowed the name O. *Henry* from one of the guards at the prison. He spent some of his prison time writing stories, but he wrote most of his stories in New York City later.

When Porter died, it just happened that his life ended with a surprise, too. As friends arrived at the church for his funeral, they found that a wedding had been scheduled for the same time.

*Rip had been hunting and he was tired.
Certainly he was in no hurry to return to his
nagging wife or the fields that needed tending.
Besides, the mountains were so quiet and
peaceful. Why not lie down to rest a little while?*

Rip Van Winkle

WASHINGTON IRVING

WHOEVER HAS MADE a voyage up the Hudson must remember the Kaatskill mountains. They are a dismembered branch of the great Appalachian family, and are seen away to the west of the river, swelling up to a noble height, and lording it over the surrounding country. Every change of season, every change of weather, indeed, every hour of the day, produces some change in the magical hues and shapes of these mountains, and they are regarded by all the good wives, far and near, as perfect barometers. When the weather is fair and settled, they are clothed in blue and purple, and print their bold outlines on the clear evening sky; but, sometimes, when the rest of the landscape is cloudless, they will gather a hood of gray vapors about their summits, which, in the last days of the setting sun, will glow and light up like a crown of glory.

At the foot of these fairy mountains, the voyager may have descried the light smoke curling up from a village, whose shingle roofs gleam among the trees, just where the blue tints of the upland melt away into the fresh green of the nearer landscape. It is a little village, of great antiquity, having been founded by some of the Dutch colonists, in the early times of the province, just about the beginning of the government of the good Peter Stuyvesant[1] (may he rest in peace!), and there were some of the houses of the original settlers standing within a few years, built of small yellow bricks brought from Holland, having latticed windows and gable fronts, surmounted with weathercocks.

In that same village, and in one of these very houses (which, to tell the precise truth, was sadly timeworn and weather-beaten), there lived many years since, while the country was yet a province of Great Britain, a simple good-natured fellow, of the name of Rip Van Winkle. He was a descendant of the Van Winkles who figured so gallantly in the chivalrous days of Peter Stuyvesant, and accompanied him to the siege of Fort Christina.[2] He inherited, however, but little of the martial character of his ancestors. I have

---

1 **Peter Stuyvesant** (stī′ və zənt) 1592–1672: last governor of the Dutch colony making up what is now New York, New Jersey, and Delaware.
2 **Fort Christina:** Stuyvesant seized this fort from the Swedish in 1655.

observed that he was a simple good-natured man; he was, moreover, a kind neighbor, and an obedient henpecked husband. Indeed, to the latter circumstance might be owing that meekness of spirit which gained him such universal popularity; for those men are most apt to be obsequious[3] and conciliating abroad who are under the discipline of shrews[4] at home. Their tempers, doubtless, are rendered pliant and malleable in the fiery furnace of domestic tribulation; and a curtain lecture is worth all the sermons in the world for teaching the virtues of patience and long-suffering. A termagant[5] wife may, therefore, in some respects, be considered a tolerable blessing; and if so, Rip Van Winkle was thrice blessed.

Certain it is, that he was a great favorite among all the good wives of the village, who, as usual, with the amiable sex, took his part in all family squabbles; and never failed, whenever they talked those matters over in their evening gossipings, to lay all the blame on Dame Van Winkle. The children of the village, too, would shout with joy whenever he approached. He assisted at their sports, made their playthings, taught them to fly kites and shoot marbles, and told them long stories of ghosts, witches, and Indians. Whenever he went dodging about the village, he was surrounded by a troop of them, hanging on his skirts, clambering on his back, and playing a thousand tricks on him with impunity;[6] and not a dog would bark at him throughout the neighborhood.

The great error in Rip's composition was an insuperable aversion[7] to all kinds of prof-itable labor. It could not be from the want of assiduity[8] or perseverance; for he would sit on a wet rock, with a rod as long and heavy as a Tartar's[9] lance, and fish all day without a murmur, even though he should not be encouraged by a single nibble. He would carry a fowling piece[10] on his shoulder for hours together, trudging through woods and swamps, and up hill and down dale, to shoot a few squirrels or wild pigeons. He would never refuse to assist a neighbor even in the roughest toil, and was a foremost man at all country frolics for husking Indian corn, or building stone fences; the women of the village, too, used to employ him to run their errands, and to do such little odd jobs as their less obliging husbands would not do for them. In a word Rip was ready to attend to anybody's business but his own; but as to doing family duty, and keeping his farm in order, he found it impossible.

In fact, he declared it was of no use to work on his farm; it was the most pestilent little piece of ground in the whole country; everything about it went wrong, and would go wrong, in spite of him. His fences were continually falling to pieces; his cow would either go astray or get among the cabbages; weeds were sure to grow quicker in his fields than anywhere else; the rain always made a point of setting in just as he had some outdoor work to do; so that though his patrimonial estate[11] had dwindled away under his management, acre by acre, until there was little more left than a mere patch of Indian corn and potatoes; yet it was the

---

3 **obsequious** (ob sē′ kwē əs): servile; obedient or polite from hope of some gain or from fear.
4 **shrews**: bad-tempered women.
5 **termagant** (tėr′ mə gənt): violent; scolding.
6 **impunity** (im pyü′ nə tē): freedom from punishment.
7 **insuperable aversion** (in süp′ ėr ə bəl ə vėr′ zhən): dislike that cannot be surpassed.

8 **assiduity** (as′ ə dü′ ə tē): diligence, careful and steady attention to what one is doing.
9 **Tartar**: member of one of the tribes that overran Asia and eastern Europe during the Middle Ages.
10 **fowling piece**: old-fashioned gun for shooting fowl; the gun had a long barrel that ended in a shape like a bell.
11 **patrimonial estate** (pat rə mō′ ni əl ə stāt): land belonging to one's ancestors.

worst-conditioned farm in the neighborhood.

His children, too, were as ragged and wild as if they belonged to nobody. His son Rip, an urchin begotten in his own likeness, promised to inherit the habits, with the old clothes of his father. He was generally seen trooping like a colt at his mother's heels, equipped in a pair of his father's castoff galligaskins,[12] which he had much ado to hold up with one hand, as a fine lady does her train in bad weather.

Rip Van Winkle, however, was one of those happy mortals, of foolish, well-oiled dispositions, who take the world easy, eat white bread or brown, whichever can be got with least thought or trouble, and would rather starve on a penny than work for a pound.[13] If left to himself, he would have whistled life away in perfect contentment; but his wife kept continually dinning in his ears about his idleness, his carelessness, and the ruin he was bringing on his family. Morning, noon, and night, her tongue was incessantly going, and everything he said or did was sure to produce a torrent of household eloquence. Rip had but one way of replying to all lectures of the kind, and that, by frequent use, had grown into a habit. He shrugged his shoulders, shook his head, cast up his eyes, but said nothing. This, however, always provoked a fresh volley from his wife; so that he was fain[14] to draw off his forces, and take to the outside of the house—the only side which, in truth, belongs to a henpecked husband.

Rip's sole domestic adherent was his dog Wolf, who was as much henpecked as his master; for Dame Van Winkle regarded them as companions in idleness, and even looked upon Wolf with an evil eye, as the cause of his master's going so often astray. True it is, in all points of spirit befitting an honorable dog, he was as courageous an animal as ever scoured the woods—but what courage can withstand the everduring and all-besetting terrors of a woman's tongue? The moment Wolf entered the house his crest fell, his tail drooped to the ground, or curled between his legs, he sneaked about with a gallows air, casting many a sidelong glance at Dame Van Winkle, and at the least flourish of a broomstick or ladle, he would fly to the door with yelping precipitation.

Times grew worse and worse with Rip Van Winkle as years of matrimony rolled on; a tart temper never mellows with age, and a sharp tongue is the only edged tool that grows keener with constant use. For a long while he used to console himself, when driven from home, by frequenting a kind of perpetual club of the sages, philosophers, and other idle personages of the village; which held its sessions on a bench before a small inn, designated by a rubicund[15] portrait of His Majesty George the Third.[16] Here they used to sit in the shade through a long lazy summer's day, talking listlessly over village gossip, or telling endless sleepy stories about nothing. But it would have been worth any statesman's money to have heard the profound discussions that sometimes took place, when by chance an old newspaper fell into their hands from some passing traveler. How solemnly they would listen to the contents, as drawled out by Derrick Van Bummel, the schoolmaster, a dapper, learned little man, who was not to be daunted by the most

---

12 **galligaskins** (gal' ə gas' kənz): knee breeches.
13 **pound:** British monetary unit. Today, the pound equals about $2.25.
14 **fain** (fān): willing, but not eager.

15 **rubicund** (rü' bə kənd): reddish; ruddy.
16 **George the Third:** King of England from 1760 to 1820.

gigantic word in the dictionary; and how sagely they would deliberate upon public events some months after they had taken place.

The opinions of this junto[17] were completely controlled by Nicholas Vedder, a patriarch of the village, and landlord of the inn, at the door of which he took his seat from morning till night, just moving sufficiently to avoid the sun and keep in the shade of a large tree; so that the neighbors could tell the hour by his movements as accurately as by a sundial. It is true he was rarely heard to speak, but smoked his pipe incessantly. His adherents, however (for every great man has his adherents), perfectly understood him, and knew how to gather his opinions. When anything that was read or related displeased him, he was observed to smoke his pipe vehemently, and to send forth short, frequent and angry puffs; but when pleased, he would inhale the smoke slowly and tranquilly, and emit it in light and placid clouds; and sometimes, taking the pipe from his mouth, and letting the fragrant vapor curl about his nose, would gravely nod his head in token of perfect approbation.

From even this stronghold the unlucky Rip was at length routed by his termagant wife, who would suddenly break in upon the tranquillity of the assemblage and call the members all to naught; nor was that august personage, Nicholas Vedder himself, sacred from the daring tongue of this terrible virago,[18] who charged him outright with encouraging her husband in habits of idleness.

Poor Rip was at last reduced almost to despair; and his only alternative, to escape from the labor of the farm and clamor of his wife, was to take gun in hand and stroll away into the woods. Here he would sometimes seat himself at the foot of a tree, and share the contents of his wallet with Wolf, with whom he sympathized as a fellow sufferer in persecution. "Poor Wolf," he would say, "thy mistress leads thee a dog's life of it; but never mind, my lad, whilst I live thou shalt never want a friend to stand by thee!" Wolf would wag his tail, look wistfully in his master's face, and if dogs can feel pity I verily believe he reciprocated the sentiment with all his heart.

In a long ramble of the kind on a fine autumnal day, Rip had unconsciously scrambled to one of the highest parts of the Kaatskill mountains. He was after his favorite sport of squirrel shooting, and the still solitudes had echoed and re-echoed with the reports of his gun. Panting and fatigued, he threw himself, late in the afternoon, on a green knoll, covered with mountain herbage, that crowned the brow of a precipice. From an opening between the trees he could overlook all the lower country for many a mile of rich woodland. He saw at a distance the lordly Hudson, far, far below him, moving on its silent but majestic course, with the reflection of a purple cloud, or the sail of a lagging bark, here and there sleeping on its glassy bosom, and at last losing itself in the blue highlands.

On the other side he looked down into a deep mountain glen, wild, lonely, and shagged, the bottom filled with fragments from the impending cliffs, and scarcely lighted by the reflected rays of the setting sun. For some time Rip lay musing on this scene; evening was gradually advancing; the mountains began to throw their long blue shadows over the valleys; he saw that it would be dark long before he could reach the village, and he heaved a heavy sigh when he

---

17 junto (jun′ tō): clique; ruling body.
18 virago (və rā′ gō): a scolding; bad-tempered woman.

thought of encountering the terrors of Dame Van Winkle.

As he was about to descend, he heard a voice from a distance, hallooing, "Rip Van Winkle! Rip Van Winkle!" He looked round, but could see nothing but a crow winging its solitary flight across the mountain. He thought his fancy must have deceived him, and turned again to descend, when he heard the same cry ring through the still evening air; "Rip Van Winkle! Rip Van Winkle!" At the same time Wolf bristled up his back, and giving a low growl, skulked to his master's side, looking fearfully down into the glen. Rip now felt a vague apprehension stealing over him; he looked anxiously in the same direction, and perceived a strange figure slowly toiling up the rocks, and bending under the weight of something he carried on his back. He was surprised to see any human being in this lonely and unfrequented place, but supposing it to be someone of the neighborhood in need of his assistance, he hastened down to yield it.

On nearer approach he was still more surprised at the singularity of the stranger's appearance. He was a short square-built old fellow, with thick bushy hair, and a grizzled beard. His dress was of the antique Dutch fashion—a cloth jerkin strapped round the waist—several pair of breeches, the outer one of ample volume, decorated with rows of buttons down the sides, and bunches at the knees. He bore on his shoulder a stout keg that seemed full of liquor and made signs for Rip to approach and assist him with the load. Though rather shy and distrustful of this new acquaintance, Rip complied with his usual alacrity; and mutually relieving one another, they clambered up a narrow gully, apparently the dry bed of a mountain torrent. As they ascended, Rip every now and then heard long rolling peals, like distant thunder, that seemed to issue out of a deep ravine, or rather cleft, between lofty rocks, toward which their rugged path conducted. He paused for an instant, but supposing it to be the muttering of one of those transient thundershowers which often take place in mountain heights, he proceeded. Passing through the ravine, they came to a hollow, like a small amphitheater,[19] surrounded by perpendicular precipices, over the brinks of which impending trees shot their branches, so that you only caught glimpses of the azure sky and the bright evening cloud. During the whole time Rip and his companion had labored on in silence; for though the former marveled greatly what could be the object of carrying a keg of liquor up this wild mountain, yet there was something strange and incomprehensible[20] about the unknown that inspired awe and checked familiarity.

On entering the amphitheater, new objects of wonder presented themselves. On a level spot in the center was a company of odd-looking personages playing at ninepins.[21] They were dressed in a quaint outlandish fashion; some wore short doublets, others jerkins, with long knives in their belts, and most of them had enormous breeches, of similar style with that of the guide's. Their visages, too, were peculiar: one had a large beard, broad face, and small piggish eyes: the face of another seemed to consist entirely of nose, and was surmounted by a white sugar-loaf hat, set off with a little red cock's tail. They all had beards, of various shapes and colors. There was one who seemed to be the

---

19 **amphitheater** (am′ fə thē′ ə tər): an open theater, the seats for which are built on a hillside in a semicircle.
20 **incomprehensible** (in kom prē hen′ sə bəl): impossible to understand.
21 **ninepins**: a bowling game with nine pins.

commander. He was a stout old gentleman, with a weather-beaten countenance; he wore a laced doublet, broad belt and hanger,[22] high crowned hat and feather, red stockings, and high-heeled shoes, with roses[23] in them. The whole group reminded Rip of the figures in an old Flemish painting, in the parlor of Dominic Van Shaick, the village parson, and which had been brought over from Holland at the time of the settlement.

What seemed particularly odd to Rip was, that though these folks were evidently amusing themselves, yet they maintained the gravest faces, the most mysterious silence, and were, withal,[24] the most melancholy party of pleasure he had ever witnessed. Nothing interrupted the stillness of the scene but the noise of the balls, which, whenever they were rolled, echoed along the mountains like rumbling peals of thunder.

As Rip and his companion approached them, they suddenly desisted from their play, and stared at him with such fixed statuelike gaze, and such strange, uncouth,[25] lackluster countenances, that his heart turned within him, and his knees smote together. His companion now emptied the contents of the keg into large flagons, and made signs to him to

22 **hanger:** a short sword.
23 **roses:** ribbons in a rose-shaped arrangement.

24 **withal** (wi thôl'): with it all; besides; as well.
25 **uncouth** (un küth'): crude.

wait upon the company. He obeyed with fear and trembling; they quaffed the liquor in profound silence, and then returned to their game.

By degrees Rip's awe and apprehension subsided. He even ventured, when no eye was fixed upon him, to taste the beverage, which he found had much of the flavor of excellent Hollands.[26] He was naturally a thirsty soul, and was soon tempted to repeat the draught. One taste provoked another; and he reiterated his visits to the flagon so often that at length his senses were overpowered, his eyes swam in his head, his head gradually declined, and he fell into a deep sleep.

On waking, he found himself on the green knoll whence he had first seen the old man of the glen. He rubbed his eyes—it was a bright sunny morning. The birds were hopping and twittering among the bushes, and the eagle was wheeling aloft, and breasting the pure mountain breeze. "Surely," thought Rip, "I have not slept here all night." He recalled the occurrences before he fell asleep. The strange man with a keg of liquor—the mountain ravine—the wild retreat among the rocks—the woebegone party at ninepins—the flagon—"Oh! that flagon! that wicked flagon!" thought Rip—"what excuse shall I make to Dame Van Winkle!"

He looked round for his gun, but in place of the clean well-oiled fowling piece, he found an old firelock lying by him, the barrel incrusted with rust, the lock falling off, and the stock worm-eaten. He now suspected that the grave roysters[27] of the mountain had put a trick upon him, and, having dosed him with liquor, had robbed him of his gun. Wolf, too, had disappeared, but he might have strayed away after a squirrel or partridge. He whistled after him and shouted his name, but all in vain; the echoes repeated his whistle and shout, but no dog was to be seen.

He determined to revisit the scene of the last evening's gambol, and if he met with any of the party, to demand his dog and gun. As he rose to walk, he found himself stiff in the joints, and wanting in his usual activity. "These mountain beds do not agree with me," thought Rip, "and if this frolic should lay me up with a fit of the rheumatism, I shall have a blessed time with Dame Van Winkle." With some difficulty he got down into the glen: he found the gully up which he and his companion had ascended the preceding evening; but to his astonishment a mountain stream was now foaming down it, leaping from rock to rock, and filling the glen with babbling murmurs. He, however, made shift to scramble up its sides, working his toilsome way through thickets of birch, sassafras, and witch hazel, and sometimes tripped up or entangled by the wild grapevines that twisted their coils or tendrils from tree to tree, and spread a kind of network in his path.

At length he reached to where the ravine had opened through the cliffs to the amphitheater; but no traces of such opening remained. The rocks presented a high, impenetrable wall over which the torrent came tumbling in a sheet of feathery foam, and fell into a broad deep basin, black from the shadows of the surrounding forest. Here, then, poor Rip was brought to a stand. He again called and whistled after his dog; he was only answered by the cawing of a flock of idle crows, sporting high in air about a dry tree that overhung a sunny precipice; and who, secure in their elevation, seemed to look down and scoff at the poor man's perplexities. What was to be done? The morning was passing away, and Rip felt famished for

---

26 **Hollands**: gin made in Holland.
27 **roysters**: roisterers; noisy revelers.

want of his breakfast. He grieved to give up his dog and gun; he dreaded to meet his wife; but it would not do to starve among the mountains. He shook his head, shouldered the rusty firelock, and, with a heart full of trouble and anxiety, turned his steps homeward.

As he approached the village he met a number of people, but none whom he knew, which somewhat surprised him, for he had thought himself acquainted with everyone in the country round. Their dress, too, was of a different fashion from that to which he was accustomed. They all stared at him with equal marks of surprise, and whenever they cast their eyes upon him, invariably stroked their chins. The constant recurrence of this gesture induced Rip, involuntarily, to do the same, when, to his astonishment, he found his beard had grown a foot long!

He had now entered the skirts of the village. A troop of strange children ran at his heels, hooting after him, and pointing at his gray beard. The dogs, too, not one of which he recognized for an old acquaintance, barked at him as he passed. The very village was altered; it was larger and more populous. There were rows of houses which he had never seen before, and those which had been his familiar haunts had disappeared. Strange names were over the doors—strange faces at the windows—everything was strange. His mind now misgave him; he began to doubt whether both he and the world around him were not bewitched. Surely this was his native village, which he had left but the day before. There stood the Kaatskill mountains—there ran the silver Hudson at a distance—there was every hill and dale precisely as it had always been—Rip was sorely perplexed—"That flagon last night," thought he, "has addled my poor head sadly!"

It was with some difficulty that he found the way to his own house, which he approached with silent awe, expecting every moment to hear the shrill voice of Dame Van Winkle. He found the house gone to decay—the roof fallen in, the windows shattered, and the doors off the hinges. A half-starved dog that looked like Wolf was skulking about it. Rip called him by name, but the cur snarled, showed his teeth, and passed on. This was an unkind cut indeed—"My very dog," sighed poor Rip, "has forgotten me!"

He entered the house, which, to tell the truth, Dame Van Winkle had always kept in neat order. It was empty, forlorn, and apparently abandoned. This desolateness overcame all his connubial[28] fears—he called loudly for his wife and children—the lonely chambers rang for a moment with his voice, and then all again was silence.

He now hurried forth, and hastened to his old resort, the village inn—but it too was gone. A large rickety wooden building stood in its place, with great gaping windows, some of them broken and mended with old hats and petticoats, and over the door was painted, "The Union Hotel, by Jonathan Doolittle." Instead of the great tree that used to shelter the quiet little Dutch inn of yore, there now was reared a tall naked pole, with something on the top that looked like a red nightcap, and from it was fluttering a flag, on which was a singular assemblage of stars and stripes—all this was strange and incomprehensible. He recognized on the sign, however, the ruby face of King George, under which he had smoked so many a peaceful pipe; but even this was singularly metamorphosed.[29] The red coat was changed for one

---

28 **connubial** (kə nü′ bē əl): having to do with marriage.
29 **metamorphosed** (met′ ə môr′ fōzd): changed in form, structure, or substance.

of blue and buff, a sword was held in the hand instead of a scepter, the head was decorated with a cocked hat, and underneath was painted in large characters,

GENERAL WASHINGTON

There was, as usual, a crowd of folk about the door, but none that Rip recollected. The very character of the people seemed changed. There was a busy, bustling, disputatious tone about it, instead of the accustomed phlegm and drowsy tranquillity. He looked in vain for the sage Nicholas Vedder, with his broad face, double chin, and fair long pipe, uttering clouds of tobacco smoke instead of idle speeches; or Van Bummel, the schoolmaster, doling forth the contents of an ancient newspaper. In place of these, a lean, bilious-looking fellow, with his pockets full of handbills, was haranguing vehemently[30] about rights of citizens—elections—members of congress—liberty—Bunker's Hill—heroes of seventy-six—and other words, which were a perfect Babylonish[31] jargon to the bewildered Van Winkle.

The appearance of Rip, with his long grizzled beard, his rusty fowling piece, his uncouth dress, and an army of women and children at his heels, soon attracted the attention of the tavern politicians. They crowded round him, eyeing him from head to foot with great curiosity. The orator bustled up to him, and drawing him aside, inquired "on which side he voted?" Rip stared in vacant stupidity. Another short but busy little fellow pulled him by the arm, and, rising on tiptoe, inquired in his ear, "Whether he was Federal or Democrat?"

Rip was equally at a loss to comprehend the question; when a knowing, self-important old gentleman, in a sharp cocked hat, made his way through the crowd, putting them to the right and left with his elbows as he passed, and planting himself before Van Winkle, with one arm akimbo, the other resting on his cane, his keen eyes and sharp hat penetrating, as it were, into his very soul, demanded in an austere tone, "what brought him to the election with a gun on his shoulder, and a mob at his heels, and whether he meant to breed a riot in the village?"—"Alas! gentlemen," cried Rip, somewhat dismayed, "I am a poor, quiet man, a native of the place, and a loyal subject of the king, God bless him!"

Here a general shout burst from the bystanders—"A tory! a tory! a spy! a refugee! hustle him! away with him!" It was with great difficulty that the self-important man in the cocked hat restored order; and, having assumed a tenfold austerity of brow, demanded again of the unknown culprit, what he came there for, and whom he was seeking? The poor man humbly assured him that he meant no harm, but merely came there in search of some of his neighbors, who used to keep about the tavern.

"Well—who are they?—name them."

Rip bethought himself a moment, and inquired, "Where's Nicholas Vedder?"

There was a silence for a little while, when an old man replied, in a thin piping voice, "Nicholas Vedder! why, he is dead and gone these eighteen years! There was a wooden tombstone in the churchyard that used to tell all about him, but that's rotten and gone too."

"Where's Brom Dutcher?"

"Oh, he went off to the army in the beginning of the war; some say he was killed

---

30 **vehemently** (vē′ ə mənt lē): passionately.
31 **Babylonish**: confused, incomprehensible.

at the storming of Stony Point[32]—others say he was drowned in a squall at the foot of Antony's Nose.[33] I don't know—he never came back again."

"Where's Van Bummel, the schoolmaster?"

"He went off to the wars too, was a great militia general, and is now in Congress."

Rip's heart died away at hearing of these sad changes in his home and friends, and finding himself thus alone in the world. Every answer puzzled him too, by treating of such enormous lapses of time, and of matters which he could not understand: war—Congress—Stony Point; he had no courage to ask after any more friends, but cried out in despair, "Does nobody here know Rip Van Winkle?"

"Oh, Rip Van Winkle!" exclaimed two or three, "Oh, to be sure! That's Rip Van Winkle yonder, leaning against the tree."

Rip looked, and beheld a precise counterpart of himself, as he went up the mountain: apparently as lazy, and certainly as ragged. The poor fellow was now completely confounded. He doubted his own identity, and whether he was himself or another man. In the midst of his bewilderment, the man in the cocked hat demanded who he was, and what was his name?

"God knows," exclaimed he, at his wit's end; "I'm not myself—I'm somebody else—that's me yonder—no—that's somebody else got into my shoes—I was myself last night, but I fell asleep on the mountain, and they've changed my gun, and everything's changed, and I'm changed, and I can't tell what's my name, or who I am!"

The bystanders began now to look at each other, nod, wink significantly, and tap their fingers against their foreheads. There was a whisper, also, about securing the gun, and keeping the old fellow from doing mischief, at the very suggestion of which the self-important man in the cocked hat retired with some precipitation. At this critical moment a fresh comely[34] woman pressed through the throng to get a peep at the gray-bearded man. She had a chubby child in her arms, which, frightened at his looks, began to cry. "Hush, Rip," cried she, "hush, you little fool; the old man won't hurt you." The name of the child, the air of the mother, the tone of her voice, all awakened a train of recollection in his mind. "What is your name, my good woman?" asked he.

"Judith Gardenier."

"And your father's name?"

"Ah, poor man, Rip Van Winkle was his name, but it's twenty years since he went away from home with his gun, and never has been heard of since—his dog came home without him; but whether he shot himself, or was carried away by the Indians, nobody can tell. I was then but a little girl."

Rip had but one question more to ask; but he put it with a faltering voice:

"Where's your mother?"

"Oh, she too had died but a short time since; she broke a blood vessel in a fit of passion at a New England peddler."

There was a drop of comfort, at least, in this intelligence. The honest man could contain himself no longer. He caught his daughter and her child in his arms. "I am your father!" cried he—"Young Rip Van Winkle once—old Rip Van Winkle now!—Does nobody know poor Rip Van Winkle?"

---

32 **Stony Point:** site on the Hudson River of a fort important in the Revolutionary War.

33 **Antony's Nose:** another fortified headland on the Hudson.

---

34 **comely** (kum′ lē): attractive.

All stood amazed, until an old woman, tottering out from among the crowd, put her hand to her brow, and peering under it in his face for a moment, exclaimed, "Sure enough! It is Rip Van Winkle—it is himself! Welcome home again, old neighbor—Why, where have you been these twenty long years?"

Rip's story was soon told, for the whole twenty years had been to him but as one night. The neighbors stared when they heard it; some were seen to wink at each other, and put their tongues in their cheeks: and the self-important man in the cocked hat, too, when the alarm was over, had returned to the field, screwed down the corners of his mouth, and shook his head—upon which there was a general shaking of the head throughout the assemblage.

It was determined, however, to take the opinion of old Peter Vanderdonk, who was seen slowly advancing up the road. He was a descendant of the historian of that name, who wrote one of the earliest accounts of the province. Peter was the most ancient inhabitant of the village, and well versed in all the wonderful events and traditions of the neighborhood. He recollected Rip at once, and corroborated his story in the most satisfactory manner. He assured the company that it was a fact, handed down from his ancestor the historian, that the Kaatskill mountains had always been haunted by strange beings. That it was affirmed that the great Hendrick Hudson, the first discoverer of the river and country, kept a kind of vigil there every twenty years, with his crew of the *Half Moon;* being permitted in this way to revisit the scenes of his enterprise, and keep a guardian eye upon the river, and the great city called by his name. That his father had once seen them in their old Dutch dresses playing at ninepins in a hollow of the mountain; and that he himself had heard, one summer afternoon, the sound of their balls like distant peals of thunder.

To make a long story short, the company broke up and returned to the more important concerns of the election. Rip's daughter took him home to live with her; she had a snug, well-furnished house, and a stout cheery farmer for a husband, whom Rip recollected for one of the urchins that used to climb upon his back. As to Rip's son and heir, who was the ditto of himself, seen leaning against the tree, he was employed to work on the farm; but evinced[35] an hereditary disposition to attend to anything else but his business.

Rip now resumed his old walks and habits; he soon found many of his former cronies, though all rather the worse for the wear and tear of time; and preferred making friends among the rising generation, with whom he soon grew into great favor.

Having nothing to do at home, and being arrived at that happy age when a man can be idle with impunity, he took his place once more on the bench at the inn door, and was reverenced as one of the patriarchs of the village, and a chronicle of the old times "before the war." It was sometime before he could get into the regular track of gossip, or could be made to comprehend the strange events that had taken place during his torpor.[36] How that there had been a revolutionary war—that the country had thrown off the yoke of old England—and that, instead of being a subject of His Majesty George the Third, he was now a free citizen of the United States. Rip, in fact, was no politician; the changes of states and empires made but

---

35 **evinced** (ē vinsd'): showed clearly.
36 **torpor** (tôr' pėr): suspension of activity, as in hibernation.

little impression on him; but there was one species of despotism under which he had long groaned, and that was—petticoat government. Happily that was at an end; he had got his neck out of the yoke of matrimony, and could go in and out whenever he pleased, without dreading the tyranny of Dame Van Winkle. Whenever her name was mentioned, however, he shook his head, shrugged his shoulders, and cast up his eyes; which might pass either for an expression of resignation to his fate, or joy at his deliverance.

He used to tell his story to every stranger that arrived at Mr. Doolittle's hotel. He was observed, at first, to vary on some points every time he told it, which was, doubtless, owing to his having so recently awaked. It at last settled down precisely to the tale I have related, and not a man, woman, or child in the neighborhood, but knew it by heart. Some always pretended to doubt the reality of it, and insisted that Rip had been out of his head, and that this was one point on which he always remained flighty. The old Dutch inhabitants, however, almost universally gave it full credit. Even to this day they never hear a thunderstorm of a summer afternoon about the Kaatskill, but they say Hendrick Hudson and his crew are at their game of ninepins; and it is a common wish of all henpecked husbands in the neighborhood, when life hangs heavy on their hands, that they might have a quieting draught out of Rip Van Winkle's flagon.

Discussion

1. What is there about Rip's personality and character that make him a likely person for the kind of adventure he had in the mountains?

2. How is Dame Van Winkle's personality different from Rip's?

3. What events lead to Rip's falling asleep? How does Rip determine who the persons in the amphitheater are? What is odd about their behavior?

4. When Rip awakens, what evidence is there that he has been asleep for a long time? How long has he been gone from the village? How long does Rip think he has been away?

5. In what ways has the village changed during Rip's absence? What other important changes have occurred?

6. What are the reactions of the people in the village when Rip reappears? Why?

7. What has happened to Dame Van Winkle during Rip's absence? Describe Rip's feelings about this turn of events.

Writer's Craft

Star Wars. Close Encounters of the Third Kind. Star Trek. Real life adventures?

Superman. Buck Rogers. The Bionic Woman. The Lone Ranger. The Wizard of Oz. Robin Hood. Actual flesh-and-blood individuals?

"Suppose that. . . ." "Just imagine that. . . ." It's a good bet that at sometime in his or her life, every human being has done some supposing, some imagining. Imagination lets us get away temporarily from the everyday, humdrum world. Imagination lets us experience what things might be like if only—.

Those who write stories are great ones for using imagination. Take Washington Irving, for example. At one point, he no doubt thought along these lines: It's not physically possible for anyone to sleep soundly for twenty years. But *what if* a person could? What would that person's life be like when he or she awoke? Having so triggered his imagination, Irving was off and writing a "just suppose" story. The result is "Rip Van Winkle," a story of make-believe, a story of FANTASY.

1. What words and/or phrases in the first two paragraphs give clues that this will be a story of fantasy?

2. The characters in a story of fantasy, as well as details of the setting, are often based on real-life persons and places. The fantasy lies in what happens. What are some of the happenings in "Rip Van Winkle" that are pure fantasy?

Vocabulary

While Rip Van Winkle slept, the world changed. Some English words, too, underwent either great or small changes as time passed. For example, the word *urchin,* meaning "a small, mischievous boy" as used in this Washington Irving story, originally meant "hedgehog." The word *perplex,* meaning "puzzle or confuse" could have been defined orginally as "to weave on a loom."

These and many other kinds of changes in the meanings and forms of words are recorded in their ETYMOLOGIES, or word histories. Most dictionaries give the etymology of nearly every word they contain. Some dictionaries present the etymology of a word directly after the abbreviation for its part of speech. Other dictionaries give each word's etymology after the definition has been completed. But wherever the etymology is located, it is most often enclosed in brackets [ ], which set it apart from other information in the entry.

Here is an example of the etymology of another word from "Rip Van Winkle"—*metamorphosis* ("a marked change in the form, shape, or structure"):

[Latin *metamorphosis* from Greek: *meta-* ("change") + *morphe* ("form")]

This etymology tells us that many words in English were originally drawn from Latin or Ancient Greek. Its arrangement shows that etymologies, or word histories, move backward from the most recent to the earliest form or use of the word. In the case of *metamorphosis,* the etymology shows that hardly any change has taken place since the earliest use of the word.

In order to save space, some dictionaries present their etymologies in abbreviated versions. One common way to abbreviate the etymology given above would be this:

[< L. *metamorphosis* < Gk. *meta-* ("change") + *morphe* ("form")]

In this example, *L.* stands for *Latin, Gk.* for *Greek,* and < for *taken from.* Other abbreviations that are often used include *ME* for *Middle English; OE* for *Old English; F.* for *French.*

On a separate sheet of paper, copy from a dictionary both the modern meaning and the etymology of each of the following words found in "Rip Van Winkle":

countenance
crony
torpor
tribulation
yore

Washington Irving 1783—1859

Washington Irving's parents came from Scotland to the colony of New York, and his father fought in the Revolutionary War. The youngest of eleven children, Washington Irving was named for his father's commander. After a happy childhood as the family "baby," Irving worked at business and law without much enthusiasm or success. Young Irving fell in love, but his sweetheart died before they were married. Though he later courted other women, Irving never married.

Family business sent him to England for seventeen years. There he met several important authors who influenced and encouraged his writing. After a stay in Spain (where he also wrote) he returned to New York. His books had made him famous even before he arrived.

This author is remembered most for his comical sketches of Rip Van Winkle and Ichabod Crane ("The Legend of Sleepy Hollow"). As the first American author of importance, he earned a place for America in the literature of the world.

4 THE ART OF STORYTELLING

Discussion

1. Read this story and then answer the questions following it.

The Case of the Stubborn Conductor

ANONYMOUS

The little open-air cable car sat poised on its rails at the end of San Francisco's Powell Street, ready to retrace the run it had just completed. The conductor-gripman quietly placed his right knee on the seat nearest to him as the passengers boarded, blocking it to any occupant. The car was crowded, with late arrivals standing in the aisle.

"What are we waiting for?" a woman's raspy voice complained. "Why aren't we going?"

The conductor stood with one knee up, his face expressionless, as if he had not heard.

The voice sounded again, this time more plaintive than the last, almost whining. "He has a seat blocked. Why does he do that when so many of us are standing?"

"Some people show no respect," a companion voice observed. "Look at his badge. Get his number. He ought to be reported."

The conductor continued to ignore the passengers, his posture rigid, his eyes looking forward up the street, his hands resting on the grip-lever, a faint smile now crossing his face.

And then there was a sudden hush as a small, hobbling figure approached from up the street, her shoulders bent with age, a gnarled hand picking at the concrete with a cane in an ineffectual but desperate hurry.

As she lumbered aboard, the conductor reached down gently to take her arm. Then, as she dropped breathlessly into the "reserved" seat near him, he pulled the bell cord and, with a quick, businesslike jerk, engaged the cable grip. And the car began to move.

1. a. Would you describe the mood of the story as humorous, angry, melancholy, serious, or matter-of-fact? Why?
   b. What is the writer's attitude toward the conductor? toward the waiting passengers? How do you know?
   c. What would you say is the story's theme?

2. a. Which of the stories in this unit are written from the first-person point of view? How do you know?

   b. Which of the stories in this unit are written from the omniscient point of view? How do you know?

3. Which one of the stories in this unit appealed to you the most? Why?

Composition

1. The plot of "The Gift of the Magi," as you know, has an unexpected twist—a surprise ending. Would you say that both "Charles" and "A Letter to God" also have surprise endings? In a one-page composition, give your answer to that question, and then explain why you answer as you do.

2. Something happened to you in school today (or this week) that would make a good, *brief* story—a story no longer than "The Case of the Stubborn Conductor" (page 310). Tell (write) that story from *your* point of view—that is, from the *first-person* point of view. Be sure to tell what *you* thought and felt at the time. Then rewrite your story from the *omniscient* point of view. What can you include in the second version that you couldn't in the first?

5

OLD CLOWN MAKING UP *John Sloan* The Phillips Collection, Washington D.C.

Plays

PLAYS

At festival times more than 2500 years ago, the citizens of every important city in Greece rose before dawn to attend certain special events celebrated in honor of Apollo. Thronging to their hillside amphitheaters, they would sit for hours on hard stone benches, absorbed in the plays performed there. Ever since, plays have delighted audiences the world over. There are at least two reasons: First, plays provide entertainment. Second, plays make it possible for people to see *themselves* in a variety of situations. Plays, in short, provide valuable insights into human behavior.

The plays of ancient Greece were performed by actors wearing masks, and were staged without scenery on the bare floor of those hillside amphitheaters. In contrast, the plays we see today are performed by actors wearing makeup and costumes appropriate for the time the action is supposed to occur. What's more, the plays we see today are performed in one of three places: (1) on a lighted stage in a theater before a live audience; (2) on a specially designed and equipped stage, or set, in front of motion picture cameras; or (3) on a stage, or set, in a studio in front of television cameras (and sometimes a live audience, too).

But what exactly is a play? Well, just recall some movies or television plays you have seen recently. (If you are lucky enough to have seen some stage plays, think back about them, too.) As you do so, you'll realize that a PLAY *is simply the acting out of a narrative (story) by a person or persons who move and speak in front of a live audience or a camera.* Not only do the actors—those who do the moving and speaking—pretend to be the characters in the play, they also seek to behave and speak exactly as would real-life persons in the same circumstances.

Persons who write plays—playwrights—have a task different from that of storywriters and poets. Whereas poets and storywriters can tell you directly that a character is kind and generous or heartless and cruel, playwrights can't. And whereas poets and storywriters can tell you directly that a character is happy or sad or whatever, playwrights can't. Playwrights, you see, are *not* usually on stage or on the set with the actors. But even if they are, they can't step out on the stage or in front of the camera, interrupt the action, and explain what's going on or what kind of persons the characters are. Yet every playwright must somehow supply that information. There are two ways: (a) through DIALOGUE—what the characters in the play say to one another—and (b) through STAGE DIRECTIONS. Dialogue is the verbal action in a play, and stage directions indicate the physical action.

Stage directions are the playwright's instructions to the director and to the actors. Stage directions specify what the stage or set is to look like. They indicate where the actors on the stage are to be at specific times during the play; they indicate how and where the actors are to move around; and they indicate the tone of voice in which actors are to speak certain lines. Stage directions, then, are written from the actors' point of view, not the audience's. When an actor is directed to move *right* or *left,* it is that actor's right (or left). If the actor is directed to go *upstage,* he or she moves to the back; if directed to move *downstage,* he or she moves to that part closest to the audience (or to the camera).

Every play is written to be performed—to be seen and heard by an audience. Unfortunately, however, it would be impossible for you to see every play in existence—even in the movies or on television. But to enjoy what outstanding playwrights—past and present—have written, you can *read* their plays.

Reading a play is somewhat different from seeing it performed. In the first place, you need to visualize the setting and the costumes. Then you need to "hear" the tones of voice in which the actors speak their lines. Third, you need to picture the actors' movements—indeed, all of the action. To do all of these things, you need to read the playwright's stage directions carefully. You can't afford to hurry over or miss anything.

The three plays in this unit offer three kinds of presentation. The first one—"The Pen of My Aunt"—is a stage play. The second—"Grandpa and the Statue"—is a radio play. And the third—"Flight into Danger"—is a television play.

Ready? The plays are about to begin!

For four long years during World War II—from 1940 to 1944—Adolf Hitler's armies held France in their iron grip. During those years—a time called the Occupation—the defeated French people seemed helpless. They lacked the guns and the ammunition necessary to overthrow their Nazi rulers. Yet many French patriots used other, quieter methods to weaken the enemy and hasten the day of France's liberation.

The Pen of My Aunt

JOSEPHINE TEY

Characters

Madame
Simone
Stranger
Corporal

Scene: *A French country house during the Occupation by German forces in World War II. The lady of the house is seated in her drawing-room.*

Simone[1] *(approaching).* Madame! Oh, madame! Madame, have you—

Madame. Simone.

Simone. Madame, have you seen what—

Madame. Simone!

Simone. But madame—

Madame. Simone, this may be an age of barbarism, but I will have none of it inside the walls of this house.

Simone. But madame, there is a—there is a—

Madame *(silencing her).* Simone. France may be an occupied country, a ruined nation, and a conquered race, but we will keep, if you please, the usages of civilization.

Simone. Yes, madame.

---

1 **Simone:** pronounced "sē mōn'."

Madame. One thing we still possess, thank God; and that is good manners. The enemy never had it; and it is not something they can take from *us*.

Simone. No, madame.

Madame. Go out of the room again. Open the door—

Simone. Oh, *madame!* I wanted to tell you—

Madame. —Open the door, shut it behind you—quietly—take two paces into the room, and say what you came to say. (Simone *goes hastily out, shutting the door. She reappears, shuts the door behind her, takes two paces into the room, and waits.)* Yes, Simone?

Simone. I expect it is too late now; they will be here.

Madame. Who will?

Simone. The soldiers who were coming up the avenue.

Madame. After the last few months I should not have thought that soldiers coming up the avenue was a remarkable fact. It is no doubt a party with a billeting order.[2]

Simone (crossing to the window). No, madame, it is two soldiers in one of their little cars, with a civilian between them.

Madame. Which civilian?

Simone. A stranger, madame.

Madame. A stranger? Are the soldiers from the Combatant branch?

Simone. No, they are those beasts of Administration. Look, they have stopped. They are getting out.

Madame (at the window). Yes, it is a stranger. Do you know him, Simone?

Simone. I have never set eyes on him before, madame.

Madame. You would know if he belonged to the district?

Simone. Oh, madame, I know every man between here and St. Estèphe.[3]

Madame (dryly). No doubt.

Simone. Oh, merciful God, they are coming up the steps.

Madame. My good Simone, that is what the steps were put there for.

Simone. But they will ring the bell and I shall have to—

Madame. And you will answer it and behave as if you had been trained by a butler and ten upper servants instead of being the charcoal-burner's daughter from over at Les Chênes.[4] *(This is said encouragingly, not in unkindness.)* You will be very calm and correct—

Simone. Calm! Madame! With my inside turning over and over like a wheel at a fair!

Madame. A good servant does not have an inside, merely an exterior. *(Comforting)* Be assured, my child. You have your place here; that is more than those creatures on our doorstep have. Let that hearten you—

Simone. Madame! They are not going to ring. They are coming straight in.

Madame (bitterly). Yes. They have forgotten long ago what bells are for.

---

2 **billeting order**: a written order from an authorized military officer demanding sleeping accommodations for soldiers.

3 **St. Estèphe**: pronounced ''saN tă stef′.''
4 **Les Chênes**: pronounced ''lā shen′.''

[*Door opens.*]

Stranger (*in a bright, confident, casual tone*). Ah, there you are, my dear aunt. I am so glad. Come in, my friend, come in. My dear aunt, this gentleman wants you to identify me.

Madame. Identify you?

Corporal. We found this man wandering in the woods—

Stranger. The corporal found it inexplicable that anyone should wander in a wood.

Corporal. And he had no papers on him—

Stranger. And I rightly pointed out that if I carry all the papers one is supposed to these days, I am no good to God or man. If I put them in a hip pocket, I can't bend forward; if I put them in a front pocket, I can't bend at all.

Corporal. He said that he was your nephew, madame, but that did not seem to us very likely, so we brought him here.

[*There is the slightest pause; just one moment of silence.*]

Madame. But of course this is my nephew.

Corporal. He is?

Madame. Certainly.

Corporal. He lives here?

Madame (*assenting*). My nephew lives here.

Corporal. So! (*Recovering*) My apologies, madame. But you will admit that appearances were against the young gentleman.

Madame. Alas, Corporal, my nephew belongs to a generation who delight in flouting[5] appearances. It is what they call "expressing their personality," I understand.

Corporal (*with contempt*). No doubt, madame.

Madame. Convention is anathema[6] to them, and there is no sin like conformity. Even a collar is an offense against their liberty, and a discipline not to be borne by free necks.

Corporal. Ah yes, madame. A little more discipline among your nephew's generation, and we might not be occupying your country today.

Stranger. You think it was that collar of yours that conquered my country? You flatter yourself, Corporal. The only result of wearing a collar like that is varicose veins[7] in the head.

Madame (*repressive*). Please! My dear boy. Let us not descend to personalities.

Stranger. The matter is not personal, my good aunt, but scientific. Wearing a collar like that retards the flow of fresh blood to the head, with the most disastrous consequences to the gray matter of the brain. The hypothetical gray matter. In fact, I have a theory—

Corporal. Monsieur,[8] your theories do not interest me.

Stranger. No? You do not find speculation interesting?

Corporal. In this world one judges by results.

Stranger (*after a slight pause of reflection*). I see. The collared conqueror sits in the high places, while the collarless conquered lies about in the woods. And who comes best out of that, would you say? Tell me, Corporal, as

---

5 **flouting:** scorning; intentionally disregarding.

6 **anathema** (ə nath' ə mə): something that is hated.
7 **varicose veins:** swollen veins.
8 **Monsieur** (mə syü'): the French word for sir, mister.

The Pen of My Aunt 319

man to man, do you never have a mad, secret desire to lie unbuttoned in a wood?

Corporal. I have only one desire, monsieur, and that is to see your papers.

Stranger *(taken off guard and filling in time)*. My papers?

Madame. But is that necessary, Corporal? I have already told you that—

Corporal. I know that madame is a very good collaborator[9] and in good standing—

Madame. In that case—

Corporal. But when we begin an affair we like to finish it. I have asked to see monsieur's papers, and the matter will not be finished until I have seen them.

Madame. You acknowledge that I am in "good standing," Corporal?

Corporal. So I have heard, madame.

Madame. Then I must consider it a discourtesy on your part to demand my nephew's credentials.

Corporal. It is no reflection on madame. It is a matter of routine, nothing more.

Stranger *(murmuring)*. The great god Routine.

Madame. To ask for his papers was routine; to insist on their production is discourtesy. I shall say so to your Commanding Officer.

Corporal. Very good, madame. In the meantime, I shall inspect your nephew's papers.

Madame. And what if I—

Stranger *(quietly)*. You may as well give it up, my dear. You could as easily turn a steamroller. They have only one idea at a time. If the Corporal's heart is set on seeing my papers, he shall see them. *(Moving towards the door)* I left them in the pocket of my coat.

Simone *(unexpectedly, from the background)*. Not in your *linen* coat?

Stranger *(pausing)*. Yes. Why?

Simone *(with apparently growing anxiety)*. Your cream linen coat? The one you were wearing yesterday?

Stranger. Certainly.

Simone. Merciful Heaven! I sent it to the laundry!

Stranger. To the laundry!

Simone. Yes, monsieur; this morning; in the basket.

Stranger *(in incredulous anger)*. You sent my coat, *with my papers in the pocket,* to the laundry!

Simone *(defensive and combatant)*. I didn't know monsieur's papers were in the pocket.

Stranger. You didn't know! You didn't know that a packet of documents weighing half a ton were in the pocket. An identity card, a *laisser passer,*[10] a food card, a drink card, an army discharge, a permission to wear civilian clothes, a permission to go farther than ten miles to the east, a permission to go more than ten miles to the west, a permission to—

Simone *(breaking in with spirit)*. How was I to know the coat was heavy! I picked it up

---

9 **collaborator** (kə lab′ ə rā′ tər): a person who helps the enemy.

10 *laisser passer* (les ā′ pä sā′): a military pass authorizing one to travel.

with the rest of the bundle that was lying on the floor.

Stranger (*snapping her head off*). My coat was on the back of the chair.

Simone. It was on the floor.

Stranger. On the back of the chair!

Simone. It was on the floor with your dirty shirt and your pajamas, and a towel and what not. I put my arms round the whole thing and then—woof! into the basket with them.

Stranger. I tell you that coat was on the back of the chair. It was quite clean and was not going to the laundry for two weeks yet—if then. I hung it there myself, and—

Madame. My dear boy, what does it matter? The damage is done now. In any case, they will find the papers when they unpack the basket, and return them tomorrow.

Stranger. If someone doesn't steal them. There are a lot of people who would like to lay hold of a complete set of papers, believe me.

Madame (*reassuring*). Oh, no. Old Fleureau[11] is the soul of honesty. You have no need to worry about them. They will be back first thing tomorrow, you shall see; and then we shall have much pleasure in sending them to the Administration Office for the Corporal's inspection. Unless, of course, the Corporal insists on your personal appearance at the office.

Corporal (*cold and indignant*). I have seen monsieur. All that I want now is to see his papers.

Stranger. You shall see them, Corporal, you shall see them. The whole half-ton of them. You may inspect them at your leisure. Provided, that is, that they come back from the laundry to which this idiot has consigned them.

Madame (*again reassuring*). They will come back, never fear. And you must not blame Simone. She is a good child, and does her best.

Simone (*with an air of belated virtue*). I am not one to pry into pockets.

Madame. Simone, show the Corporal out, if you please.

Simone (*natural feeling overcoming her for a moment*). He knows the way out. (*Recovering*) Yes, madame.

Madame. And Corporal, try to take your duties a little less literally in future. My countrymen appreciate the spirit rather than the letter.

Corporal. I have my instructions, madame, and I obey them. Good day, madame. Monsieur.

[*He goes, followed by* Simone—*door closes. There is a moment of silence.*]

Stranger. For a good collaborator, that was remarkably quick adoption.

Madame. Sit down, young man. I will give you something to drink. I expect your knees are none too well.

Stranger. My knees, madame, are pure gelatine. As for my stomach, it seems to have disappeared.

Madame (*offering him the drink she has poured out*). This will recall it, I hope.

Stranger. You are not drinking, madame.

Madame. Thank you, no.

---

11 **Fleureau:** pronounced "flə rō′."

Stranger. Not with strangers. It is certainly no time to drink with strangers. Nevertheless, I drink to the health of a collaborator. *(He drinks.)* Tell me, madame, what will happen tomorrow when they find that you have no nephew?

Madame *(surprised).* But of course I have a nephew. I tell lies, my friend; but not *silly* lies. My charming nephew has gone to Bonneval for the day. He finds country life dull.

Stranger. Dull? This—this heaven?

Madame *(dryly).* He likes to talk and here there is no audience. At Headquarters in Bonneval he finds the audience sympathetic.

Stranger *(understanding the implication).* Ah.

Madame. He believes in the Brotherhood of Man—if you can credit it.

Stranger. After the last six months?

Madame. His mother was American, so he has half the Balkans[12] in his blood. To say nothing of Italy, Russia and the Levant.[13]

Stranger *(half-amused).* I see.

Madame. A silly and worthless creature, but useful.

Stranger. Useful?

Madame. I—borrow his cloak.

Stranger. I see.

Madame. Tonight I shall borrow his identity papers, and tomorrow they will go to the office in St. Estèphe.

Stranger. But—he will have to know.

---

12 **Balkans:** countries of southeast Europe.
13 **Levant:** countries at the eastern end of the Mediterranean Sea.

Madame *(placidly).* Oh, yes, he will know, of course.

Stranger. And how will you persuade such an enthusiastic collaborator to deceive his friends?

Madame. Oh, that is easy. He is my heir.

Stranger *(amused).* Ah.

Madame. He is, also, by the mercy of God, not too unlike you, so that his photograph will not startle the Corporal too much tomorrow. Now tell me what you are doing in my wood.

Stranger. Resting my feet—I am practically walking on my bones. And waiting for tonight.

Madame. Where are you making for? *(As he does not answer immediately)* The coast? *(He nods.)* That is four days away—five if your feet are bad.

Stranger. I know it.

Madame. Have you friends on the way?

Stranger. I have friends at the coast, who will get me a boat. But no one between here and the sea.

Madame *(rising).* I must consult my list of addresses. *(Pausing)* What was your service?

Stranger. Army.

Madame. Which Regiment?

Stranger. The 79th.

Madame *(after the faintest pause).* And your Colonel's name?

Stranger. Delavault was killed in the first week, and Martin took over.

Madame *(going to her desk).* A "good collaborator" cannot be too careful. Now I can

consult my notebook. A charming color, is it not? A lovely shade of red.

Stranger. Yes—but what has a red quill pen to do with your notebook?—Ah, you write with it of course—stupid of me.

Madame. Certainly I write with it—but it is also my notebook—look—I only need a hair-pin—and then—so—out of my quill pen comes my notebook—a tiny piece of paper— but enough for a list of names.

Stranger. You mean that you keep that list on your desk? *(He sounds disapproving.)*

Madame. Where did you expect me to keep it, young man? In my corset? Did you ever try to get something out of your corset in a hurry? What would you advise as the ideal quality in a hiding place for a list of names?

Stranger. That the thing should be difficult to find, of course.

Madame. Not at all. That it should be easily destroyed in an emergency. It is too big for me to swallow—I suspect they do that only in books—and we have no fires to consume it, so I had to think of some other way. I did try to

memorize the list, but what I could not be sure of remembering were those that—that had to be scored off. It would be fatal to send someone to an address that—that was no longer available. So I had to keep a written record.

Stranger. And if you neither eat it nor burn it when the moment comes, how do you get rid of it?

Madame. I could, of course, put a match to it, but scraps of freshly burned paper on a desk take a great deal of explaining. If I ceased to be looked on with approval my usefulness would end. It is important there-fore that there should be no sign of anxiety on my part: no burned paper, no excuses to leave the room, no nods and becks and winks. I just sit here at my desk and go on with my letters. I tilt my nice big inkwell sideways for a moment and dip the pen into the deep ink at the side. The ink flows into the hollow of the quill, and all is blotted out. *(Consulting the list)* Let me see. It would be good if you could rest your feet for a day or so.

Stranger *(ruefully).* It would.

Madame. There is a farm just beyond the Marnay crossroads on the way to St. Estèphe—*(She pauses to consider.)*

Stranger. St. Estèphe is the home of the singleminded Corporal. I don't want to run into him again.

Madame. No, that might be awkward; but that farm of the Cherfils[14] would be ideal. A good hiding-place, and food to spare, and fine people—

Stranger. If your nephew is so friendly with

---

14 **Cherfils:** pronounced "sher fē'."

the invader, how is it that the Corporal doesn't know him by sight?

Madame (*absently*). The unit at St. Estèphe is a noncommissioned one.

Stranger. Does the Brotherhood of Man exclude sergeants, then?

Madame. Oh, definitely. Brotherhood does not really begin under field rank, I understand.

Stranger. But the Corporal may still meet your nephew somewhere.

Madame. That is a risk one must take. It is not a very grave one. They change the personnel every few weeks, to prevent them becoming too acclimatized. And even if he met my nephew, he is unlikely to ask for the papers of so obviously well-to-do a citizen. If you could bear to go *back* a little—

Stranger. Not a step! It would be like—like denying God. I have got so far, against all the odds, and I am not going a yard back. Not even to rest my feet!

Madame. I understand; but it is a pity. It is a long way to the Cherfils farm—two miles east of the Marnay crossroads it is, on a little hill.

Stranger. I'll get there; don't worry. If not tonight then tomorrow night. I am used to sleeping in the open by now.

Madame. I wish we could have you here, but it is too dangerous. We are liable to be billeted on at any moment, without notice. However, we can give you a good meal, and a bath. We have no coal, so it will be one of those flat-tin-saucer baths. And if you want to be very kind to Simone you might have it somewhere in the kitchen regions and so save her carrying water upstairs.

Stranger. But of course.

Madame. Before the war I had a staff of twelve. Now I have Simone. I dust and Simone sweeps, and between us we keep the dirt at bay. She has no manners but a great heart, the child.

Stranger. The heart of a lion.

Madame. Before I put this back you might memorize these: Forty Avenue Foch, in Crest, the back entrance.

Stranger. Forty Avenue Foch, the back entrance.

Madame. You may find it difficult to get into Crest, by the way. It is a closed area. The pot boy[15] at the Red Lion in Mans.

Stranger. The pot boy.

Madame. Denis the blacksmith at Laloupe. And the next night should take you to the sea and your friends. Are they safely in your mind?

Stranger. Forty Avenue Foch in Crest; the pot boy at the Red Lion in Mans; and Denis the blacksmith at Laloupe. And to be careful getting into Crest.

Madame. Good. Then I can close my notebook—or roll it up, I should say—then—it fits neatly, does it not? Now let us see about some food for you. Perhaps I could find you other clothes. Are these all you—

[*The* Corporal's *voice is heard mingled in fury with the still more furious tones of* Simone. *She is yelling: 'Nothing of the sort, I tell you, nothing of the sort,' but no words are clearly distinguishable in the angry row. The door is flung open, and the*

---

15 **pot boy**: dishwasher.

Corporal *bursts in dragging a struggling* Simone *by the arm.*]

Simone *(screaming with rage and terror)*. Let me go, you foul fiend, you murdering foreigner, let me go. *(She tries to kick him.)*

Corporal *(at the same time)*. Stop struggling, you lying deceitful little bit of no-good.

Madame. Will someone explain this extraordinary—

Corporal. This creature—

Madame. Take your hand from my servant's arm, Corporal. She is not going to run away.

Corporal *(reacting to the voice of authority and automatically complying)*. Your precious servant was overheard telling the gardener that she had never set eyes on this man.

Simone. I did not! Why should I say anything like that?

Corporal. With my own ears I heard her, my own two ears. Will you kindly explain that to me if you can.

Madame. You speak our language very well, Corporal, but perhaps you are not so quick to understand.

Corporal. I understand perfectly.

Madame. What Simone was saying to the gardener, was no doubt what she was announcing to all and sundry at the pitch of her voice this morning.

Corporal *(unbelieving)*. And what was that?

Madame. That she *wished* she had never set eyes on my nephew.

Corporal. And why should she say that?

Madame. My nephew, Corporal, has many charms, but tidiness is not one of them. As

you may have deduced from the episode of the coat. He is apt to leave his room—

Simone *(on her cue; in a burst of scornful rage)*. Cigarette ends, pajamas, towels, bedclothes, books, papers—all over the floor like a *flood.* Every morning I tidy up, and in two hours it is as if a bomb had burst in the room.

Stranger *(testily)*. I told you already that I was sor—

Simone *(interrupting)*. As if I had nothing else to do in this enormous house but wait on you.

Stranger. Haven't I said that I—

Simone. And when I have climbed all the way up from the kitchen with your shaving water, you let it get cold; but will you shave in cold? Oh, no! I have to bring up another—

Stranger. I didn't ask you to climb the stairs, did I?

Simone. And do I get a word of thanks for bringing it? Do I indeed? You say: "*Must* you bring it in that hideous jug; it offends my eyes."

Stranger. So it does offend my eyes!

Madame. Enough, enough! We had enough of that this morning. You see, Corporal?

Corporal. I could have sworn—

Madame. A natural mistake, perhaps. But I think you might have used a little more common sense in the matter. *(Coldly)* And a great deal more dignity. I don't like having my servants manhandled.

Corporal. She refused to come.

Simone. Accusing me of things I never said!

Madame. However, now that you are here again you can make yourself useful. My nephew wants to go into Crest the day after tomorrow, and that requires a special pass. Perhaps you would make one out for him.

Corporal. But I—

Madame. You have a little book of permits in your pocket, haven't you?

Corporal. Yes, I—

Madame. Very well. Better make it valid for two days. He is always changing his mind.

Corporal. But it is not for me to grant a pass.

Madame. You sign them, don't you?

Corporal. Yes, but only when someone tells me to.

Madame. Very well, if it will help you, I tell you to.

Corporal. I mean, permission must be granted before a pass is issued.

Madame. And have you any doubt that a permission will be granted to my nephew?

Corporal. No, of course not, madame.

Madame. Then don't be absurd, Corporal. To be absurd twice in five minutes is too often. You may use my desk—and my own special pen. Isn't it a beautiful quill, Corporal?

Corporal. Thank you, madame, no. *We* Germans have come a long way from the geese.

Madame. Yes?

Corporal. I prefer my fountain pen. It is a more efficient implement. *(He writes.)* "For the 15th and 16th. Holder of identity card number"—What is the number of your identity, monsieur?

Stranger. I have not the faintest idea.

Corporal. You do not know?

Stranger. No. The only numbers I take an interest in are lottery numbers.

Simone. I know the number of monsieur's card.

Madame *(afraid that she is going to invent one).* I don't think that likely, Simone.

Simone *(aware of what is in her mistress's mind, and reassuring her).* But I really *do* know, madame. It is the year I was born, with two "ones" after it. Many a time I have seen it on the outside of the card.

Corporal. It is good that someone knows.

Simone. It is—192411.

Corporal. 192411. *(He fills in the dates.)*

Madame *(as he nears the end).* Are you going back to St. Estèphe now, Corporal?

Corporal. Yes, madame.

Madame. Then perhaps you will give my nephew a lift as far as the Marnay crossroads.

Corporal. It is not permitted to take civilians as passengers.

Stranger. But you took me here as a passenger.

Corporal. That was different.

Madame. You mean that when you thought he was a miscreant you took him in your car, but now that you know he is my nephew you refuse?

Corporal. When I brought him here it was on service business.

Madame *(gently reasonable).* Corporal, I think you owe me something for your general lack of tact this afternoon. Would it be too much to ask you to consider my nephew a miscreant for the next hour while you drive him as far as the Marnay crossroads?

Corporal. But—

Madame. Take him to the crossroads with you and I shall agree to forget your—your lack of efficiency. I am sure you are actually a very efficient person, and likely to be a sergeant any day now. We won't let a blunder or two stand in your way.

Corporal. If I am caught giving a lift to a civilian, I shall *never* be a sergeant.

Madame (*still gentle*). If I report on your conduct this afternoon, tomorrow you will be a private.

Corporal (*after a long pause*). Is monsieur ready to come now?

Stranger. Quite ready.

Corporal. You will need a coat.

Madame. Simone, get monsieur's coat from the cupboard in the hall. And when you have seen him off, come back here.

Simone. Yes, madame.

[*Exit Simone.*]

Corporal. Madame.

Madame. Good day to you, Corporal.

[*Exit Corporal.*]

Stranger. Your talent for blackmail is remarkable.

Madame. The place has a yellow barn. You had better wait somewhere till evening, when the dogs are chained up.

Stranger. I wish I had an aunt of your caliber.[16] All mine are authorities on crochet.[17]

---

16 **caliber**: quality.
17 **crochet** (krō shā′): a kind of knitting.

Madame. I could wish you were my nephew. Good luck, and be careful. Perhaps one day, you will come back, and dine with me, and tell me the rest of the tale.

[*The sound of a running engine comes from outside.*]

Stranger. Two years today, perhaps?

Madame. One year today.

Stranger (*softly*). Who knows? (*He lifts her hand to his lips.*) Thank you, and *au revoir*. (*Turning at the door*) Being sped on my way by the enemy is a happiness I had not anticipated. I shall never be able to repay you for that. (*He goes out.*) (*Off stage*) Ah, my coat—thank you, Simone.

[*Sound of car driving off.* Madame *pours out two glasses. As she finishes,* Simone *comes in, shutting the door correctly behind her and taking two paces into the room.*]

Simone. You wanted me, madame?

Madame. You will drink a glass of wine with me, Simone.

Simone. With you, madame!

Madame. You are a good daughter of France and a good servant to me. We shall drink a toast together.

Simone. Yes, madame.

Madame (*quietly*). To Freedom.

Simone (*repeating*). To Freedom. May I add a bit of my own, madame?

Madame. Certainly.

Simone (*with immense satisfaction*). And a very bad end to that Corporal!

[*Curtain*]

1. When the Stranger asks Madame to identify him as her nephew, what is Madame's almost immediate response? What does that response suggest about her?
2. What purpose does Madame have for telling her first lie to the Corporal?
3. What would probably happen to the Stranger if the Corporal had any doubt that Madame was in good standing as a collaborator?
4. At first Simone appears to be an unsophisticated, immature country girl. But what evidence is there that she isn't at all as simple and as inexperienced as she seems?
5. How does Simone's argument with the Corporal lead to Madame's words of praise: "You are a good daughter of France . . ."?
6. What do you think is Madame's boldest action?
7. Why do you think the play is titled "The Pen of My Aunt"?

Writer's Craft

From your reading of the stories in Units 3 and 4, you know that plot and character are two essential elements of every narrative. As you have probably also guessed, they are essential elements of plays, too. What's more, from your work in Units 3 and 4, you discovered something else about literature. There are three important ways that storywriters—and playwrights, too—have of letting you know what kind of person each CHARACTER is:

—Telling what the character says
—Indicating what the character does
—Telling what others say about the character.

The author of "The Pen of My Aunt" uses all three methods.

1. In the opening scene Madame says to Simone: "One thing we still possess . . . is good manners. The enemy never had it; and it is not something they can take from *us*." What do Madame's words tell you about the kind of person she is?
2. What sentences spoken by the Corporal characterize him as an efficient, obedient, disciplined soldier who prides himself on strict observance of military regulations? Find at least three such sentences.
3. What characteristic of Simone's is revealed by each of the following things she *does?*
   a. Simone rushes into the drawing room without heeding the instructions that Madame has previously given her.

b. On the spur of the moment Simone pretends to have sent the nephew's linen coat to the laundry.
c. Simone tells the gardener that she has never before seen the Stranger, who claims to be Madame's nephew.
d. Simone recalls the number of the nephew's identity card.

4. One character who does not appear at all on the stage is characterized by *what* the *other characters say about* that person.
a. Who is that character?
b. What kind of person do you find that character to be? Name at least three characteristics.
c. What lines spoken by other characters in this play support your description of that person? Find a total of at least three such lines.

Composition

1. Shortly before leaving with the Corporal for the Marnay crossroads, the Stranger says to Madame: "I wish I had an aunt of your caliber. All mine are authorities on crochet." What does the Stranger mean? Do you share his point of view, or do you disagree with it? Why?

In a composition of three paragraphs, write your answers to those three questions. First, briefly explain what the Stranger's remark means. Second, state whether you agree or disagree with his point of view. Finally, supply at least two reasons for your agreement or disagreement.

2. Suppose that instead of losing World War II, the Axis Powers—Germany, Italy, and Japan—had won. Suppose, too, that today these countries have occupation forces in the United States. Finally, suppose that you have considered all of the following courses of action as possibilities for your own behavior:

—ACTIVE OPPOSITION, like that of Madame in "The Pen of My Aunt";
—COLLABORATION, like that of Madame's real nephew;
—ESCAPE, to join "Free U.S. Forces" in Central America, like the Stranger's efforts to join the Free French armies;
—NEUTRALITY, like that of the Stranger's aunts; that is, going about your own personal affairs and letting others worry about the foreign occupation of your country.

In a composition of two paragraphs:
—tell which course of action is the "right" one for you;
—explain why you have chosen that course of action. Give at least three reasons.

Vocabulary

In "The Pen of My Aunt," the Nazi Army causes the problems that face Madame, Simone, and the Stranger. Like any other organization or institution, armies use a SPECIALIZED VOCABULARY. The term *specialized vocabulary* means a list of words used only—or mostly—in one specific profession or job.

Many terms that are part of most specialized vocabularies are multiple-meaning words. That is, they are words that have one meaning in the specialized vocabulary itself, but one or more other meanings when used outside it. For example, in the specialized vocabulary of the army, *occupation* means "the holding and control of a region by a foreign military force." But outside this special vocabulary, *occupation* means "the trade, work, or activity through which a person earns a living."

Each sentence below contains an *italicized* multiple-meaning word that is part of an army's specialized vocabulary. Here, however, the word is used with one of its other meanings. On a separate sheet of paper, copy this word. Write the definition for the word as it is used in the army. Then write a sentence of your own for each word, using the word in the sense you just defined.

1. The school principal did not believe in spanking or in any other form of *corporal* punishment.

2. Your *arms* are badly sunburned.

3. My room is a *mess,* and I'm going to straighten it up right now.

4. Their telephone has been out of *order* for a week.

5. A couple of *taps* of the teacher's ruler on the desk was the signal to put all pencils down.

Josephine Tey (Elizabeth Mackintosh) 1897—1952

Novelist and playwright Elizabeth Mackintosh was born and raised in Inverness, Scotland.

Mackintosh used her great-great-grandmother's name (Tey) when she wrote detective stories featuring Inspector Grant. His first case, *The Man in the Queue,* was about a man who was murdered in a crowd waiting outside a fashionable London theater. One critic has said the Tey detective novels are "as congenial as a witty friend and a hearth fire on a snowy day."

handle and make a sword out of it for me. Naturally, I wasn't very old before he began working on me about the statue.

[Sound. *High wind.*]

Child Monaghan (*softly, as though Grandpa is in bed*). Grampa?

Monaghan (*awakened*). Heh? What are you doin' up?

Child Monaghan. Ssssh! Listen!

[Sound. *Wind rising up and fading . . . rising higher and fading.*]

Monaghan (*gleefully*). Aaaaaaaah! Yes, yes. This'll do it, boy. This'll do it! First thing in the morning we'll go down to the docks, and I'll bet you me life that Mr. Sheean's statue is smashed down and layin' on the bottom of the bay. Go to sleep now; we'll have a look first thing.

[Music. *Up and down.* Sound. *Footsteps.*]

Child Monaghan. If it fell down, all the people will get their dimes back, won't they, Grampa? Slow down; I can't walk so fast.

Monaghan. Not only will they get their dimes back, but Mr. Sheean and the whole crew that engineered the collection are going to rot in jail. Now mark my words. Here, now, we'll take a shortcut around this shed.

[Sound. *Footsteps continue a moment, then gradually disappointedly they come to a halt.*]

Child Monaghan. She's—she's still standing, Grampa.

Monaghan. She is that. (*Uncomprehending*) I don't understand it. That was a terrible wind last night. Terrible.

Child Monaghan. Maybe she's weaker, though. Heh?

Monaghan. Why . . . sure, that must be it. I'll wager she's hangin' by a thread. (*Realizing*) Of course! That's why they put her out there in the water so when she falls down she won't be flattening out a lot of poor innocent people. Hey—feel that?

Child Monaghan. The wind! It's starting to blow again!

Monaghan. Sure, and look at the sky blackening over!

[Sound. *Wind rising.*]

Feel it comin' up! Take your last look at the statue, boy. If I don't mistake me eyes, she's takin' a small list to Jersey[2] already!

[Music. *Up and down.*]

Young Monaghan. It was getting embarrassing for me on the block. I kept promising the other kids that when the next wind came, the statue would come down. We even had a game. Four or five kids would stand in a semicircle around one kid who was the statue. The statue kid had to stand on his heels and look right in our eyes. Then we'd all take a deep breath and blow in his face. He'd fall down like a stick of wood. They all believed me and Grampa . . . until one day. We were standing around throwing rocks at an old milk can. . . .

[Sound. *Banging of rocks against milk can.*]

George. What're you doin'?

Child Monaghan. What do we look like we're doin'?

George. I'm going someplace tomorrow.

Charley. I know: church. Watch out, I'm throwin'.

[Sound. *Can being hit.*]

2 **list to Jersey**: leaning a little toward New Jersey.

George. I mean after church.

Jack. Where?

George. My old man's going to take me out on the Statue of Liberty boat.

[Sound. *Banging against can abruptly stops.*]

Child Monaghan. You're not going out on the statue, though, are you?

George. Sure, that's where we're going.

Child Monaghan. But you're liable to get killed. Supposing there's a high wind tomorrow?

George. My old man says that statue couldn't fall down if all the wind in the world and John L. Sullivan[3] hit it at the same time.

Child Monaghan. Is that so?

George. Yeh, that's so. My old man says that the only reason your grandfather's saying that it's going to fall down is that he's ashamed he didn't put a dime in for the pedestal.

Child Monaghan. Is that so?

George. Yeh, that's so.

Child Monaghan. Well, you tell your old man that if he gets killed tomorrow not to come around to my grandfather and say he didn't warn him!

Jack. Hey, George, would your father take me along?

George. I'll ask him, maybe he—

Child Monaghan. What, are you crazy, Jack?

---

3 **John L. Sullivan:** world heavyweight boxing champion, 1882–1892.

Mike. Ask him if he'd take me too, will ya, George?

Child Monaghan. Mike, what's the matter with you?

Joe. Me too, George, I'll ask my mother for money.

Child Monaghan. Joe! Didn't you hear what my grampa said?

Joe. Well . . . I don't really believe that any more.

Child Monaghan. You don't be—

Mike. Me neither.

Jack. I don't really think your grampa knows what he's talkin' about.

Child Monaghan. He don't, heh? *(Ready to weep)* Okay . . . okay. *(Bursting out)* I just hope that wind blows tomorrow, boy! I just hope that wind blows!

[Music. *Up and down.* Sound. *Creaking of a rocking chair.*]

Grampa?

Monaghan. Huh?

Child Monaghan. Can you stop rocking for a minute? *(Rocking stops.)* Can you put down your paper? *(Rustle of paper)* I—I read the weather report for tomorrow.

Monaghan. The weather report. . . .

Child Monaghan. Yeh. It says fair and cool.

Monaghan. What of it?

Child Monaghan. I was wondering. Supposing you and me we went on a boat tomorrow. You know, I see the water every day when I go down to the docks to play, but I never sat on it. I mean in a boat.

Monaghan. Oh. Well, we might take the ferry on the Jersey side. We might do that.

Child Monaghan. Yeh, but there's nothing to see in Jersey.

Monaghan. You can't go to Europe tomorrow.

Child Monaghan. No, but couldn't we go toward the ocean? Just . . . *toward* it?

Monaghan. Toward it. What—what is it on your mind, boy? What is it now?

Child Monaghan. Well, I. . . .

Monaghan. Oh, you want to take the Staten Island ferry. Sure, that's in the direction of the sea.

Child Monaghan. No, Grampa, not the Staten Island ferry.

Monaghan. You don't mean—*(Breaks off)* Boy!

Child Monaghan: All the kids are going tomorrow with Georgie's old man.

Monaghan. You don't believe me any more.

Child Monaghan. I do, Grampa, but. . . .

Monaghan. You don't. If you did, you'd stay clear of the Statue of Liberty for love of your life!

Child Monaghan. But, Grampa, when is it going to fall down? All I do is wait and wait.

Monaghan *(with some uncertainty)*. You've got to have faith.

Child Monaghan. But every kid in my class went to see it, and now the ones that didn't are going tomorrow. And they all keep talking about it, and all I do. . . . Well, I can't

keep telling them it's a swindle. I—I wish we could see it, Grampa. It don't cost so much to go.

Monaghan. As long as you put it that way, I'll have to admit I'm a bit curious meself as to how it's managed to stand upright so long. Tell you what I'll do. Barrin' wind, we'll chance it tomorrow!

Child Monaghan. Oh, Gramp!

Monaghan. But! If anyone should ask you where we went, you'll say—Staten Island. Are y' on?

Child Monaghan. Okay, sure. Staten Island.

Monaghan *(secretively)*. We'll take the early boat, then. Mum's the word, now. For if old man Sheean hears that I went out there, I'll have no peace from the thief the rest of m' life.

[Music. *Up and down.* Sound. *Boat whistles.*]

Child Monaghan. Gee, it's nice ridin' on a boat, ain't it, Grampa?

Monaghan. Never said there was anything wrong with the boat. Boat's all right. You're sure now that Georgie's father is takin' the kids in the afternoon.

Child Monaghan. Yeh, that's when they're going. Gee, look at those two sea gulls. Whee! look at them swoop! They caught a fish!

Monaghan. What I can't understand is what all these people see in that statue that they'll keep a boat like this full makin' the trip, year in year out. To hear the newspapers talk, if the statue was gone we'd be at war with the nation that stole her the followin' mornin' early. All it is, is a big pile of French copper.

Child Monaghan. The teacher says it shows us that we got liberty.

Monaghan. Bah! If you've got liberty, you don't need a statue to tell you you got it; and if you haven't got liberty, no statue's going to do you any good tellin' you you got it. It was a criminal waste of the people's money. *(Quietly)* And just to prove it to you, I'll ask this feller sitting right over there what he sees in it. You'll see what a madness the whole thing was. Say, mister?

Alf. Hey?

Monaghan. I beg your pardon. I'm a little strange here, and curious. Could you tell me why you're going to the Statue of Liberty?

Alf. Me? Well, I tell ya. I always wanted to take an ocean voyage. This is a pretty big boat—bigger than the ferries—so on Sundays, sometimes, I take the trip. It's better than nothing.

Monaghan. Thank you. *(To the kid)* So much for the great meaning of that statue, me boy. We'll talk to this lady standing at the rail. I just want you to understand why I didn't give Sheean me dime. Madam, would you be good enough to—oh, pardon me. *(To boy)* Better pass her by; she don't look so good. We'll ask that girl there. Young lady, if you'll pardon the curiosity of an old man, could you tell me in a few good words what it is about that statue that brings you out here?

Girl. What statue?

Monaghan. Why, the Statue of Liberty up 'head. We're coming up to it.

Girl. Statue of Liberty! Is this the Statue of Liberty boat?

Monaghan. Well, what'd you think it was?

Girl. Oh, my! I'm supposed to be on the Staten Island ferry! Where's the ticket man?

(*Going away*) Ticket man! Where's the ticket man?

Child Monaghan. Gee whiz, nobody seems to want to see the statue.

Monaghan. Just to prove it, let's see this fellow sitting on this bench here. Young man, say—

Young man. I can tell you in one word. For four days I haven't had a minute's peace. My kids are screaming, my wife is yelling, upstairs they play the piano all day long. The only place I can find that's quiet is a statue. That statue is my sweetheart. Every Sunday I beat it out to the island and sit next to her, and she don't talk.

Child Monaghan. I guess you were right, Grampa. Nobody seems to think it means anything.

Monaghan. Not only doesn't mean anything, but if they'd used the money to build an honest roomin' house on that island, the immigrants would have a place to spend the night, their valises wouldn't get robbed, and they—

Megaphone Voice. Please keep your seats while the boat is docking. Statue of Liberty— all out in five minutes!

Child Monaghan. Look down there, Gramp! There's a peanut stand! Could I have some?

Monaghan. I feel the wind comin' up. I don't think we dare take the time.

[Music. *Up and down.*]

Child Monaghan: Sssssseuuuuuuww! Look how far you can see! Look at that ship way out in the ocean!

Monaghan. It is; it's quite a view. Don't let go of me hand now.

Child Monaghan. I betcha we could almost see California.

Monaghan. It's probably that grove of trees way out over there. They do say it's beyond Jersey.

Child Monaghan. Feels funny. We're standing right inside her head. Is that what you meant, July IV, MDC . . .?

Monaghan. That's it. That tablet in her hand. Now shouldn't they have put "Welcome All" on it instead of that foreign language? Say! Do you feel her rockin'?

Child Monaghan. Yeah, she's moving a little bit. Listen, the wind!

[Sound. *Whistling of wind.*]

Monaghan. We better get down; come on! This way!

Child Monaghan. No, the stairs are this way! Come on!

[Sound. *Running. Then quick stop.*]

Monaghan. No, I told you they're the other way! Come!

Veteran (*calm, quiet voice*). Don't get excited, Pop. She'll stand.

Monaghan. She's swayin' awful.

Veteran. That's all right. I been up here thirty, forty times. She gives with the wind, flexible. Enjoy the view, go on.

Monaghan. Did you say you've been up here forty times?

Veteran. About that many.

Monaghan. What do you find here that's so interesting?

Veteran. It calms my nerves.

Monaghan. Ah. It seems to me it would make you more nervous than you were.

Veteran. No, not me. It kinda means something to me.

Monaghan. Might I ask what?

Veteran. Well . . . I was in the Philippine War,[4] back in ninety-eight. Left my brother back there.

Monaghan. Oh, yes. Sorry I am to hear it. Young man, I suppose, eh?

Veteran. Yeh. We were both young. This is his birthday today.

Monaghan. Oh, I understand.

Veteran. Yeh, this statue is about the only stone he's got. In my mind I feel it is, anyway. This statue kinda looks like what we believe. You know what I mean?

Monaghan. Looks like what we believe—I—I never thought of it that way. I—I see what you mean. It does look that way. *(Angrily)* See now, boy? If Sheean had put it

that way, I'd a give him me dime. *(Hurt)* Now, why do you suppose he didn't tell me that! Come down now. I'm sorry, sir, we've got to get out of here.

[Music. *Up and down.* Sound. *Footsteps under.*]

Hurry now; I want to get out of here. I feel terrible. I do, boy. That Sheean, that fool. Why didn't he tell me that? You'd think—

Child Monaghan. What does this say?

[Sound. *Footsteps halt.*]

Monaghan. Why, it's just a tablet, I suppose. I'll try it with me spectacles, just a minute. Why, it's a poem, I believe. "Give me your tired, your poor, your huddled masses yearning to breathe free, the wretched refuse[5] of your teeming[6] shore. Send these, the homeless, tempest-tost[7] to me, I lift . . . my lamp beside . . . the golden door!" Oh, dear. *(Ready to weep)* It had "Welcome All" on it all the time. Why

---

4 **Philippine War:** Spanish American War, 1898–1899.

5 **refuse** (ref' yūs): here, unwanted people.
6 **teeming:** bustling with people.
7 **tempest-tost:** storm-tossed.

didn't Sheean tell me? I'd a given him a quarter! Boy, go over there and here's a nickel and buy yourself a bag of them peanuts.

Child Monaghan (astonished). Gramp!

Monaghan. Go on now, I want to study this a minute. And be sure the man gives you full count.

Child Monaghan. I'll be right back.

[Sound. *Footsteps running away.*]

Monaghan (to himself). "Give me your tired, your poor, your huddled masses. . . ."

[Music. *Swells from a sneak to full, then under to background.*]

Young Monaghan. I ran over and got my peanuts and stood there cracking them open, looking around. And I happened to glance over to Grampa. He had his nose right up to that bronze tablet, reading it. And then he reached into his pocket and kinda spied around over his eyeglasses to see if anybody was looking, and then he took out a coin and stuck it in a crack of cement over the tablet.

[Sound. *Coin falling onto concrete.*]

It fell out, and before he could pick it up I got a look at it. It was a half a buck. He picked it up and pressed it into the crack so it stuck. And then he came over to me and we went home.

[Music. *Changes to stronger, more forceful theme.*]

That's why, when I look at her now through this window, I remember that time and that poem, and she really seems to say, "Whoever you are, wherever you come from, Welcome All. Welcome Home."

[Music. *Flares up to finish.*]

Discussion

1. As described in the conversation between Young Monaghan and August, which one of Grandpa's characteristics stands out in Young Monaghan's memory? Why?

2. Even after seeing the Statue of Liberty in the warehouse, Grandpa refuses to contribute to the pedestal fund. What excuses does he give for his refusal?

3. Why does Grandpa hope that the Statue will be blown down?

4. What suspicion of Grandpa's seems confirmed by the three strangers he talks to on the boat?

5. Do you consider Grandpa's change in attitude toward the Statue believable or unbelievable? Why?

6. Why does Grandpa give his grandson a nickel to buy peanuts?

7. Near the end of the play, Grandpa reads lines from a poem inscribed on the Statue of Liberty. Using your own words, rephrase those lines to show that you understand their meaning.

Like any other play, "Grandpa and the Statue" is made up almost entirely of DIALOGUE. Dialogue is the literary term for any oral exchange—talk—that involves two or more persons.

A playwright uses dialogue for at least two important reasons: (1) to unfold the plot of the play and (2) to characterize the persons involved. Since plot and characterization make up two basic ingredients of every play, dialogue might well be considered a play's "life blood."

1. In "Grandpa and the Statue," the opening dialogue between Young Monaghan and August focuses attention on (a) a person, (b) an object, and (c) a location—all of which are important elements in the plot. Name that person, that object, and that location. Then quote at least one line of dialogue that shows how *each* of those important elements is introduced.

2. In the scene on Grandpa Monaghan's front porch, Sheean explains the plan for providing a base for the Statue of Liberty (page 335). What lines from the dialogue show that Sheean tries to shame Grandpa into contributing a dime to the cause? How is this part of the dialogue essential to the unfolding of the plot?

3. Below are a few lines of dialogue from the play:

   Monaghan. How am I to get back to Butler Street from here?
   Sheean. You've got legs to walk.
   Monaghan. . . . I come on the trolley.
   Sheean. . . . I paid your fare and I'm not repeating the kindness.
   Monaghan. Sheean? You've stranded me!

   Which one of Grandpa's personal characteristics does this bit of dialogue emphasize?

1. Dialogue in plays is printed in a way that is different from the form used for dialogue in other types of literature. For example, if the first story in this book—"The Most Dangerous Game"—were printed as a play, the opening lines of dialogue would look something like this:

   Whitney. Off there to the right—somewhere—is a large island. It's rather a mystery—
   Rainsford. What island is it?
   Whitney. The old charts call it "Ship-Trap Island." A suggestive name, isn't it?

   Compare these lines of dialogue with the dialogue in the original story on page 5. You can see that the dialogue in play form is different from story dialogue in at least two ways: First, the play dialogue has no quotation marks at the beginning or at the end of what each speaker says. Second, the play dialogue contains no explanatory remarks such as *said Whitney* or *Rainsford asked* or *Whitney replied.* You can also see one other important difference. Story dialogue calls for a new paragraph each time there is a change of speaker; play dialogue does not. Rewrite at least ten lines of dialogue from *Grandpa and the Statue* as it would be printed if it were a story instead of a play.

2. Nearly everyone can remember at least one interesting elderly person who would make a good central character for a story or a play. Such a person might be memorable for his or her talkativeness, crabbiness, stinginess, generosity, or some other outstanding trait. Think of an elderly person whom you knew when you were in the first or second grade. Imagine that you had gone to this person with a problem or that you wanted to know why he or/she refused to fly in an airplane. Write a short dialogue that you might have had with this person. Use the form in which play dialogue is written.

Arthur Miller 1915 —

Arthur Miller, playwright and novelist, has not always been interested in literature. He explains that in school, "I was more interested in football, hockey, and just plain fooling around. I was a poor student and failed many subjects—algebra three times.

"The book that changed my life was *The Brothers Karamazov,* which I picked up, I don't know how or why, and all at once I believed I was born to be a writer." He read that book on the New York subway going to and from his warehouse job. Even though his high school record was not promising, Miller managed to get into college. He wrote his first play in ten days of spring vacation. "I had seen but one play in my life and had read the tragedies of Shakespeare. The play won several prizes and made me confident I could go ahead from there."

In 1949, Miller won a Pulitzer Prize for *Death of a Salesman.* This play, like much of Miller's work, is about how the past affects people's lives, catching them in the tangles they have created themselves. Miller says, "The story of any play is how the birds come home to roost."

Delayed in leaving Winnipeg, Charter Flight 714 is at last airborne.
Destination: Vancouver, British Columbia
Altitude: 16,000 feet

Air speed: 210 knots (about 240 miles per hour)
Weather: Ground fog; otherwise, perfect.
Flight pattern: Routine
Flight conditions: TERRIFYING!

Flight into Danger

a television play

ARTHUR HAILEY

Characters

Aboard Flight 714:

The passengers:
George Spencer
Dr. Frank Baird
Eight Male Passengers
Two Women Passengers

The crew:
Captain
First Officer
Stewardess

At Vancouver Airport:
Captain Martin Treleaven
Airport Controller
Harry Burdick
Switchboard Operator
Radio Operator
Tower Controller
Teletype Operator

At Winnipeg Airport:
First Passenger Agent
Second Passenger Agent

Act I

[Fade In. *The passenger lobby of Winnipeg Air Terminal at night. At the departure counter of Cross-Canada Airlines, a male passenger agent in uniform (First Agent) is checking a manifest.[1] He reaches for P.A. mike.*]

First Agent. Flight 98, direct fleetliner service to Vancouver, with connections for Victoria, Seattle, and Honolulu, leaving im-

mediately through gate four. No smoking. All aboard, please.

[*During the announcement George Spencer enters through the main lobby doorway. About thirty-five, he is a senior factory salesman for a motor-truck manufacturer. Spencer pauses to look for the Cross-Canada counter, then hastens toward it, arriving as the announcement concludes.*]

Spencer. Is there space on Flight 98 for Vancouver?

---

1 **manifest** (man′ ə fest): a list of passengers.

First Agent. Sorry, sir, that flight is full. Did you check with reservations?

Spencer. Didn't have time. I came straight out on the chance you might have a "no show" seat.

First Agent. With the big football game on tomorrow in Vancouver, I don't think you'll have much chance of getting out before tomorrow afternoon.

Spencer. That's no good. I've got to be in Vancouver tomorrow by midday.

First Agent (hesitates). Look, I'm not supposed to tell you this, but there's a charter flight in from Toronto. They're going out to the coast for the game. I did hear they were a few seats light.

Spencer. Who's in charge? Where do I find him?

First Agent. Ask at the desk over there. They call themselves Maple Leaf Air Charter. But mind, I didn't send you.

Spencer (smiles). Okay, thanks.

[Spencer *crosses to another departure counter which has a cardboard sign hanging behind it—Maple Leaf Air Charter. Behind the desk is an agent in a lounge suit. He is checking a manifest.*]

Spencer. Excuse me.

Second Agent. Yes?

Spencer. I was told you might have space on a flight to Vancouver.

Second Agent. Yes, there's one seat left. The flight's leaving right away, though.

Spencer. That's what I want.

Second Agent. Very well, sir. Your name, please?

Spencer. Spencer—George Spencer.

Second Agent. That'll be fifty-five dollars for the one-way trip.

Spencer. Will you take my air travel card?

Second Agent. No, sir. Just old-fashioned cash.

Spencer. All right. (*Produces wallet and counts out bills*)

Second Agent (handing over ticket). Do you have any bags?

Spencer. One. Right here.

Second Agent. All the baggage is aboard. Would you mind keeping that with you?

Spencer. Be glad to.

Second Agent. Okay, Mr. Spencer. Your ticket is your boarding pass. Go through gate three and ask the commissionaire for Flight 714. Better hurry.

Spencer. Thanks a lot. Good night.

Second Agent. Good night.

[*Exit* Spencer. *Enter* Stewardess.]

Second Agent. Hi, Janet. Did the meals get aboard?

Stewardess. Yes, they've just put them on. What was the trouble?

Second Agent. Couldn't get service from the regular caterers here. We had to go to some outfit the other side of town. That's what held us up.

Stewardess. Are we all clear now?

Second Agent. Yes, here's everything you'll need. (*Hands over papers*) There's one more passenger. He's just gone aboard. So that's fifty-six souls in your lovely little hands.

Stewardess. I'll try not to drop any.

Second Agent (*reaching for coat*). Well, I'm off for home.

Stewardess (*as she leaves*). 'Night.

Second Agent (*pulling on coat*). 'Night, Janet. (*Calls after her*) Don't forget to cheer for the Blue Bombers tomorrow.

[*The* Stewardess *waves and smiles.*]

[*Dissolve To. The passenger cabin of a DC-4 airliner. There is one empty aisle seat. Seated next to it is Dr. Frank Baird, 55. George Spencer enters, sees the unoccupied seat, and comes toward it.*]

Spencer. Pardon me, is this anyone's seat?

Baird. No.

Spencer. Thanks.

[Spencer *sheds his topcoat and puts it on the rack above the seats. Meanwhile the plane's motors can be heard starting.*]

[Cut To. *Film insert of four-engined airplaine exterior. Night, the motors starting.*]

[Cut To. *The passenger cabin.*]

Baird. I presume you're going to the big game like the rest of us.

Spencer. I'm ashamed to admit it, but I'd forgotten about the game.

Baird. I wouldn't say that too loudly if I were you. Some of the more exuberant fans might tear you limb from limb.

Spencer. I'll keep my voice down. (*Pleasantly*) Matter of fact, I'm making a sales trip to the coast.

Baird. What do you sell?

Spencer. Trucks.

Baird. Trucks?

Spencer. That's right. I'm what the local salesmen call the son-of-a-gun from head office with the special prices. . . . Need any trucks? How about forty? Give you a real good discount today.

Baird (*laughs*). I couldn't use that many, I'm afraid. Not in my line.

Spencer. Which is?

Baird. Medicine.

Spencer. You mean you're a doctor?

Baird. That's right. Can't buy one truck, leave alone forty. Football is the one extravagance I allow myself.

Spencer. Delighted to hear it, Doctor. Now I can relax.

[*As he speaks, the run-up of the aircraft engines begins, increasing to a heavy roar.*]

Baird (*raising his voice*). Do you think you can in this racket? I never can figure out why they make all this noise before take-off.

Spencer (*shouting, as noise increases*). It's the normal run-up of the engines. Airplane engines don't use battery ignition like you have in your car. They run on magneto ignition, and each of the magnetos is tested separately. If they're okay and the motors are giving all the power they should—away you go!

Baird. You sound as if you know something about it.

Spencer. I'm pretty rusty now. I used to fly fighters in the air force. But that was ten years ago. Reckon I've forgotten most of it. . . . Well, there we go.

[*The tempo of the motors increases. Baird and Spencer lean toward the window to watch the take off, although it is dark outside.*]

[Cut To. *Film insert of airplane taking off, night.*]

[Cut To. *The passenger cabin. The noise of the motors is reduced slightly, and the two men relax in their seats. Spencer reaches for cigarettes.*]

Spencer. Smoke?

Baird. Thank you.

[*They light up. The* Stewardess *enters from aft[2]*

2 **aft**: the back.

of airplane and reaches for two pillows from the rack above.*]

Stewardess. We were held up at Winnipeg, sir, and we haven't served dinner yet. Would you care for some?

Spencer. Yes, please.

[*The* Stewardess *puts a pillow on his lap.*]

Stewardess *(to* Baird*).* And you, sir?

Baird. Thank you, yes. *(To* Spencer*)* It's a

bit late for dinner, but it'll pass the time away.

Stewardess. There's lamb chop or grilled halibut.

Baird. I'll take the lamb.

Spencer. Yes, I'll have that, too.

Stewardess. Thank you, sir.

Baird (*to* Spencer). Tell me . . . By the way, my name is Baird.

Spencer. Spencer, George Spencer.

[*They shake hands.*]

Baird. How'd 'do. Tell me, when you make a sales trip like this, do you. . . .

[*Fade voices and pan with the* Stewardess, *returning aft. Entering the airplane's tiny galley,*[3] *she picks up a telephone and presses a call button.*]

Voice of First Officer. Flight deck.

Stewardess. I'm finally serving the dinners. What'll "you all" have—lamb chops or grilled halibut?

Voice of First Officer. Just a minute. (*Pause*) Skipper says he'll have the lamb . . . Oh, hold it! . . . No, he's changed his mind. Says he'll take the halibut. Make it two fish, Janet.

Stewardess. Okay. (*The* Stewardess *hangs up the phone and begins to arrange meal trays.*)

[Cut To. Spencer *and* Baird.]

Spencer. No, I hadn't expected to go west again this quickly.

Baird. You have my sympathy. I prescribe my travel in small doses.

[*The* Stewardess *enters and puts meal tray on pillow.*]

Baird. Oh, thank you.

Stewardess. Will you have coffee, tea, or milk, sir?

Baird. Coffee, please.

Stewardess. I'll bring it later.

Baird. That'll be fine. (*To* Spencer) Tell me do you follow football at all?

Spencer. A little. Hockey's my game, though. Who are you for tomorrow?

Baird. The Argos, naturally. (*As the* Stewardess *brings second tray*) Thank you, dear.

Stewardess. Will you have coffee, tea, or—

Spencer. I'll have coffee, too. No cream.

[*The* Stewardess *nods and exits.*]

Spencer (*to* Baird). Must be a calm night outside. No trouble in keeping the dinner steady.

Baird (*looking out of window*). It is calm. Not a cloud in sight. Must be a monotonous business flying these things, once they're off the ground.

Spencer. It varies, I guess.

[Audio. *Fade up the roar of motors.*]

[Dissolve To. *Film insert of airplane in level flight, night.*]

[Dissolve To. *The aircraft flight deck. The* Captain *is seated on left, the* First Officer *on right. Neither is touching the controls.*]

First Officer (*into radio mike*). Height 16,000 feet. Course 285 true. ETA[4] Vancouver 0505 Pacific Standard. Over.

---

3 **galley:** place where food is prepared for serving.

4 **ETA:** estimated time of arrival.

Voice on Radio. Flight 714. This is Winnipeg Control. Roger.[5] Out.

[*The* First Officer *reaches for a log sheet and makes a notation, then relaxes in his seat.*]

First Officer. Got any plans for Vancouver?

Captain. Yes, I'm going to sleep for two whole days.

[*The Stewardess enters with a meal tray.*]

Stewardess. Who's first?

Captain. You take yours, Harry.

[*The Stewardess produces a pillow and the* First Officer *slides back his seat, well clear of the control column. He places the pillow on his knees and accepts the tray.*]

First Officer. Thanks, honey.

Captain. Everything all right at the back, Janet? How are the football fans?

Stewardess. They tired themselves out on the way from Toronto. Looks like a peaceful, placid night.

First Officer (*with mouth full of food, raising fork for emphasis*). Aha! Those are the sort of nights to beware of. It's in the quiet times that trouble brews. I'll bet you right now that somebody's getting ready to be sick.

Stewardess. That'll be when you're doing the flying. Or have you finally learned how to hold this thing steady? (*To* Captain) How's the weather?

Captain. General fog east of the mountains, extending pretty well as far as Manitoba. But it's clear to the west. Should be rockaby smooth the whole way.

---

5 **Roger:** aviation talk meaning "message received and understood."

Stewardess. Good. Well, keep junior here off the controls while I serve coffee. (*Exits*)

First Officer (*calling after her*). Mark my words, woman! Stay close to that mop and pail.

Captain. How's the fish?

First Officer (*hungrily*). Not bad. Not bad at all. If there were about three times as much it might be a square meal.

[Audio. *Fade voices into roar of motors.*]

[Dissolve To. *The passenger cabin.* Spencer *and* Baird *are concluding their meal.* Baird *puts down a coffee cup and wipes his mouth with a napkin. Then he reaches up and presses a call button above his head. There is a soft "ping," and the* Stewardess *enters.*]

Stewardess. Yes, sir?

Baird. That was very enjoyable. Now, if you'll take the tray I think I'll try to sleep.

Stewardess. Surely. (*To* Spencer) Will you have more coffee, sir?

Spencer. No, thanks.

[*The* Stewardess *picks up the second tray and goes aft.* Spencer *yawns.*]

Spencer. Let me know if the noise keeps you awake. If it does, I'll have the engines stopped.

Baird (*chuckles*). Well, at least there won't be any night calls—I hope.

[Baird *reaches up and switches off the overhead reading lights so that both seats are in semi-darkness. The two men prepare to sleep.*]

[Dissolve To. *Film insert of airplane in level flight, night.*]

[Dissolve To. *The passenger cabin. The* Captain *emerges from the flight deck and strolls aft, saying "Good evening" to one or two people who glance up as he goes by. He passes* Spencer *and* Baird, *who are sleeping. As the* Captain *progresses, the* Stewardess *can be seen at the rear of the cabin. She is bending solicitously over a woman passenger, her hand on the woman's forehead. The* Captain *approaches.*]

Captain. Something wrong, Miss Burns?

Stewardess. This lady is feeling a little unwell. I was going to get her some aspirin. *(To the* Woman Passenger*)* I'll be back in a moment.

Captain. Sorry to hear that. What seems to be the trouble?

[*The* Woman Passenger *has her head back and her mouth open. A strand of hair has fallen across her face, and she is obviously in pain.*]

First Woman Passenger *(speaking with an effort)*. I'm sorry to be such a nuisance, but it hit me all of a sudden . . . just a few minutes ago . . . dizziness and nausea and a sharp pain . . . *(indicating abdomen)* down here.

Captain. Well, I think the Stewardess will be able to help you.

[Stewardess *returns.*]

Stewardess. Now, here you are; try these. *(She hands over two aspirins and a cup of water. The passenger takes them, then puts her head back on the seat rest.)*

First Woman Passenger. Thank you very much. *(She smiles faintly at the* Captain.*)*

Captain *(quietly, taking the* Stewardess *aside)*. If she gets any worse you'd better let me know and I'll radio ahead. But we've still five hours' flying to the coast. Is there a doctor on board, do you know?

Stewardess. There was no one listed as a

doctor on the manifest. But I can go round and ask.

Captain *(looks around)*. Well, most everybody's sleeping now. We'd better not disturb them unless we have to. See how she is in the next half hour or so. *(He bends down and puts a hand on the woman's shoulder.)* Try to rest, madam, if you can. Miss Burns will take good care of you.

[*The* Captain *nods to the* Stewardess *and begins his return to the flight deck. The* Stewardess *arranges a blanket around the* Woman Passenger. Spencer *and* Baird *are still sleeping as the* Captain *passes.*]

[Dissolve To. *Film insert of airplane in level flight, night.*]

[Dissolve To. *The passenger cabin.* Spencer *stirs and wakes. Then he glances forward to where the* Stewardess *is leaning over another section of seats, and her voice can be heard softly.*]

Stewardess. I'm sorry to disturb you, but we're trying to find out if there's a doctor on board.

First Male Passenger. Not me, I'm afraid. Is something wrong?

Stewardess. One of the passengers is feeling unwell. It's nothing too serious. *(Moving on to the next pair of seats)* I'm sorry to disturb you, but we're trying to find out if there's a doctor on board.

[*There is an indistinct answer from the two people just questioned, then* Spencer *sits forward and calls the* Stewardess.]

Spencer. Stewardess! *(Indicating* Baird, *who is still sleeping)* This gentleman is a doctor.

Stewardess. Thank you. I think we'd better wake him. I have two passengers who are quite sick.

Spencer. All right. *(Shaking Baird's arm)* Doctor! Doctor! Wake up!

Baird. Um . . . Um . . . What is it?

Stewardess. Doctor. I'm sorry to disturb you. But we have two passengers who seem quite sick. I wonder if you'd take a look at them.

Baird *(sleepily)*. Yes . . . yes . . . of course.

[Spencer *moves out of the seat to permit* Baird *to reach the aisle.* Baird *then follows the* Stewardess *aft to the* First Woman Passenger. *Although a blanket is around her, the woman is shivering and gasping, with her head back and eyes closed. The doctor places a hand on her forehead, and she opens her eyes.*]

Stewardess. This gentleman is a doctor. He's going to help us.

First Woman Passenger. Oh, Doctor! . . .

Baird. Now, just relax.

[*He makes a quick external examination, first checking pulse, then taking a small pen-type flashlight from his pocket and looking into her eyes. He then loosens the blanket and the woman's coat beneath the blanket. As he places a hand on her abdomen, she gasps with pain.*]

Baird. Hurt you there? *(With an effort she nods.)* There?

First Woman Passenger. Oh, yes! Yes!

[Baird *replaces the coat and blanket, then turns to the* Stewardess.]

Baird *(with authority)*. Please tell the captain we must land at once. This woman has to be gotten to a hospital immediately.

Stewardess. Do you know what's wrong, Doctor?

Baird. I can't tell. I've no means of making a proper diagnosis. But it's serious enough to

land at the nearest city with hospital facilities. You can tell your captain that.

Stewardess. Very well, Doctor. (*Moving across the aisle and forward*) While I'm gone will you take a look at this gentleman here? He's also complained of sickness and stomach pains.

[Baird *goes to a male passenger indicated by the* Stewardess. *The man is sitting forward and resting his head on the back of the seat ahead of him. He is retching.*[6]]

Baird. I'm a doctor. Will you put your head back, please?

[*The man groans, but follows the doctor's instruction. He is obviously weak.* Baird *makes another quick examination, then pauses thoughtfully.*]

Baird. What have you had to eat in the last twenty-four hours?

Second Male Passenger (*with effort*). Just the usual meals . . . breakfast . . . bacon and eggs . . . salad for lunch . . . couple of sandwiches at the airport . . . then dinner here.

[*The* Stewardess *enters, followed by the* Captain.]

Baird (*to the* Stewardess). Keep him warm. Get blankets around him. (*To the* Captain) How quickly can we land, Captain?

Captain. That's the trouble. I've just been talking to Calgary. There was a light fog over the prairies earlier, but now it's thickened and everything is closed in this side of the mountains. It's clear at the coast, and we'll have to go through.

Baird. Is that faster than turning back?

Captain. It would take us longer to go back now than to go on.

Baird. Then, how soon do you expect to land?

Captain. At about 5 A.M. Pacific time. (*As* Baird *glances at his watch*) You need to put your watch on two hours because of the change of time. We'll be landing in three hours forty-five minutes from now.

Baird. Then, I'll have to do what I can for these people. Can my bag be reached? I checked it at Toronto.

Captain. We can get it. Let me have your tags, Doctor.

[Baird *takes out a wallet and selects two baggage tags which he hands to the* Captain.]

Baird. There are two tags. It's the small overnight case I want.

[*As he finishes speaking, the airplane lurches violently.* Baird *and the* Stewardess *and the* Captain *are thrown sharply to one side. Simultaneously the telephone in the galley buzzes several times. As the three recover their balance the* Stewardess *answers the phone quickly.*]

Stewardess. Yes?

First Officer's Voice (*under strain*). Come forward quickly. I'm sick!

Stewardess. The First Officer is sick. He says come forward quickly.

Captain (*to* Baird). You'd better come too.

[*The* Captain *and* Baird *move quickly forward, passing through the flight deck door.*]

[Cut To. *The flight deck. The* First Officer *is at the controls on the right-hand side. He is retching and shuddering, flying the airplane by will power and nothing else. The* Captain *promptly slides into the left-hand seat and takes the controls.*]

---

6 retching: vomiting.

Captain. Get him out of there!

[*Together* Baird *and the* Stewardess *lift the* First Officer *from his seat, and as they do, he collapses. They lower him to the floor, and the* Stewardess *reaches for a pillow and blankets.* Baird *makes the same quick examination he used in the two previous cases. Meanwhile the* Captain *has steadied the aircraft, and now he snaps over a button to engage the automatic pilot. He releases the controls and turns to the others, though without leaving his seat.*]

Captain. He must have been changing course when it happened. We're back on auto pilot now. Now, Doctor; what is it? What's happening?

Baird. There's a common denominator in these attacks. There has to be. And the most likely thing is food. *(To the* Stewardess*)* How long is it since we had dinner?

Stewardess. Two and a half to three hours.

Baird. Now, then, what did you serve?

Stewardess. Well, the main course was a choice of fish or meat.

Baird. I remember that, I ate meat. *(Indicating the* First Officer*)* What did he have?

Stewardess *(faintly, with dawning alarm).* Fish.

Baird. Do you remember what the other two passengers had?

Stewardess. No.

Baird. Then, go back quickly, and find out, please.

[*As the* Stewardess *exits,* Baird *kneels beside the* First Officer, *who is moaning.*]

Baird. Try to relax. I'll give you something in a few minutes to help the pain. You'll feel better if you stay warm.

[Baird *arranges the blanket around the* First Officer. *Now the* Stewardess *reappears.*]

Stewardess *(alarmed)*. Doctor, both those passengers had fish. And there are three more cases now. And they ate fish too. Can you come?

Baird. Yes, but I need that bag of mine.

Captain. Janet, take these tags and get one of the passengers to help you. *(Hands over* Baird's *luggage tags)* Doctor, I'm going to get on the radio and report what's happening to Vancouver. Is there anything you want to add?

Baird. Yes. Tell them we have three serious cases of suspected food poisoning, and there appear to be others. When we land we'll want ambulances and medical help waiting, and the hospitals should be warned. Tell them we're not sure, but we suspect the poisoning may have been caused by fish served on board. You'd better suggest they put a ban on serving all food which originated wherever ours came from until we've established the source for sure.

Captain. Right. *(He reaches for the radio mike, and* Baird *turns to go aft. But suddenly a thought strikes the* Captain.*)* Doctor, I've just remembered. . . .

Baird. Yes.

Captain *(quietly)*. I ate fish.

Baird. When?

Captain. I'd say about half an hour after he did. *(Pointing to the* First Officer*)* Maybe a little longer. Is there anything I can do?

Baird. It doesn't follow that everyone will be affected. There's often no logic to these things. You feel all right now?

Captain. Yes.

Baird. You'd better not take any chances. Your food can't be completely digested yet. As soon as I get my bag I'll give you something to help you get rid of it.

Captain. Then, hurry, Doctor. Hurry! *(Into mike)* Vancouver control. This is Maple Leaf Charter Flight 714. I have an emergency message. Do you read? Over.

Voice on Radio *(Vancouver* Operator*)*. Go ahead, 714.

Captain. We have serious food poisoning on board. Several passengers and the First Officer are seriously ill. . . .

[Dissolve To. *The luggage compartment below the flight deck. A passenger is hurriedly passing up bags to the* Stewardess. Baird *is looking down from above.*]

Baird. That's it! That's it down there! Let me have it!

[Fade Out.]

1. Fairly early in Act I (page 351), the First Officer makes this casual remark: "It's in the quiet times that trouble brews." How is this innocent remark closer to the truth than the First Officer realizes?

2. Where did the meals served aboard Flight 714 originally come from?

3. Just before Flight 714 leaves Winnipeg, George Spencer explains to Dr. Baird why propeller planes are so noisy during take-off. What past experience enables Spencer to give this explanation? How could Spencer's past experience be important later?

4. By the end of Act I, three separate conditions or situations show that Flight 714 is in very serious trouble. What are those conditions or situations?

Act II

[*Fade In. The control room, Vancouver Airport. At a radio panel an operator, wearing headphones, is transcribing a message on a typewriter. Partway through the message he presses a button on the panel and a bell rings stridently, signaling an emergency. At once an Airport Controller appears behind the operator and reads the message as it continues to come in. Nearby is a telephone switchboard manned by an Operator, and a battery of teletypes clattering noisily.*]

Controller (*over his shoulder, to the* Switchboard Operator). Get me Area Traffic Control, then clear the teletype circuit to Winnipeg. Priority message. (*Stepping back to take phone*) Vancouver Controller here. I've an emergency report from Maple Leaf Charter Flight 714, ex-Winnipeg for Vancouver. There's serious food poisoning among the passengers, and the First Officer is down too. They're asking for all levels below them to be cleared, and priority approach and landing. ETA is 0505 . . . Roger. We'll keep you posted. (*To a* Teletype Operator *who has appeared*) Got Winnipeg? (*As the* Teletype Operator *nods*) Send this message. Controller Winnipeg. Urgent. Maple Leaf Charter Flight 714 reports serious food poisoning among passengers believed due to fish dinner served on flight. Imperative check source and suspend all other food service originating same place. That's all. (*To the* Switchboard Operator) Get me the local agent for Maple Leaf Charter. Burdick's his name—call his home. And after that, I want the city police—the senior officer on duty. (*Controller crosses to radio control panel and reads message which is just being completed. To the* Radio

Operator) Acknowledge. Say that all altitudes below them are being cleared, and they'll be advised of landing instructions here. Ask them to keep us posted on condition of the passengers.

Switchboard Operator. Mr. Burdick is here at the airport. I have him on the line now.

Controller. Good. Controller here. Burdick, we've got an emergency on one of your flights—714, ex-Toronto and Winnipeg. (*Pause*) No, the aircraft is all right. There's food poisoning among the passengers, and the First Officer has it too. You'd better come over. (*Replaces phone. Then to the* Switchboard Operator) Have you got the police yet? (*As the* Operator *nods*) Right, put it on this line.

Hullo, this is the Controller, Vancouver Airport. Who am I speaking to, please? (*Pause*) Inspector, we have an emergency on an incoming flight. Several of the passengers are seriously ill, and we need ambulances and doctors out here at the airport. (*Pause*) Six people for sure, maybe more. The flight will be landing at five minutes past five local time—that's about three and a half hours. Now, will you get the ambulances, set up traffic control, and alert the hospitals? Right. We'll call you again as soon as there's anything definite.

[*During the above,* Harry Burdick, *local manager of Maple Leaf Air Charter, has entered.*]

Burdick. Where's the message?

[*The* Radio Operator *hands him a copy which* Burdick *reads.*]

Burdick (*to* Radio Operator). How's the weather at Calgary? It might be quicker to go in there.

Controller. No dice! There's fog down to the deck everywhere east of the Rockies. They'll have to come through.

Burdick. Let me see the last position report. (*As* Controller *passes a clipboard*) You say that you've got medical help coming?

Controller. The city police are working on it now.

Burdick. That message! They say the First Officer is down. What about the Captain? Ask if he's affected, and ask if there's a doctor on board. Tell them we're getting medical advice here in case they need it.

Controller. I'll take care of that.

Burdick (*to the* Switchboard Operator). Will you get me Doctor Knudsen, please? You'll find his home number on the emergency list.

Controller (*into radio mike*). Flight 714, this is Vancouver.

[Dissolve To. *The airplane passenger cabin.* Baird *is leaning over another prostrate passenger. The main lighting is on in the cabin, and other passengers, so far not affected, are watching, with varying degrees of concern and anxiety. Some have remained in their seats, others have clustered in the aisle. The doctor has obtained his bag and it is open beside him. The* Stewardess *is attending to another passenger nearby.*]

Baird (*to the* Stewardess). I think I'd better talk to everyone and tell them the story. (*Moving to center of cabin, he raises his voice.*)

Ladies and gentlemen, may I have your attention, please? If you can't hear me, perhaps you would come a little closer. (*Pause, as passengers move in*) My name is Baird, and I am a doctor. I think it's time that everyone knows what is happening. So far as I can tell, we have several cases of food poisoning, and we believe that the cause of it was the fish which was served for dinner.

Second Woman Passenger (*with alarm, to man beside her*). Hector! We both had fish!

Baird. Now, there is no immediate cause for alarm or panic, and even if you did eat fish for dinner, it doesn't follow that you are going to be affected too. There's seldom any logic to these things. However, we are going to take some precautions, and the Stewardess and I are coming around to everyone, and I want you to tell us if you ate fish. If you did we'll tell you what to do to help yourselves. Now, if you'll go back to your seats we'll begin right away. (*To the* Stewardess, *as passengers move back to their seats*) All we can do now is to give immediate first aid.

Stewardess. What should that be, Doctor?

Baird. Two things. First, everyone who ate fish must drink several glasses of water. That will help dilute the poison. After that we'll give an emetic.[7] I have some emetic pills in my bag, and if there aren't enough we'll have to rely on salt. Do you have salt in the galley?

Stewardess. A few small packets which go with the lunches, but we can break them open.

Baird. All right. We'll see how far the pills will go first. I'll start at the back here. Meanwhile you begin giving drinking water

---

7 emetic (i met′ ik): medicine causing one to vomit.

to the passengers already affected and get some to the First Officer too. I'll ask someone to help you.

First Male Passenger. Can I help, Doc?

Baird. What did you eat for dinner—fish or meat?

First Male Passenger. Meat.

Baird. All right. Will you help the Stewardess bring glasses of water to the people who are sick? I want them to drink at least three glasses each—more if they can.

Stewardess (going to galley). We'll use these cups. There's drinking water here and at the rear.

First Male Passenger. All right, let's get started.

Baird (to the Stewardess). The Captain! Before you do anything else you'd better get him on to drinking water, and give him two emetic pills. Here. (Takes bottle from his bag and shakes out the pills) Tell him they'll make him feel sick, and the sooner he is, the better.

Stewardess. Very well, Doctor.

Second Woman Passenger (frightened). Doctor! Doctor! I heard you say the pilots are ill. What will happen to us if they can't fly the plane? (To husband) Hector, I'm frightened.

Third Male Passenger. Take it easy, my dear. Nothing has happened so far, and the doctor is doing all he can.

Baird. I don't think you'll have any reason to worry, madam. It's quite true that both of the pilots had the fish which we believe may have caused the trouble. But only the first officer is affected. Now, did you and your husband eat fish or meat?

Third Male Passenger. Fish. We both ate fish.

Baird. Then, will you both drink at least three—better make it four—of those cups of water which the other gentleman is bringing around. After that, take one of these pills each. (Smiling) I think you'll find there are little containers under your seat. Use those. (Goes to rear of plane)

Fourth Male Passenger (in broad English Yorkshire accent). How's it commin', Doc? Everything under control?

Baird. I think we're holding our own. What did you have for dinner?

Fourth Male Passenger. Ah had the bloomin' fish. Didn't like it neither. Fine how d'you do this is. Coom all this way t'see our team win, and now it looks like ah'm headed for a mortuary slab.

Baird. It really isn't as bad as that, you know. But just as a precaution, drink four cups of water—it's being brought around now—and after that take this pill. It'll make you feel sick.

Fourth Male Passenger (pulls carton from under seat and holds it up): It's the last time I ride on a bloomin' airplane! What service! They give you your dinner and then coom round and ask for it back.

Baird. What did you have for dinner, please—meat or fish?

Fifth Male Passenger. Meat, Doctor.

Sixth Male Passenger. Yes, I had meat too.

Baird. All right, we won't worry about you.

Seventh Male Passenger. I had meat, Doctor.

Eighth Male Passenger. I had fish.

Doctor. Very well, will you drink at least four cups of water please? It'll be brought round to you. Then take this pill.

Sixth Male Passenger (*slow speaking*). What's caused this food poisoning, Doctor?

Baird. Well, it can either be caused through spoilage of the food, or some kind of bacteria—the medical word is staphylococcus poisoning.

Sixth Male Passenger (*nodding knowledgeably*). Oh yes . . . staphylo . . . I see.

Baird. Either that, or some toxic substance may have gotten into the food during its preparation.

Seventh Male Passenger. What kind do you think this is, Doctor?

Baird. From the effect I suspect a toxic substance.

Seventh Male Passenger. And you don't know what it is?

Baird. We won't know until we make laboratory tests. Actually, with modern food-handling methods—the chances of this happening are probably a million to one against.

Stewardess (*entering*). I couldn't get the First Officer to take more than a little water, Doctor. He seems pretty bad.

Baird. I'll go to him now. Have you checked all the passengers in the front portion?

Stewardess. Yes, and there are two more new cases—the same symptoms as the other passengers.

Baird. I'll attend to them—after I've looked at the First Officer.

Stewardess. Do you think. . . .

[*Before the sentence is completed the galley telephone buzzes insistently. Baird and the Stewardess exchange glances quickly, then, without waiting to answer the phone, race to the flight deck door.*]

[*Cut To. The flight deck. The Captain is in the left-hand seat. Sweat pouring down his face, he is racked by retching, and his right hand is on his stomach. Yet he is fighting against the pain and attempting to reach the radio transmitter mike. But he doesn't make it, and as Baird and the Stewardess reach him, he falls back in his seat.*]

Captain (*weakly*). I did what you said . . . guess it was too late. . . . You've got to give me something, Doctor . . . so I can hold out . . . till I get this airplane on the ground. . . . You understand? . . . It'll fly itself on this course . . . but I've got to take it in . . . Get on the radio . . . Tell control. . . .

[*During the above Baird and the Stewardess have been helping the Captain from his seat. Now he collapses into unconsciousness, and Baird goes down beside him. The Doctor has a stethoscope now and uses it.*]

Baird. Get blankets over him. Keep him warm. There's probably a reaction because he tried to fight it off so long.

Stewardess (*alarmed*): Can you do what he said? Can you bring him round long enough to land?

Baird (*bluntly*). You're part of this crew, so I'll tell you how things are. Unless I can get him to a hospital quickly, I'm not even sure I can save his life. And that goes for the others too.

Stewardess. But—

Baird. I know what you're thinking, and I've thought of it too. How many passengers are there on board?

Stewardess. Fifty-six.

Baird. And how many fish dinners did you serve?

Stewardess *(composing herself)*. Probably about fifteen. More people ate meat than fish, and some didn't eat at all because it was so late.

Baird. And you?

Stewardess. I had meat.

Baird *(quietly)*. My dear, did you ever hear the term "long odds"?

Stewardess. Yes, but I'm not sure what it means.

Baird. I'll give you an example. Out of a total field of fifty-five, our chances of safety depend on there being one person back there who not only is qualified to land this airplane, but who didn't choose fish for dinner tonight.

[*After her initial alarm the* Stewardess *is calm now, and competent. She looks* Baird *in the eye and even manages a slight smile.*]

Stewardess. Then, I suppose I should begin asking.

Baird *(thoughtfully)*. Yes, but's there's no sense in starting a panic. *(Decisively)* You'd better do it this way. Say that the First Officer is sick and the Captain wondered if there's someone with flying experience who could help him with the radio.

Stewardess. Very well, Doctor. *(She turns to go.)*

Baird. Wait! The man who was sitting beside me! He said something about flying in the war. And we both ate meat. Get him first! But still go round to the others. There may be someone else with more experience.

[*The* Stewardess *exits and* Baird *busies himself with the* First Officer *and the* Captain. *After a moment,* George Spencer *enters.*]

Spencer. The Stewardess said—*(then, as he sees the two pilots)* . . . No! Not both pilots!

Baird. Can *you* fly this airplane—and land it?

Spencer. No! No! Not a chance! Of course not!

Baird. But you told me you flew in the war.

Spencer. So I did. But that was fighters—little combat airplanes, not a great ship like this. I flew airplanes which had one engine. This has four. Flying characteristics are different. Controls don't react the same way. It's another kind of flying altogether. And besides that, I haven't touched an airplane for over ten years.

Baird *(grimly)*. Then, let's hope there's someone else on board who can do the job . . . because neither of these men can.

[*The* Stewardess *enters and pauses.*]

Stewardess *(quietly)*. There's no one else.

Baird. Mr. Spencer, I know nothing of flying. I have no means of evaluating what you tell me. All I know is this: that among the people on this airplane who are physically able to fly it, you are the only one with any kind of qualification to do so. What do you suggest?

Spencer *(desperately)*. Isn't there a chance— of either pilot recovering?

Baird. I'll tell you what I just told the Stewardess here. Unless I can get them to a hospital quickly, I can't even be sure of saving their lives.

[*There is a pause.*]

Spencer. Well—I guess I just got drafted. If either of you are any good at praying, you can start any time. *(He slips into the left-hand seat.)* Let's take a look. Altitude 16,000. Course 290. The ship's on automatic pilot—we can be thankful for that. Air speed 210 knots. *(Touching the various controls)* Throttles, pitch, mixture, landing gear, flaps, and the flap indicator. We'll need a check list for landing, but we'll get that on the radio. . . . Well, maybe we'd better tell the world about our problems. *(To the* Stewardess*)* Do you know how to work this radio? They've added a lot of gismos since my flying days.

Stewardess *(pointing)*. It's this panel up here they use to talk to the ground, but I'm not sure which switches you have to set.

Spencer. Ah, yes, here's the channel selector. Maybe we'd better leave it where it is. Oh, and here we are—"transmit." *(He flicks a switch, and a small light glows on the radio control panel.)* Now we're in business. *(He picks up the mike and headset beside him, then turns to the other two.)* Look, whatever happens I'm going to need another pair of hands here. Doc, I guess you'll be needed back with the others, so I think the best choice is Miss Canada here. How about it?

Stewardess. But I know nothing about all this!

Spencer. Then that'll make us a real good pair. But I'll tell you what to do ahead of time. Better get in that other seat and strap yourself in. That all right with you, doc?

Baird. Yes, do that. I'll take care of things in the back. And I'd better go there now. Good luck!

Spencer. Good luck to *you.* We're all going to need it.

[Baird *exits.*]

Spencer. What's your first name?

Stewardess. Janet.

Spencer. Okay, Janet. Let's see if I can remember how to send out a distress message. . . . Better put on that headset beside you. *(Into mike)* May Day! May Day! May Day![8] *(To the* Stewardess*)* What's our flight number?

Stewardess. 714.

Spencer *(into mike)*. This is Flight 714, Maple Leaf Air Charter, in distress. Come in anyone. Over.

Voice on Radio *(immediately, crisply)*. This is Calgary, 714. Go ahead!

Voice on Radio *(Vancouver* Operator*)*. Vancouver here, 714. All other aircraft stay off the air. Over.

Spencer. Thank you, Calgary and Vancouver. This message is for Vancouver. This aircraft is in distress. Both pilots and some passengers—*(To the* Stewardess*)* How many passengers?

Stewardess. It was seven a few minutes ago. It may be more now.

Spencer. Correction. At least seven passengers are suffering from food poisoning. Both pilots are unconscious and in serious condition. We have a doctor on board who says that neither pilot can be revived. Did you get that, Vancouver? *(Pause)* Now we come to the interesting bit. My name is Spencer, George Spencer. I am a passenger on this airplane. Correction: I was a passenger. I have about a thousand hours' total flying time, but

---

8 **May Day:** emergency call for help. The expression comes from the French *m'aidez* (me dā'), meaning "Help me!"

all of it was on single-engine fighters. And also, I haven't flown an airplane for ten years. Now, then, Vancouver, you'd better get someone on this radio who can give me some instructions about flying this machine. Our altitude is 16,000, course 290 magnetic, air speed 210 knots. We are on automatic pilot. Your move, Vancouver. Over. *(To the* Stewardess*)* You want to make a bet that that stirred up a little flurry down below?

[*The* Stewardess *shakes her head, but does not reply.*]

[Dissolve To. *The control room, Vancouver. The* Controller *is putting down a phone as the* Radio Operator *brings a message to him. He reads the message.*]

Controller. Oh, no! *(To the* Radio Operator*)* Ask if—No, let me talk to them.

[*The* Controller *goes to panel and takes the transmitter mike. The* Radio Operator *turns a switch and nods.*]

Controller *(tensely).* Flight 714. This is Vancouver control. Please check with your doctor on board for any possibility of either pilot recovering. Ask him to do everything possible to revive one of the pilots, even if it means neglecting other people. Over.

Spencer's Voice on Radio. Vancouver, this is 714, Spencer speaking. I understand your message. But the doctor says there is no possibility whatever of either pilot recovering to make the landing. He says they are critically ill and may die unless they get hospital treatment soon. Over.

Controller. All right, 714. Stand by, please. *(He pauses momentarily to consider the next course of action. Then briskly to the* Switchboard Operator*)* Get me Area Traffic Control—fast. *(Into phone)* Vancouver controller. The emergency we had! . . . Right now it looks like it's shaping up for a disaster.

[Fade Out.]

Discussion

1. At about what time of day or night (Pacific Time) does Act II take place? Explain briefly how you arrived at your answer.

2. When Dr. Baird and the Stewardess are alone, Dr. Baird confides the real seriousness of the sick passengers' condition. How serious is it?

3. For the most part, Act II focuses on Dr. Baird and the Stewardess and their efforts to comfort the sick passengers. It is not until almost the end of the act that attention turns to George Spencer. Yet George is not sick; he had meat for dinner. Why is he involved in what is going on?

4. When George Spencer and the Stewardess take over the controls of the plane, their situation affords them one thing they can be thankful for. What one advantage do they have? At what point in the flight will that advantage become useless?

Act III

[Fade In. *The control room, Vancouver. The atmosphere is one of restrained pandemonium. The* Radio Operator *is typing a message. The teletypes are busy. The* Controller *is on one telephone, and* Harry Burdick *on another. During what follows, cut back and forth from one to the other.*]

Controller *(into phone)*. As of right now, hold everything taking off for the East. You've got forty-five minutes to clear any traffic for South, West, or North. After that, hold everything that's scheduled outward. On incoming traffic, accept anything you can get on the deck within the next forty-five minutes. Anything you can't get down by then for sure, divert away from this area. Hold it. *(A messenger hands him a message which he scans. Then to messenger)* Tell the security officer. *(Into phone)* If you've any flights coming in from the Pacific, divert them to Seattle. And any traffic inland is to stay well away from the east-west lane between Calgary and Vancouver. Got that? Right.

Burdick *(into phone)* Is that Cross-Canada Airlines? . . . Who's on duty in operations? . . . Let me talk to him. *(Pause)* Mr. Gardner, it's Harry Burdick of Maple Leaf Charter. We have an incoming flight that's in bad trouble, and we need an experienced pilot to talk on the radio. Someone who's flown DC-4's. Can you help us? *(Pause)* Captain Treleaven? Yes, I know him well.

(Pause) You mean he's with you now? *(Pause)* Can he come over to control right away? *(Pause)* Thank you. Thank you very much. *(To the* Switchboard Operator*)* Get me Montreal. I want to talk with Mr. Barney Whitmore. You may have to try Maple Leaf Air Charter office first, and someone there'll have his home number. Tell them the call is urgent.

Switchboard Operator. Right. *(To the* Controller*)* I've got the fire chief.

Controller *(into phone)*. Chief, we have an emergency. It's Flight 714, due here at 0505. It may be a crash landing. Have everything you've got stand by. If you have men off duty, call them in. Take your instructions from the tower. They'll tell you which runway we're using. And notify the city fire department. They may want to move equipment into this area. Right. *(To the* Switchboard Operator*)* Now get me the city police again—Inspector Moyse.

Switchboard Operator. I have Seattle and Calgary waiting. They both received the message from Flight 714 and want to know if we got it clearly.

Controller. Tell them thank you, yes, and we're working the aircraft direct. But ask them to keep a listening watch in case we run into any reception trouble. *(Another message is handed him. After reading, he passes it to* Burdick.*)* There's bad weather moving in.

That's all we need. (*To the* Switchboard Operator) Have you got the police? Right! (*Into phone*) It's the Airport Controller again, Inspector. We're in bad trouble, and we may have a crash landing. We'll need every spare ambulance in the city out here—and doctors and nurses too. Will you arrange it? (*Pause*) Yes, we do—fifty-six passengers and a crew of three. (*Pause*) Yes, the same time—0505. That's less than three hours.

Burdick (*to the* Switchboard Operator). Is Montreal on the line yet? . . . Yes, give it to me . . . Hullo. Hullo. Is that you, Barney? . . . It's Harry Burdick in Vancouver. I'll give you this fast, Barney. Our flight from Toronto is in bad trouble. They have food poisoning on board, and both pilots and a lot of the passengers have passed out. There's a doctor on board, and he says there's no chance of recovery before they get to a hospital. (*Pause*) It's a passenger doing the flying. He's just been on the radio. (*Pause*) No, he isn't qualified. He flew single-engine fighters in the war, nothing since. (*Pause*) I've asked him that. This doctor on board says there isn't a chance. (*Pause*) What else can we do? We've got to talk him down. Cross-Canada is lending us a pilot. It's Captain Treleaven, one of their senior men. He's here now, just arrived. We'll get on the radio with a check list and try to bring him in. (*Pause*) We'll do the best we can. (*Pause. Then impatiently*) Of course it's a terrible risk, but can you think of something better? (*Pause*) No, the papers aren't on to it yet, but don't worry, they will be soon. We can't help that now. (*Pause. Anxious to get off phone*) That's all we know, Barney. It only just happened. I called you right away. ETA is 0505 Pacific time; that's just under three hours. I've got a lot to do, Barney. I'll have to get on with it. (*Pause. Nodding impatiently*)

I'll call you. I'll call you as soon as I know anything more . . . G'bye.

[*During the foregoing* Captain Martin Treleaven, *forty-five, has entered. He is wearing an airline uniform. As* Burdick *sees* Treleaven, *he beckons him, indicating that he should listen.*]

Burdick (*to* Treleaven). Did you get that?

Treleaven (*calmly*). Is that the whole story?

Burdick. That's everything we know. Now, what I want you to do is get on the horn and talk this pilot down. You'll have to help him get the feel of the airplane on the way. You'll have to talk him round the circuit. You'll have to give him the cockpit check for landing, and—so help me—you'll have to talk him onto the ground.

[*Captain* Treleaven *is a calm man, not easily perturbed. While* Burdick *has been talking, the Captain has been filling his pipe. Now, with methodical movements, he puts away his tobacco pouch and begins to light the pipe.*]

Treleaven (*quietly*). You realize, of course, that the chances of a man who has only flown fighter airplanes, landing a four-engine passenger ship safely are about nine to one against.

Burdick (*rattled*). Of course I know it! You heard what I told Whitmore. But do you have any other ideas?

Treleaven. No. I just wanted to be sure you knew what we were getting into, Harry. . . . All right. Let's get started. Where do I go?

Controller. Over here.

[*They cross to the radio panel, and the* Operator *hands him the last message from the aircraft. When he has read it, he takes the transmitter mike.*]

The message says you have flown single-engine fighters. What kind of airplanes were these, and did you fly multi-engine airplanes at all? Let's hear from you, George. Over.

[Cut To. *The flight deck.*]

Spencer *(into mike).* Hullo, Vancouver, this is 714. Glad to have you along, Captain. But let's not kid each other, please. We both know we need a lot of luck. About my flying. It was mostly on Spitfires and Mustangs. And I have around a thousand hours' total. And all of that was ten years ago. Over.

[Cut To. *The control room.*]

Treleaven *(into mike).* Don't worry about that, George. It's like riding a bicycle. You never forget it. Stand by.

Controller *(to Treleaven).* The air force has picked up the airplane on radar, and they'll be giving us courses to bring him in. Here's the first one. See if you can get him on that heading.

Treleaven *(nods. Then into mike).* 714, are you still on automatic pilot? If so, look for the auto pilot release switch. It's a push button on the control yoke and is plainly marked. Over.

[Cut To. *The flight deck.*]

Spencer *(into mike).* Yes, Vancouver. I see the auto pilot switch. Over.

[Cut To. *The control room.*]

Treleaven *(into mike).* Now, George, in a minute you can unlock the automatic pilot and get the feel of the controls, and we're going to change your course a little. But first, listen carefully. When you use the controls they will seem very heavy and sluggish compared with a fighter airplane. But don't worry, that's quite normal. You must take

Treleaven. How does this thing work?

Radio Operator *(turning a switch).* You're on the air now.

Treleaven *(calmly).* Hullo, Flight 714. This is Vancouver, and my name is Martin Treleaven. I am a Cross-Canada Airlines captain, and my job right now is to help fly this airplane in. First of all, are you hearing me okay? Over.

Voice of Spencer. Yes, Captain, loud and clear. Go ahead, please.

Treleaven. Where's that message? *(As Operator passes it, into mike)* I see that I'm talking to George Spencer. Well, George, I don't think you're going to have much trouble. These DC-4's handle easily, and we'll give you the drill for landing. But first of all, please tell me what your flying experience is.

care, though, to watch your air speed carefully, and do not let it fall below 120 knots while your wheels and flaps are up. Otherwise you will stall. Now, do you have someone up there who can work the radio to leave you free for flying? Over.

[Cut To. *The flight deck.*]

Spencer (*into mike*). Yes, Vancouver. I have the Stewardess here with me, and she will take over the radio now. I am now going to unlock the automatic pilot. Over. (*To the Stewardess as he depresses the auto pilot release*) Well, here we go. (*Feeling the controls,* Spencer *eases into a left turn. Then, straightening out, he eases the control column slightly forward and back.*)

[Cut To. *The control room.*]

Treleaven's Voice. Hullo, 714. How are you making out, George? Have you got the feel of her yet?

[Cut To. *The flight deck.*]

Spencer. Tell him I'm on manual now and trying out some gentle turns.

Stewardess (*into mike*). Hullo, Vancouver. We are on manual now and trying out some gentle turns.

[Cut To. *The control room.*]

Treleaven (*into mike*). Hullo, George Spencer. Try the effect on fore-and-aft control on your air speed. To begin with, close your throttles slightly and bring your air speed back to 160. Adjust the trim as you go along. But watch that air speed closely. Remember to keep it well above 120. Over.

[Cut To. *The flight deck.*]

Spencer (*tensely. Still feeling out the controls*). Tell him okay.

Stewardess (*into mike*). Okay, Vancouver. We are doing as you say.

Treleaven's Voice (*after a pause*). Hullo, 714. How does she handle, George?

Spencer (*disgustedly*). Tell him sluggish like a wet sponge.

Stewardess. Sluggish like a wet sponge, Vancouver.

[Cut To. *The control room. There is a momentary relaxing of tension as* Captain Treleaven *and the group around him exchange grins.*]

Treleaven (*into mike*). Hullo, George Spencer. That would be a natural feeling, because you were used to handling smaller airplanes. The thing you have got to remember is that there is a bigger lag in the effect of control movements on air speed, compared with what you were used to before. Do you understand that? Over.

[Cut To. *The flight deck.*]

Spencer. Tell him I understand.

Stewardess (*into mike*). Hullo, Vancouver. Yes, he understands. Over.

[Cut To. *The control room.*]

Treleaven (*into mike*). Hullo, George Spencer. Because of that lag in air speed you must avoid any violent movements of the controls, such as you used to make in your fighter airplanes. If you *do* move the controls violently, you will over-correct and be in trouble. Is that understood?

[Cut To. *The flight deck.*]

Spencer (*nodding, beginning to perspire*). Tell him—yes, I understand.

Stewardess (*into mike*). Yes, Vancouver. Your message is understood. Over.

[Cut To. *The control room.*]

Treleaven *(into mike)*. Hullo, George Spencer. Now I want you to feel how the ship handles at lower speeds when the flaps and wheels are down. But don't do anything until I give you the instructions. Is that clear? Over.

[Cut To. *The flight deck.*]

Spencer. Tell him okay; let's have the instructions.

Stewardess *(into mike)*. Hullo, Vancouver. Yes, we understand. Go ahead with the instructions. Over.

Treleaven's Voice. First of all, throttle back slightly, get your air speed steady at 160 knots, and adjust your trim to maintain level flight. Then tell me when you're ready. Over.

Spencer. Watch that air speed, Janet. You'll have to call it off to me when we land, so you may as well start practicing.

Stewardess. It's 200 now . . . 190 . . . 185 . . . 180 . . . 175 . . . 175 . . . 165 . . .155 . . . 150 . . . *(Alarmed)* That's too low! He said 160!

Spencer *(tensely)*. I know. I know. Watch it! It's that lag on the air speed I can't get used to.

Stewardess. 150 . . . 150 . . . 155 . . . 160 . . . 160 . . . It's steady on 160.

Spencer. Tell them.

Stewardess *(into mike)*. Hullo, Vancouver. This is 714. Our speed is steady at 160. Over.

[Cut To. *The control room.*]

Treleaven *(into mike)*. Okay, 714. Now, George, I want you to put down twenty degrees of flap. But be careful not to make it any more. The flap lever is at the base of the control pedestal and is plainly marked. Twenty degrees will mean moving the lever down to the second notch. Over.

[Cut To. *The flight deck.*]

Spencer. Janet, *you'll* have to put the flaps down. *(Pointing)* There's the lever.

Treleaven's Voice. Can you see the flap indicator, George? It's near the center of the main panel.

Spencer. Here's the indicator he's talking about. When I tell you, push the lever down to the second notch and watch the dial. Okay?

Stewardess. Okay. *(Then with alarm)* Oh, look at the air speed! It's down to 125!

[Spencer *grimaces*[9] *and pushes the control column forward.*]

Spencer *(urgently)*. Call off the speed! Call off the speed!

Stewardess. 140 . . . 150 . . . 160 . . . 170 . . . 175 . . . Can't you get it back to 160?

Spencer *(straining)*. I'm trying! I'm trying! *(Pause)* There it is.

[Cut To. *The passenger cabin.*]

Second Woman Passenger *(frightened)*. Hector! We're going to crash! I know it! Oh, do something! Do something!

Baird *(appears at her elbow)*. Have her take this. It'll help calm her down. *(Gives pill and cup to the* Third Male Passenger*)* Try not to worry. That young man at the front is a very experienced pilot. He's just what they call "getting the feel" of the airplane. *(He moves aft in the cabin.)*

First Male Passenger. Doctor!

Baird. Yes.

First Male Passenger. Tell us the truth, Doctor. Have we got a chance? Does this fellow know how to fly this thing?

Baird. We've got all kinds of chances. He's a very experienced pilot, but it's just that he's not used to flying this particular type and he's getting the feel of it.

Fourth Male Passenger. You didn't need none of them pills to make me sick. Never mind me dinner. Now ah'm workin' on yesterday's breakfast.

[Cut To. *The flight deck.*]

---

9 **grimaces** (grə mãs′ əz): twists the face in dislike and fear.

Stewardess *(into mike)*. Hullo, Vancouver. Air speed is 160, and we are ready to put down the flaps. Over.

[Cut To. *The control room.*]

Treleaven *(into mike)*. Okay, 714. Go ahead with your flaps. But be careful—only twenty degrees. Then, when you have twenty degrees down, bring back the air speed to 140, adjust your trim, and call me again. Over.

[Cut To. *The flight deck.*]

Spencer. Okay, Janet—flaps down! Twenty degrees.

[*The* Stewardess *pushes down the flap lever to its second notch.*]

Spencer. Tell them we've got the flaps down, and the air speed's coming to 140.

Stewardess *(into mike)*. Hullo, Vancouver. This is 714. The flaps are down, and our air speed is 140.

[Cut To. *The control room.*]

Treleaven. All right, 714. Now, the next thing is to put the wheels down. Are you still maintaining level flight?

[Cut To. *The flight deck.*]

Spencer. Tell him—more or less.

Stewardess *(into mike)*. Hullo, Vancouver. More or less.

[Cut To. *The control room.*]

Radio Operator. This guy's got a sense of humor.

Burdick. That's a *real* help.

Treleaven *(into mike)*. Okay, 714. Try to keep your altitude steady and your speed at

140. Then, when you *are* ready, put down the landing gear and let your speed come back to 120. You will have to advance your throttle setting to maintain that air speed, and also adjust your trim. Is that understood? Over.

[Cut To. *The flight deck.*]

Spencer. Ask him—what about the propeller controls and mixture?

Stewardess (*into mike*). Hullo, Vancouver. What about the propeller controls and mixture? Over.

[Cut To. *The control room.*]

Controller. He's thinking, anyway.

Treleaven (*into mike*). Leave them alone for the time being. Just concentrate on holding that air speed steady with the wheels and flaps down. Over.

[Cut To. *The flight deck.*]

Spencer. Wheels down, Janet, and call off the air speed.

Stewardess (*selects landing gear down*). 140 . . . 145 . . . 140. . . 135 . . . 130 . . . 125 . . . 120 . . . 115 . . . The speed's too low!

Spencer. Keep calling it!

Stewardess. 115 . . . 120 . . . 120 . . . Steady on 120.

[Cut To. *The control room.*]

Treleaven (*into mike*). Hullo, George Spencer. Your wheels should be down by now, and look for three green lights to show that they're locked. Over.

[Cut To. *The flight deck.*]

Spencer. Are they on?

Stewardess. Yes—all three lights are green.

Spencer. Tell them.

Stewardess (*into mike*). Hullo, Vancouver. Yes, there are three green lights.

[Cut To. *The control room.*]

Treleaven. Okay, 714, now let's put down full flap so that you can feel how the airplane will handle when you're landing. As soon as full flap is down, bring your air speed back to 110 knots and trim to hold it steady. Adjust your throttle setting to hold your altitude. Is that understood? Over.

[Cut To. *The flight deck.*]

Spencer. Tell him yes.

Stewardess (*into mike*). Yes, Vancouver. That is understood.

Spencer. Full flap, Janet! Push the lever all the way down, and call off the air speed.

Stewardess. 120 . . . 115 . . . 115 . . . 110 . . . 110 . . .

Spencer. Okay, tell 'em we've got full flap and air speed 110, and she still handles like a sponge, only more so.

Stewardess (*into mike*). Hullo, Vancouver. We have full flap, and air speed is 110. And the pilot says she still handles like a sponge, only more so.

[Cut To. *The control room. Again there is a momentary sense of relief.*]

Treleaven (*into mike*). That's nice going, George. Now I'm going to give you instructions for holding your height and air speed while you raise the flaps and landing gear. Then we'll run through the whole procedure again.

[Cut To. *The flight deck.*]

Spencer. Again! I don't know if my nerves'll stand it. (*Pause*) All right. Tell him okay.

[Dissolve To. *Control room clock showing 2:55.*]

[Dissolve To. *Control room clock showing 5:20.*]

[Dissolve To. *The control room. Captain Treleaven is still seated in front of the transmitter, but has obviously been under strain. He now has his coat off and his tie loosened, and there is an empty carton of coffee beside him. Burdick and the Controller are in the background, watching tensely. A phone rings and the Controller answers it. He makes a note and passes it to Treleaven.*]

Treleaven (*into mike*). Hullo, Flight 714. Our flying practice has slowed you down, and you are later than we expected. You are now twelve minutes flying time from Vancouver Airport, but it's getting light, so your landing will be in daylight. You should be able to see us at any minute. Do you see the airport beacon? Over.

Stewardess's Voice. Yes, we see the airport beacon. Over.

Treleaven. Okay, George, now you've practiced everything we need for a landing. You've flown the ship with wheels and flaps down, and you know how she handles. Your fuel feeds are checked, and you're all set to come in. You won't hear from me again for a few minutes because I'm moving to the control tower so I'll be able to see you on the circuit and approach. Is that clear? Over.

Stewardess's Voice. Yes, Vancouver, that is understood. Over.

Treleaven. All right, George. Continue to approach at two thousand feet on your present heading and wait for instructions. We'll let you know the runway to use at the last minute, because the wind is shifting. Don't forget, we want you to do at least one dummy run, and then go round again so you'll have practice in making the landing approach. Over. *(He mops his forehead with a crumpled handkerchief.)*

[Cut To. *The flight deck.* Spencer, *too, has his coat off and tie loosened. His hair is ruffled, and the strain is plainly beginning to tell on him. The* Stewardess *is still in the copilot's seat, and* Baird *is standing behind them both. The* Stewardess *is about to acknowledge the last radio message, but* Spencer *stops her.*]

Spencer. I'll take it, Janet. *(Into mike)* No dice, Vancouver. We're coming straight in and the first time is "it." Dr. Baird is here beside me. He reports two of the passengers and the First Officer are in critical condition, and we must land in the next few minutes. The doctor asks that you have stomach pumps and oxygen equipment ready. Over.

[Cut To. *The control room.*]

Burdick. He mustn't! We need time!

Treleaven. It's his decision. By all the rules he's in command of the airplane. *(Into mike)* 714, your message is understood. Good luck to us all. Listening out. *(To* Burdick *and the* Controller*)* Let's go.

[Dissolve To. *The flight deck.*]

Spencer. This is it, Doctor. You'd better go back now and make sure everybody's strapped in tight. Are both the pilots in seats?

Baird. Yes.

Spencer. How about the passengers who aren't sick? Are they worried?

Baird. A little, but there's no panic. I exaggerated your qualifications. I'd better go. Good luck.

Spencer *(with ironic grin).* Thanks.

[Dissolve To. *The control tower, Vancouver Airport. It is a glass-enclosed area, with radio panels and other equipment, and access is by a stairway from below. It is now daylight and the* Tower Controller *is looking skyward, using binoculars. There is the sound of hurried feet on the stairway and* Treleaven, *the* Controller, *and* Burdick *emerge in that order.*]

Tower Controller. There he is!

[Treleaven *picks up a second pair of binoculars, looks through them quickly, then puts them down.*]

Treleaven. All right—let's make our decision on the runway. What's it to be?

Tower Controller. Zero eight. It's pretty well into wind now, though there'll be a slight crosswind from the left. It's also the longest.

Treleaven *(into mike).* Hullo, Flight 714. This is Martin Treleaven in Vancouver Tower. Do you read me? Over.

[Cut To. *The flight deck.*]

Stewardess *(into mike).* Yes, Vancouver Tower. Loud and clear. Over.

[Cut To. *The tower.*]

Treleaven *(crisply, authoritatively, yet calmly).* From here on, do not acknowledge any further transmissions unless you wish to ask a question. You are now ready to join the airport circuit. The runway for landing is zero eight. That means you are now crosswind and will shortly make a left turn on to the downwind leg. Begin now to lose height to one thousand feet. Throttle back slightly and make your descent at 400 feet a minute.

Let your air speed come back to 160 knots and hold it steady there . . . Air speed 160.

Controller (*reaching for phone*). Runway is zero eight. All vehicles stand by near the extreme south end. Do not, repeat not, go down the runway until the aircraft has passed by you, because it may swing off. Is that clear? (*Pause*) Right.

[Cut To. *Film insert of fire trucks and ambulances. They are manned and move away with sirens wailing.*]

[Cut To. *The flight deck. Spencer is pushing the throttles forward, and the tempo of the motors increases.*]

Spencer. Tell them we're at one thousand feet and leveling off.

Stewardess (*into mike*). Vancouver Tower. We are now at one thousand feet and leveling off. Over.

Treleaven's Voice. Now let's have twenty degrees of flap. Do not acknowledge this message.

Spencer. Twenty degrees of flap, Janet.

[*The* Stewardess *reaches for flap lever and pushes it down while she watches the flap indicator.*]

Treleaven's Voice. When you have your flaps down, bring your air speed back slowly to 140 knots, adjust your trim, and begin to make a left turn onto the downwind leg. When you have turned, fly parallel with the runway you see on your left. I repeat—air speed 140 and begin a left turn.

[Cut To. *Close-up of an instrument panel showing artificial horizon and air-speed indicator. The air speed first comes back to 130, goes slightly below it, then returns to 130. The artificial horizon tilts so that the airplane symbol is banked to the left.*]

[Cut To. *The flight deck. Spencer has control yoke turned to the left and is adjusting the throttles.*]

[Cut To. *The tower.*]

Treleaven. Watch your height! Don't make that turn so steep! Watch your height! More throttle! Keep the air speed on 140 and the nose up! Get back that height! You need a thousand feet!

[Cut To. *The flight deck. Spencer eases the throttle open, and the tempo of the motors increases. He eases the control column forward, then pulls back again.*]

[Cut To. *Close-up of climb and descent indicator. The instrument first shows a descent of 500 feet per minute, then a climb of 600 feet, and then gradually begins to level off.*]

[Cut To. *The control tower. Captain Treleaven is looking out through binoculars, the others anxiously behind him.*]

Treleaven (*angrily*). He can't fly the bloody thing! Of course he can't fly it! You're watching fifty people going to their deaths!

Burdick (*shouting*). Keep talking to him! Keep talking! Tell him what to do!

Treleaven (*urgently, into mike*). Spencer, you can't come straight in! You've got to do some circuits, and practice that approach. You've enough fuel left for three hours' flying. Stay up, man! Stay up!

[Cut To. *The flight deck.*]

Spencer. Give it to me! (*Taking the mike. Then tensely*) Listen, down there! I'm coming in! Do you hear me? . . . I'm coming in. There are people up here who'll die in less than an hour, never mind three. I may bend your precious airplane a bit, but I'll get it down. Now, get on with the landing check. I'm putting the gear down now. *(To the* Stewardess*)* Wheels down, Janet!

[*The* Stewardess *selects landing gear "down," and* Spencer *reaches for the throttles.*]

[Cut To. *Film insert of airplane in flight, day. Its landing wheels come down.*]

[Cut To. *The flight deck.*]

Stewardess *(looks out of window, then back to* Spencer*).* Wheels down and three green lights.

[Cut To. *The tower.*]

Burdick. He may not be able to fly, but he's sure got guts.

Treleaven *(into mike).* Increase your throttle slightly to hold your air speed now that the wheels are down. Adjust your trim and keep that height at a thousand feet. Now check your propeller setting and your mixture—propellers to fully fine; mixture to full rich. I'll repeat that. Propellers to fully fine; mixture to full rich.

[Cut To. *The flight deck.*]

Spencer *(to himself, as he moves controls).* Propellers fully fine. Mixture full rich. *(To the* Stewardess*)* Janet, let me hear the air speed.

Stewardess. 130 . . . 125 . . . 120 . . . 125 . . . 130 . . .

[Cut To. *The tower.*]

Treleaven *(into mike).* You are well downwind now. You can begin to make a left turn on the crosswind leg. As you turn, begin losing height to 800 feet and let your air speed come back to 120. I'll repeat that. Start a left turn. Lose height to 800. Air speed 120. *(He picks up binoculars, then puts them down*

hurriedly, and takes mike again.) You are losing height too fast! You are losing height too fast! Open up! Open! Hold your height, now! Keep your air speed at 120.

[Cut To. *The flight deck.*]

Stewardess. 110 . . . 110 . . . 105 . . . 110 . . . 110 . . . 120 . . . 120 . . . Steady at 120.

Spencer. What a blasted insensitive wagon this is! It doesn't respond! It doesn't respond at all!

Stewardess. 125 . . . 130 . . . 130 . . . Steady on 130.

[Cut To. *The tower.*]

Treleaven. Start your turn into wind now to line up with the runway. Make it a gentle turn—you've plenty of time. As you turn, begin losing height, about 400 feet a minute. But be ready to correct if you lose height too fast. Adjust your trim as you go . . . That's right! . . . Keep turning! As soon as you've completed the turn, put down full flap and bring your air speed to 115. I'll repeat that. Let down 400 feet a minute. Full flap. Then air speed 115. *(To the others)* Is everything ready on the field?

Controller. As ready as we'll ever be.

Treleaven. Then, this is it. In sixty seconds we'll know.

[Cut To. *The flight deck.*]

Spencer *(muttering).* Not quite yet . . . a little more . . . that should do it. *(As he straightens out of the turn)* Janet, give me full flap!

[*The* Stewardess *reaches for the flap control, pushes it down, and leaves it down.*]

Spencer. Height and air speed!

Stewardess. 700 feet, speed 130 . . . 600 feet, speed 120 . . . 500 feet, speed 105 . . . We're going down too quickly!

Spencer. I know! I know! (*He pushes throttles forward, and the tempo of the motors increases.*) Keep watching it!

Stewardess. 450 feet, speed 100 . . . 400 feet, speed 100 . . .

[Cut To. *Film insert of airplane (DC-4) with wheels and flaps down, on a landing approach.*]

[Cut To. *The tower.*]

Treleaven (*urgently into mike*). Open up! Open up! You're losing height too fast! (*Pause*) Watch the air speed! Your nose is too high! Open up quickly or she'll stall! Open up, man! Open up!

Burdick. He heard you. He's recovering.

Treleaven (*into mike*). Maintain that height until you get closer into the runway. But be ready to ease off gently . . . You can start now . . . Let down again . . . That looks about right . . . But watch the air speed. Your nose is creeping up . . . (*More steadily*) Now, listen carefully, George. There's a slight crosswind on the runway, and your drift is to the right. Straighten up just before you touch down, and be ready with your right rudder as soon as you are down. And remember to cut the switches if you land too fast. (*Pause*) All right, your approach is good . . . Get ready to round out—now! (*Pause. Then urgently*) You're coming in too fast! Lift the nose up!

[Cut To. *The flight deck.*]

Treleaven's Voice. Lift the nose up! Back on the throttles! Throttles right back! Hold her off! Not too much! Not too much! Be ready for that crosswind! Ease her down, *now!* Ease her down!

[Cut To. *Film insert of a landing wheel skimming over a runway and about to touch down. As it makes contact, rock picture to show instability.*]

[Cut to. *The flight deck. There is a heavy thud, and Spencer and the Stewardess are jolted in their seats. There is another, another, and another. Everything shakes.*]

Spencer (*shouting*). Cut the switches! Cut the switches!

[*The Stewardess reaches upward and pulls down the cage of the master switches. Instantly the heavy roar of motors stops, but there is still a whistling because the airplane is traveling fast. Spencer stretches out his legs as he puts his full strength into applying the airplane toe brakes, at the same time pulling back on the control column. There is a screaming of rubber on pavement, and Spencer and the Stewardess are thrown violently to the left. Then, except for the hum of the radio and gyros, there is a silence as the airplane stops.*]

Spencer (*disgustedly*). I ground looped! I did a lousy stinking ground loop! We're turned right around the way we came!

Stewardess. But we're all right! We're all right! You did it! You did it!

[*She leans over and kisses him. Spencer pulls off his radio headset. Outside there is a rising note of approaching sirens. Then, from the headset we hear* Captain Treleaven's *voice.*]

Treleaven's Voice (*exuberantly*). Hullo, George Spencer. That was probably the lousiest landing in the history of this airport. So don't ever ask us for a job as a pilot. But there are some people here who'd like to shake you by the hand, and later on we'll buy you a drink. Stay right where you are, George! We're coming over.

[Fade Out.]

1. What preparation does the Vancouver controller make for what seems likely to be the crash landing of Flight 714?

2. Why does Captain Treleaven begin his communication with George Spencer by suggesting that George will have little difficulty in flying and landing the four-motor plane? Why does George Spencer have a hard time handling the controls of the plane?

3. On more than one occasion during George Spencer's piloting of the plane, the Stewardess, who is acting as radio operator, calls off the rapid changes in their air speed. What is the purpose of her giving this information?

4. Do you think that George Spencer's faulty but safe landing of Flight 714 is believable or unbelievable? Why?

5. Perhaps you noted that the other two plays in this unit have just one act. The principal reason is that each of those plays focuses on only *one* concern—only *one* event in the lives of the characters. "Grandpa and the Statue," for example, focuses on Grandpa's finally accepting the Statue of Liberty as something worthwhile. "The Pen of My Aunt" focuses on Madame's and Simone's actions to insure the Stranger's escape from the custody of the enemy corporal.

   But "Flight into Danger" has *three* acts. Not only does the play focus on *more than one concern—more than one conflict*—but it also affects more people in more complicated ways. In developing the plot of the play, each act has its own special job to do. What do you think is the job, or the purpose, of each act in this play?

6. There are actually two stories—two conflicts—in this play. What are those two conflicts? Which one do you consider more important? Why?

7. Most of the action of this play takes place inside an airplane in flight. How does that setting affect the characters and what they do? How did the setting affect you?

8. "Flight into Danger" is a suspense play.
   a. Where does the climax occur?
   b. In Act I, what first arouses your uncertainty and anxiety about the fate of Flight 714?
   c. What events in Act II add to the suspense?
   d. In Act III, by what means does the author continue to develop suspense right up to the point of the climax?

9. "Flight into Danger" is a television play. Do you think it would be more effective or less effective if it were performed as a stage play? Why? if it were performed as a radio play? Why?

Composition

1. Recall the different ways each of the following characters reacts during the crisis aboard Flight 714:

   —Dr. Baird and the Stewardess remain calm and businesslike, doing all they can to comfort and help the sick passengers.
   —George Spencer becomes nervous and irritable; yet he performs his task courageously.
   —The Fourth Male Passenger resorts to wisecracks to hide his discomfort and fear.
   —The Second Woman Passenger seems ready at any minute to become hysterical.

   Of these five characters, whose behavior is closest to the way you would have acted if you had been aboard Flight 714?
   a. Write that person's name near the left margin at the top of your paper.
   b. Imagine that you *are* the character whose name you have written down. Imagine, too, that it is now two days after the flight. In the words of the character you have chosen, write a letter to a friend, describing the *important events* on Flight 714 as *you* experienced them. Keep in mind that you could not possibly have seen and known everything that occurred. Limit your account to only those events that *you* (as the character you are pretending to be) saw and experienced.

2. When Captain Treleaven tells Spencer to circle the Vancouver Airport for practice prior to landing, Spencer refuses. In fact, he insists on landing immediately. Do you think that Spencer is right or wrong to take the extra risk of killing everyone aboard the plane on the chance of saving the critically sick passengers? Write a composition expressing your point of view. First, indicate whether you think Spencer's decision was right or wrong. Then support your opinion with at least three reasons for thinking as you do.

Vocabulary

How an airplane flight ends is obviously far more interesting than how a word ends. But how a word ends can be very important. Assume that your mother told you to bring "your friend" home for dinner, but you thought she said to bring "your friend*s*." No lives would be in danger, but everybody involved could be hungry when you showed up with half a dozen hungry teenagers instead of one.

The meanings of many words change greatly with the addition of one or more letters. Any letter or group of letters added at the end of a word to change its meaning is called a SUFFIX.

Probably the most often-used suffix in our language is the letter *s*. As shown below, an *s* added to a noun (naming word) changes the noun from a singular word (one) to a plural (more than one). For example:

flight (singular) + *s* = *flights* (plural)
plane (singular) + *s* = *planes* (plural)

But this same suffix, *-s,* added to a present tense verb (action word) has the opposite effect. Adding the suffix *-s* to a verb makes it singular instead of plural. For example:

One flight take*s* off (singular); but two or more flight*s* *take* off (plural).
One plane land*s* (singular); but two or more plane*s* *land* (plural).

Note: In these examples, the verbs are in the present tense (going on now). This rule does not apply to the past or future tense. In addition, the rule applies only to third-person verbs (those following nouns or *he, she, it,* or *they*), not to first-person ones (following *I* or *we*) or to second-person ones (following *you*).

In each sentence below, choose the verb form in parentheses ( ) that fits correctly with the noun—which is its subject. Write your answers on a separate sheet of paper.

1. Mr. Spencer (arrive, arrives) at the airport too late to catch Flight 98.
2. Two passenger agents (arrange, arranges) a seat for Mr. Spencer on a charter flight.
3. He (seat, seats) himself beside Dr. Baird.
4. The two of them (talk, talks) about Mr. Spencer's air force experiences.
5. The Stewardess (give, gives) them a choice of dinners: lamb or halibut.
6. While the Stewardess (fix, fixes) the dinners, the Captain and First Officer (comment, comments) on the flight's smoothness.
7. Then one passenger (become, becomes) sick.
8. As others (grow, grows) ill, Dr. Baird (distinguish, distinguishes) the sick from the well according to the dinners they have eaten.
9. Mr. Spencer (assume, assumes) control of the plane when both the Captain and the First Officer (fall, falls) ill.

5 PLACES

Discussion

1. The three selections making up this unit represent different ways of presenting plays. "The Pen of My Aunt" is a typical one-act stage play, "Grandpa and the Statue" is a radio play, and "Flight into Danger" is a full-length television play. Which one would you most like to see (or hear) performed by professional actors? Why?

2. What, in your opinion, was the most exciting moment you experienced in the three plays? What was the most affecting or touching moment?

3. In a word or two, or in a short phrase, characterize each of the following:
   a. Madame
   b. Simone
   c. The Stanger
   d. The Corporal
   e. Grandpa Monaghan
   f. Sheean
   g. George Spencer
   h. Dr. Baird
   i. The Stewardess
   j. Captain Martin Treleaven

4. In writing stage directions, a playwright seeks to make sure that his or her meaning comes across clearly. Below are three passages, each from one of the plays in this unit. What is the purpose of the stage directions in each passage?
   a. **Stranger** [*in a bright, confident, casual tone*]. Ah, there you are, my dear aunt. I am so glad. Come in, my friend, come in. My dear aunt, this gentleman wants you to identify me."
      (from "The Pen of My Aunt")
   b. [MUSIC: *Up and down.* SOUND. *Boat whistles.*]
      (from "Grandpa and the Statue")
   c. **Spencer** [*shaking* Baird's *arm*]. Doctor! Doctor! Wake up!
      (from "Flight into Danger")

5. Each of the passages on the next page is a bit of dialogue from one of the plays in this unit. After reading each passage, explain—
   a. who the speaker is;
   b. how the dialogue helps you understand the kind of person that speaker is.

A.

I'm coming in! Do you hear me? I'm coming in. There are people up here who'll die in less than an hour, never mind three. I may bend your precious airplane a little, but I'll get it down. (From "Flight into Danger")

B.

Take him to the crossroads with you and I shall agree to forget your—your lack of efficiency. I am sure you are actually a very efficient person, and likely to be a sergeant any day now. We won't let a blunder or two stand in your way. (From "The Pen of My Aunt")

C.

Looks like what we believe—I—I never thought of it that way. I—I see what you mean. It does look that way. (*Angrily*) See now, boy? If Sheean had put it that way, I'd a give him me dime. (*Hurt*) Now, why do you suppose he didn't tell me that! Come down now. I'm sorry, sir, we've got to get out of here. . . . Hurry now; I want to get out of here. I feel terrible. I do, boy. That Sheean, that fool. Why didn't he tell me that? You'd think—(From "Grandpa and the Statue")

Composition

1. The *medium* (stage, radio, television) for which a play is written influences the way it is printed on a page. What if "Grandpa and the Statue" had been written for television presentation rather than for radio? Or what if "The Pen of My Aunt" had been written for radio rather than for the stage? In each case, there would have to be certain changes made in the printing of each play. Choose ONE of the following scenes and rewrite it according to the instructions given:
   a. From "Grandpa and the Statue": Grandpa talks with the veteran and then sends Child Monaghan away to buy peanuts (page 343). Rewrite the scene for television presentation.
   b. From "The Pen of My Aunt": The Corporal drags Simone into the house, exclaiming to Madame that the girl claimed never to have seen the Stranger before (page 326). Rewrite the scene for radio presentation.

2. When you write dialogue, you need to suit that dialogue to the characters—to the kinds of persons who are speaking.

   Write a short dialogue of your own—a dialogue that might well take place between characters of your own choosing in a situation of your own choosing. Be sure to include appropriate stage directions.

6

FLOWERS *Odilon Redon* Collection, the Solomon R. Guggenheim Museum

Poems

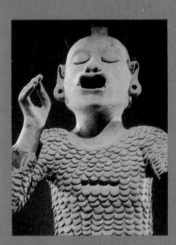

POEMS

Long before ancient peoples invented writing, they sang—and spoke—what we today know as poems. A festival celebrating the harvest, for example, the birth of a child, a hero's triumphant return from battle, a marriage, the dedication of a new temple, a death—all were occasions marked by recitation and song. Those who did the reciting and the singing just naturally fit their words into rhythmic patterns. In short, they sang and spoke POEMS.

In poems, words and meanings are closely joined. That is, poems say a lot in very little space. Every poem is like a little world of its own; its words and phrases have been pulled tightly together. If you change one line—often, one word—you change the meaning, the intent, the effect of the whole poem.

Poems can help us see ordinary things in a new light. Poems can help us see and feel in new ways we might not otherwise experience. Poems can trigger our imaginations! Poems can make us wonder! Poems can—well, just see for yourself.

Narrative Poems

There are many kinds of poems. Some describe what poets see; some describe what poets remember. Some express how poets feel about a person, a place, or an event. Thus, they convey mood. Some poems are humorous, deliberately designed to make you laugh. And some poems tell stories.

This section focuses on poems that tell stories—or NARRATIVE POEMS. Like each of the prose stories you have read in previous units, a narrative poem has a setting, one or more characters, a plot that builds to a climax, and even suspense. And again like prose stories, the tale that a narrative poem tells can be about almost anything.

The Cremation of Sam McGee

ROBERT W. SERVICE

There are strange things done in the midnight sun
    By the men who moil[1] for gold;
The Arctic trails have their secret tales
    That would make your blood run cold;
The Northern Lights have seen queer sights,   5
    But the queerest they ever did see
Was the night on the marge[2] of Lake Lebarge
    I cremated Sam McGee.

---

1 **moil**: work; toil.
2 **marge**: shore.

Now Sam McGee was from Tennessee, where the cotton blooms and blows.
Why he left his home in the South to roam 'round the Pole, God only knows. 10
He was always cold, but the land of gold seemed to hold him like a spell;
Though he'd often say in his homely way that "he'd sooner live in hell."

On a Christmas Day we were mushing our way over the Dawson trail
Talk of your cold! through the parka's fold it stabbed like a driven nail.
If our eyes we'd close, then the lashes froze till sometimes we couldn't see; 15
It wasn't much fun, but the only one to whimper was Sam McGee.

And that very night, as we lay packed tight in our robes beneath the snow,
And the dogs were fed, and the stars o'erhead were dancing heel and toe,
He turned to me, and "Cap," says he, "I'll cash in this trip, I guess;
And if I do, I'm asking that you won't refuse my last request." 20

Well, he seemed so low that I couldn't say no; then he says with a sort of moan:
"It's the cursèd cold, and it's got right hold till I'm chilled clean through to the bone.
Yet 'taint being dead—it's my awful dread of the icy grave that pains;
So I want you to swear that, foul or fair, you'll cremate my last remains."

A pal's last need is a thing to heed, so I swore I would not fail; 25
And we started on at the streak of dawn; but God! he looked ghastly pale.
He crouched on the sleigh, and he raved all day of his home in Tennessee;
And before nightfall a corpse was all that was left of Sam McGee.

There wasn't a breath in that land of death, and I hurried, horror-driven,
With a corpse half hid that I couldn't get rid, because of a promise given; 30
It was lashed to the sleigh, and it seemed to say: "You may tax your brawn and brains,
But you promised true, and it's up to you to cremate those last remains."

Now a promise made is a debt unpaid, and the trail has its own stern code.
In the days to come, though my lips were dumb, in my heart how I cursed that load.
In the long, long night, by the lone firelight, while the huskies, round in a ring, 35
Howled out their woes to the homeless snows—O God! how I loathed the thing.

And every day that quiet clay seemed to heavy and heavier grow;
And on I went, though the dogs were spent and the grub was getting low;
The trail was bad, and I felt half mad, but I swore I would not give in;
And I'd often sing to the hateful thing, and it hearkened with a grin. 40

Till I came to the marge of Lake Lebarge, and a derelict[3] there lay;
It was jammed in the ice, but I saw in a trice it was called the "Alice May."
And I looked at it, and I thought a bit, and I looked at my frozen chum;
Then "Here," said I, with a sudden cry, "is my cre-ma-tor-eum."

---

3 **derelict** (der' ə likt): abandoned ship.

Some planks I tore from the cabin floor, and I lit the boiler fire;   45
Some coal I found that was lying around, and I heaped the fuel higher;
The flames just soared, and the furnace roared—such a blaze you seldom see;
And I burrowed a hole in the glowing coal, and I stuffed in Sam McGee.

Then I made a hike, for I didn't like to hear him sizzle so;
And the heavens scowled, and the huskies howled; and the wind began to blow.   50
It was icy cold, but the hot sweat rolled down my cheeks, and I don't know why;
And the greasy smoke in an inky cloak went streaking down the sky.

I do not know how long in the snow I wrestled with grisly fear;
But the stars came out and they danced about ere again I ventured near;
I was sick with dread, but I bravely said: "I'll just take a peep inside.   55
I guess he's cooked, and it's time I looked;" . . . then the door I opened wide.

And there sat Sam, looking cool and calm, in the heart of the furnace roar;
And he wore a smile you could see a mile, and he said: "Please close that door.
It's fine in here, but I greatly fear you'll let in the cold and storm—
Since I left Plumtree, down in Tennessee, it's the first time I've been warm."   60

                    There are strange things done in the midnight sun
                        By the men who moil for gold;
                    The Arctic trails have their secret tales
                        That would make your blood run cold;
                    The Northern Lights have seen queer sights,   65
                        But the queerest they ever did see
                    Was that night on the marge of Lake Lebarge
                        I cremated Sam McGee.

Discussion

1. What is the setting of the poem? the mood of the poem? How does the poet create that mood?

2. What is Sam's predicament? Why does he want to be cremated?

3. How does the narrator cremate Sam? What is the result of that cremation?

4. Why can "The Cremation of Sam McGee" be called a narrative poem?

When writing prose, an author uses paragraphs to show when ideas, subjects, or situations change. When writing poetry, poets often use STANZAS to indicate such changes. When a poet divides a poem into stanzas, each stanza—as a rule—has the same number of lines as each of the other stanzas. What's more, each line of each stanza is likely to have the same number of syllables. It is this repeated pattern of lines and syllables that gives a poem its beat—its RHYTHM. And rhythm, of course, dictates the pulse of a poem—how it is read.

Then, in addition to establishing the poem's rhythm, a poet is likely to use RHYME. That is, he or she will end each line of the poem with a syllable (or word) that sounds like the end syllable (or word) of one or more of the other lines. And sometimes—as in "The Cremation of Sam McGee"—the poet will use rhyming words *within* a single line. Note, for example, the first line of the poem: "There are strange things done in the midnight sun." The words *done* and *sun* are rhyming words within that one line.

It is through the combination of rhythm and rhyme that a poet and a poem create a pleasing musical effect.

1. Look back at the second through fourteenth stanzas. How many lines are there in each of those stanzas? What rhymes are made by the last syllables (or words) of the lines in each stanza? What pattern of rhymes is repeated?

2. What other examples of internal rhyme can you find—that is, of rhyming words within the same line?

3. The first and last stanzas have a form that's different from the other thirteen stanzas. What is different about the *form* of those two stanzas? What rhyme pattern of end words do you find in those stanzas? What examples of internal rhyme do you find?

4. Why, do you suppose, did Robert Service, the poet, make the first and last stanzas different from the others? In what way are they like the other stanzas?

Vocabulary

CONTEXT CLUES are hints about the meaning of an unknown word given by the known words that surround it. The more successful you become at making context clues work for you, the more effectively you will read, and the faster your vocabulary will grow.

Read the sentences on the next page. From the context clues in each sentence, choose a word (or a small group of words) that could fill in the blank to complete the meaning of the sentence. Then, on a separate sheet of paper, (a) write your word(s). (b) Go back to "The Cremation of Sam McGee," and copy the word the author originally used in the same position. (c) Use a dictionary or the glossary to find the definition of the author's original word, and copy it on your paper.

EXAMPLE: On Christmas Day we were _____ our way over the
               Dawson trail.
ANSWERS: (a) traveling
               (b) mushing
               (c) traveling over snow with a dog sled

1. There are strange things done in the midnight sun
    By the men who _____ for gold.

2. A pal's last need is a thing to _____, so I swore I would not fail.

3. In the long, long night, by the lone firelight, while the huskies, round in a ring,/Howled out their woes to the homeless snows—O God! how I _____ the thing.

4. A derelict there lay;/It was jammed in the ice, but I saw in a _____ it was called the "Alice May."

5. I do not know how long in the snow I wrestled with _____ fear.

Robert W. Service 1874–1958

Robert W. Service was not recognized as a serious poet, but he was very popular for his rhythmic verses about the rugged Yukon frontier. His melodramatic poem "The Shooting of Dan McGrew" is one of the most often imitated poems in English.

Service was born in England and grew up in Scotland. He became bored with his banking job and set off to see the New World. He took the cheapest boat to Canada, arriving in Victoria, B.C., in 1905, with only five dollars. He said, "For the next seven years, I took a course in the College of Hard Knocks, graduating without enthusiasm." After traveling and working all along the Pacific coast, he spent eight years working at banks in the Yukon.

He began writing poetry in the style of his favorite poet, Rudyard Kipling. His first volume of poetry, *Songs of a Sourdough,* was an immediate success.

When Elizabeth Blackwell told people what she wanted to do, they were shocked. No American woman had ever done that before. Why did she want to be different?

Elizabeth Blackwell

EVE MERRIAM

What will you do when you grow up,
nineteenth-century-young-lady?
Will you sew a fine seam and spoon dappled cream
under an apple tree shady?

Or will you be a teacher   5
in a dames' school[1]
and train the little dears
by the scientific rule
that mental activity
may strain   10
the delicate female brain;
therefore let
the curriculum stress music, French, and especially
etiquette:
teach how to set   15
a truly refined banquet.
Question One:
What kind of sauce
for the fish dish,
and pickle or lemon fork?   20
Quickly, students,
which should it be?

Now Elizabeth Blackwell, how about you?
Seamstress or teacher, which of the two?

---

1 **dames' school:** a school in a woman's home.

You know there's not much else that a girl can do.   25
Don't mumble, Elizabeth. Learn to raise your head.
"I'm not very nimble with a needle and thread.
I could teach music—if I had to," she said,
"But I think I'd rather be a doctor instead."

"Is this some kind of joke?"   30
asked the proper menfolk.
"A woman be a doctor?
Not in our respectable day!
A doctor? An M.D.! Did you hear what she said?
She's clearly and indubitably out of her head!"   35

"Indeed, indeed, we are thoroughly agreed,"
hissed the ladies of society all laced in and prim,
"it's a scientific fact a doctor has to be a him.
Yes, sir,
'twould be against nature   40
if a doctor were a her."

Hibble hobble bibble bobble
widdle waddle wag
tsk tsk
    twit twit   45
        flip flap flutter
              mitter matter mutter
moan groan wail and rail
    Indecorous!
        Revolting!!   50
          A scandal
            A SIN
their voices pierced the air like a jabbing hat-pin.
But little miss Elizabeth wouldn't give in.

To medical schools she applied.   55
In vain.
And applied again
and again
and again
and one rejection offered this plan: 60
why not disguise herself as a man?
If she pulled back her hair, put on boots and pants,
she might attend medical lectures in France.
Although she wouldn't earn a degree,
they'd let her study anatomy.   65

Elizabeth refused to hide
her feminine pride.
She drew herself up tall
(all five feet one of her!)
and tried again.   70
And denied again.
The letters answering no
mounted like winter snow.

Until the day
when her ramrod will   75
finally had its way.
After the twenty-ninth try,
there came from Geneva, New York
the reply
of a blessed   80
Yes!

Geneva,
Geneva,
how sweet the sound;
Geneva,   85
Geneva,
sweet sanctuary found . . .
. . . and the ladies of Geneva
passing by her in the street
drew back their hoopskirts   90
so they wouldn't have to meet.

   Psst, psst,
   hiss, hiss
   this sinister scarlet miss.
   Avoid her, the hoyden, the hussy,   95
   lest we all be contaminated!
   If your glove so much as touch her, my dear,
   best go get it fumigated!

When Elizabeth came to table,
their talking all would halt;   100
wouldn't so much as ask her
please to pass the salt.

In between classes
without a kind word,
Elizabeth dwelt   105
like a pale gray bird.

In a bare attic room
cold as stone,
far from her family,
huddled alone   110

studying, studying
throughout the night
warming herself
with an inner light:

don't let it darken,   115
the spark of fire;
keep it aglow,
that heart's desire:

the will to serve,
to help those in pain—   120
flickered and flared
and flickered again—

until
like a fairy tale
(except it was true!)   125
Elizabeth received
her honored due.

The perfect happy ending
came to pass:
Elizabeth graduated . . .   130
. . . at the head of her class.

And the ladies of Geneva
all rushed forward now to greet
that clever, dear Elizabeth,
so talented, so sweet!   135

Wasn't it glorious
she'd won first prize?

Elizabeth smiled
with cool gray eyes

and she wrapped her shawl   140
against the praise:

how soon there might come
more chilling days.

Turned to leave
without hesitating.   145

She was ready now,
and the world was waiting.

Discussion

1. What was it Elizabeth Blackwell wanted to do? How did most people react to her choice of vocation? Why do you think they acted as they did?

2. Although medical school after medical school rejected Elizabeth Blackwell's application for admission, one offered a plan. What was it? What was Elizabeth's reaction? Where was Elizabeth Blackwell finally accepted as a medical student?

3. What was the "perfect happy ending"? At this point, how did people treat Elizabeth Blackwell? How do you explain their treatment?

4. Explain the meaning of the last two lines of the poem.

Writer's Craft

In "The Cremation of Sam McGee," the character is a fictional person and the narrative is a fantasy. That is, it is wholly imagined. In this poem, Elizabeth Blackwell is an actual person in an actual setting. But there is another important difference between the two poems. In "The Cremation of Sam McGee," the RHYME follows a regular pattern, and each line is the same length and has the same number of syllables. In "Elizabeth Blackwell," however, the lines are long and short and in-between. And the rhyme is there, but it is not a regularly patterned rhyme scheme. Instead, there is considerable variety in line length and in rhyme. Because poems can have so much variety, many readers consider poetry to be the most creative form of literature. Part of the appeal and charm of poetry comes from the fact that poems do not have to be as structured as prose. What's more, part of the appeal of poetry comes from the fact that even the poem's appearance on the page can arouse the reader's interest.

1. In "Elizabeth Blackwell," point out some examples of rhyme. Where does most of the rhyme occur?

2. Some of the words Eve Merriam uses may not be found in the dictionary, but their very sounds no doubt provoke a response from you. How does the combination of words and sounds beginning "Hibble hobble" help you understand what is happening?

Composition

1. Today it is not unusual for a woman to aspire to become a doctor, and certainly many female doctors now have successful practices. But, as indicated in the poem "Elizabeth Blackwell," a little more than a hundred years ago, it was unheard of for a woman to study to be a physician. The poem suggests that in the 19th century only

certain occupations were considered suitable for women. The poem also suggests that a number of obstacles blocked the path of any woman who had other-than-ordinary occupational hopes. In a short composition, explain what you understand by those "certain suitable occupations" and by "the number of obstacles" in the paths of those who had other hopes.

2. Even today there are some occupations considered to be better suited to one sex than to the other. For example, until recently, there were few, if any, male nurses. What's more, there were few female engineers or mechanics. Do you think that occupations of all kinds should or should not be available to both men and women? In a short composition, state your position on that question. Then support your position by giving at least three reasons for thinking as you do.

Eve Merriam 1916—

Eve Merriam was born in Philadelphia and has always loved cities. She lives in New York now and says, "I expect to be the last living inhabitant of Manhattan when everyone else has quit for sub- or exurbia."

She enjoys writing, especially poetry. Her favorite pastimes are browsing in libraries and secondhand bookstores and traveling. As for athletics, she says, "In my dreams I am a proficient ice skater—in real life, I am wobbly but willing."

Merriam uses her talents as author and lecturer to speak out against problems she sees in society. Her book *The Inner City Mother Goose* is a collection of rhymes which present the not-too-pleasant world that today's city children see. Her poems speak more to adults than to children. One short poem about political corruption says, "There was a crooked man/And he did very well." Merriam also concentrates on women's issues, lecturing and writing about equal education for girls and boys.

Ghent, is a city in northwest Belgium. Almost due east about a hundred miles lies the German city of Aachen (ä'kən), known in former times as Aix-la-Chapelle (aks lä sha pel'). It is between these two cities that three horsemen rode on an imaginary mission during one of the many wars fought in that part of Europe in the 1600s.

How They Brought the Good News from Ghent to Aix

ROBERT BROWNING

I sprang to the stirrup, and Joris, and he;
I galloped, Dirck galloped, we galloped all three;
"Good speed!" cried the watch, as the gate bolts undrew;
"Speed!" echoed the wall to us galloping through;
Behind shut the postern,[1] the lights sank to rest,   5
And into the midnight we galloped abreast.

Not a word to each other; we kept the great pace
Neck by neck, stride by stride, never changing our place;
I turned in my saddle and made its girths tight,
Then shortened each stirrup, and set the pique[2] right,   10
Rebuckled the cheek strap, chained slacker the bit,
Nor galloped less steadily Roland a whit.

'Twas moonset at starting; but while we drew near
Lokeren, the cocks crew and twilight dawned clear.
At Boom, a great yellow star came out to see;   15
At Düffeld, 'twas morning as plain as could be;
And from Mecheln church steeple we heard the half-chime,
So Joris broke silence with, "Yet there is time!"

---

1 **postern:** back gate.
2 **pique** (pēk): the saddle blanket.

At Aershot, up leaped of a sudden the sun,
And against him the cattle stood black every one,   20
To stare through the mist at us galloping past,
And I saw my stout galloper Roland at last,
With resolute shoulders, each butting away
The haze, as some bluff river headland its spray:

And his low head and crest, just one sharp ear bent back   25
For my voice, and the other pricked out on his track;
And one eye's black intelligence,—ever that glance
O'er its white edge at me, his own master, askance![3]
And the thick heavy spume-flakes which aye and anon
His fierce lips shook upwards in galloping on.   30

By Hasselt, Dirck groaned; and cried Joris, "Stay spur!
Your Roos galloped bravely, the fault's not in her,
We'll remember at Aix"—for one heard the quick wheeze
Of her chest, saw the stretched neck and staggering knees,
And sunk tail, and horrible heave of the flank,   35
As down on her haunches she shuddered and sank.

So, we were left galloping, Joris and I,
Past Looz and past Tongres, no cloud in the sky;
The broad sun above laughed a pitiless laugh,
'Neath our feet broke the brittle bright stubble like chaff;[4]   40
Till over by Dalhem a dome-spire sprang white,
And "Gallop," gasped Joris, "for Aix is in sight!"

"How they'll greet us!"—and all in a moment his roan
Rolled neck and croup over, lay dead as a stone;
And there was my Roland to bear the whole weight   45
Of the news which alone could save Aix from her fate,
With his nostrils like pits full of blood to the brim,
And with circles of red for his eye-sockets' rim.

Then I cast loose my buffcoat, each holster let fall,
Shook off both my jack boots, let go belt and all,   50
Stood up in the stirrup, leaned, patted his ear,
Called my Roland his pet name, my horse without peer;[5]
Clapped my hands, laughed and sang, any noise, bad or good,
Till at length into Aix Roland galloped and stood.

---

3 **askance** (ə skans'): with suspicion.
4 **chaff**: husks of grains separated from the seed by
threshing.
5 **peer**: equal.

And all I remember is—friends flocking round   55
As I sat with his head 'twixt my knees on the ground;
And no voice but was praising this Roland of mine,
As I poured down his throat our last measure of wine,
Which (the burgesses voted by common consent)
Was no more than his due who brought good news from Ghent.   60

Discussion

1. Why is it important that the narrator and his two companions reach Aix? Why didn't two of the horsemen reach their destination?

2. How does the narrator help his horse, Roland, complete the final part of the journey? What is Roland's reward?

3. How does the poet indicate the passing of time and the progress of the journey?

4. In telling his story, the poet has deliberately left you, the reader, to supply many details for yourself: who the sender of the message is, for example, and who in Aix is the intended receiver of that message. In fact, you don't ever know what the message itself is. Why is it *not* important to your understanding and enjoyment of the poem to know what the "good news" is?

Writer's Craft

RHYTHM, you will recall from page 391, refers to the regular repetition of the *beat* in the lines of a poem. That is, the lines of a poem are made up of *accented* and *unaccented* syllables. And when the pattern of those accented and unaccented syllables is repeated with regularity, rhythm results. Take, for example, this line from "How They Brought the Good News from Ghent to Aix":

Not a wórd to each óther; we képt the great páce

Notice that there are two *unaccented* syllables followed by one accented syllable and that this pattern is repeated four times in that one line. Of course, this is only one of many rhythmic patterns that poets can use. But from this example you can see how rhythm helps to make pleasing musical sounds—how it therefore helps make poems so appealing to the ear.

1. You know that in each line of this poem there are four instances where two *unaccented* syllables are followed by an *accented*

syllable. In other words, there are four beats to the line. What does that rhythm suggest—a leisurely ride or a ride characterized by urgency and haste? What familiar sound does that rhythm suggest?

2. Suppose that the poem begins like this:

> At midnight in the town of Ghent
> Three riders on their horses bent.
> Brave Dirck and I,—and Joris, too,—
> For Aix with news so good and true,
> Prepared to ride through thick and thin.
> "Good speed!" the watch cried from within.
> The iron gate he opened wide
> And out we flew with measured stride.

How does the rhythm of those eight lines compare with the rhythm Browning uses in his poem? Which rhythm—Browning's or that in the above eight lines—is the more appropriate for telling the story? Why?

3. Note line 19: "At Aershot, up leaped of a sudden the sun." Why, do you think, did Browning phrase the sentence that way?

Robert Browning 1812—1889

London-born writer Robert Browning was a lively, robust, healthy man. He has been described as having the style of Teddy Roosevelt, but "with far better mental equipment." When he was seventeen, he asked his parents if the family income allowed him to live "a life of pure culture." With their consent, he set out to be a poet rather than work for a steady salary.

In 1846, he was introduced to the frail Elizabeth Barrett whose poems he already loved. Eighteen months later they eloped, knowing that Elizabeth's father would not consent to their marriage. They lived very happily for sixteen years in Florence, Italy.

When Elizabeth died, Robert Browning was overcome with grief and went into seclusion in London for two years. Finally his natural optimism returned, and he rejoined society. With his renewed writing, he became more popular than he had been. For the rest of his life, Browning was one of the most popular poets and personalities of London.

The Princess of Pure Delight

IRA GERSHWIN

The Prince in Orange and the Prince in Blue
And the Prince whose raiment was of Lavender hue—
They sighed and they suffered and they tossed at night
For the neighboring Princess of Pure Delight. . . .
    (Who was secretly in love with a Minstrel)   5

Her father, the King, didn't know which to choose;
There were two charming suitors he'd have to refuse.
So he called for the Dean of his Sorcerers and
Inquired which one was to win her hand.
    (Which they always did in those days)   10

"My King, here's a riddle—you test them tonight:
What word of five letters is never spelled right?
What word of five letters is always spelled wrong?
The one who can answer will be wedded ere long.
    That will be twenty gulden,[1] please!"   15

The King called the three and he told them the test,
The while his fair daughter kept beating her breast.
He put them the riddle. They failed (as he feared).
Then all of a sudden the Minstrel appeared!
    (Quite out of breath)   20

"I'll answer that riddle," cried the singer of song.
"What's never spelled 'right' in five letters is 'wrong'
And it's right to spell 'wrong'—w-r-o-n-g!
Your Highness, the Princess belongeth to me!
    And I love her, anyway!"   25

"Be off with you, villain!" the King cried in rage,
"For my Princess a Prince—not a man from the stage!"
"But, Sire!" said the Minstrel, "'tis love makes me say
No King who's a real King treats lovers this way!
    It isn't sporting.   30

---

1 **gulden:** gold coins.

And if you're no real King, no Princess is she—
And if she's no Princess then she can wed me!"
"By gad," cried His Highness, "you handsome young knave,
I fear me you're right!" and his blessing he gave,
    As a trumpeter began to trumpet.   35

The Princess then quickly came out of her swoon
And she looked at her swain² and her world was in tune.
And the castle soon rang with cheer and with laughter
And of course they lived happily ever after.   40

---

2 **swain**: lover.

Discussion

1. What suitors does the King think are eligible to wed his daughter? Why does he look upon them as eligible?

2. Whom does the Princess love? Who loves the Princess?

3. What plan does the Dean of Sorcerers suggest to the King to help decide who is to wed the Princess?

4. Explain the riddle put to all of the Princess's suitors. Who answers the riddle satisfactorily?

5. What reasoning does the Minstrel use to persuade the King that it is he, the Minstrel, who is entitled to wed the Princess?

Writer's Craft

An 18th-century English poet once said, "Variety's the very spice of life." And ever since then, people the world over have taken him at his word. Writers certainly have! For example, take Ira Gershwin. In writing "The Princess of Pure Delight," he knew that giving the poem some VARIETY would give it some spice—some extra appeal—and so he did.

As you can see, each stanza in the poem consists basically of four lines, each with four beats. You can see, too, that in each stanza, the first and second lines rhyme, as do the third and fourth lines. So far, so good. Nothing out of the ordinary yet.

But now comes the variety—the spice. To every stanza except the last one, the poet has added a fifth line. Notice that in none of those stanzas does that fifth line rhyme with any of the preceding four lines. Notice, too, that each fifth line breaks the rhythm of the preceding four. Some fifth lines have three beats; some have two. (There is even variation—spice—in the variation!)

Why the variety? Well, breaking the rhythm of the basic four lines is in itself a humorous variation. But even more to the point, those fifth lines serve two other important purposes: First, three of them give the poet a chance to let characters in the story make unexpected remarks. Second, four of those fifth lines give the poet himself a chance to make a humorous comment about the story he's telling.

1. Which of the seven "fifth lines" in the poem permit a character to make a remark you don't expect?
2. Which of the seven "fifth lines" in the poem give the poet himself a chance to comment on the story?

Ira Gershwin 1896—

Ira Gershwin became famous as the lyricist for music written by his brother George Gershwin and several other composers. Separately and together, the Gershwins produced many songs now familiar to everyone. Sometimes George would write the music first, and Ira wrote words to fit. Other times Ira wrote the lyrics first, and George's melody would follow. They were an effective team.

Porgy and Bess is one of the team's best known works. This folk opera about Black life was one of the few American works allowed to be performed in Nazi-occupied Denmark during World War II. The song "It Ain't Necessarily So" from this folk opera became something like a hymn for the Danish resistance effort.

Ballads

One of the oldest forms of poetry is a special kind of narrative poem known as the BALLAD. As a rule, ballads are concerned with sharp conflicts and deep human emotion. Once in a while, however, a ballad will deal with the funny side of life.

The first ballads were songs made up by bards and minstrels who traveled from town to town, earning their living by singing their stories to entertain groups of people—common people in town marketplaces, as well as nobles in manor houses and castles. Sometimes listeners would join in on the refrain (repeated lines), and sometimes listeners would dance to the music of the ballad.

The minstrels who composed the early ballads were, as a rule, uneducated persons. As a result, the language of the early ballads is quite simple. The ballads were passed on orally from one minstrel to another and from one generation to another. And so, there are often several variations of the same ballad. But even though names and details may differ, the basic story remains unchanged. Interestingly enough, it wasn't until the middle of the 1700s that scholars began to write down the early ballads in the forms in which we read them today.

Ballads differ from ordinary narrative poems in these ways: (1) They usually involve common, everyday people (although there are ballads about nobles, too). (2) They ordinarily deal with physical courage and/or tragic love. (3) They contain little characterization or description; the action moves forward mainly through dialogue. (4) Much of the story is told indirectly; that is, you, the reader, have to fill it in from what the words imply—suggest.

A final characteristic that distinguishes ballads from other narrative poems is this: Traditionally, ballads tell their stories in BALLAD STANZAS. Each stanza has four lines, and the fourth line usually rhymes with the second. As a rule, the rhythm comes from the repetition of one unaccented sound followed by one accented sound. The first and third lines of the ballad stanza usually have four accented sounds (syllables); the second and fourth lines have three each. Occasionally, to hold the rhythm to the regular beat, you'll need to slur over some sounds or run two syllables together to make them sound like one.

Detail from an illuminated manuscript.

This ancient Scottish ballad is one of the most famous ballads in literature. Variations of it are known throughout Europe, as well as the English-speaking countries.

Lord Randal

"O where ha you been, Lord Randal, my son?
And where ha you been, my handsome young man?"
"I ha been at the greenwood, mother, mak my bed soon,
For I'm wearied wi huntin and fain wad[1] lie down."

"An wha met ye there, Lord Randal, my son?   5
And wha met you there, my handsome young man?"
"O I met wi my true-love, mother, mak my bed soon,
For I'm wearied wi huntin and fain wad lie down."

"And what did she give you, Lord Randal, my son?
And what did she give you, my handsome young man?"   10
"Eels fried in a pan, mother, mak my bed soon,
For I'm wearied wi huntin, and fain wad lie down."

"And wha gat your leavins, Lord Randal, my son?
And wha gat your leavins, my handsome young man?"
"My hawks and my hounds, mother, mak my bed soon,   15
For I'm wearied wi hunting and fain wad lie down."

"And what becam of them, Lord Randal, my son?
And what becam of them, my handsome young man?"
"They stretched their legs out an died, mother, mak my bed soon,
For I'm wearied wi hunting and fain wad lie down."   20

"O I fear you are poisoned, Lord Randal, my son.
I fear you are poisoned, my handsome young man."
"O yes, I am poisoned, mother, mak my bed soon,
For I'm sick at the heart and I fain wad lie down."

---

1 **fain wad:** would like to.

"What d' ye leave to your mother, Lord Randal, my son? 25
What d' ye leave to your mother, my handsome young man?"
"Four and twenty milk kye², mother, mak my bed soon,
For I'm sick at the heart and I fain wad lie down."

"What d' ye leave to your sister, Lord Randal, my son?
What d' ye leave to your sister, my handsome young man?" 30
"My gold and my silver, mother, mak my bed soon,
For I'm sick at the heart and I fain wad lie down."

"What d' ye leave to your brother, Lord Randal, my son?
What d' ye leave to your brother, my handsome young man?"
"My houses and my lands, mother, mak my bed soon, 35
For I'm sick at the heart and I fain wad lie down."

"What d' ye leave to your true-love, Lord Randal, my son?
What d' ye leave to your true-love, my handsome young man?"
"I leave her hell and fire, mother, mak my bed soon,
For I'm sick at the heart and I fain wad lie down." 40

---

2 **kye**: cattle.

Discussion

1. What is the situation at the opening of the poem?

2. How does the story unfold? (That is, by what means do you learn about what happens?)

3. Who is responsible for Lord Randal's being poisoned? How do you know?

4. In your own words, briefly retell the story of the ballad.

Writer's Craft

As a rule, ballads deal with love and honor and death. In "Lord Randal" you read of love (which had apparently turned to hate) and of approaching death. In addition, ballads present action directly and swiftly. Almost all descriptive details are left out. In "Lord Randal," the action is recounted rapidly in a direct question-and-answer dialogue between Lord Randal and his mother.

Another feature characteristic of many ballads is the REFRAIN. Though a refrain may be an entire stanza, it is usually a line or a phrase repeated at the end of each stanza. Because, at first, ballads were sung, the refrain became a device for involving the listeners in the performance. That is, the audience had a part in the telling of the story by joining in on the refrain at appropriate times.

1. In "Lord Randal," the refrain takes two forms. What are they? Where does the first change to the second? Why, do you think, does that change occur?

2. How much of the story is told directly by the dialogue? How much of the story is implied (hinted at)?

Detail from an illuminated manuscript.

Bonny Barbara Allan

It was in and about the Martinmas[1] time,
    When the green leaves were a falling,
That Sir John Graeme,[2] in the West Country,
    Fell in love with Barbara Allan.

He sent his men down through the town,   5
    To the place where she was dwelling:
"O haste and come to my master dear,
    Gin[3] ye be Barbara Allan."

O hooly, hooly[4] rose she up,
    To the place where he was lying,   10
And when she drew the curtain by,[5]
    "Young man, I think you're dying."

"O it's I'm sick, and very, very sick,
    And 't is a' for Barbara Allan."
"O the better for me ye's never be,   15
    Tho your heart's blood were a spilling.

"O dinna ye mind, young man," said she,
    "When ye was in the tavern a drinking,
That ye made the healths[6] gae[7] round and round,
    And slighted Barbara Allan?"   20

---

1 **Martinmas:** November 11; feast of St. Martin.
2 **Graeme:** pronounced "grēm."
3 **Gin:** if.
4 **hooly:** slowly, softly.
5 **by:** aside.
6 **healths:** toasts (drinks) to one's health.
7 **gae:** go.

Detail from an illuminated manuscript.

He turned his face unto the wall,
  And death was with him dealing:
"Adieu, adieu, my dear friends all,
  And be kind to Barbara Allan."

And slowly, slowly raise she up,   25
  And slowly, slowly left him,
And sighing said, she could not stay,
  Since death of life had reft[8] him.

She had not gane a mile but twa,
  When she heard the dead-bell ringing,   30
And every jow[9] that the dead-bell geid,[10]
  It cry'd, Woe to Barbara Allan!

"O mother, mother, make my bed.
  O make it saft and narrow.
Since my love died for me today,   35
  I'll die for him tomorrow."

---

8 **reft**: robbed.
9 **jow**: stroke.
10 **geid** (gēd): gave.

Discussion

1. How does the time of the year in which this ballad is set help to establish the mood for the poem? How does the mood emphasize the character of Barbara Allan?

2. How does Barbara Allan respond to the fact that Sir John Graeme is dying? What reason does she give for her actions?

3. Why does Sir John send for Barbara Allan? Why does he die? Why does Barbara Allan say that she will die? In your opinion, if each loved the other, why did they behave so cruelly toward each other?

Robin Hood and Alan a Dale

Come listen to me, you gallants so free,
    All you that love mirth for to hear,
And I will you tell of a bold outlaw,
    That lived in Nottinghamshire.

As Robin Hood in the forest stood,   5
    All under the greenwood tree,
There was he ware of a brave young man,
    As fine as fine might be.

The youngster was clothed in scarlet red,
    In scarlet fine and gay,   10
And he did frisk it over the plain,
    And chanted a roundelay.[1]

As Robin Hood next morning stood,
    Amongst the leaves so gay,
There did he espy[2] the same young man   15
    Come drooping along the way.

The scarlet he wore the day before,
    It was clean cast away;
And every step he fetch a sigh,
    "Alack and a well a day!"[3]   20

Then stepped forth brave Little John,
    And Much the miller's son,
Which made the young man bend his bow,
    When as he saw them come.

"Stand off, stand off!" the young man said,   25
    "What is your will with me?" —
"You must come before our master straight,
    Under yon greenwood tree."

---

1 **roundelay:** a song with a refrain.
2 **espy** (ə spī'): caught sight of.
3 **alack and well a day:** alas.

And when he came bold Robin before,
    Robin askt him courteously,   30
"O hast thou any money to spare,
    For my merry men and me?"

"I have no money," the young man said,
    "But five shillings and a ring;
And that I have kept this seven long years,   35
    To have it at my wedding.

"Yesterday I should have married a maid,
    But she is now from me tane,[4]
And chosen to be an old knight's delight,
    Whereby my poor heart is slain."   40

"What is thy name?" then said Robin Hood,
    "Come tell me, without any fail."—
"By the faith of my body," then said the young man,
    "My name it is Alan a Dale."

"What wilt thou give me," said Robin Hood,   45
    "In ready gold or fee,
To help thee to thy true-love again,
    And deliver her unto thee?"

"I have no money," then quoth the young man,
    "No ready gold nor fee,   50
But I will swear upon a book
    Thy true servant for to be."—

"But how many miles to thy true-love?
    Come tell me without any guile."—[5]
"By the faith of my body," then said the young man,   55
    "It is but five little mile."

Then Robin he hasted over the plain,
    He did neither stint nor lin,[6]
Until he came unto the church
    Where Alan should keep his wedding.   60

"What dost thou do here?" the Bishop he said,
    "I prithee now tell to me:"
"I am a bold harper," quoth Robin Hood,
    "And the best in the north countrey."

---

4 **tane:** taken.
5 **guile:** deceit; trickery.
6 **lin:** stop.

"O welcome, O welcome!" the Bishop he said,   65
   "That musick best pleaseth me." —
"You shall have no musick," quoth Robin Hood,
   "Till the bride and the bridegroom I see."

With that came in a wealthy knight,
   Which was both grave and old,   70
And after him a finikin[7] lass,
   Did shine like glistering gold.

"This is no fit match," quoth bold Robin Hood,
   "That you do seem to make here;
For since we are come unto the church,   75
   The bride she shall chuse her own dear."

Then Robin Hood put his horn to his mouth,
   And blew blasts two or three;
When four and twenty bowmen bold
   Come leaping over the lee.   80

And when they came into the churchyard,
   Marching all on a row,
The first man was Alan a Dale,
   To give bold Robin his bow.

"This is thy true-love," Robin he said,   85
   "Young Alan, as I hear say;
And you shall be married at this same time,
   Before we depart away."

"That shall not be," the Bishop he said,
   "For thy word it shall not stand;   90
They shall be three times askt[8] in the church,
   As the law is of our land."

Robin Hood pull'd off the Bishop's coat,
   And put it upon Little John;
"By the faith of my body," then Robin said,   95
   "This cloath doth make thee a man."

When Little John went into the quire,[9]
   The people began for to laugh;
He askt them seven times in the church,
   Least three should not be enough.   100

---

7 finikin: dainty.
8 **askt**: The marriage intentions of a couple had to be
announced in the church on three separate occasions.
9 **quire**: choir; the part of the church where the singers sit.

"Who gives me this maid?" then said Little John;
    Quoth Robin, "That do I!
And he that doth take her from Alan a Dale
    Full dearly he shall her buy."

And thus having ended this merry wedding,   105
    The bride lookt as fresh as a queen,
And so they return'd to the merry greenwood,
    Amongst the leaves so green.

Discussion

1. In the third stanza (lines 9–12) what is the mood of the young man? What is his mood in the fourth and fifth stanzas (lines 13–20)? What causes the change in his mood?

2. What agreement do Robin Hood and Alan a Dale make? How does Robin help Alan a Dale?

3. How does Robin overcome the Bishop's objections to the marriage of the maid and Alan a Dale?

4. Point out examples of internal rhyme.

Writer's Craft

The BALLAD RHYTHM in "Robin Hood and Alan a Dale" is typical of that used in ballads. That is, the first and third lines of every stanza have four beats each, and the second and fourth have three each. But did you notice the variation in the number of sounds/syllables making up each beat? Look again at line 1:

    Come listen to me, you gallants so free,

The first beat consists of two syllables, the second beat has three, the third beat goes back to two syllables, and the fourth has three again. If we use a short, concave line (˘) to indicate the *un*accented syllables and a diagonal mark (´) to indicate the accented syllables, we can show the rhythm like this:

    Cŏme lístĕn tŏ mé, yŏu gállăñts sŏ frée,

Many lines in the ballad are made up of this kind of combination of two- and three-syllable beats.
    But look again at line 8: "As fine as fine might be." How many syllables does each beat have?

From this brief discussion, you can see that the balladeers of old liked to put a little variation into the rhythm of their ballads. Variation, you see, adds interest.

1. In "Robin Hood and Alan a Dale," find at least five lines in which the rhythm consists of a combination of two- and three-syllable beats.

2. Find at least five lines in the ballad that are made up exclusively of two-syllable beats.

3. Look at lines 43 and 55. How do they vary from the others in the number of syllables per beat?

Vocabulary

Language changes. Two hundred years from now, your great-great-great-great grandchildren will be puzzled when they see some words that you use every day. Even if you had never heard of Robin Hood until you read "Robin Hood and Alan a Dale," some of its words would tell you it was written long ago. Words like that, words that are no longer in use, are called ARCHAIC.

Sometimes, context clues alone are enough to tell you the meaning of an archaic word. ("I have no money," then *quoth* the young man,/"No ready gold nor fee. . . .") At the other times, you need to look at footnotes, the glossary, or a dictionary to find out what an archaic word means. ("He did neither stint not *lin*/Until he came to the church.") Draw upon all these resources as you do this exercise.

Below are several excerpts from "Robin Hood and Alan a Dale." In each, one or more archaic words are printed in *italics*. On a separate sheet of paper, paraphrase (that is, rewrite in your own words) each excerpt. In your paraphrase, replace all archaic words with familiar modern ones. Use a dictionary to do this exericse.

EXAMPLE: "You must come before our *master straight,*
Under *yon* greenwood tree."
ANSWER: We must take you to our leader right away under the nearby greenwood tree.

1. "What *wilt thou* give me?" said Robin Hood.
2. Then Robin he *hasted* over the plain.
3. "That *musick best pleaseth* me."
4. With that came in a wealthy knight,
  Which was both grave and old,
And after him a *finikin* lass,
  Did shine like *glistering* gold.

As a rule, ballads tell of serious matters in people's lives—about love and death. But as you have seen in "Robin Hood and Alan a Dale," some ballads are concerned with the lighter side of life. Where do you think this ballad fits in?

Get Up and Bar the Door

It fell about the Martinmas[1] time,
    And a gay time it was then,
When our goodwife got puddings to make,
    And she's boiled them in the pan.

The wind so cold blew south and north,   5
    And blew into the floor;
Quoth our goodman to our goodwife,
    "Get up and bar the door."

"My hand is in my household work,
    Goodman, as ye may see;   10
And it will not be barred for a hundred years,
    If it's to be barred by me!"

They made a pact between them both,
    They made it firm and sure,
That whosoe'er should speak the first,   15
    Should rise and bar the door.

Then by there came two gentlemen,
    At twelve o'clock at night,
And they could see neither house nor hall,
    Nor coal nor candlelight.   20

"Now whether is this a rich man's house,
    Or whether is it a poor?"
But never a word would one of them speak,
    For barring of the door.

---

1 **Martinmas:** the feast of St. Martin on November 11.

The guests they ate the white puddings,   25
   And then they ate the black;
Tho' much the goodwife thought to herself,
   Yet never a word she spake.

Then said one stranger to the other,
   "Here, man, take ye my knife;   30
Do ye take off the old man's beard,
   And I'll kiss the goodwife."

"There's no hot water to scrape it off,
   And what shall we do then?"
"Then why not use the pudding broth,   35
   That boils into the pan?"

O up then started our goodman,
   An angry man was he;
"Will ye kiss my wife before my eyes?
   And with pudding broth scald me?"   40

Then up and started our goodwife,
   Gave three skips on the floor;
"Goodman, you've spoken the foremost word.
   Get up and bar the door."

Discussion

1. Does this ballad belong with the serious ballads or with ballads on the lighter side? Why?

2. What reason does the goodwife give for refusing to "get up and bar the door"? What pact do the husband and wife then make?

3. When neither the wife nor the husband will speak, what do the "guests" decide to do? What reaction is then forthcoming from the goodman? In turn, how does the goodwife behave?

4. What personality trait can be said to describe both the goodman and the goodwife?

5. In review, how does "Get Up and Bar the Door" illustrate what you have learned about the ballad?

Composition

1. You know that a ballad usually tells its story by means of dialogue. You, the reader, must "fill in the gaps"—that is, use your imagination to complete what is implied. Choose one of the five ballads you have just read and, using your own words, summarize the story that the ballad tells. Feel free to include what you think is implied—or even is needed—for understanding the story.

2. You know that ballads usually tell of love, death, or physical courage. You know, too, that ballads can be humorous as well as serious. Choose a topic that interests you, and write a modern-day ballad of at least five stanzas. As much as possible in your ballad, use dialogue to tell your story.

Descriptive Poems

The poems and the ballads you have read so far are narrative poems—poems that tell stories. Not all poems, however, are intended to tell stories. A large number of them—perhaps most of them—have a different purpose.

Suppose that your school has just won the basketball championship, and you want to share your excitement and your joy with someone else. Of course, you could just simply shout, "We're number one!" But how do you communicate your enthusiasm to someone in another town? And how can you make it possible to relive your enthusiasm in years to come? One good way is to write a poem!

Or suppose that on a hike in the mountains, you sit for a while on a rock overlooking a lush green valley. You listen to the wind in the pines; you mark the lazy passage of fleecy clouds across the sapphire-blue sky; you feel a warm, personal closeness with nature. How can you tell someone else how you feel? You can share your experience in a poem.

Or again, suppose you want to let another person know just how much you value his or her friendship. One effective way of doing so is to write a poem.

These examples represent the kinds of experiences poets write about in DESCRIPTIVE POEMS—brief, melodic poems that express the writers' feelings about a scene or a situation or an occasion.

Descriptive poems are usually very personal poems about ideas and experiences that interest most people: the beauty of nature, love and friendship, the enjoyment of life, patriotism, the effects of the passing of time, death. Descriptive poems, you see, enable you to look at familiar things in a way you may never have thought about before.

BEACH GIRL *Morris Hirshfield 1937*

*Descriptive poems concern those things that
people have found to be worthwhile in life.*

Mama Is a Sunrise

EVELYN TOOLEY HUNT

When she comes slip-footing through the door,
   she kindles us
    like lump coal lighted,
    and we wake up glowing.
She puts a spark even in Papa's eyes   5
and turns out all our darkness.

When she comes sweet-talking in the room,
   she warms us
    like grits and gravy,
    and we rise up shining.   10
Even at night-time Mama is a sunrise
that promises tomorrow and tomorrow.

Discussion

1. What effect does Mama have on those around her? What phrases in the poem indicate that effect?

2. Note the hyphened word in the first line of each stanza. What do those two words suggest about Mama?

3. In line 6, the speaker uses these words: "and turns out all our darkness." What's unusual about that phrase? What do you think it means?

4. What is the importance of the last two lines of the poem?

The speaker in "Mama Is a Sunrise" expresses
the love and the trust a child accords a parent. In
this poem, the speaker—a Scottish poet—expresses
his feeling for his "only luve" (love).

A Red, Red Rose

ROBERT BURNS

O, my luve is like a red, red rose,
   That's newly sprung in June.
O, my luve is like the melodie,
   That's sweetly played in tune.

As fair art thou, my bonie lass,   5
   So deep in luve am I,
And I will luve thee still, my dear,
   Till a' the seas gang dry.

Till a' the seas gang dry, my dear,
   And the rocks melt wi' the sun!   10
And I will luve thee still, my dear,
   While the sands o' life shall run.

And fare thee weel, my only luve,
   And fare thee weel a while!
And I will come again, my luve,   15
   Tho' it were ten thousand mile!

1. Does the poet's love for his "bonie lass" seem to you to be genuine or trivial? Why? Refer to specific lines in the poem to support your answer.

2. In your own words, state what the poet is saying in the last stanza (lines 13–16).

Writer's Craft

> O, my luve is like a red, red rose
>   That's newly sprung in June.

That's how Robert Burns describes his true love. But suppose he had written this instead:

> O, my luve is a fair young maid
>   Who is beautiful indeed.

Which passage is more effective in *showing* you his true love's beauty? Obviously, the first one—the one that Burns wrote. Why? Well, he *compares* his true love (someone you don't know) to a glorious (red, red) spring rose just opening its petals. Because the rose is something that you *are* familiar with, you can picture it in your mind. And in doing so, you, in effect, say to yourself something like this: "Ah, I see. She's as beautiful as a red rose that's just starting to bloom."

It's in using words and phrases that form *pictures* in your mind that poets can help you share their experiences. One effective way to create a word picture is to make a COMPARISON—to say that something is *like* something else in a certain way. Robert Burns, for example, says that his "luve is *like* a red, red rose." This kind of comparison is a SIMILE (sim′ ə lē). That is, the comparison is stated, or expressed directly by using the word *like* or *as*.

In "Mama Is a Sunrise" (page 422) the poet uses a simile in lines 8 and 9 by saying: "she warms us like grits and gravy,"

Here, the poet compares the effect Mama has on her children to the way eating grits and gravy actually does make a person warm.

You, too, use similes every day in talking with others. For instance, you may have said that something is "as old as the hills" or that someone is "skinny as a rail," or that someone "looks like a ghost."

Poets use similes—picture-making comparisons expressed through the use of *like* or *as*—to add interest and effectiveness to what they write.

1. What other similes do you find in "A Red, Red Rose"?

2. What other similes do you find in "Mama Is a Sunrise"?

3. Select one of the similes you have found and explain how it adds to your understanding of what the poet is saying.

Composition

1. The two poems, "Mama Is a Sunrise," and "A Red, Red Rose" tell of the speakers' feelings for loved ones. In each case, the poet uses comparisons to prove the depth of his or her love. Which poem, through its comparisons, do you think does the better job of describing the feelings of the speaker? In a paragraph, write your answer to that question. Be sure to give your reasons for thinking as you do.

2. In "Mama Is a Sunrise," the reader learns about a woman who, through her unique personality, is an inspiration to the people around her. Upon walking into a room, people react to her presence. Somehow she emits a sense of warmth and brightness. Write a paragraph or two in which you describe Mama. Use the ideas in the poem, but expand and elaborate. You might tell how you think Mama looks or how she would act in a certain situation. You may wish to use some dialogue showing how she would respond in an imagined circumstance. Try to choose descriptive words that give the reader of your paper a clear picture of Mama.

Robert Burns 1759—1796

Robert Burns was born in Ayrshire, Scotland, the oldest of seven children in a farming family. His father encouraged his children to be well read, but the hard farm life didn't allow much time or money for formal education. Burns spent much of his youth doing strenuous farm work on poor soil. In his teen years Burns began writing songs. He could not sing them himself, however, because he was tone-deaf.

After the breakup of a romance, Burns decided to leave for Jamaica. He published a book of poems to raise money for the trip and became a success. Edinburgh society accepted him as the "peasant poet." But his charming conversation could not hide differences of opinion and lifestyles. So Burns's popularity with society did not last long.

Burns continued to write, but lack of money made him work beyond his strength. His difficult situation didn't stop his writing, but it shortened his life considerably.

As Scotland's greatest poet, Burns refined the peasants' ballads into beautiful lyrics. He gave all the world his most famous song, the song we sing to welcome the New Year, "Auld Lang Syne."

To be sure, the person in this poem is a human being. Yet he's more than that. He represents an idea.

Abou Ben Adhem

LEIGH HUNT

Abou Ben Adhem (may his tribe increase!)
Awoke one night from a deep dream of peace,
And saw, within the moonlight in his room,
Making it rich, and like a lily in bloom,
An angel writing in a book of gold:—   5
Exceeding[1] peace had made Ben Adhem bold,
And to the presence in the room he said,
"What writest thou?"—The vision raised its head,
And with a look made of all sweet accord,[2]
Answered, "The names of those who love the Lord."   10
"And is mine one?" said Abou. "Nay, not so,"
Replied the angel. Abou spoke more low,
But cheerly still; and said, "I pray thee then,
Write me as one that loves his fellow men."

   The angel wrote, and vanished. The next night   15
It came again with a great wakening light,
And showed the names whom love of God had blessed,
And lo! Ben Adhem's name led all the rest.

---

1 **Exceeding:** great; unlimited.
2 **accord:** agreement; harmony.

1. How does it happen that on the second night Abou Ben Adhem's name heads the list "of those who love the Lord"?
2. What idea does Abou Ben Adhem represent?
3. What simile do you find in the poem? What two things are compared?

(James Henry) Leigh Hunt 1784—1859

Leigh Hunt was born in England to a family who had been driven from the American colonies because of their sympathy for the British. He was a frail, sensitive child who suffered at school because he felt sorry for boys who were beaten. He was not healthy enough to go to the university, but he managed to meet literary people who encouraged his writing.

In 1808, Hunt and his brother began their colorful life as journalists by founding the *Examiner*. This paper was consistently outspoken against the government. Hunt was often put on trial for the paper's political remarks, and usually he was released. But one article insulting the Prince Regent sent both brothers to separate jails for three years. Hunt's life in jail was not too difficult. His wife was with him most of the time and writers and poets visited often. Lord Byron, the poet, even gave a dinner party at the jail in Hunt's honor. Hunt continued to edit the *Examiner* from the jail, but the paper did not last many years after that.

Besides showing how a person feels toward another or toward others, a descriptive poem can focus on personal traits that seem worthy of consideration.

Direction

ALONZO LOPEZ

I was directed by my grandfather
To the East,
   so I might have the power of the bear;
To the South,
   so I might have the courage of the eagle;   5
To the West,
   so I might have the wisdom of the owl;
To the North,
   so I might have the craftiness of the fox;
To the Earth,   10
   so I might receive her fruit;
To the Sky,
   so I might lead a life of innocence.

Discussion

1. The title of the poem—"Direction"—can be said to have two meanings. Explain.
2. What useful personal characteristics will the speaker acquire if he does as "directed" by his grandfather? Why are those characteristics considered valuable?

430 *Poems*

"I'll tell you how the Sun rose"

EMILY DICKINSON

I'll tell you how the Sun rose—
A ribbon at a time.
The steeples swam in amethyst,[1]
The news like squirrels ran.

The hills untied their bonnets,   5
The bobolinks begun.
Then I said softly to myself,
"That must have been the sun!"

But how he set, I know not.
There seemed a purple stile   10
Which little yellow boys and girls
Were climbing all the while

Till when they reached the other side,
A dominie[2] in gray
Put gently up the evening bars   15
And led the flock away.

---

1 **amethyst** (am' ə thist): violet.
2 **dominie** (dom' ə nē): schoolmaster.

Discussion

1. What two times of the day is Emily Dickinson describing?

2. What colors does she use to describe each of those times of day? Which lines do you think paint the most vivid word pictures?

3. Notice in line 3 that the "steeples *swam*" and in line 4 that "the news like squirrels *ran*." What do you think the verbs *swam* and *ran* suggest about this time of day?

4. It is true that this poem concerns two specific times during the day. But what is the larger subject—the broader focus—of this descriptive poem?

Writer's Craft

As you know, poets—and other writers, too—can create vivid pictures in your mind by making comparisons. For example, a writer can paint a word picture by saying that something is *like* another in a certain way, or by saying that something is *as . . . as* something else. This kind of comparison, of course, is a *simile* (page 424).

But sometimes in making a comparison, a writer will be more subtle. Rather than stating that something is like something else, the writer *suggests* or *implies* that something *is* like something else. For example, when the poet says, "Mama is a sunrise" (page 422) she is comparing the positive, cheering effect that Mama has on her family to the reassuring, cheering effect that a sunrise has after the night's darkness.

Here, then, is a second way poets have of creating vivid pictures in your mind; they compare one thing to another by suggesting that one thing *is* the other. We call this kind of comparison a METAPHOR (met′ ə fôr).

1. Here are the first two lines of Emily Dickinson's poem:

   I'll tell you how the sun rose—
   A ribbon at a time.

   Explain the metaphor in the line "A ribbon at a time."

2. Line 5 of the poem contains a metaphor. What comparison is the poet making?

3. Find at least three other metaphors in the poem. Explain why each is a metaphor.

Many descriptive poems reflect real-life human experiences and feelings. By choosing and arranging their words carefully, poets describe their feelings so effectively that you might well exclaim, "I've felt exactly the same way!" The next group of poems focus on various kinds of human experiences.

"The days and months do not last long"

PAI TA-SHUN

The days and months do not last long
The springs and autumns follow one by one,
And when I watch the fall of the flowers
And of the leaves and of the trees,
I know that even the loveliest person
Little by little must change.

Discussion

1. What reminds the poet of the rapid passing of time?
2. What does that reminder lead the poet to realize?

Aztec Poem

ANONYMOUS

But even if it were so,
if it were true that suffering is our only lot,
if things are this way on earth,
must we always be afraid?
Will we always have to live with fear?   5
Must we always be weeping?

For we live on earth,
there are lords here,
there is authority, there is nobility,
there are eagles and tigers.   10

And who then goes about always saying
that this is the way it is on earth?
Who is it that forces death upon himself?
There is commitment, there is life,
there is struggle, there is work!   15

Discussion

1. To whom do you think the poet is speaking?
2. What are the questions the speaker asks?
3. In the second stanza, the speaker refers to the earth, to lords, to nobility, and to eagles and tigers. Why?
4. In the third stanza, how does the speaker answer the questions asked in the first stanza?

"Blow, blow, thou winter wind"

WILLIAM SHAKESPEARE

Blow, blow, thou winter wind,
Thou art not so unkind
  As man's ingratitude.
Thy tooth is not so keen,
Because thou art not seen,   5
  Although thy breath be rude.[1]
Heigh-ho, sing heigh-ho, unto the green holly!
Most friendship is feigning,[2] most loving mere folly:[3]
  Then, heigh-ho, the holly!
  This life is most jolly.   10

Freeze, freeze, thou bitter sky,
That dost not bite so nigh
  As benefits forgot.
Though thou the waters warp,
Thy sting is not so sharp   15
  As friend rememb'red not.
Heigh-ho, sing heigh-ho, unto the green holly!
Most friendship is feigning, most loving mere folly:
  Then, heigh-ho, the holly!
  This life is most jolly.   20

1 **rude:** here, harsh.
2 **feigning** (fān' ing): pretending.
3 **folly:** foolishness.

1. What human experience is this poem concerned with?

2. What attitude does the poet seem to take toward that human experience? Which lines best reflect his attitude?

3. The metaphor in the first stanza compares human ingratitude to what? What metaphor do you find in the second stanza? What two things are compared?

Writer's Craft

Part of the appeal of "Blow, blow, thou winter wind" lies in Shakespeare's use of phrases that are pleasant to listen to. Two such phrases are "winter wind" and "heigh-ho, the holly." They are pleasing to the ear because the important words making up each phrase begin with the same consonant sound. The REPETITION of the same initial sound gives the poem a certain musical quality.

Chances are that you use this same kind of repetition pattern—a succession of similar sounds—in your own speech. For example, you may have invited a friend to play Ping-Pong. Or you may have used expressions like "sink or swim," "rant and rave," "spick and span," "hale and hearty," "might and main," and "wrack and ruin." And finally, you've probably had fun attempting tongue-twisters like "Peter Piper picked a peck of pickled peppers" or "She sells seashells at the seashore" or "Rubber baby buggy bumpers."

1. In the first stanza of the poem, what other phrases are made up of words that begin with the same consonant sound?

2. What examples of this same kind of repetition pattern do you find in the second stanza?

William Shakespeare 1564—1616

William Shakespeare is regarded as the greatest writer of the English language. Shakespeare was a popular success throughout his career. He and several other actors formed an acting company. Shakespeare was the principal playwright, an actor, and a shareholder. He wrote thirty-seven plays (romantic comedies, tragedies, and histories) for their theater, the Globe. Shakespeare wrote sonnets and longer poems when the theaters were closed because of the plague.

"Oh, when I was in love with you"

A. E. HOUSMAN

Oh, when I was in love with you,
   Then I was clean and brave,
And miles around the wonder grew
   How well did I behave.

And now the fancy passes by,
   And nothing will remain,
And miles around they'll say that I
   Am quite myself again.

Discussion

1. What has happened to the speaker in the poem?
2. In the first stanza, how does the speaker behave? Why?
3. In the second stanza, how does the speaker behave? Why?
4. What human experience is this poem concerned with?

Alfred Edward Housman 1859–1936

A. E. Housman was best known for his first book of poems, *A Shropshire Lad*. After studying at Oxford University, Housman took a job with a patent office and spent his spare time translating and writing articles about Latin classics. He gained recognition as a scholar and eventually became a Latin professor at Cambridge University in England. He was a perfectionist in his own studies and writings, and he severely criticized scholars whom he considered sloppy or careless. His colleagues respected and feared him.

Housman was equally hard on himself as a poet. In his concern to present only his best poems to the public, he destroyed more poems than he published. His second volume of poems was titled *Last Poems*. Others were published after his death.

In this poem the speaker looks out at falling snow. As he does so, the snow comes to represent both sorrow and consolation. The poem divides into two parts: one about the actual snowfall and one about what the snow represents.

The First Snowfall

JAMES RUSSELL LOWELL

The snow had begun in the gloaming,
  And busily all the night
Had been heaping field and highway
  With a silence deep and white.

Every pine and fir and hemlock   5
  Wore ermine too dear for an earl,
And the poorest twig on the elm tree
  Was ridged inch deep with pearl.

From sheds new-roofed with Carrara[1]
  Came Chanticleer's[2] muffled crow,   10
The stiff rails softened to a swan's-down,
  And still fluttered down the snow.

I stood and watched by the window
  The noiseless work of the sky,
And the sudden flurries of snowbirds,   15
  Like brown leaves whirling by.

I thought of a mound in sweet Auburn[3]
  Where a little headstone stood;
How the flakes were folding it gently,
  As did robins the babes in the wood.   20

1 **Carrara:** white marble.
2 **Chanticleer's** (chan' tə klirz): the rooster's.
3 **Auburn:** Mount Auburn Cemetery in Cambridge, Massachusetts.

Up spoke our own little Mabel,
  Saying, "Father, who makes it snow?"
And I told of the good All-father
  Who cares for us here below.

Again I looked at the snowfall,   25
  And thought of the leaden sky
That arched o'er our first great sorrow,
  When that mound was heaped so high.

I remembered the gradual patience
  That fell from that cloud like snow,   30
Flake by flake, healing and hiding
  The scar that renewed our woe.

And again to the child I whispered,
  "The snow that husheth all,
Darling, the merciful Father   35
  Alone can make it fall!"

Then, with eyes that saw not, I kissed her,
  And she, kissing back, could not know
That *my* kiss was given to her sister,
  Folded close under deepening snow.   40

Discussion

1. Which stanzas are concerned with the actual snowfall?

2. As the poet watches "by the window," what does he think about?

3. What is "our first great sorrow" (line 27)?

4. What is the poet saying in the last stanza?

5. How is the snowfall like the poet's sorrow? In what sense is the snow also a consolation?

6. What simile do you find in the fourth stanza? in the fifth stanza? in the eighth stanza?

7. In the first three stanzas there are four metaphors. Identify at least two of them and explain what things are being compared. Why is the phrase "leaden sky" (line 26) a metaphor?

8. Why do you think the poet titled the poem "The First Snowfall"? What does he mean by *First*?

Vocabulary

A WORD-SERIES CONTEXT CLUE enables you to figure out the general meaning of an unfamiliar word. That word is included in a list of familiar words that tell about the same kind of thing. For example:

John enjoyed solving riddles, puzzles, and *conundrums*.

You can figure out that *conundrums* must mean some kind of game or brain-teaser because it is listed in a word series with riddles.

The following sentences and phrases have one *italicized* word. Using the word-series context clue, find the general meaning of the *italicized* word. Write your answers on a separate sheet of paper.

1. During our visit to the zoo, we saw monkeys hanging from bars, baboons making faces, and tiny *marmosets*.
2. The lawyer's lecture to the group was about trust agreements, wills, and *codicils*.
3. The painting was done in shocking pink, teal blue, and *heliotrope*.
4. Every pine and fir and *hemlock*
5. And tangerines and *mangoes* and grapefruit

James Russell Lowell 1819—1881

James Russell Lowell was born in Cambridge, Massachusetts, a son of an old, important New England family. He earned three degrees at Harvard but apparently was not an entirely serious student. During his senior year, was sent away from campus for a while because he was not studying seriously and had been "cutting up" during chapel.

Lowell had not been especially interested in social causes as a student, but he changed when he met and married Maria White. She was a dedicated abolitionist. At her encouragement, Lowell began to write articles against slavery, sometimes using the Yankee folk speech he often used in poetry. Lowell "had thought of his writing as a 'fencing stick' and was surprised to find that it could be used as a weapon."

This next group of poems focuses on what has long been a favorite subject for writers of descriptive poems—nature. The wonders of nature, the beauty of nature, nature's creatures, nature's moods, the effects nature has on us human beings—all have been celebrated in verse.

What picture(s) form in your mind when you hear or see the word September? *How similar is your September to Helen Hunt Jackson's?*

September

HELEN HUNT JACKSON

The goldenrod is yellow;
   The corn is turning brown;
The trees in apple orchards
   With fruit are bending down.

The gentian's bluest fringes   5
   Are curling in the sun;
In dusty pods the milkweed
   Its hidden silk has spun.

The sedges flaunt their harvest
   In every meadow nook;   10
And asters by the brookside
   Make asters in the brook.

From dewy lanes at morning
   The grapes' sweet odors rise;
At noon the roads all flutter   15
   With yellow butterflies.

By all these lovely tokens
   September days are here,
With summer's best of weather,
   And autumn's best of cheer.   20

Discussion

1. In what sense is this poem a poem of nature?

2. What are some of the things that the poet has chosen to describe about nature in September? If you were to describe the Septembers you have experienced, what objects would you include?

3. What do lines 11 and 12 mean?

4. What meaning do you get from lines 19 and 20?

5. What colors do you find throughout this poem?

6. Which lines in each stanza rhyme? What rhythm do you find in each stanza?

Composition

1. Using descriptive language in poem form, Helen Hunt Jackson has pictured her favorite time of year. Her poem is carefully structured: There are four lines to a stanza, the second and fourth lines rhyme, and there is a definite and orderly rhyme pattern. In a paragraph or two, describe Mrs. Jackson's "September" in your own words. What idea will you use for your topic sentence? What details will support that topic sentence?

2. Each of us probably has a favorite time of year. What is your favorite month of the year? In a paragraph or two, identify your favorite month, and then give reasons for your choice. In supplying your reasons, you'll want to refer to objects and colors and other sensory impressions that typify "your" time of year.

Helen Hunt Jackson 1830–1885

Helen Hunt Jackson was best known for her novel *Ramona* about Native American life in California.

She was born in Amherst, Massachusetts, and was a lifelong friend of Emily Dickinson. She traveled extensively throughout the United States. While living in Colorado, Jackson became concerned about the unfair treatment of Native Americans. At her own expense, she sent copies of her first major project, *A Century of Dishonor,* to all members of Congress. However, no changes came about as a result of her book.

Jackson hoped that a fictional account of the Native Americans' problems would arouse public interest. And so she wrote *Ramona.*

For most of us, taking nature for granted is all too easy. Perhaps that's one reason why we need poets—to bring nature's beauty to our attention.

Daffodils

MAY SWENSON

Yellow telephones
in a row in the garden
are ringing,
shrill with light.

Old-fashioned spring   5
brings earliest models out
each April the same,
naïve and classical.

Look into the yolk-
colored mouthpieces   10
alert with echoes.
Say hello to time.

Discussion

1. The poet compares the daffodils in her garden to what?
2. The entire poem is actually a long metaphor. Do you agree or disagree? Why?
3. Explain lines 5 and 6: "Old-fashioned spring/brings earliest models out."
4. What is the meaning of the last line?

Rain

FRANK MARSHALL DAVIS

Today the rain
is an aged man
a gray old man
a curious old man
in a music store   5

Today houses
are strings of a harp
soprano harp strings
bass harp strings
in a music store   10

The ancient man
strums the harp
with thin long fingers
attentively picking
a weary jingle   15
a soft jazzy jangle
then dodders away
before the boss comes 'round. . . .

1. How is the rain like a man in a music store? How are houses like the strings of a harp?
2. What is the mood of the poem? What words suggest that mood?
3. In the poem there are two sound-meaning words. That is, the sound of each word is the same as its meaning. What are those two words?
4. In saying that the ancient man "dodders away" (line 17), what does the poet mean?
5. What do you understand by the last line?

Composition

1. Like "Daffodils" (page 444), the poem "Rain" is one long metaphor. In a paragraph or two explain why.
2. Using the idea expressed in "Rain," write a poem of your own about a rainstorm. In planning your poem, there are some things you'll want to consider: (a) Should the storm be a violent one or a light one? (b) Should you compare the storm to a person or to something else? (c) If you use a person for comparison, what kind of person should he or she be? In writing your poem, try to keep the lines as short as they are in "Rain." Limit your poem to three stanzas.

Vocabulary

A HOMONYM is a word that sounds the same as another word, but it sometimes has a different spelling and always a different meaning from the word it sounds like. For example, the words *rain* and *rein* are homonyms.

A. Each of the following sentences contains an *italicized* word. On a separate sheet of paper, list the *italicized* words. After each one write a homonym for that word. Then write an original sentence which uses the homonym correctly.

1. A puppy had *hair* that was flowing.
2. *No*, I will not go.
3. Lonnie has a new *pair* of shoes.
4. *Sew* the seams straight.
5. He rose out of *sight*.

B. List three more sets of homonyms. Then write a sentence for each word, using the homonym correctly.

"A trout leaps high"

ONITSURA

A trout leaps high—
  Below him, in the river bottom,
    Clouds flow by.

Discussion

1. Explain how this poem is a snapshot in words.
2. How can it be that "in the river bottom/Clouds flow by"?

Onitsura (Kawajima Onitsura) 1661–1738

The Japanese poet Onitsura was a Samurai by birth who did not want to become a soldier (as was expected). He composed his first poem when he was eight. Eventually he became a monk of Zen so that he could study with the great poet Basho.

Onitsura believed that in order to be a poet a person must see the world through the eyes of a child. He was famous in his time and was an important guide for later poets.

Each of these six short poems is an example of Haiku or—as Richard Wright calls his word poems—Hokku. Of Japanese origin, both refer to a three-line poem that describes a single image.

Hokku Poems

RICHARD WRIGHT

I am nobody
A red sinking autumn sun
Took my name away

Make up your mind snail!
You are half inside your house
And halfway out!

Keep straight down this block
Then turn right where you will find
A peach tree blooming

The spring lingers on
In the scent of a damp log
Rotting in the sun

Whose town did you leave
O wild and drowning spring rain
And where do you go?

The crow flew so fast
That he left his lonely caw
Behind in the fields

Writer's Craft

HAIKU (or *Hokku*) is one of the simplest forms a descriptive poem can take. But though the form is simple, the act of composing *Haiku* is not.

As explained above, the purpose of *Haiku* is to use words so effectively that in just three lines they paint a single picture in your mind. But those three lines must follow a prescribed pattern: The first must have five *syllables*—no more, no fewer. The second must have seven syllables. The third line—like the first—must have five. Thus, in a total of only seventeen syllables, the *Haiku* writer must describe something so vividly that only one sharp mental picture results.

1. Which one of these *Hokku* poems appeals to you most? Why?

2. In what way are these *Hokku* poems descriptive poems of nature?

Composition

1. The sensory image—the mental picture—in each of Richard Wright's "Hokku Poems" appeals to one or more of our five senses. In a paragraph, point to which of the five senses each poem appeals to.

2. Write one or two *Haiku* poems of your own. For your subject(s), choose some aspect of nature that appeals to you. (All six of Richard Wright's *Hokku* Poems are concerned with nature.) Remember that each poem you write can have only three lines with five, seven, and five syllables, respectively. Try to use sensory words that create a sharp mental picture.

Vocabulary

Keep straight down this *block*
Then turn right where you will find
A peach tree blooming.

In this Haiku, the word *block* means "a section of city." However, as you know, *block* can mean several other things as well, including "a solid piece of wood." The word *block* is a HOMONYM. Homonyms are words that have the same pronunciation and sometimes the same spelling, but have different meanings.

Below, you will find five word problems. Each one gives you two different meanings. Can you think of a homonym for each pair of meanings? Write all your answers on a separate sheet of paper.

1. the lower part of a tree __*or*__ a large piece of luggage

2. a row __*or*__ a string on which cloths are hung outdoors

3. an up-and-down motion of the hand __*or*__ a swell of water

4. a person who has guests __*or*__ a huge number

5. a fallen tree trunk __*or*__ a ship's record of progress

Descriptive poems help us see ourselves and our world in fresh and original ways. They do so because their writers—poets who look sharply and listen carefully—react forcefully to what they experience. In no area of human affairs have poets reacted more vigorously than that which concerns the love for one's country. The five poems that follow prove the point.

My Native Land

SIR WALTER SCOTT

Breathes there the man, with soul so dead,
Who never to himself hath said,
   This is my own, my native land?
Whose heart hath ne'er within him burned,
As home his footsteps he hath turned   5
   From wandering on a foreign strand?[1]
If such there breathe, go, mark him well;
For him no minstrel raptures swell;
High though his titles, proud his name,
Boundless his wealth as wish can claim,—   10
Despite those titles, power, and pelf,[2]
The wretch, concentered all in self,
Living, shall forfeit fair renown,
And, doubly dying, shall go down
To the vile dust from whence he sprung,   15
Unwept, unhonored, and unsung.

---

1 **strand:** shore.
2 **pelf:** riches.

1. Why would a person have a greater appreciation for his or her native land after being away for a while?
2. What *cannot* take the place of one's native land?
3. What do you understand by the expression "doubly dying" (line 14)?
4. Why is a person who puts personal power and riches ahead of the well-being of his or her country likely to die "unwept, unhonored, and unsung"?
5. The poem contains several expressions made up of words beginning with the same sound. Identify at least five of them.

Sir Walter Scott 1771—1832

Sir Walter Scott's first literary success was his long poem *The Lady of the Lake.* His first novel, *Waverly,* was published anonymously because he did not want his poetry fame to be tied to a novel which might fail. The novel was an instant success. Readers were so curious about the anonymous author that Scott signed his next novels "by the Author of Waverly."

In 1826, Scott's publishing company lost a large sum because a bank collapsed. Scott could have declared bankruptcy and given his estate to the creditors, but he chose to pay off the debt. Although in weak health, he wrote thirty pages daily for the next eighteen months. He paid half the debt but his health failed. He was unable to work much more before he died. Fifteen years later, sales of his books had repaid the entire debt.

A familiar patriotic song begins with these words: "This is my country!" My country? How so?

My Land Is Fair for Any Eyes to See

JESSE STUART

My land is fair for any eyes to see—
Now look, my friends—look to the east and west!
You see the purple hills far in the west—
Hills lined with pine and gum and black-oak tree—
Now to the east you see the fertile valley!   5
This land is mine, I sing of it to you—
My land beneath the skies of white and blue.
This land is mine, for I am part of it.
I am the land, for it is part of me—
We are akin and thus our kinship be!   10
It would make me a brother to the tree!
And far as eyes can see this land is mine.
Not for one foot of it I have a deed—
To own this land I do not need a deed—
They all belong to me—gum, oak, and pine.   15

Discussion

1. By what right does the speaker call the country "*my* land"?
2. Why does the speaker *not* need a deed to own the land?
3. What passages give a feeling of the expanse of the country?
4. What significance, if any, do you find in the use of the word *any* in the title?

THE DRUMMER BOY *William Morris Hunt* Museum of Fine Arts. Boston. Ellen Gardner Fund.

Freedom! From 1620 to the present day, America has meant and means freedom. What assurance is there that America will continue to be "the land of the free"?

Song of the Settlers

JESSAMYN WEST

Freedom is a hard-bought thing—
A gift no man can give,
For some, a way of dying,
For most, a way to live.

Freedom is a hard-bought thing—   5
A rifle in the hand,
The horses hitched at sunup,
A harvest in the land.

Freedom is a hard-bought thing—
A massacre, a bloody rout,   10
The candles lit at nightfall,
And the night shut out.

Freedom is a hard-bought thing—
An arrow in the back,
The wind in the long corn rows,   15
And the hay in the rack.

Freedom is a way of living,
A song, a mighty cry.
Freedom is the bread we eat;
Let it be the way we die!   20

Discussion

1. Who were—and who are—the "settlers"? What was their song? In what way is their song still sung today?

2. What does the statement "Freedom is a hard-bought thing" mean?

3. What do you understand by the statement, "Freedom is a way of living"?

4. Those who settled America thought freedom was worth fighting for. Do you think so? Why? Do you think that the struggle for freedom is over, or does the struggle continue today? Why?

One of America's strengths lies in the fact that people of widely different backgrounds have been able to work together—and are still striving to work together—toward common goals.

I, Too

LANGSTON HUGHES

I, too, sing America.

I am the darker brother.
They send me to eat in the kitchen
When company comes,
But I laugh,   5
And eat well,
And grow strong.

Tomorrow,
I'll be at the table
When company comes.   10
Nobody'll dare
Say to me,
"Eat in the kitchen,"
Then.

Besides,   15
They'll see how beautiful I am
And be ashamed—

I, too, am America.

Discussion

1. Who is the "I" in the poem?
2. What do you understand by the line, "They send me to eat in the kitchen" (line 3)?
3. What do you understand by the phrase "And grow strong" (line 7)?
4. Which two lines of the poem are almost identical? What effect does the repetition and the position of these lines have?

On September 13, 1814, British warships in Chesapeake Bay began a bombardment of Fort McHenry, which protected the city of Baltimore. The bombardment lasted all through the night. But at seven o'clock on the morning of September 14, the guns stopped firing. Suddenly a break in the smoke and mist revealed the stars and stripes still flying proudly over the fort! So excited was Francis Scott Key, an American lawyer who had been detained aboard a British vessel, that from his pocket he took an unfinished letter and on the back of it immediately wrote down these verses.

The Star-Spangled Banner

FRANCIS SCOTT KEY

Oh! say, can you see, by the dawn's early light,
What so proudly we hailed at the twilight's last gleaming?
Whose broad stripes and bright stars, thro' the perilous fight,
O'er the ramparts we watched were so gallantly streaming?
And the rockets' red glare, the bombs bursting in air,   5
Gave proof thro' the night that our flag was still there.
Oh! say, does that star-spangled banner yet wave
O'er the land of the free and the home of the brave?

On the shore, dimly seen thro' the mist of the deep,
Where the foe's haughty host in dread silence reposes,   10
What is that which the breeze, o'er the towering steep,
As it fitfully blows, half conceals, half discloses?
Now it catches the gleam of the morning's first beam,
In full glory reflected, now shines on the stream.
'Tis the star-spangled banner. Oh! long may it wave   15
O'er the land of the free and the home of the brave!

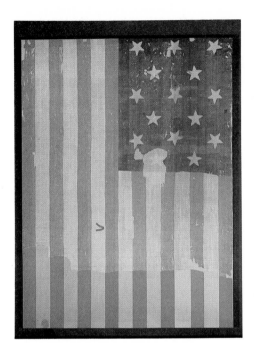

And where is that band who so vauntingly swore
That the havoc of war and the battle's confusion
A home and a country should leave us no more?
Their blood has washed out their foul footstep's pollution.   20
No refuge could save the hireling and slave
From the terror of flight or the gloom of the grave,
And the star-spangled banner in triumph doth wave
O'er the land of the free and the home of the brave.

Oh! thus be it ever when freemen shall stand   25
Between their loved home and the war's desolation,
Blest with vict'ry and peace, may the Heav'n-rescued land
Praise the Pow'r that hath made and preserved us a nation.
Then conquer we must, when our cause it is just,
And this be our motto, "In God is our trust."   30
And the star-spangled banner in triumph shall wave
O'er the land of the free and the home of the brave.

Discussion

1. What do you understand by the first four lines of the third stanza?
2. Although the refrain—the last two lines of each stanza—is similar, each differ somewhat from the other three. What significance do you see in that difference?
3. What characteristics of America do you find emphasized in our National Anthem?

Vocabulary

Here are eight words that appear in the patriotic poems in this part of the book:

akin	pomp
astride	ramparts
minstrel	renown
perilous	rout

On a separate sheet of paper, copy these words and define each one. Use a dictionary as needed. On the same sheet, tell which of the words you have defined fits best into the blank in each of the following sentence contexts:

1. A sad song of longing for home was sung by the lonely _____.
2. The founders of the United States wanted our leaders to be simple, down-to-earth people with none of the elegance and _____ of European royalty.
3. Regardless of their race or religion, all Americans should realize that they are _____ to one another.
4. The pioneers' covered-wagon journey was made _____ by lack of roads, sudden storms, and dwindling food supplies.
5. Davy Crockett died defending the _____ of the Alamo in Texas.
6. The general, _____ his magnificent horse, led the troops into battle.
7. The _____ of Abraham Lincoln is not limited to the United States; people in every land admire him.
8. At the end of World War II, the Nazis suffered a complete _____ at the hands of the Allied Forces.

Humorous Poems

Chances are that you've never thought much about how versatile poems are. They can be long; they can be short; they can be neither. They can use rhyme, but they don't have to. They can use a definite, regular rhythm or no rhythm at all. They often use words to form sharp pictures in your mind, but sometimes they don't.

Poems can tell stories. Some of those stories—particularly those about the long ago—are ballads. Using very few words, poems can describe any situation or any condition. They can express joy or sorrow or any feeling in between. And they can be funny. In fact, some poems exist for the sole purpose of making you laugh.

Sarah Cynthia Sylvia Stout Would Not Take the Garbage Out

SHEL SILVERSTEIN

Sarah Cynthia Sylvia Stout
Would not take the garbage out!
She'd scour the pots and scrape the pans,
Candy the yams and spice the hams,
And though her daddy would scream and shout,   5
She simply would not take the garbage out.
And so it piled up to the ceilings:
Coffee grounds, potato peelings,
Brown bananas, rotten peas,
Chunks of sour cottage cheese.   10
It filled the can, it covered the floor,
It cracked the window and blocked the door
With bacon rinds and chicken bones,
Drippy ends of ice cream cones,
Prune pits, peach pits, orange peel,   15
Gloppy glumps of cold oatmeal,
Pizza crusts and withered greens,

Soggy beans and tangerines,
Crusts of black burned buttered toast,
Gristly bits of beefy roasts . . .   20
The garbage rolled on down the hall,
It raised the roof, it broke the wall . . .
Greasy napkins, cookie crumbs,
Globs of gooey bubble gum,
Cellophane from green baloney,   25
Rubbery blubbery macaroni,
Peanut butter, caked and dry,
Curdled milk and crusts of pie,
Moldy melons, dried-up mustard,
Eggshells mixed with lemon custard,   30
Cold french fries and rancid meat,
Yellow lumps of Cream of Wheat.
At last the garbage reached so high
That finally it touched the sky.
And all the neighbors moved away,   35
And none of her friends would come to play.
And finally Sarah Cynthia Stout said,
"OK, I'll take the garbage out!"
But then, of course, it was too late . . .
The garbage reached across the state,   40
From New York to the Golden Gate.
And there, in the garbage she did hate,
Poor Sarah met an awful fate,
That I cannot right now relate
Because the hour is much too late.   45
But children, remember Sarah Stout
And always take the garbage out!

Discussion

1. What do you think happened to "Poor Sarah"? Why, do you think, does the speaker not reveal the "awful fate" that befell "Poor Sarah"? Does his *not* telling you what Sarah's fate is add to or detract from the fun of the poem? Why?

2. What is the moral—or the lesson—of the poem? Do you think the lesson is to be taken seriously, or not? Why?

3. What examples of exaggeration do you find in the poem? What is the effect of those exaggerations?

4. What combinations of words having the same initial sounds do you find in the poem? Do these word-combinations add to or detract from the humor of the poem? Why?

5. In using phrases like "Drippy ends of ice cream cones" and "Soggy beans" and "Gristly bits of beefy roasts," the poet creates sharp sensory images. What other phrases create sharp sensory images like those? To which ones of our five senses do those images appeal?

Shel Silverstein 1932——

Shel Silverstein is a well-muscled man in blue jeans and cowboy hat. He hates interviews but loves to talk. Besides writing prose and poetry, he "also writes songs, draws cartoons, sings, plays guitar, and has a good time."

His greatest success as a songwriter was "A Boy Named Sue," recorded by Johnny Cash and other singers. Silverstein also writes and draws cartoons for magazines. Although he did not eagerly go into children's literature, he has written and illustrated several books for children and is not surprised that they are successful. Silverstein says of his work, "What I do is good. I wouldn't let it out if I didn't think it was."

Silverstein has a busy life, traveling often from his houseboat in Sausalito, California. He says, "I want to go everywhere, look at and listen to everything. You can go crazy with some of the wonderful stuff there is in life."

The Porcupine

OGDEN NASH

Any hound a porcupine nudges
Can't be blamed for harboring grudges.
I know one hound that laughed all winter
At a porcupine that sat on a splinter.

Ogden Nash 1902—1971

Ogden Nash was the best-known humorous poet of his time. After
unsuccessful attempts at teaching and business, Nash got his first
writing job, creating ads for streetcars. He worked in the editorial
department of a publishing company then, and he began writing
serious verse in his free time. He did not feel satisfied with his serious
poetry, though, and decided he should "laugh at myself before anyone
laughed at me."

One summer afternoon at work, he wrote a "silly" verse and tossed
it in the wastebasket. But a few minutes later, he dug it out and sent it
to a magazine which bought it. Soon he was making more money on
his spare-time poems than on his job. He quit his job to write
full-time.

Nash often misspelled words to make unexpected rhymes.
Describing a green plant he did not like, he wrote "Parsley/Is gharsly."
He also varied the length of his lines greatly. Each line of poetry, he
said, was "like a horse running up to a hurdle but you don't know
when it'll jump."

Limericks

A puppy whose hair was so flowing
There really was no means of knowing
    Which end was his head,
    Once stopped me and said,
"Please, sir, am I coming or going?"

               —OLIVER HERFORD

Writer's Craft

The five-line verse you have just read is a special kind of poem called a LIMERICK. (The name probably comes from a song about the old town of Limerick in Ireland.) People write limericks for one reason only—for fun! A limerick is usually a nonsense verse—that is, it concerns something ridiculous. Even so, every limerick follows a distinct—and distinctive—pattern. As you can see, a limerick has five lines. The first, second, and fifth lines have the same length—that is, they have nine syllables each—and they rhyme. The third and fourth lines are shorter in that each has only five syllables, and they, too, rhyme. Sometimes, to maintain the limerick rhythm, you may have to slur two syllables into one sound.

1. How many lines does "A Puppy" have?
2. Which lines contain nine syllables each and rhyme?
3. Which lines contain five syllables each and rhyme?

Oliver Herford 1863–1935

Oliver Herford, a poet, illustrator, and wit, was one of the most quoted persons of his time. He was born in England but came to the United States with his family when he was six. He had a long and brilliant career as a versifier and artist for leading magazines.

He wrote and illustrated fifty books of "artistic nonsense." His special talent lay in making animals and things seem human. One night as he strolled past a one-room schoolhouse, he thought of the dreary day ahead tomorrow for pupils and teacher. He let himself in and spent two hours covering the blackboard with a droll mural of wild animals. The next day, teacher and pupils were delighted.

Once, when several of Herford's poems had been rejected by a magazine, he bundled them together and sent them to the editor again with this note: "Sir: Your office boy has been continually rejecting these masterpieces. Kindly see that they receive the attention of the editor." That time several of the poems were accepted.

There was an old man of Nantucket
Who kept all his cash in a bucket;
  But his daughter, named Nan,
  Ran away with a man,
And as for the bucket, Nantucket.

Pa followed the pair to Pawtucket
(The man and the girl with the bucket)
  And he said to the man,
  "You're welcome to Nan."
But as for the bucket, Pawtucket.

ANONYMOUS

A decrepit old gas man named Peter,
While hunting around for the meter,
  Touched a leak with his light;
  He rose out of sight,
And, as everyone who knows anything
  about poetry can tell you, he also
  ruined the meter.

Discussion

1. Would you say that the limericks about Nantucket and Pawtucket conform to the typical limerick pattern, or not? Why?
2. What's unusual about the last limerick? What joke do you find there?

You know, of course, that dialogue can tell a story. In this one, which takes place during the Civil War, a captain in the Union Army exchanges some words with a young sentry.

Achilles Deatheridge

EDGAR LEE MASTERS

"Your name is Achilles Deatheridge?
How old are you, my boy?"
"I'm sixteen past and I went to the war
From Athens, Illinois."

"Achilles Deatheridge, you have done   5
A deed of dreadful note."
"It comes of his wearing a battered hat,
And a rusty, wrinkled coat."

"Why, didn't you know how plain he is?
And didn't you ever hear   10
He goes through the lines by day or night
Like a sotty cannoneer?

"You must have been half dead for sleep,
For the dawn was growing bright."
"Well, Captain, I had stood right there   15
Since six o'clock last night.

"I cocked my gun at the swish of the grass,
And how am I at fault
When a dangerous-looking man won't stop
When sentry hollers Halt?   20

"I cried out Halt and he only smiled
And waved his hand like that.
Why, any Johnnie could wear the coat
And any fellow the hat.

"I hollered Halt again and he stopped   25
And lighted a fresh cigar.
I never noticed his shoulder badge,
And I never noticed a star."

"So you arrested him? Well, Achilles,
When you hear the swish of the grass,   30
If it's General Grant inspecting the lines,
Hereafter let him pass."

SKETCH OF A YOUNG SOLDIER *Winslow Homer*

Discussion

1. What happened?
2. According to the captain and Achilles Deatheridge, what kind of person was General Grant?
3. Why, in your opinion, is this poem included in a section about humorous poems?

Ode to a Violin

LOUIS OMAR SALINAS

Six lessons
in six weeks

I leave
you

on a bench
wounded

THE VIOLIN *Juan Gris*

Discussion

1. How well do you think a person would play the violin after only six lessons?
2. Why, do you think, does the speaker call the violin "wounded"?
3. An ode is a dignified poem on a serious subject. Does the speaker's calling the poem an ode add to or detract from the humor? Why?

Luis Omar Salinas 1937——

Luis Omar Salinas was born in Robstown, Texas. He attended grammar school there and spent several years in Monterrey, Mexico. He then went to live with an aunt and an uncle in Bakersfield, California. He graduated from the local high school and worked his way through college as a dishwasher, construction worker, shoe salesman, and copy boy.

Salinas has been active for the Chicano cause in Southern California. He was part of the beginning of the *Teatro Campesinos,* an informal theater for farm workers. Besides writing, Salinas teaches at colleges in California.

6   POEMS

Discussion

Read the poem below and then answer the questions following it.

The Open Door

ELIZABETH COATSWORTH

Out of the dark
To the sill of the door
Lay the snow in a long
Unruffled floor,
And the lamplight fell   5
Narrow and thin
Like a carpet unrolled
For the cat to walk in.
Slowly, smoothly,
Black as the night,   10

With paws unseen
White upon white,
Like a queen who walks
Down a corridor,
The black cat paced   15
The cold smooth floor
And left behind her,
Bead upon bead,
The track of small feet
Like dark fern-seed.   20

1. Would you say that "The Open Door" is a narrative poem, a descriptive poem, a ballad, or a humorous poem? Why?

2. What is the *basic* rhythm pattern of the poem?

3. What pattern of rhyme, if any, do you find in the poem?

4. What kinds of comparisons do you find in lines 3 and 4, and in lines 5–7? What things are compared? How are they alike?

5. Find at least three lines in the poem that create vivid images.

Composition

1. In this unit, which narrative poem and which ballad did you find most interesting? Which descriptive poem or poems had the greatest appeal for you? Which humorous poem gave you the most enjoyment? In a brief composition, identify the poems you liked best. Then explain why they appealed to you.

2. Look back at the four limericks on pages 465 and 467 and note their five-line structure. Then write a limerick of your own.

Myths, Fables, and Folktales

MYTHS, FABLES, AND FOLKTALES

Naturally, you know what narratives are. They are simply accounts of events or experiences. For example, the short stories you have read—stories like "The Most Dangerous Game," "The Pacing Goose," "Through the Tunnel," and "The Gift of the Magi"—are narratives. Then, too, you know that events and experiences can be recounted as narrative poems and ballads. "The Cremation of Sam McGee" and "Lord Randal" are examples. And when you come right down to it, plays like "Flight into Danger" are narratives in dramatic form.

But that's not all. There are other kinds of narratives—narratives that have come to us from the ancient past. Like us, the peoples of those times wanted to understand their world and to explain occurrences in nature. Like us, they wanted to understand themselves and to find happiness. And like us, they sought to honor their heritage and keep the ways of living that were distinctly theirs. Although they didn't have our scientific knowledge or our written records of long human experience, they were able to satisfy their wants because they had the human gift of imagination. As a result of their curiosity and their creative minds, they told imaginative stories—narratives that were passed on by word of mouth from teller to teller and from generation to generation. It is these narratives that we today know as MYTHS and FABLES and FOLKTALES.

Myths

The rumble of thunder heralds an approaching storm. In the spring, nature awakens with new life. Some areas of the world are barren and hot; others are bitter cold and snow-covered. How so?

To explain natural phenomena like these, we today turn to science. But how did the ancients explain them—the people of early civilizations who didn't have our modern science to turn to? In their wonderings and imaginings about the world around them, those people fixed the responsibility for the workings of nature on beings with superhuman powers—on gods and goddesses. Many stories grew up about those gods and goddesses and their activities. It is these stories that we call MYTHS.

Greek Myths

Every ethnic-cultural group has its myths. Even we in the United States today have our myths. Santa Claus's bringing toys to good boys and girls every Christmas is an example. But probably the best-known myths are those of ancient Greece and Rome.

The Greco-Roman myths—called Classical myths—have had an important influence on our Western civilization. The planets, for example, are named after Greek/Roman gods and goddesses. And so are five months of our year. The moon landings, together with the NASA space projects preceding and following them, bear the names of Greek/Roman gods. And so do many commercial trade names. Finally, such words as *jovial, martial, cupidity,*

saturnine, vulcanize, cereal, and *mercurial* come from the names of Greek/Roman gods.

The chart below lists the names of the principal Greek gods. The names in parentheses are the Roman names. At the right of the name is given the sphere of influence of each god or goddess.

CHART OF THE GREEK GODS

The Titans
Cronus (Saturn)—ruler of the Titans until Zeus dethroned him
Ocean—river encircling the earth
Atlas—bore the world on his shoulders
Prometheus (prǝ mē′thē ǝs)—savior of human-kind

The Olympians (lived on Mount Olympus in Thessaly, in the northeast part of Greece)
Zeus (züs) **(Jupiter)**—king of the gods
Hera (Juno)—queen of the gods
Poseidon (pō sī′dǝn) **(Neptune)**—god of the sea
Hades (Pluto)—god of the underworld
Hestia (Vesta)—goddess of the hearth and home
Ares (âr′ēz) **(Mars)**—god of war
Pallas Athene (pāl′ǝs ǝ thē′nǝ) **(Minerva)**—goddess of wisdom
Apollo (Phoebus Apollo)—god of the sun
Aphrodite (ǎf′rǝ dī′ tī) **(Venus)**—goddess of love and beauty
Hermes (hûr′mēz) **(Mercury)**—messenger of the gods; presided over any event which required skill and dexterity
Artemis (är′tǝ mǐs) **(Diana)**—goddess of the moon
Hephaestus (hē fěs′ tǝs) **(Vulcan)**—artist; made weapons for the gods
Demeter (Ceres)—goddess of agriculture and the harvest

"In the beginning God created the heavens and the earth." That's how the Book of Genesis begins the ancient Hebrew account of The Creation. Other ancient civilizations, however, had other versions. Here is the account of The Creation according to the ancient Greeks.

Prometheus and Pandora

THOMAS BULFINCH

THE CREATION OF THE WORLD is a problem naturally fitted to excite the liveliest interest of man, its inhabitant. The ancient pagans[1] had their own way of telling the story, which is as follows:

Before earth and sea and heaven were created, all things wore one aspect, to which we give the name of Chaos—a confused and shapeless mass, nothing but dead weight, in which, however, slumbered the seeds of things. Earth, sea, and air were all mixed up together; so the earth was not solid, the sea was not fluid, and the air was not transparent. God and Nature at last interposed, and put an end to this discord, separating earth from sea, and heaven from both. The fiery part, being the lightest, sprang up, and formed the skies; the air was next in weight and place. The earth, being heavier, sank below; and the water took the lowest place, and buoyed up the earth.

Here some god—it is not known which—gave his good offices in arranging and disposing the earth. He appointed rivers and bays their places, raised mountains, scooped out valleys, distributed woods, fountains, fertile fields, and stony plains. The air being cleared, the stars began to appear, fishes took possession of the sea, birds of the air, and four-footed beasts of the land.

But a nobler animal was wanted, and Man was made. It is not known whether the creator made him of divine materials, or whether in the earth, so lately separated from heaven, there lurked still some heavenly seeds.

Prometheus took some of this earth, and kneading it up with water, made man in the image of the gods. He gave him an upright stature, so that while all animals turn their faces downward, and look to the earth, he raises his to heaven, and gazes on the stars.

Prometheus was one of the Titans, a gigantic race, who inhabited the earth before the creation of man. To him and his brother

---

1 **pagans** (pā′ gəns): people who are not Christians, Jews, or Mohammedans.

Epimetheus was committed the office of making man, and providing him and all other animals with the faculties necessary for their preservation. Epimetheus undertook to do this, and Prometheus was to overlook his work, when it was done. Epimetheus accordingly proceeded to bestow upon the different animals the various gifts of courage, strength, swiftness, sagacity;[2] wings to one, claws to another, a shelly covering to a third, etc.

But when man came to be provided for, who was to be superior to all other animals,

2 **sagacity** (sə gas′ə te): wisdom.

Epimetheus had been so prodigal[3] of his resources that he had nothing left to bestow upon him. In his perplexity he resorted to his brother Prometheus, who, with the aid of Minerva, went up to heaven, and lighted his torch at the chariot of the sun, and brought down fire to man. With this gift man was more than a match for all other animals. It enabled him to make weapons wherewith to subdue them; tools with which to cultivate the earth; to warm his dwelling, so as to be comparatively independent of climate; and to introduce the arts and to coin money, the means of trade and commerce.

Woman was not yet made. The story (absurd enough!) is that Jupiter made her, and sent her to Prometheus and his brother, to punish them for their presumption[4] in stealing fire from heaven; and man, for accepting the gift. The first woman was named Pandora. She was made in heaven, every god contributing something to perfect her. Venus gave her beauty, Mercury persuasion, Apollo music, etc. Thus equipped, she was conveyed to earth, and presented to Epimetheus, who gladly accepted her, though cautioned by his brother to beware of Jupiter and his gifts. Epimetheus had in his house a jar, in which were kept certain noxious[5] articles for which, in fitting man for his new abode, he had had no occasion.

Pandora was seized with an eager curiosity to know what this jar contained; and one day she slipped off the cover and looked in. Forthwith there escaped a multitude of plagues for hapless[6] man—such as gout, rheu-matism, and colic for his body, and envy, spite, and revenge for his mind—and scattered themselves far and wide. Pandora hastened to replace the lid; but, alas! the whole contents of the jar had escaped, one thing only excepted, which lay at the bottom, and that was *hope*. So we see at this day, whatever evils are abroad, hope never entirely leaves us; and while we have *that*, no amount of other ills can make us completely wretched.

Prometheus has been a favorite subject with the poets. He is represented as the friend of mankind, who taught them civilization and the arts. But as, in so doing, he transgressed[7] the will of Jupiter, he drew down on himself the anger of the ruler of gods and men. Jupiter had him chained to a rock on Mount Caucasus. This state of torment might have been brought to an end at any time by Prometheus, if he had been willing to submit to his oppressor; for he possessed a secret which involved the stability[8] of Jove's throne, and if he would have revealed it, he might have been at once taken into favor. But that he disdained[9] to do. He has therefore become the symbol of magnanimous[10] endurance of unmerited suffering, and strength of will resisting oppression.

"I would not quit
This bleak ravine, these unrepentant[11]
    pains. . . .
Pity the self-despising slaves of Jove,
Not me, within whose mind sits peace
    serene."

Shelley

---

3 **prodigal** (prod'ə gəl): wasteful; lavish.
4 **presumption** (pri zump' shən): bold venture going beyond the limits or rules imposed by the gods.
5 **noxious** (nok' shəs): harmful.
6 **hapless** (hap' lis): unlucky.

7 **transgressed** (trans gresd'): disobeyed.
8 **stability** (stə bil'ə tē): firmness.
9 **disdained**: proudly refused.
10 **magnanimous** (mag nan'ə məs): honorable; noble.
11 **unrepentant** (un ri pen' tənt): not showing sorrow or remorse for wrongdoing.

Discussion

1. Besides explaining the creation of the earth and of human beings, what else does the Prometheus myth explain?

2. The word *chaos* is often used to describe confusion. What does Chaos represent in this myth?

3. According to this myth, in what ways do human beings differ from the animals of the earth?

4. In what ways does Prometheus's gift of fire benefit humankind? Why might this gift have violated the will of Jupiter?

5. In Greek mythology Pandora is the first woman on earth. Among her characteristics is one that proves disastrous. Explain.

6. Why is it significant that *hope* is the only thing left in the jar Pandora opens? What is another human quality that might be considered important?

7. The lines quoted at the end of the selection are from a long poem, "Prometheus Unbound," by Percy Bysshe Shelley, a 19th-century English poet. Who do you think is speaking these lines? What do you think they mean?

Vocabulary

A SUFFIX is a letter or a small group of letters that you can add to the end of a word to change its meaning. One suffix that speakers and writers of English use every day is *-ed*. This suffix serves two major purposes:

1. To change many verbs that express present action (action going on right now) into verbs that express past action:

PRESENT				PAST
look	+	-ed	=	looked
hope	+	-d	=	hoped

2. To change some nouns ("naming words") into adjectives ("describing words"):

NOUN				ADJECTIVE (plus a noun described)
vein	+	-ed	=	veined (hands)
flower	+	-ed	=	flowered (dress)

   (In the example *hope*, notice that when *-ed* is added to a word that ends in *e*, the suffix *-d* alone is added.)

A. In each of the following sentences, based on "Prometheus and Pandora," one word ending with the suffix *-ed* is *italicized*. On a separate sheet of paper, copy these words. After each one, tell which purpose for using the *-ed* suffix is involved.

1. The myth "Prometheus and Pandora" tells what ancient peoples *believed* about the creation of the earth.

2. First, God and Nature *separated* heaven, earth, and water.

3. Before people were made, fishes took possession of the water; birds took possession of the air; and four-*footed* beasts took possession of the land.

4. Epimetheus gave gifts to all the other creatures, but Prometheus made humans the most *gifted* by providing them with fire.

5. Pandora's curiosity *released* sickness, envy, revenge, and other kinds of evil upon the world.

B. Not every word that ends in *-ed* uses those two letters as a suffix. Sometimes *e* and *d* are simply the last letters of a word itself. Make two columns on your paper. In the column at the left, copy from the list below all words that have *-ed* as a suffix. In the column at the right, copy the words that ordinarily end in the letters *-ed*.

red	overfed
excited	contributed
limited	wed
bobsled	wedded

Thomas Bulfinch 1796—1867

Thomas Bulfinch was a quiet, retiring man who enjoyed having free time to study and write. He was not ambitious or lucky in business, and he held several jobs before he found the one which suited his needs. Finally, he became a clerk in a Boston bank and stayed at that position until he died thirty years later. Bulfinch was satisfied with the bank job because it provided a steady income and still left time for writing and other interests. *The Age of Fable* was Bulfinch's best known work.

Some areas of the earth are bleak deserts, whereas other areas are fertile gardens. How so? Well, the ancient Greeks had an explanation.

Phaëthon, Son of Apollo

OLIVIA E. COOLIDGE

THOUGH APOLLO always honored the memory of Daphne, she was not his only love. Another was a mortal, Clymene,[1] by whom he had a son named Phaëthon.[2] Phaëthon grew up with his mother, who, since she was mortal, could not dwell in the halls of Olympus or in the palace of the sun. She lived not far from the East in the land of Ethiopia, and as her son grew up, she would point to the place where Eos, goddess of the dawn, lighted up the sky and tell him that there his father dwelt. Phaëthon loved to boast of his divine father as he saw the golden chariot riding high through the air. He would remind his comrades of other sons of gods and mortal women who, by virtue of their great deeds, had themselves become gods at last. He must always be first in everything, and in most things this was easy, since he was in truth stronger, swifter, and more daring than the others. Even if he were not victorious, Phaëthon always claimed to be first in honor. He could never bear to be beaten, even if he must risk his life in some rash way to win.

Most of the princes of Ethiopia willingly paid Phaëthon honor, since they admired him greatly for his fire and beauty. There was one boy, however, Epaphos,[3] who was rumored to be a child of Zeus himself. Since this was not certainly proved, Phaëthon chose to disbelieve it and to demand from Epaphos the deference[4] that he obtained from all others. Epaphos was proud too, and one day he lost his temper with Phaëthon and turned on him, saying, "You are a fool to believe all that your mother tells you. You are all swelled up with false ideas about your father."

Crimson with rage, the lad rushed home to his mother and demanded that she prove to him the truth of the story that she had often told. "Give me some proof," he implored her, "with which I can answer this insult of Epaphos. It is a matter of life and death to me, for if I cannot, I shall die of shame."

"I swear to you," replied his mother solemnly, "by the bright orb of the sun itself that you are his son. If I swear falsely, may I

---

1 **Clymene** (klim′ ə nē).
2 **Phaëthon** (fā′ə thon).

3 **Epaphos** (ep′ə fəs).
4 **deference** (def′ər əns): respect.

never look on the sun again, but die before the next time he mounts the heavens. More than this I cannot do, but you, my child, can go to the eastern palace of Phoebus Apollo—it lies not far away—and there speak with the god himself."

The son of Clymene leaped up with joy at his mother's words. The palace of Apollo was indeed not far. It stood just below the eastern horizon, its tall pillars glistening with bronze and gold. Above these it was white with gleaming ivory, and the great doors were flashing silver, embossed with pictures of earth, sky, and sea, and the gods that dwelt therein. Up the steep hill and the bright steps climbed Phaëthon, passing unafraid through the silver doors, and stood in the presence of the sun. Here at last he was forced to turn away his face, for Phoebus sat in state on his golden throne. It gleamed with emeralds and precious stones, while on the head of the god was a brilliant diamond crown upon which no eye could look undazzled.

Phaëthon hid his face, but the god had recognized his son, and he spoke kindly, asking him why he had come. Then Phaëthon plucked up courage and said, "I come to ask you if you are indeed my father. If you are so, I beg you to give me some proof of it so that all may recognize me as Phoebus's son."

The god smiled, being well pleased with his son's beauty and daring. He took off his crown so that Phaëthon could look at him, and coming down from his throne, he put his arms around the boy, and said, "You are indeed my son and Clymene's, and worthy to be called so. Ask of me whatever thing you wish to prove your origin to men, and you shall have it."

Phaëthon swayed for a moment and was dizzy with excitement at the touch of the god. His heart leaped; the blood rushed into his face. Now he felt that he was truly divine, unlike other men, and he did not wish to be counted with men any more. He looked up for a moment at his radiant father. "Let me drive the chariot of the sun across the heavens for one day," he said.

Apollo frowned and shook his head. "I cannot break my promise, but I will dissuade you if I can," he answered. "How can you drive my chariot, whose horses need a strong hand on the reins? The climb is too steep for you. The immense height will make you dizzy. The swift streams of air in the upper heaven will sweep you off your course. Even the immortal gods could not drive my chariot. How then can you? Be wise and make some other choice."

The pride of Phaëthon was stubborn, for he thought the god was merely trying to frighten him. Besides, if he could guide the sun's chariot, would he not have proved his right to be divine rather than mortal? For that he would risk his life. Indeed, once he had seen Apollo's splendor, he did not wish to go back and live among men. Therefore, he insisted on his right until Apollo had to give way.

When the father saw that nothing else would satisfy the boy, he bade the Hours bring forth his chariot and yoke the horses. The chariot was of gold and had two gold-rimmed wheels with spokes of silver. In it there was room for one man to stand and hold the reins. Around the front and sides of it ran a rail, but the back was open. At the end of a long pole there were yokes for the four horses. The pole was of gold and shone with precious jewels: the golden topaz, the bright diamond, the green emerald, and the flashing ruby. While the Hours were yoking the swift, pawing horses, rosy-fingered Dawn hastened to the gates of heaven to draw them open. Meanwhile Apollo anointed his son's face with a magic ointment, that he might be able to bear the heat of the firebreathing horses and the golden chariot. At last Phaëthon mounted the chariot and grasped the reins, the barriers were let down, and the horses shot up into the air.

At first the fiery horses sped forward up the accustomed trail, but behind them the chariot was too light without the weight of the immortal god. It bounded from side to side and was dashed up and down. Phaëthon was too frightened and too dizzy to pull the reins, nor would he have known anyway whether he was on the usual path. As soon as the horses felt that there was no hand controlling them, they soared up, up with fiery speed into the heavens till the earth grew pale and cold beneath them. Phaëthon shut his eyes, trembling at the dizzy, precipitous[5] height. Then the horses dropped down, more swiftly than a falling stone, flinging themselves madly from side to side in panic because they were masterless. Phaëthon dropped the reins entirely and clung with all his might to the chariot rail. Meanwhile as they came near the earth, it dried up and cracked apart. Meadows were reduced to white ashes, cornfields smoked and shriveled, cities perished in flame. Far and wide on the wooded mountains the forests were ablaze, and even the snow-clad Alps were bare and dry. Rivers steamed and dried to dust. The great North African plain was scorched until it became the desert that it is today. Even the sea shrank back to pools and caves, until dried fishes were left baking upon the white-hot sands. At last the great earth mother called upon Zeus to save her from utter destruction,

and Zeus hurled a mighty thunderbolt at the unhappy Phaëthon, who was still crouched in the chariot, clinging desperately to the rail. The dart cast him out, and he fell flaming in a long trail through the air. The chariot broke in pieces at the mighty blow, and the maddened horses rushed snorting back to the stable of their master, Apollo.

Unhappy Clymene and her daughters wandered over the whole earth seeking the body of the boy they loved so well. When they found him, they took him and buried him. Over his grave they wept and could not be comforted. At last the gods in pity for their grief changed them into poplar trees, which weep with tears of amber in memory of Phaëthon.

---

5 **precipitous** (pri sip′ə təs): steep.

Discussion

1. Why does Phaëthon demand proof that Apollo is his father?

2. Well pleased with his son, Apollo makes a rash promise. What is it? Why does Phaëthon insist that Apollo keep that promise?

3. What effects does Phaëthon's efforts to drive the sun chariot have on the earth?

4. What happened to Clymene, Phaëthon's mother?

5. What qualities or characteristics of human behavior does this myth illustrate?

Vocabulary

A SYNONYM is a word that means nearly the same as another word. An ANTONYM is a word that means nearly the opposite of another word.

Look at each pair of words below and decide which are synonyms and which are antonyms:

1. strong—weak   4. tall—short

2. hate—love   5. quiet—silent

3. cute—pretty   6. comrades—friends

If your decision is that, 2, and 4 are antonyms and that the rest are synonyms, you are ready to move on. If not, go back again and review the definitions.

A. The following are some pairs of words from "Phaëthon, Son of Apollo." Tell whether the words in each pair are related as synonyms or as antonyms. Write your answers on a separate paper. Whenever you are in doubt about a word's meaning, check the dictionary.

1. mortal—immortal   6. amber—golden

2. god-like—divine   7. precious—worthless

3. brilliant—dull   8. victorious—defeated

4. immense—small   9. implored—begged

5. ointment—salve   10. precipitous—steep

B. Each sentence below contains one *italicized* word. Think of a synonym to replace that word. Write the synonym on your paper.

1. Since Clymene was a mortal, she could not *dwell* in the halls of Olympus.

2. Phaëthon loved to boast of his divine father as he saw Phoebus's golden *chariot* riding through the sky.

3. Phaëthon could never bear to be beaten, even if he must risk his life in some *rash* way to win.

4. Epaphos told Phaëthon, "You are a *fool* to think that Apollo is your father."

5. *Crimson* with rage, Phaëthon rushed home to his mother and demanded the truth.

C. In this exercise, for each *italicized* word, write an *antonym* on your paper.

1. Clymene claimed *falsely* that Apollo was Phaëthon's father.

2. She *discouraged* a visit to the god himself.

3. Phaëthon was *frightened* to enter Apollo's palace.

4. Apollo was *pleased* when Phaëthon asked to drive the golden chariot across the sky.

5. Phaëthon's ride proved to be a huge *success* for him as well as for the earth below.

Olivia E. Coolidge 1908—

As a child, Olivia E. Coolidge made up long stories with her sister. Once they decided to put them in a book and recruited their mother's help for the actual writing. "But it soon turned out," Coolidge remembers, "that a story which sounded splendid in bed or by candlelight was less exciting when dictated slowly to a patient grownup."

Coolidge studied classics at Oxford University and then came to the United States. In teaching and telling stories to her own children, she found what children like to learn about. She began writing for children with the attitude that history should let the lives and ideas of people speak for themselves.

"Somewhere over the rainbow . . ." "Wishing will make it so. . . ." Those phrases from popular songs of a few years back are relatively new. But the idea behind them isn't. Wishing is as old as the human race. But it was the Greek sculptor Pygmalion who discovered that wishing could actually make it so!

Pygmalion and Galatea

MIRIAM COX

ON THE ISLAND OF CYPRUS[1] lived a talented young sculptor named Pygmalion[2]. The statues he carved were so lifelike that they seemed actually to breathe; yet they were far more beautiful than real human beings.

Travelers came from great distances to admire his work. But if the visitors were women, they were certain to be turned away abruptly. For Pygmalion was a woman-hater. Not only had he decided never to marry, but he scorned even to talk to girls.

Naturally the pretty maidens of the village tried to change this harsh attitude and dreamed up all kinds of little tricks to attract his attention, for Pygmalion was handsome as well as gifted. But all their efforts were useless; he would have nothing to do with any of them, preferring to toil from morning until night upon one beautiful work of art after another.

Oddly enough, however, when an unusually fine piece of ivory came into his possession one day, he decided to fashion it into the statue of a woman. After all, he couldn't go on forever making sculptures only of men and animals. In this statue he would express all his ideals of supreme beauty. It would be interesting to show misguided men that living women were quite inferior, by comparison!

Long before the statue was completed, Pygmalion knew that it would be his masterpiece. The mellow ivory seemed to welcome the lightest touch of his delicate chisels, and it was as if his very soul were being molded into his new creation. He could hardly wait to finish it. Often he worked all through the night, and felt cheated when at last he had to stop for food and sleep.

At last the statue was complete, and Pygmalion stood in awe before it. He had achieved his goal; here truly was matchless beauty; this was perfection. The figure glowed with an inner radiance that made the

---

1 Cyprus (sī′ prəs).
2 Pygmalion (pig mā′ lē ən).

softly curved lips seem about to open into a welcoming smile. It was as if a living maiden would descend gracefully from the marble pedestal at any moment.

For several days Pygmalion could not bear to leave his statue for a moment, so entranced was he by her beauty. Then he began to search the shops for trinkets, pretty robes, and jewels. Lovingly he adorned his statue with them, almost imagining that he could hear her happy laughter as she accepted his gifts.

She became so real to him that he gave her a name, Galatea,[3] and told her of his hopes and sorrows just as if she was a living woman. Finally he had to admit the truth to himself: he had fallen in love at last, but with a cold ivory statue of his own making. What could be more hopeless? Gradually his joy in her began to turn to deep sadness. If only she were real!

Now each year a great festival was held in honor of Aphrodite,[4] the goddess of love and beauty. The people of Cyprus especially loved this day because it was to their island that the goddess had first been blown by the breezes after rising from the ocean foam.

All day long her temple was thronged with worshipers who offered incense at the altar, decked her statue with garlands, and presented gifts. In the crowd were many unhappy lovers who had come to ask for her aid, because it was well known that Aphrodite was interested in the course of true love. Occasionally she would even lend mortals her magic belt, which enabled its wearer to inspire love in others.

Pygmalion had always felt deep devotion for Aphrodite, for he worshiped beauty. But as he approached her shrine, he was troubled. Could he tell her of the deep desire in his heart? Would she listen to such a plea as his, knowing that he had always hated women? Hesitantly he placed his offerings on her altar and pleaded, "Grant me, O Goddess of Love and Beauty, the greatest of all gifts: let me have a maiden like the ivory Galatea for my wife. Or better still. . . ." But at that moment the flames of the altar leaped high into the air. Could this mean that Aphrodite favored his prayer?

Pygmalion was excited as he hurried home, flung open his door, and went to his lovely Galatea. He touched her delicately chiseled hand; it felt warm and soft! As he watched spellbound, scarlet flooded into her lips and a breeze from the open doorway caressed hair that fell like a golden fountain over her white shoulders.

With a happy cry, Pygmalion stepped forward to embrace her; then he stopped. So often he had imagined that this was happening, only to awake to cruel disappointment. But this time it was not a dream. Violet eyes shining with love, Galatea stepped down from her marble pedestal into his eager arms. Aphrodite had answered the prayer in his heart: his statue had been granted the gift of life and was his to adore forever.

Aphrodite riding a swan.
Detail from a Greek vase painting.

---

3 **Galatea** (ga lə tē′ə).
4 **Aphrodite** (af′rə dī′tē).

1. Why did Pygmalion decide to carve a statue of a woman?

2. What was Pygmalion's wish? How did it happen that he made such a wish? Why did he express his wish at the temple of Aphrodite? What do you infer from his unfinished thought "Or better still . . ."?

3. How did things turn out for Pygmalion? Do you or do you not think that he deserved what he got? Why?

Composition

1. What implications does the myth about Pygmalion have for young people today? In a paragraph, explain what you think the myth suggests for helping young people realize their ambitions.

2. *My Fair Lady*, a musical comedy by Alan Jay Lerner and Frederic Loewe, had its opening performance on Broadway in 1956. Since then, it has been performed in countries the world over. In 1964, the motion picture version won the Academy Award as best picture. It may surprise you to learn that *My Fair Lady* is based on a play by the noted Irish dramatist George Bernard Shaw. The title: *Pygmalion.* From sources in the library or from persons who have seen *My Fair Lady,* find out what the plot is about. Then, in a composition of one or more paragraphs—
   a. Briefly summarize the plot of *My Fair Lady;*
   b. Show how it is related to the myth about Pygmalion and Galatea.

Miriam Stewart Cox

Miriam Stewart Cox was born in Logan, Utah, and she has spent most of her life in the West. She earned degrees from Utah State University and the University of Idaho. Cox was taught in a wide variety of situations—nursery school, kindergarten, high school, and college. Presently, she teaches English at California State University at Fullerton.

Cox has published books about the myths of Japan and Greece. She is involved in several professional organizations and contributes articles to several journals. In her spare time, she enjoys opera and social dancing.

If you say that your cousin Mac is a Hercules, would you expect him to shake your hand or punch you in the nose? Or if you say that a person has done a Herculean (her kyə lē′ ən) task, would you expect that person to feel complimented or insulted? You can find the answers in this ancient Greek myth.

Hercules

EDITH HAMILTON

THE GREATEST HERO of Greece was Hercules. He was a personage of quite another order from the great hero of Athens, Theseus.[1] He was what all Greece except Athens most admired. The Athenians were different from the other Greeks and their hero therefore was different. Theseus was, of course, bravest of the brave as all heroes are, but unlike other heroes he was as compassionate[2] as he was brave and a man of great intellect as well as great bodily strength. It was natural that the Athenians should have such a hero because they valued thought and ideas as no other part of the country did. In Theseus their ideal was embodied. But Hercules embodied what the rest of Greece most valued. His qualities were those the Greeks in general honored and admired. Except for unflinching courage, they were not those that distinguished Theseus.

Hercules was the strongest man on earth and he had the supreme self-confidence magnificent physical strength gives. He considered himself on an equality with the gods—and with some reason. They needed his help to conquer the giants. In the final victory of the Olympians over the brutish sons of Earth, Hercules's arrows played an important part. He treated the gods accordingly. Once when the priestess at Delphi gave no response to the question he asked, he seized the tripod she sat on and declared that he would carry it off and have an oracle of his own. Apollo, of course, would not put up with this, but Hercules was perfectly willing to fight him and Zeus had to intervene. The quarrel was easily settled, however. Hercules was quite good-natured about it. He did not want to quarrel with Apollo, he only wanted an answer from his oracle. If Apollo would give it, the matter was settled as far as he was concerned. Apollo on his side, facing this undaunted person, felt an admiration for his boldness and made his priestess deliver the response.

Throughout his life Hercules had this perfect confidence that no matter who was

---

1 **Theseus** (thē süs′).
2 **compassionate** (kəm pash′ ə nit): sympathetic.

against him he could never be defeated, and facts bore him out. Whenever he fought with anyone the issue was certain beforehand. He could be overcome only by a supernatural force. Hera used hers against him with terrible effect and in the end he was killed by magic, but nothing that lived in the air, sea, or on land ever defeated him.

Intelligence did not figure largely in anything he did and was often conspicuously absent. Once when he was too hot he pointed an arrow at the sun and threatened to shoot him. Another time when the boat he was in was tossed about by the waves he told the waters that he would punish them if they did not grow calm. His intellect was not strong. His emotions were. They were quickly aroused and apt to get out of control, as when he deserted the *Argo* and forgot all about his comrades and the Quest of the Golden Fleece in his despairing grief at losing his young armor-bearer, Hylas. This power of deep feeling in a man of his tremendous strength was oddly endearing, but it worked immense harm, too. He had sudden outbursts of furious anger which were always fatal to the often innocent objects. When the rage had passed and he had come to himself he would show a most disarming penitence[3] and agree humbly to any punishment it was proposed to inflict on him. Without his consent he could not have been punished by anyone—yet nobody ever endured so many punishments. He spent a large part of his life expiating[4] one unfortunate deed after another and never rebelling against the almost impossible demands made upon him. Sometimes he punished himself when others were inclined to exonerate[5] him.

It would have been ludicrous[6] to put him in command of a kingdom as Theseus was put; he had more than enough to do to command himself. He could never have thought out any new or great idea as the Athenian hero was held to have done. His thinking was limited to devising a way to kill a monster which was threatening to kill him. Nevertheless he had true greatness. Not because he had complete courage based upon overwhelming strength, which is merely a matter of course, but because, by his sorrow for wrongdoing and his willingness to do anything to expiate it, he showed greatness of soul. If only he had had some greatness of mind as well, at least enough to lead him along the ways of reason, he would have been the perfect hero.

He was born in Thebes and for a long time was held to be the son of Amphitryon,[7] a distinguished general. In those earlier years he was called Alcides,[8] or descendant of Alcaeus[9] who was Amphitryon's father. But in reality he was the son of Zeus. His mother, Alcmena,[10] bore two children, Hercules to Zeus and Iphicles[11] to Amphitryon. The difference in the boys' descent was clearly shown in the way each acted in face of a great danger which came to them before they were a year old. Hera, as always, was furiously jealous and she determined to kill Hercules.

One evening Alcmena gave both the children their bath and their fill of milk and laid them in their crib, caressing them and saying, "Sleep, my little ones, soul of my soul. Happy

---

3 **disarming penitence:** sincere regret for his sin.
4 **expiating** (ek′spē āt ing): atoning for; making up for.
5 **exonerate** (eg zon′ ə rāt′): pardon.

6 **ludicrous** (lü də krəs): ridiculous.
7 **Amphitryon** (am fit′rē on).
8 **Alcides** (al′sə dēz).
9 **Alcaeus** (al kē əs).
10 **Alcmena** (alk mē′nə).
11 **Iphicles** (if′ ə klēz).

be your slumber and happy your awakening." She rocked the cradle and in a moment the babies were asleep. But at darkest midnight when all was silent in the house two great snakes came crawling into the nursery. There was a light in the room and as the two reared up above the crib, with weaving heads and flickering tongues, the children woke. Iphicles screamed and tried to get out of bed, but Hercules sat up and grasped the deadly creatures by the throat. They turned and twisted and wound their coils around his body, but he held them fast. The mother heard Iphicles's screams and, calling to her husband, rushed to the nursery. There sat Hercules laughing, in each hand a long limp body. He gave them gleefully to Amphitryon. They were dead. All knew then that the child was destined to great things. Teiresias,[12] the blind prophet of Thebes, told Alcmena: "I swear that many a Greek woman as she cards the wool at eventide shall sing of this your son and you who bore him. He shall be the hero of all mankind."

Great care was taken with his education, but teaching him what he did not wish to learn was a dangerous business. He seems not to have liked music, which was a most important part of a Greek boy's training, or else he disliked his music master. He flew into a rage with him and brained him with his lute.[13] This was the first time he dealt a fatal blow without intending it. He did not mean to kill the poor musician; he just struck out on the impulse of the moment without thinking, hardly aware of his strength. He was sorry, very sorry, but that did not keep him from doing the same thing again and

again. The other subjects he was taught, fencing, wrestling and driving, he took to more kindly, and his teachers in these branches all survived. By the time he was eighteen he was full-grown and he killed, alone by himself, a great lion which lived in the woods of Cithaeron, the Thespian lion. Ever after he wore its skin as a cloak with the head forming a kind of hood over his own head.

His next exploit was to fight and conquer the Minyans, who had been exacting a burdensome tribute from the Thebans. The grateful citizens gave him as a reward the hand of the Princess Megara. He was devoted to her and to their children and yet this marriage brought upon him the greatest sorrow of his life as well as trials and dangers such as no one ever went through, before or after. When Megara had borne him three sons he went mad. Hera, who never forgot a wrong, sent the madness upon him. He killed his children and Megara, too, as she tried to protect the youngest. Then his sanity returned. He found himself in his bloodstained hall, the dead bodies of his sons and his wife beside him. He had no idea what had happened, how they had been killed. Only a moment since, as it seemed to him, they had all been talking together. As he stood there in utter bewilderment the terrified people who were watching him from a distance saw that the mad fit was over, and Amphitryon dared to approach him. There was no keeping the truth from Hercules. He had to know how this horror had come to pass and Amphitryon told him. Hercules heard him out; then he said, "And I myself am the murderer of my dearest."

"Yes," Amphitryon answered trembling. "But you were out of your mind."

---

12 **Teiresias** (tī rē′sē əs).
13 **lute** (lüt): ancient stringed instrument.

Hercules. Detail from a Greek vase painting.

Hercules paid no attention to the implied excuse.

"Shall I spare my own life then?" he said. "I will avenge upon myself these deaths."

But before he could rush out and kill himself, even as he started to do so, his desperate purpose was changed and his life was spared. This miracle—it was nothing less—of recalling Hercules, from frenzied feeling and violent action to sober reason and sorrowful acceptance, was not wrought by a god descending from the sky. It was a miracle caused by human friendship. His friend Theseus stood before him and stretched out his hands to clasp those bloodstained hands. Thus according to the common Greek idea he would himself become defiled and have a part in Hercules's guilt.

"Do not start back," he told Hercules. "Do not keep me from sharing all with you. Evil I share with you is not evil to me. And hear me. Men great of soul can bear the blows of heaven and not flinch."

Hercules said, "Do you know what I have done?"

"I know this," Theseus answered. "Your sorrows reach from earth to heaven."

"So I will die," said Hercules.

"No hero spoke those words," Theseus said.

"What can I do but die?" Hercules cried. "Live? A branded man, for all to say, 'Look. There is he who killed his wife and sons!' Everywhere my jailers, the sharp scorpions of the tongue!"

"Even so, suffer and be strong," Theseus answered. "You shall come to Athens with me, share my home and all things with me. And you will give to me and to the city a great return, the glory of having helped you."

A long silence followed. At last Hercules spoke, slow, heavy words. "So let it be," he said. "I will be strong and wait for death."

The two went to Athens, but Hercules did not stay there long. Theseus, the thinker, rejected the idea that a man could be guilty of murder when he had not known what he was doing and that those who helped such a one could be reckoned defiled. The Athenians agreed and welcomed the poor hero. But he himself could not understand such ideas. He could not think the thing out at all; he could only feel. He had killed his family. Therefore he was defiled and a defiler of others. He deserved that all should turn from him with loathing. At Delphi where he went to consult the oracle, the priestess looked at the matter just as he did. He needed to be purified, she told him, and only a terrible penance[14] could do that. She bade him go to his cousin Eurystheus, King of Mycenae[15] (of Tiryns in some stories) and submit to whatever he demanded of him. He went willingly, ready to do anything that could make him clean again. It is plain from the rest of the story that the priestess knew what Eurystheus was like and that he would beyond question purge[16] Hercules thoroughly.

Eurystheus was by no means stupid, but of a very ingenious turn of mind, and when the strongest man on earth came to him humbly prepared to be his slave, he devised a series of penances which from the point of view of difficulty and danger could not have been improved upon. It must be said, however, that he was helped and urged on by Hera. To the end of Hercules's life she never forgave him for being Zeus's son. The tasks Eurystheus gave him to do are called "the Labors of Hercules." There were twelve of them and each one was all but impossible.

The first was to kill the lion of Nemea, a

---

14 **penance** (pen′ əns): atonement; punishment.
15 **Eurystheus, King of Mycenae** (yūr is′thūs, mī sē′nē).
16 **purge** (pėrj): cleanse; purify.

beast no weapons could wound. That difficulty Hercules solved by choking the life out of him. Then he heaved the huge carcass up on his back and carried it into Mycenae. After that, Eurystheus, a cautious man, would not let him inside the city. He gave him his orders from afar.

The second labor was to go to Lerna and kill a creature with nine heads called the Hydra, which lived in a swamp there. This was exceedingly hard to do, because one of the heads was immortal and the others almost as bad, inasmuch as when Hercules chopped off one, two grew up instead. However, he was helped by his nephew Iolaus[17] who brought him a burning brand with which he seared[18] the neck as he cut each head off so that it could not sprout again. When all had been chopped off he disposed of the one that was immortal by burying it securely under a great rock.

The third labor was to bring back alive a stag with horns of gold, sacred to Artemis, which lived in the forests of Cerynitia. He could have killed it easily, but to take it alive was another matter and he hunted it a whole year before he succeeded.

The fourth labor was to capture a great boar which had its lair on Mount Erymanthus. He chased the beast from one place to another until it was exhausted; then he drove it into deep snow and trapped it.

The fifth labor was to clean the Augean stables in a single day. Augeas had thousands of cattle and their stalls had not been cleared out for years. Hercules diverted the courses of two rivers and made them flow through the stables in a great flood that washed out the filth in no time at all.

The sixth labor was to drive away the Stymphalian birds, which were a plague to the people of Stymphalus because of their enormous numbers. He was helped by Athena to drive them out of their coverts,[19] and as they flew up he shot them.

The seventh labor was to go to Crete and fetch from there the beautiful savage bull that Poseidon had given Minos. Hercules mastered him, put him in a boat, and brought him to Eurystheus.

The eighth labor was to get the man-eating mares of King Diomedes of Thrace. Hercules slew Diomedes first and then drove off the mares unopposed.

The ninth labor was to bring back the girdle[20] of Hippolyta,[21] the Queen of the Amazons. When Hercules arrived she met him kindly and told him she would give him the girdle, but Hera stirred up trouble. She made the Amazons think that Hercules was going to carry off their queen, and they charged down on his ship. Hercules, without a thought of how kind Hippolyta had been, without any thought at all, instantly killed her, taking it for granted that she was responsible for the attack. He was able to fight off the others and get away with the girdle.

The tenth labor was to bring back the cattle of Geryon, who was a monster with three bodies living on Erythia, a western island. On his way there Hercules reached the land at the end of the Mediterranean and he set up as a memorial of his journey two great rocks, called the Pillars of Hercules (now Gibraltar and Ceuta). Then he got the oxen and took them to Mycenae.

The eleventh labor was the most difficult

---

17 **Iolaus** (ī ō lā′ əs).
18 **seared** (sird): burned.

19 **coverts** (kuv′ərts): shelters.
20 **girdle** (gėr′dl): belt; sash.
21 **Hippolyta** (hi pol′ ə tə).

of all so far. It was to bring back the Golden Apples of the Hesperides, and he did not know where they were to be found. Atlas, who bore the vault of heaven upon his shoulders, was the father of the Hesperides, so Hercules went to him and asked him to get the apples for him. He offered to take upon himself the burden of the sky while Atlas was away. Atlas, seeing a chance of being relieved forever from his heavy task, gladly agreed. He came back with the apples, but he did not give them to Hercules. He told Hercules he could keep on holding up the sky, for Atlas himself would take the apples to Eurystheus. On this occasion Hercules had only his wits to trust to; he had to give all his strength to supporting that mighty load. He was successful, but because of Atlas's stupidity rather than his own cleverness. He agreed to Atlas's plan, but asked him to take the sky back for just a moment so that Hercules could put a pad on his shoulders to ease the pressure. Atlas did so, and Hercules picked up the apples and went off.

The twelfth labor was the worst of all. It took him down to the lower world, and it was then that he freed Theseus from the Chair of Forgetfulness. His task was to bring Cerberus, the three-headed dog, up from Hades. Pluto gave his permission provided Hercules used no weapons to overcome him. He could use his hands only. Even so, he forced the terrible monster to submit to him. He lifted him and carried him all the way up to the earth and on to Mycenae. Eurystheus very sensibly did not want to keep him and made Hercules carry him back. This was his last labor.

Hercules brings Cerebrus to King Eurytheus. Detail from a Greek vase painting.

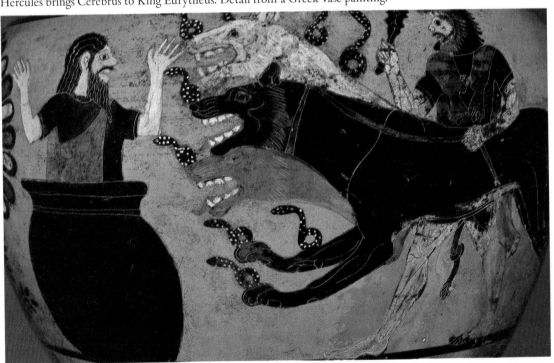

1. What incident in Hercules' childhood indicates that he is destined to do great things?

2. How is Hercules saved from killing himself in remorse over the death of his wife and children?

3. The qualities demonstrated by Hercules are those that the ancient Greeks honored and admired. What *are* those qualities that make Hercules a great hero?

4. The selection you have read here is only part of the story of Hercules. Do you think that he became a more thoughtful person upon the completion of his twelve labors, or do you think he probably committed additional rash actions? Why? To what extent, do you think, do people learn by their mistakes?

Composition

1. To atone for the murder of his wife and children, Hercules must perform twelve labors. In a paragraph, briefly describe each of those labors.

2. It is true that Hercules was a great hero. But was he or was he not *the perfect hero*? What, if any, flaws do you find in his character? In a short composition, give your answers to those questions. Be sure to give reasons for responding as you do. You can base your reasons on passages you find in this selection.

Edith Hamilton 1867–1963

After earning degrees at Bryn Mawr College, Edith Hamilton continued to study classics at the University of Munich. Because she was the first woman ever admitted to that university, officials decided that she should sit in a special chair on the lecturer's platform. Hamilton felt very conspicuous at first, but she appreciated having such a choice seat for the lectures.

Edith Hamilton was "a citizen of two worlds, the ancient and the modern—and equally at home with the best of both." Just before her ninetieth birthday, the people of Athens proclaimed her a citizen of that city. It was an appropriate reward for someone who had shown readers that the ancient world was as lively as our own.

Norse Myths

Like the people of ancient Greece, the Germanic clans and tribes of northern Europe worshiped gods and goddesses, too. But unlike Greece, where the skies are sunny most of the year, northern Europe often has bitter cold winters and gray, rainy summers. Life in northern Europe was a good deal harsher than that in the Mediterranean countries, and the myths of the north—Norse Myths—reflect that fact.

Like the North people themselves, Norse gods and goddesses were considered large, rugged, warlike individuals who prized loyalty and courage above all else. Norse heroes were usually fierce but honest warriors who slew all evil-doers and who died on the battlefield. They were then swooped up by the Valkyries (val′ ki rēz), fierce warrior maidens, and taken to Valhalla, a kind of paradise where the warriors feasted endlessly and engaged in mock battles. Following is a list of the principal Norse gods and goddesses.

Odin (also **Woden, Wotan**): the all-father and chief of the gods. (Our word *Wednesday* comes from his name.)

Frigga (also **Fricka**): Odin's wife (Our word *Friday* comes from her name.)

Freya (also **Freyja**): the daughter of Odin and Frigga; goddess of love and beauty; goddess of the spring

Baldur: son of Odin and Frigga; god of sunlight, spring, and joy

Loki: god of fire; god of mischief

Tiu (also **Tyr**): god of the sky. (Our word *Tuesday* comes from his name.)

Thor: god of war. (Our word *Thursday* comes from his name.)

Hel: goddess of the realm of the dead

Hoder (also **Hoth, Hothr**): blind son of Odin.

Frost Giants: spirits of the frost and of the icy mountains

The Norse gods and goddesses live in **Asgard,** a place built especially for them.

The Building of the Wall

PADRAIC COLUM

ALWAYS THERE HAD been war between the giants and the gods— between the giants who would have destroyed the world and the race of men, and the gods who would have protected the race of men and would have made the world more beautiful.

There are many stories to be told about the gods, but the first one that shall be told to you is the one about the building of their city.

The gods had made their way up to the top of a high mountain and there they decided to build a great city for themselves that the giants could never overthrow. The city they would call Asgard, which means "the place of gods." They would build it on a beautiful plain that was on the top of that high mountain. And they wanted to raise round their city the highest and strongest wall that had ever been built.

Now one day when they were beginning to build their halls and their palaces a strange being came to them. Odin,[1] the father of the gods, went and spoke to him. "What dost thou want on the mountain of the gods?" he asked the Stranger.

"I know what is in the mind of the gods," the Stranger said. "They would build a city here. I cannot build a city here. I cannot build palaces, but I can build great walls that can

never be overthrown. Let me build the wall round your city."

"How long will it take you to build a wall that will go round our city?" said the father of the gods.

"A year, O Odin," said the Stranger.

Now Odin knew that if a great wall could be built around it the gods would not have to spend all their time defending their city, Asgard, from the giants, and he knew that if Asgard were protected, he himself could go amongst men and teach them and help them. He thought that no payment the Stranger could ask would be too much for the building of that wall.

That day the Stranger came to the council of the gods, and he swore that in a year he would have the great wall built. Then Odin made oath that the gods would give him what he asked in payment if the wall was finished to the last stone in a year from that day.

The Stranger went away and came back on the morrow. It was the first day of summer when he started work. He brought no one to help him except a great horse.

Now the gods thought that this horse would do no more than drag blocks of stone for the building of the wall. But the horse did more than this. He set the stones in their places and mortared them together. And day and night and by light and dark the horse

---

1 **Odin** (ō′dən): chief of the Norse gods.

Detail from a Norwegian tapestry.

worked, and soon a great wall was rising round the palaces that the gods themselves were building.

"What reward will the Stranger ask for the work he is doing for us?" the gods asked one another.

Odin went to the Stranger. "We marvel at the work you and your horse are doing for us," he said. "No one can doubt that the great wall of Asgard will be built up by the first day of summer. What reward do you claim? We would have it ready for you."

The Stranger turned from the work he was doing, leaving the great horse to pile up the blocks of stone. "O father of the gods," he said, "O Odin, the reward I shall ask for my work is the Sun, and the Moon, and Freya,[2]

who watches over the flowers and grasses, for my wife."

Now when Odin heard this he was terribly angered, for the price the Stranger asked for his work was beyond all prices. He went amongst the other gods who were then building their shining palaces within the great wall and he told them what reward the Stranger had asked. The gods said, "Without the Sun and the Moon the world will wither away." And the goddesses said, "Without Freya all will be gloom in Asgard."

They would have let the wall remain unbuilt rather than let the Stranger have the reward he claimed for building it. But one who was in the company of the gods spoke. He was Loki,[3] a being who only half

2 **Freya** (frā′yə): Norse goddess of love and beauty.

3 **Loki** (lō′kē): Norse god of mischief.

belonged to the gods; his father was the Wind Giant. "Let the Stranger build the wall round Asgard," Loki said, "and I will find a way to make him give up the hard bargain he has made with the gods. Go to him and tell him that the wall must be finished by the first day of summer, and that if it is not finished to the last stone on that day the price he asks will not be given to him."

The gods went to the Stranger and they told him that if the last stone was not laid on the wall on the first day of the summer not Sol or Mani, the Sun and the Moon, nor Freya would be given him. And now they knew that the Stranger was one of the giants.

The giant and his great horse piled up the wall more quickly than before. At night, while the giant slept, the horse worked on and on, hauling up stones and laying them on the wall with his great forefeet. And day by day the wall around Asgard grew higher and higher.

But the gods had no joy in seeing that great wall rising higher and higher around their palaces. The giant and his horse would finish the work by the first day of summer, and then he would take the Sun and the Moon, Sol and Mani, and Freya away with him.

But Loki was not disturbed. He kept telling the gods that he would find a way to prevent him from finishing his work, and thus he would make the giant forfeit the terrible price he had led Odin to promise him.

It was three days to summertime. All the wall was finished except the gateway. Over the gateway a stone was still to be placed. And the giant, before he went to sleep, bade his horse haul up a great block of stone so that they might put it above the gateway in the morning, and so finish the work two full days before summer.

It happened to be a beautiful moonlit night. Svadilfare,[4] the giant's great horse, was hauling the largest stone he ever hauled when he saw a little mare come galloping towards him. The great horse had never seen so pretty a little mare and he looked at her with surprise.

"Svadilfare, slave," said the little mare to him and went frisking past.

Svadilfare put down the stone he was hauling and called to the little mare. She came back to him. "Why do you call me 'Svadilfare, slave'?" said the great horse.

"Because you have to work night and day for your master," said the little mare. "He keeps you working, working, working, and never lets you enjoy yourself. You dare not leave that stone down and come and play with me."

"Who told you I dare not do it?" said Svadilfare.

"I know you daren't do it," said the little mare, and she kicked up her heels and ran across the moonlit meadow.

Now the truth is that Svadilfare was tired of working day and night. When he saw the little mare go galloping off he became suddenly discontented. He left the stone he was hauling on the ground. He looked round and he saw the little mare looking back at him. He galloped after her.

He did not catch up on the little mare. She went on swiftly before him. On she went over the moonlit meadow, turning and looking back now and again at the great Svadilfare, who came heavily after her. Down the mountainside the mare went, and Svadilfare, who now rejoiced in his liberty

_____

4 **Svadilfare** (svä′dəl fär).

and in the freshness of the wind and in the smell of the flowers, still followed her. With the morning's light they came near a cave and the little mare went into it. They went through the cave. Then Svadilfare caught up on the little mare and the two went wandering together, the little mare telling Svadilfare stories of the Dwarfs and the Elves.

They came to a grove and they stayed together in it, the little mare playing so nicely with him that the great horse forgot all about time passing. And while they were in the grove the giant was going up and down, searching for his great horse.

He had come to the wall in the morning, expecting to put the stone over the gateway and so finish his work. But the stone that was to be lifted up was not near him. He called for Svadilfare, but his great horse did not come. He went to search for him, and he searched all down the mountainside and he searched as far across the earth as the realm of the giants. But he did not find Svadilfare.

The gods saw the first day of summer come and the gateway of the wall stand unfinished. They said to each other that if it were not finished by the evening they need not give Sol and Mani to the giant, nor the maiden Freya to be his wife. The hours of the summer day went past and the giant did not raise the stone over the gateway. In the evening he came before them.

"Your work is not finished," Odin said. "You forced us to a hard bargain and now we need not keep it with you. You shall not be given Sol and Mani nor the maiden Freya."

"Only the wall I have built is so strong I would tear it down," said the giant. He tried to throw down one of the palaces, but the gods laid hands on him and thrust him outside the wall he had built. "Go, and trouble Asgard no more," Odin commanded.

Then Loki returned to Asgard. He told the gods how he had transformed himself into a little mare and had led away Svadilfare, the giant's great horse. And the gods sat in their golden palaces and behind the great wall and rejoiced that their city was now secure, and that no enemy could ever enter it or overthrow it. But Odin, the father of the gods, as he sat upon his throne was sad in his heart, said that the gods had got their wall built by a trick; that oaths had been broken, and that a blow had been struck in injustice in Asgard.

Discussion

1. What is the trick that Loki plays on the Stranger and on Svadilfare?

2. Who is the Stranger? What is the reason for the hostility between the giants and the gods?

3. For what reasons does Odin want a wall built around Asgard?

4. Why is Odin unhappy about the way the Stranger has been tricked? But at the beginning, does or does not the Stranger intend to trick the gods?

5. With what in Greek mythology can Asgard be compared? With whom in Greek mythology can Odin be compared?

Vocabulary

Many English words have been built by putting ROOT WORDS together with one or more PREFIXES and SUFFIXES.

A root word is a group of letters whose spelling and meaning are both drawn from some other language, like Latin or Greek. An example of a root word is *construct*, which was drawn from Latin. In Latin, the root of this word means "to pile up; to make; or to build." Some roots can stand alone as words.

A prefix is a letter or group of letters placed before a word to change the word's meaning. An example of a prefix is *re-*, meaning "again, or back." When you add the prefix *re-* to the root word *construct*, you get *reconstruct*, meaning "to build again, or to build back."

Like a prefix, a suffix consists of one or more letters added to the end of a word to change the word's meaning. A suffix is always added to the end of a word. Prefixes and suffixes cannot stand alone as words but must be attached to root words. An example of a suffix is *-ed* which can change a present-tense verb to a past-tense one:

reconstruct ("to build again now") + *-ed* ("past") = reconstructed ("built again, in the past")

Sometimes the same suffix, *-ed*, can change a verb into an adjective. For example:

un- ("not") + protect ("shield") + *-ed* = unprotected ("not shielded")

A. Make three columns on a separate sheet of paper. Label the column at the left *Prefixes*. Label the second column in the middle *Root Words*. Label the column at the right *Suffixes*. Then separate the parts of the following words and write each part under its proper heading:

undefended   unfinished   discontented   repayment

B. If the answers you gave in Exercise A were as follows, you are ready to go forward: first column—*un-*, *un-*, *dis-*, and *re-*; second column—*defend*, *finish*, *content*, and *pay*; third column, *-ed*, *-ed*, *-ed*, and *-ment*. If your answers were different from these, reread the definitions and examples above before you continue. From the columns on the next page, take one prefix, one root word, and one suffix at a time. Add the three together to build as many English words as you can. Write your answers on your paper. There are at least fifteen words to be found in this group.

EXAMPLE: re- appoint -ment
ANSWER: reappointment

PREFIXES	ROOT WORDS	SUFFIXES
un–	define	-ed (or *-s*)
re–	charge	-es (or *-d*)
dis–	appoint	-ment

Padraic Colum 1881—1972

Padraic Colum was born and raised in Ireland. His father managed a workhouse for poor people who had nowhere else to go. As a boy, Colum especially enjoyed hearing the tales of the one-night visitors who were traveling artists, fiddlers, or singers. At home and at his grandmother's house in the next county, Colum absorbed the legends and lore of Ireland which he later wrote about.

When Colum married the critic Mary Gunning Maguire, his aunt in Philadelphia sent them two tickets to the United States as her wedding gift. They had already rented a house in Ireland, but a year later they came to America.

Living in New York, Colum spent some time each day translating a long Irish folk story into English. When the editor of the New York *Tribune* needed something for a children's page, Colum showed him the Irish tale. The story was published as a serial. Colum later wrote several collections of folktales for children.

Of all the gods, Baldur came closest to being perfect. All the world loved him. All the world? Everybody? Well, almost everybody!

Baldur, the Beautiful

OLIVIA E. COOLIDGE

"ARISE, GREAT PROPHETESS!" trumpeted a voice in the misty dark. Far over the barren plains rang the loud summons, and the damp, invisible rocks re-echoed, "Arise!"

Nothing stirred in the darkness, and no light showed, save that which gleamed on the spear of the rider and on the flanks of his cloud-grey horse. From the back grave mound before which he stood the muffled voice of the sleeper answered his cry. "Let me rest," it complained. "I have been snowed on, wetted with rain, and drenched with cold dew. I have long been dead. Why rouse me again to feeling?"

"Awake!" cried the rider once more, and he lifted his spear so that the light which shone from it fell on his blue mantle, his dress of grey, and his long, white beard. "I who call you am Odin, Allfather, and I come to learn tidings of Hel."

There was a little movement in the mist on the grave mound, and the voice answered again, nearer now. "I have been long in the kingdom of Hel, grim queen of the dead. What would you learn of that terrible goddess?

"Why does Hel haunt the dream of Bal- dur, the radiant one, the most glorious of the gods? Why should she come to him in whose pure presence nothing unclean or ugly has ever till now appeared? What power has Hel over Baldur that she should bring gloom to his brow and dismay to the whole race of gods, whose happiness depends on him?"

"Hel lays claim to bright Baldur," replied the toneless voice of the prophetess. "She bids her servants brew meat for the welcoming feast. She strews her benches with rings and her dais with gold, for she says that Baldur will surely descend to her kingdom, and that she will keep him with her until the Day of Doom."

"Hel must never have Baldur," cried Odin. "Baldur is the treasure of the world. He is beauty and unclouded joy, pure goodness that knows no evil."

"Let me go," moaned the misty shape. "I have answered your question, and to be here in my body is torment. I must return to the dead."

"Sleep again, dread prophetess," said Odin. "Feel no longer the rain and the snow. Hel strews her rings in vain for my son, for we shall know how to keep him from harm."

The mist was still again now, and the

grave mound was quiet. Odin set spurs to the great horse, who rose through the air swifter than wind, his mane and tail streaming behind him like grey clouds. The light from the god's spear grew small and vanished in the distance. Silence fell again on the dark land, broken only by the dripping of water from the rocks.

All the gods were saddened by the strange dreams of Baldur and the new look of gloom on his bright face. When, however, Odin brought to Asgard the words of the prophetess, their dismay deepened to black despair. The happiness of Asgard depended upon Baldur, the wisest and most lovely of gods. None could endure the thought of losing him, yet there seemed no way to avoid what the Fates had planned. For a long while there was silence.

"Hel shall not take my son!" cried Odin's wife, Frigga, at last. "I will not endure it! All things on earth shall give me an oath that they will do Baldur no harm."

Frigga hastened out from Asgard, and first she went to the stones and the rocks. All these made oath not to trip her son, Baldur, nor to cut him, nor bruise him, nor hit him. Then she went to the trees and the bushes, who swore not to pierce him, or beat him, or touch him to do any harm. Next she asked the plants which are poisonous, and then the birds and the beasts. Every animal from huge bear to tiny ant promised to spare Baldur, but still the queen of goddesses was not content. She took oaths from the rivers, lest they drown him, from the earth lest it bury him, from fire, snow, and ice, and everything harmful. All things did her bidding gladly for love of the radiant god.

When at last Frigga returned to Asgard, everything had sworn her oath. Even leaves slipped sideways in air, lest they fall upon Baldur. A god, idly flinging a twig near him, saw it check and drop harmless. Intrigued by the sight, he threw a little stone, which glanced aside as though hitting some invisible wall around Baldur. The other gods shouted with glee and tried sticks, stones, spears, and great clubs, none of which would touch him. Some bounced back, some curved in the air, some dropped suddenly right at his feet. Each thing that they threw behaved differently, but none of them harmed him. One whole summer morning the gods amused themselves watching the many things they flung at the smiling Baldur. Each god thought of something new for his turn, and the crowd laughed loudly at every trick.

Loki, the father of mischief, strolled away from the merry circle. He alone hated Baldur, since his evil nature found no delight in the god who was perfectly pure and good. For a long time he had cunningly hidden his thoughts, so that none suspected that he wished Baldur harm. Loki glanced up at Frigga, who sat smiling down on the sport from the window of her bower. "This is a fine game," he said earnestly, "but is it not dangerous? Surely amid so many things there must be some you have forgotten."

"I went through the whole earth," said Frigga, "and now in my mind I can think of only one thing I have missed. I am certain there are no more."

"But if you have missed one thing," cried Loki, "should not all the gods be warned?"

"Oh, that is only the mistletoe," replied Frigga smiling. "It is such a little shrub that I do not see there is anything it can do."

"I think Baldur must be safe," said Loki walking off with a careless air. "You have indeed relieved my heart."

Loki went out into the forest to search for the mistletoe. It is such a small bush that it was hard for him to find a piece large enough to make a dart. He did so, however, at last, and he sharpened it well. With this in his hand he came back to the courtyard, where the fun was dying down somewhat, though there was still shouting and laughter whenever a new weapon was tried.

Hoder, the brother of Baldur, stood sadly aside from the rest, for he was blind, and all had neglected him, absorbed in their new game. Loki took him by the elbow. "Come, join in the sport," he said.

"How can I?" asked Hoder sadly.

"Come with me and let me guide you." He led Hoder to the circle, planting him straight in front of the smiling Baldur. He put the mistletoe dart in Hoder's hand. "Now strike," he said, "and show them your strength." Hoder, pleased to have entered the game, lunged forward with all his might.

There was a loud cry, and then a terrible silence. The blind god stood puzzled, turning his head from side to side, as though listening for laughter and applause. "Baldur, the beautiful, is dead!" cried someone behind him in a high voice. Still he could not comprehend it, but merely repeated in a dull, questioning tone: "Baldur the beautiful . . .?"

They shouldered him aside and bent over Baldur. The blind god clutched at them insistently, but they pushed him away. He heard them walking off slowly, as though they were carrying something. They were gone, leaving him alone in his darkness with no one to answer his call.

"We must bury Baldur gloriously," said Odin, "and send him down in fitting splendor to the gloomy kingdom of Hel. Yet while we mourn him, we will not despair. I have given my own untiring horse to Hermod, my messenger, and he has gone down through the mist to beg Hel for Baldur's life."

The gods sent Baldur to sea in a blazing pyre on the deck of his Viking ship. He had weapons and bright garments to take with him, and Odin gave him a ring, his greatest treasure, from which eight new rings dropped on each ninth night. All the gods and the Valkyries[1] and even the frost giants watched the vessel sail with its flaming burden straight out to the setting sun. But while they sorrowed for Baldur, Hermod was riding Odin's wind-swift horse down through the darkness nine nights long, until the green earth above him seemed a vague and distant dream. At last in a gleam of light he saw the deep, black river which bounded Hel's kingdom, and over it a bridge roofed with shining gold.

"Who rides my bridge?" cried the maiden who sat guarding it. "Five troops of dead who passed over yesterday did not shake it as does the tread of this one man."

"Has Baldur passed this way?" called Hermod.

"Baldur, the beautiful, rode downward and northward, where lies the palace of Hel."

Hermod set spurs to Sleipnir, and the tireless horse rushed on over the grey rocks and the echoing valleys where nothing grew. They leaped the great wall around Hel's palace, and Hermod alighting, strode through her yawning doors.

Vast and grey was the palace of Hel, and the flames of her fire burned chilly blue. The goddess sat in a chair of bone. Her pale face was ghastly in the strange light, and her eyes stared like the eyes of the dead. Down the long table beside her sat shadowy hosts of men, some clothed in faint scarlet and misty gold, some in dim rags, all pale. Here the

---

1 **Valkyries** (val′kə rēs): warrior maidens who took slain warriors to Valhalla, the eternal home of heroes.

table they sat at was Famine, and the beds that they slept in were Care.

By the dreadful goddess sat Baldur, his golden hair faint and dull, yet still he turned to the messenger with the ghost of his lovely smile. He thanked him in tones like those of his own voice far away.

"Great goddess," cried Hermod loudly in the full voice of the living, "in pity give us back Baldur, without whom the whole world is forlorn."

Hel neither spoke nor moved her set eyes, but she turned her head around on him in a pitiless glare.

"Give us back Baldur," pleaded Hermod. "Never before has a living god or hero dared to make this ride."

His voice echoed through the great hall and died away into silence. All the ranks of grey dead sat staring at him, and Hel answered never a word.

"In the name of Allfather Odin, who sent you here," cried Hermod again, "answer me and grant me Baldur, the darling of the earth."

"If all the world so loves Baldur," said Hel in a voice hoarse from long disuse, "then let all the earth weep. If all things mourn for Baldur, he may go free; but if one refuses, he shall remain."

The shade of Baldur rose from his place and accompanied Hermod to the door. "Give my greeting to Asgard," said he in his far-off, gentle voice. "It is a long way thence, and Hel will keep me, but when the Day of Doom and Destruction has passed over the earth, I shall arise to behold a new and more beautiful world."

"We shall deliver you," cried Hermod. "Be very sure that everything will weep."

"Take his ring to my father, Odin," said the shade, "in memory of me." He put the ring into Hermod's hand, where it glowed as bright and golden as it had done in Odin's hall. "Farewell, and remember Baldur."

All the earth wept for Baldur in running stream of tears. The trees and plants dripped gently, flowers folded, the air was misty, and the clouds dropped rain. All the birds fell silent, save the mourning dove and the melancholy nightingale. As the messengers of Odin went from place to place, the very stones oozed moisture, as they do in the spring thaw. At last, however, the gods came to a cave in the hills, in the mouth of which sat Loki, disguised as an aged hag. "Weep for Baldur!" cried they. "Only the tears of the whole world may unloose him from the bonds of Hel."

The hag looked up. "Why should I weep for Baldur?" she croaked. "What did he do for me?"

"Baldur, the beautiful, is the source of the whole world's joy. Weep for him, lest he vanish forever and leave sorrow and pain on earth."

"When did I ever rejoice?" cried Loki in the voice of the aged hag. "Let Hel keep what she has. Why should I care?" With a screech he sprang up and fled into the darkness of the cave, nor would he come forth again, no matter how the messengers implored.

Thus Hel kept her hold on Baldur, even as he had foreseen. With him pure goodness and joy vanished from earth. What remained was mixed with evil and haunted by care. Nevertheless, it was said that after the Day of Doom a new world would come. Then Baldur would arise from the dead and sit in the meadows with Hoder, no longer blind. The sons of Thor and Odin would dwell on the plains where Asgard had risen before, and a new, fair race would people the earth in the light of a brighter sun.

Discussion

1. What steps does Frigga take to prevent Baldur from dying and going to the underworld?
2. What games do the gods play when they know that Baldur cannot be harmed?
3. Who is it that does not love Baldur? Why? How does he trick Frigga into revealing the one way in which Baldur can be harmed?
4. How is Baldur killed?
5. At one point Hel says, "If all things mourn for Baldur, he may go free; but if one refuses, he shall remain." And then Hermod cries, "We shall deliver you. Be very sure that everything will weep." In spite of these statements, the reader knows that Baldur will never be released. Why?

Vocabulary

Context clues are hints given about the general meaning of an unfamiliar word by surrounding words. Among the many different types of context clues are those in which an author tells you directly what an unfamiliar word means. This is called the DIRECT-EXPLANATION CONTEXT CLUE. For example:

Hel was the grim queen of the dead.
Hel, the grim queen of the dead, wanted Baldur.
Hel, who was the grim queen of the dead, wanted Baldur.

Each sentence above tells you directly and specifically who Hel is. However, each one tells you in a different way. Which sentence uses commas and words which are synonyms for *Hel* to explain the name? Which sentence uses the words *who was* plus synonyms for *Hel* to identify her? Which sentence tells you who she is by using a direct definition only?

Direct-explanation context clues are useful for many unfamiliar words, but they are especially helpful when you want to learn about the characters in a story.

Copy the sentences below on a separate sheet of paper. In each sentence, circle the direct-explanation context clue (or clues) that can help identify the character whose name is *italicized.*

1. *Baldur* is the treasure of the world. He is beauty and unclouded joy, pure goodness that knows no evil.
2. "Hel shall not take my son!" cried Odin's wife, *Frigga*, at last.
3. *Loki*, the father of mischief, strolled away from the merry circle.
4. *Hoder*, the brother of Baldur, stood sadly aside from the rest.

Every ethnic-cultural group has its myths. Even the original inhabitants of what we know today as North America had their myths. Though less well known than the Classical or the Norse myths, the myths of the early Native Americans accurately reflect their beliefs and their ways of living. The story of "The Creation" is as old as the human race. But just as there are many nationalities and races of human beings, so there are many accounts of the beginning of the world. Here is the story of "The Creation" as told by people of the Cheyenne tribes.

The Cheyenne Account of How the World Was Made

as told by MARY LITTLE BEAR INKANISH

IN THE BEGINNING there was nothing, and Maheo,[1] the All Spirit, lived in the void.[2] He looked around him, but there was nothing to see. He listened, but there was nothing to hear. There was only Maheo, alone in nothingness.

Because of the greatness of his Power, Maheo was not lonesome. His being was a Universe. But as he moved through the endless time of nothingness, it seemed to Maheo that his Power should be put to use. What good is Power, Maheo asked himself, if it is not used to make a world and people to live in it?

With his Power, Maheo created a great water, like a lake, but salty. Out of this salty water, Maheo knew, he could bring all life that ever was to be. The lake itself was life, if Maheo so commanded it. In the darkness of nothingness, Maheo could feel the coolness of the water and taste on his lips the tang of the salt.

---

1 **Maheo** (mə hā′ō).
2 **void**: empty nothingness.

"There should be water beings," Maheo told his Power. And so it was. First the fish, swimming in the deep water, and then the mussels and snails and crawfish, lying on the sand and mud Maheo had formed so his lake should have a bottom.

Let us also create something that lives on the water, Maheo thought to his Power.

And so it was. For now there were snow geese and mallards and teal and coots and terns and loons living and swimming about on the water's surface. Maheo could hear the splashing of their feet and the flapping of their wings in the darkness.

I should like to see the things that have been created, Maheo decided.

And, again, so it was. Light began to grow and spread, first white and bleached in the east, then golden and strong till it filled the middle of the sky and extended all around the horizon. Maheo watched the light, and he saw the birds and fishes, and the shellfish lying on the bottom of the lake as the light showed them to him.

How beautiful it all is, Maheo thought in his heart.

Then the snow goose paddled over to where she thought Maheo was, in the space above the lake. "I do not see You, but I know that You exist," the goose began. "I do not know where You are, but I know You must be everywhere. Listen to me, Maheo. This is good water that You have made, on which we live. But birds are not like fish. Sometimes we get tired swimming. Sometimes we would like to get out of the water."

"Then fly," said Maheo, and he waved his arms, and all the water birds flew, skittering

along the surface of the lake until they had speed enough to rise in the air. The skies were darkened with them.

"How beautiful their wings are in the light," Maheo said to his Power, as the birds wheeled and turned, and became living patterns against the sky.

The loon was the first to drop back to the surface of the lake. "Maheo," he said, looking around, for he knew that Maheo was all about him, "You have made us sky and light to fly in, and You have made us water to swim in. It sounds ungrateful to want something else, yet still we do. When we are tired of swimming and tired of flying, we should like a dry solid place where we could walk and rest. Give us a place to build our nests, please, Maheo."

"So be it," answered Maheo, "but to make such a place I must have your help, all of you. By myself, I have made four things: the water, the light, the sky air, and the peoples of the water. Now I must have help if I am to create more, for my Power will only let me make four things by myself."

"Tell us how we can help You," said all the water peoples. "We are ready to do what You say."

Maheo stretched out his hand and beckoned. "Let the biggest and the swiftest try to find land first," he said, and the snow goose came to him.

"I am ready to try," the snow goose said, and she drove herself along the water until the white wake behind her grew and grew to a sharp white point that drove her up into the air as the feathers drive an arrow. She flew high into the sky, until she was only a dark spot against the clearness of the light. Then the goose turned, and down she plunged, faster than any arrow, and dived into the water. She pierced the surface with her beak as if it were the point of a spear.

The snow goose was gone a long time. Maheo counted to four four hundred times before she rose to the surface of the water and lay there floating, her beak half open as she gasped for air.

"What have you brought us?" Maheo asked her, and the snow goose sighed sadly, and answered, "Nothing. I brought nothing back."

Then the loon tried, and after him, the mallard. Each in turn rose until he was a speck against the light, and turned and dived with the speed of a flashing arrow into the water. And each in turn rose wearily, and wearily answered, "Nothing," when Maheo asked him what he had brought.

At last there came the little coot, paddling across the surface of the water very quietly, dipping his head sometimes to catch a tiny fish, and shaking the water beads from his scalp lock whenever he rose.

"Maheo," the little coot said softly, "when I put my head beneath the water, it seems to me that I see something there, far below. Perhaps I can swim down to it—I don't know. I can't fly or dive like my sister and brothers. All I can do is swim, but I will swim down the best I know how, and go as deep as I can. May I try, please, Maheo?"

"Little brother," said Maheo, "no man can do more than his best, and I have asked for the help of all the water peoples. Certainly you shall try. Perhaps swimming will be better than diving, after all. Try, little brother, and see what you can do."

"Hah-ho!" the little coot said. "Thank you, Maheo," and he put his head under the water and swam down and down and down and down, until he was out of sight.

The coot was gone a long, long, long time.

Then Maheo and the other birds could see a little dark spot beneath the water's surface, slowly rising toward them. It seemed as if they would never see the coot himself, but at last the spot began to have a shape. Still it rose and rose, and at last Maheo and the water peoples could surely see who it was. The little coot was swimming up from the bottom of the salty lake.

When the coot reached the surface, he stretched his closed beak upward into the light, but he did not open it.

"Give me what you have brought," Maheo said, and the coot let his beak fall open, so a little ball of mud could fall from his tongue into Maheo's hand, for when Maheo wanted to, he could become like a man.

"Go, little brother," Maheo said. "Thank you, and may what you have brought always protect you."

And so it was and so it is, for the coot's flesh still tastes of mud, and neither man nor animal will eat a coot unless there is nothing else to eat.

Maheo rolled the ball of mud between the palms of his hands, and it began to grow larger, until there was almost too much mud for Maheo to hold. He looked around for a place to put the mud, but there was nothing but water or air anywhere around him.

"Come and help me again, water peoples," Maheo called. "I must put this mud somewhere. One of you must let me place it on his back."

All the fish and all the other water creatures came swimming to Maheo, and he tried

to find the right one to carry the mud. The mussels and snails and crawfish were too small, although they all had solid backs, and they lived too deep in the water for the mud to rest on them. The fish were too narrow, and their back fins stuck up through the mud and cut it to pieces. Finally only one water person was left.

"Grandmother Turtle," Maheo asked, "do you think that you can help me?"

"I'm very old and very slow, but I will try," the turtle answered. She swam over to Maheo, and he piled the mud on her rounded back, until he had made a hill. Under Maheo's hands the hill grew and spread and flattened out, until the Grandmother Turtle was hidden from sight.

"So be it," Maheo said once again. "Let the earth be known as our Grandmother, and let the Grandmother who carries the earth be the only being who is at home beneath the water, or within the earth, or above the ground; the only one who can go anywhere by swimming or by walking as she chooses."

And so it was, and so it is. Grandmother Turtle and all her descendants must walk very slowly, for they carry the whole weight of the whole world and all its peoples on their backs.

Now there was earth as well as water, but the earth was barren. And Maheo said to his Power, "Our Grandmother Earth is like a woman; she should be fruitful. Let her begin to bear life. Help me, my Power."

When Maheo said that, trees and grass sprang up to become the Grandmother's hair. The flowers became her bright ornaments, and the fruits and the seeds were the gifts that the earth offered back to Maheo. The birds came to rest on her hands when they were tired, and the fish came close to her sides. Maheo looked at the Earth Woman and he thought she was very beautiful; the most beautiful thing he had made so far.

She should not be alone, Maheo thought. Let me give her something of myself, so she will know that I am near her and that I love her.

Maheo reached into his right side, and pulled out a rib bone. He breathed on the bone, and laid it softly on the bosom of the Earth Woman. The bone moved and stirred, stood upright and walked. The first man had come to be.

"He is alone with the Grandmother Earth as I once was alone with the void," said Maheo. "It is not good for anyone to be alone." So Maheo fashioned a human woman from his left rib, and set her with the man. Then there were two persons on the Grandmother Earth, her children and Maheo's. They were happy together, and Maheo was happy as he watched them.

After a year, in the springtime, the first child was born. As the years passed, there were other children. They went their ways, and founded many tribes.

From time to time, after that, Maheo realized that his people walking on the earth had certain needs. At those times, Maheo, with the help of his Power, created animals to feed and care for the people. He gave them deer for clothing and food, porcupines to make their ornaments, the swift antelopes on the open plains, and the prairie dogs that burrowed in the earth.

At last Maheo thought to his Power, Why, one animal can take the place of all the others put together, and then he made the buffalo.

Maheo is still with us. He is everywhere, watching all his people, and all the creation he has made. Maheo is all good and all life; he is the creator, the guardian, and the teacher. We are all here because of Maheo.

1. When Maheo decided his Power should be put to use, what was his first creation? What life forms did the first creation accommodate? What were Maheo's later creations?

2. Which creature was successful in bringing back the mud from which the earth was formed? What is the significance of Maheo's saying ". . . and may what you have brought always protect you"?

3. In what ways was Grandmother Turtle the only appropriate creature to carry the mud which became earth?

4. What passages prove the faith earthly creatures had in Maheo?

5. The knowledge that this is a Native American myth gives the next-to-last paragraph added importance. How so?

Mary Little Bear Inkanish 1875—1963

Mary Little Bear Inkanish was born in a Cheyenne tipi in the Indian Territory which is now Oklahoma. Her ancestry was mixed, and she was named Vee-hay-kay, "White Girl." She attended an Indian agency school where the principal called her Mary. She took part of the name of her mother, Little Bear Woman. In her twenties, she married a Caddo man, Jim Inkanish, who had been a student at the school. Mary Little Bear Inkanish became renowned as a craftswoman who kept alive the arts and lore of her tribe.

The Seven Stars

(CHEYENNE)

JOHN STANDS IN TIMBER *and* MARGOT LIBERTY

ONE TIME LONG AGO a man and wife and their only child, a beautiful girl, lived in a big village in a valley. When the girl was old enough, her mother began teaching her how to use porcupine quills, sewing them onto deerskin clothing and blankets in lovely designs. The girl became good at this. Her work was among the finest done by all the people.

One day she began to work on an outfit of buckskin clothing for a man, decorating it with her best designs in dyed quills. It took her a month to finish it. When she was done she started on another, and that took a month also. And then she kept on until she had finished seven outfits in the same way. When the work was done she told her mother and father, "There are seven young men living a long journey from here. They are brothers. Since I have no brothers or sisters of my own I am going out to find them and take them for my brothers and live with them, and someday they will be known to all the people on earth."

They did not try to stop her. The girl's mother said, "I will go with you as far as the trail that leads to the lodge of the seven young men." The next morning she helped her daughter make two bags to pack the clothing in. They put three of the outfits in each of these and packed them on two dogs. The last and smallest outfit the girl carried herself.

They traveled until they came to the trail. Here the girl's mother stopped. She watched her daughter until she was out of sight and then turned and headed home. The girl kept going with the two dogs until she came to a wide river with a large tepee on its bank. As she approached, a little boy came running out, saying, "I am the youngest of the seven brothers. The rest are hunting and will be back by sundown."

The girl said, "I came to find you all. I am going to take you for my brothers." They led the dogs to the tepee and unloaded the packs. Then the girl spoke to the dogs and turned them loose, and they ran off, going home. Next she unwrapped the smallest buckskin outfit and gave it to the little boy, saying, "My brother, this is a gift from me." Right away he put on his new moccasins and leggings and shirt and a little blanket, and he was happy because of their beautiful designs.

Inside the tepee the little boy pointed to each of the beds in turn, telling to which of the brothers it belonged; and on each she put one of the buckskin outfits. Then she prepared a meal and waited until they should appear. At sundown they approached the camp, and the youngest ran out to meet them, throwing himself on the ground and kicking his legs in the air so they would be sure to see his new moccasins and leggings.

"Where did you get those things?" they asked.

"You said not to let anyone near the tepee," he said, "but a girl came, and before I could tell her to stay out she said she had brought us all some new clothes and she is taking us for brothers. She is a beautiful girl."

They were pleased with the news and went on in. In those days brothers and sisters did not talk to one another, but since the smallest had already spoken to the girl he kept on and acted as interpreter, telling the girl what the others wanted and giving them her answers. And they lived together, and were happy to have someone prepare their meals.

One morning, when the older brothers were again hunting, a yellow buffalo calf came running up to the tepee and stopped a little distance from it, looking all around.

"Buffalo Calf," said the little boy, "what do you want?"

"I am sent by the buffaloes," the calf answered. "They want your sister, and I am to take her back with me."

"No, you cannot have her," said the boy. "The older brothers are hunting and you must wait until they come back." So the calf ran away, kicking and jumping until he was out of sight. In a little while a two-year-old heifer came running up the same way and stopped outside the tepee.

"Two-Year-Old Heifer," said the little boy, "what do you want?"

"I am sent by the buffaloes," she answered. "They want your sister and I will take her back with me. If you don't let her go the Old Buffalo is coming."

"No," said the little boy. "Go back and tell them they cannot have her." So she ran away like the calf, kicking and jumping until she was out of sight. And in a little while a third buffalo came—a big cow.

"Buffalo Cow," said the little boy, "what do you want? Why are you bothering us?"

"I am sent by the buffaloes," said the cow. "They want your sister. If you don't let her go the herd is coming here after her, and you will all be killed."

"Well, you cannot have her," said the little boy. "Go back and tell them." So the buffalo cow ran away, kicking and jumping like the others. Soon the brothers returned from hunting, and when the little boy told them what had happened they were afraid. Before long they heard a noise like the earth shaking, and saw a great herd of buffalo coming toward the tepee with a big bull in the lead.

"Hurry!" cried one of the six brothers to the youngest. "You have power that can keep anything from touching you. Use it and save us!" So the little boy ran and got his bow and arrows. He aimed into the top of a tree nearby, and when the arrow hit it the tree began to grow until the top was almost out of sight. The brothers lifted the girl into the lowest branches and climbed after her, and in a minute the ground below them was covered with buffalo. All they could hear was snorting and bawling. Then the lead bull came forward and started to circle the tree trunk down below. He was angry, shaking his head and pawing the ground. Soon he charged at the tree and stopped just short of it. He did this three times, but the fourth time he struck it and cut a big piece out of it with his horn.

Four times he did the same thing, hitting the tree on the fourth charge, and cutting out a bigger piece of the trunk each time. The fourth time it swayed and then began to topple and fall.

"Hurry!" cried the brothers to the little boy. "Save us!" Quickly he aimed and shot another arrow far into the sky. It vanished from sight and they felt the tree growing upwards after it. At last it hit the sky. They all climbed out of the branches and stayed there and turned into stars. They can still be seen at night as the Seven Stars, called by the white people the Big Dipper.

When they were all through telling that story, we boys would go out with them and look up at those stars, and we believed it. It was a story supposed to make us go to sleep, but I would lie awake thinking about those seven brothers for quite awhile, and what happened to them. I never did hear what became of the girl.

Discussion

1. According to this myth, who are the seven stars?

2. What power did the youngest brother have? How did he save the girl and his brothers from the angry buffalo?

3. What, if any, significance do you find in the last sentence?

John Stands In Timber 1884–1967

John Stands in Timber was a Cheyenne whose grandfather died at the battle with General Custer. He attended a mission school where the priests tried to rename him Forrest, but he kept his original name.

A native American song says, "My friends, only the stones stay on earth forever. Use your best ability." With that thought, Stands in Timber resolved to become a collector and keeper of his tribe's oral literature. He could describe battles and whole histories without notes. He sought out other storytellers to add their tales to his own. Working with Margot Liberty, he put his memories into a book, but he died before it was actually printed. The book, *Cheyenne Memories, A Folk History,* contains not only all the lore and tribal history he remembered, but also his own personal memories—for example, the six weeks he spent acting for the original movie, "The Oregon Trail."

Margot Pringle Liberty

Born in the early 1920s, Margot Pringle Liberty is the daughter of a well-known historical author. She was teaching for the Bureau of Indian Affairs when she met John Stands in Timber. He was eager to write his book, so they began sorting his woodshed full of notes and clippings. He would talk for as much as eight hours, pausing only while Liberty changed the tape reel. Then Liberty typed, edited, and annotated the text. After the book was finished in 1967, Liberty earned a degree in anthropology. Now she teaches at the University of Pittsburgh.

Fables

As you have seen, myths are stories that grew out of the efforts of ancient people to explain their world. Myths involve supernatural beings and events and are often concerned with the mysteries of nature.

FABLES are close cousins to myths. Though they don't involve supernatural beings, most involve animals that talk. Instead of describing supernatural events, fables deal with everyday situations that most of us face at some time or other. Instead of explaining the workings of nature, fables teach useful lessons about life and how to live it.

Probably the most famous teller of fables was a Greek slave named Aesop (ē'sop), who is supposed to have lived in ancient Athens from 620 B.C. to 560 B.C. Though some authorities doubt that there was such a person, other scholars believe that Aesop was a legendary figure—a man who probably did live in ancient Greece at one time, although no one can prove it.

Fables of Aesop

The Lion and the Mouse

ONCE WHEN A LION was asleep a little mouse began running up and down upon him; this soon wakened the lion, who placed his huge paw upon him, and opened his big jaws to swallow him. "Pardon, O King," cried the little mouse; "forgive me this time, I shall never forget it: who knows but what I may be able to do you a turn some of these days?" The lion was so tickled at the idea of the mouse being able to help him, that he lifted up his paw and let him go. Some time after the lion was caught in a trap, and the hunters, who desired to carry him alive to the king, tied him to a tree while they went in search of a wagon to carry him on. Just then the little mouse happened to pass by, and seeing the sad plight[1] in which the lion was, went up to him and soon gnawed away the ropes that bound the king of the beasts. "Was I not right?" said the little mouse.

"Little friends may prove great friends."

---
1 plight: situation; condition.

520

The Milkmaid and Her Pail

PATTY, THE MILKMAID, was going to market carrying her milk in a pail on her head. As she went along she began calculating what she would do with the money she would get for the milk. "I'll buy some fowls from Farmer Brown," said she, "and they will lay eggs each morning, which I will sell to the parson's wife. With the money that I get from the sale of these eggs I'll buy myself a new dimity frock and a chip hat; and when I go to market, won't all the young men come up and speak to me! Polly Shaw will be that jealous; but I don't care. I shall just look at her and toss my head like this." As she spoke, she tossed her head back, the pail fell off it and all the milk was spilt. So she had to go home and tell her mother what had occurred.

"Ah, my child," said her mother,

"Do not count your chickens before they are hatched."

The Jay and the Peacocks

A JAY VENTURING into a yard where peacocks used to walk, found there a number of feathers which had fallen from the peacocks when they were molting.[1] He tied them all to his tail and strutted down toward the peacocks. When he came near them they soon discovered the cheat, and striding up to him pecked at him and plucked away his borrowed plumes. So the jay could do no better than go back to the other jays, who had watched his behavior from a distance; but they were equally annoyed with him, and told him:

"It is not only fine feathers that make fine birds."

---

1 **molting**: shedding their feathers.

The Fox and the Crow

A FOX ONCE SAW A CROW fly off with a piece of cheese in its beak and settle on a branch of a tree. "That's for me, as I am a fox," said Master Reynard, and he walked up to the foot of the tree. "Good day, Mistress Crow," he cried. "How well you are looking today: how glossy your feathers; how bright your eye. I feel sure your voice must surpass that of other birds, just as your figure does; let me hear but one song from you that I may greet you as the queen of birds." The crow lifted up her head and began to caw her best, but the moment she opened her mouth the piece of cheese fell to the ground, only to be snapped up by Master Fox. "That will do," said he. "That was all I wanted. In exchange for your cheese I will give you a piece of advice for the future—

"Do not trust flatterers."

The Hare and the Tortoise

A HARE JEERED at a tortoise for the slowness of his pace. But he laughed and said, that he would run against her and beat her any day she should name. "Come on," said the hare, "you shall soon see what my feet are made of." So it was agreed that they should start at once. The tortoise went off jogging along, without a moment's stopping, at his usual steady pace. The hare, treating the whole matter very lightly, said she would first take a little nap, and that she should soon overtake the tortoise. Meanwhile the tortoise plodded on, and the hare oversleeping herself, arrived at the goal, only to see that the tortoise had got in before her.

Slow and steady wins the race.

1. The italicized sentence at the end of each fable is its truth or moral or lesson. In your own words, explain the lesson taught by each of the five fables.

2. On page 520, you read that fables "teach useful lessons about life and how to live it." In what way is the lesson taught by each of these five fables useful today?

3. You know that fables (a) usually involve animals that talk, (b) deal with everyday situations, and (c) point up truths about life. What other characteristics, if any, do you find that make fables enjoyable to read?

Composition

1. The moral of "The Milkmaid and Her Pail," you will recall, is this: "Do not count your chickens before they are hatched." Suppose, however, that instead of a milkmaid as the central character, the fable involved a cowboy driving a herd of cattle to market. Rewrite the fable in such a way that the same moral applies. Give your fable an appropriate title. Be prepared to share your fable with the class.

2. Every fable, as you know, has a moral. Choose a familiar general truth—"Honesty is the best policy," for example, or "A rolling stone gathers no moss," or any other that appeals to you. (If you wish, choose a moral from the fables you've read here.) Then write a fable of your own—a fable that illustrates the moral you've chosen. Be sure to state the moral at the end of your fable. Give your fable an appropriate title. Finally, be prepared to share your fable with the class.

Vocabulary

Context clues are words or ideas that accompany an unfamiliar word and that help the reader understand the general meaning of that word. One type of context clue which is found in Aesop's fables is the EXAMPLE CONTEXT CLUE. When an author uses a word that he or she thinks might be unfamiliar to the reader, the author often places an example context clue nearby to make its meaning clearer. Study this example context clue:

> The man's job was to *enhance* the crown. He worked slowly and carefully to set diamonds and rubies into its golden border.

If you saw the word *enhance* in the first sentence alone, you would not be able to figure out what the word meant. The author has added the second sentence as an example of what people do when they *enhance.*

The author may put this example either before or after the unfamiliar word.

Use example context clues to find the general meaning of each *italicized* word below. Write your answers on a separate sheet of paper. After each general definition, write the example or examples that helped you find it.

1. The milkmaid began *calculating* what she would do with the money she would get for the milk. "I'll buy some fowls from Farmer Brown," she said, "and they will lay eggs each morning, which I will sell to the parson's wife."

2. A hare *jeered* at a tortoise for the slowness of his pace. "At that speed," she laughed scornfully, "you'll never reach your goal!"

3. The hunters tied up the lion and went to find a wagon. Just then the mouse came along and saw the lion's *plight*.

4. The jay found a number of feathers which had fallen from the peacocks when they were *molting*.

5. The fox said to the crow: "I feel sure your voice must *surpass* that of other birds. Your song must be far more beautiful than theirs. Let me hear one of your songs so that I may hail you as queen of the birds."

Aesop 620?—564 B.C.

Aesop was a Greek storyteller of animal fables, and a slave. His owner granted him freedom as a reward for his wit, learning, and storytelling. Aesop became interested in public affairs and traveled widely. He told fables everywhere he went. Often his stories thinly disguised his opinions of the politics of a city.

King Croesus welcomed the famous storyteller into his court and made him an ambassador. The former slave was successful in settling many arguments by telling his entertaining and wise fables.

Some of the stories attributed to Aesop actually came from other sources, some older, some more recent than Aesop. But he is recognized throughout the world as the person who perfected the art of the animal fable.

Aesop wasn't the only person who told fables. Through the years, persons in a number of countries have told them. One such person—an American writer—is James Thurber, who wrote a book titled Fables for Our Time. Here is one of them.

The Tortoise and the Hare

JAMES THURBER

THERE WAS ONCE a wise young tortoise who read in an ancient book about a tortoise who had beaten a hare in a race. He read all the other books he could find but in none of them was there any record of a hare who had beaten a tortoise. The wise young tortoise came to the natural conclusion that he could outrun a hare, so he set forth in search of one. In his wanderings he met many animals who were willing to race him: weasels, stoats, dachshunds, badger-boars, short-tailed field mice, and ground squirrels. But when the tortoise asked if they could outrun a hare, they all said no, they couldn't (with the exception of a dachshund named Freddy, and nobody paid any attention to him). "Well, I can," said the tortoise, "so there's no use wasting time on you." And he continued his search.

After many days, the tortoise finally encountered a hare and challenged him to a race. "What are you going to use for legs?" asked the hare. "Never mind that," said the tortoise. "Read this." He showed the hare the story in the ancient book, complete with the moral about the swift not always being so terribly fast. "Tosh," said the hare. "You couldn't go fifty feet in an hour and a half, where as I can go fifty feet in one and a fifth seconds." "Posh," said the tortoise. "You probably won't even finish second." "We'll see about that," said the hare. So they marked off a course fifty feet long. All the other animals gathered around. A bull-frog sat them on their marks, a gun dog fired a pistol, and they were off.

When the hare crossed the finish line, the tortoise had gone approximately eight and three-quarter inches.

Moral: *A new broom may sweep clean, but never trust an old saw.*

Discussion

1. How is it that the tortoise decides he can win a race with a hare? Why could the tortoise find nothing in books about a hare that had won a race with a tortoise?

2. Why did the tortoise not race with weasels and field mice and squirrels?

3. How does the moral of Thurber's fable suggest his attitude toward the lesson of Aesop's fable?

4. What is Thurber's moral? What humor do you see in it?

James Thurber 1894–1961

James Thurber was as famous for his comic drawings of pudgy dogs as for his humorous writing. He drew before he wrote and doodled constantly on envelopes, tablecloths, or any other surface.

Thurber grew up in Columbus, Ohio. A childhood accident with a bow and arrow made him blind in one eye. Eventually, he became totally blind. Thurber studied at Ohio State University. After World War I, he became a code clerk for the State Department. Then he worked as a reporter for several years. Thurber met E. B. White, who offered to help him find some kind of job at *The New Yorker* magazine. Thurber received the very big job of managing editor, but after six months he went happily to the less important job of writing a column.

Thurber's cartoons of all shapes of dogs and people were quite popular in *The New Yorker* magazine. These cartoons and Thurber's character Walter Mitty (a timid man with valiant daydreams) are the Thurber creations that America remembers most.

Folktales

"Cinderella." "The Ugly Duckling." "Snow White." "Pinocchio." These are FOLKTALES that almost every English-speaking girl and boy has read and enjoyed.

Like ballads (page 406), folktales were first told centuries ago and then handed down from teller to teller and from generation to generation. When they were finally written down, there were often several versions of the same basic story. Folktales, then, have become an important part of our literary heritage.

Why have folktales had such wide appeal? For one thing, they are concerned mostly with everyday people—with the common folk, not with great heroes. What's more, they focus on situations that human beings in general have experienced. And finally, they reflect the life of the people of a particular region or of a particular country.

In every region of the world where people share a heritage of similar customs and beliefs, there are sure to be folktales. Folktales from three such regions follow.

African Folktales

A spider a spinner of tales? Of course! What could be more natural?

All Stories Are Anansi's

ASHANTI

IN THE BEGINNING, all tales and stories belonged to Nyame, the Sky God. But Kwaku Anansi, the spider, yearned to be the owner of all the stories known in the world, and he went to Nyame and offered to buy them.

The Sky God said: "I am willing to sell the stories, but the price is high. Many people have come to me offering to buy, but the price was too high for them. Rich and powerful families have not been able to pay. Do you think you can do it?"

Anansi replied to the Sky God: "I can do it. What is the price?"

"My price is three things," the Sky God said. "I must first have Mmoboro, the hornets. I must then have Onini, the great python. I must then have Osebo, the leopard. For these things I will sell you the right to tell all stories."

Anansi said, "I will bring them."

He went home and made his plans. He first cut a gourd from a vine and made a small hole in it. He took a large calabash[1] and filled it with water. He went to the tree where the hornets lived. He poured some of the water over himself, so that he was dripping. He threw some water over the hornets, so that they too were dripping. Then he put the calabash on his head, as though to protect himself from a storm, and called out to the hornets: "Are you foolish people? Why do you stay in the rain that is falling?"

The hornets answered, "Where shall we go?"

"Go here, in this dry gourd," Anansi told them.

The hornets thanked him and flew into the gourd through the small hole. When the last of them had entered, Anansi plugged the hole with a ball of grass, saying, "Oh, yes, but you are really foolish people!"

He took his gourd full of hornets to Nyame, the Sky God. The Sky God accepted them. He said, "There are two more things."

Anansi returned to the forest and cut a long bamboo pole and some strong vines. Then he walked toward the house of Onini, the python, talking to himself. He said: "My wife is stupid. I say he is longer and stronger. My wife says he is shorter and weaker. I give him more respect. She gives him less respect. Is she right or am I right? I am right, he is longer. I am right, he is stronger."

When Onini, the python, heard Anansi talking to himself, he said, "Why are you arguing this way with yourself?"

The spider replied: "Ah, I have had a dispute with my wife. She says you are shorter and weaker than this bamboo pole. I say you are longer and stronger."

---

1 **calabash** (kal' ə bash): a gourdlike fruit whose dried shell is used to make bottles, bowls, drums, pipes, and rattles.

Onini said: "It's useless and silly to argue when you can find out the truth. Bring the pole and we will measure."

So Anansi laid the pole on the ground, and the python came and stretched himself out beside it.

"You seem a little short," Anansi said.

"I can stretch no more," Onini said.

"When you stretch at one end, you get shorter at the other end," Anansi said. "Let me tie you at the front so you don't slip."

He tied Onini's head to the pole. Then he went to the other end and tied the tail to the pole. He wrapped the vine all around Onini, until the python couldn't move.

"Onini," Anansi said, "it turns out that my wife was right and I was wrong. You are shorter than the pole and weaker. My opinion wasn't as good as my wife's. But you were even more foolish than I, and you are now my prisoner."

Anansi carried the python to Nyame, the Sky God, who said, "There is one thing more."

Osebo, the leopard, was next. Anansi went into the forest and dug a deep pit where the leopard was accustomed to walk. He covered it with small branches and leaves and put dust on it, so that it was impossible to tell where the pit was. Anansi went away and hid. When Osebo came prowling in the black of night, he stepped into the trap Anansi had prepared and fell to the bottom. Anansi heard the sound of the leopard falling, and he said, "Ah, Osebo, you are half-foolish!"

When morning came, Anansi went to the pit and saw the leopard there.

"Osebo," he asked, "what are you doing in this hole?"

"I have fallen into a trap," Osebo said. "Help me out."

"I would gladly help you," Anansi said. "But I'm sure that if I bring you out, I will have no thanks for it. You will get hungry, and later on you will be wanting to eat me and my children."

"I swear it won't happen!" Osebo said.

"Very well. Since you swear it, I will take you out," Anansi said.

He bent a tall green tree toward the ground, so that its top was over the pit, and he tied it that way. Then he tied a rope to the top of the tree and dropped the other end of it into the pit.

"Tie this to your tail," he said.

Osebo tied the rope to his tail.

"Is it well tied?" Anansi asked.

"Yes, it is well tied," the leopard said.

"In that case," Anansi said, "you are not merely half-foolish, you are all-foolish."

And he took his knife and cut the other rope, the one that held the tree bowed to the ground. The tree straightened up with a snap, pulling Osebo out of the hole. He hung in the air head downward, twisting and turning. And while he hung this way, Anansi killed him with his weapons.

Then he took the body of the leopard and carried it to Nyame, the Sky God, saying: "Here is the third thing. Now I have paid the price."

Nyame said to him: "Kwaku Anansi, great warriors and chiefs have tried, but they have been unable to do it. You have done it. Therefore, I will give you the stories. From this day onward, all stories belong to you. Whenever a man tells a story, he must acknowledge that it is Anansi's tale."

In this way Anansi, the spider, became the owner of all stories that are told. To Anansi all tales belong.

Discussion

1. What is the price for which Nyame, the Sky God, is willing to sell all tales and stories?

2. How does Anansi capture the hornets? the python? the leopard? When Anansi has captured each of them, what does he say about them?

3. What qualities, if any, does Anansi share with the Norse god Loki and with the Fox in the fable "The Fox and the Crow"?

4. In your opinion, does it seem appropriate or inappropriate for a spider to be the owner of all tales and stories? Why?

Vocabulary

Words that have more than one definition are called MULTIPLE-MEANING WORDS. Each sentence below, taken from the story "All Stories Are Anansi's," contains an *italicized* word which has at least one other meaning besides the one in the sentence. For each *italicized* word, do the following on a separate sheet of paper:

1. Write the definition as the word is used in the sentence.

2. Write another definition of the word. (You may need to use a dictionary to find another definition.)

3. Write a sentence using the word as you defined it in 2, above.

EXAMPLE: "I *swear* it won't happen!" Osebo said.
ANSWER: swear—to promise; to vow
　　　　swear—to curse
　　　　The minister was upset when he heard the man *swear*.

1. He covered it with small *branches* and leaves and put dust on it.

2. Is she *right* or am I right?

3. The tree straightened up with a *snap*, pulling Osebo out of the hole.

4. *Rich* and powerful families have not been able to pay.

5. Why do you *stay* in the rain that is falling?

The Third Gift

JAN CAREW

I N LONG-TIME-PAST DAYS there was a black prophet named Amakosa who was the leader of the Jubas—a clan of herdsmen and wanderers. When Amakosa felt age nesting inside his tired limbs, and was certain that the soft footsteps he heard following him were those of Mantop, Death's messenger boy, he summoned the elders of the clan to a palaver.[1] It was a time when endless seasons of drought and dust were scattering the Jubas and their herds like silk cotton blossoms in the wind, and the clan was threatened with extinction.

The elders gathered in a circle and drank libations. As the sacred gourd was passed around, dark hands, lean and veined, trembled like leaves.

Amakosa, with his old and cunning eyes gleaming in nests of wrinkled flesh, said calmly, "We must find green pastures, and places where the wind brings rain, and where the vampire sun is no longer king."

"Ai! Ai!" the people said in a chorus, "lead us there and we will follow you."

So the Jubas picked up their belongings and followed Amakosa across the parched savannahs[2] where the wind had bent the thorn trees like old men's backs and where the stunted elephant grass hissed like snakes. Through endless seasons of waxing and waning moons, they left a trail of bones picked clean by vultures and bleached by the sun. One evening, when the gloaming[3] was giving way to starlight and pale lightnings, they came to the foot of a mountain whose peak was lost in the stars. They washed their dirty limbs in cool streams and threw themselves down on the innocent grass, wherever sleep surprised them.

They woke up at day—clean refreshed, and stretching themselves like ocelots, they asked, "What is this mountain called, Amakosa?"

"It has no name, so we will call it Nameless Mountain," Amakosa said.

"And what is this place called, Amakosa?"

"We will call it Arisa, the place of springs."

The Jubas settled in Arisa, and when Mantop, Death's messenger boy, finally knocked on his door, Amakosa called the Jubas together and said,

"Listen well to what I have to say. My face has beaten against many years, and now Mantop has sent for me. You must choose a

---

1 **palaver** (pə lav′ ər): conference.
2 **savannahs** (sə van′ əz): treeless plains.

3 **gloaming** (glō′ ming): evening twilight.

leader to succeed me. When I have gone, all the young men must make their way up Nameless Mountain. The one that climbs the highest and brings back a gift of the wonders that he saw, him you must make your leader."

The Jubas were silent when Mantop led their prophet away. When sunset was casting long shadows, they saw the two—a headless man with a flute stuck in his throat and the old man Amakosa, bent with the weight of his years—walking towards the River of Night. And at day-clean even the wind was heavy with lamentation.[4]

Then all the young men set out up Nameless Mountain—up past the orchids and wild vines on the mossy face of the rocks, up to where the wild mango stripes the slopes with white blossoms, up to where secret springs gurgle into rivers. Up and up they climbed until all they could hear was the wind in the stranger-trees and the echoes of drums on the plains. Towards evening one man came back weary and sleepy as mud, and the others followed dragging their feet. But the one that climbed the highest came running deer-speed down the mountainside holding something in his hand high above his head. He didn't stop until he reached the village square. The Jubas crowded around him and chorused, "Show us the wonderful thing you brought, Brother-Man!"

And the young man said, "Come closer and see." He opened his hand and declared, "This is what I have brought. Eye never saw and hand never touched a gift like this."

And the women cried out with wonder, "Look at the curve of it and the way it catches the light! It is truly a wondrous thing!"

4 **lamentation** (lam′ ən tā′ shən): wailing.

The gift that the young man brought was a stone, and when this stone caught the light, it had all the colors of mountain orchids and rainbows and more.

"But what is the message in this stone?" the people asked.

"This stone brings us the gift of Work," the young man said. "Since we wandered into this green country we have become idle, and idleness is a more terrible threat than drought or hunger."

And looking at the stone all of the Jubas had a vision of ploughshares and axe blades, endless fields of maize and cassava, and harvest times filled with the songless singing of their drums.

Jawa, the man who had brought the gift of Work, ruled for a long time. The Juba nation multiplied, and the memory of hunger and laziness was pushed far away from them.

But the time came when Mantop, Death's messenger boy, knocked on Jawa's door of reeds, and he, too, had to walk the trail to the River of Night. The lamentation weighed heavy on the hearts of those he left behind.

So, once again at fore-day-morning, the young men set out up Nameless Mountain. And Kabo, the man who climbed the highest this time, came down the mountainside soft-softly. He could not hurry because the gift he brought was a mountain flower. When he stood in the center of the village square holding this marvelous flower in his hand, it was clear for all to see that he had brought his people the gift of Beauty. They crowded around him to marvel at the curve of the petals and the colors and the way the pistil caught the light and made the pollen glitter like jewels. The singing drums and the song-makers sang Kabo's praises far into the night.

Kabo ruled through many moons, and the Juba country became a place to wonder at.

The door of every house had flowers painted on it in bright vermilion colors; the girls wore flowers in their hair; flowers without number were carved out of wood and stone, and every canoe was built with a flower sculpted on its prow.

But the Jubas grew dissatisfied. They had Work and Beauty and yet they wanted more. Some began to mutter that they were thinking of moving to another country down the river and across the plains. So when Mantop sent for Kabo everyone knew that his successor would have to bring back a powerful gift from Nameless Mountain to hold the nation together.

Kabo went on his journey to the River of Night quietly, and for the third time the young men set out up Nameless Mountain. Amongst them was a dreaming, sad-faced son of Tiho the Hunter who was called Ika, the Quiet One. Ika always looked as if he was gnawing at the bones of everlasting griefs.

He took a trail on the far side of Nameless Mountain where none of the others dared follow. When night fell and the fireflies brightened the fields and forests like fallen stars, everyone returned except Ika.

And the weary ones who had returned said, "We saw him parting the clouds and climbing up and up, and none of us had the strength to follow him."

When Ika did not return by the next morning, the Jubas sent search parties to look for him and posted lookouts on the mountainside. Sun and Moon lengthened many shadows; still Ika did not return. There was plenty of talk about him and how he had gone his lonesome way to die on Nameless Mountain.

But one morning bright with dew and singing birds, Ika came running down the mountainside, parting the long grass and leaping from rock to rock. He was clenching his fist and holding his hand high above his head. He reached the river bank and crossed the cassava fields, trampling down the young plants. When he came to the village square he did not stop.

And the people said, "Aye, aye, Ika, you're home, man! We were waiting for you until our hearts were becoming weary with waiting."

But he kept on running, and again they shouted, "You're home, man! Ika, you're home!"

Ika would have run right across the village square and away towards the fields of elephant grass if he had not tripped on a piece of firewood. He fell and lay panting as though his chest was going to burst, still keeping his fist clenched.

"What gift have you brought us, Brother-Man? Talk to us. What did you see above the clouds on Nameless Mountain?"

For a long time Ika could find no words to answer them. But Leza, the Healer, came and anointed him with kuru oil. The men could not wait to see the gift he had brought; so they pried his fist open. But when they opened Ika's hand, it was empty.

When Ika found his tongue again, he said, "I went up to the clouds and over and above them, and I don't know how long it took because past the clouds was a brightness that blinded my eyes. Then there came a time when all I felt was a soft carpet under my feet, and when I breathed in the mountain air, it was like drawing knife blades up my nostrils. When my sight came back I found myself on the mountain top. . . ."

"Lord! You must've seen the whole world from there, Ika!" a young man exclaimed.

"Yes, and while I stood up there a soft white thing like rain started to fall . . . and yet it wasn't rain because it fell like leaves when there is no wind. I gathered this downy whiteness in my hand, but the farther down the mountainside I ran, the less of it I was holding, so I went back for more and ran down the mountain again. Four times I did this, and every time I was heading for home bird-speed, this magic thing melted in my hand. All I bring with me now is the memory of it, the feel of the sky and the bite of the wind—and the fire and ice burning my hand."

And the people listening believed, for this quiet young man, when he did speak, could warble like singing-birds-sweet, and when he spoke, his words would grow inside your head like seeds.

Ika became prophet of the Jubas, for he had brought the best gift of all, the gift of Fantasy, of Imagination and of Faith. So, with the gifts of Work and Beauty and Imagination, the Jubas became poets and bards and creators, and they live at the foot of Nameless Mountain to this day.

Discussion

1. What were the gifts that the first two young men brought back from Nameless Mountain? What did those gifts represent? In what way did they help the Jubas?

2. Why did it take Ika so long to return to the village? What was it that he held in his hand? What did this gift represent? Why?

3. For what reason(s) was Ika's gift called "the gift of Fantasy, of Imagination, and of Faith"?

Writer's Craft

All of us use language, but some of us use it more effectively than others. Take Jan Carew, for instance. He's the author who wrote down the folktale "The Third Gift." Much of the appeal of that folktale lies in Carew's EFFECTIVE USE OF LANGUAGE. For example, consider this passage: ". . . Amakosa felt age nesting inside his tired limbs . . ." (page 531). The metaphor in that passage creates a vivid picture in your mind: *Old age, like a bird nesting in a tree, has found a refuge in Amakosa's arms and legs.* This is an unusual, appealing, and gentle way of saying that Amakosa was growing old.

And then take this passage: ". . . endless seasons of drought and dust were scattering the Jubas and their herds like silk cotton blossoms in the wind . . ." (page 531). What an effective simile!

Finally, note the unusual way Carew indicates a common occurrence: "My face has beaten against many years . . ." (page 531). Here is a fresh, original way of showing the passing of time. What's more, the expression is particularly appropriate for this folktale about the Juba people.

1. As you look through "The Third Gift," find at least five metaphors that strike you as examples of the effective use of language.

2. Similarly, find five similes that appeal to you.

3. What other interesting or unusual word-combinations that suggest the passing of time can you find?

Jan Carew 1925——

An international man of many accomplishments in varied fields, Jan Carew was born in Agricola, British Guiana, which later became Guyana. His ancestors were Black, Indian, Dutch, and Portuguese. After graduating from the local high school, Carew taught at that school. Then he worked as a customs official in British Guiana and Trinidad.

Carew came to the United States to attend two universities. Later, he studied in Prague and at the Sorbonne in Paris. His own paintings were exhibited in London in 1948. He edited a multi-lingual poetry magazine in Holland for a while. Then he went to London to act with Sir Laurence Olivier's company.

Since then, Carew has been working as a consultant on race relations and as a writer. His jobs have been in England, Latin America, Ghana, Canada, and the United States. He has written for the Canadian Broadcasting Company and has published verse, novels, and plays.

Mexican Folktales

It's often surprising how experience can change a person.

The Three Counsels

as told by RILEY AIKEN

THIS WAS A BOY who ran away from home. Though at heart not bad, he had three habits that were by no means good, for he would stick to no purpose, was always asking about people's affairs, and would not control his temper.

Sí señor, he ran away from home, but, do you know, he was hardly beyond the horizon when he left the highway for a trail, called to an old man to know his business, and flew into a rage when the latter did not answer.

Presently, however, the *viejito*[1] spoke. "I am a peddler of advice," said he.

"What kind of advice?" asked the boy.

"It will cost you one peso to find out," was the answer.

The boy had only three pesos, but curiosity induced him to give one to the *viejito*.

"First," said the old man, "don't leave a highway for a trail."

"Is that what you call advice?" asked the boy. "You are a fraud."

"Don't you like that one?" asked the *viejito*. "Then give me another peso and lend an ear."

The boy reluctantly handed over the second of his three pesos and waited. "Second,"

said the *viejito*, "don't ask about things that don't pertain to you."

"*Mal ladrón,*"[2] shouted the boy, "for one peso I would kill you."

"Calm yourself, *hijito*,"[3] said the old man. "I have among my wares one more bit of advice you need. Will you buy it or not?"

The boy's curiosity was too much for him. He gave his last peso to the stranger and listened attentively for the third time.

"Don't lose your temper," laughed the old man, and before the boy could gather his wits, he had vanished into the chaparral.[4]

Sad and empty of pocket, the youth continued on his way.

He took to the road again just as a stranger mounted on a large black horse galloped up.

"Where to, *joven*?"[5] called he.

"To the city," said the boy.

"Then you need advice," responded the man. "Look, I will help you. One league up the road you will find a short cut. You will recognize it by my horse's tracks. It will save you many miles."

The boy thanked him and continued on

---

1 viejito (vē yə hē′ tō): little old man.

2 mal ladron (mäl la drōn′): thief; robber.
3 hijito (ē hē′tō): sonny.
4 chaparral (chap′ ə ral): thicket of shrubs and dwarf trees.
5 joven (hō′ven): young person; here, young man.

The Three Counsels **537**

his journey with the purpose of leaving the highway for the path. However, never being able to keep to a purpose, he disregarded the path.

At noon he came to a ranch house. A bandit sat beneath an arbor in front of it.

"*Pase,*[6] *joven,*" he called. "You are just in time for dinner."

The boy entered the house and took a chair at the table. He had waited no time when a servant placed before him a dish containing the head of a man. He was at the point of asking a question when he remembered suddenly one of his three costly bits of advice. "I had better ask no question," thought he.

---

6 **Pase** (pä′ sā): pass along; here, come in.

"Young man," said the bandit, "what do you think of this head?"

"It is a good head," replied the boy.

"Have you no questions?" queried the bandit.

"No, señor, none."

"Would you like to see some of my keepsakes?" asked the bandit.

"If it is your pleasure to show them," said the boy, "then it will be my pleasure to see them."

A closet was opened and the boy was shown many skeletons hanging by the neck.

"How do you like my men?" asked the host.

"They are good men," answered the boy.

"*Joven,*" said the bandit, "I kill all my guests. These men, like you, each in his turn stepped across my threshold to have dinner with me. Each was shown a head, but different from you, they wanted to know all about it. Their curiosity brought them to their present condition. You, however, have asked nothing about things that do not concern you, and for that reason my servants will conduct you safely from the ranch. In my corral there are three mules and a horse. The mules will be loaded with gold, and the horse will be saddled. These are yours."

Six bags of gold were tied *mancornado* (in pairs) and placed on the mules. The boy mounted the horse and with the help of the servants was soon on the highway again. "Indeed," he said to himself, "it pays to keep to the main road and it pays to ask no questions about things that do not concern one. Now I am rich."

"Halt!" called a voice from the roadside.

There stood a bandit with his arms crossed.

"What have you in those sacks?" he asked.

The boy was on the point of cursing with

rage when he recalled the third bit of advice.

"It is a secret I prefer not to tell," he answered calmly.

"Speak or I shall kill you," threatened the bandit.

"If you feel that is best," said the boy, "then follow your conscience."

"Ha!" said the man, "you are a wise boy. *Adios;* may you have a pleasant journey."

This *joven* entered the city. Before many weeks had passed he had built and stocked the best store in town and was making barrels of money. Furthermore, he met and married a wealthy girl. However, the best of all was that she, too, did not leave the main road for a path, asked no questions about things that did not pertain to her, and always kept her temper.

Discussion

1. In what way does the second paragraph of the folktale emphasize the boy's three habits "that were by no means good. . ."? How does the old man's advice further emphasize the boy's bad habits?

2. Does the boy heed the old man's advice, or doesn't he? How do you know? What is the outcome of the course of action the boy takes?

3. Narratives are often said to have a beginning, a middle, and an end. This folktale seems to follow such a pattern precisely. Explain.

4. Like fables, this folktale has a lesson or a moral. In fact, it has four morals. In your own words, state what you see as those four morals.

Composition

1. The old man in the folktale, "The Three Counsels" gives three pieces of advice. In a brief composition, identify the advice that seems most important to you. Tell why it is important.

2. Have you ever begun cleaning your room, only to run across something you have been meaning to read—with the result that the cleaning comes to a halt? Or have you ever been so curious about something that you asked a question that was none of your businesss? Or have you ever flared up, perhaps at some good-natured teasing, only to feel sort of foolish at becoming angry about nothing? To have any or all of these experiences is only natural. In a composition of one or more pages, relate an experience in which you either *did* or *did not* heed one of the three pieces of advice given in "The Three Counsels." Be sure to reveal the consequences! Be sure, too, to tell how you felt as a result of your heeding or not heeding the advice.

Popocatepetl (pō pō kə tā′ pə təl), an active volcano in northern Mexico, has not erupted in years. Yet smoke still rises from its crater. Why?

Popocatepetl and Ixtlaccihuatl

retold by JULIET PIGGOTT

THERE WAS ONCE an Aztec emperor in Tenochtitlan.[1] He was very powerful. Some thought he was wise as well, whilst others doubted his wisdom. He was both a ruler and a warrior and he kept at bay those tribes living in and beyond the mountains surrounding the Valley of Mexico, with its huge lake called Texcoco in which Tenochtitlan was built. His power was absolute and the splendor in which he lived was very great.

It is not known for how many years the Emperor ruled Tenochtitlan, but it is known that he lived to a great age. However, it was not until he was in his middle years that his wife gave him an heir, a girl. The Emperor and Empress loved the princess very much and she was their only child. She was a dutiful daughter and learned all she could from her father about the art of ruling, for she knew that when he died she would reign in his stead in Tenochtitlan.

Her name was Ixtlaccihuatl.[2] Her parents and her friends called her Ixtla. She had a pleasant disposition and, as a result, she had many friends. The great palace where she lived with the Emperor and Empress rang with their laughter when they came to the parties her parents gave for her. As well as being a delightful companion Ixtla was also very pretty, even beautiful.

Her childhood was happy and she was content enough when she became a young woman. But by then she was fully aware of the great responsibilities which would be hers when her father died and she became serious and studious and did not enjoy parties as much as she had done when younger.

Another reason for her being so serious was that she was in love. This in itself was a joyous thing, but the Emperor forbade her to marry. He wanted her to reign and rule alone when he died, for he trusted no one, not even his wife, to rule as he did except his much loved only child, Ixtla. This was why there were some who doubted the wisdom of the Emperor, for, by not allowing his heiress to marry, he showed a selfishness and short-sightedness towards his daughter and his empire which many considered was not truly wise. An emperor, they felt, who was not truly wise could not also be truly great. Or even truly powerful.

---

1 Tenochtitlan (tā nok′tē tlän′).
2 Ixtlaccihuatl (ēs′ tlä sē′ wä təl).

The man with whom Ixtla was in love was also in love with her. Had they been allowed to marry their state could have been doubly joyous. His name was Popocatepetl[3] and Ixtla and his friends all called him Popo. He was a warrior in the service of the Emperor, tall and strong, with a capacity for gentleness, and very brave. He and Ixtla loved each other very much and while they were content and even happy when they were together, true joy was not theirs because the Emperor continued to insist that Ixtla should not be married when the time came for her to take on her father's responsibilities.

This unfortunate but moderately happy relationship between Ixtla and Popo continued for several years, the couple pleading with the Emperor at regular intervals and the Emperor remaining constantly adamant. Popo loved Ixtla no less for her father's stubborness and she loved him no less while she studied, as her father demanded she should do, the art of ruling in preparation for her reign.

When the Emperor became very old he also became ill. In his feebleness he channeled all his failing energies towards instructing Ixtla in statecraft, for he was no longer able to exercise that craft himself. So it was that his enemies, the tribes who lived in the mountains and beyond, realized that the great Emperor in Tenochtitlan was great no longer, for he was only teaching his daughter to rule and not ruling himself.

The tribesmen came nearer and nearer to Tenochtitlan until the city was besieged. At last the Emperor realized himself that he was great no longer, that his power was nearly gone and that his domain was in dire peril.

Warrior though he long had been, he was now too old and too ill to lead his fighting men into battle. At last he understood that, unless his enemies were frustrated in their efforts to enter and lay waste to Tenochtitlan, not only would he no longer be Emperor but his daughter would never be Empress.

Instead of appointing one of his warriors to lead the rest into battle on his behalf, he offered a bribe to all of them. Perhaps it was that his wisdom, if wisdom he had, had forsaken him, or perhaps he acted from fear. Or perhaps he simply changed his mind. But the bribe he offered to whichever warrior succeeded in lifting the siege of Tenochtitlan and defeating the enemies in and around the Valley of Mexico was both the hand of his daughter and the equal right to reign and rule, with her, in Tenochtitlan. Furthermore, he decreed that directly he learned that his enemies had been defeated he would instantly cease to be Emperor himself. Ixtla would not have to wait until her father died to become Empress and, if her father should die of his illness or old age before his enemies were vanquished, he further decreed that he who overcame the surrounding enemies should marry the princess whether he, the Emperor, lived or not.

Ixtla was fearful when she heard of her father's bribe to his warriors, for the only one whom she had any wish to marry was Popo and she wanted to marry him, and only him, very much indeed.

The warriors, however, were glad when they heard of the decree: there was not one of them who would not have been glad to have the princess as his wife and they all relished the chance of becoming Emperor.

And so the warriors went to war at their ruler's behest, and each fought trebly hard, for each was fighting not only for the safety of Tenochtitlan and the surrounding valley,

---

3 Popocatepetl (pō pō kä tā′ pət əl).

but for the delightful bride and for the right to be the Emperor himself.

Even though the warriors fought with great skill and even though each one exhibited a courage he did not know he possessed, the war was a long one. The Emperor's enemies were firmly entrenched around Lake Texcoco and Tenochtitlan by the time the warriors were sent to war, and as battle followed battle the final outcome was uncertain.

The warriors took a variety of weapons

Detail from an Aztec codex.

with them; wooden clubs edged with sharp blades of obsidian,[4] obsidian machets, javelins which they hurled at their enemies from troughed throwing boards, bows and arrows, slings and spears set with obsidian fragments, and lances, too. Many of them carried shields woven from wicker and covered in tough hide and most wore armor made of thick quilted cotton soaked in brine.

The war was long and fierce. Most of the warriors fought together and in unison, but some fought alone. As time went on, natural leaders emerged and, of these, undoubtedly Popo was the best. Finally it was he, brandishing his club and shield, who led the great charge of running warriors across the valley, with their enemies fleeing before them to the safety of the coastal plains and jungles beyond the mountains.

The warriors acclaimed Popo as the man most responsible for the victory and, weary though they all were, they set off for Tenochtitlan to report to the Emperor and for Popo to claim Ixtla as his wife at last.

But a few of those warriors were jealous of Popo. Since they knew none of them could rightly claim the victory for himself (the decision among the Emperor's fighting men that Popo was responsible for the victory had been unanimous), they wanted to spoil for him and for Ixtla the delights which the Emperor had promised.

These few men slipped away from the rest at night and made their way to Tenochtitlan ahead of all the others. They reached the capital two days later, having traveled without sleep all the way, and quickly let it be known that, although the Emperor's warriors had been successful against his enemies, the warrior Popo had been killed in battle.

4 **obsidian** (ob sid′ ē ən): a hard, dark, glassy rock that is formed when lava cools.

It was a foolish and cruel lie which those warriors told their Emperor, and they told it for no reason other than that they were jealous of Popo.

When the Emperor heard this, he demanded that Popo's body be brought to him so that he might arrange a fitting burial. He knew the man his daughter had loved would have died courageously. The jealous warriors looked at one another and said nothing. Then one of them told the Emperor that Popo had been killed on the edge of Lake Texcoco and that his body had fallen into the water and no man had been able to retrieve it. The Emperor was saddened to hear this.

After a little while he demanded to be told which of his warriors had been responsible for the victory but none of the fighting men before him dared claim the successful outcome of the war for himself, for each knew the others would refute him. So they were silent. This puzzled the Emperor and he decided to wait for the main body of his warriors to return and not to press the few who had brought the news of the victory and of Popo's death.

Then the Emperor sent for his wife and his daughter and told them their enemies had been overcome. The Empress was thoroughly excited and relieved at the news. Ixtla was only apprehensive. The Emperor, seeing her anxious face, told her quickly that Popo was dead. He went on to say that the warrior's body had been lost in the waters of Lake Texcoco, and again it was as though his wisdom had left him, for he spoke at some length of his not yet being able to tell Ixtla who her husband would be and who would become Emperor when the main body of warriors returned to Tenochtitlan.

But Ixtla heard nothing of what he told her, only that her beloved Popo was dead. She went to her room and lay down. Her

Popocatepetl and Ixtlaccihuatl **543**

mother followed her and saw at once she was very ill. Witch doctors were sent for, but they could not help the princess, and neither could her parents. Her illness had no name, unless it was the illness of a broken heart. Princess Ixtlaccihuatl did not wish to live if Popocatapetl was dead, and so she died herself.

The day after her death Popo returned to Tenochtitlan with all the other surviving warriors. They went straight to the palace and, with much cheering, told the Emperor that his enemies had been routed and that Popo was the undoubted victor of the conflict.

The Emperor praised his warriors and pronounced Popo to be the new Emperor in his place. When the young man asked first to see Ixtla, begging that they should be married at once before being jointly proclaimed Emperor and Empress, the Emperor had to tell Popo of Ixtla's death, and how it had happened.

Popo spoke not a word.

He gestured the assembled warriors to follow him and together they sought out the few jealous men who had given the false news of his death to the Emperor. With the army of warriors watching, Popo killed each one of them in single combat with his obsidian studded club. No one tried to stop him.

That task accomplished, Popo returned to the palace and, still without speaking and still wearing his stiff cotton armor, went to Ixtla's room. He gently lifted her body and carried it out of the palace and out of the city, and no one tried to stop him doing that either. All the warriors followed him in silence.

When he had walked some miles he gestured to them again and they built a huge pile of stones in the shape of a pyramid. They all worked together and they worked fast while Popo stood and watched, holding the body of the princess in his arms. By sunset the mighty edifice was finished. Popo climbed it alone, carrying Ixtla's corpse with him. There, at the very top, under the heap of stones, he buried the young woman he had loved so well and for so long, and who had died for the love of him.

That night Popo slept alone at the top of the pyramid by Ixtla's grave. In the morning he came down and spoke for the first time since the Emperor had told him the princess was dead. He told the warriors to build another pyramid, a little to the south-east of the one which held Ixtla's body and to build it higher than the other.

He told them too to tell the Emperor on his behalf that he, Popocatepetl, would never reign and rule in Tenochtitlan. He would keep watch over the grave of the Princess Ixtlaccihuatl for the rest of his life.

The messages to the Emperor were the last words Popo ever spoke. Well before the evening the second mighty pile of stones was built. Popo climbed it and stood at the top, taking a torch of resinous pine wood with him.

And when he reached the top he lit the torch and the warriors below saw the white smoke rise against the blue sky, and they watched as the sun began to set and the smoke turned pink and then a deep red, the color of blood.

So Popocatepetl stood there, holding the torch in memory of Ixtlaccihuatl, for the rest of his days.

The snows came and, as the years went by, the pyramids of stone became high white capped mountains. Even now the one called Popocatepetl emits smoke in memory of the princess whose body lies in the mountain which bears her name.

1. What is the setting of the folktale?
2. The story concerns three *major* problems to be solved. What are they?
3. What is the reward the Emperor offers his warriors?
4. By whom and in what manner is Popo's victorious homecoming spoiled?
5. According to the folktale, how were two of the white-capped mountains of Mexico formed?
6. What human emotions do you find clearly expressed in this folktale?

Vocabulary

A HOMONYM is a word which sounds the same as another word but has a different meaning and often is spelled differently. For example:

in—inn   great—grate
reign—rain   know—no
there—their—they're

A. On a separate sheet of paper, copy the sentences below. Choose the correct homonyms from above to complete each sentence.

   1. The weary travelers stopped their horses _____ front of the _____, where the travelers rented rooms for the night.
   2. The king of the small farming country claimed that the gods favored him highly; however, the crops were dying because so little _____ had fallen during his _____.
   3. Please tell those players that _____ to put all _____ belongings over _____ in the gym.
   4. The sewer workers found that a _____ amount of garbage had plugged up the _____ which covers the entrance to the pipes.
   5. _____, I don't _____ anybody by that name.

B. On the same paper, write four sentences of your own. In each sentence, use correctly one of the following sets of homonyms. Underline each homonym you use.

   1. plane—plain
   2. to—too—two
   3. or—ore
   4. heard—herd

Like Pandora, Urashima was curious. Was he also too curious?

Urashima

retold by MIRIAM COX

THE FISHER LAD URASHIMA[1] caught a tortoise on his line one day. A pity to harm it, he thought, for these creatures are said to live a thousand years. He allowed it to slip back into the sea, and again baited his hook for a fish. But the day was warm, and the youth soon fell fast asleep as his boat drifted idly on the quiet waters.

"Urashima, Urashima!" Through his dreams came the sound of his name being called again and again. He awoke to find the tortoise by his boat. "You were kind to me," it said. "Let me repay by taking you down to the Palace of the Dragon King where the Sea Princess herself may thank you."

Here was adventure! Eagerly Urashima climbed on the creature's broad back and down they glided through the sea lanes into the shining depths.

It was not long before he could see the delicate tracery of towers, pillars, and bridges spiraling up through the emerald waters. Then it seemed as if the rainbow had fallen into the sea, for a magnificent procession of fish—silver, green, gold, red—formed on either side to escort them to the Dragon King's palace.

When the pearled gates swung open, the lad drew back in awe. Before him was a land of enchantment. Here all the four seasons presented their glories at once: spring with its blossoming cherry and silken-winged butterflies; summer's gardenias bending over shimmering pools; autumn's blaze of maple leaves; winter's white embroidery on tree and fern.

But the beauty of the Sea Princess who came forward to greet him eclipsed all of these wonders, and when she spoke it was as if every singing bird had given her its sweetest note. "You were kind to my messenger, the tortoise," she said. "Stay with us as long as you wish in this land of eternal youth that we may show our gratitude." She clapped her hands, and a great company of fishes glided in bearing on their fins coral trays heaped with delicacies. While the princess and Urashima feasted, other merry little fishes entertained them with song and dance.

For three years he stayed in the Palace of the Dragon King, finding new delights with every hour. But then he began to worry about his aged parents. How they must be grieving at his strange disappearance!

---

1 Urashima (ü rə shē′mə).

"Let me return for one day to my home," he said to the Sea Princess. "Then I will come back to dwell forever in this beautiful realm."

"I had hoped to make you so happy that you would never leave," she answered sadly, for she had fallen in love with the gentle lad from the great world above the waters. "But if you must go, take this gift." She handed him a small box. "It contains a valuable treasure—one that should not be seen by mortal eyes. Take it as a token of my love, but I entreat you, do not open it!"

Bewildered, he stopped an old woman and asked, "Where is Urashima's home? What has become of his parents?"

She stared at him suspiciously. "Urashima? I have lived here eighty years and never have I heard of Urashima." She started to hobble away and then turned back. "Wait! Vaguely I remember hearing my old grandmother tell about a fisher lad by that name who was drowned at sea. But that was three hundred years ago!"

Detail from a Japanese screen.

Urashima promised, and mounting the tortoise, was swiftly borne upward to earth. But as he stepped upon the beach, he found to his amazement that everything had changed. Where was the old tree under which he had dozed so often? Where was his father's house? The stream ran through the village as always, but now it was spanned by a new bridge that he had never seen before.

Tears welled into Urashima's eyes. How could he have forgotten that in the country of the Sea King one day was like a hundred years! Now everyone he loved on earth was gone! He would go back at once to his dear princess in the place where the four seasons displayed their glories at once, and where fishes danced on their tails and played musical instruments with their fins.

But where was the tortoise? How could he return? What if he were never to see his princess again! The box! Surely in the box he could discover the secret of returning to the sea. Perhaps she had given it to him for that very reason.

With trembling fingers he lifted the lid. A wreath of white smoke coiled out, wove itself into a delicate column above his head for a moment, and then drifted out over the sea.

Now Urashima felt a change come over him. His limbs suddenly felt stiff and tired; his eyes became so dim that shore and sea faded away into a vague mist; the wind caught at a long white beard that fell to his waist.

"The princess had sealed my youth in the box, and I have let it go!" He staggered forward, lifted his arms imploringly to the sea, and then fell upon the sand. Urashima was dead.

Discussion

1. What is in the box that the Sea Princess gives Urashima? Why does she warn Urashima not to open the box? What happens when he does?

2. What do the people back in Urashima's village think happened to him? When Urashima returns to his village, what changes does he find? How long has he actually been away? How long does he think he has been away?

3. What is unusual about the seasons at the Palace of the Dragon King?

4. What similarity, if any, do you find between this folktale and the Greek myth about Pandora? What similarity, if any, do you find between this folktale and "Rip Van Winkle"?

In Japan a skilled wrestler is a V.I.P. (very important person). Forever-Mountain was truly a skilled wrestler. What could three women—even three strong women—teach him?

Three Strong Women

CLAUS STAMM

LONG AGO, IN JAPAN, there lived a famous wrestler, and he was on his way to the capital city to wrestle before the Emperor.

He strode down the road on legs thick as the trunks of small trees. He had been walking for seven hours and could, and probably would, walk for seven more without getting tired.

The time was autumn, the sky was a cold, watery blue, the air chilly. In the small bright sun, the trees along the roadside glowed red and orange.

The wrestler hummed to himself, "Zun-zun-zun," in time with the long swing of his legs. Wind blew through his thin brown robe, and he wore no sword at his side. He felt proud that he needed no sword, even in the darkest and loneliest places. The icy air on his body only reminded him that few tailors would have been able to make expensive warm clothes for a man so broad and tall. He felt much as a wrestler should: strong, healthy, and rather conceited.

A soft roar of fast-moving water beyond the trees told him that he was passing above a river bank. He "zun-zunned" louder; he loved the sound of his voice and wanted it to sound clearly above the rushing water.

He thought: They call me Forever-Mountain because I am such a good strong wrestler—big, too. I'm a fine, brave man and far too modest ever to say so. . . .

Just then he saw a girl who must have come up from the river, for she steadied a bucket on her head.

Her hands on the bucket were small, and there was a dimple on each thumb, just below the knuckle. She was a round little girl with red cheeks and a nose like a friendly button. Her eyes looked as though she were thinking of ten thousand funny stories at once. She clambered up onto the road and walked ahead of the wrestler, jolly and bounceful.

"If I don't tickle that fat girl, I shall regret it all my life," said the wrestler under his breath. "She's sure to go 'squeak' and I shall laugh and laugh. If she drops her bucket, that will be even funnier—and I can always run and fill it again and even carry it home for her."

He tiptoed up and poked her lightly in the ribs with one huge finger.

"Kochokochokocho!" he said, a fine, ticklish sound in Japanese.

The girl gave a satisfying squeal, giggled, and brought one arm down so that the wrestler's hand was caught between it and her body.

"Ho-ho-ho! You've caught me! I can't move at all!" said the wrestler, laughing.

"I know," said the jolly girl.

He felt that it was very good-tempered of her to take a joke so well, and started to pull his hand free.

Somehow, he could not.

He tried again, using a little more strength.

"Now, now—let me go, little girl," he said. "I am a very powerful man. If I pull too hard I might hurt you."

"Pull," said the girl. "I admire powerful men."

She began to walk, and though the wrestler tugged and pulled until his feet dug great furrows in the ground, he had to follow. She couldn't have paid him less attention if he had been a puppy—a small one.

Ten minutes later, still tugging while trudging helplessly after her, he was glad that the road was lonely and no one was there to see.

"Please let me go," he pleaded. "I am the famous wrestler Forever-Mountain. I must go and show my strength before the Emperor"—he burst out weeping from shame and confusion—"and you're hurting my hand!"

The girl steadied the bucket on her head with her free hand and dimpled sympathetically over her shoulder.

"You poor, sweet little Forever-Mountain," she said. "Are you tired? Shall I carry you? I can leave the water here and come back for it later."

"I do not want you to carry me. I want you to let me go, and then I want to forget I ever saw you. What do you want with me?" moaned the pitiful wrestler.

"I only want to help you," said the girl, now pulling him steadily up and up a narrow mountain path. "Oh, I am sure you'll have no more trouble than anyone else when you come up against the other wrestlers. You'll win, or else you'll lose, and you won't be too badly hurt either way. But aren't you afraid you might meet a really *strong* man someday?"

Forever-Mountain turned white. He stumbled. He was imagining being laughed at throughout Japan as "Hardly-Ever-Mountain."

She glanced back.

"You see? Tired already," she said. "I'll walk more slowly. Why don't you come along to my mother's house and let us make a strong man of you? The wrestling in the capital isn't due to begin for three months. I know, because Grandmother thought she'd go. You'd be spending all that time in bad company and wasting what little power you have."

"All right. Three months. I'll come along," said the wrestler. He felt he had nothing more to lose. Also, he feared that the girl might become angry if he refused, and place him in the top of a tree until he changed his mind.

"Fine," she said happily. "We are almost there."

She freed his hand. It had become red and a little swollen. "But if you break your promise and run off, I shall have to chase you and carry you back."

Soon they arrived in a small valley. A simple farmhouse with a thatched roof stood in the middle.

"Grandmother is at home, but she is an old

lady and she's probably sleeping." The girl shaded her eyes with one hand. "But Mother should be bringing our cow back from the field—oh, there's Mother now!"

She waved. The woman coming around the corner of the house put down the cow she was carrying and waved back.

She smiled and came across the grass, walking with a lively bounce like her daughter. "These mountain paths are full of stones. They hurt the cow's feet. And who is the nice young man you've brought, Maru-me?"[1]

The girl explained. "And we have only three months!" she finished anxiously.

"Well, it's not long enough to do much, but it's not so short a time that we can't do something," said her mother, looking thoughtful. "But he does look terribly feeble. He'll need a lot of good things to eat. Maybe when he gets stronger he can help Grandmother with some of the easy work about the house."

"That will be fine!" said the girl, and she called her grandmother—loudly, for the old lady was a little deaf.

"I'm coming!" came a creaky voice from inside the house, and a little old woman leaning on a stick and looking very sleepy tottered out of the door. As she came toward them she stumbled over the roots of a great oak tree.

"Heh! My eyes aren't what they used to be. That's the fourth time this month I've stumbled over that tree," she complained and, wrapping her skinny arms about its trunk, pulled it out of the ground.

"Oh, Grandmother! You should have let me pull it up for you," said Maru-me.

"Hm. I hope I didn't hurt my poor old back," muttered the old lady. She called out.

"Daughter! Throw that tree away like a good girl, so no one will fall over it. But make sure it doesn't hit anybody."

"You can help Mother with the tree," Maru-me said to Forever-Mountain. "On second thought, you'd better not help. Just watch."

Her mother went to the tree, picked it up in her two hands, and threw it—clumsily and with a little gasp. . . . Up went the tree, sailing end over end, growing smaller and smaller as it flew. It landed with a faint crash far up the mountainside.

"Ah, how clumsy," she said. "I meant to throw it *over* the mountain. It's probably blocking the path now, and I'll have to get up early tomorrow to move it."

The wrestler was not listening. He had very quietly fainted.

"Oh! We must put him to bed," said Maru-me.

"Poor, feeble young man," said her mother.

"I hope we can do something for him. Here, let me carry him, he's light," said the grandmother. She slung him over her shoulder and carried him into the house, creaking along with her cane.

The next day they began the work of making Forever-Mountain over into what they thought a strong man should be. They gave him the simplest food to eat, and the toughest. Day by day they prepared his rice with less and less water, until no ordinary man could have chewed or digested it.

Every day he was made to do the work of five men, and every evening he wrestled with Grandmother. Maru-me and her mother agreed that Grandmother, being old and feeble, was the least likely to injure him accidentally. They hoped the exercise might be good for the old lady's rheumatism.

He grew stronger and stronger but was

---

hardly aware of it. Grandmother could still throw him easily into the air—and catch him again—without ever changing her sweet old smile.

He quite forgot that outside this valley he was one of the greatest wrestlers in Japan and was called Forever-Mountain. His legs had been like logs; now they were like pillars. His big hands were hard as stones, and when he cracked his knuckles the sound was like trees splitting on a cold night.

Sometimes he did an exercise that wrestlers do in Japan—raising one foot high above the ground and bringing it down with a crash. Then people in nearby villages looked up at the winter sky and told one another that it was very late in the year for thunder.

Soon he could pull up a tree as well as the grandmother. He could even throw one—but only a small distance. One evening, near the end of his third month, he wrestled with Grandmother and held her down for half a minute.

"Heh-heh!" She chortled and got up, smiling with every wrinkle. "I would never have believed it!"

Maru-me squealed with joy and threw her arms around him—gently, for she was afraid of cracking his ribs.

"Very good, very good! What a strong man," said her mother, who had just come home from the fields, carrying, as usual, the cow. She put the cow down and patted the wrestler on the back.

They agreed that he was now ready to show some *real* strength before the Emperor.

"Take the cow along with you tomorrow when you go," said the mother. "Sell her and buy yourself a belt—a silken belt. Buy the fattest and heaviest one you can find. Wear it when you appear before the Emperor, as a souvenir from us."

"I wouldn't think of taking your only cow.

You've already done too much for me. And you'll need her to plow the field, won't you?"

They burst out laughing, Maru-me squealed, her mother roared. The grandmother cackled so hard and long that she choked and had to be pounded on the back.

"Oh, dear," said the mother, still laughing. "You didn't think we used our cow for anything like *work*! Why, Grandmother here is stronger than five cows!"

"The cow is our pet," Maru-me giggled. "She has lovely brown eyes."

"But it really gets tiresome having to carry her back and forth each day so that she has enough grass to eat," said her mother.

"Then you must let me give you all the prize money that I win," said Forever-Mountain.

"Oh, no! We wouldn't think of it!" said Maru-me. "Because we all like you too much to sell you anything. And it is not proper to accept gifts of money from strangers."

"True," said Forever-Mountain. "I will now ask your mother's and grandmother's permission to marry you. I want to be one of the family."

"Oh! I'll get a wedding dress ready!" said Maru-me.

The mother and grandmother pretended to consider very seriously, but they quickly agreed.

Next morning Forever-Mountain tied his hair up in the topknot that all Japanese wrestlers wear, and got ready to leave. He thanked Maru-me and her mother and bowed very low to the grandmother, since she was the oldest and had been a fine wrestling partner.

Then he picked up the cow in his arms and trudged up the mountain. When he reached the top, he slung the cow over one shoulder and waved good-bye to Maru-me.

At the first town he came to, Forever-Mountain sold the cow. She brought a good price because she was unusually fat from never having worked in her life. With the money, he bought the heaviest silken belt he could find.

When he reached the palace grounds, many of the other wrestlers were already there, sitting about, eating enormous bowls of rice, comparing one another's weight, and telling stories. They paid little attention to Forever-Mountain, except to wonder why he had arrived so late this year. Some of them noticed that he had grown quiet and took no part at all in their boasting.

All the ladies and gentlemen of the court were waiting in a special courtyard for the wrestling to begin. They wore many robes, one on top of another, heavy with embroidery and gold cloth, and sweat ran down their faces and froze in the winter afternoon. The gentlemen had long swords so weighted with gold and precious stones that they could never have used them, even if they had known how. The court ladies, with their long black hair hanging down behind, had their faces painted dead white, which made them look frightened. They had pulled out their real eyebrows and painted new ones high above the place where eyebrows are supposed to be, and this made them all look as though they were very surprised at something.

Behind a screen sat the Emperor—by himself, because he was too noble for ordinary people to look at. He was a lonely old man with a kind, tired face. He hoped the wrestling would end quickly so that he could go to his room and write poems.

The first two wrestlers chosen to fight were Forever-Mountain and a wrestler who was said to have the biggest stomach in the country. He and Forever-Mountain both threw some salt into the ring. It was understood that this drove away evil spirits.

Then the other wrestler, moving his stomach somewhat out of the way, raised his foot and brought it down with a fearful stamp. He glared at Forever-Mountain as if to say, "Now *you* stamp, you poor frightened man!"

Forever-Mountain raised his foot. He brought it down.

There was a sound like thunder, the earth shook, and the other wrestler bounced into the air and out of the ring, as gracefully as any soap bubble.

He picked himself up and bowed to the Emperor's screen.

"The earth-god is angry. Possibly there is something the matter with the salt," he said. "I do not think I shall wrestle this season." And he walked out, looking very suspiciously over one shoulder at Forever-Mountain.

From then on, Forever-Mountain brought his foot down lightly. As each wrestler came into the ring, he picked him up very gently, carried him out, and placed him before the Emperor's screen, bowing most courteously every time.

The court ladies' eyebrows went up even higher. The gentlemen looked disturbed and a little afraid. They loved to see fierce, strong men tugging and grunting at each other, but Forever-Mountain was a little too much for them. Only the Emperor was happy behind his screen, for now, with the wrestling over so quickly, he would have that much more time to write his poems. He ordered all the prize money handed over to Forever-Mountain.

"But," he said, "you had better not wrestle any more." He stuck a finger through his screen and waggled it at the other wrestlers, who were sitting on the ground weeping with disappointment like great fat babies.

Forever-Mountain promised not to wrestle any more. Everybody looked relieved. The wrestlers sitting on the ground almost smiled.

"I think I shall become a farmer," Forever-Mountain said, and left at once to go back to Maru-me.

Maru-me was waiting for him. When she saw him coming, she ran down the mountain, picked him up, together with the heavy bags of prize money, and carried him halfway up the mountainside. Then she giggled and put him down. The rest of the way she let him carry her.

Forever-Mountain kept his promise to the Emperor and never fought in public again. His name was forgotten in the capital. But up in the mountains, sometimes, the earth shakes and rumbles, and they say that is Forever-Mountain and Maru-me's grandmother practicing wrestling in the hidden valley.

Discussion

1. Forever-Mountain is "strong, healthy, and rather conceited." He is proud that he is a famous wrestler. But after his meeting with Maru-me, how do his feelings about himself change?

2. Why is it the grandmother who is chosen to wrestle with Forever-Mountain?

3. At the palace, in what way does Forever-Mountain dispose of each competitor? Why?

4. At the end of the folktale, Forever-Mountain is a happy man, even though "his name was forgotten in the capital." Why is it that he no longer needs to "wrestle before the Emperor"?

5. What examples of exaggeration do you find in the author's descriptions of the three strong women?

6. What exaggeration do you find in what the author tells you about Forever-Mountain—especially after his special training by Maru-me and the other women?

7. What examples of exaggeration do you find in the author's description of what happened at court?

8. What is the overall effect of the author's use of exaggeration?

7 MYTHS, FABLES, AND FOLKTALES

Discussion

1. What did the term *hero* seem to mean to the ancient Greeks? What do *you* understand by the word *hero?* How are heroes unlike ordinary people? What persons would you name as modern heroes?

2. The names of many commercial products that we use every day have come from the names of Greek or Roman gods and goddesses. Which of those names are you familiar with?

3. As you know, a fable makes an observation about life or gives some advice about how to live your life. To what situations today might you apply the general advice given in "The Fox and the Crow"? in "The Lion and the Mouse"?

4. In the "Folktales" section of this unit, you have read six folktales. Take time now to look back briefly at each one. Which one of those folktales appeals to you most? Why?

5. From your reading and discussion of the six folktales, you can form some idea of what a folktale is. What do you think are the folktale's outstanding characteristics?

Composition

1. In the first section of the unit, you read four Greek myths, two Norse myths, and two Native American myths. Take time now to look back at each one. Then, in a one-page composition, (a) tell which myth you liked best, and (b) explain why it appeals to you. Give at least three reasons for choosing the myth you select.

2. Myths that explain a condition or a feature of nature are known as "nature myths" or "science myths" ("Prometheus and Pandora," "Phaëthon, Son of Apollo.") *In a brief composition, write your own original nature myth.* Such a myth might explain why there are high and low tides, or why thunder accompanies a rainstorm, or why the sky is blue or why grasshoppers hop, or why leopards have spots, or. . . . Use a Greek, Norse, or Native American God or Goddess in your myth.

The Novel

THE NOVEL

There are more NOVELS published every year than any other kind of book. A novel is a type of literature having these features: First it is a long narrative—usually too long to be completed at one sitting. Second, it is written not in verse (poem form), but in prose—the straightforward kind of expression we ordinarily use in talking to one another. Third, it usually involves fictional (imagined) characters and events.

A novel is a much more fully developed narrative than any of the stories you've already read in this book. If you were to look back at those stories, you'd find that each one focuses (a) on just one major character and (b) on just one main incident or episode in the life of that character. Anything that does not concern the specific conflict presented in that one incident or episode is strictly *excluded*. A novel, on the other hand, ranges over a much longer period of time in the lives of the main characters. And because it does so, it tells about many incidents or episodes in their lives. It examines those incidents or episodes in some detail so that you, the reader, can see them from a number of points of view. Furthermore, notice that we've used the word *characters*. Although a novel can—and often does—focus on one main character, the writer of the novel (the novelist) can introduce other characters who influence the main character in many important ways. And because the novel covers a fairly long period of time—the novelist can examine the lives of all these characters in great detail. Thus it is that the major concern of a novel is on *lives*, not on fragments of lives.

Winter Thunder, the novel presented here, is a short novel—known as a NOVELLA. It is shorter than some other novels you may have read. Nonetheless, *Winter Thunder* involves you in the lives of several young people whose efforts to resolve their problems could spell the difference between life and death.

Winter Thunder

MARI SANDOZ

THE SNOW BEGAN quietly this time, like an afterthought to the gray Sunday night. The moon almost broke through once, but toward daylight a little wind came up and started white curls, thin and lonesome, running over the old drifts left from the New Year storm. Gradually the snow thickened, until around eight-thirty the two ruts of the winding trails were covered and undisturbed except down in the Lone Tree district, where an old yellow bus crawled heavily along, feeling out the ruts between the choppy sand hills.

As the wind rose the snow whipped against the posts of a ranch fence across the trail, and caked against the bus windows, shutting in the young faces pressed to the glass. The storm increased until all the air was a powdery white and every hill, every trace of road, was obliterated. The bus wavered and swayed in its direction, the tracks filling in close upon the wheels as they sought out the trail lost somewhere far back, and then finally grasped at any footing, until it looked like some great snowy, bewildered bug seen momentarily through the shifting wind. But it kept moving, hesitating here, stalling there in the deepening drifts, bucking heavily into them, drawing back to try once more while the chains spun out white fans that were lost in the driving snow which seemed almost as thick, as dense. Once the bus had to back down from a steep little patch that might have led into a storm-lost valley with a ranch house and warmth and shelter. It started doggedly around, slower now, but decisive, feeling cautiously for traction[1] on the drifted hillside. Then the wheels began to slip, catch, and then slip again, the bus tipping precariously in the push of the wind, a cry inside lost under the rising noise of the storm.

For a long time it seemed that the creeping bus could not be stopped. Even when all discernible[2] direction or purpose was finally gone, it still moved, backing, starting again, this way and that, plowing the deepened slope, swaying, leaning until it seemed momentarily very tall and held from toppling only by the thickness of the flying snow. Once more a wheel caught and held under the thunder of the red-hot smoking exhaust. It slipped, and held again, but now the force of the wind was too great. For a moment the tilting bus seemed to lift. Then it pivoted into a slow skid and turned half around, broadside. Slowly it went over, almost as though without weight at all, settling lightly against a drift, to become a part of it at that thickening place where the white storm turned to snowbanks, lost except that there were frightening cries from inside, and a hiss of steam and smoke from the hot engine against the snow.

---

1 **traction:** the pulling force or friction between wheels and a surface, enabling a vehicle to move.
2 **discernible** (də zėr′ nə bəl): capable of being seen.

In a moment the door was forced outward, the wind catching a puff of smoke as dark, muffled heads pushed up and were white in an instant. They were children, mostly in snowsuits and in sheepskin coats, thrust down over the bus side, coughing and gasping as the force of the blizzard struck them, the older ones hunching their shoulders to shield themselves and some of the rest.

Once more the engine roared out and the upper back wheel spun on its side, free and foolish in its awkward caking of snow. Then the young woman who had handed the children down followed them, her sheepskin collar up about her head, her arms full of blankets and lunch boxes.

"You'll have to give it up, Chuck," she called back into the smoking interior. "Quick! Bring the rest of the lunches—"

With Chuck, sixteen and almost as tall as a man, beside her, Lecia Terry pushed the frightened huddle of children together and hurried them away downwind into the wall of storm. Once she tried to look back through the smother of snow, wishing that they might have taken a rope and shovel from the toolbox. But there was no time to dig for them on the under side now.

Back at the bus thick smoke was sliding out the door into the snow that swept along the side. Flames began to lick up under the leaning windows, the caking of ice suddenly running from them. The glass held one moment and burst, and the flames whipped out, torn away by the storm as the whole bus was suddenly a wet, shining yellow that blistered and browned with the heat. Then there was a dull explosion above the roar of the wind, and down the slope the fleeing little group heard it and thought they saw a dark fragment fly past overhead.

"Well, I guess that was the gas tank going," Chuck shouted as he tried to peer back under his shielding cap. But there was only the blizzard closed in around them, and the instinctive fear that these swift storms brought to all living creatures, particularly the young.

There was sobbing among the children now, a small one crying out, "Teacher! Teacher!" inside the thick scarf about her face, clutching for Lecia in her sudden panic.

"Sh-h, Joanie. I'm right here," the young woman soothed, drawing the six-year-old to her, looking around for the others, already so white that she could scarcely see them in the powdery storm.

"Bill, will you help Chuck pack all the lunches in two, three boxes, tight, so nothing gets lost? Maggie's big sirup bucket'll hold a lot. Throw all the empties away. We'll have to travel light—" she said, trying to make it sound a little like an old joke.

"My father will be coming for me soon—" the eight-year-old Olive said primly. "So you need not touch my lunch."

"Nobody can find us here," Chuck said shortly, and the girl did not reply, too polite to argue. But now one of the small boys began to cry. "I want my own lunch box too, Teacher," he protested, breathless from the wind. "I—I want to go home!"

His older brother slapped him across the ear muffs with a mittened hand. "Shut up, Fritz," he commanded. "You can't go home. The bus is—" Then he stopped, looking toward the teacher, almost lost only an arm's length away, and the full realization of their plight struck him. "We can't go home," he said, so quietly that he could scarcely be heard in the wind. "The bus is burned and Chuck and Miss Lecia don't know where we are—"

"Sure we know!" Chuck shouted against him without looking up from the lunch packing, his long back stooped protectively over his task. "Don't we know, Lecia? Anyway, it won't last. Radio this morning said just light snow flurries, or Dad wouldn't have let me take the bus out 'stead of him, even sick as he was." The tall boy straightened up, the lunch boxes strung to the belt of his sheepskin to bang together in the wind until they were snow-crusted. "Baldy Stever'll be out with his plane looking for his girl friend soon's it clears a little, won't he, Lecia?" he said. "Like he came New Year's, with skis on it."

But the bold talk did not quiet the sobbing, and the teacher's nod was lost in the storm as she tied scarves and mufflers across the faces of the younger children, leaving only little slits for the eyes, with the brows and lashes already furred with snow. Then she lined up the seven, mixing the ages from six-year-old Joanie to twelve-year-old Bill, who limped heavily as he moved in the deepening snow. One of the blankets she pinned around the thinly dressed Maggie, who had only a short outgrown coat, cotton stockings, and torn overshoes against the January storm. The other blanket she tied around herself, ready to carry Joanie on her back, Indian fashion, when the short little legs were worn out.[3]

Awkwardly, one after another, Lecia pulled the left arm of each pupil from the sleeve, buttoned it inside the coat and then tied the empty sleeve to the right arm of the one ahead. She took the lead, with little Joanie tied to her belt, where she could be helped. Chuck was at the tail end of the clumsy little queue, just behind Bill with the steel-braced ankle.

"Never risk getting separated," Lecia remembered hearing her pioneer grandfather say when he told of burying the dead from the January blizzard of 1888 here, the one still called the school children's storm. "Never get separated and never stop moving until you find shelter—"

The teacher squinted back along the line, moving like some long snowy winter-logged animal, the segmented back bowed before the sharpening blizzard wind. Just the momentary turn into the storm took her breath and frightened her for these children hunched into themselves, half of them crying softly, hopelessly, as though already lost. They must hurry. With not a rock anywhere and not a tree within miles to show the directions, they had to seek out the landmark of the ranch country—the wire fence. So the girl started downwind again, breaking the new drifts as she searched for valley ground where fences were most likely, barbed-wire fences that might lead to a ranch, or nowhere except around some hay meadow. But it was their only chance the girl from the sand hills knew. Stumbling, floundering through the snow, she kept the awkward string moving, the eyes of the older ones straining through frozen lashes for even the top of one fence post, those of the small ones turned in upon their fear as the snow caked on the mufflers over their faces and they stumbled blindly to the pull from ahead.

Once there was a bolt of lightning, milky white in the blizzard, and a shaking of thunder, ominous[4] winter thunder that stopped the moving feet. Almost at once the wind grew sharper, penetrating even Chuck's

---

3 **The other** . . . **worn out:** Lecia was ready to carry Joanie on her back as an Indian mother would carry her baby.

4 **ominous** (om'ə nəs): menacing; threatening.

heavy sheepskin coat, numbing the ears and feet as panting, sobbing, the children plowed on again, the new drifts soon far above Lecia's boots, and no visibility, no way to avoid them.

With their hands so awkwardly useless, someone stumbled every few steps, but the first to fall was the crippled Bill, the others, the crying ones too, standing silent in the storm, not even able to slap one frozen hand against another while the boy was helped up. After that others went down, and soon it was all that the teacher and the boy Chuck could do to keep the children moving as they pushed through the chop hills and found themselves going up what seemed a long wind-swept, wind-frozen slope, Lecia carrying Joanie on her back most of the time now. But they kept moving somehow, barely noticing even the jack rabbit that burst out among their feet and was gone into the storm. Otherwise there was nothing.

After a long, long time they reached what seemed a high ridge of hills standing across the full blast of the north wind that bent them low and blinded. Suddenly Chuck's feet slid off sideways into a hole, a deep-cupped blowout hidden by the storm. Before he could stop, he had drawn the rest tumbling in after him, with an avalanche of snow. Crying, frightened, the smaller ones were set to their feet and brushed off a little. Then they all crouched together under the bank to catch their breath out of the wind, shivering, wet from the snow that had fallen inside their clothes, which were already freezing hard as board.

"With the blowouts always from the northwest to the southeast," Chuck shouted into the teacher's covered ear, "the wind's plainly from the north, so we're being pushed about due south. That direction there can't

be a house for five, six miles, even if we could find it—unless we got clear out of our home country—"

The girl shivered, empty with fear. "—So that's why we haven't found a fence," she said slowly. "We're probably in the old Bar M summer range, miles and miles across. But we can't go any other direction—"

"I could alone; I could make it out alone!" Chuck shouted suddenly, angrily.

For a moment the teacher was silent, waiting, but when he added nothing more, she said: "You can't leave these little ones now, Chuck. Even if you were sure you could find a ranch—"

There was no reply, except that the crippled boy began to cry, a reddening from his ankle coming up through the snow that was packed into his overshoes around the brace. Others were sobbing too, and shaking with cold, but the younger ones were very quiet now, already drowsing, and so the young teacher had to get to her feet and help lift the children out of the blowout. Slapping the muffler-covered cheeks, shaking the smaller ones so hard that the caked snow fell from them, she got the line moving again, but very slowly. She was worn out too, from the path-breaking and with Joanie in her arms to warm the child, keep her from the sleep of freezing that came upon her on Lecia's back, with only the thin blanket against the ice of the wind.

They seemed to be going down now, through a long deep-drifted slope, plowing into buried yucca clumps, the sharp spears penetrating the snowsuits, even the boot tops. Here a few head of cattle passed them, less than three feet away and barely to be seen. They were running, snow-caked, blinded, bawling, and Lecia squinted anxiously back into the storm for others, for a herd that might be upon them, trample them as surely as stampeding buffaloes. But there were no more now, and she could see that Chuck was shouting, "Little chance of its clearing up soon, with that snow thunder and those cattle already drifting so fast—all the way from the winter range!"

Yes, drifting fast with the force and terror of the storm, even hardy, thick-haired range cattle running!

Then suddenly one of the younger boys cried out something. "Teacher!" he repeated, "I saw a post!"

But it must have been a trick of the wind, for there was only the driving snow, except that the sharp-eyed Maggie saw one too, ahead and to the right—a snowy post with only the upper foot or so out of the drifts, holding up a strand of gray wire taut and humming in the cold.

For a moment Lecia could not see through the blurring of her eyes. At least this was something to follow, but which way? To her signal Chuck lifted his arm and dropped it. He didn't recognize the fence either, and so the teacher took the easier direction, left-ward, only sideface to the wind, although it might lead to the hills, to some final drift as the fleeing cattle would end.

Moving slowly along the fence, Lecia knew that it could not be much farther anyway. Her arms were wooden with cold and the weight of the child, her legs so weary in the deepening drifts that with each step it seemed that she could never lift a snow-caked boot again.

Then suddenly Chuck was doubling up the line. "I think I know where we are! That old split post just back there's where we made a take-down running coyotes with Dad's hounds this fall. If I'm right, this is Miller's north meadow, and there's a strip of willows down ahead there, off to the right—"

For a moment the girl set Joanie into the deep snow, panting, and even when she caught her breath, she was afraid to speak.

"How far to a house?" she finally asked, her lips frozen.

"There's no house along this fence if it's the Miller," Chuck had to admit. "It just goes around the meadow, three, four miles long."

"You're sure—" the teacher asked slowly, "—sure there's no cross fence to the ranch? You might get through, find help in time—"

The boy could only shake his snowy head and then, thinking that the storm hid this, he shouted the words on the wind. No, no cross fence, and the ranch was five miles south. Not even a haystack left in the valley here. Miller had had his hay balers in this fall, hauled it all out for his fancy Angus herd.

Then they must take a chance on the willows, with Bill hardly able to limp along, Joanie too heavy to carry, and several others worn out. So they wallowed through the drifted fence and tried to keep parallel to its direction, but far enough in the meadow to see any willows. There must be willows now.

Suddenly Lecia went down in what must have been a deep gully, the ground gone, the girl sinking into soft powdery snow to her shoulder. Panting, choking, she managed to get Joanie and the rest back out and the frightened ones quieted a little. Then she swung off right along the barer edge of the gully, seeking a place to cross. The wind was blowing in powerful gusts now, so that she could scarcely stand up. Bent low she dragged at the line behind her, most of the children crawling in the trench she plowed for them. There was no crying now—only the slow, slow moving. Perhaps they should dig into the snow here below the gully bank. Indians and trappers had done that and survived. But they had thick-furred buffalo robes to shut out the cold and snow, and they were grown men, tough, strong—not helpless, worn-out children, their frozen feet heavy as stone, with only an overgrown boy and a twenty-three-year-old girl to lead them, keep them alive.

More and more often Lecia had to stop, her head down, her arms dropping the weight of the little girl. But there seemed to be a shallowing in the gully now, and so it was time she tried to break a path through it and turned back toward the fence if they were not to wander lost as so many did that other time, long ago, when a teacher and her nine pupils were lost, finally falling to die on the prairie. They must cling to the fence here, if it went no farther than around the meadow. At least it was proof that something existed on the earth except the thick, stinging blizzard, with a white, freezing, plodding little queue caught in the heart of it, surrounded.

Once when the girl looked up from the running snow it seemed there was something darkish off to the right, little farther than arm's reach away. She saw it again, something rounded, perhaps a willow clump, low, snow filled, and possibly with more near by. Signaling to Chuck, Lecia turned down to it—a willow covered as in sleep, but with at least two more bushes just beyond, larger, darker, and standing closer together, their longer upper arms snow-weighted, entwined over the drifts. There, between the clumps, out of the worst of the storm, she left the children squatted close, the blankets held over them. With the belts of her coat and Chuck's, they tied the longer brushy tops of the two clumps together as solidly as they could. Then, fighting the grasping wind, they managed to fasten the blankets across the gap between the willows, to hold awhile. Behind this protection Lecia dug through the snow to the frozen ground while Chuck gathered

dead wood. Inside a close little kneeling circle of children they built a fire pile with some dry inner bark and a piece of sandwich paper for the lighting. Awkwardly, with freezing hands the teacher and Chuck hurried, neither daring to think about matches, dry ones, in any pocket after this stumbling and falling through the snow.

The two smaller children were dropping into the heavy sleep of exhaustion and cold and had to be held in their places by the older ones while Chuck dug swiftly through his pockets, deeper, more awkwardly, then frantically, the circle of peering eyes like those of fearful young animals, cornered, winter-trapped.

Down to his shirt, Chuck found some in his pocket, six in a holder made of two rifle cartridges slipped together. Hurrying clumsily he struck one of the matches. It sputtered and went out, the flames sucked away. They had to try again, making a closer circle, with the coattails of the children thrown up over their heads to shut out the storm. This time the match caught on the waxed paper and the diamond willow began to snap and sizzle in the snow, throwing a dancing light up to the circle of crouching children.

But it seemed even colder now that they had stopped walking and Lecia thought of the night ahead, with the temperature surely down to twenty-five or thirty below zero. Beyond that she would not look now; but to get through this night they must have a great pile of wood, and they must have shelter even to hold the fire.

"We can't both go out at one time," the teacher told Chuck in their planning, somehow making it seem as for a long, long time. "It's too risky for the children. We might not get back."

The boy looked around from the fire he was nursing, and upward, but there was still no thinning of the storm, the area of snowy visibility almost as small as the confines of their new meat-freeze room[5] at the ranch. Even so he gave the girl no sign of agreement.

Lecia set willow poles into the snowbanks as she went to look for wood, none farther apart than the outstretched reach of her arms. She found more willows, each clump sitting alone in the isolation of the driving storm, so cold now that the green wood snapped off like glass. Each time it was only by the row of sticks in the drifts that she managed to stagger her blinded and panting way back against the wind with her load of wood.

The brushier portions she piled behind the blankets of the shelter to catch the snow and shut out the wind. Some, long as fish poles, she pushed through the willow clumps and across the opening between, in a sort of lattice inside the bellying blankets that Eddie and Calla tried to hold in place. They were the first of the children to separate themselves from the snowy composite, the enforced co-ordinate that had been the queue driven by the storm, the circle that shielded the sprouting fire. Now they were once more individuals who could move alone, hold the blankets from blowing inward, pile the dry powdery snow from the ground against and between the sticks, trying to work it like plaster, building a wall between the clumps of willows. Even Bill helped a little, as far as he could reach without moving the bad ankle. They worked slowly, clumsily, pounding their freezing hands at the fire, but returning.

By one o'clock the north wind was cut off so that the fire fattened and burned higher, softening the ice caked to the clothing until it

could be knocked off, and softening the face of the drift reached by the wind-blown heat. The children packed this against the north wall too, and into the willow clumps both ways, drawing the rounded wall inward toward the top along the bend of the willows, making what looked like half of an Indian snow shelter, or the wickiup Calla had seen at the county fair, just high enough at the center for a seven-year-old to stand up, the snow walls glistening rosy in the firelight as the wind was shut off.

"That's a good job!" Chuck shouted over the roar of the storm as he tried to rub circulation into Joanie's waxen feet. The small girl was beginning to cry out of her sleep with the first pain; others began too, their ears and hands swollen and purpling, their toes painful as their boots thawed. But it seemed that the feet of nine-year-old Maggie must be lost, the ragged old overshoes and cotton stockings so frozen that she had to cut them away with Eddie's knife. Under them her feet were like stone, dead white stone, although the girl was working hard to rub life into them. She worked silently and alone, as had become natural long ago, her thin face pinched and anxious with the pain and the alarm.

Of them all only Olive seemed untouched. She was dry in her heavy waterproofed snowsuit with attached rubber feet inside the snow boots. And she was still certain that her father would soon come for her.

"He would not care to leave me in such an unpleasant place—"

When they had the semicircular wall of the shelter drawn in as far as the snow would hold, Lecia decided to pull the blankets away from the outside and use one over the top, with the belt-tied willows sticking through a smoke hole cut in the center. But as the

---

5 **meat-freeze room**: a place for freezing and keeping meat until the time comes to cook it.

blankets came down, part of the loose snow wall was blown in by the force of the blizzard, the huddle of children suddenly white again, the fire almost smothered. So the wall had to be rebuilt in discouragement, but with care, using more brush and sticks, more fire-softened snow to freeze in place as soon as it was struck by the storm. Lecia had to stop several times for her hands too, pounding them hard, holding them over the fire, the diamond sparkling. She tried to turn the ring off before the swelling became too great and then gave it up. The wall must be finished, and when it was solid, Calla came to whisper under the roar of the wind. "Bill's been eating the lunch," she said.

"Oh, Bill! That's not fair to the others, to your own little sister Joanie!" Lecia cried. Suddenly not the good teacher, she grabbed up the containers and hung them on high branches out in plain sight for watching, for reminders and derision from the other children. "Why, it may be days before we are found!" she scolded, in her exasperation saying what should have been kept hidden in silence.

Before the boy could defend himself with a plea of hunger or his usual complaint about the crippled foot, some realization of their plight had struck the others. Even little Fritz, with the security of an older sister and brother like Calla and Eddie along, began to sob. Only the round-cheeked Olive was calm, the others angered to see it, wanting to shout against her outsider's assurance, to tell her she was too stupid and green to know that her father could not come for her in such a blizzard, that he would never find her if he could get through. But they were silent under the teacher's admonitory eye. And, as in the schoolhouse and on the playground, Bill had withdrawn, except that now it could not be more than a foot or two.

As the frozen earth between the willow humps became soggy, Calla and Eddie helped move the others around so that there was room to draw the fire first one way and then another, to dry and warm the ground. Lecia watched to see that they set no one afire and then bowed her head out into the storm again. Chuck was dragging in willows for the night. They drove sticks into the hardening drifts around the front of the shelter and piled brush against them to catch the snow. It filled in as fast as they worked until there was no more than a little crawling hole left. Then Chuck laid a mat of brushy sticks on the ground and packed soft snow into them to freeze, making a handled slab big enough to close the low doorway. Now, so long as the blanket with the smoke hole stayed tied over the top they could be as warm as they wished in the little shelter that was scarcely longer than a tall man—a close cramping for the teacher, Chuck, and the seven pupils, but easily warmed with a few fingers of wood, an Indian fire.[6] Safe and warm so long as the shelter stood against the rising ferocity of the blizzard, and the willows lasted.

---

6 **Indian fire:** a small fire near which a person can huddle for warmth.

1. The story begins with a detailed description of the setting. Why is it important for you, the reader, to become well aware of that setting?

2. When do you first see the characters? Who are those characters? Who seems to be the main character? Why was Chuck, a sixteen-year-old boy, driving the school bus?

3. During the search for shelter, Lecia remembers some advice given her by her pioneer grandfather. What is that advice? Why is it important? How does Lecia follow that advice?

4. What evidence do you find that Chuck may cause a problem? How is Olive different from the other children in the group? What special problems do Bill and Maggie have?

5. Briefly explain how the willow clumps were used to provide shelter for the group. In what way was the ground of the shelter dried out? How was the low doorway closed?

6. Who is Baldy Stever? What do you know about him at this point in the story? Of what importance do you think this information might be?

By now the cold stung the nose and burned the lungs, the snow turned to sharp crystals that drew blood from the bare skin. It drove the teacher and Chuck in to the fire, shaking, unable, it seemed, ever to be warmed through again. Lecia opened her sheepskin coat, hung up her frozen scarf and cap and shook out her thick brown hair that gleamed in the firelight. Even with her tawny skin red and swollen, her gold-flecked hazel eyes bloodshot, she was still a pretty girl, and the diamond on her hand flashed as she hunted for her stick of white salve to pass around for the raw, bleeding lips. It was all she could do.

Now they tried to plan for what was to come, but here they were as blind as in the flight through the storm. There would be sickness, with the noses already running, Joanie coughing deep from her chest, and, worst of all, Maggie's feet that seemed to be dying. Besides, the fire must be kept going and the food spread over three, perhaps four, days.

Here Bill raised his complaining voice. "You ain't our boss outside of school! We'll do what we want to. There ain't enough to eat for everybody."

"You mean *isn't,* not *ain't,*" the teacher corrected firmly. "And talking like that—

when you've barely missed one lunch time!"

"You ain't never my boss," Chuck said casually, "—only about the kids while in the bus, like you do with my dad when he's driving. I sure can do what I want to here, and I'll do it."

Slowly the girl looked around the ring of drowsy, firelit eyes upon her, some uneasy at this bold talk to their teacher, but some smaller ones aping the defiance of the big boys. Chuck, who sat almost a head taller than Lecia, grinned down at the pretty young teacher but with an arrogance that was intended to remind her he saw nothing here as his responsibility, nothing this side of the bus except saving himself.

Unable to reply in words that would not frighten the children more, the teacher looked past the fire into the boy's broad, defiant face, into his unblinking, storm-red eyes, the look commanding at first, then changing to something else in spite of herself, into a sort of public test, until it seemed she dared not turn her gaze away or at that instant the sixteen-year-old boy must assert his victory by plunging out into the storm and perhaps destroy himself, perhaps bring death to all of them.

Before this silent, incomprehensible struggle the children were uneasy and afraid, even the coughing stilled, so that the storm seemed very loud outside the smoke hole. But little Fritz was too young to be held so for long. "I'm hungry!" he shouted against the restraining hand of his sister. "I want my lunch!"

As though freed, released, Chuck sat back and grinned a little at the small boy. Matter of factly the teacher washed her raw hands with snow and held them over the fire. Then she spread her napkin on her lap and set out all there was in the eight lunches now:

fourteen sandwiches, most of them large, six pieces of Sunday cake, a handful of cookies, a few pieces of candy, and six apples and two oranges, frozen hard. There were two thermos bottles of milk, and these Lecia pushed away into the snow wall.

"If somebody gets sick and can't eat solid food," she said to the owners, their eyes following her hands in consternation.[7] Even with the best management, there would be no food of any kind in a few days, but this the small owners could not yet understand.

The frozen fruit she handed to Chuck and, without meeting the girl's eyes, he set it around the coals for toasting, to be eaten now because it would not keep well, and might sicken leaner stomachs. In the meantime Lecia set one lunch box filled with snow near the fire and packed away all except four of the big sandwiches into the others, the eyes of the children following her hands here too, even as she hung the containers back above her head. Then she divided the four sandwiches into halves and passed them around.

"Eat very slowly," she cautioned. "Blizzards usually last three days, so we must make what we have here last too, probably clear to Thursday, or longer."

But Bill seemed not to be listening. "Chuck's eating!" he suddenly protested. "He ain't, *isn't*, in on the lunches."

For a moment the teacher looked sternly at the boy. "After Chuck carried them all from the bus, helped you through the bad places, and helped to make the shelter and the fire!" the girl said in astonishment. "Now we'll have no more of this bickering and complaint. Here we are equal partners, and not one of us will get out of this alive unless

we keep working together. Even your comic books should have taught you that much! And don't think this is play. You remember what the storm of 1888 was called in your history book—because so many school children died in it. That storm was short, not over two days most places, nothing for length like the one we had holiday time this year, and no telling about this one. Most of the children in 1888 died because somebody got panicky, didn't think, or they didn't stick together—"

There was silence all around the fire now, the storm seeming to rise, the children edging closer to each other, glancing fearfully over their shoulders as though toward night windows with terrible things stalking outside.

"Oh, we're O.K.," Chuck said optimistically. "We can last three days easy here—" the rebellion gone from him, or hidden for the moment.

Thinking of a five-day storm, the teacher looked around the frightened, sooty faces, the children coughing and sniffling, their pocket tissue gone, the few handkerchiefs hung to dry and wondered if any, even the man-tall Chuck, would be here by then.

But Olive, the newcomer, was unconcerned. "I should like another sandwich, Miss Terry. From my own lunch, please," she said, with the formality of an old-fashioned boarding school for eight-year-olds. "I won't need the remainder. My father will come for me when it is time."

"He won't find you—" Maggie said as she rubbed at her feet, color seeping into them now, an angry gray-splotched purple, with pain that twisted the thin face.

"My father will come," Olive repeated, plainly meaning that he was not like the fathers of the others here, particularly Maggie's, who had done nothing since the war

---

7 **consternation** (kon stər nā′ shən): a combination of amazement and dismay that brings confusion.

except make a little South Pacific bug juice,[8] as he called it, for himself from chokecherries, wild grapes, or raisins in the way they did in the war. He had only a little piece of copper tubing, and so he couldn't make more than enough for himself, yet he got into jail just the same, for crashing his old truck through the window of the county assistance office.[9] But things had not been good before that. Often this fall Maggie was at school when the bus arrived, not waiting at the stop near their crumbling old sod shack but walking the three miles. Sometimes her face was bruised, but she was silent to any questioning. If Maggie lost her feet now, it was because she had no warm snowsuit and high boots like the others, only the short old coat above her skinny knees, the broken overshoes with the soles flopping.

But there was still a cheerful face at the fire. Although little Fritz's cheeks seemed swollen to bursting and his frosted ears stood away under the flaps of his cap, he could still show his gap-toothed grin in mischief.

"If we don't get home till Thursday, Teacher, Baldy'll be awful mad at you when he comes flying out Wednesday—"

The rest laughed a little, drowsily. "Maybe Baldy won't be flying around that soon," Eddie said, and was corrected by Calla's sisterly concern. "Don't say Baldy. Say Mr. Stever."

But the teacher busied herself hanging up everything loose. Then with Chuck's knife she slit the remaining blanket down the middle and fastened half around each side against the snow wall, like a tipi lining. By the time the white blizzard darkness came,

the smaller children had all been taken outside for the last time and lay in fretful, uneasy sleep. Olive had been the last, waiting stubbornly for her father until she toppled forward. Calla caught her and made room for the girl still murmuring, "Papa—"

Finally the last sob for parent and home was stilled, even Joanie asleep, her feverish head in the teacher's lap, her throat raw and swelling, with nothing except hot snow water to ease the hollow cough. There were half a dozen lozenges in Lecia's pocket but these must be saved for the worse time that would surely come.

The children were packed around the fire like little pigs or puppies on a very cold night. Chuck was at the opposite side from Lecia, the boys on his side, the girls on hers, with Calla and her brothers around the back. The older ones lay nearer the wall, their arms over the younger to hold their restlessness from the fire.

But Bill was still up, drawn back under the willows, his head pulled into his sheepskin collar, his ankle bent to him. He watched the teacher doze in fatigue, met her guilty waking gaze sullenly. But finally he reached down into his pocket and drew out something in waxed paper.

"I didn't eat the piece you gave me—" he said, holding out his half of the sandwich.

"Bill! That was fine of you," the girl said, too worn out for more as she reached up to put it away.

"No—no, you eat it. I guess you didn't take any."

A moment Lecia looked at the boy, but he avoided her as he edged himself around Chuck closer to the fire, turning his chilled back to the coals, and so she ate the buttered bread with the thick slice of strengthening cold beef, while more snow was driven in

---

8 **South Pacific bug juice:** homemade brandy with a high alcoholic content.
9 **county assistance office:** the county department responsible for unemployment benefits.

through the smoke hole and settled in sparkling dust toward the little fire. There were white flashes too, and the far rumble of winter thunder.

"Is—is there lots of willows left?" the crippled boy asked.

The teacher knew what he meant—how many clumps, and if so far out that someone might get lost.

"I think there are quite a few," she replied, needing to reassure the boy, but unable to make it a flat lie.

A long time he sat silent. Finally he pulled his cap off and shook the long yellowish hair back from his petulant face. "I wonder what Mother's doing—" he said slowly, looking away, his hand seeking out the tortured ankle. Lecia motioned him to hold it over to her and so she did not need to reply, to ask what all the mothers of these children must be doing, with the telephone lines still down from the other storm and surely nobody foolish enough to try bucking this one, unless it might be Olive's father, the new Eastern owner of the little Box Y ranch.

With snow water heated in the lunch tin, Lecia washed the poor stick that was the boy's ankle, gently sponging the bone laid almost bare where the frozen snow and the iron brace wore through the scarred and unhealthy skin.

"It looks pretty bad, Bill, but you probably won't have to put the brace back on for days—" Lecia started to comfort, but it was too late, and she had to see fear and anger and self-pity darken the face in the firelight. Because nothing could be unsaid, the girl silently bandaged the ankle with half of the boy's handkerchief. "Now get a little sleep if you can," she said gently.

The boy crawled in next to Eddie as though Ed were the older, and for a long time the teacher felt the dark eyes staring at her out of the shadowy coat collar as though she had deliberately maneuvered this plunge into the blizzard.

Discussion

1. Once the crude shelter is built, the group seems relatively safe for the moment. What problems still confront Lecia, Chuck, and the children? What food does the group have? What decision about the food does Lecia make?

2. Again, Lecia meets defiance, this time from two members of the group. Who are they? Describe their actions. How does Lecia deal with their behavior?

3. In what way does Olive again demonstrate that she is different from the other children? What more do you learn about Maggie's background? What role does little Fritz seem to play in the group?

4. After everyone finally settles down for the night, Bill shows another side to his personality. Explain. What does Lecia say that seems to make Bill revert to his usual conduct?

Several times before midnight the girl started to doze but jerked herself awake at the frozen creak of the willow shelter, to push the out-tossed arms back and replenish the fire.

Eddie's cough began to boom deep as from a barrel. He turned and moaned, digging at his chest, Calla helpless beside him, her sleep-weighted eyes anxious on the teacher. Maggie too was finally crying now. Her feet had puffed up and purpled dark as jelly bags, with the graying spots that would surely break and slough off, perhaps spread in gangrene. Yet all Lecia could do was turn the girl's feet from the fire and push them behind the blanket against the snow to relieve the pain and itching a little. Perhaps only freeze them more. Lecia touched the girl's forehead to calm her but felt her stiffen and start to pull away from this unaccustomed kindly touch. Then Maggie relaxed a little and as the teacher stroked the hot temples, she wondered how many days it might be before help could get through. Suddenly their plight here seemed so hopeless, the strength and wisdom of her twenty-three years so weak and futile, that she had to slip out into the storm for calm. And finally Maggie slept, worn out, but still tearing at her feet.

To the weary girl watching, half asleep, at the fire, the roar of the storm rose and fell like the panting of a great live thing, sometimes a little like many great planes warming up together. If only she had married Dale Stever New Year's, they would be in the Caribbean now, these children all safe at home, with probably no other teacher available so soon. Once Lecia turned her swollen hand to the fire, watching the ring catch and break the light into life, and tried to recall the fine plans Dale had made for them. He wasn't a rancher's son like those who usually took her to parties and dances—like Joe, or Wilmo, or even Ben, of the local bank. Dale had come from outside last summer and bought up the sale pavilion in town. Since then he flew all around the surrounding ranch country in a plane the color of a wild canary rising from a plum thicket, gathering stock for the sales. Fairtime he took Lecia and her friend Sallie down to the state fair, and several times on long trips since, to Omaha to the ballet and to Denver. At first it seemed he was all jolly big-talk, with windy stories of his stock in an oil company down in Dallas and in a Chicago commission house. He had a touch of gray at his temples that he thought made him look distinguished when he had his hat on, and to their fathers he called himself the Dutch uncle of the two girls. But gradually he concentrated on Lecia, and at Christmas there was the big diamond and the plane ready to fly south. He even took her to the school board to ask for a release from her contract.

"No," the old school director told the girl. "Bill Terry was a friend of mine, brought me into the country. I can't help his granddaughter marry no man in a rush hurry."

Dale laughed confidently and put his arm about the girl's shoulder as they left, but somehow Lecia couldn't break her contract. They must wait until school was out. Dale had been angry. "This is no life for a girl as pretty as you," he said. Truly he was right. Today it was no life for any girl.

Soon after midnight Lecia was startled out of a doze by the sound of cattle bawling somewhere in the roar of the storm, like the herds that passed her home in the night of the May blizzard three years ago, when so many died in the drifts and lakes that the whole region was a stench far into the summer. Then suddenly the girl realized where she was, and hurried bareheaded out into the storm. The bawling was very close; any moment hundreds of storm-blinded cattle might be running over the little willows, over their own two clumps.

Lecia dragged burning sticks from the fire, but in an instant the storm had sucked their flame away. So, with her arms up to shield her eyes from the snow that was sharp as steel dust, she stood behind the shelter shouting the "Hi-ah! Hi-ah!" she had learned when she helped the cowboys push cattle[10] to market. It was a futile, lost little sound against cattle compelled to run by an instinct that could not be denied, compelled to flee for survival before the descent of the arctic storm, never stopping until trapped in some drift, or boldly overtaken in some open fence corner to freeze on their feet, as Lecia had seen them stand.

Realizing her danger as a warmth crept over her, the girl stumbled back into the shelter and crouched at the fire. She barely noticed the sting of returning blood in her ears and face while she listened until the drifting herd was surely past, made more afraid by the knowledge of this thing that drove cattle galloping through the night, the power of it, and how easily it could overcome the little circle of children here if it were not for the handful of fire, for the walls of the storm's own snow.

Toward morning the weary girl knew that she could not keep awake. She had stirred Chuck to sit up a while, but he was unable to shake off the weight of sleep so heavy on an overgrown boy. Trying to remember how the Indians carried their fire—something about moss and damp, rotted wood—Lecia pulled old dead roots from the willow butts and laid them into the coals with the ends sticking far out. Even with waxed paper handy it would be a desperate chance. Willows burned fast as kindlings and there were only five matches, including the one from Eddie's pocket, and no telling how many spoiled by dampness.

Even so it was sweet to let herself sink into darkness, but it seemed that she awoke at once, stiff and cold from the nightmare that reached into the waking black, even the ashes of the fire spot cold. With the waxed paper held ready, the girl blew on the ends of the unburnt roots her hands found, carefully, breathless in her fear. At last a red spark glowed deep in one, and when the fire was going again, she slipped outside for calm in the cold that was like thin, sharp glass in the nose.

There was still no earth and no sky, only the white storm of late dawn blowing hard. But the wood had lasted and now Lecia put on a few extra sticks and heated water to wash the goose mush from the inflamed eyes of the children. She started a rousing song: "Get up! Get up, you sleepyhead!" but even before it was done, Joanie began to whimper, "I'm hungry—"

So the teacher laid out four sandwiches on sticks over the coals and then added another half for herself when she saw Bill watching. "There won't be anything more today except a pinch of cake unless the sun breaks through."

"If it does, we can stomp out a message on the snow," Calla said cheerfully.

"Yes, even if people can't travel for a whole week, Baldy'll come flying over to see about his girl friend," Bill said, boldly.

The younger boys laughed a little, but Chuck was more serious. "If the sky lightens at all and there's no blowing. I'll do the stomping before I leave."

"You'd run away now?" the teacher asked

---

10 **push cattle:** herd or drive cattle.

softly as she combed at Joanie's fine brown hair.

"Somebody's got to get help," he defended in loud words.

The children around the fire were suddenly quiet, turning their eyes to follow the tall boy as he pulled up his sheepskin collar and crawled out into the storm. And silent a long time afterward—all except Joanie, who sobbed softly, without understanding. Even Olive looked up once, but Maggie grated her feet hard along the snow wall and tore at their congestion as though she heard nothing.

Then suddenly there was stomping outside and Chuck came back in, snowy, thick frost all over his collar and cap, his brows and lashes in ice, the children pushing over toward him, as to one gone, lost. He brought more wood, and the teacher seemed to have forgotten that he had said anything about leaving. But the children watched him now, even when they pretended they didn't, and watched Lecia too, for suspicion had come in.

The teacher started as for a school day, except that the arithmetic was rote learning of addition and multiplication tables and a quick run through some trick problems: "If I had a fox, a goose, and some corn to get across a river in a boat—" and then, "If I had a dollar to buy a hundred eggs—no, I should take something that won't make us hungry."

"Like a hundred pencils?"

"Well, yes, let's take pencils. I want to buy a hundred for a dollar. Some are five cents each, poor ones two and a half cents, and broken ones half a cent. How many of each kind must I buy?"

In history and nature study they talked about the Indians that still roamed the sand hills when Lecia's grandfather came into the country. They lived the winter long in skin tipis something like the shelter here, and almost as crowded, but with piles of thick-

furred buffalo robes for the ground and the beds. The girls sat on one side, the boys on the other.

"Like we are here—" Fritz said, his eyes shining in the discovery. "We're Indians. Whoo-oo-oo!" he cried, slapping his mouth with his palm.

They talked about the food too, the piles of dried and pounded meat, the winter hunts, how the village and lodges were governed, and what the children did, their winter games, one almost like "button, button." The boys learned from the men—such things as arrow-making, and later bullet-making, hunting, fighting; and particularly the virtues of resourcefulness, courage, fortitude, and responsibility for all the people. A girl learned from the women—beading, tanning hides, and all the other things needed to live well with modesty, steadfastness, and generosity, and with courage and fortitude and responsibility too, for it was thought that the future of the people lay in the palms of the women, to be cherished or thrown away.

"What does that mean, Teacher?" Fritz asked, hitting out in mischief at his brother Eddie, despite Calla and the teacher both watching, then shouting he was hungry again.

The rest tried to laugh a little as Calla whispered to her small brother, trying to make herself heard against the storm, while Lecia taught them a poem about Indians. Even Joanie repeated a few lines for her, although the child leaned weak and feverish against Calla while Bill comforted his bound ankle and Maggie tried hard to pull herself out of the curious drowsiness that had the teacher frightened.

After a while the children played "button, button," and tried to tell each other poems. When Eddie got stuck on "Snowbound,"[11] Bill nudged Fritz and they laughed as easily at his discomfiture as at school, perhaps because Chuck was back and this was the second day of the storm, with tomorrow the third. Then it would clear up and somebody with a scoop shovel would get his horse along the barer ridges to a telephone.

"Maybe somebody'll just come running over the hills to find us," Eddie teased, looking at Olive, turning his face from the teacher.

"Well, even if nobody came and Baldy couldn't find a place to land with skis on his plane, he would have sacks of food and blankets and stuff dropped like in the movies and the newspapers."

"I saw it in a movie once, I did," Joanie cried.

So they talked, pretending no one was looking up at the hanging lunch buckets, or sick and afraid. But Lecia did not hear them.

"Oh-oo, Teacher's sleeping like one of those old Indian women up to Gordon, just sitting there!" Eddie exclaimed.

"Sh-h," Calla said, in her way. "Let her stretch out here," and with a polite smile Olive moved aside.

---

11 "**Snowbound**": a poem written by John Greenleaf Whittier (1809–1892) an American poet.

1. Until now, you know very little about Dale Stever, Lecia's fiancé. What do you learn about him in this part of the story? If Lecia had married Dale on New Year's, how would events be different?

2. Explain Lecia's fears when she hears the bawling of the cattle. What is the "thing" that drives the cattle?

3. Once again, Chuck says he is going to leave the group. What effect does this announcement have on the children?

4. Lecia makes an effort to treat the day as a school day. What subjects does the group discuss? What did the children learn that was more meaningful to them because of their situation?

5. The severe storm and the intense cold are described through the use of similes. Point out the similes that describe the cold and storm in this section of the story.

That night Joanie was delirious, and once Maggie slipped past the teacher out into the storm to relieve the fire of her feet. By midnight she couldn't stand on them, and the grayish spots were yellow under the thick skin of a barefoot summer, the swelling creeping above the girl's thin ankles, with red streaks reaching almost to the knees. Her eyes glistened, her cheeks were burning, and she talked of wild and dreadful things.

Lecia tried to remember all that she had read of frost-bite, all that her grandfather had told, but she knew that the inflammation spreading past the frozen area was like the cold overtaking the fleeing cattle, and she had to make a desperate decision. She dug two holes deep into the snow wall and laid Maggie with her feet in them almost to her knees, wishing they had something waterproof for covering. The cold would probably freeze the girl more, but it would numb the nerves and perhaps slow the congestion and tissue starvation. Later, when the girl was restless again and crying, Lecia found the yellow spots spreading, painful and hard as boils. She burned the end of a safety pin and while Maggie's frightened eyes became caverns in her thin face, Lecia opened one of the spots. Bloody pus burst down over her hand. Holding the foot aside she wiped it away on the snow, from her ring too, and then slipped it from her shrunken finger and hung it on a twig overhead, where it swayed a little, like a morning dewdrop while she opened the rest of the festering.

When the girl's feet were bathed and bound in the sleeves torn from Lecia's white shirt blouse, she thrust them back into the snow. Then she gave Maggie half a cup of the milk, very quietly, hoping none would

awaken to see, although none needed it more. Almost at once the girl was asleep, to rest until the pus gathered again. But the first time Lecia returned with firewood she saw the thermos bottle half out. She jerked it from the hole. The milk was all gone, and across the little fire Olive stared at her teacher.

"It was mine," the girl said flatly.

So the time had come when the little food left must be hidden. Now, with all but Olive sleeping, was the time. When Lecia came back in, the girl held out something—the ring that had been left hanging on the twig and forgotten.

The next day and the next were the same, only colder, the drifts deeper and harder along the willows, the wind so sharp with snow that it froze the eyeballs. Lecia and Chuck covered their faces as they fought

their way back against it, the wood dragging from their shoulders, tied by a strap of cloth cut off around the bottom of Lecia's coat. One at a time they went out and came back, a hand stretched ahead feeling for the next guide pole in the snow before the other let go of the last, the covered face turned from the storm to save the breath from being torn away by the wind.

All the third day there was watching out of the smoke hole for the sky that never appeared. When night finally came without star or stillness, even Lecia, who had tried to prepare herself for this eventuality, felt that she could not face another day of blizzard. Maggie no longer sat up now and both Joanie and Eddie were so sick—their fever high, their chests filling—that the teacher had to try something. She seemed to remember that the early settlers used willow bark to break a fever, so she steeped a handful in Maggie's tin cup until the liquid was strong and dark. She made the two children drink it, first experimentally, then more, and after a while they began to sweat. When they awoke they were wet, their hair clinging to their vulnerable young foreheads, but they seemed better all the next day, except weak. Then at night it was the same with Joanie.

The fourth day was like the rest, colder, with the same white storm outside, the children hunching silent upon themselves inside. Sometimes a small one sobbed a little in sickness and hunger, but it was no more than a soft moaning now, even when Lecia divided most of the little food that was left. The children, even Chuck, took it like animals, and then sat silent again, the deep-socketed eyes watching, some slyly gnawing at willow sticks and roots hidden in the palm.

Everybody around the fire was coughing and fevered now, it seemed to Lecia, the bickering going beyond childish things to quarrels about real or fancied animosities between their families. Once even Calla spoke angrily to Bill, defending her brothers.

"At least they aren't mama babies like you!"

"Mama babies! I wouldn't talk if everybody knew that my family got a start in cattle by stealing calves—"

"You can't say such things!" Calla cried, up and reaching for Bill, caught without his brace and unable to flee into the storm, Joanie crying: "Don't! Don't hit my brother!"

When Lecia returned, Chuck was holding the two apart, shaking them both. The teacher spoke in anger and impatience too now, and Bill's face flushed with embarrassment and shame, the sudden red like fever in his hunger-grayed cheeks.

Only Maggie with her poor feet was quiet, and Olive, sitting as though stunned or somewhere far away. The teacher knew that she should do something for this girl, only eight yet apparently so self-contained. Olive never spoke of her father now, as none of the boys teased Lecia about Baldy any more. Olive was as remote about him as everything else since the night she drank the milk, and found the ring on a twig.

Too weary to think about it, and knowing she must keep awake in the night, Lecia stretched out for a nap. When she awoke Olive was sitting exactly the same, but the places of Chuck and Eddie were empty—Eddie out in the blizzard after his night of sweating. Then the boys returned with wood, weak, dragging, almost frozen, and with something that Lecia had to be told outside. There seemed only one willow clump left.

One clump? Then they must start digging at the frozen butts, or even pull down their shelter to keep the fire alive, for now the boys too were believing that the storm would blow forever. Yet toward evening there was a thinning above the smoke hole, the sun suddenly there like a thin disk of milky ice from the bottom of a cup. It was almost a promise, even though the storm swept the sun away in a few minutes and the wind shifted around to the south, whipping in past the block the boys had in the hole of the shelter. The children shivered, restless. Once Eddie rose from his sleep and fought to get out, go home. When he finally awakened, he lay down in a chill, very close to the fire, and would not move until a stench of burning cloth helped rouse him. Then he drank the bitter willow bark tea too and finally he slept.

Friday morning the sun came out again toward ten o'clock, the same cold, pale disk, with the snow still running along the earth, running higher than the shelter or Chuck, shutting out everything except the veiled sun. The boy came in, looked around the starved, listless circle at the fire, at the teacher too, with her face that had been so pretty Monday morning gaunt and sooty now.

He laid two red-tipped matches, half of all he had, in the girl's lap. "I'm getting out," he said, and without a protest from anyone crawled through the hole and was gone.

The children were almost past noticing his desertion now, barely replying when spoken to. If the colds got worse or pneumonia struck, it would be over in a few hours. Maggie hadn't sat up since yesterday, lying flat, staring at the white storm blowing thin above the smoke hole. If any of them wondered how Lecia could keep the fire going alone, with nothing much except the willow butts left, none spoke of it. The teacher sat with her arms hanging between her knees, hopeless.

She finally stirred and put the matches away in waxed paper in her shirt pocket where her ring lay, buttoning the flap down carefully now. Joanie started to cough again, choking, turned red and then very white under the grime and grayness of her face, lying very still. Now Bill made the first gesture toward his small sister.

"Come here, Doll," he said gently, drawing her awkwardly from Lecia's lap, the child lifting her head slowly, holding herself away, looking up at him as a baby might at a stranger, to be weighed and considered. Then she snuggled against him and in a moment she was asleep.

Discussion

1. As the blizzard rages on, sickness becomes more and more serious. What remedies does Lecia recall that give the ailing children some relief?

2. The bickering among the children takes on a different tone from what went on earlier in their ordeal. In your opinion, what causes this "different tone?" Which two children remain quiet throughout the bickering?

3. What responses does Olive make when Lecia discovers the milk is gone? Although Olive still remains isolated from the group, in what one way has she changed? In your opinion, should there be as much concern about Olive as about the children who have physical illnesses? Explain.

4. On Friday, Chuck says, "I'm getting out." How does the response of Lecia and the children differ from when Chuck has threatened leaving other times? In your opinion, why is the response different?

5. What unusual action does Bill take? How does Joanie react to Bill's gesture?

After a long time there seemed a dull sound outside, and then Chuck was suddenly back, crawling in almost as though he had not left, panting in his weakness from the fight against the wind that had turned north again, and colder.

"Scared an eagle off a drift out there," he finally managed to say. "And there's a critter stuck in the snow—beyond the far willows. Small spring calf. Froze hard, but its meat—"

Then the realization that Chuck was back struck the teacher. She was not alone with the children, and he too was safe for now. But there was something more. The boy who had resented them and his involvement in their plight—he had escaped and come back.

"Oh, Chuck!" the girl exclaimed. Then what he said reached her mind. "A calf? Maybe we could build a fire there so we can cut some off, if we can't get it all out." She reached for her boots. "But we'll have to go work at it one at a time—" looking around the firelit faces that were turned toward her as before, but the eyes alert, watching as though a morsel might be dropped, even thrown.

"I'll go with Chuck, Miss Lecia," Bill said softly. "He can show me and I'll show you. Save time hunting—"

The teacher looked at the crippled boy, already setting Joanie gently aside and reaching for his brace. She felt pride in him, and unfortunate doubt.

"He can probably make it," Chuck said, a little condescending. "It's not over an eighth of a mile, and I found more willows farther along the way, the drifts mostly frozen hard too. I blazed the willows beyond our poles—"

"You'll be careful—mark everything," the girl pleaded.

"We've got to. It's snowing again, and the sun's gone."

It seemed hours since the boys went out and finally the teacher had to go after them, appalled that the younger ones had to be left alone, yet it must be done. She moved very carefully, feeling her way in the new storm, going sideways to it, from pole to pole. Then she came to a place where the markers were gone, probably blown down and buried by the turning wind. The boys were out there, lost, in at least fifteen, perhaps twenty, below zero. Without sticks to guide her way back, the girl dared go no farther but she crouched there, bowed before the wind, cupping her mouth with her mittens, shouting her hopeless: "Boys! Chuck! O-hoo!" the wind snatching it away. She kept calling until she was shaking and frozen and then to a frightening warmth.

But now she had to keep on, for it seemed that she heard something, a vague, smothered sound, and yet a little like a reply. Tears freezing on her face she called again and again until suddenly the boys were at her feet, there before she could see them, so much like the snow, like white dragging animals, one bowed, half carrying the other. For a few minutes they crouched together in desperate relief, the snow running over them as something immovable, like an old willow butt. Then, together, they pulled themselves up and started back. When they finally reached the shelter, out of breath and frozen, they said nothing of what had happened, nor spoke at all for a while. Yet all, even little Joanie, seemed to sense that the boys had almost been lost.

As soon as the teacher was warmed a little, she started out alone, not certain that she could make it against the storm, but knowing that she must try to get meat. She took Chuck's knife, some dry bark, waxed paper, the two matches in her shirt pocket, and a

bundle of poles pulled from their shelter. Moving very carefully beyond the gap in the willow markers, she set new sticks deep, and tipped carefully with the new storm. She found the farther willow clumps with Chuck's blazing, and the brush pile the boys had made, and beside it the ice-covered head of the calf still reaching out of the snow. The hole they had dug around the red hindquarters was drifted in loosely, but easily dug out. Lecia set a fire pile there and felt for a match with her numb fingers, fishing in the depths of her pocket, something round in the way, her ring. But she got the match and lighted the fire under her shielding sheepskin coat. For a long time she crouched protectively over the flame, the wind carrying away the stench of burning calf hair. As the skin thawed, she hacked at it the way Indians must have done here a thousand years ago, their stone knives sharper and more expertly handled.

At a sound she looked over her shoulder and saw a coyote not three feet away, gaunt-bellied too, and apparently no more afraid than a hungry dog. But suddenly he caught the human smell, even against the wind, and was gone. He would have made a soft rug at the fire, Lecia thought, and wondered if he might not return to watch just beyond the wall of storm. But she was too busy to look. As the heat penetrated the meat, she cut off one slice after another until she had a little smoky pile, not much for nine people who had lived five days on one lunch apiece, but enough to bring tears that were not all from the storm. In this meat, perhaps three pounds, might lie the life of her pupils.

Lecia scattered the fresh ashes over the calf to keep the coyotes away and piled brush into the fire hole. Then she headed sideways into the storm, so violent that it was a good thing she had the strength of a little cautious meat inside her, for it seemed no one could face the wounding snow. Numb and frightened, she managed to hold herself, not get hurried, panicked, never move until the next broken willow, the next marker was located. So she got back, to find Chuck out near the shelter digging wood from the old clumps, watching, uneasy.

It was hard for the children to wait while the thinner slices of meat roasted around the sticks. When the smell filled the little shelter, Lecia passed out toasted bits to be chewed very slowly and well. It tasted fine and none asked for bread or salt—not even Olive, still silent and alone. She accepted the meat, but returned only distant gravity for the teacher's smile.

By now the white blizzard darkness was coming back, but before they slept there was a little piece of boiled veal for each and a little hot broth. It was a more cheerful sleeping time, even a confident one, although in the night they were struck by the diarrhea that Lecia had expected. But that was from the fresh meat and should not last.

By now Lecia could build a coal bed with rotten wood and ashes to hold a fire a long time, even with diamond willows, and so she dressed Maggie's feet, the girl light as a sack of bird bones, and prepared the night fire. For a while Chuck and Eddie kept each other awake with stories of coyote hunts and with plans for another morning of storm, the sixth. The two boys met the day with so much confidence that Lecia had to let them go out into the storm. Eddie, only ten, suddenly became a little old man in his seriousness as he explained their plans carefully. They would make a big brush pile so that they could settle out of the wind and work the fire until they got a whole hindquarter of the calf hacked off. So the teacher watched them go out very full of hope, the hope of meat, one of the half blankets along to drag their prize in over the snow, like great hunters returning.

Bill had looked sadly after the disappearing boot soles, but without complaint. He helped Lecia with the smaller children, washing at the grime of their faces that would never yield except to soap, and took them out into the storm and back while the teacher soaked Maggie's great swollen feet and tried to keep the girl from knowing that the bone ends of her toes could be seen in the suppurating pits of dying flesh. There were holes on the tops of the toes too, along the edges of her feet, and up the heels as high as the ankle. But above there the swelling seemed looser, the red streaks perhaps no farther up the bony legs. Once Bill looked over the teacher's shoulder and then anxiously into her face. Others had chilblains— his own feet were swollen from yesterday— but not like this.

"Will she lose—" he started to whisper, but he could not put the rest into words, not with a crippled foot himself.

Discussion

1. Chuck again returns to the group after saying, "I'm getting out." What has he discovered while away? What does this discovery mean to the group? Explain the meaning of this sentence: "The boy who had resented them and his involvement in their plight—he had escaped and come back" (page 581).

2. What causes Chuck and Bill to lose their way in their hunt for the frozen calf? How does Lecia help them? How does Lecia make it to the frozen calf and back to the shelter? What does Lecia do to keep the coyotes away from the calf? How does Lecia prepare the meat?

3. Why was Bill unable to finish his question about Maggie's feet?

The air was thick and white with new snow whipped by a northwest wind when Lecia went out for a little wood and to watch for the boys. But they were once more within touching distance before she could see them—very cold and backing awkwardly into the storm through the soft, new drifts, but dragging a whole hindquarter of the calf. It was a lot of meat, and surely the wind must finally blow itself out, the clouds be drained.

By the time Eddie and Chuck were warm they knew they had eaten too much roasted veal while they worked. Next Olive became sick, and Fritz, their deprived stomachs refusing the sudden meat, accepting only the broth. During the night the nausea struck Lecia too, and left her so weak that she could scarcely lift her head all the next day. That night Chuck lost his voice for a while, and Joanie was worse again, her mind full of terrors, the cough so deep, so exhausting that Bill made a little tent over her face with the skirt of his coat to carry steam from a bucket of boiling snow water to her face. Then sometime toward morning the wind turned and cut into the southeast corner of the shelter, crumbling the whole side inward.

The boys crawled out to patch it with brush and snow softened at the fire, Lecia helping dry off the children, as much as she could. Then when they were done and she laid her swimming head down, she heard a coyote's thin, high howl and realized that the wind was dying. Through the smoke hole she saw the running snow like pale windrows of cloud against the sky, and between them stars shining, far pale stars. As one or another awoke, she directed sleepy eyes to look up. Awed, Joanie looked a second time. "You mean they're really stars—?"

"Yes, and maybe there will be sunshine in the morning."

Dawn came early that eighth day, but it seemed that nothing could be left alive in the cold whiteness of the earth that was only frozen scarves of snow flung deep and layered over themselves. The trailing drifts stretched down from the high ridge of hills in the north, so deep that they made a long, sliding slope of it far over the meadow and up the windwhipped hills beyond, with not a dark spot anywhere to the horizon—not a yucca or fence post or willow above the snow. In the

first touch of the sun the frozen snow sparkled in the deep silence following a long, long storm. Then out of the hills a lone grouse came cackling over the empty meadow, gleaming silver underneath as she flew, her voice carrying loud in the cold stillness.

But the meadow was not completely empty, for out of a little white mound of drifted willows a curl of smoke rose and spread thin and blue along the hill. There was another sound too, farther, steadier than the cackle of the grouse, a sound seeming to come from all around and even under the feet.

"A plane!" Chuck shouted hoarsely, bursting into the blinding sunlight.

Several other dark figures crept out behind him into the frosty air, their breath a cloud about them as they stood looking northward. A big plane broke from the horizon over the hills, seeming high up, and then another, flying lower. Foolishly Chuck and Eddie started to shout. "Help! Hello! Help!" they cried, waving their arms as they ran toward the planes, as though to hasten their sight, their coming.

But almost at once the sky was empty, the planes circling and gone. For a long time the boys stared in the broad, cold sky, pale, with nothing in it except wind streaks that were stirring along the ground too, setting feather curls of snow to running.

"Quick! Let's make a big smudge!" Lecia called out, her voice loud in the unaccustomed quiet, and fearful. She threw water on the fire inside, driving smoke out of the hole while the boys set the snowy woodpile burning.

Before the smoke could climb far, there were planes up over the north hills again, coming fast. Now even Fritz got out into the stinging cold—everybody except Joanie, held back by Lecia, and Olive, who did not move from her place. Maggie was lifted up by the teacher to watch through the smoke hole as something tumbled from the higher plane, came falling down. Then it opened out like the waxy white bloom of the yucca, and settled toward the snow, with several other smaller chutes, bright as poppies, opening behind.

There was shouting and talk outside the shelter and while Lecia was hurrying to get the children into their caps and boots, a man came crawling into the shelter with a bag—a doctor. In the light of the fire and a flashlight he looked swiftly at Joanie and then at Olive, considered her unchanging face, lifted the lids of her eyes, smiled, and got no response. Then he examined the poor feet of Maggie, the girl like a skin-bound skeleton in this first sharp light, her eyes dark and fearful on the man's face.

The doctor nodded reassuringly to Lecia, and smiled down at Maggie.

"You're a tough little girl!" he said. "Tough as the barbed wire you have out in this country. But you're lucky somebody thought to try snow against the gangrene—" He filled a little syringe and fingered cotton as he looked around to divert the child.

"All nine of you alive, the boys say. Amazing! Somebody got word to a telephone during the night, but we had no hope for any of you. Small children lost eight days without food, with fifty inches of snow at thirty-eight below zero. Probably a hundred people dead through the country. The radio in the plane picked up a report that six were found frozen in a car stalled on the highway—not over five miles from town. I don't see how you managed here."

The doctor rubbed the punctured place in the child's arm a little, covered it, smiling into her fearful eyes, as men with a stretcher broke into the front of the shelter.

When they got outside, the air was loud with engine roar, several planes flying around overhead, two with skis already up toward the shelter and a helicopter, hovering like a brownish dragonfly, settling. Men in uniform were running toward the children, motioning where they should be brought.

They came along the snow trail broken by the stretcher men, but walking through it as through the storm. Lecia, suddenly trembling, shaking, her feet unsteady on the frozen snow, was still in the lead, the others behind her, and Chuck once more at the end. Bill, limping awkwardly, carried little Joanie, who clung very close to her brother. They were followed by Calla and Eddie, with Fritz between them, and then the stretcher with Maggie. Only Olive of all the children walked alone, just ahead of Chuck, and brushing aside all help.

There were men running toward the bedraggled, sooty little string now, men with cameras and others, among them some who cried, joyous as children, and who must be noticed, must be acknowledged soon—Olive's father and Dale Stever of the yellow plane—

But for now, for this little journey back from the smoke-holed shelter of snow, the awkward queue stayed together.

Discussion

1. By what method does Bill attempt to aid Joanie overcome her cough?

2. What happens to the shelter toward morning of the eighth day? What encouraging signs does Lecia notice?

3. After the plane flies over the shelter, what do Lecia and the others do to attract attention? On hearing the planes approach, all leave the shelter except which children? Who is the first "outsider" to enter the shelter?

4. As the doctor works with Maggie, he keeps up a constant chatter. From him, what do you learn about the storm?

5. The ordeal of weathering the storm leaves its mark on each member of the group—with the possible exception of one person. Who is that person? In what way is that person's behavior at the end of the story much the same as it was at the beginning?

6. Just as at the beginning of the story, the little group—at the end of their ordeal—fall into formation as they walk toward their rescuers. What is that formation? What is different about it now?

8 THE NOVEL

Discussion

A. About the plot:
1. *Winter Thunder* has a principal or main plot and several less important plots, or subplots.
   a. Describe the main plot by telling what the story is about.
   b. One subplot (that is an orderly sequence of incidents involving a minor problem/conflict) has to do with Bill and his coming to accept some responsibility for his sister, Joanie. There are five other subplots in the novel. Identify them.
2. The plot of every story, you will recall, is based on conflict.
   a. What are the opposing forces that produce the main conflict in the novel?
   b. What other conflicts—subconflicts—do you find?
3. What conditions and incidents add suspense to the story?
4. Where, in your opinion, does the climax occur?

B. About the characters:
1. Who is the main character in the novel? How do you know?
2. What would you say are that main character's outstanding personal traits?
3. Which of the other eight characters does the author develop in depth? What are some important things you learn about each?

Composition

1. Which character, in your opinion, changes the most during the eight-day ordeal? In a composition of a page or so, identify the person who, from your point of view, exhibits the greatest change in personality. Use examples from the novel to support your choice.
2. Some of those who have read *Winter Thunder* maintain that Lecia is brave because she has no other choice: the children depend upon her. Do you think that, as a rule, people who exhibit bravery and courage do so because they have to? In a composition of one or more paragraphs, give your answer to that question. Then explain briefly why you believe as you do.

Literary Terms Handbook

attitude: (page 247) the feelings an author expresses concerning the subject or the characters written about; also, the feelings a character expresses about a subject or another character. Some attitudes an author may reveal are, for example, admiration, dislike, amusement, affection, pity, and anger. Writers convey attitude by the descriptive terms they use. For example, in "The Pacing Goose" (page 81), the author reveals her attitude of good-natured amusement toward the goose Samantha when she describes how the goose grew: "She swelled, almost at once, like a slack sail which gets a sudden breeze, into a full-rounded convexity." And in the same story, Eliza (the main character) reveals her attitude toward geese by describing them as "pretty as swans." Eliza's husband, on the other hand, reveals his dislike by calling geese "shifty-eyed birds."

ballad: (page 406) a narrative poem made up of four-line stanzas in which the second and the fourth lines rhyme. Ballads have a characteristic rhythm: an unaccented syllable (sound) is followed by an accented syllable (sound), and that combination makes one beat. As a rule, the first and the third lines of the stanza each have four beats, whereas the second and the fourth lines have three each.

Ballads first appeared in the British Isles during the Middle Ages. Originally sung by wandering minstrels, they were passed on from generation to generation by word of mouth. It was not until about 200 years ago that ballads were written down.

Ordinarily, ballads tell of physical courage or tragic love. Though they may occasionally be concerned with the nobility, they usually involve common folk. Ballads contain little characterization or description. The plot unfolds by means of dialogue. Readers/listeners must generally use imagination to fill in the gaps in the stories told by ballads. For examples of typical ballads, see pages 407; 410; 412; 418.

ballad rhythm: See **ballad.**

ballad stanza: See **ballad.**

central character: See **character.**

character: (pp. 146; 161; 329) a person (occasionally, an animal) who participates in the events that occur in a story or a narrative poem or a play. Although every character in a work of literature has some importance, the reader has the greatest interest in the **central** (or main) **character.** George Spencer, for example, is the central character in *Flight into Danger* (page 346).

characterization: (page 229) the method by which a writer shows what kind of person each character is. Writers can **characterize** a person by means of direct description. For example, the author of "The Most Dangerous Game" characterizes General Zaroff as follows: "He was a tall man past middle age, for his hair was a vivid white; but his thick eyebrows and pointed military mustache were as black as the night . . ." (page 9). More often, however, writers characterize a person by showing what he or she thinks and says and does. For example, Squeaky in "Raymond's Run" (page 250) brags that "There's no track meet I don't win the first place medal." Finally, a writer can characterize a person by showing how others feel about him or her. For example, the author of "Mary McLeod Bethune: Woman of Courage" (page 32) points out that President Franklin Delano Roosevelt appointed Mrs. Bethune to several important positions.

characterize: See **characterization.**

climax: (page 183) the turning point in a story or play; the point at which the outcome of the narrative or play is determined. The reader's interest and suspense are highest at this point. The climax in *Flight into Danger* (page 378) occurs when George Spencer cries, "Cut the switches!" and the stage directions indicate that the airplane touches down on the runway.

comparison: (page 424) an examination of two or more persons, ideas, animals, or objects to discover how they are alike or different. (See also **metaphor, simile.**)

conflict (page 156) the struggle between opposing forces, causing the events that occur in a narrative. Conflict is the essential ingredient of every narrative and every play. Conflict can consist of a struggle (fight) between one character and another—as in "The Most Dangerous Game" (page 5) and in "David and Goliath" (page 38). Conflict can also occur between a person and some aspect of nature (a force beyond his or her control). That's the case in "How Whirlwind Saved Her Cub" (page 54) and in "The Sea Devil" (page 147). Finally, conflict can occur between a person and himself or herself—that is, in a person's mind. That's the case in "The Apprentice" (page 212) and in "Weep No More, My Lady" (page 264). Occasionally, a story will have more than one conflict. "Top Man" (page 92), for example, has two important struggles. The mountain-climbers strive to reach the mountain peak (person versus nature), and Osborn and Nash strongly disagree about how best to reach their goal (person versus person).

descriptive poem: (page 421) a poem about a person, scene, situation, or occasion which reveals the poet's feelings. "I'll tell you how the sun rose" (page 431), for example, describes Emily Dickinson's feelings about the sunrise and the sunset.

dialogue: (pp. 315; 344) words spoken by the characters in a story or a play.

effective use of language (page 535) the skillful use of words; saying what you mean and meaning what you say.

exaggeration: (page 283) stretching the facts beyond the actual truth. Exaggeration usually has a humorous effect. Consider these lines from "Sarah Cynthia Sylvia Stout Would Not Take the Garbage Out" (page 462):

> The garbage reached across the state,
> From New York to the Golden Gate.
> And there, in the garbage she did hate,
> Poor Sarah met an awful fate.

fable: (page 520) a short, imaginative narrative that teaches a useful lesson about life and how to live it. The characters in a fable are usually animals that talk. The jay in the fable "The Jay and the Peacocks" (page 521), for example, learns that it is not wise to pretend to be something one is not.

fantasy: (page 307) a work of literature that deals with an unreal world. Though events in the plot—and perhaps some of the characters—may not be true to life as we know it, the author usually supplies enough recognizable details to make the story or the play believable. Science fiction, for example, is based on fantasy. And "Rip Van Winkle" (page 293) is based on fantasy. A story or a play that deals in fantasy is, in effect, saying something like this: Events like these cannot and do not happen in the real world, but if they could happen, they might well happen in this way.

first-person point of view: See **point of view.**

folktale: (page 527) a story that reflects the life of the people of a particular region. Before being written down, many folktales were passed on orally from person to person—probably for many generations. Folktales are usually concerned with everyday people who experience typical human situations. In "Popocatepetl and Ixtaccihuatl" (page 540), for example, a young Aztec couple must contend with the girl's father's objections to their marrying.

Haiku: (page 449) a three-line poem that describes a single image in no more than seventeen syllables. The first line has five syllables, the second line has seven, and the third line has five. The Haiku originated in Japan.

limerick: (page 466) a humorous five-line poem. The first, second, and fifth lines have three beats each, and they rhyme. The third and fourth lines have two beats each, and they rhyme. (Several limericks appear on pages 465, 467.)

metaphor: (page 432) a suggested or implied comparison between two unlike things. A metaphor suggests that something is something else.

A metaphor in "I'll tell you how the sun rose (page 431) compares sunlit hilltops to bright bonnets (hats) that women wore in the 19th century:

"The hills untied their bonnets"

The poem title "Mama Is a Sunrise" (page 422) is also a metaphor. Here, the poet is comparing the effect Mama has on her family to the anticipation and good feelings that the sunrise brings after the night's darkness.

mood: (page 240) the atmosphere or feeling that a work of literature conveys. The setting of a story or a drama or a poem helps create the mood. For example, the isolated island with its rocky coast and thick jungle established the mood of mystery and tension in "The Most Dangerous Game" (page 5). Details about how things look, sound, feel, taste, and smell also contribute to the mood of a work of literature. Dan'l Webster, the frog in "The Celebrated Jumping Frog of Calaveras County" (pages 280–282), is described as looking "like a solid gob of mud" and "mighty baggy." Details such as these give the story a light, humorous mood.

motivation: (page 209) the reasons for a character's acting as he or she does. In *The Pen of My Aunt* (page 316), the motivation for both Madame and Simone is their wish to protect the stranger from the enemy.

myth: (page 475) a story about superhuman beings—gods, goddesses, or heroes. Myths are often imaginative explanations of natural occurrences. The myth of Prometheus and Pandora (page 476), for example, explains why human beings must contend with diseases.

narrative poem: (page 387) a poem that tells a story. "Elizabeth Blackwell" (page 393) is a narrative poem about a woman's struggle to become a doctor. A **ballad** is a special kind of narrative poem. (See also **ballad.**)

narrator: (page 257) the person who tells a story or a narrative poem. The narrator may be the author or a character in the story. (See also **point of view.**)

novel: (page 558) a long prose narrative that involves fictional or imagined characters and events. Because of its length, a novel involves more characters, complications, and conflicts than a short story does. A narrative like *Winter Thunder* (page 559) is called a **novella,** or short novel.

omniscient point of view: See **point of view.**

play: (page 314) the acting out of a narrative (story) by a person or persons who move and speak on a stage in front of a live audience or a camera. Plays vary in length and type. For example, *The Pen of My Aunt* (page 316) is a stage play; "Grandpa and the Statue" (page 333) is a radio play; and *Flight into Danger* (page 346) is a television play. A person who writes stage, radio, and television plays is called a **playwright.**

playwright: See **play.**

plot: (page 146) the arrangement or sequence of events in a story, play, or narrative poem. In general, every plot (sequence of events) unfolds as follows: (1) confronting the central character with a problem (conflict); (2) detailing the important ways in which that character deals with the problem; (3) resolving the problem. If, in that resolution, the central character successfully solves the problem and attains his or her goal, the plot is said to be comic. If, on the other hand, the forces opposing the main character prevent him/her from attaining the goal, the plot is said to be tragic. The plot of "Raymond's Run" (page 250), for example, is comic. But the plot of "The Telltale Heart" (page 235) is tragic.

point of view: (page 257) the position or viewpoint from which a narrative is recounted. The author, of course, is actually the person telling the story. But sometimes an author will tell the story from the viewpoint of one of the characters in the story. That is, the author will pretend to be a participant in the events. Such a story is told from a **first-person point of view.** The term "first person" refers to the pronouns "I" and "we"; the narrator is the "I" of a story. The events and the other characters are seen through the narrator's eyes. Paul Annixter is the author of "Last Cover" (page 223), but the character Stan tells the story of his artistic brother, Colin. The narrator does not have to be the central character, or even a major character; Colin, not Stan, is the central character in "Last Cover."

Often, rather than having a character tell the story, the author himself or herself will assume the role of narrator, who knows everything that goes on and sees into the minds of all the characters. In this case, the story has an **omniscient point of view.** "Omniscient" means "all-knowing," that is, "knowing everything." "Weep No More, My Lady" (page 264) is written from the omniscient point of view. The writer can thus let the reader know that My Lady is a valuable Basenji long before any character in the story gains that information. Also, the author lets us know what the characters—Skeeter, Jesse, and Cash—think and feel.

refrain: (page 408) a line or phrase repeated at regular points in a poem, usually at the end of each stanza. A refrain can also be an entire stanza repeated at certain points in a poem. The refrain in "Lord Randal" (page 407) consists of one line.

> *"For I'm wearied wi' huntin' and fain wad lie down."*

repetition: (page 436) a succession of the same consonant sound at the beginnings of words close together in a poem. Repetition can give a poem a musical quality. It can also emphasize the words having the same initial sound. Note the repeated *s* sounds in these lines from "The First Snowfall" (page 439):

> *The stiff rails softened to a swan's-down,*
> *And still fluttered down the snow.*

rhyme: (pp. 391; 397) the repetition of words or syllables with similar sounds. This repetition occurs at specific places in a poem, usually at the end of lines. Rhyming usually follows a consistent pattern within a poem. In each stanza of "Robin Hood and Alan a Dale" (page 412), for example, the second and fourth lines rhyme:

> *"Stand off, stand off" the young man said,*
> *"What is your will with me?"—*
> *"You must come before our master straight,*
> *Under yon greenwood tree."*

In "The Cremation of Sam McGee" (page 389) the first and second lines of each stanza rhyme, as also do the third and fourth lines. But within each line there is **internal rhyme:**

> *"On Christmas Day we were mushing our way*
> *over the Dawson trail.*
> *Talk of your cold! through the parka's fold*
> *it stabbed like a driven nail.*
> *If our eyes we'd close, then the lashes froze till*
> *sometimes we couldn't see;*
> *It wasn't much fun, but the only one*
> *to whimper was Sam McGee.*

rhythm: (pp. 391; 401) the pattern in which accented and unaccented syllables are repeated in each line of a poem; the beat of a poem. For example, the first and third lines of "A Red, Red Rose" (page 423) have four unaccented syllables alternating with four accented syllables. In other words, there are four beats in the first and third lines. The second and the fourth lines each have three unaccented syllables alternating with three accented syllables. Thus there are three beats in each of those lines:

> *Ănd faře thĕe wеél, mў ońlў lúve,*
> *Ănd faře thĕe wéel ă while!*
> *Ănd I will cóme ăgaín, mў lúve,*
> *Thŏ' it wеře tĕn thoúsănd míle!*

sensory images: (pp. 424; 432) words that cause or help you to take in an experience through one or more of your five senses: sight, sound, touch, smell, taste. In the poem, "To James" (page 62), for example, these lines contain sensory images:

> *"How your spikes*
> *Ripped the cinders"*

The verb *ripped* appeals not only to your sense of sight but also to your senses of hearing and of touch. That one word helps you hear and feel the crunch of the spikes on the cinders.

setting: (page 193) the time and place in which a narrative or drama takes place. The setting of "Rip Van Winkle" (page 293), for example, is the Catskill Mountains of New York shortly before and during the American Revolution.

simile: (page 424) an expressed comparison; the

comparison of two unlike things, using the word *like* or *as*. "A Red, Red Rose" (page 423), for example, contains this simile: "O, my luve is *like* the melodie/That's sweetly played in tune." "I'll tell you how the sun rose" (page 431), contains this simile: "The news *like* squirrels ran" (line 4). Finally, in "Blow, blow, thou winter wind" (page 435), there is this simile: "thou art not so unkind/*As* man's ingratitude" (lines 2 and 3).

stage directions: (page 315) the playwright's instructions to the director and actors. Stage directions vary in purpose. They are used to specify what the stage or set should look like. They also indicate how and where actors are to move during the play (for example, *upstage left* or *downstage right*). Stage directions can also tell the tones of voice in which actors are to speak certain lines.

stanza: (page 391) a division in a poem consisting of a group of related lines. Every stanza in a poem usually has the same number of lines, as well as the same pattern of rhyme and rhythm. "How They Brought the Good News from Ghent to Aix" (page 399), for example, has stanzas of six lines each.

surprise ending: (page 290) an unexpected conclusion to a work of literature. In "The Inspiration of Mr. Budd" (page 173), the surprise comes when the escaped murderer's dyed hair turns green, thus allowing him to be recognized and captured.

suspense: (page 171) a feeling of excitement, anxiety, and curiosity about what will happen in a story or play. It is suspense that keeps readers interested in a story or play until they find out what happens. Readers of "The Small Miracle" (page 129) are in suspense about two things in the story. They are curious about whether Pepino will be able to take Violetta into the crypt of St. Francis of Assisi. They also wonder whether Violetta will get well.

theme: (page 276) the central idea in a work of literature. The theme of the poem, "Lucinda Matlock" (page 110), for example, is: *In order to live well, a person must be brave, energetic, and joyous.* Not all literary works have themes.

variety: (page 404) changes in the rhyme pattern or rhythm pattern of a poem, or an out-of-the ordinary way of expressing an idea. Variety can make a work of literature more interesting and can emphasize certain features of the work. Variety can also add humor to a poem, as in the last line of the limerick "A decrepit old gas man named Peter" (page 467).

Index of Literary Terms

Glossary

The glossary includes unfamiliar words used in this anthology. In most cases words that are footnoted in the text are not included here. The order and kinds of information given in an entry are shown below:

1. The defined word is divided into syllables. For example: **mo·not·o·nous.**

2. Pronunciation. The pronunciation of each defined word is given. For example: **te·di·ous** (tē′ dē əs).

3. Accents. The mark ′ is placed after a syllable with primary or heavy accent, and the mark ′ after a syllable shows a secondary or lighter accent, as in **ap·pre·hen·sive** (ap′ ri hen′siv).

4. The part of speech and, when useful, information about the singular or plural form.

5. Usage labels. For example: **reck·on** . . . INFORMAL. think.

6. Definition. The words are always defined according to their use in the book; in addition, other commonly used meanings are frequently given.

7. Derivative parts of speech. Other commonly used parts of speech derived from an entry are frequently given. For example: **dis·cern** . . . **—discernible,** *adj.*

The following abbreviations are used:

adj.	adjective
adv.	adverb
n.	noun
pl.	plural
v.	verb

Pronunciation Key

a, hat, cap; **ā**, age, face; **ä**, father, far; **b**, bad, rob; **ch**, child, much; **d**, did, red; **e**, let, best; **ē**, equal, be; **ėr**, term, learn; **f**, fat, if; **g**, go, bag; **h**, he, how; **i**, it, pin; **ī**, ice, five; **j**, jam, enjoy; **k**, kind, seek; **l**, land, coal; **m**, me, am; **n**, no, in; **ng**, long, bring; **o**, hot, rock; **ō**, open, go; **ô**, order, all; **oi**, oil, voice; **ou**, house, out; **p**, paper, cup; **r**, run, try; **s**, say, yes; **sh**, she, rush; **t**, tell, it; **th**, thin, both; **ŦH**, then, smooth; **u**, cup, butter; **u̇**, full, put; **ü**, rule, move; **v**, very, save; **w**, will, woman; **y**, young, yet; **z**, zero, breeze; **zh**, measure, seizure; **ə** represents: a in about, e in taken, i in pencil, o in lemon, u in circus.

Y as in Fr. *du*; **à** as in Fr. *ami*; **œ** as in Fr. *peu*; **N** as in Fr. *bon*; **H** as in Ger. *ach*.

ac·ces·si·ble (ak ses′ə bəl), *adj.* **1.** easy to reach, enter, or use; convenient or attainable. **2.** that can be entered or reached; approachable.

ac·cli·mate (ə klī′mit), *v.* accustom or become accustomed to a new climate, surroundings, or conditions.

ac·rid (ak′rid), *adj.* sharp, bitter, or stinging to the mouth, eyes, skin, or nose.

a·cute (ə kyüt′), *adj.* **1.** acting keenly on the senses; sharp, intense. **2.** coming quickly to a crisis; brief and severe. **3.** crucial; critical. **4.** quick in perceiving and responding to impressions. **5.** quick in discernment; sharp-witted; clever.

ad·a·mant (ad′ə mənt), *adj.* not giving in readily; firm and unyielding; immovable.

a·lac·ri·ty (ə lak′rə tē), *n.* brisk and eager action; liveliness.

am·bro·sia (am brō′zhə), *n.* **1.** (in Greek and Roman myths) the food of the gods. **2.** anything especially delightful to taste or smell.

a·men·i·ties (ə men′ə tēs), *n., pl.* pleasant ways; polite acts. Saying "Thank you" and holding the door open for a person are amenities.

a·mi·a·ble (ā′mē ə bəl), *adj.* having a good-natured and friendly disposition; pleasant and agreeable.

am·i·ca·ble (am′ə kə bəl), *adj.* friendly.

an·ti·so·cial (an′ti sō′shəl), *adj.* not sociable, not friendly.

ar·dor (är′dər), *n.* passion; great enthusiasm; eagerness; zeal.

ar·du·ous (är′jü əs), *adj.* **1.** hard to do; requiring much effort; **2.** using up energy; strenuous.

ap·pre·hen·sion (ap′ri hen′shən), *n.* expectation of misfortune; dread of impending danger.

ap·pre·hen·sive (ap′ri hen′siv), *adj.* afraid that some misfortune is about to occur; anxious about the future; fearful.

as·cer·tain (as′ər tān′), *v.* find out for certain by trial and research; make sure of; determine.

au·da·cious (ô dā′shəs), *adj.* **1.** having the courage to take risks; recklessly daring; bold. **2.** rudely bold; impudent.

awe·some (ô′səm), *adj.* causing a feeling of wonder and reverence.

be·hest (bi hest′), *n.* command; order.

be·lat·ed (bi lā′tid), *adj.* happening or coming late or too late; delayed.

bi·zarre (bə zär′), *adj.* strikingly odd in appearance or style; grotesque.

brev·i·ty (brev′ə tē), *n.* **1.** shortness in time. **2.** shortness in speech or writing; conciseness.

brogue (brōg), *n.* **1.** an Irish accent or pronunciation of English. **2.** a strongly marked foreign accent or pronunciation of English.

can·dor (kan′dər), *n.* saying openly what one really thinks; honesty in giving one's view or opinion; frankness and sincerity.

ca·price (kə prēs′), *n.* **1.** a sudden change of mind without reason; unreasonable notion or desire; whim. **2.** tendency to change suddenly and without reason.

chor·tle (chôr′tl), *v., n.* —*v.* chuckle or snort with glee. —*n.* a gleeful chuckle or snort. [blend of *chuckle* and *snort;* coined by Lewis Carroll]

com·bat·ant (kəm bat′nt), *n., adj.* —*n.* one that takes part in combat; fighter. —*adj.* **1.** fighting. **2.** ready to fight.

com·pe·tent (kom′pə tənt), *adj.* properly qualified; able; fit.

con·de·scend·ing (kon′di sen′ding), *adj.* characterized by exaggerated politeness toward and concern for younger persons or one's social inferiors.

con·found (kon found′), *v.* confuse.

con·sole (kən sōl′), *v.* ease the grief or sorrow of; comfort.

con·spic·u·ous (kən spik′yü əs), *adj.* easily seen; clearly visible.

con·spic·u·ous·ly (kən spik′yü əs lē), *adj.* **1.** in a manner easily seen or clearly visible. **2.** remarkably; worthy of notice.

---

hat, āge, fär, let, ēqual, tėrm;
it, īce; hot, ōpen, ôrder;
oil, out; cup, pùt, rüle;
ch, child; ng, long; sh, she;
th, thin; ŦH, then; zh, measure;

ə represents *a* in about, *e* in taken,
i in pencil, *o* in lemon, *u* in circus.

---

con·ster·na·tion (kon′stər nā′shən), *n.* great dismay; paralyzing terror.

con·vul·sive (kən vul′siv), *adj.* **1.** violently disturbing. **2.** characterized by violent muscle spasms.

cred·i·ble (kred′ə bəl), *adj.* worthy of belief; believable.

cu·mu·la·tive (kyü′myə lə tive), *adj.* increasing or growing in amount or force, by additions; accumulated.

curt (kėrt), *adj.* rudely brief; short; abrupt.

da·is (dā′is), *n.* a raised platform at one end of a hall or large room for a throne, seats of honor, a lectern.

dap·per (dap′ər), *adj.* **1.** neat, trim, or spruce. **2.** small and active.

de·jec·tion (di jek′shən), *n.* lowness of spirits; sadness; discouragement.

des·o·la·tion (des′ə lā′shən), *n.* **1.** devastation. **2.** a ruined, lonely, or deserted condition. **3.** a desolate place. **4.** lonely sorrow; sadness.

di·lem·ma (də lem′ə), *n.* situation requiring a choice between two alternatives, which are or appear to be equally unfavorable; difficult choice.

dis·cern (də zėrn′), *v.* see clearly; perceive the difference between (two or more things); distinguish or recognize. —**discernible,** *adj.*

dis·dain·ful (dis dān′fəl), *adj.* feeling or showing scorn; scornful.

dis·suade (di swād′), *v.* **1.** persuade not to do something. **2.** advise against.

dis·traught (dis trôt′), *adj.* mentally upset by doubt and confusion; crazed.

di·vine (də vīn′), *adj.* **1.** of God or a god. **2.** given by or coming from God; sacred; holy. **3.** like God or a god; heavenly.

du·bi·ous (dü′bē əs), *adj.* **1.** doubtful; uncertain. **2.** feeling doubt; wavering or hesitating. **3.** of questionable character.

e·clipse (i klips′), *n., v.* —*n.* a complete or partial blocking of light passing from one heavenly body to another. A solar eclipse occurs when the moon passes between the sun and the earth. A lunar eclipse occurs when the moon enters the earth's shadow. —*v.* **1.** cut off or dim the light from; darken. **2.** cast a shadow upon; obscure. **3.** surpass; outshine.

ec·sta·sy (ek′stə sē), *n.* condition of great joy; thrilling or overwhelming delight.

e·la·tion (i lā′shən), *n.* high spirits; joy.

el·o·quence (el′ə kwəns), *n.* **1.** vivid, moving, effective manner of expression. **2.** power to win by speaking; the art of using language so as to stir the feelings.

eq·ua·ble (ek′wə bəl), *adj.* uniform; even.

ex·hil·ra·tion (eg zil′ə rā′shən), *n.* **1.** sense of feeling well, happy, and vigorous. **2.** high spirits.

ex·tinc·tion (ek stingk′shən), *n.* a condition when something no longer exists. The dodo, for example, no longer exists; thus it has suffered extinction.

ex·u·ber·ant (eg zü′bər ənt), *adj.* abounding in health and spirits; overflowing with good cheer.

fer·vent (fėr′vənt), *adj.* **1.** showing great warmth of feeling; very earnest; ardent. **2.** hot; glowing; intense.

flur·ry (flėr′ē), —*n.* **1.** a sudden gust. **2.** a light fall of rain or snow. **3.** a sudden commotion.

for·lorn (fôr lôrn′), *adj.* **1.** left alone and neglected; deserted; abandoned. **2.** wretched in feeling or looks; unhappy. **3.** hopeless; desperate.

gar·ru·lous (gar′ə ləs), *adj.* talking too much; talkative.

gen·ial (jē′nyəl), *adj.* smiling and pleasant, cheerful and friendly; kindly.

gid·dy (gid′ē), *adj.* **1.** characterized by a whirling feeling in one's head; dizzy. **2.** never or rarely serious; frivolous; fickle.

gi·gan·tic (ji gan′tik), *adj.* huge; enormous.

gin·ger·ly (jin′jər lē), *adv., adj.* —*adv.* with extreme care or caution. —*adj.* extremely cautious or wary.

gris·ly (griz′lē), *adj.* frightful; horrible; ghastly.

gro·tesque (grō tesk′), *adj.* odd or unnatural in shape, appearance, manner.

hy·po·thet·i·cal (hī′pə thet′ə kəl), *adj.* assumed; supposed.

im·mi·nent (im′ə nənt), *adj.* likely to happen soon; about to occur.

---

hat, āge, fär, let, ēqual, tėrm;
it, īce; hot, ōpen, ôrder;
oil, out; cup, pùt; rüle;
ch, child; ng, long; sh, she;
th, thin; ᴛʜ, then; zh, measure;

ə represents *a* in about, *e* in taken,
i in pencil, *o* in lemon, *u* in circus.

im·mo·bile (i mō′bəl), *adj.* not movable; firmly fixed; not changing; motionless.

im·mor·tal (i môr′tl), *adj.* living forever; never dying.

im·per·a·tive (im per′ə tiv), *adj., n.* —*adj.* **1.** not to be avoided; absolutely necessary; urgent. —*n.* command.

im·plore (im plôr′), *v.* **1.** beg or pray earnestly for. **2.** beg (a person) to do something.

im·pru·dent (im prüd′nt), *adj.* not carefully planned; rash; unwise; not discreet.

im·pulse (im′puls), *n.* **1.** a sudden, driving force or influence; thrust; push. **2.** the effect of a sudden, driving force or influence. **3.** a sudden inclination or tendency to act.

im·pu·ni·ty (im pyü′nə tē), *n.* freedom from punishment, injury, or disadvantage.

in·ces·sant (in ses′nt), *adj.* never stopping; continued or repeated without interruption; ceaseless.

in·cred·u·lous (in krej′ə ləs), *adj.* not ready to believe; doubting; skeptical.

in·dif·fer·ent (in dif′ər ənt), *adj.* **1.** having or showing no interest or attention. **2.** impartial; neutral. **3.** not mattering much; unimportant. **4.** neither good nor bad; just fair; mediocre. —**indifferently,** *adv.*

in·dig·nant (in dig′nənt), *adj.* angry at something that seems unworthy, unjust, or unfair. —**indignation,** *n.*

in·do·lent·ly (in′dl ənt lē), *adv.* disliking work; lazily; idly.

in·du·bi·ta·bly (in dü′bə tə blē), *adv.* without doubt; certainly; unquestionably.

in·duce (in düs′), *v.* lead on; influence; persuade.

in·ert (in èrt′), *adj.* **1.** having no power to move or act; lifeless. **2.** inactive; slow; sluggish.

in·ex·plic·a·ble (in′ik splik′ə bəl), *adj.* incapable of being explained or understood; mysterious.

in·ex·tri·ca·ble (in ek′strə kə bəl), *adj.* forming a mess or tangle from which it is impossible to get free; incapable of being disentangled or untied.

in·fec·tious (in fek′shəs), *adj.* easily communicated or spread to others.

in·ter·mi·na·ble (in tèr′mə nə bəl), *adj.* **1.** never stopping; unceasing; endless. **2.** so long as to seem endless; very long and tiring.

in·ter·pose (in′tər pōz′), *v.* **1.** put or come between; insert. **2.** interrupt. **3.** interfere in order to help; intervene; intercede.

in·val·id (in′və lid), *n.* person who is weak because of sickness or injury; infirm or sickly person.

ir·res·o·lut·ly (i rez′ə lüt lē), *adv.* unable to make up one's mind; vacillating.

jeer (jir), *v., n.* —*v.* make fun rudely or unkindly; mock; scoff. —*n.* a mocking or insulting remark; rude, sarcastic comment.

li·ba·tion (lī bā′shən), *n.* **1.** a pouring out of wine or water as an offering to a god. **2.** the wine or water offered in this way.

loath (lōth), *adj.* unwilling, reluctant.

mal·ice (mal′is), *n.* active ill will; wish to hurt or make suffer.

ma·lig·nant (mə lig′nənt), *adj.* **1.** evil, hateful. **2.** having an evil influence; very harmful. **3.** very dangerous; causing or threatening to cause death.

mal·le·a·ble (mal′ē ə bəl), *adj.* **1.** capable of being hammered, rolled, or extended into various shapes without being broken. Gold, silver, copper, and tin are malleable; they can be beaten into thin sheets. **2.** adaptable. Persons who adjust easily to various situations or who can be influenced toward certain actions are said to be malleable.

mar·tial (mär′shəl), *adj.* **1.** warlike. **2.** associated with war. **3.** of or having to do with the army and navy.

mis·cre·ant (mis′krē ənt), *adj., n.* —*adj.* wicked; base. —*n.* a base or wicked person; villain.

mo·not·o·nous (mə not′n əs), *adj.* **1.** continuing in the same tone or pitch. **2.** wearing because of its sameness; tedious; tiresome.

mor·tal (môr′tl), *adj., n.* —*adj.* **1.** sure to die sometime. **2.** human. **3.** causing death; lethal; fatal. **4.** to the death; implacable; relentless. —*n.* **1.** a being that is sure to die sometime. All living creatures are mortals. **2.** human being.

mor·ti·fy (môr′tə fī), *v.* hurt the feelings of; humiliate.

na·ïve (nä ēv′), *adj.* deficient in worldly wisdom; not sophisticated; unaffectedly simple and natural.

ne·go·ti·ate (ni gō′shē āt), *v.* **1.** talk over and arrange terms; confer; consult. **2.** arrange for. **3.** INFORMAL: get past or over, as *The car negotiated the sharp curve by slowing down.*

non·cha·lant (non′shə lənt), *adj.* coolly unconcerned.

ob·scure (əb skyur′), *adj.* **1.** not well known. **2.** not easily discovered.

om·i·nous (om′ə nəs), *adj.* unfavorable; threatening.

o·paque (ō pāk′), *adj.* **1.** not letting light through; not transparent or translucent. **2.** not shining; dark; dull.

op·pres·sor (ə pres′ər), *n.* one who is cruel or unjust to others.

pal·pa·ble (pal′pə bəl), *adj.* **1.** readily seen or heard and recognized. **2.** that which can be touched or felt.

pan·de·mo·ni·um (pan′də mō′nē əm), *n.* wild disorder; lawless confusion.

pa·tent (pāt′nt), *adj.* evident; obvious.

pen·sive (pen′siv), *adj.* thoughtful in a serious way.

per·turb (pər tėrb′), *v.* disturb greatly; make uneasy or troubled; distress.

pes·ti·lent (pes′tl ənt), *adj.* harmful; destroying; troublesome; annoying.

pi·ous (pī′əs), *adj.* **1.** active in worship or prayer; religious. **2.** seeming; pretending to be religious or interested in a worthy cause.

plac·id (plas′id), *adj.* pleasantly calm or peaceful; quiet.

pli·ant (plī′ənt), *adj.* **1.** bending easily; flexible; supple. **2.** easily influenced. **3.** adaptable.

pre·dic·tion (pri dik′shən), *n.* **1.** act of announcing or telling beforehand. **2.** prophecy.

pre·dom·i·nat·ing (pri dom′ə nāt ing), *adj.* most noticeable; prevailing.

prod·i·gy (prod′ə jē), *n.* person endowed with amazing brilliance, talent, especially a remarkably talented child.

pros·trate (pros′trāt), *adj.* lying out flat; overcome and helpless.

pru·dence (prüd′ns), *n.* wisdom; good judgment.

quirk (kwėrk), *n.* a peculiar way of acting.

---

hat, āge, fär, let, ēqual, tėrm;
it, īce; hot, ōpen, ôrder;
oil, out; cup, pùt, rüle;
ch, child; ng, long; sh, she;
th, thin; ᴛH, then; zh, measure;

ə represents *a* in about, *e* in taken,
i in pencil, *o* in lemon, *u* in circus.

reck·on (rek′ən), *v.* **1.** consider; judge. **2.** INFORMAL. think; suppose.

re·fec·tor·y (ri fek′tər ē), *n.* a room for meals, especially in a monastery, convent, or school.

re·fute (ri fyüt′), *v.* prove wrong; disprove.

re·luc·tant (ri luk′tənt), *adj.* showing unwillingness; unwilling.

re·morse (ri môrs′), *n.* deep, painful regret for having done wrong.

ru·mi·na·tion (rü′mə nā′shən), *n.* meditation; reflection.

sa·vor (sā′vər), *v.* enjoy the taste and smell of. —**sa·vor,** *n.*

scru·ti·ny (skrüt′n ē), *n.* close examination; careful inspection.

se·rene (sə rēn′), *adj.* peaceful; calm.

si·mul·ta·ne·ous·ly (sī′məl tā′nē əs lē), *adv.* at the same time.

sin·ews (sin′yüz), *n., pl.* **1.** nerves. **2.** tendons that connect nerves and muscles.

smug (smug), *adj.* obviously pleased with one's own goodness, cleverness, respectability; self-satisfied; complacent.

sol·ace (sol′is), *n.* comfort, consolation.

stac·ca·to (stə kä′tō), *adj.* **1.** disconnected; detached. **2.** abrupt.

stu·di·ous (stü′dē əs), *adj.* **1.** fond of study. **2.** showing careful consideration; careful; thoughtful; zealous.

su·cu·lent (suk′yə lənt), *adj.* full of juice; juicy.

sul·len (sul′ən), *adj.* **1.** silent because of bad humor or anger. **2.** showing bad humor or anger. **3.** gloomy in disposition.

tan·gi·ble (tan′jə bəl), *adj.* **1.** real; actual; definite. **2.** capable of being felt when touched; capable of being accurately appraised for its value.

te·di·ous (tē′dē əs), *adj.* long and tiring; boring; wearisome.

teem (tēm), *v.* be full (of); abound; swarm.

te·na·cious (ti nā′shəs), *adj.* **1.** holding fast. **2.** stubborn; persistent; obstinate. **3.** able to remember; retentive.

terse (tėrs), *adj.* brief and to the point.

tes·ty (tes′tē), *adj.* easily irritated; impatient.

trac·tion (trak′shən), *n.* friction between a body and the surface on which it moves, enabling the body to move without slipping.

tran·quil (trang′kwəl), *adj.* free from agitation or disturbance; calm; peaceful; quiet.

tran·sient (tran′shənt), *adj., n.* —*adj.* **1.** passing soon; fleeting; not lasting. **2.** passing through and not staying long. —*n.* visitor or boarder who stays for a short time.

trem·u·lous (trem′yə ləs), *adj.* **1.** shaking; quivering. **2.** timid; fearful.

tri·fling (trī′fling), *adj.* **1.** having little value; not important. **2.** frivolous; shallow.

u·nan·i·mous (yü nan′ə məs), *adj.* in complete accord or agreement.

un·can·ny (un kan′ē), *adj.* **1.** strange and mysterious; weird. **2.** so far beyond what is normal or expected as to have some special power.

un·daunt·ed (un dôn′tid), *adj.* not dismayed or discouraged; fearless.

ur·bane (ėr′bān′), *adj.* **1.** courteous, refined, or elegant. **2.** smoothly polite.

vague (vāg), *adj.* **1.** not definitely or precisely expressed. **2.** indefinite; indistinct.

veer (vir), *v., n.* —*v.* change in direction; shift; turn. —*n.* a change of direction.

ve·he·ment·ly (vē′ə mənt lē), *adv.* **1.** in a manner showing strong feeling; eagerly; passionately. **2.** forcefully; violently.

ver·mil·ion (vər mil′yən), *n., adj.* —*n.* **1.** a bright red. **2.** a bright-red coloring matter. —*adj.* bright red.

vex (veks), *v.* **1.** anger by trifles; annoy; provoke. **2.** worry; trouble; harass.

Index by Types of Literature

Index of Authors and Titles

Acknowledgments *continued from page iv.*

Brown and Co. Also for "Hercules" by Edith Hamilton. Copyright 1942 by Edith Hamilton. Copyright renewed © 1969 by Dorian Fielding Reid and Doris Fielding Reid, executrix of the will of Edith Hamilton. Slightly adapted from *Mythology* by Edith Hamilton, by permission of Little, Brown and Co. Also for "First Crossing of the Atlantic" by Samuel Eliot Morison. Copyright 1942, © 1955 by Samuel Eliot Morison. Abridged from *Christopher Columbus, Mariner* by Samuel Eliot Morison, by permission of Little, Brown and Co. in association with The Atlantic Monthly Press. Also for the poem "The Porcupine" by Ogden Nash. Copyright 1944 by Ogden Nash. From *Verses from 1929 On* by Ogden Nash, by permission of Little, Brown and Co. Also for two poems by May Swenson—"Daffodils" excerpted from "A City Garden in April": Copyright © 1966 by May Swenson. Originally appeared in *The New Yorker;* and "Fable for When There's No Way Out": Copyright © 1967 by May Swenson. Both from *New & Selected Things Taking Place* by May Swenson, by permission of Little, Brown and Co. in association with The Atlantic Monthly Press. Also for the poems "Hope" and "I'll tell you how the Sun rose" from *The Complete Poems of Emily Dickinson* edited by Thomas H. Johnson; Little, Brown and Company, 1960.

Macmillan Publishing Co., Inc., for "The Building of the Wall" by Padraic Colum. Reprinted with permission of Macmillan Publishing Co., Inc. from *The Children of Odin* by Padraic Colum. Copyright 1920 by Macmillan Publishing Co., Inc., renewed 1948 by Padraic Colum. Also for the poem "The Open Door" by Elizabeth Coatsworth. Reprinted with permission of Macmillan Publishing Co., Inc. from *Away Goes Sally* by Elizabeth Coatsworth. Copyright 1934 by Macmillan Publishing Co., Inc., renewed 1962 by Elizabeth Coatsworth Beston. Also for "Prometheus and Pandora" from *A Book of Myths* by Thomas Bulfinch (New York: Macmillan, 1942). Also for the poem "Abou Ben Adhem" from *Collected Poems of Leigh Hunt,* published by Macmillan Publishing Co., Inc.

G. P. Putnam's Sons for the poem "The Microscope" by Maxine Kumin. Reprinted by permission of G. P. Putnam's Sons from *Wonderful Babies of 1809 and Other Years* by Maxine Kumin. Copyright © 1968 by Maxine Kumin.

Random House, Inc., for "Raymond's Run" by Toni Cade Bambara. Copyright © 1970 by Toni Cade Bambara. Reprinted from *Gorilla, My Love,* by Toni Cade Bambara, by permission of Random House, Inc. Also for "Mary McLeod Bethune" by Dorothy Nathan. Condensed by permission of Random House, Inc., from *Women of Courage,* by Dorothy Nathan. Copyright © 1964 by Dorothy Nathan. Also for the poems "I, Too" and "Mother to Son" by Langston Hughes. Copyright 1954 by Langston Hughes. Reprinted from *Selected Poems of Langston Hughes,* by Langston Hughes, by permission of Alfred A. Knopf, Inc.

Paul R. Reynolds, Inc., for "My Furthest Back Person—'The African'" by Alex Haley, adapted from his article in *The New York Times Magazine,* July 16, 1972. Copyright © 1972 by Alex Haley. Also for "Hokku Poems" by Richard Wright. Copyright © by Richard Wright. All reprinted by permission of Paul R. Reynolds, Inc., 12 East 41st Street, New York, N.Y. 10017.

Charles Scribner's Sons for "Popocatepetl and Ixtlaccihuatl" abridged and slightly adapted from *Mexican Folk Tales* by Juliet Piggott. Copyright © 1973 Juliet Piggott. Used by permission of Charles Scribner's Sons.

Viking Penguin Inc. for *Three Strong Women* by Claus Stamm. Copyright © 1962 by Claus Stamm and Kazue Mizumura. Reprinted by permission of Viking Penguin Inc.

A. S. Barnes & Company, Inc., for the poems "Bonny Barbara Allan" and "Lord Randall." By permission of the publisher. Copyright © 1955 Harper & Brothers. Publisher A. S. Barnes. From *The Ballad Book,* editor, MacEdward Leach. All rights reserved.

Curtis Brown Ltd, London, for "Through the Tunnel" from *The Habit of Loving* by Doris Lessing. Reprinted by permission.

Witter Bynner Foundation for Poetry, Inc., for the poem beginning "The days and months do not last long" by Pai Ta-Shun, originally titled "Changes" from *Canticle of Pan* by Witter Bynner. Copyright 1920 by Alfred A. Knopf, Inc. Copyright renewed 1948 by Witter Bynner. Reprinted with permission of the Witter Bynner Foundation for Poetry, Inc.

Cohen & Grossberg for the poem "The Princess of Pure Delight" from *Lady in the Dark* by Ira Gershwin and Moss Hart. Copyright 1941 by Random House. Reprinted by permission of the Estate of Moss Hart.

Current History, Inc., for the limerick "A puppy whose hair was so flowing" by Oliver Herford. From *The Century Magazine,* copyright 1912. Reprinted by permission of Current History, Inc.

Frank Marshall Davis for his poem "Rain." Reprinted by permission of the author.

Dodd, Mead & Company, Inc., for the adaptation of "How Whirlwind Saved Her Cub" by Dorothy M. Johnson. Reprinted by permission of Dodd, Mead & Company, Inc. from *Buffalo Woman* by Dorothy M. Johnson. Copyright © 1977 by Dorothy M. Johnson. Also for the poem "The Cremation of Sam McGee" by Robert Service. Reprinted by permission of Dodd, Mead & Company, Inc. from *The Collected Poems of Robert Service.*

Norma Millay Ellis for the poem "The Courage That My Mother Had" by Edna St. Vincent Millay. From *Collected Poems,* Harper & Row. Copyright 1954 by Norma Millay Ellis. Reprinted by permission.

Ambrose Flack for his story "The Strangers That Came to Town," which appeared originally in *Woman's Home Companion,* July 1952. Reprinted by permission of the author.

Angel Flores for "A Letter to God" by Gregorio Lopez y Fuentes, from Angel Flores (ed.): *Great Spanish Short Stories.* New York: Dell, 1962, © Angel Flores, 1962. Reprinted by permission.

Ginn and Company for "The Case of the Stubborn Conductor" from *New Voices 3 in Literature, Language, and Composition* by Jay Cline and others, © Copyright, 1978, by Ginn and Company (Xerox Corporation). Reprinted by permission.

Arthur Gordon for his story "The Sea Devil." Appeared originally in the April 11, 1953, issue of *The Saturday Evening Post.* Copyright, 1953, by Curtis Publishing Company. Used by permission of the author.

Arthur Hailey for the adaptation of his play, "Flight into Danger," copyright 1956, 1957, 1960 by Arthur Hailey. Used by permission of the author.

Harvard University Press for the poem "I'll tell you how the Sun rose" by Emily Dickinson. Reprinted by permission of the publishers and the Trustees of Amherst College from *The Poems of Emily Dickinson,* edited by Thomas H. Johnson, Cambridge, Mass.: The Belknap Press of Harvard University Press, Copyright © 1951, 1955, 1979 by the President and Fellows of Harvard College.

David Higham Associates Limited, London, for "The Inspiration of Mr. Budd" from *In the Teeth of the Evidence* by Dorothy Sayers, published by Victor Gollancz Ltd. Also for the play "The Pen of My Aunt" by Josephine Tey, published by Peter Davis Ltd. Both reprinted by permission.

Lawrence Hill & Co. Publishers, Inc., for "Last Cover" by Paul

Annixter. Reprinted by permission of Lawrence Hill & Co., Westport, Conn. from *The Best Nature Stories of Paul Annixter* copyright 1974 by Jane and Paul Annixter.

Evelyn Tooley Hunt for her poem "Mama Is a Sunrise" from *The Lyric* (1972). Reprinted by permission of the author.

Mrs. Edgar Lee Masters for the poem "Achilles Deatheridge" from *The Great Valley* by Edgar Lee Masters. Copyright 1916 by The Macmillan Company. Also for the poem "Lucinda Matlock" from *Spoon River Anthology* by Edgar Lee Masters. Published by The Macmillan Company. Copyright © 1914, 1915, 1916, 1942, 1944 by Edgar Lee Masters. Both reprinted by permission of Mrs. Edgar Lee Masters.

Harold Matson Company, Inc., for "Good-by, Grandma" from *Dandelion Wine* by Ray Bradbury. Copyright © 1957 by Ray Bradbury. Reprinted by permission of the Harold Matson Co., Inc. Also for "Weep No More, My Lady" by James Street. Copyright © 1941 by James Street, copyright renewed 1969 by Lucy Nash Street. Reprinted by permission of the Harold Matson Co., Inc. Also for "Top Man" from *Island of the Blue Macaws* by James Ramsey Ullman. Copyright © 1940 by James Ramsey Ullman, copyright renewed 1967. Reprinted by permission of the Harold Matson Co., Inc.

McGraw-Hill Ryerson Limited, Canada, for the poem "The Cremation of Sam McGee" from *The Collected Poems of Robert Service*. Reprinted by permission of McGraw-Hill Ryerson Limited.

The New York Times Company for the adaptation of "My Furthest Back Person—'The African'" by Alex Haley, from *The New York Times* Sunday Magazine, July 16, 1972. © 1972 by the New York Times Company. Reprinted by permission.

Gloria Safier, Inc., and Molly Picon for "I'll Give You Law," (Chapter 8) from *So Laugh A Little* by Molly Picon. Copyright © 1962, by Molly Picon. Used by permission of the author.

Luis Omar Salinas for his poem "Ode to a Violin." Copyright © 1974 by Luis Omar Salinas. Reprinted by permission of the author.

The Society of Authors, London, for the poem "Oh, when I was in love with you" from "A Shropshire Lad"—Authorized Edition— by A. E. Housman. Reprinted by permission of The Society of Authors as the literary representative of the Estate of A. E. Housman and Jonathan Cape Ltd., publishers of A. E. Housman's *Collected Poems*.

Jesse Stuart for the poem "My Land Is Fair for Any Eyes to See" from his book *Man with a Bull-Tongue Plow*. Published by E. P. Dutton. Reprinted by permission of the author.

Texas Folklore Society for "The Three Counsels" edited by Riley Aiken, PTFS XXVI, *Texas Folk and Folklore*, Mody C. Boatright, Wilson Hudson, and Allen Maxwell, eds. Reprinted by permission.

Third World Press for the poem "Courage" from *More to Remember* by Dudley Randall. Reprinted by permission of Third World Press, 7524 South Cottage Grove, Chicago, Illinois 60019.

Mrs. James Thurber for "The Tortoise and the Hare" by James Thurber. Copyright © 1940 James Thurber. Copyright © 1968 Helen Thurber. From *Fables for Our Time*, published by Harper and Row. New York. Originally printed in *The New Yorker*.

Charles E. Tuttle Co., Inc., Tokyo, for "Muddy Road" from *Zen Flesh, Zen Bones*, edited by Paul Reps. Reprinted by permission of the publisher.

The University of North Carolina Press for "The Street of the Three Crosses" from *Mexican Village* by Josephina Niggli. Copyright 1945 The University of North Carolina Press. Reprinted by permission of the publisher.

The Vanguard Press for quotations from Mary McLeod Bethune as included in *Women of Courage* by Dorothy Nathan. Quotations are reprinted from *Mary McLeod Bethune* by Catherine Owens Peare by permission of the publisher, Vanguard Press, Inc. Copyright 1951; Copyright © renewed 1979 by Catherine Owens Peare.

The Westminster Press for *Winter Thunder* by Mari Sandoz. Copyright, MCMLI by The Curtis Publishing Co. Copyright, MCMLIV by Mari Sandoz. Published by The Westminster Press. Reprinted by permission of the publisher.

Yale University Press for "The Seven Stars" from *Cheyenne Memories* by John Stands in Timber and Margot Liberty. Reprinted by permission of the publisher, Yale University Press.

Every effort has been made to trace the ownership of all copyrighted material in this book and to obtain permission for its use.

Footnote respellings and definitions are from *Scott, Foresman Advanced Dictionary* E. L. Thorndike and Clarence L. Barnhart. Copyright © 1979 by Scott, Foresman and Company. Reprinted by permission of the publisher.

Credits

Design, Art Direction, Production, Photograph Research and Editing

DESIGN OFFICE / San Francisco

Illustration

JUDITH CHENG / Raymond's Run
DICK COLE / Winter Thunder
KINUKO CRAFT / The Apprentice; The Third Gift
KEITH CRISS / A Letter to God; The Pen of My Aunt
DAVID CUNNINGHAM / Flight into Danger
JACK DESROCHER / David and Goliath
TOM DURFEE / "A puppy whose hair was so flowing"
KEN HAMILTON / I'll Give You Law
ALETA JENKS / Charles
CHRISTA KIEFFER / The Strangers That Came to Town
JEN-ANN KIRCHMEIER / The Celebrated Jumping Frog of Calaveras County
JAMES McCONNELL / The Most Dangerous Game; The Inspiration of Mr. Budd
HEATHER PRESTON / The Small Miracle; Robin Hood and Allan-a-Dale; The Lion and the Mouse
JENNY RUTHERFORD / Weep No More, My Lady
JACLYNE SCARDOVA / Good-by, Grandma
KAREN SCOTT / The Pacing Goose; Grandpa and the Statue
ARVIS STEWART / The Telltale Heart; The Three Counsels
CHRIS WALKER / The Street of the Three Crosses
JAN WILLS / How Whirlwind Saved Her Cub; Top Man; The Sea Devil

Photographs, Paintings, Prints, Drawings, Sculpture

COVER *detail from* "Schooner at Sunset", Winslow Homer/Fogg Art Museum

Page
ii   "Schooner at Sunset" Winslow Homer/Fogg Art Museum
2   BOTTOM "Hound and Hunter" Winslow Homer/National Gallery of Art, Washington, D.C.
3   TOP © Johnson Publishing Company
3   BOTTOM © Claus Meyer/Black Star
8   © Roy King/Icon
26   © Johnson Publishing Company
33   Bettmann Archive
36   © John Running
43   © Michael McKenzie/Bruce Coleman
47   New York Public Library
63   © Claus Meyer/Black Star
72   BOTTOM "Dancers" Edgar Degas/National Gallery of Art, Washington, D.C.
73   LEFT The Kortebein Collection
90   "Stairs, Provincetown" Charles Demuth, 1920, gouache and pencil, 23½ x 19½ inches/ Museum of Modern Art, New York
111   "Gravestone Rubbing; Abigail Muzzy"/Cleveland Museum of Art
120   Maryland Historical Society
123   Robert Eckert/EKM Nepenthe
124   The Kortebein Collection
127   © Runk & Schoenberger/Grant Heilman
144   BOTTOM "Family of Saltimbanques" Pablo Picasso/National Gallery of Art, Washington, D.C.
164   "Figure on Porch" Richard Deibenkorn/Oakland Museum, gift of the Anonymous Donor Program of the American Federation of Arts

612

BCDEFGHIJ 0854321

Printed in the United States of America